PERSONS AND THEIR WORLD

PERSONS AND THEIR WORLD

An Introduction to Philosophy

Jeffrey Olen
University of Wisconsin at Stevens Point

RANDOM HOUSE NEW YORK

To Sam and Belle Olen

First Edition

98765432

Copyright © 1983 by Random House, Inc.

Library of Congress Cataloging in Publication Data

Olen, Jeffrey.
  Persons and their world.

  Bibliography: p.
  Includes index.
  1. Philosophy—Introductions.   I. Title.
BD21.0375 1983   100   82–21511
ISBN 0–394–32545–1

Manufactured in the United States of America

Text design: Levavi & Levavi
Cover design: Carol Grobe

PERMISSIONS ACKNOWLEDGMENTS

Aristotle, "Metaphysics," translated by W. D. Ross. From *The Oxford Translation of Aristotle*, edited by W. D. Ross (2nd ed., 1928). Reprinted by permission of Oxford University Press.

D. M. Armstrong, "The Nature of Mind," pp. 67–73, from *The Mind/Brain Identity Theory* by C. V. Borst. Reprinted by permission of Macmillan, London and Basingstoke, and the author.

From *The Philosophical Works of Descartes*, Haldane and Ross, translators; Meditations I, from "Meditations on First Philosophy." Reprinted by permission of Cambridge University Press.

From Curt Ducasse, "In Defense of Dualism." Reprinted by permission of New York University Press from *Dimensions of the Mind*, edited by Sidney Hook. Copyright © 1960 by New York University.

From *Leibniz: Selections*, edited by Philip P. Wiener. Copyright © 1951 Charles Scribner's Sons; copyright renewed (New York: Charles Scribner's Sons, 1951). Reprinted with the permission of Charles Scribner's Sons.

Norman Malcolm, "Knowledge and Belief," *Mind*, LXI, 242 (April 1952), pp. 183–187. Reprinted by permission of Basil Blackwell, Publisher.

From *Karl Marx: Selected Writings*, edited by David McLellan, © David McLellan 1977. Reprinted by permission of Oxford University Press.

George Pitcher, *A Theory of Perception*. Copyright © 1971 by Princeton University Press. Excerpt, pp. 684–691, reprinted by permission of Princeton University Press.

Pages 773–777 from *The Dialogues of Plato* translated by Benjamin Jowett (3rd ed., 1892). Reprinted by permission of Oxford University Press.

From *The Right and the Good* by W. D. Ross (1930). Reprinted by permission of Oxford University Press.

From *Being and Nothingness* by Jean-Paul Sartre. Reprinted by permission of Philosophical Library Publishers.

From *Beyond Freedom and Dignity*, by B. F. Skinner. Copyright © 1971 by B. F. Skinner. Reprinted by permission of Alfred A. Knopf, Inc.

PREFACE

In 1977, some members of a university philosophy department were interviewing me for a job. One asked me what I would teach in an introductory course in the theory of knowledge. My answer included some of the topics covered in Parts V and VI of this book—topics such as how we justify our beliefs, how we perceive, and whether we can have certain knowledge. The interviewer was dissatisfied. "Why teach that old stuff?" he asked. "Students aren't interested in any of that."

I don't remember the details of my response, but it was a long and impassioned one. Roughly (and in grossly abbreviated form), it went like this: "I love philosophy. I love it enough to spend my professional life writing and teaching it. I love it enough to want to introduce it to students and get them to share some of my enthusiasm for it. And many of my students do share my enthusiasm for it. No course can fascinate everybody, but enough students have enjoyed wrestling with questions they've never before asked, challenging beliefs they've always taken for granted, finding themselves turned every which way by equally compelling arguments to conflicting conclusions—in short, grappling with the very same issues that have fascinated philosophers from ancient times to today—that I refuse to believe it's time for us to abandon the tradition from Plato to Quine in favor of something more 'interesting'. That isn't why I chose to become a philosophy professor."

I did not get the job.

A year or so later when Jane Cullen of Random House approached me about writing an introductory text, I thought back to that interview. I also thought about many of the introductory texts currently on the market, and about the various directions that introductory courses throughout the country were taking. I was not all that comfortable with some of my conclusions, and I soon realized that a certain sort of text was needed—one that could engage students in philosophical thinking about issues that are not marginal to the concerns of professional philosophers today, but form the heart of contemporary discussion. I do not know whether I have written such a book, but I have tried, within certain limits, to do so.

Here's how.

First, I decided that the views of such eminent contemporary American philosophers as W. V. Quine, Hilary Putnam, and Wilfrid Sellars should be included. Such philosophers have provided us with a profound rethinking of many traditional questions. Unfortunately, due to the remarkable sophistication of their methods, their influence has largely been ignored in introductory texts. So I set out to find a way to correct that flaw.

Second, I decided that the continuity between classical and contemporary philosophers should be firmly established. The way to do that, I felt, was to pit Sellars against Locke and Berkeley, Quine and Putnam against Descartes, and so forth, not as thinkers separated by centuries, but, as far as possible, as contemporaries engaged in current battles.

This approach necessitated a substantial rethinking of the standard divisions in most introductory texts. For example, it is the norm to approach the theory of knowledge by way of the controversy between rationalism and empiricism—between the view that our knowledge rests on secure foundations *not* provided by observation and the view that it rests on secure foundations that *are* provided by observation. According to this division, Descartes, Spinoza and Leibniz are martialed on the rationalist side; Locke, Berkeley and Hume on the empiricist side. But in current debate, the issue is not *what* these secure foundations are, but *whether* any such foundations exist. Are any beliefs so certain that they cannot be given up come what may? Or are all beliefs discardable in the light of new observations and theory? And if all beliefs are discardable, are we forced into skepticism? Is knowledge unattainable? Is the goal of science something other than truth? These are the questions that I chose to emphasize, and the contributions to them made by Descartes and others that I chose to stress.

Third, I decided that even though this book would reflect contemporary views of traditional issues, it should avoid the more unfortunate trends associated with "analytic" philosophy, the movement that turned such questions as "What is right?" to "What do we mean by the word *right?*" On my office door hangs the following limerick:

Some new philosophical herds
Talk not about things but of words.
As for me give me please
The birds and the bees
Instead of the "bees" and the "birds."

I have kept that limerick in mind throughout the entire writing of this book. In Chapter 4, "The Nature of Moral Knowledge," for example, my concern is whether the truth of moral principles is relative to one's culture. In some texts, it would be standard to approach the question by asking what the words "good" and "right" mean. I chose otherwise.

Fourth, I determined that the book should be as free as possible of technical jargon. Since the labeling of positions is unavoidable, words like "relativism" and "epiphenomenalism" cannot comfortably be banished from books such as this. Still, it took only a small bit of thought to realize that I could write three chapters on the theory of knowledge without using such expressions as "the analytic-synthetic distinction."

Fifth, I decided that there should be no artificial barriers between philosophy and, say, physics, anthropology, or psychology. Readers of this book will learn as much about Einstein as about Aristotle, which is the way I think it should be. The search for knowledge is a cooperative enterprise, and no philosophy text should ignore this point.

It is my hope, then, that I have written an interesting and readable contemporary book that accurately reflects philosophy today, without shortshrifting the remarkable accomplishments of the past.

In selecting topics for this book, I have been guided by two criteria. First, the selected topic should be one that has engaged both the great figures in the history of philosophy and the best minds in contemporary philosophy. Second, it should be a topic that can be suitably treated in an introductory textbook of this type. Although the first criterion is a fairly easy one to apply, the second is far more problematic. The troublesome part is the phrase "of this type." Of *what* type?

My goal in this book has been to present philosophy not as a history of positions or movements, but as a particular sort of enterprise. I wanted the book to be more than a book *about* philosophy. I wanted it to be a book that *exemplifies* philosophy by being a book *of* philosophy. Therefore, I adopted the following procedure: Ideally, every chapter would present two opposing viewpoints on the same topic. Is the truth of moral principles relative to one's culture or not? Are human beings purely physical or not? Can we know anything for certain or not? Are the worlds of experience and science compatible or not? The advantage of organizing the chapters in this way would be to allow me to focus on the arguments for these positions. That is, such an organization would allow me to show not only *what* philosophers think about, but *how* they think about it. It would enable me to show how the battle lines among philosophers are drawn, how the battles are fought, and how they are won. It would enable me to display the nature of philosophical *activity*. Moreover, it would allow me to present philosophers separated by many centuries as talking *to* one another rather than *past* one another, as engaging in an extended conversation about the same issues.

To achieve this goal, I had to pick topics with great care. Most important, I had to be sure that the most significant and interesting arguments in support of the contested positions could be fairly treated in an introductory text. Although this method of organization has forced me to sacrifice some topics that I would otherwise have liked to include, I think that the tradeoff was well worth it.

Let me make some final comments about a book "of this type." First, in emphasizing arguments as opposed to history, I do not refer in the main body of the chapters to many thinkers who have addressed the issues at hand. This lack is made up by the sections titled "For Further Reading," which follow each part. These sections are not mere lists of readings, but include remarks on the views expressed by their authors.

Second, in treating each topic in the context of two competing positions, I was often forced to omit positions and arguments that are interesting in their own right but peripheral to the flow of the chapter. This lack is made up by the boxed sections that appear in many of the chapters.

Third, since this is a book *of* philosophy, I do not remain above the battle. Although I have tried to present all arguments and positions fairly, if one side seems more compelling to me than the other, I say so, and explain why. Still, the reader should keep in mind that my final words on each topic are provisional. Philosophers have challenged my views and changed my mind before, and they will no doubt continue to do so. Thus, I add a humble question mark to the section that ends the main body of each chapter: "The Final Word?"

Fourth, since this is for many of you the first book of philosophy you have ever read, it is important that it contain some examples of philosophy written by philosophers *for* philosophers. Thus, each of the seven parts ends with short selections by two philosophers, so that Aristotle, Descartes, and others can speak for themselves.

Finally, some instructors who have read this book have expressed regret that one philosopher or another has not been given enough attention. That, I fear, is inevitable in a book of this type. The history of philosophy is a long one, and all of us who teach philosophy have our particular fondnesses. I could not include them all. (I was even forced to exclude some of my own.) I hope that individual instructors will find it easy to work theirs in during classroom lectures and discussions.

There was one regret, however, that caused me some concern. Although Plato and Aristotle are mentioned about as much as any other philosopher, some instructors felt that the philosophers of ancient Greece deserved more attention. I decided that they were right. There are some important views of Plato and Aristotle that do not bear directly on the issues of this book but do deserve mention in an introductory text. Also, the philosophers of ancient Greece were

the first philosophers. That makes their story an inherently interesting and instructive one. How did philosophy begin? How did it develop into a mature
discipline? How did humankind first become interested in philosophical questions? How did humankind first answer them?

For students who are interested in these questions, and for instructors who
feel that exploring them with their students is the best way to begin a course in
the introduction to philosophy, I have provided a second introductory chapter.

I have one more point to make before proceeding to my expressions of gratitude. This book was written at a peculiar time in the evolution of our language.
Women have rightly taken exception to the use of such expressions as "a philosopher, when he . . ." (as contrasted to "a nurse, when she . . ."), yet in many
cases it is difficult to find a replacement that is not awkward. My solution to this
problem (borrowed from the contemporary philosopher Daniel Dennett), is to
use "he" sometimes and "she" sometimes, but never the awkward "he or she"
or the ungrammatical "they." No method determines when one is used rather
than the other. My only concern is that they are used approximately the same
number of times.

When Charlton Heston accepted his Academy Award for his performance in
Ben Hur, he said something like this: "It's really true. When you get up here you
do want to thank everybody."

I do not want to make too many comparisons between winning an Oscar and
writing a book, but this much they have in common: I could not have written a
book of this type without having incurred numerous debts along the way.

That I have managed to write so many words on so many topics is a testament
to the graduate education I received at Temple University. I am grateful to the
members of the philosophy department there, many of whom continue to be
my friends.

I am grateful also to my colleagues at Stevens Point, who have allowed me to
juggle my schedule so as to complete this book in time. I owe particular thanks
to John Bailiff, Richard Feldman, Arthur Herman, Tom Overholt and John
Zawadsky for reading portions of the manuscript, and to John Vollrath, who
read almost all of it and provided me with many useful comments. Vollrath is
also responsible for the instructor's manual.

Although I do not mention my students by name in this book, I often refer to
them as a group. Every chapter in this book has in one way or another been
partially shaped by my interaction with them, in and out of the classroom.
More direct help came from Deb Foat and Tim Rode, philosophy majors at
Stevens Point, who assisted me in various ways.

Special thanks go to one student I have never seen in the classroom—Susan
Olen, who traveled from Florida to Wisconsin during the summer between her
high-school graduation and college matriculation to visit her much-older
brother, and who read a half-dozen chapters of this book and was kind enough
to laugh only in the right places.

Judi Opiola, Patty Stendahl and Carolee Cote deserve copious thanks for preparing my final typescript, and for helping me hunt down bibliographical information.

Finally, I want to thank the editors at Random House—particularly David Follmer and John Sturman, for their welcome help in the final stages of this book's preparation; and Jane Cullen, for suggesting that I write this book and for being such an understanding, supportive editor. During one of the many delightful lunches Jane and I had together, we were interrupted by a friend of mine who writes nonacademic books and who marveled aloud at the friendship that existed between this writer and his editor. If it is really unusual, I am all the more grateful.

J. O.
Stevens Point, Wisconsin
October 1982

CONTENTS

PART II: POLITICS AND THE INDIVIDUAL

PART III: FREEDOM, ACTION, AND RESPONSIBILITY

PART V: KNOWLEDGE AND SCIENCE

PART VI: THE SENSES AND REALITY

PART VII: RELIGIOUS BELIEF

INTRODUCTION

Chapter 1

THE
PHILOSOPHER'S
TASK

The history of philosophy reads like a long family saga. In the beginning there were the great patriarch and matriarch, the searches for knowledge and wisdom, who bore a large number of children. Mathematics, physics, ethics, psychology, logic, political thought, metaphysics (the search for knowledge of the ultimate nature of reality), and epistemology (the study of knowledge itself)—all belonged to the same family. Philosophers were not *just* philosophers, but mathematicians and physicists and psychologists as well. Indeed, in the beginning of the family's history, no distinction was made between philosophy and these other disciplines.

Pythagoras, for example, whose name you may recognize from geometry's Pythagorean theorem, was not only one of the first philosophers, but also one of the first mathematicians, beginning his work in the sixth century B.C. And Aristotle, who lived in the fourth century B.C., wrote works on psychology and physics as well as ethics and metaphysics. In fact, Aristotelian physics dominated the western world for two thousand years, when it was finally replaced by Newtonian physics.

In the beginning, then, all systematic search for knowledge was philosophy. This fact is still reflected in the modern university, where the highest degree granted in all of the sciences and humanities is the Ph.D.—the doctor of philosophy.

But the children gradually began to leave home. First to leave were physics and astronomy, as they began to develop experimental techniques of their own. This exodus, led by Galileo (1564–1642), Isaac Newton (1642–1727), and Johannes Kepler (1571–1630), created the first of many great family crises, all centering on the same question: What is left for philosophy to do? René Descartes (1596–1650), after whom we call a graph's x and y axes "Cartesian coordinates," was the first great philosopher to grapple seriously with the question, and because of this, he is now considered the father of modern philosophy.

Descartes took philosophy's major task to be the establishment of a secure foundation for scientific knowledge. What can be known for certain, he asked himself, and how can we build up our knowledge of the world from these certain foundations? These questions led him to examine the human mind and its relation to the human body. Since then, psychology, philosophy of science, and epistemology have been central to the philosophical enterprise. How is knowledge possible? What features of the human mind enable it to have knowledge? How can and do we come to have scientific knowledge, ethical knowledge, everyday practical knowledge?

Although such questions came to be central, many of the other questions that had perplexed the family since ancient Greece have continued to puzzle succeeding generations. How should we live our lives? How should we treat others? What is the best form of society? Moreover, many philosophers continued to speculate about a deeper reality than the one the physicist explored. Is reality at bottom physical, nonphysical, or both? Is the universe united by factors other than physical laws—by divine providence, perhaps, or a universal moral order? Does life on earth have any meaning?

Eventually, psychology left home. As late as the end of the nineteenth century, the same man—William James (1842–1910)—could be known as both the president of the American Psychology Association and the most eminent philosopher in America. Still, when James built the nation's first experimental psychology laboratory, he helped pave the way for psychology's maturity, and another child was soon gone.

This produced another great crisis, which was dealt with in two different ways. In the English-speaking world, under the influence of Bertrand Russell (1872–1969) and Ludwig Wittgenstein (1889–1951), philosophy turned to the study of logic and language, spawning the movement known as analytic philosophy. Analytic philosophers were somewhat embarrassed by the history of philosophy. It seemed to them that as soon as reliable methods for answering certain types of questions were devised, the questions were no longer deemed philosophical. Philosophy, it seemed to them, was becoming the last bastion of unanswerable questions.

To make philosophy as scientifically respectable as such long-gone offspring as mathematics and physics, they declared that the job of philosophy was to analyze language and thereby show that many traditional philosophical questions and theories were based on a confusion about the workings of language. After completing this task, philosophy would continue as a clarifying enterprise, which philosophers, because of their training in logic, were singularly qualified to carry out.

On the European continent, under the influence of Edmund Husserl (1859–1938) and Søren Kierkegaard (1813–1855), phenomenology and existentialism became dominant. Although there are important differences between the two movements, both emphasized the examination of human reality from the inside. The phenomenologist attempted to understand the workings of human consciousness. The existentialist concentrated on describing and analyzing what it is like to be a human being, not from the objective viewpoint of the psychologist, but from the personal viewpoint of the human being.

Although these three movements—analytic philosophy, phenomenology and existentialism—still exert some influence, they appear to have run their respective courses. The reasons for the decline of analytic philosophy are particularly instructive. For one thing, many philosophers began to feel that the analytic program was excessively limiting. They wanted to do more than merely dismiss confusions and analyze language. For another, linguistics as a separate science had begun to reach a high degree of sophistication, developing various techniques for understanding human language. Thus, another child left home, leading to a familiar family crisis. What was left for philosophy to do?

This time, the crisis seemed more serious than before, as it became obvious that disciplines other than linguistics were beginning to encroach on philosophical preserves. Anthropologists, psychologists, and members of a new science called sociobiology turned their attention to the study of ethics. Psychologists began to broaden their perspective and theorize about the workings of the mind in such activities as perception and memory. And a new discipline arose, artificial intelligence, in which researchers make use of computer techniques to ask such traditional questions as "How is intelligence possible?"

What, then, is philosophy?

It is my hope, of course, that a careful reading of this book will provide a suitable answer to this question, since it is intended to exemplify philosophical thinking about many topics that philosophers have found to be of philosophical importance. But I can provide some preliminary thoughts about the nature of philosophical reasoning, philosophical questions, and, finally, the task of philosophy.

Philosophical reasoning proceeds mainly by clarification and argument. That is, philosophers generally begin by sorting out different issues and questions that are not always clearly distinguished in the ordinary course of things, and then reach and defend conclusions concerning these issues. Although it is undeniable that philosophers present their own opinions on various matters, they do not present naked opinions. They *argue* for their opinions. They present *reasons*, statements they hope will be relatively noncontroversial, and then try to show that, once we accept these statements, it is more reasonable than not to accept some further statements—their conclusions.

These arguments are both positive and negative. Philosophers try to show not only that their own views are reasonable, but that they are more reasonable than competing views. Thus, they use arguments to criticize the views of their opponents. In this way, philosophy can be seen as a continuing conversation among philosophers. One philosopher sorts through various issues and questions and then presents arguments in favor of his own positions regarding these issues and questions. Another comes along and criticizes the arguments of the first and offers another position supported by new arguments. Further criticism is then applied to the views and arguments of the second. Perhaps a third position will be developed; perhaps the first will be saved from the arguments of the second philosopher. At any rate, out of such conversations, new theories are developed, old theories resurrected, new approaches to old problems found, and sometimes problems (at least provisionally) solved.

So far, my characterization of philosophical reasoning does not distinguish it from scientific reasoning, moral reasoning, or ordinary practical reasoning. Scientific journals, for example, are filled with clarifications, arguments and criticisms. What, then, is the difference? As far as the *kind* of reasoning is concerned, there is, I think, none. The major difference is not in kind, but in emphasis. For one thing, philosophers, being trained in the rules of argument (that is, in logic), tend to be more self-consciously argumentative. They tend to pay more attention to the form of their arguments, to present them in a more formal way. Second, scientific journals are filled with details about experiments. The sciences have their own sophisticated experimental techniques for answering questions, and their theories and conclusions are supported by statements gleaned from laboratory and field research.

Although philosophers often refer to the findings of the special sciences, they do not ordinarily perform such research themselves. A philosopher's lab is her study, her library, her office, or the ordinary conversation around her. If a philosopher performs an experiment, it is more often than not a "thought" experiment. That is, she imagines various possibilities and uses the techniques of logic to see what follows from these possibilities.

But even this difference is not absolute. Not all physicists, for example, do laboratory research. Albert Einstein (1879–1955), the great theoretical physicist, developed his special theory of relativity while working in a patent office! And some philosophers do field work similar to that of, say, linguists.

Let us turn, then, from philosophical reasoning to philosophical questions. What is a philosophical question? The short answer is this: any question a philosopher finds worth pursuing. And that short answer is not far from the mark. Consider the following questions, which have engaged and continue to engage the attention of philosophers:

When we see something, do we form mental images of what we see?

Can the "truths" of mathematics be proved wrong by experience?

Can the existence of human misery be reconciled with the existence of a perfectly good God?

Can human behavior be explained by the same kinds of laws as the rest of nature?

How do we determine the right thing to do?

Does science lead to truth?

It is difficult to determine what, if anything, these questions have in common to make them distinctively philosophical, other than the interest they hold for philosophers. Besides, none of them is the sole preserve of the philosopher. Natural and social scientists, theologians, poets, popular essayists, mathematicians—all have turned their professional attention to at least one of them.

This fact is, in part, a consequence of the family saga of philosophy. Take the first question on our list. Aristotle, Descartes, Russell, and most other great figures in the history of philosophy have grappled with various issues concerning human perception, and even though the special sciences have begun to apply their experimental techniques to these issues, philosophers have not abandoned them.

If anything distinguishes the interest of the philosopher in these issues from the interest of the special sciences, it is this: The concern of the philosopher is more wide-ranging. The philosopher strives to combine individual answers into a unified whole.

We have returned, it seems, to the nature of the philosopher's task, and the rather vague answer I have just given suggests that whatever philosophers do, generality is somehow crucial. Let me expand on that a bit.

The contemporary American philosopher W. V. Quine once said that science is self-conscious common sense and philosophy is self-conscious science. There is, I think, much truth to that aphorism. Common sense is the great repository of human learning, and it is contained in the shared beliefs and conversations of us all. Science sharpens common-sense reasoning, subjects common-sense beliefs to scrutiny, seeks more reliable explanations for the phenomena that common-sense beliefs explain, alters our beliefs about these phenomena and thereby increases the store of human knowledge. Philosophy, in turn, reflects on both common sense and science, subjecting both to careful scrutiny. What picture of humankind in the world does physics give us? Psychology? Anthropology? How do these pictures relate to one another? To our common-sense pictures?

Another contemporary American philosopher, Wilfrid Sellars, has suggested that the task of the philosopher is to help us find our way about the world, to give as far as possible a total picture of humankind and its place in the world. The psychologist studies the tasks performed by the brain when we perceive something; the sociologist studies the effects of society on our perceptions; the neurophysiologist studies the chemical changes in our brains; the physicist studies the path of light and the particles of which we and our environments are composed. The philosopher, through familiarity with what these scientists say, sifts and compares and hopes to find a coherent picture of the person through it all.

Thus, we find the same philosopher writing about perception, the relation between mind and body, explanations of human behavior, our interactions with others and the possibility of certain knowledge. Sometimes he will report the findings of one or several special sciences. Sometimes he will enter into debates with members of these sciences, in professional journals and conferences. In that way the conversation expands to include thinkers other than philosophers.

In a sense, then, the family saga is beginning to come full circle. Or, more correctly, we might say something like this: Instead of wondering what to do now that the children have all grown up and left home, the parents have decided to return to their old tasks—not as full-fledged physicists, psychologists, and mathematicians, of course, but as interested and informed observers of, and occasionally participants in, their endeavors.

Thus, philosophy does not have its own domain of knowledge. Its domain is, in effect, the sum of all domains. But that is not to say that philosophy is a superfluous discipline. On the contrary. As the special sciences become more numerous and specialized, as various aspects of traditional philosophical questions are parceled out piecemeal to these sciences, as our view of humankind's place in the world becomes more fractured, the need for a discipline that keeps an informed eye on the whole grows rather than diminishes.

In saying the above, I have been expressing a particular point of view. Not every philosopher would agree with what I have said, since the question "What is philosophy?" is itself a philosophical question, and different schools of philosophy have offered different answers to it. For example, existentialism, which I have already mentioned and to which I devote a chapter in this book, tends to eschew scientific understandings of human reality in favor of an examination of human reality as experienced from the inside. Still, the point of view I have expressed is, I think, in the best tradition of philosophy, from the ancient Greeks to the present.

At any rate, this book has been written with this point of view in mind. Its emphasis is on the human person, as an acting, choosing, perceiving and learning creature, engaged in social interaction with others and the search for knowledge, understanding, and a place in the world. Although the book is divided into seven distinct parts, with each part further divided into three chapters, I hope that a unified view of the person and the philosophical enterprise emerges.

Chapter 2

THE BEGINNINGS
OF PHILOSOPHY

In Chapter 1, I compared the history of philosophy to a family saga. I also gave a very brief and highly schematic account of that saga. In this chapter, we shall take a closer look at the beginnings of that saga. We shall see how in the course of a few generations philosophy emerged as a mature discipline. Our focus will be the *metaphysics* of ancient Greece—the beginnings of the western world's systematic search for the ultimate nature of reality.

SOME EARLY QUESTIONS

You will probably find nothing remarkable about the following statements:

1. There are many things in the world.
2. Things come into and go out of existence.
3. While they exist, things undergo change.
4. Things are similar to one another in some respects and different from one another in other respects.

Why do you find such statements unremarkable? Because you take their truth for granted. You are probably sitting on a chair as you read this book. That makes three things—you, the chair, and the book. There was a time when none of the three existed. All have changed and all will continue to change. The book, for example, came into existence when it was printed and bound. It will be written in, dog-eared, torn, splashed with coffee or some other liquid and otherwise mangled. Eventually, it will be thrown into the trash and then destroyed. But during the course of its existence it will remain the same book.

That change, similarity, and difference exist is a fact of your life. If you are interested in such matters, your interest is far more likely to be a *specific* one than a *general* one. You are more likely to be interested in why some *particular* change occurred than in why change occurs at all. You are more likely to be interested in *particular* similarities and differences than in the fact that there are similarities and differences at all. Thus, you ask questions like these: Why won't my car start? Why does my food taste funny? What made me sick? You do not ask how change, difference, and similarity are possible.

But the ancient Greeks did. Some of their answers will strike you as surprising, no doubt, perhaps even naive. But remember this. It is not just philosophy that began with the ancient Greeks, but science as well. Unlike ourselves, the ancient Greeks did not have twenty-five hundred years of investigation to build upon. Their answers mark the beginning. Seen in that light, some of their answers are remarkably on target.

THE BASIC STUFF

Our story begins in Ionia, an ancient Greek region of Asia Minor, in the sixth century B.C. There a man named Thales decided that there must be some underlying basis to reality that would explain the world of our senses. It would explain the relative stability and order of the world. How can things remain the same through change? How can different things be similar to one another? They are all made of the same stuff. And that stuff, Thales claimed, is water.

Why water? It is difficult to say precisely what Thales' reasons were for choosing water, since he left no writings behind him. But most historians attribute the following two reasons to him. First, water is of prime importance to the maintenance of life. Second, there seems to be some observational evidence. When we dig deeply enough into the earth, for example, we strike water.

What about change? Change occurs because water, the basic stuff, contains in itself a principle of change. Thales is noted for saying that all things are filled with gods. He did not mean that individual gods live in all the things of the world. He meant that the things of the world are composed of a stuff that itself has the power to cause change.

Speculation about the basic stuff did not stop with Thales. He became the founder of a school of philosophy known as the Ionian school. The other members of the school accepted his claim that there must be some basic stuff, but they disagreed on the identity of that stuff. It is important to note that they did not *merely* disagree with Thales. They used *arguments* against him. They tried to show that their views were more *reasonable* than his. In doing so, they began the history of philosophical argument and debate.

Anaximander, a contemporary of Thales, argued this way. If reality were ultimately composed of water, everything would be wet. But some things are dry. Therefore, water cannot be the basic stuff. Moreover, if we pick any other familiar stuff as the basic stuff, we will run into a similar problem. The world is far too varied to be composed of any one familiar stuff. Therefore, the basic stuff must be something other than any particular kind of stuff. It must have no characteristics that limit its ability to take on the characteristics of the familiar object of the world. It must, that is, be nothing in particular. He called this stuff "the boundless."

Change, he thought, is the result of eternal motion. Originally, the basic stuff was in eternal motion, rather like an eddy in a river, and out of that motion came this and many other worlds. Continued motion brought continued change, including the evolution of life.

Anaximenes, the youngest member of the Ionian school, criticized Anaximander. How could "the boundless" break up into all the different individual things of this world? How could nothing in particular account for all the particular somethings? Anaximenes was certain that it could not. So, like Thales, he turned to a familiar stuff. His choice was air.

If we take air as the basic stuff, he claimed, we can easily explain change and difference. The key can be found in condensation. Condensation, he said, is a process by which air thickens into moisture. If air becomes even denser, he continued, it becomes solid. Therefore, we can explain all differences as differences in density, and we can explain all changes as changes in density.

Appearance and Reality

The acceptance of one basic stuff posed the following problem for the three thinkers we have considered. How can *one* stuff be the *many* varied things we find in the world? How can we reconcile the seemingly contradictory existence of the one and the many?

Two other thinkers born in the sixth century B.C. gave two radical and radically different answers. The first, Heraclitus, claimed that *fire* was the basic constituent of reality. What sets his answer apart from the previous ones is that fire is not a *stuff*, like air and water, but a *process*, what we now know to be rapid oxidation. Fire is in a constant state of flux, constantly changing. Therefore, the world is itself in a constant state of flux, is itself constantly changing. According to Heraclitus, the permanence and stability we observe are misleading. They are the result of change and movement, not some deeper permanence and stability. He used the example of a river. We cannot step into the same river twice, he said, because the water is constantly flowing and changing. Similarly, the basis of all things in the world is flowing and changing. The order and unity we observe are not due to the permanence and stability of the basic stuff, but to the *patterns* of flux and change. What is basic to unity, then, is change.

What is striking about this view is that it distinguishes reality as it *is* from reality as it *appears.* What *appears* to be stability and permanence is in *reality* patterned flux. This distinction between appearance and reality was made even more forcefully by another thinker, Parmenides. But unlike Heraclitus, Parmenides declared that it is the appearance of change and motion that is misleading—not just misleading, but illusory. Reality is eternal and perfectly stable. Nothing changes, nothing moves, nothing comes into existence and nothing goes out of existence.

It is impossible for something to come *into* existence, he argued, because it would have to come either from nothing or from something. Obviously, something cannot come from nothing. But if it comes from something then it must have already existed in that something. It is impossible for something to go *out* of existence, because to go out of existence is to become nothing, but there is no such thing as nothing. What is not, Parmenides said, is not. Similarly, it is impossible for something to *change.* To change is to become something else. Therefore, the old thing must go out of existence to be replaced by the new thing. But that is impossible.

Zeno, Parmenides' most famous pupil, presented a number of paradoxes to show that a particular kind of change, motion, is impossible. Suppose, to use a modern example, that you are trying to pass the car ahead of you. Let's say that it takes you ten seconds to reach the point where the car was when you began to pass it. In those ten seconds it will have moved ahead to another point. Let's say it now takes you five seconds to reach that point. By then the car will have moved again. If you reach the new point in two and a half seconds, the car will still be ahead of you, because it has again moved. If we continue this line of reasoning, we see that you can never overtake the car, no matter how much faster than it you are traveling.

Or suppose you are trying to reach a door. First you must travel half the distance to it, then half that distance, then half that distance, then half that distance, and so on. Since we can continue dividing the remaining distances in half, you can never reach the door. What such paradoxes show, Zeno claimed, is that our perception of motion must be illusory.

Numbers and Atoms

The views we have considered so far are likely to sound odd to the modern ear. The view we will consider next, that of Pythagoras, is likely to sound oddest of all, even though one aspect of it is strikingly modern.

According to Pythagoras, the world is made up of numbers. Numbers? What could that possibly mean? For one thing, it means that all relationships can be expressed mathematically. This aspect of his view was suggested by his interest in music and his discovery that musical relationships can be expressed mathematically. Consider the guitar. If you strum an open string you get one tone. If you press the first fret while strumming the string you get a higher tone. If you press the second you get a still higher one. The further down the neck you press, the higher the tone. This can be expressed as a mathematical ratio—two tones are related to each other as two lengths of a string. Pythagoras claimed that all relationships can be expressed in similar ways.

He also claimed that the analogy between musical relationships and others can be pressed even further. Just as there are harmonious and disharmonious musical relationships, so are all relationships either harmonious or disharmonious. Thus, he spoke of "the music of the spheres," or the cosmic harmony to be found in the world's orderly, harmonious relationships.

This emphasis on mathematical descriptions is, of course, a modern one. But when Pythagoras said that the world is composed of numbers he meant more than that. He quite literally meant that numbers are the building blocks of ordinary objects. How could that be? Well, we are in the habit of using numerals to refer to numbers—the numeral 2, for example, to refer to the number two. Pythagoras used a different notation—patterns of dots. Each number had its own pattern. By using this notation, he could think of numbers as geometrical patterns. But he also thought of physical objects as being composed of such patterns. Lines, surfaces, and solids are composed of points, he thought, and the patterns of these points matched the patterns of the numbers.

Far less odd to the modern ear is the view of the atomists, originating with Leucippus in the fifth century B.C. and developing with Democritus into the fourth. The atomists were impressed by Parmenides' arguments for the impossibility of change, creation, and destruction. But they were reluctant to give up the facts of ordinary experience. The result was *atomism*, the view that reality is composed of small, indivisible atoms that can be neither created nor destroyed. These atoms move through empty space, colliding with one another and forming patterns. Ordinary objects, including human beings, are composed of these atoms. And change, including the behavior of human beings, is the result of their movement and the new patterns that result. Thus, what changes and comes into existence are patterns of atoms.

These atoms do not have the qualities we ordinarily observe in objects. They are not, for example, colored. How, then, can the objects of experience have color? According to Democritus, they can't. Color is a sensation in *us*, he claimed. It is produced when atoms are thrown free of objects and strike us in the eye. It is not out there in the objects we see.

SOCRATES VERSUS THE SOPHISTS

With such a variety of views about the ultimate nature of reality, it is not surprising that some skepticism arose concerning the ability of the human mind to reach the truth. This skepticism was directed not only toward metaphysics, but toward ordinary matters as well.

It was personified by the Sophists. The Sophists were wandering teachers of rhetoric, the art of argument and persuasion. But they did more than teach rhetoric. They also held, in the words of the Sophist Protagoras, that "man is the measure of all things." By that they meant that there is no objective truth. There is, for example, no objective moral truth. We are all inclined to do what is in our own interest. The morality of any society is merely what is in the interest of the most powerful group in that society. Nor is there any objective truth about the external world. When we use our senses to learn about the world, we observe only how things appear to us. But things appear differently to different people. So all truth is subjective.

One man was horrified by the Sophists. That man was Socrates, an Athenian philosopher of the fifth century B.C. and one of the most important figures of ancient Greece. He was opposed to the Sophists' doctrines and to their teaching of rhetoric. In place of rhetoric he introduced *dialectic*. Dialectic was not a method of *persuasion*, but his method of getting at *truth*. First he asked people to provide definitions of such notions as justice and goodness. Then he questioned them about their definitions. Gradually the definitions were altered and sharpened until the essence of the notion was reached. As we shall see, the dialectic of Socrates was a crucial step in the development of philosophy. Indeed, it was so important that historians consider him *the* pivotal figure of the period, and they mark his importance by referring to the philosophers who came before— Thales, Pythagoras, and so on—as "pre-Socratics."

PLATO

Socrates' main concern was morality—objective and universal definitions of justice and goodness. But his great student Plato, who was deeply impressed by the dialectic of Socrates, applied it to other areas as well, including metaphysics. In doing so, he brought philosophy to its maturity.

One of Plato's most important contributions to philosophy is his theory of *Forms*, a very powerful theory that allowed him to deal with many of the problems debated by earlier thinkers.

What are Forms? Perhaps the best way to begin to understand them is in terms of Socrates' definitions. According to Socrates, we can grasp the essence of a notion by arriving at a proper definition of it. According to Plato, this essence exists *apart* from our idea of it and *apart* from the ordinary objects of this world. We have, for example, an idea of goodness. Answering to the correct *idea* of goodness is the *quality* goodness. This quality is an abstract entity. It is not a particular individual thing that exists in the world of the senses, but something that is shared by the objects of that world. Nor does it exist in our minds. But it can be grasped by our minds. This entity is the Form of the Good. There are also Forms answering to our correct mathematical notions, and to our notions of shapes, plants, animals, and so on.

Although these Forms are not in the world of sense experience, it would be a mistake to think that they are therefore less real than the objects in that world. Indeed, Plato claimed that the Forms are *more* real than the objects of sense experience. What reality ordinary objects have comes from the Forms. It is because of the Form of the Good that we can be good. It is because of the Form of roundness that oranges are round. It is because of the Form of horseness (that quality of being a horse) that horses are horses. The objects of this world "participate in" or "share in" the Forms, and it is through this participation that they are what they are.

Why did Plato believe in the existence of Forms? For one thing, the Forms explain how the objects of this world can be similar to one another. Round things are similar to one another because they have something in common—the quality roundness. But when we look at round things we do not see roundness itself, we see only round things. Therefore, roundness must be apart from round things.

Also, if the Forms did not exist, knowledge would be impossible. Plato believed this for the following three reasons:

1. Plato accepted Heraclitus' view that the world of sense experience is in constant flux. But he also believed that knowledge cannot be about what changes. It can be about only what is eternal and unchanging. Therefore, the objects of knowledge must be apart from the world of sense experience. The Forms were such objects. Round things come and go and change, but roundness itself, the Form of the round, is an eternal and unchanging essence.

2. In geometry we deal with perfect circles, squares, straight lines, and so forth. But there are no such things in the world of the senses. Therefore, our knowledge of them must be of the Forms of these figures.

3. Each of our senses has its own objects. Colors and shapes are the objects of sight, for instance. Sounds are the objects of hearing. Knowledge and opinion, he believed, are faculties much like the senses. Because they are different from each other, they must have different objects. The objects of opinion are the objects in the world of sense experience. Therefore, the object of knowledge must be something else—the Forms.

Finally, Plato, like Socrates, was concerned to combat the moral skepticism of the Sophists, and the Form of the Good guarantees the universality and objectivity of Socratic definitions.

Plato's Achievement

It is easy to regard Plato's theory of Forms as a compromise between the views of Heraclitus and Parmenides. The world of the senses is, as Heraclitus said, in constant flux. But that which is most real is, as Parmenides said, eternal and unchanging. It is also easy to find a bit of the Sophists in Plato. Like them, he believed that sense perception could not result in knowledge. But unlike them he believed that reason, through its grasp of the Forms, could. Plato was also influenced by Pythagoras. At one time, he seriously considered the view that the Forms might be numbers. But Plato's achievement does not rest in what he took from his predecessors. Earlier, I said that he brought philosophy to its maturity as a discipline. Let us take a brief look at how he accomplished that.

First, Plato made the world of the Forms the basis of a broad and carefully worked out metaphysical system. Here, for example, is how he developed his view of human persons. If knowledge is of the Forms, and if it does not come from the senses, then there must be some organ apart from our physical organs that can grasp the Forms. This organ is a nonphysical mind, or soul. So the human person must be made up of two things, a physical body and a nonphysical soul. Moreover, this soul must be eternal, because our knowledge of the Forms is innate. That is, we do not learn about the Forms in our earthly existence, but are born already knowing about them. As children, we can learn that oranges are round because we have an innate knowledge of roundness. But this innate knowledge is possible only if our souls already existed. Therefore, our souls are immortal.

Second, Plato applied Socrates' dialectic to matters of morality, politics, art, and psychology as well as metaphysics and human knowledge. His confidence in human reason was so strong that he felt it could uncover the truth about the good life and the perfect state as well as the ultimate nature of reality.

Third, Plato proceeded by careful, step-by-step argumentation. Most of his works were written as dialogues between Socrates and other figures, and the positions that Plato finally accepted were the product of careful consideration and criticism of alternative views. It is as much through his arguments as his views that Plato affected the history of philosophy.

Fourth, Plato's dialectical skill was aimed at his own views as well as the views of others. In more than twenty works he continued to refine and develop his views. At one point he even provides what many people take to be one of the strongest criticisms of his own theory of Forms. The criticism goes like this. Oranges are round and balls are round because they have something in common, roundness, which they have in virtue of the Form of the Round. But the Form of the Round must have roundness in common with them. Therefore, using the same reasoning, we conclude that there must be another Form of the Round, in virtue of which the first Form and other round things are round. But if the two Forms share roundness, there must be a third Form. And then a fourth, and a fifth, and so on indefinitely. Thus, Plato's argument leads to an infinite regress of Forms.

ARISTOTLE

The leap from Plato's predecessors to Plato is an extraordinary one. The leap from Plato to his brilliant student Aristotle is no less extraordinary. What is most extraordinary about Aristotle is his startling modernity. In individual books of logic, metaphysics, biology, physics, psychology, ethics, art and politics, he presents a strikingly modern figure as he pays close attention to mundane details, as he painstakingly catalogs what he observes, and as he carefully repeats and criticizes the views of his predecessors. Whereas Plato directs our attention away from the physical world of change, Aristotle directs it back with a previously unheard-of scientific precision.

Aristotle was dissatisfied with Plato's theory of Forms because he believed that it did not explain enough. The world of Forms seemed to him an unnecessary doubling of the world of the senses. If we want to understand various aspects of the visible world, it is no help to know that there is some invisible world in which this one shares. Indeed, it is not even clear what Plato could have meant by "share." Moreover, an important part of our understanding of this world concerns change, and a world of stable, unchanging Forms cannot help us to understand change. Rather than posit such a world, then, we should turn our attention to a careful study of the world of the senses.

When Aristotle turned his attention to this world, he decided that what is most real is the concrete individual object—this person, this animal, this chair, this tree. Although we can make a *logical* distinction between roundness and the round things of this world, that does not mean that roundness can exist apart from round things. Roundness is to be found only in round things. Thus, roundness is not *more* real than round things. Rather, it is *less* real. Its existence depends on the existence of individual things. Thus, Aristotle called individual things primary substances. Roundness, like all forms (and I use the small *f* to stress the point), has only a dependent reality. Also, since the forms belong to the world of the senses, observation of that world can bring knowledge.

For Aristotle, some forms are more important for our understanding than others. Most important are the forms that define what it is to belong to a certain genus or species, such as human being, tree, or horse. These are most important because they are essential to the individuals that have them, whereas other forms, such as color, are merely accidental. To use Aristotle's own example, Socrates was essentially a human being. It is his humanity that defines him. He was also snub-nosed, but that is only an accidental fact about him. It does not define him.

Aristotle on Change and Explanation

As a scientist, Aristotle was interested in understanding particular kinds of changes. But he was also interested in understanding how change is possible. His answer goes like this. Just as we can logically distinguish an object's *form* from the object itself, so can we logically distinguish an object's *matter* from the object itself. By "matter" here, Aristotle meant *bare* matter, matter without any qualities whatever. Of course, bare matter cannot exist by itself any more than greenness can—because it is nothing but pure potentiality. It is what can become green or red, a tree or a human being. Since every *potential* something is an *actual* something else, as a potential oak is an actual acorn, bare matter is nowhere to be found. But it is the potentiality of matter that allows for change.

Aristotle was also interested in the *kinds* of explanation we can give for changes. In a famous passage, he discusses the four kinds of explanation that we can give to any change. The first involves the *material* make-up of the thing that changes. For example, if we want to explain how a statue came to be, we must include in our explanation what it is made of—bronze, say, or marble. The second involves the *form* that the thing takes on when it changes. What are the object's defining characteristics? What distinguishes it from other things? In the case of the statue, an explanation of this type would say that it is a statue of such and such a shape. The third involves what Aristotle called the *primary source* of the change. An explanation of this kind refers to what initiated the change, its *efficient cause.* In the case of the statue, the reference would be to its sculptor. The fourth involves the *final* cause of the change, meaning the goal or purpose of the change. In the case of the statue, it would be the purposes of the sculptor. It is important to note, however, that the goal or purpose will not always be a human purpose. Aristotle believed that everything in nature has a goal toward which it naturally strives. Thus, one way of explaining an acorn's change into an oak is to say that the acorn had the natural goal of becoming an oak.

Aristotle's Achievement

Plato's achievement, we saw, was to bring philosophy to its maturity. Aristotle's achievement was to rethink the questions raised by Plato and to develop a metaphysical system no less original, no less well thought out, no less complex than his teacher's. Crucial to his rethinking were his rejection of Plato's theory of Forms and his own scientific bent.

Nowhere does the difference between Aristotle and Plato come through more clearly than in Aristotle's discussion of the soul. Unlike Plato, Aristotle saw the subject as a continuation of biology. The soul is not something unique to humans. It is the principle of life in all living things. Nor is it a separate entity spending part of its eternal existence in the human body. Rather, it is a capacity of the body, analogous to an axe's capacity to chop wood.

Aristotle's method was to treat individually each of the soul's functions—nutrition, growth, movement, perception, desire, imagination, and the various kinds of thought and knowledge. In each case he attempted to explain how the function is carried out and how it relates to the others.

A brief look at his discussion of sense perception will help us appreciate how his disagreement with Plato on the Forms affected his other views. When we perceive something, the appropriate sense organ receives what Aristotle called the *sensible form* of the object. In the case of sight, for example, the organ is the eye and the sensible forms are shape and color. This is possible because the forms are in the perceived objects, and because the separate sense organs naturally have the appropriate capacities to receive them. It is possible also because there is an appropriate medium—light in the case of sight—that transmits the sensible forms. Aristotle was unable to describe the process in detail, but he suggested that the forms are stamped onto the organ, somewhat as an impression can be stamped onto clay. Memory, he says, is the retention of these sensible forms, and imagination is a movement initiated by sense perception.

Abstract reasoning, on the other hand, involves what Aristotle called *intelligible forms.* Intelligible forms are the essences of objects, the forms that define them. They are not, strictly speaking, perceived by sense organs. To use Aristotle's examples, the eye can perceive straightness, but not *what it is* to be straight. The hand can perceive the warmth of flesh, but not *what it is* to be flesh. These forms, or definitions, can be understood, but they cannot be perceived. But they must be received in some way, Aristotle thought. There must be some receiving organ and there must be some medium of transmission. The receiving organ Aristotle called the *passive reason.* He called the transmitting medium the *active reason.*

The passive reason receives intelligible forms much as the eye receives sensible forms. Because the ancient Greeks did not know of the role of the brain, Aristotle was not able to identify any part of the body as the receiving organ. Still, he believed that the passive reason cannot survive the death of the body. The active reason, on the other hand, is eternal. But in saying that, Aristotle was not accepting Plato's view of the immortality of the soul. Thought and memory require images, Aristotle believed, and images require sense perception, and sense perception requires the body. That, apparently, is why Aristotle believed that the passive reason could not survive the death of the body. At any rate, he clearly stated that there can be no thought without the passive reason, which is not eternal. Thus, the active reason is not a personal soul. It is an impersonal medium that transmits intelligible forms in a way similar to the way that light transmits sensible ones. Its survival of the body's death is not to be identified with the survival of the person.

What we find in Aristotle's discussion of the soul, then, is his extreme this-worldliness. The human soul, like the forms, belongs to this world and is open to scientific investigation. With plants and other animals it shares the functions of nutrition, growth, and reproduction. With other animals it shares desire, sense perception, appetite, and imagination. It alone can reason abstractly, but its ability to do so is dependent on its other functions. And these functions are dependent on the body.

WHAT NEXT?

The history of philosophy does not, of course, stop with Aristotle. But with Aristotle we have come to an important point. We now have a mature discipline with two carefully worked out but competing points of view. It has been said that all philosophy is a footnote to Plato and Aristotle. Like all such catchy sayings, this one can be misleading if pressed too far. But there is some truth to it. By laying out the issues and carefully arguing for their own views, Plato and Aristotle provided the groundwork for much that came after them.

If this book were a history of philosophy, we would trace their influence from their immediate followers to the present. But it is not. Our concern in the remainder of the book will be specific philosophical questions and the arguments that philosophers have used in support of their answers.

The purpose of this second chapter, then, is not to begin a detailed account of the entire family saga. In part, it is to broaden your understanding of what philosophy is by showing you how it began and developed in its earliest stages—how humankind's early wonder at matters we now take for granted blossomed into sophisticated theories about the nature of reality, and how these theories led to speculation about the human mind, human knowledge, and their place in nature. Its purpose has also been to introduce you to some of the concerns of the coming chapters by showing you how humankind first became interested in them. The way that philosophers have treated these concerns has, of course, changed throughout the centuries. Still, the concerns themselves can be found in the ideas of the ancient Greeks—the ultimate nature of reality, the human mind, knowledge, perception, morality, and justice.

Although none of the seven parts of this book is titled Metaphysics, many deal with the metaphysical concerns we have touched upon in this chapter. In Part VI, for example, we discuss the relationship between the way the world appears and the way it really is. Modern physics describes the world much as Democritus did. How can we reconcile such a world with the world as it appears to us? Different answers to this question lead to different views of the ultimate nature of reality. We shall take a close look at some of these views, including the view that reality is ultimately mental rather than physical.

In Part IV, we discuss the human mind. We shall look at two views that are closely related to the views of Plato and Aristotle. According to one, the human mind is a substance distinct from the human body. According to the other, the human mind is identical with the brain or its functions. We shall also look at the question of personal identity. What makes me the same person I was thirty years ago? Although this question was not directly posed by Aristotle, our discussion of his views on the human soul does touch upon the question. Can *I* continue to exist if my thoughts and memories do not?

In Part III, we discuss human behavior. Much of the discussion involves different ways of explaining human behavior. We shall focus on two kinds of explanation, both noted by Aristotle—explanation in terms of efficient causes and explanations in terms of purpose. If I say that I opened the window because I wanted some fresh air, have I *really* explained my behavior? Or is the real explanation to be found in causal mechanisms—in the activities of my nervous system, for instance? The discussion hinges on the question of free will. Do we have free will? Or are we complex machines of a certain sort? Democritus, who thought that human behavior, like all change, is the product of the mechanistic activity of atoms, thought that we are. In Part III, we shall look at other reasons for thinking so.

In Part VII, we return to the question of purpose. In nature we seem to find evidence of purposiveness. Everything seems to have been put here for some purpose. Does this show that the world was designed by God? Are the purposes we seem to find God's? We also ask about the purpose of human life. Is there some purpose to our lives beyond our own individual purposes? If not, does that mean that our lives are meaningless?

In our discussion of human knowledge, we again address some of the concerns of the ancient Greeks. For example, Part V begins with a discussion of skepticism. Can we know anything for certain? Or can we be wrong about anything we claim to know? We also ask about the relationship between knowledge and sense perception. Plato, we saw, believed that knowledge did not come from the senses, while Aristotle put great trust in the ability of his observations to yield knowledge. Today, of course, most of us believe that the senses play an important role in knowledge. But how important is that role? Does all knowledge depend on sense perception? Or is some knowledge, like our knowledge of mathematics, independent of it?

Our discussion of sense perception continues in Part VI. When we look at objects in the world, do we form mental images of what we see? Aristotle believed that vision involves images, but not mental ones. When he said that the eye receives an object's sensible forms, he meant that part of the eye actually takes on the shape and color of the viewed object. Thus, the images he spoke of were physical images, rather like the images that light casts on the retina. But are there mental images as well? We shall also take a look at some contemporary theories on the psychology of perception. These theories are, of course, far more advanced than Aristotle's, but our interest in them is much in the spirit of Aristotle.

The book begins with discussions of morality and justice. Part I deals with ethics. Part II deals with political philosophy. We have not yet focused on the ancient Greeks' discussions of these matters, but some views of Socrates, Plato, and Aristotle will be discussed in these two parts. We shall, for example, discuss Plato's reasons for believing that it is unreasonable not to be moral. We shall discuss Socrates' reason for obeying the law even if it meant accepting his own execution. We shall also discuss the nature of moral knowledge, including Aristotle's arguments for the objectivity and universality of his own moral views. And we shall discuss other topics that arose among the ancient Greeks, including what makes an action right or wrong and what kind of government we should have.

Forms and Universals

One topic that we *have* focused on will not be discussed in later chapters—forms. My reason for excluding it is not that philosophers have lost interest. They have not. Rather, I have omitted it because the discussions since Plato and Aristotle have grown too technical and complex to be treated adequately in an introductory text. Still, I can give some indication of how the topic has fared.

Since Aristotle, philosophers have usually referred to forms as *universals*, in order to distinguish them from *individual* objects. A blade of grass, for example, is a particular individual. Greenness, on the other hand, is a quality shared by individual blades of grass. Similarly, Lassie and Rin-Tin-Tin are particular dogs, while the quality of being a dog is shared by them and other dogs.

That, at any rate, is what a *realist* would say. A realist is someone who believes that universals actually exist. A *nominalist*, on the other hand, believes that universals do not exist. To a nominalist, only individuals exist. Some nominalists believe that individual bits of greenness exist, but that there is no such thing as the universal "greenness." They believe that there is such a thing as the greenness of this blade of grass and that there is such a thing as the greenness of this shirt or this leaf, but not that there is one thing, greenness, that all these particular bits of greenness share. Other nominalists go even further. They deny that there are individual bits of greenness. To them, there are only green things. According to these nominalists, the word "green" does not name any quality, for there are no qualities to be named. When we say that green is a color, we are not saying that there is such a *thing* as green. We are really saying that all green things are colored.

The dispute between realists and nominalists has been going on from medieval times to the present. Nominalists argue that no one can have a clear idea as to what universals are. What kind of thing could greenness be? Moreover, they do not think that there is any good reason to believe in their existence. If we say that greenness exists, we have not explained why green things are green. In fact, that green things are green *needs* no explanation, except when we want to explain how an individual or group of individuals came to be green. And that is not to be explained by universals.

Realists think otherwise. Why is it that the word "green" applies to many things? Because they share a universal—greenness. It is not enough merely to say that they are green as the nominalists do. Some realists also claim that we must assume the existence of universals to understand certain scientific laws. When the scientist says that heat is the motion of molecules, she is talking about universals. She is saying that what we thought to be two universals, heat and the motion of molecules, are really one. She is not just saying that things with so much heat also have so much molecular motion.

Despite their differences about universals, Plato and Aristotle both fall into the realist camp. Both believed that universals exist. Still, realists are more in the spirit of Plato, and nominalists are more in the spirit of Aristotle. Unlike Plato, Aristotle thought that individual things are the most real. Nominalists press the point further. They argue that individual things are *all* that is real. And as we have just seen, their arguments have a genuine Aristotelian flavor.

STUDY QUESTIONS

1. What questions were responsible for the beginning of philosophy? How are those questions related to one another?
2. Why did Thales believe that there must be some basic stuff underlying all of physical reality? Why did he believe that it was water? What alternatives were posed by Anaximander and Anaximenes? Why?
3. Heraclitus believed that reality was in a constant state of flux. Parmenides

believed that change was impossible. What is the source of their disagreement?

4. What did Pythagoras mean by the assertion that reality is composed of numbers?

5. What is atomism? Why did the atomists believe that their views provided an answer to Parmenides' arguments against the possibility of change?

6. What did Socrates mean by dialectic? How does it differ from the rhetoric of the Sophists? How did it influence Plato?

7. What was Plato's theory of Forms? What were his reasons for accepting it? What changes did Aristotle make in the theory? Why did he make them?

8. How did the views of Plato and Aristotle on the soul differ? How were these differences shaped by other metaphysical views?

9. Today I made pancakes and sausage for breakfast. Can you provide four explanations of that event according to Aristotle's four kinds of explanation?

10. What is a realist? A nominalist? What are the arguments in favor of realism and nominalism? Where would you place Plato and Aristotle in the dispute?

GLOSSARY

Active reason. According to Aristotle, the impersonal medium that transmits *intelligible forms* to the human soul's *passive reason.*

Atomism. The view that reality is composed of small, indivisible atoms that can be neither created nor destroyed.

Dialectic. Socrates' method of arriving at the essence of a notion by successive sharpening of definitions.

Forms. According to Plato, abstract qualities that exist apart from both the world of sense experience and the mind. These qualities, such as goodness and roundness, are eternal and unchanging, and observable objects are good or round by sharing in these Forms. According to Aristotle, these qualities do not exist apart from the world of sense experience. Rather, roundness is found *in* round things.

Intelligible forms. To Aristotle, *Forms* that are thought but not perceived. These forms are the defining qualities of objects.

Nominalism. The view that *universals* do not exist. To a nominalist, green and round things exist, but not greenness and roundness.

Passive reason. According to Aristotle, the organ of the soul that receives *intelligible forms.*

Realism. The view that *universals* exist. To a realist, greenness and roundness exist apart from green and round things.

Sophists. Traveling teachers of ancient Greece (during the fifth and early fourth centuries B.C.). The Sophists were most noted for their teaching of rhetoric (the art of argument and persuasion) and the claim that there is no objective truth.

Universals. Abstract qualities shared by individual things. Roundness, for example, is a universal shared by round things.

SELECTIONS

The first selection is from Book VI of Plato's Republic. It is a dialogue between Socrates, the first speaker, and Glaucon. (Socrates
is the "I" of the passage, and Glaucon is the "he.")

In this famous passage, Socrates compares the world of the
senses to shadows cast on a cave wall, and he compares the Form
of the Good to the sun outside. The metaphor vividly portrays
Plato's view that the Forms exist apart from the world of the
senses and that they are more real than the objects of that world.
It also portrays the supreme importance of one Form, the Form of
the Good, which is characterized as the source of all that is beautiful, right and true. In this passage we also find Plato's view that
knowledge of the Forms is innate.

When reading this selection, keep this in mind. When Plato
refers to the world of becoming, he refers to the world of
change—the world of the senses. When he refers to the world of
being, he refers to the eternal, unchanging world of the Forms.

In stark contrast is our second selection, from Book XIII of Aristotle's Metaphysics. In this passage, Aristotle criticizes Plato's theory of Forms. The passage is much drier and less poetic than
Plato's. Notice Aristotle's concern for the world of the senses. Notice also how he faults Plato for being too metaphorical in his description of the relationship between Forms and the individual
objects of this world.

Also, keep in mind the following points: First, when Aristotle
uses the terms "Ideas" and the "ideal theory" he means "Forms"
and "the theory of Forms." And the supporters of the ideal theory
he mentions are, of course, Plato and his followers. (Plato is the
author of the Phaedo, mentioned in the last paragraph of the selection.) Second, when Aristotle refers to the "one over many" argument, he refers to Plato's argument that there must be one
thing (roundness, for example) that many things (balls, oranges,
and so forth) have in common. Third, when he refers to "the third
man," he means the argument that Plato used against himself,
which we looked at earlier.

PLATO

The Myth of the Cave

And now, I said, let me show in a figure how far our nature is enlightened or
unenlightened:—Behold! human beings living in an underground den,
which has a mouth open towards the light and reaching all along the den;
here they have been from their childhood, and have their legs and necks

chained so that they cannot move, and can only see before them, being prevented by the chains from turning round their heads. Above and behind
them a fire is blazing at a distance, and between the fire and the prisoners
there is a raised way; and you will see, if you look, a low wall built along the
way, like the screen which marionette players have in front of them, over
which they show the puppets.

I see.

And do you see, I said, men passing along the wall carrying all sorts of
vessels, and statues and figures of animals made of wood and stone and various materials, which appear over the wall? Some of them are talking, others
silent.

You have shown me a strange image, and they are strange prisoners.

Like ourselves, I replied; and they see only their own shadows, or the
shadows of one another, which the fire throws on the opposite wall of the
cave?

True, he said; how could they see anything but the shadows if they were
never allowed to move their heads?

And of the objects which are being carried in like manner they would only
see the shadows?

Yes, he said.

And if they were able to converse with one another, would they not suppose that they were naming what was actually before them?

Very true.

And suppose further that the prison had an echo which came from the
other side, would they not be sure to fancy when one of the passers-by
spoke that the voice which they heard came from the passing shadow?

No question, he replied.

To them, I said, the truth would be literally nothing but the shadows of
the images.

That is certain.

And now look again, and see what will naturally follow if the prisoners are
released and disabused of their error. At first, when any of them is liberated
and compelled suddenly to stand up and turn his neck round and walk and
look towards the light, he will suffer sharp pains; the glare will distress him,
and he will be unable to see the realities of which in his former state he had
seen the shadows; and then conceive some one saying to him, that what he
saw before was an illusion, but that now, when he is approaching nearer to
being and his eye is turned towards more real existence, he has a clearer vision,—what will be his reply? And you may further imagine that his instructor is pointing to the objects as they pass and requiring him to name
them,—will he not be perplexed? Will he not fancy that the shadows which
he formerly saw are truer than the objects which are now shown to him?

Far truer.

And if he is compelled to look straight at the light, will he not have a pain
in his eyes which will make him turn away to take refuge in the objects of

vision which he can see, and which he will conceive to be in reality clearer than the things which are now being shown to him?

True, he said.

And suppose once more, that he is reluctantly dragged up a steep and rugged ascent, and held fast until he is forced into the presence of the sun himself, is he not likely to be pained and irritated? When he approaches the light his eyes will be dazzled, and he will not be able to see anything at all of what are now called realities.

Not all in a moment, he said.

He will require to grow accustomed to the sight of the upper world. And first he will see the shadows best, next the reflections of men and other objects in the water, and then the objects themselves; then he will gaze upon the light of the moon and the stars and the spangled heaven; and he will see the sky and the stars by night better than the sun or the light of the sun by day?

Certainly.

Last of all he will be able to see the sun, and not mere reflections of him in the water, but he will see him in his own proper place, and not in another; and he will contemplate him as he is.

Certainly.

He will then proceed to argue that this is he who gives the season and the years, and is the guardian of all that is in the visible world, and in a certain way the cause of all things which he and his fellows have been accustomed to behold?

Clearly, he said, he would first see the sun and then reason about him.

And when he remembered his old habitation, and the wisdom of the den and his fellow-prisoners, do you not suppose that he would felicitate himself on the change, and pity them?

Certainly, he would.

And if they were in the habit of conferring honours among themselves on those who were quickest to observe the passing shadows and to remark which of them went before, and which followed after, and which were together; and who were therefore best able to draw conclusions as to the future, do you think that he would care for such honours and glories, or envy the possessors of them? Would he not say with Homer,

'Better to be the poor servant of a poor master,'

and to endure anything, rather than think as they do and live after their manner?

Yes, he said, I think that he would rather suffer anything than entertain these false notions and live in this miserable manner.

Imagine once more, I said, such an one coming suddenly out of the sun to be replaced in his old situation; would he not be certain to have his eyes full of darkness?

To be sure, he said.

And if there were a contest, and he had to compete in measuring the shadows with the prisoners who had never moved out of the den, while his sight was still weak, and before his eyes had become steady (and the time which would be needed to acquire this new habit of sight might be very considerable), would he not be ridiculous? Men would say of him that up he went and down he came without his eyes; and that it was better not even to think of ascending; and if any one tried to loose another and lead him up to the light, let them only catch the offender, and they would put him to death.

No question, he said.

This entire allegory, I said, you may now append, dear Glaucon, to the previous argument; the prison-house is the world of sight, the light of the fire is the sun, and you will not misapprehend me if you interpret the journey upwards to be the ascent of the soul into the intellectual world according to my poor belief, which, at your desire, I have expressed—whether rightly or wrongly God knows. But, whether true or false, my opinion is that in the world of knowledge the idea of good appears last of all, and is seen only with an effort; and, when seen, is also inferred to be the universal author of all things beautiful and right, parent of light and of the lord of light in this visible world, and the immediate source of reason and truth in the intellectual; and that this is the power upon which he who would act rationally either in public or private life must have his eye fixed.

I agree, he said, as far as I am able to understand you.

Moreover, I said, you must not wonder that those who attain to this beatific vision are unwilling to descend to human affairs; for their souls are ever hastening into the upper world where they desire to dwell; which desire of theirs is very natural, if our allegory may be trusted.

Yes, very natural.

And is there anything surprising in one who passes from divine contemplations to the evil state of man, misbehaving himself in a ridiculous manner; if, while his eyes are blinking and before he has become accustomed to the surrounding darkness, he is compelled to fight in courts of law, or in other places, about the images or the shadows of images of justice, and is endeavouring to meet the conceptions of those who have never yet seen absolute justice?

Anything but surprising, he replied.

Any one who has common sense will remember that the bewilderments of the eyes are of two kinds, and arise from two causes, either from coming out of the light or from going into the light, which is true of the mind's eye, quite as much as of the bodily eye; and he who remembers this when he sees any one whose vision is perplexed and weak, will not be too ready to laugh; he will first ask whether that soul of man has come out of the brighter life, and is unable to see because unaccustomed to the dark, or having turned from darkness to the day is dazzled by excess of light. And he will count the one happy in his condition and state of being, and he will pity the other; or, if he have a mind to laugh at the soul which comes from below into the light, there will be more reason in this than in the laugh which greets him who returns from above out of the light into the den.

That, he said, is a very just distinction.

But then, if I am right, certain professors of education must be wrong when they say that they can put a knowledge into the soul which was not there before, like sight into blind eyes.

They undoubtedly say this, he replied.

Whereas, our argument shows that the power and capacity of learning exists in the soul already; and that just as the eye was unable to turn from darkness to light without the whole body, so too the instrument of knowledge can only by the movement of the whole soul be turned from the world of becoming into that of being, and learn by degrees to endure the sight of being, and of the brightest and best of being, or in other words, of the good.

ARISTOTLE

Criticisms of Plato

The supporters of the ideal theory were led to it because on the question about the truth of things they accepted the Heraclitean sayings which describe all sensible things as ever passing away, so that if knowledge or thought is to have an object, there must be some other and permanent entities, apart from those which are sensible; for there could be no knowledge of things which were in a state of flux. But when Socrates was occupying himself with the excellences of character, and in connexion with them became the first to raise the problem of universal definition . . . [he] did not make the universals or the definitions exist apart; they, however, gave them separate existence, and this was the kind of thing they called Ideas. Therefore it followed for them, almost by the same argument, that there must be Ideas of all things that are spoken of universally, and it was almost as if a man wished to count certain things, and while they were few thought he would not be able to count them, but made more of them and then counted them; for the Forms are, one may say, more numerous than the particular sensible things, yet it was in seeking the causes of these that they proceeded from them to the Forms. For to each thing there answers an entity which has the same name and exists apart from the substances, and so also in the case of all other groups there is a one over many, whether these be of this world or eternal.

Again, of the ways in which it is proved that the Forms exist, none is convincing; for from some no inference necessarily follows, and from some arise Forms even of things of which they think there are no Forms. For according to the arguments from the sciences there will be Forms of all things of which there are sciences, and according to the argument of the 'one over many' there will be Forms even of negations, and according to the argument that thought has an object when the individual object has perished, there will be Forms of perishable things; for we have an image of these. Again, of the most accurate arguments, some lead to Ideas of relations, of which they say there is no independent class, and others introduce the 'third man.'

. . .

Above all one might discuss the question what in the world the Forms contribute to sensible things, either to those that are eternal or to those that come into being and cease to be; for they cause neither movement nor any change in them. But again they help in no wise either towards the knowledge of other things (for they are not even the substance of these, else they would have been in them), or towards their being, if they are not *in* the individuals which share in them; though if they were, they might be thought to be causes, as white causes whiteness in a white object by entering into its composition. But this argument, which was used first by Anaxagoras, and later by Eudoxus in his discussion of difficulties and by certain others, is very easily upset; for it is easy to collect many and insuperable objections to such a view.

But, further, all other things cannot come from the Forms in any of the usual senses of 'from.' And to say that they are patterns and the other things share in them is to use empty words and poetical metaphors. For what is it that works, looking to the Ideas? And any thing can both be and come into being without being copied from something else, so that, whether Socrates exists or not, a man like Socrates might come to be. And evidently this might be so even if Socrates were eternal. And there will be several patterns of the same thing, and therefore several Forms; e.g. 'animal' and 'two-footed,' and also 'man-himself,' will be Forms of man. Again, the Forms are patterns not only of sensible things, but of Forms themselves also; i.e. the genus is the pattern of the various forms-of-a-genus; therefore the same thing will be pattern and copy.

Again, it would seem impossible that substance and that whose substance it is should exist apart; how, therefore, could the Ideas, being the substances of things, exist apart?

In the *Phaedo* the case is stated in this way—that the Forms are causes both of being and of becoming. Yet though the Forms exist, still things do not come into being, unless there is something to originate movement; and many other things come into being (e.g. a house or a ring) of which they say there are no Forms. Clearly therefore even the things of which they say there are Ideas can both be and come into being owing to such causes as produce the things just mentioned, and not owing to the Forms. But regarding the Ideas it is possible, both in this way and by more abstract and accurate arguments, to collect many objections like those we have considered.

FOR FURTHER READING

Each of the seven parts of this book will be followed by a detailed bibliography. In this bibliographic section, I shall note some general works, plus some material relating to the second introductory chapter.

The most important reference book in philosophy is *The Encyclopedia of Philosophy* (New York: Macmillan, 1967), Paul Edwards, editor in chief. This eight-volume work contains articles on all major philosophers, philosophical movements, and philosophical issues. Most articles are written by philosophers, and all are followed by bibliographies. The articles vary widely in their difficulty and sophistication, but many are useful to the introductory student. Another important reference is *The Philosophers' Index*, which contains a listing of papers published in many philosophy journals as well as abstracts of most listed papers. It is available in most, if not all, college and university libraries.

There are many histories of philosophy on the market. Probably the most detailed is the multivolume *History of Philosophy* by Frederick Copleston, widely available in a Doubleday Image paperback series. Shorter histories include W. T. Jones' four-volume *History of Western Philosophy* (New York: Harcourt, Brace & World) and Bertrand Russell's one-volume *History of Western Philosophy* (New York: Simon and Schuster, 1945).

There are also many introductory anthologies on the market. Among the most commonly used are *The Problems of Philosophy* (Boston: Allyn and Bacon, 1978), edited by William Alston and Richard Brandt; *A Modern Introduction to Philosophy* (New York: The Free Press, 1973), edited by Paul Edwards and Arthur Pap; *Reason and Responsibility* (Encino and Belmont, Cal.: Dickenson, 1978), edited by Joel Feinberg.

Three series of books are also of interest. First, there is the *Foundations of Philosophy* series (Englewood Cliffs: Prentice-Hall), edited by Elizabeth and Monroe Beardsley. At last count, the series numbered seventeen volumes, but it is still growing. Each volume is by a noted contemporary philosopher and most provide an excellent introduction to the particular branch of philosophy covered.

The other two series are more difficult. The first is the *Oxford Readings in Philosophy* series (New York: Oxford University Press), edited by G. J. Warnock. Each of the volumes contains papers by contemporary philosophers on a major branch of philosophy. The other is the *Modern Studies in Philosophy* series, edited by Amelie Rorty, originally published by Doubleday and since reissued by University of Notre Dame Press. Each volume in this series contains papers on a major philosopher. The philosophers covered extend from the ancient Greeks to those of the twentieth century.

For the writings of the ancient Greeks before Socrates, see *Selections from Early Greek Philosophy* (New York: Appleton-Century-Crofts, 1964), edited by Milton C. Nahm; John Mansley Robinson's *Introduction to Early Greek Philosophy* (New York: Houghton Mifflin, 1968); and *The Presocratics* (New York: Odyssey, 1966), edited by Philip Wheelright.

Unfortunately, there is no place to go for the writings of Socrates—because he never wrote anything. However, he is the main character in most of Plato's dialogues, and the early dialogues are fairly faithful to the Socratic dialectic. See especially the *Crito*, *Euthyphro*, *Apology*, *Gorgias*, and the early parts of the *Republic*.

All of Plato's dialogues can be found in *The Dialogues of Plato* (New York: Random House, 1937), translated by B. Jowett. In addition, many are available in either Bobbs-Merrill or Penguin editions. The *Republic* gives the best view of Plato's philosophy as a whole, including as it does discussions of ethics, politics, psychology, metaphysics, knowledge, and art. The *Theaetetus* contains Plato's most detailed discussion of knowledge, and the *Parmenides* contains his criticisms of his own theory of the Forms.

For Aristotle's works, see *The Basic Works of Aristotle* (New York: Random House, 1941), edited by Richard McKeon. Aristotle's criticisms of Plato's theory of Forms can be found in *Metaphysics*. His discussion of explanations can be found in *Physics*. His psychology can be found in *De Anima (On the Soul)*. *Metaphysics* is available in an Ann Arbor paperback edition (Ann Arbor: University of Michigan Press, 1952); *Physics*, in a University of Nebraska Press paperback; and an abridged *De Anima* in an Oxford University Press paperback.

The debate between realists and nominalists was perhaps most heated in medieval times—with Augustine and Aquinas the most important realists and Ockham and Abelard the most important nominalists. Volumes II and III of the Copleston series give a good account of this dispute. For the current debate, see Michael J. Loux's *Universals and Particulars* (Notre Dame: University of Notre Dame Press, 1976), which contains important readings by many contemporary philosophers.

Part I

ETHICS

Chapter 3

FOUNDATION
OF MORALS

"You shouldn't have . . ."
"I ought to . . ."
"It would be wrong to . . ."
"The right thing to do is . . ."

The above phrases are familiar ones, but have you ever stopped to consider how familiar they really are? If you have, then you are aware of the important role that *moral judgments* play in your life.

Consider how often we make moral judgments. Usually, moral judgments concern what we, as individuals, *ought* to do. The frequency with which we make such judgments is often hidden from us because we make them automatically, as when we suddenly remember that we made a promise and immediately set out to keep it. But if we decide to keep the promise because we feel that we *ought* to, we are making a moral judgment. Of course, decisions concerning what we ought to do are not always that simple. Sometimes they require a good deal of thought, as when a roommate asks to turn in one of your papers as his own.

Decisions regarding our own behavior do not exhaust the range of moral judgments we make. We also make moral judgments when we pass judgment on the acts of others. Moreover, we are often called on to give moral advice. So we are not only concerned with what *we* ought to do, but with what *others* ought to do as well. In fact, if we think carefully about the importance of moral judgments, we come to see that they guide our behavior in all aspects of our lives—at school, at work, with our friends and family, when we cast our votes. Indeed, that is one of the crucial features of moral judgments—they guide our behavior in all aspects of our lives.

MORAL JUDGMENTS AND MORAL PRINCIPLES

Philosophers who have come to reflect on moral judgments have been struck by a number of other things about them. First, moral judgments are *universalizable.* That is, if I say that it is right for me to perform a particular action, then I must say that it would be right for any other person in the same position to do the same thing. Similarly, if I say that it is wrong for someone else to perform a particular action, then I must say that it would be wrong for anyone in the same position (including myself) to do the same thing.

Second, moral judgments are based on *moral principles.* That is, if I say that it is wrong for John to turn in Mary's paper as his own, I am prepared to justify my judgment by saying something like, "To turn in another person's work as your own is cheating, and cheating is wrong." In other words, I arrive at a *particular* moral judgment by applying a *general* principle to a particular situation. This second feature of moral judgments helps to explain the first. If particular moral judgments are always based on moral principles, that means that there is a certain rule that applies to the case at hand. And if there is any other case at hand that is similar to that one, the same rule must apply. If the rule does not apply, then there must be some relevant difference between the two cases. Moreover, this second feature of moral judgments applies not only to judgments about particular cases, but also to many moral principles themselves. Why is cheating wrong? Because it is a form of dishonesty, and dishonesty is wrong.

Philosophers do not assume, though, that this process of justification can go on indefinitely. Eventually our chain of justification must end at some *basic* moral principle (or principles). Eventually, we must come to some general principle (or principles) that we accept on its own merits and that we can show to be the basis of all other moral principles.

Third, these moral principles that justify particular moral judgments are *overriding.* That is, whenever we decide what to do, if there are moral principles that apply to our behavior, they provide us with the most important reasons for acting. In other words, moral reasons take precedence over all other reasons. If considerations of self-interest, for example, lead us to favor one course of action, but some moral principle requires that we take another course of action, we should opt for the latter. Moral reasons, then, are those reasons meant to serve as the final arbiter in our decisions to act.

These three features of moral judgments are *logical* features. That is, they say nothing about the *content* of particular judgments or principles. They tell us that moral judgments are those judgments based on universalizable principles meant to take precedence over all other reasons for acting. They do not tell us what these principles actually are.

It is, however, a sociological or psychological fact about ourselves that we display a great amount of agreement when making moral judgments. Even when we disagree on particular moral judgments, we generally agree on the principles that apply to the case at hand. All other things being equal, we oppose killing, rape, armed robbery, lying, and so forth, just as we approve of loyalty, promise-keeping, helping others in need, and so forth. And when we do disagree about a particular case, it is generally because we disagree on the facts of the case or because we rank the principles differently. Take the example in which John wants to turn in Mary's work as his own. Assuming that they are very close friends, most of us would agree that there are two principles that apply here—loyalty and honesty. Loyalty to John requires that Mary give him the paper. Honesty requires that she not give him the paper. If we disagree about what Mary ought to do, it is not because we disagree on these principles. It is because we disagree on which should take precedence.

If we do agree on our moral principles, and if many of these principles are themselves based on moral principles, then it is reasonable to suppose that we agree on these more basic principles. And if we then suppose that eventually there must be some one or few basic moral principles, then it is reasonable to suppose that we also agree on it (or them). Accordingly, one of the chief enterprises of the moral philosopher has been to attempt to discover our basic moral principle (or principles). This enterprise can be characterized as the search for the *foundation* of our morals.

Of course, that is not the only concern of moral philosophers. They are also concerned with comparisons between moral judgments and other kinds of judgment, such as scientific judgments. Also, they are concerned with the relationship between morality and self-interest. In addition, moral philosophers are interested in questions of moral responsibility. When should we be held morally accountable for our actions? Under what circumstances should we not be held accountable? We will turn to such issues in later chapters. But first, let us turn to the search for the foundation of morals.

WHAT MAKES AN ACTION RIGHT?

To seek the foundation of our morals is, in effect, to ask the following question: What is it that makes an action right or wrong? Another way of asking the question is this: What do all right actions have in common, and what do all wrong actions have in common? If we can find one basic feature shared by all right actions, then we have answered our question. If there is no one feature, but a small (or perhaps large) number of them, such that every right action has at least one such feature, then we must settle on more than one basic moral principle.

Notice that the questions are framed in terms of the *rightness* or *wrongness* of *actions.* Generally, philosophers distinguish between *rightness* versus *wrongness*, on the one hand, and *goodness* versus *badness*, on the other. Actions (and decisions to act) are said to be right or wrong, while the persons who act, their motives for acting, and the consequences of their actions are said to be good or bad.

Although it is often the case that good persons do the right thing and bad persons do the wrong thing, it is not difficult to think of cases in which it does not work out that way. Suppose that a politician wants to become dictator of America and realizes that to do so he must first be elected president and realizes further that to be elected president he must pass himself off as a decent, concerned, humane citizen. In that case, he may do only the right things throughout his life (so as not to be discovered as the tyrant he is), but he would not be considered a good person by those who knew his motives. Although his actions are right, his motives are bad.

Similarly, we can imagine a passerby thinking that a woman is being attacked on the street and, at the cost of injury to the supposed attacker, pulling him away from her. If it turns out that the woman was not being attacked, the would-be protector did the wrong thing when he injured the other man. Still, given his motive for acting, we would not consider him a bad person because of it.

Having distinguished between rightness and goodness, we can now begin our search for the basic moral principle.

UTILITARIAN ETHICS

What is it that ultimately makes an action right? One answer that has attracted numerous philosophers throughout the history of philosophy is that it is the *consequences* of our actions that make them right or wrong. An action is right if it creates the greatest amount of good—if its consequences are better than the consequences of the alternatives. Otherwise, it is wrong. Philosophers who reason this way are called *utilitarians,* and their position is called *utilitarianism.*

Of course, we have so far supplied only half an answer. We still have to know what makes some consequences better than others. The best-known answer to this question is supplied by John Stuart Mill (1806–1873). Mill said that goodness and badness are a matter of happiness and unhappiness. Happiness is the only thing that is *intrinsically* good, or good in itself. Similarly, unhappiness is the only thing that is intrinsically bad. If we consider anything else to be good, it is only because of the happiness it gives to someone. All other goods, then, are *instrumental* goods. Their value lies only in their ability to give happiness.

Thus, Mill offers as the foundation of morals what he calls the *greatest happiness principle,* also called the *principle of utility.* We may paraphrase this principle as follows: The right action among the alternatives open to us is the action that results in the greatest happiness for all concerned.

But what, we may wonder, is happiness? Happiness, Mill says, is pleasure and the absence of pain, where pleasure and pain include not only such physical pleasures and pains as the pleasure of a dive into a cold lake on a hot day or the pain of a headache, but nonphysical ones as well, such as the pleasure derived from seeing a good film or the pain caused by being insulted by a friend. The more pleasure we feel (physical and nonphysical) and the less pain we feel (physical and nonphysical), the happier we are. Therefore, the feature that all right actions have in common is that they produce the greatest balance of pleasure over pain for all concerned, where everybody concerned is counted equally in the calculations.

To illustrate how the principle of utility works, let us assume that pleasure and pain can be easily measured, and that there is a unit of pleasure and pain called a *utile*, analogous to inches, ounces, and so forth. A positive utile is a unit of pleasure. A negative utile is a unit of pain. Let us also assume that I am faced with three alternative courses of action and that three other people stand to be affected by the course I choose. In that case, I am to calculate the number of utiles each of us would gain from each alternative, and then choose the alternative resulting in the greatest total. Thus, we might imagine the following chart, where the column headings stand for the alternatives, the row headings for the people involved, and the numbers for utiles.

	A	B	C
Groucho	+15	−15	+25
Chico	+10	−10	−10
Harpo	+10	−10	−10
Zeppo	+10	−10	−25
Total	+45	−45	−20

Inspecting the totals, we find that A is the right thing to do.

Of course, matters are rarely as simple as this. For one thing, it is not clear that we really can measure all forms of pleasure and pain. If, say, we arbitrarily give 50 utiles to eating a good pizza, how many utiles should we give to falling in love? Moreover, there will often be many more than four people involved, and we cannot always be sure how much pleasure or pain they will get. Also, it is difficult, if not impossible, to predict *all* the consequences of any of our actions.

Thus, Mill does not recommend that we apply the principle of utility directly whenever we decide what to do. In most cases, we can get by if we choose what to do on the basis of certain *rules of thumb*. More often than not, we can *maximize utility* (that is, produce the greatest happiness) if we refrain from lying, stealing, and so forth, and if we keep our promises, help others in need, and so forth. So in most cases we need only appeal to such rules of thumb as "It is wrong to lie" before we act.

Usually, it is only when these rules of thumb conflict that we have to apply the principle of utility directly. If, for example, we find ourselves at a children's music recital, and the proud mother of one of the performers asks us what we thought of her child's (unfortunately atrocious) performance, we have just such a conflict. One rule of thumb advises us to tell the truth, another to spare the mother's feelings. Applying the principle of utility, we usually decide that telling a small white lie is the right thing to do.

There are two major reasons why many philosophers have been attracted to utilitarianism. First, it does seem to mirror the way we often think when we make moral decisions. Don't we often ask ourselves whom we will hurt and whom we will help and how much we will hurt or help them before we make a decision? That is, don't we often consider the consequences before we act? Second, if we ask ourselves what the purpose of morality might be, it seems reasonable to suppose that it is to make a better world, and it seems equally reasonable to suppose that the more happiness there is, the better the world is. Utilitarianism tells us to try to make such a world. So utilitarianism does have a great initial appeal. Even so, many philosophers have rejected it, for reasons that we shall now consider.

Testing the Principle of Utility

How should we test utilitarianism? Well, if the principle of utility really is our basic moral principle, then any particular moral judgment based on that principle should agree with the moral judgment we would intuitively make. By saying that we make these judgments intuitively, I do not mean to say that we have some sixth sense about moral matters. It may be that we do (although few philosophers today would agree). It may be that these intuitions are the product of social conditioning. It may be that they are imbedded in our genetic heritage through eons of evolution. We shall leave the question open until the following chapter. But whatever may be the truth about these intuitions, we do have them. And if the principle of utility is in fact our basic moral principle, then it should agree with them.

So let us run a few thought experiments. Let us imagine certain cases and apply the principle of utility to them. If the principle of utility does not agree with our intuitions (if these cases provide counterexamples to utilitarianism), let us then ask what moral principles will provide the correct answers.

Let us begin by returning to our "utile chart," this time with different numbers in the boxes.

	A	B	C
Groucho	+90	+24	+ 75
Chico	0	+24	+ 50
Harpo	0	+24	+ 50
Zeppo	0	+24	− 75
Total	+90	+96	+100

Notice that the total in column C is the highest. Yet it is not at all clear that alternative C is the one we ought to choose. On the face of it, it does not seem that

C is as *fair* as B. That is, B spreads the utiles around evenly, whereas C gives a good deal of pleasure to three people at the expense of a good deal of pain to a fourth. Which is right then—B or C? As matters stand, the question cannot be answered. The problem is that we do not know what actions C and B are. Intuitively, we are inclined to say that sometimes it is acceptable to cause a bit of pain to produce a greater good (as when we discipline a small child), and at other times it is not. That we are unsure about the proper answer to our question suggests, then, that perhaps the consequences are not the *only* thing we must take into account before determining whether an action is right. Depending on the situation, we may have to consider other factors as well.

But before we make any final judgments, let us fill in the details with some clearly described cases.

Case 1. Six of us are driving along the highway when our car gets stuck in a snow bank. Obviously, we will have to push the car out. One person stays behind the wheel and the rest of us get out to push. As I take my place I think to myself, "Why should I push along with the others? If I only pretend to push, nobody will notice. After all, the difference between four people pushing and five people pushing is minimal, so my pretending to push will not make anybody else's task more difficult. But if I do push, it will cause me a good deal of discomfort." My calculations might look something like this:

	Push	Pretend
Groucho	− 25	− 0
Chico	− 25	− 26
Harpo	− 25	− 26
Zeppo	− 25	− 26
Gummo	− 25	− 26
Total	−125	−104

Thus, it seems that on utilitarian grounds it is perfectly all right for me to pretend to push. But should I?

Case 2. I am a physician working in a hospital emergency room, when three people arrive at the same time. All three were involved in an automobile accident. The first is so badly injured that it is certain that he will die whether he receives attention or not. The second has only minor cuts and bruises. The third is seriously injured but will survive if given immediate attention. Otherwise, he will die. The principle of utility requires that I tend first to the third person. Should I?

Case 3. A woman is dying of terminal cancer. At the most, she has a month to live. Perhaps she will last no longer than a week. There are three other people in the hospital who are in immediate need of organ transplants. One needs a heart, and the other two need a kidney each. The cancer victim's organs are in perfect condition. There are no other organs available. If I, as physician, transplant her heart and kidneys to the other patients, they will live, but she will lose a week to a month of her life. According to the principle of utility, it appears that I should perform the transplants. Do you agree?

Case 4. I am in the army, in a battlefield trench with four other soldiers. Suddenly, a grenade is thrown into the trench. I can fall on the grenade myself, sacrificing my life to save the lives of my companions, I can throw the man standing next to me on the grenade, thereby sacrificing his life to save the rest of us, or I can let the grenade go off, killing all four of us. Because of certain skills that only I have, I am needed to lead the survivors back to safety. The man next to me is not. According to the principle of utility, it seems that I should throw him on the grenade. Should I?

Case 5. After the disastrous Chinese earthquake of 1976, a man's wife and children were trapped in the rubble of their home. As he worked at digging them out, he heard the moans of the town leader beneath another pile of rubble. He stopped trying to save his family and went immediately to the rescue of the leader and his family. The leader and his family survived; the rescuer's family did not. Asked about his decision the next day, the man said that he had no regrets. The town leader was needed for the preservation of order, the direction of rescue attempts, distribution of supplies, and so forth. The leader's survival meant the survival of many other people, all of whom would have died had he saved his own family instead. It also meant a great reduction in suffering for the survivors. Thus, the man acted on good utilitarian grounds. But did he do the right thing?

The great majority of my own students accepted the utilitarian answer in the second case, but disagreed with it in the others. It is my guess that those of you reading this agree with my students. Where, then, has the utilitarian gone wrong? What moral principles does utilitarianism seem to neglect?

If we consider the first case, we seem to be back to the question of *fairness*. It doesn't seem fair for me to get the benefits of the ride without sharing in the work. Cases such as this have led many philosophers to claim that the principle of utility, if it is to be accepted at all, must be tempered with another basic moral principle—*be fair*.

Cases two and three have this much in common: In each case, there is one person who is going to die in any case and at least one person whose life can be saved by immediate attention but will otherwise die. Why is it, then, that we are inclined to save the life of such a person in case two but not case three? The difference seems to be the difference between passively letting someone die and actively hastening the death. That is, in the third case I would be *causing* harm were I to perform the transplants, while I would only be *permitting* it were I not to perform them. This feature is missing in the second case, in which I am causing direct harm to no one. The same reasoning is behind our intuitions in the fourth case. Even though three lives would be saved were I to throw the man next to me on the grenade, it seems wrong to pick him out as a sacrifice. If we try to formulate the moral principle at work in the third and fourth cases, we might conclude that it is something like this: *Do no direct harm.*

But what about our fifth case? Here there is no question of actively causing

UTILITARIAN ALTERNATIVES TO MILL

Mill's utilitarianism is often described as *hedonistic,* meaning that it says that pleasure is the only thing that is intrinsically good, or good in itself. If we consider anything else to be good, it is because of the pleasure it gives to somebody. That is, all other goods are *instrumental* goods. Why is a beautiful painting better than an ugly one? Because it gives us greater pleasure. Why is a virtuous person better than a nonvirtuous one? Because the virtuous person creates pleasure for others rather than pain.

But it is possible to be an *ideal* utilitarian instead, as was G. E. Moore (1873–1958). Moore believed that, besides pleasure, there are a number of other *states of mind* that are intrinsically good, and that, besides states of mind, a number of *aesthetic* values are intrinsically good. Although Moore is hazy on what states of mind have intrinsic value, we may suppose that he means such things as love, the desire for knowledge, and the appreciation of beauty. Such states are valuable whether they lead to pleasure or not. Similarly, if we imagine two far-off worlds, neither of which will ever be visited by a conscious creature, and if one of the worlds is more beautiful than the other, that world is the better of the two—even though it will never give anyone any pleasure whatever.

Mill's utilitarianism may also be described as *act-utilitarianism.* That is, the principle of utility is applied directly to alternative acts. The individual act that maximizes utility is the right one.

It is possible, however, to apply the principle of utility to *rules* instead of acts. That is, one might require that in any given case we act according to the rule that, if generally followed, would produce the greatest amount of good for all concerned. Such a position is called *rule-utilitarianism.* According to rule-utilitarianism, such principles as "keep your promises" are not rules of thumb, to be discarded whenever utility can be maximized by doing so. Rather, they are rules to be followed even when they do not lead to the greatest good.

This is not to say that rule-utilitarianism requires that we never break a promise. According to rule-utilitarianism, such rules have certain exceptions built into them. The principle of utility, when applied to rules rather than to acts, does not yield exceptionless rules. It yields rules of the form, "Keep your promises except under the following conditions...." The point is that we are not free to break them merely because utility can be maximized by doing so. The principle of utility is meant to justify rules, not individual acts.

Another form of utilitarianism we might mention is *egoistic* utilitarianism. Mill's form of utilitarianism may be called *altruistic,* because it requires us to take into account the pleasure and pain of everyone concerned. But someone might claim that it is only one's own pleasure and pain that must be considered. Such a person is an egoist.

Although some philosophers have claimed that a policy of rational self-interest will not differ greatly from a policy of altruistic utilitarianism, such a view is difficult to defend. In general, discussions of egoism have focused on whether egoism has any claim to being considered a moral position at all. Philosophers who say that it does not argue that egoism cannot be consistently *universalized.* That is, an egoist cannot say that it is right for others to

> follow their own self-interest without compromising his own self-interest. Other philosophers have countered by saying that the egoist can *privately* agree that others are right to follow their own self-interest without *publicly* admitting it. Although egoists are *logically* committed to thinking it right that others follow their own self-interest, they are not logically committed to *saying* so. They are, however, *morally* committed to saying the opposite.

anyone's death. Rather, a man is forced to choose which lives to save and which lives to allow to be lost through forces beyond his control. No doubt, such circumstances are the most difficult to deal with, because they force us to play God. Still, there are times when people are forced to deal with them, as was the poor father, and when they are, they must make a choice.

But why are we troubled by this man's choice? If you are like my students, you no doubt feel that the man had a special obligation to his family. Or, more generally, you feel that there are a number of people to whom we have special relationships, and because of these special relationships we have *special duties* toward them. Such relationships may include not only family ties, but friendships, doctor-patient relationships, relationships between teacher and student, lawyer and client, and so forth. Didn't our utilitarian father ignore his special duty? Let us say, then, that the principle of utility must be tempered by still another principle: Fulfill your duties arising out of *morally significant relations.*

DEONTOLOGICAL ETHICS

We will return to utilitarianism to see whether it has any defense against our counterexamples, but let us first examine the alternative system we have devised. It has four basic principles: (1) act according to the principle of utility; (2) be fair in our dealings with others; (3) do no direct harm; and (4) fulfill our duties arising from morally significant relations.

Notice that the three principles we have added are *nonconsequentialist.* That is, they do not require that we look at the effects of our actions. Rather, they tell us to perform or refrain from performing certain *types* of actions. Principles of this kind are called *deontological* principles, and many moral philosophers, called *deontologists,* believe that our basic moral principles are deontological. Is it possible to revise the principle of utility so as to capture its crucial insight in a deontological way? If so, we can have a purely deontological ethical system. And it seems that we can do just that, if we replace the principle of utility with the following: *do good for others.*

Our system of basic moral principles is similar to the moral system of W. D. Ross (1877–1971), a widely influential deontologist. Ross explains the failure of utilitarianism this way. Utilitarianism does not, he says, take account of the *personal* nature of duty. That is, our relations with others are far more complicated than the utilitarian allows. How do we make moral decisions? Not by giving everybody a row in a utile chart and counting all utiles equally. Rather, we take into account the special relationships we have with each individual and choose accordingly.

Suppose I have made a promise to somebody and am deciding whether to keep it. Do I first try to determine whether keeping the promise will maximize utility? Or do I decide to keep the promise because I made it? According to Ross, I do the latter. I do not think *forward* and try to foresee the consequences of keeping the promise. Instead, I think *backward.* I did make the promise, and I have an obligation to keep it. Thus, the relationship between me (the promisor) and the person to whom I made the promise (the promisee) is a morally significant one. I have a special duty to that person because I made the promise. The same holds for someone from whom I've borrowed money, for someone who has done me many favors, for someone I have injured, and so forth. I have a special duty to each of them. If John lends me money, I have a duty to repay him. If I have harmed Mary, I have a duty to make amends. If she has done me a favor, I have a duty to return it.

Ross calls these special duties *prima facie* duties. What is a prima facie duty? Consider these two moral principles: "Do not lie" and "Do not hurt the feelings of others." Certainly, we feel that we should do our best to follow these principles, but in certain cases we cannot follow both. Moral principles often conflict. To allow for potential conflict we might say something like this: All other things being equal, do not lie, and, all other things being equal, do not hurt another's feelings. When phrased that way, the principles do not say that we must *always* tell the truth and avoid hurting the feelings of others. Instead, they tell us how to act *if* no other principle takes precedence in a particular situation.

We might say that such principles are the basis of *conditional* duties—duties that hold in a particular situation *if* no other conditional duty takes precedence. We can then contrast them with *actual* duties, which are the duties we do have in particular situations. Prima facie duties, then, are akin to moral principles prefaced by the words "all other things being equal." They are general principles that may or may not take precedence in particular situations. When one of them does take precedence, it becomes our actual duty.

How are we to tell whether a prima facie duty is our actual duty in a particular situation? How do we decide which of two or more conflicting principles to follow? Unlike the utilitarian, Ross does not provide a method of decision, except to say that we are to consider the situation as carefully as we can, taking into account as many factors as seem to be relevant, and then come upon a reasoned decision as to which is our actual duty. We may be wrong in our decision, but that is the best that we can do. If this answer seems a weak one in comparison with the utilitarian's answer, it is wise to keep in mind two things. First, if we apply the principle of utility at such times, we can never be sure that we have predicted the consequences accurately. Second, it may be a point in Ross's favor that he recognizes that moral dilemmas do not always admit of easy answers.

DEONTOLOGICAL ALTERNATIVES TO ROSS

Ross's form of deontological ethics gives us seven types of prima facie duties, or seven basic moral principles. They are: (1) duties of *fidelity* (promise-keeping, honesty, etc.); (2) duties of *reparation* (making amends for wrongs committed); (3) duties of *gratitude;* (4) duties of *justice;* (5) duties of *beneficence* (doing good for others); (6) duties of *self-improvement;* (7) duties of *nonmaleficence* (refraining from injuring others). But it is possible to have a deontological ethical system with only one basic moral principle. It might be said, for example, that the *golden rule* ("Do unto others as you would have them do unto you") provides the basis of such a system.

Immanuel Kant (1724–1804), perhaps the most influential of all deontologists, has claimed that the foundation of morality is what he called the *categorical imperative.* (He called the principle an *imperative* because it is phrased as a command. He called it *categorical* because it is meant to be followed without regard to any other ends. That is, whatever interests we may have in a particular situation, we are to follow the basic moral principle rather than those interests.) Kant's categorical imperative may be paraphrased as follows: Whenever you choose a particular action, ask yourself whether you would be willing to accept your principle for making the choice as a universal law of nature governing the actions of everyone. If so, choose that action. If not, don't.

Suppose, for example, that I am about to break a promise because keeping it would be inconvenient. In that case, I am to ask myself whether I would will a world in which everyone broke a promise whenever keeping it was inconvenient. Not only *would* I not will such a world, Kant claimed, but I *could* not do so. Such a world is impossible, because if everyone were to break promises for such a reason, the institution of promising would disappear.

The problem with Kant's categorical imperative is that it is possible to provide different principles for the same action. It is also possible that one principle will pass the test of the categorical imperative, while the other will not. Suppose, for example, that by telling a lie I can save my brother from being unjustly killed. The principle behind the choice may be "Tell a lie whenever you can save your brother from being unjustly killed," but it might also be "Tell a lie whenever it is in someone's interest to do so." Although I would not be inclined to will the latter as a natural law governing everyone's behavior, the former seems eminently more acceptable. Thus, in many cases the categorical imperative can give conflicting results. If I decide to act on one principle, I ought to do what I have decided. If I decide to act in the same way on a different one, I ought not to do it.

Finally, Ross's ethics may be characterized as *rule-deontologism.* That is, the rightness of an act is determined by certain prima facie duties, or general principles, or general rules. Some philosophers, however, have taken positions which might be termed *act-deontologism.* According to such a view, the rightness of an act is determined independently of any moral principle. Act-deontologists, then, deny what we claimed in the beginning of this chapter, namely, that all particular moral judgments are based on moral principles.

How, then, are moral judgments made? There seem to be two possibilities. First, an act-deontologist might claim that we must *intuit* what is right in each individual case. We are forced to do this because each case is different from all others and, consequently, no general rules can be of more than provisional help. This view is often called *situation ethics.* In its most extreme form it holds that every individual situation makes its own demands, and we must choose what is right for that situation without the help of moral principles.

Second, an act-deontologist may say that the rightness of an act is not something to be discovered by the use of general principles *or* by any such faculty as intuition. Rather, whether an act is right depends on our own *decision* that it is right. This seems to be the view of some (but not all) philosophers called *existentialists,* including Jean-Paul Sartre (1905–1980). Such philosophers argue that the central fact about human beings is human freedom. The price we must pay for this freedom is the necessity of constantly choosing who we will be. And to choose who we will be is, in part, to create our own values. Although we try to mask this freedom by appealing to the authority of other persons or general principles of action, the source of all values is our own freedom. Thus, it is finally our own decision in a particular case that makes an action right.

Act-deontological ethics raises a number of questions about the nature of moral judgments and our knowledge of right and wrong. We shall turn to such questions in the following chapter. For now, it is sufficient to say that few philosophers have been convinced that there are *no* relevant similarities among individual cases, such that these cases cannot be covered by a general moral principle. Besides, if a judgment is *not* made on principle, it is difficult to see how it can be considered a *moral* judgment. That is, individual moral judgments seem to require *some* standard of rightness and wrongness.

THE UTILITARIAN RESPONSE

It may seem that the deontologist has the better claim to have captured our basic moral principles, but we should not conclude our discussion without considering how the utilitarian might respond to what has been said so far.

Beginning with the objection that we usually reason backward instead of forward when deciding, say, to keep a promise, we should note that few utilitarians would disagree with that. Once again, utilitarians recognize the need for general rules of thumb to facilitate moral decision-making. Since it is inconvenient to apply the principle of utility directly before making every decision, we reason that certain kinds of behavior will more often than not maximize utility and then behave accordingly. Thus, it might be said that what Ross calls prima facie duties are nothing but utilitarian rules of thumb. Only when they conflict do we apply the principle of utility directly. The deontologist, of course, denies that we appeal to utility in cases of conflict. But is he right?

One way of attempting to settle the matter is to follow Ross's advice. Let us abstractly describe a case of conflicting prima facie duties. I am on my way to keep a promise when I come upon someone in distress. Assuming that it is impossible both to keep the promise and help the person, what am I to do? Keep the promise or help the person? Obviously, we cannot answer the question on the basis of such a meager description. So let us ask ourselves what else we need to know. What questions must we ask before we can decide what to do? What, exactly, must we consider when we fully examine the situation?

Well, we certainly want to know what the nature of the promise is, and also what the nature of the distress is. Did I promise, say, to stop downtown to look at a Christmas display someone thought I might like, or did I promise to deliver urgently needed medical supplies? Is the distress minor, such as a cinder in the eye, or is it more serious, such as a heart attack?

But there is much more we want to know. Can I get someone else to keep the promise? Can someone else relieve the stress? Can I make it up to the promisee later? Will the promisee understand? Am I capable of relieving the distress? Does the promise involve more people than just me and the promisee? To whom did I make the promise? A friend? My daughter? A stranger?

When we consider such questions, we notice that it is easy to construe them as attempts to determine the consequences of the alternatives. Each of them seems to be seeking information concerning the potential damage to be done by either breaking the promise or leaving the person in distress.

Does this hold for the questions about the identity of the promisee? At first glance it might seem that it does not. It seems, rather, that we are trying to determine whether the promisee and I stand in a morally significant relation. But the utilitarian can respond as follows:

Why is it important to determine whether the promisee is a friend, say, or a daughter? Isn't it because of the difference in consequences that might result? Consider the importance of keeping a promise to your own child. It is crucial that a daughter be able to trust her parents. Without that trust, it is likely that a number of problems will arise. Moreover, a young child is often unable to understand why a promise has been broken, and is therefore likely to feel especially hurt when one is.

Similarly, why does it make a difference if the promisee is a friend? Perhaps it is because we are concerned that a broken promise will disrupt the friendship. On the other hand, it may be because we can count on the friend to be more understanding than someone else and not be as offended by the broken promise as someone else might be. In either case, we are concerned with the consequences.

In fact, if we consider the question of morally significant relations, and the related charge that utilitarianism oversimplifies our relations to others, we see that the utilitarian may have a case. What, after all, is it that makes a relation morally significant? Why, for example, do I have a special duty to my daughter? Isn't it because she depends on me in a way that others do not? If I don't feed her, she does not eat. If I do not feed her friends, they go home to eat. But notice. If her friend is spending the week with us, that friend is as much dependent on me as my daughter, in which case I seem to have exactly the same special duty to the friend.

The point is that such relations are morally significant because they put us in a unique position to do harm. All other things being equal, the same thing done to my daughter and to someone else will have very different consequences. And once we recognize this, we can say that utilitarianism may not be guilty of oversimplification. When I determine what good or harm will come to my daughter, the fact that she is my daughter is crucial in my deliberations. And in that case I am taking into account morally significant relations.

The same seems to hold true in the case of the relation between promisee and promisor. What makes such a relation morally significant? When I make a promise, I put myself in a unique position to do harm. If asked to do something for another and I refuse, that person can always ask somebody else. But once I accept, that person is dependent upon me. If I don't keep the promise or arrange for someone else to keep it, it does not get done. And if it is a serious promise, serious harm can result from my failure to keep it. That is the moral significance of the relation, the utilitarian might say. And in counting the damage done by breaking the promise, I am considering whatever is morally significant in the promise.

Deontologists counter such arguments by saying that if we follow such reasoning, we will often break promises when we should not. Consider a promise made to a dying man on a desert island. He asks that his fortune be left to his cat and we, in order to make his last moments as comfortable as possible, promise to honor his wishes. The man dies and we are picked up the next day. Should we relay the man's wishes or say instead that he asked that half his fortune go to his family and the rest to various charities? Utility is certainly maximized by breaking the promise here, but does that mean that we should? Many deontologists say that we should not break the promise. My own students are divided on the issue, but more think that the promise should be kept. Still, it does not seem obviously wrong to say that, since no one is hurt by the *breaking* of such a promise, while many people will be helped, and since the man's family will be hurt by the *keeping* of the promise, it is right to break it.

Similarly, the utilitarian has a response to the charge that he does not adequately take fairness into account. What, after all, is fairness? Suppose we have a pie to be distributed four ways. How should it be cut? One answer is that it should be divided equally. Someone who answers this way has an *egalitarian* conception of fairness. But someone else might say that the fair thing to do is to divide it according to need. If four pieces of pie are to be distributed, cut the pie unevenly and give the largest piece to the one who is hungriest. Someone who answers this way has what we may call a *Marxist* conception of fairness—to each according to need. Still a third person might say that the fair thing to do is to divide the pie such that the person who has done the most to earn it gets a larger share than the others. Such a person has a *merit* conception of fairness. The important point here is that although the three people disagree on how the pie should be cut and distributed, and although each might accuse the others of being unfair, each has as good a claim as the others to taking fairness into account. Thus, the entire question of fairness is far murkier than it first appears. When two people disagree, it is not always the case that one is being fair and the other not. It may simply be a matter of differing conceptions of fairness.

Let us see how this applies to utilitarianism. Might not the utilitarian say that he is being just as fair as the deontologist? After all, when deciding on the right course of action, the utilitarian takes everybody into account and weighs the benefit and harm that might come to each individual with perfect equality. Nobody counts more than anyone else. Everyone is treated evenly. What could be more fair than that? Utilitarians have a more difficult time when it comes to the matter of causing direct harm. Here, it seems, they are forced to say that our intuitions are wrong. In our third case, for example, they must say that the right thing to do is to perform the transplant. But it is always open to the utilitarian to provide the following defense:

"Our intuitions are wrong, and I can explain why they are wrong. It is impossible for small children to apply the principle of utility directly. They cannot predict the consequences of their actions, nor can they realize what causes pain and pleasure in a number of cases. Besides, they are too self-centered to apply the principle correctly. So, if little Mary throws her building blocks at little Johnny, we don't tell her that she should only hit someone else when she can achieve a greater good by doing so. We just tell her that it's wrong to hurt others. Of course, this is just a utilitarian rule of thumb, but through constant repetition and conditioning it takes on a stronger role in the child's moral conscience. As we grow older, we become aware of exceptions to the rule, but when it comes to hard cases such as the transplant case, we fail to recognize that performing the transplants is the right thing to do."

What about our final case, in which the father allowed his own family to die in order to save the town leader and his family? Once again, the utilitarian must hold that our intuitions are wrong. And, once again, he can attempt to explain why they are wrong. The explanation might go like this:

"It is not that we really believe that it was the father's *duty* to save his family rather than the town leader and his family. Rather, it is that we are horrified that the man even stopped to *ask* himself what was right in such a situation. There are times when we hope that a person would instinctively act out of love, without stopping to consider whether the decision is the right one. At such times, even to consider such matters seems cold and calculating. But if we do stop to consider, we must concede that the father did the right thing."

THE FINAL WORD?

Has the utilitarian adequately defended himself? Or do the deontological criticisms of utilitarianism still hold? Although most contemporary moral philosophers are deontologists, the matter remains far from closed.

For one thing, some philosophers inclined toward utilitarianism are currently attempting to revise utilitarianism in such a way as to avoid the objections we have considered. Whether they will be successful remains to be seen.

For another, some utilitarians argue that we should not take our intuitions as the final word. Such philosophers argue that it is not the job of the moral philosopher to provide us with the basic principles that *actually* underlie our moral judgments, but to provide us with the principles that *should* underlie them. That is, they argue that even if we are not utilitarians, we should be. Whether this line of argument will prove successful also remains to be seen.

STUDY QUESTIONS

1. What are some of the distinguishing features of moral judgments?
2. What is the principle of utility? Why does Mill also call it the greatest happiness principle?
3. What are the chief reasons for accepting utilitarianism?
4. Ross accuses the utilitarian of ignoring the personal nature of duty. Why does he make that charge? How can the utilitarian respond?
5. Why is the distinction between permitting harm and causing harm morally important? Is the utilitarian sufficiently sensitive to the distinction?
6. Both the utilitarian and deontologist accept the principle that we ought to keep our promises. The utilitarian characterizes it as a utilitarian rule of thumb, while the deontologist characterizes it as a prima facie duty. What's the difference?
7. It is often said that utilitarians will sometimes consider unfair actions to be right. Why? How can the utilitarian respond?
8. The utilitarian and deontologist give different views about the direction of moral reasoning. How do they differ? Which better captures the way that *you* reason when you reason morally?
9. We considered utilitarian alternatives to Mill's views and deontological alternatives to Ross's. What are the distinguishing features of these alternatives? Which do you prefer? Why?

GLOSSARY

Act-utilitarianism. (See *utilitarianism.*)

Categorical imperative. In the moral philosophy of Immanuel Kant, the basic moral command. It requires that, before we choose an action, we ask ourselves whether we can accept our principle for acting as an exceptionless law determining the actions of all people. If we cannot, we are not to choose that action.

Counterexample. An example demonstrating the inadequacy of a theory, hypothesis, or definition.

Deontological ethics. The view that the rightness or wrongness of actions is not determined by their consequences.

Ethical egoism. The view that it is always right to do what is in one's own self-interest and never right to do what is not in one's own self-interest.

Ethical hedonism. The view that pleasure is the only thing that is intrinsically good.

Existentialism. A philosophical movement dating back to Søren Kierkegaard (1813–1855). Typically, existentialists examine human reality from a subjective point of view and emphasize human freedom and responsibility, in addition to such phenomena as anxiety and guilt.

Greatest happiness principle. John Stuart Mill's fundamental moral principle: An action is right if, among the alternatives, it creates the greatest happiness for everybody concerned, where everybody concerned is counted equally. Also called the *principle of utility.*

Ideal utilitarianism. Form of utilitarianism according to which there are other intrinsic goods in addition to pleasure.

Instrumental value. The value that something has because of its ability to bring about some goal. Instrumental value is contrasted with *intrinsic value,* which is the value that something has for its own sake, without regard to any further goal.

Intrinsic value. (See *instrumental value.*)

Maximization of utility. The creation of the greatest balance of good over bad.

Prima facie duty. A conditional duty. To say that an action is our prima facie duty is to say that we ought to do it unless some other duty takes precedence.

Principle of utility. (See *greatest happiness principle.*)

Rule-utilitarianism. (See *utilitarianism.*)

Situation ethics. The view that the rightness of an action is not determined by the application of general principles, but by the unique features of the situation in which an individual must act.

Universalizability. That feature of moral judgments according to which any person making a moral judgment in a particular case must be willing to make the same judgment in all relevantly similar cases. If, for example, it is right for me to perform a certain action, it is right for anyone else in the same circumstances to do the same thing.

Utilitarianism. The view that the rightness and wrongness of actions is determined by their consequences. According to *act-utilitarianism,* an action is right if it produces a greater balance of good over bad. According to *rule-utilitarianism,* an action is right if it is required by a rule that would produce the greatest balance of good over bad if generally followed.

Utilitarian rule of thumb. A convenient guide to action adopted by act-utilitarians. Since, for example, the consequences of keeping a promise will usually be better than the consequences of breaking one, act-utilitarians will usually keep promises without first considering the consequences. But if they have any reason to think that, in a given case, the consequences of breaking a promise might be greater, they will add up the consequences of breaking it and those of keeping it and then choose the alternative with the best consequences.

Chapter 4

THE NATURE
OF MORAL
KNOWLEDGE

"Columbus sailed to America in 1492."

"There are electrons."

"The sun will rise tomorrow."

"There is a book in front of me."

"Stealing is wrong."

Most of us would claim to *know* what is expressed by the above sentences. That is, we would claim that the above statements are *true*. Moreover, in the case of the first four statements we would also say that anyone who expressed the opposite point of view is *wrong*. If Columbus did in fact sail to America in 1492, then the claim that he did not sail to America in 1492 must be *false*. And if anyone claimed to know that Columbus did not sail to America in 1492, we would rightly reply that the speaker knew no such thing. The speaker believes it, but believes falsely.

How do we know that Columbus sailed to America in 1492? Most of us learned it from teachers, books, parents, and the like. That is, we learned it from a reliable source, who, in turn, learned it from another reliable source. All of these reliable sources lead, eventually, to an eyewitness account of Columbus's sailing. Similarly, we learned of the existence of electrons through a chain of reliable sources terminating in the experiments of experimental physicists.

In the case of our third and fourth statements, our knowledge is firsthand. We have seen the sun rise every morning over many years and infer that the sun will rise tomorrow because it has risen every other morning. And each of you knows that there is a book in front of you because you are now observing it.

What about our fifth statement: "Stealing is wrong"? Although, once again, most of us would claim that it is true, we may nevertheless feel that it is different from the others. First of all, the source of our knowledge is somewhat mysterious. We have learned it from a number of sources, but the chain of sources does not seem to terminate in any observation. No one can *see* that stealing is wrong in the way that one can see that there is a book in front of one. Nor does there seem to be any experiment that can provide telling *evidence* that stealing is wrong. Thus, although we can be *taught* that stealing is wrong, we do not seem able to *discover* it through observation.

There is another reason why our final statement may strike us as different from the others. Suppose that someone had grown up in a culture where stealing under certain circumstances was not only permitted, but required. Suppose that, in this culture, anyone who had been offended by another was required to steal from that person or a member of that person's family. In that case, the person reared in that culture would deny that stealing is wrong. Would such a person be making a mistake, like someone who denied that Columbus sailed to America in 1492? If such a person claimed to know that stealing is often the right thing to do, would we be justified in telling him that he knows no such thing?

The problem is this: Although we are confident in many of our moral judgments, and claim to know that they are true, we are not always prepared to grant them universal validity. Sometimes we feel that they are valid only in a particular culture. Some people go even further, and claim that moral judgments are valid only for the individuals who express them.

These two features separating our fifth statement from the others are, of course, related. In part, it is the belief that differences in opinion regarding moral judgments cannot be settled by observation that tempts us to deny the universal validity of such judgments.

It is this temptation that will concern us in the present chapter. But before turning our attention to it, we should clear up one possible source of confusion. To question whether moral judgments are universally valid is *not* to question the claim made in the preceding chapter—that moral judgments are *universalizable*. To say that moral judgments are universalizable is to say that all cases that are relevantly similar must be judged in the same way. If I judge it wrong for someone else to steal a book from the university book store, I must say that it would be wrong for me to steal a book in the same circumstances. But that is not to say, for example, that someone raised in a different culture must judge the same way that I do. Universalizability is a matter of *consistency* in one's own judgments; it is not a matter of *agreement* among judgers.

ETHICAL RELATIVISM

To deny that moral judgments are universally valid is to deny that such statements as "Stealing is wrong" and "Stealing is not wrong" must always contradict each other. "Columbus sailed to America in 1492" and "Columbus did not sail to America in 1492" do contradict each other. Both statements cannot be true. But matters are different with moral judgments, some have argued. Two moral judgments that seem to contradict each other can both be true. But how can that be?

Consider the following two sentences:

"John eats meat."
"John does not eat meat."

Assuming that "John" refers to the same person in both cases, the above sentences contradict each other. Both claims, as they stand, cannot be true. But it is not difficult to remove the contradiction. Suppose we add a few words to the sentences, to make them read as follows:

"John eats meat Saturday through Thursday."
"John does not eat meat on Friday."

The two amended sentences do not contradict each other. We have removed the contradiction by *flagging* our original sentences. That is, we have added to each a phrase tying the claim to a particular time. We have *time-flagged* our original claims.

Sentences can be flagged in a number of ways. We can, for instance, *culture-flag* sentences. Take the following contradictory sentences:

"Polygamy is legal."
"Polygamy is not legal."

The contradiction can be removed by tying the claims to different cultures, as follows:

"Polygamy is legal in Saudi Arabia."
"Polygamy is not legal in the United States."

We can also *person-flag* sentences, as when we change:

"John is in love," and

"John is not in love"

to the following:

"John is in love with Mary," and

"John is not in love with Jane."

Some philosophers feel that moral judgments *must* be flagged before we can say that they are true or false. That is, they feel that such statements as "Stealing is wrong" must be read as something like "Stealing violates the norms of such and such a culture," or "Stealing violates the principles of behavior of such and such a person." And only when we know what culture or person is being referred to can we know whether the claim is true.

Such people are called *ethical relativists*, because they hold that moral judgments are true or false relative to a particular reference point. Thus, "Stealing is wrong" will be true or false depending on who says it, where it is said, or when it is said.

Cultural Relativism

Perhaps the most plausible form of relativism is the form that requires that moral judgments be culture-flagged. This view is called *cultural relativism*. Why would anyone be a cultural relativist? We can readily pick out two reasons.

First, it appears to be undeniable that morals do vary from culture to culture. This variation is probably most apparent in sexual morality. In some cultures, as we have noted, polygamy is morally acceptable. Beyond that, there are cultures in which homosexuality is accepted and others where it is not. Furthermore, there are cultures that restrict sex to married couples and others in which pre- and extra-marital sex are not only accepted but encouraged.

But cultural variation is hardly restricted to sexual morality. Anthropologist Ruth Benedict (1887–1948), perhaps the most vigorous defender of cultural relativism, has marshaled a wide range of cases in support of her view. Included among her cases is a practice that existed among the Kwakiutl, a Pacific Northwest tribe, at the end of the nineteenth century. When a relative died, by whatever means, members of the mourning family would "avenge" the death by killing arbitrarily selected members of another tribe. More recently, there are the Ik of Uganda, a people constantly on the brink of starvation. Among the Ik, there is a minimal sense of parental obligation, and children reaching the age of three are made to fend for themselves.

The second consideration in favor of cultural relativism is this. Morality, it has been claimed, is a purely social institution. It comes about only when society comes about. Outside of society, humans live in a *state of nature*, in which there are no common ways of life, no norms of behavior, no moral obligations and no distinction between right and wrong. In a state of nature, the only guide to behavior is self-interest. Only when society is introduced does the distinction between right and wrong come to exist.

But in that case, the argument continues, morality is merely a matter of social convention. It is as much a cultural norm as etiquette or traffic regulations. What makes something right or wrong are the conventions of the particular culture. Societies need morality, just as they need rules of the road, but in both cases all that matters is that the system maintain order. It makes no difference whether, as in America, we drive on the right side of the road, or, as in England, on the left, just as long as the procedure is generally followed. It would be absurd for us to go to England and attempt to overturn their traffic conventions, just as it would be absurd for us to condemn the British for using a knife and fork differently than we do. The situation is similar with morality, it is argued. Morality is a mere matter of convention. Whether we have one or more spouses is merely a cultural norm.

It is the purely conventional nature of morality, on this view, that explains why moral knowledge is simply a matter of transmission from one generation to the next, and does not find its source in the observation of any distinct moral facts. According to cultural relativism, there are no moral facts apart from the conventions of one's culture. Many people have been troubled by cultural relativism, though. To see why, let us shift our attention from sexual morality to other aspects of morality.

In America, it is fairly common and certainly morally permissible to eat fresh lobster. In many restaurants, the procedure is this. One steps over to a lobster tank, selects a live lobster of one's choosing and then returns to the table while the lobster is thrown live into boiling water.

But suppose that, in some other culture, the procedure is a bit different. Suppose that there is a playpen, instead of a tank, and that it is filled, not with lobsters, but with live babies. In this imagined culture, one walks to the playpen, selects a baby, and then returns to the table while the baby is thrown live into boiling water. If morality is simply a matter of social convention, like etiquette, we should be no more justified in interfering with this practice than we would be justified in interfering with the British way of using a knife and fork. Indeed, should we decide to "rescue" the babies from their fate, we would be guilty of a crime analogous to cattle rustling. But is this really a case in which we would be content to "do as the Romans do"?

But notice—that we find such a situation abhorrent does not mean that relativism is a mistaken view of morality. That we don't like a view is one thing; that it is false is something else entirely. Still, our abhorrence does lessen our inclination to accept it. Can we find any arguments in support of our new inclination?

We can begin by re-examining the arguments *for* cultural relativism. The first argument, it will be recalled, is that different cultures do in fact have different moralities. Cultures do vary in their beliefs as to what is right and wrong. But this argument is not by itself compelling. Just because there is disagreement, that is no reason to conclude that one culture or more cannot be wrong about its beliefs. Suppose that some cultures still believed that the earth is the center of the universe. Cultural differences regarding such matters would not lead us to adopt cultural relativism regarding astronomy. Such cultures, we would maintain, are wrong. If cultural differences would not lead us to accept cultural relativism in astronomy, why should we accept cultural relativism in ethics?

The second argument begins with the claim that morality is just a social institution. Since morality is created by a culture, it is the culture that determines what is right and wrong. There can be no higher appeal. But we can grant that morality arises only within a society without accepting relativism.

Let us agree that the awareness of moral obligation arises only within society. Let us also agree that no one can have any conception of morality before being introduced to the morality of some society. In that case, to first learn about morality is to learn the morality of a particular society. But it may still be possible that, once we do develop a sense of right and wrong, we can then come to know of some higher morality, by which we can judge the morality of any particular society. That is, we may discover some universal moral principles that ought to hold everywhere, despite the disagreements among cultures. If there really are such universal principles, we can say that even though eating babies is permissible according to the moral principles of our imagined culture, the practice is decidedly immoral according to these universal principles.

Of course, merely raising the possibility of such universal moral principles does nothing to defeat the relativist. Are there such principles? How can we come to know of them? Who is to say that the morality of any particular culture does not measure up to them? What is moral knowledge if not the knowledge of the morals of one's own culture?

ETHICAL INTUITIONISM

In the beginning of this chapter, we contrasted ethical judgments with four statements most of us would consider true. Each of the four, it was said, first came to be known through some form of observation. But aren't there some things we can know in some other way? Consider the following:

"Equals added to equals are equal."

"Everything is what it is."

The first statement, of course, is one of Euclid's axioms of geometry. It says that if line A is equal in length to line B, and if line C is equal in length to line D, then the line composed of A and C is equal to the line composed of B and D. How can we know that this is true? Well, we can take two five-inch lines and add each to a three-inch line, measure the totals to see if they are equal, and then repeat the process for a very large number of pairs. But that is entirely unnecessary. Mere reflection on the axiom is enough to assure us of its truth.

Similarly, we can assure ourselves that the second statement is true by mere reflection. This statement, known as the law of identity, says the following of anything at all: If it is a certain sort of thing, then it is that sort of thing. If it's a ball, then it's a ball; if it's a duck, then it's a duck; if it's a lamp, then it's a lamp, and so forth. How, one may wonder, could this possibly be false? Such statements are often said to be *self-evident* truths, meaning that they require no proof or evidence. Their truth is obvious to anyone who understands them.

Many philosophers have claimed that our knowledge of basic moral principles is of the same kind. According to them, the basic moral truths are also self-evident. Such philosophers are often called *ethical intuitionists.*

It is important to note that ethical intuitionists do not claim that we are born believing these basic moral truths. Nor do they claim that we are born knowing the distinction between right and wrong. Nor do they claim that we have some special moral faculty in addition to reason and the five senses. They claim, rather, that once we have learned the relevant moral concepts and reached a certain level of maturity and instruction, we can then assure ourselves by reflection that certain moral principles are true. Once again, there is an analogy to Euclid's axiom. One must learn the relevant geometric concepts before one can tell that the axiom is self-evident. It is not a truth known or available to infants.

Thus, the ethical intuitionist has an answer to the cultural relativist. Even though we must learn about morality from others, even though there is no awareness of the distinction between right and wrong without a society, that does not mean that there can be no moral principles apart from those of individual cultures. Nor does it mean that there can be no universal morality by which we might judge the morality of any particular culture.

It is fair to say, I think, that in our daily lives most of us behave like ethical intuitionists. Whatever our basic moral commitments, they do strike us as self-evident, and we see neither a need to defend them nor a way of doing so. If someone does not accept them, we do not try to convince that person by rational argument. Rather, we assume that the person is insane, or some sort of moral monster. Think, for example, of how we tend to view Hitler. Think also of how, when confronted by a particularly heinous crime, we say and hear such things as "The killer must be insane!"

But there are difficulties with intuitionism. First, there is an important difference between ethical judgments and Euclid's axiom. Although it appears that we do not *need* evidence in support of the latter, we can confirm it whenever we like. That is, even if we can *know* that it is true without observing that it is true, it is still possible to observe that the axiom holds up in a particular case. Remember, it was said earlier that it may be unnecessary to examine individual cases before coming to accept its truth. It was not said that such examination is impossible.

In the case of ethical judgments, however, observation seems entirely beside the point. We cannot, for example, watch somebody commit armed robbery and *see* the wrongness of the act. But in that case, how can we decide who is right when intuitions conflict? Or, for that matter, how can we ever know that there is anything to intuit? How can we know that our "intuitions" are anything other than the product of social conditioning? Without answers to such questions, intuitionism must remain suspect.

Moreover, how can we *explain* conflicting intuitions? One noted intuitionist, W. D. Ross, claims that it is self-evident that in most cases it is wrong to lie. Suppose that someone else were to respond as follows:

"I always lie when it's easier to do so than to tell the truth. And why shouldn't I? After all, what's wrong with lying if no one gets hurt? Nothing at all that I can think of. The only reason you think lying is wrong is because your parents beat it into your head when you were a child. But why did they do that? Because they couldn't keep an eye on you all the time, so they decided to turn you into their own little FBI. They tell you not to play with Johnny. But if you lie about where you've been, they can never know whether you're obeying them or not. So they teach you that lying is wrong, so you'll inform on yourself. That's why you think lying is wrong. But if you really think about it, there's no reason to accept it."

How can we explain the disagreement between Ross and our defender of lying? Notice, the speaker seems rational enough, and he certainly seems to understand the relevant concepts, just as he seems to have reflected on the matter a good deal. How is it that he denies what Ross takes to be self-evident, even though he would not deny that equals added to equals are equal, or that everything is what it is?

The intuitionist can have recourse only to a notion of some sort of moral blindness, akin to color blindness. But there are problems with this move. When people are color blind, we can point to defective parts of their visual apparatus responsible for the condition. But in the case of "moral blindness" we can point to no such apparatus responsible for the discrimination of right and wrong; hence, we can point to no defects responsible for the "blindness."

It seems, then, that ethical intuitionism is not an adequate response to ethical relativism. Is there someplace else to turn?

VALUES, CRITERIA, AND FUNCTION

Perhaps it is best at this point to step back briefly from ethics in order to examine some other value judgments that do not seem to be relative. Consider the following:

"This is a good carving knife."
"John is a good baseball player."
"Mary is a good surgeon."

Presumably, if two people knew all the facts about the knife, Mary, and John, chances are very high that they would not disagree. In the first case, if the knife has a strong blade that can hold a sharp edge longer than most knives, and if it has a comfortable handle that can be gripped securely, and if its construction is such that the knife can be expected to last a reasonable length of time, it is a good carving knife. Similarly, if John maintains a batting average of .300 and manages to knock in over a hundred runs a season, and if he is charged with few errors in the field, he is a good baseball player. And if Mary performs her operations successfully, does not lose her patients on the operating table, and works quickly and without error, she is a good surgeon.

This does not mean that disagreement is never possible. The possibility of disagreement is most pronounced in some comparative cases. Suppose, for example, that we are comparing a shortstop who consistently bats around .320 but is weak when it comes to home runs and runs batted in, to a centerfielder who is always near the top of the league in home runs and runs batted in but maintains a .250 batting average. Depending on whether we think that power or batting average is more important, we might argue that either is better. But nobody familiar with their respective records and the game of baseball could reasonably deny that both are good baseball players.

Why not? Because terms like "baseball player," "carving knife," and "surgeon" are what we may call *function words*. That is, if someone is a baseball player, he has a certain function to perform, and that function is defined by the rules of baseball. Baseball is a game in which the side having the most runs at the end wins. Therefore, a player's function is to help his team score runs and to prevent the other team from scoring runs. And he performs this dual function by getting on base, scoring other runners, and fielding and throwing the baseball. So someone is a good baseball player if he gets on base, knocks in runs, and catches and throws without error. Similarly, the function of a carving knife is to cut meat, and the sharper and stronger the blade, the better able the knife to perform the function. So something is a good carving knife if it has a sharp, strong blade. Finally, surgeons have their purpose as well, and there are certain characteristics that people must have to perform that function, and if they have them they are good surgeons.

The above tells us something about judgments that something is "a good such-and-such." We call something good if it meets certain standards, or *criteria*, and at least in a good many cases, these criteria are determined by the function the thing is intended to serve.

Similar remarks apply to judgments about what people *ought* to do, or what it is *right* for them to do. Consider a game of chess, the point of which is to checkmate the opponent's king before the opponent can checkmate one's own king. Thus, in chess, one *ought* to protect one's king and penetrate the opponent's defense. Also, it is *right* to make the moves that lead to these goals. Therefore, judgments about what one ought to do or what it is right for someone to do are also closely related to function.

Let us now turn our attention back to moral judgments. When we say that someone is morally good, or that it is morally right to do something, or that someone ought morally to behave in a certain way, our judgments are of a very *general* sort. That is, we are judging the person not as a ball player or surgeon or performer of any other narrow role. We are judging that person *as a person.* To be morally good is to be a good person. To do the morally right thing is to do what one ought to do as a person.

Generally, we think it morally right to perform our narrow functions. Generally, we think it morally right for ball players to hit home runs, farmers to grow crops, lawyers to defend their clients, and so forth. There are times, however, when the situation is reversed. Such was the case with the Watergate cover-up, many people feel. Although it is generally right for a member of the White House staff to serve the interests of the president, the moral duties of Nixon's staff did not coincide with their duties as members of the staff. And, in such cases, our moral duties are expected to take precedence. As stressed in the previous chapter, moral principles are *overriding* principles. They take precedence over all others.

We now have a possible response to the ethical relativist. If we have, as persons, a specifiable function, then we can hope that this function will generate a set of criteria that determines a universal morality for all people. Do we, as persons, have a specifiable function? At first, the answer would seem to be no. We are not artifacts, like a carving knife. Nor does life strike us as a game, like baseball, that has predefined rules that give each of us a role to play. But let us take a closer look.

Theological Ethics

Although it would be misleading to say that the great world religions view human beings merely as God's artifacts, or that they view life as a game bearing the same relationship to God that baseball does to its inventor, Abner Doubleday, it would be correct to say that *many* of them do view us as God's creatures, and that they all conceive of human life as having a role to play in some larger design. Since this view of human beings is central to most religions, it is not surprising that an important part of religious teaching includes morality. To accept a religion is to accept a view of humanity's essential nature and purpose on earth. Hence, it is also to accept certain criteria of goodness and certain standards of right and wrong. And it is also not surprising that the great world religions have been among the most forceful opponents of ethical relativism.

In light of our current concern, then, might we not say this: Since God has created us and put us here for a purpose, there is a universal morality created by God by which we must judge the moralities of individual cultures. Such a view may be called *theological ethics.*

There are, however, three important objections to such a claim. First, even if God did put us here for a certain purpose, why must we accept God's purpose for us as our own? We are not, after all, mere artifacts. We are responsible and rational human agents, free to set our own goals and define our own purposes. We are not bound to accept those given by God.

The force of this response may be illustrated by two considerations. Suppose, for example, that we are able to create intelligent life in the laboratory, and that our creations were virtually indistinguishable from ourselves. Would our creations be bound by the functions we assign to them, whatever those functions might be? If, for example, we were to decide to make them our slaves, would they be morally bound to accept their chains?

Or suppose that the world is the creation of some bloodthirsty god. Suppose further that this god created us to be like the gladiators of ancient Rome, and that he expects us to fight among ourselves to the death. Would we be morally bound to kill each other off? Once again, the answer seems to be no. But in that case, the mere fact that God has put us here for a purpose, if it is a fact, is not enough to provide a universal morality.

The second objection to theological ethics is that the various religions are themselves social institutions, and that they display as much variation as other social institutions. How can we know which to accept? Is there any one that is *right* to accept? Doesn't the same problem arise here that arises in ethics?

Finally, there is a good deal of controversy over whether there *is* a God, or whether there is any grand design in which we have a predetermined place. We will deal with this controversy in later chapters. For now, it is enough to say that the theists have been unable to convince the atheists. Thus, theological ethics seems to provide no better answer to relativism than intuitionism does.

Ethics and Human Nature

There is one more response to relativism we may consider. According to this response, there is some essential nature that human beings have, and that essential nature determines what a good person is. That is, human beings naturally have certain sorts of ends in life, and the universally valid morality is the one that leads to those ends. A human being's function, then, is a part of the natural human endowment.

Many philosophers have held this view, although they have not always agreed on what the function of a human being is. Two of the most influential proponents of this view are Aristotle (384–322 B.C.) and Friedrich Nietzsche (1844–1900).

It was Aristotle's belief that everything in nature has a goal toward which it naturally strives. This goal constitutes the proper function of that thing. What is the proper function of human beings? Aristotle's answer is *eudaimonia*. Following standard practice, I will translate *eudaimonia* as "happiness." But we must understand that, for Aristotle, happiness is not just a psychological state, but total well-being.

What is happiness? It is, Aristotle says, an activity of the soul in conformity with virtue. But what is virtue? Virtue is the excellence appropriate to a particular type of thing. Since rationality is, for Aristotle, the unique defining characteristic of human beings, human virtue is activity in accord with reason. But reason plays two roles in human life. First, it has a practical role. That is, it guides our behavior in our daily lives. Second, it has a purely intellectual role. That is, it strives for understanding for its own sake.

There are, Aristotle claims, two types of virtue corresponding to these two functions of reason. Corresponding to the first, there are the moral virtues. A morally virtuous person is one whose passions are guided by practical reason. Thus, a morally virtuous person is one who is moderate in his actions, or, in Aristotle's terms, chooses the mean rather than the extremes. Corresponding to the second function of reason are the intellectual virtues. An intellectually virtuous person is one who leads a life of contemplation.

In contrast to Aristotle, Nietzsche claims that the essential element of human beings is what he calls the *will to power*. When this will is not thwarted in people, they strive to enlarge their strength and power over themselves and others. They do not concern themselves with pity for the weak, but recognize obligations only to those of equal strength and power.

Since human beings are healthy only when the will to power is not thwarted, the only acceptable morality is one in accordance with that will. Such a morality was the morality of the ancient Romans, stressing as it did the virtues of courage, nobility, and conquest. Their morality was, as Nietzsche put it, a master morality. In contrast, Christian morality, which advises us, among other things, to turn the other cheek, is viewed as a slave morality. Rather than strength, it celebrates weakness. But to celebrate weakness is to thwart the will to power and, consequently, the will to life itself. Thus it is to be rejected by the healthy.

In contemporary times, the connection between morality and human nature is being advanced by Edward Wilson, a leading figure in the controversial field of *sociobiology*, which attempts to explain social behavior in terms of evolutionary biology. Among Wilson's most controversial claims is that social and cultural institutions among all humans are in part the product of heredity. Just as our physical characteristics developed through eons of evolution, so did our social behavior. The genes that predispose us to forms of social organization beneficial to the species survived through a long process of *natural selection*. Culture, to be sure, plays a role in the determination of social institutions, but the importance of genetic determination is not to be underestimated. Thus, Wilson claims, morality is not *purely* a cultural institution, but has a genetic base as well. He supports this view by pointing to certain universal features of morality, such as the incest taboo and altruism, and arguing that such features are advantageous to the survival of the species. Of course, he does not claim that all cultures prohibit precisely the same interfamily sexual relations. Nor does he claim that all types of altruism can be found in all cultures. His claim is that some incest prohibitions and altruistic norms can be found in all cultures. We are, then, genetically predisposed to ban incest and behave altruistically. Our various cultures determine how these dispositions are worked out in daily life.

If Wilson is right, we are on our way to a deep understanding of the origin of morality. But does his theory take us any closer to a universally valid morality? Wilson thinks that it does. From the standpoint of evolutionary biology, human beings are vehicles for DNA, our genetic material, to reproduce itself. In that

MORAL UNIVERSALS

It is not only the sociobiologists who emphasize similarities across cultures. Some anthropologists have done so as well. Ralph Linton, for example, has claimed that the following are either universal or nearly universal. Regarding sexual morality, there are incest prohibitions, the ideal of lifelong marriages, and limitations on the sexual activity of spouses. Regarding the family, parents are expected to care for children and the children to care for parents in old age, the family functions as an economic unit, and it is expected to support the interests of its members. Linton also points to the recognition of personal property, economic obligations stemming from the exchange of goods and services, and prohibitions against murder and various types of physical aggression. More generally, he claims that all moral systems strive primarily to ensure the successful functioning of the society and secondarily to provide for the needs of individuals within the society. These resemblances can, Linton argues, provide the basis for a universal ethical system. Two factors now stand in the way, however. First, cultures disagree about the relative importance of values. Second, individuals tend to think of themselves primarily as members of a nation or tribe rather than of a world society. But as this narrowness diminishes in the modern world, universal agreement will become easier.

If Linton sounds overly optimistic about the prospects for a universal morality, we may turn to another argument based on resemblances among cultures. Some philosophers have argued that, at least regarding some moral principles, there is no difference in *values* among cultures, but only in beliefs about *matters of fact*. According to this view, every culture condemns and values the same *type* of behavior, but other differences in belief lead to differences about what counts as that type of behavior.

Two cases will illustrate this argument—abortion and slavery. Beginning with abortion, we all recognize that murder is wrong, but different beliefs about the fetus lead to different beliefs about whether abortion is murder. In one view, a fetus is a full-fledged human being. Hence, to abort it is to commit murder. In another view, a fetus is not a full-fledged human being. Hence, to abort it is not murder. Similarly, it can be argued that all cultures recognize that "people like us" are not to be treated like personal property. Unfortunately, there may be disagreement about what counts as people like us. During the period of slavery in America, African blacks were not considered to be relevantly like whites of European descent. The differences in their cultures and skin color were taken to justify the view that they were comparative children, morally and intellectually inferior to whites. Thus, slaveholders did not disagree with us about moral principles. They simply had mistaken beliefs about racial differences. Had they not held these mistaken beliefs, they would not have approved of slavery.

The difficulty with this view is that it assumes that we can make a clear distinction between moral beliefs and beliefs about matters of fact. Is it, for example, purely a factual matter as to whether a fetus is a full-fledged human being or not? Are beliefs about the inferiority or equality of different races purely factual? I think not. Beliefs about how the world is and how we ought to behave toward it are too closely connected to make such a sharp distinction. Therefore, we cannot say that the differences among cultures involve only one kind of belief and not the other.

case, the function of morality is the furtherance of that goal. Thus, continued study in sociobiology will provide the basis for a universal morality.

We have looked at three views of human nature and the ethical implications that have been drawn from them. What stands out is the radical disagreement among them. Indeed, there may very well be less agreement concerning the essential nature of human beings than there is concerning morality.

This lack of agreement raises an important difficulty in any attempt to base morality on a theory of human beings. Is there really such a thing as one essential function of human beings? Aristotle is clearly right that it is normal for people to strive for happiness, just as he is right that rationality is an important element of human nature. Nietzsche's claim that power is an important goal for most people also seems to have some validity. Similarly, Wilson's claim that we are vessels for keeping our DNA intact also has, from a particular perspective, a certain validity. But we may go on to characterize human nature and goals in a number of other ways as well.

But which is *the* function of human beings? Are we primarily rational creatures? Primarily driven by the will to power? Primarily the means of the survival of genes? It seems that such questions do not admit of answers. In fact, to the extent that they admit of any answer at all, it is to the extent that each individual supplies it for himself or herself. Part of being a responsible, rational agent, it seems, is to decide what one's ultimate purposes in life are. Different perspectives provide different answers. And no one perspective forces itself upon us as the only correct one.

RELATIVISM AND MORAL CRITICISM

We seem to have been drawn to two conclusions. First, there appears to be no source of moral knowledge apart from the norms of a culture. Although other sources have been suggested and continue to be accepted by some people, the arguments in support of such sources are far from compelling. In that case, to learn that something is right or wrong is to learn the mores of a particular society.

But the preceding section has led us to another conclusion. Part of being a responsible, rational agent, it was said, is to choose one's own ultimate purposes. But if purposes or functions generate criteria for the making of value judgments, that means that part of being a responsible, rational agent is the choice of moral principles. In that case, we not only learn morality from our culture, but we can criticize and alter that morality. So even if the learning of morality is the learning of some culture's morality, that culture need not supply the final word on right and wrong.

This last point is an important one, which has too often gone unnoticed by opponents of cultural relativism. Many of these opponents have claimed that, if cultural relativism is true, the moral norms of a given culture cannot be criticized. Fortunately, the cultural relativist is not forced to accept that view. Moral disputes can be waged and won by rational argument. Here's how.

First, moral judgments are not arbitrary. They are based on principles, and those principles must be applied consistently. This, once again, is the force of the universalizability requirement. Therefore, individuals can criticize their cultures by pointing out that certain principles are not being applied consistently. This line is often pursued by opponents of abortion, for example, who claim that whatever leads us to condemn the killing of a child should also lead us to condemn the aborting of a fetus.

Moreover, moral beliefs are closely connected to other beliefs. If we can change enough of these other beliefs, we can change the connected moral beliefs. In this regard, we may consider the various civil rights movements of recent times. Certain beliefs about women—that they are physically or emotionally unable to handle certain types of work, for instance—have been responsible for their being denied certain jobs. Anyone convinced that these beliefs are wrong has lost the basis for such discrimination.

Finally, even basic moral principles can be changed by rational argument. Although basic moral principles can often conflict without forcing us to give one up altogether, if it can be shown that one basic moral principle conflicts with others more often than the rest, that may lead someone to question, and reject, that principle.

Thus, to accept cultural relativism is not to accept the adage, "When in Rome, do as the Romans do." Let us return to our extreme example of the imagined culture that treats babies like lobsters. There may be many grounds for criticizing the abhorrent practice. Since the practice extends only to babies, and, presumably, only to some of them, we can accuse the culture of inconsistency. And, if certain beliefs are held by the culture to the effect that the selected babies are different from adults and other babies, we can challenge those beliefs. And if, as is highly improbable, the principle justifying the practice is taken as basic, we can argue that the principle is incongruous with other basic moral commitments of the culture.

THE SOCIAL FUNCTION OF MORALITY

In the preceding section, we looked at three grounds for criticizing the moral norms of a given culture. All turned on one fact—that moral judgments are not made in a vacuum. They are closely connected to other judgments, moral and nonmoral.

A similar point can be made about morality as a social institution. It, too, does not occur in a vacuum. It evolves among other social institutions, and, like these other institutions, it has a particular role to play in society. It is a means of maintaining social stability, of settling conflicts among individual interests, of allowing us to live together as social beings. Thus, we have another basis for criticizing the morality of a given culture. We can point out that certain norms run counter to that role. Morality may be a social convention, but, like other social conventions, it is there for a purpose.

Consider another social convention, the rules of the road. It does not matter

ARE MORAL JUDGMENTS TRUE OR FALSE?

In this chapter, I claimed that value judgments are made according to certain standards, or criteria, and that to say that Mary is a good person is to say that Mary meets the standards by which people are judged. Whether that claim is true or false depends on the standard appealed to. Many philosophers, however, have claimed that such judgments cannot be true or false. According to this view, called *noncognitivism*, to say that someone is a good person or that a certain act is right is not to say anything about the person that can be true or false.

What are we doing when we make a moral judgment? Opinions vary on this point. One type of noncognitivism, called *emotivism*, says that we are doing two things. First, we are expressing our feelings about the person or act judged. That is, we are doing something analogous to cheering or hissing a football team. When the Dallas Cowboys come onto the field, the Dallas fans express their feelings by cheering. The fans of the opposing team express theirs by hissing. Neither side is making a claim about the Cowboys. Neither is saying something about the team that can be true or false. Similarly, part of what we do when we say that stealing is wrong is to say something like "Stealing—hiss!" But we are doing something else as well. We are commanding another person to have the same feelings that we do. That is, we are saying something like, "Disapprove of stealing!" Since commands, like cheers and hisses, cannot be true or false, neither can moral judgments.

Another noncognitivist view is called *prescriptivism*. According to this view, we *are* saying something about Mary when we say she is a good person. We are, in part, claiming that she meets certain standards by which we judge people. But we are doing something else as well. We are commending her. To commend someone is to give her a pat on the back, as it were. It is to add something to the mere description. But to commend is more than to pat someone on the back. It is to guide actions as well. Although commendations are not the same as commands, they do have something in common with them. They guide a person's actions with respect to what is being judged. As prescriptivist R. M. Hare puts it, if I say that Mary is a good person, I commit myself to behaving like her in the relevant ways. Because of this extra commending feature of moral judgments, they cannot be true or false.

Why would anyone accept noncognitivism? There are two major reasons. First, if moral judgments can be true or false, there must be some moral facts that make the judgments true or false. What makes it true that emeralds are green? The fact that emeralds are green. So if it is true that Mary is a good person, it must be the fact that she is good that makes the judgment true.

But what could such a fact be like? Either it is a purely *natural* fact that anyone can observe through the senses or prove by experiment, or it is a *nonnatural* fact that cannot be observed or proved by experiment, but can be discovered only through intuition. But intuitionism is unacceptable, for reasons discussed in this chapter. So is *ethical naturalism*, the view that moral facts are natural facts. As noted in the chapter, we cannot observe moral facts. Nor can we prove that something is good or right by experiment. Therefore, there are no moral facts.

But I have claimed that there are moral facts—the norms of a particular culture. That makes me an ethical naturalist. However, I have also said that we cannot observe goodness or rightness. How can that be?

My answer is this. Moral facts are *social* facts, and the reason we can't observe rightness and goodness is the same as the reason we can't observe other features that depend on social facts. For example, we can't observe someone's United States citizenship. Nor can we observe someone's affiliation with a political party. To be a citizen or a Democrat is to have a certain place in a social network. It is not to have a particular observable trait, like brown hair. We don't learn what it is to be a citizen or a Democrat by observing citizenship or party affiliation. We learn it by being told what it is. The same holds for rightness and goodness. To do the right thing is to behave in accordance with certain social norms. We learn what these norms are by being told about them, and we determine that an action is right or wrong by applying these norms to it.

But this answer does not satisfy noncognitivists. They object to the identification of moral facts with natural facts of any sort, including social facts. This brings us to the second reason for being a noncognitivist. Natural facts, they claim, tell us how the world *is*. Ethics, on the other hand, is not about the way the world *is*, but how it *ought* to be. Its aim is not to *describe*, but to *prescribe*. It is a means of guiding action, not of describing. Therefore, such natural facts as cultural norms cannot be moral facts.

Once again, my answer involves the nature of social facts. Often, when we deal with social institutions, the line between what is the case and what ought to be the case is not a sharp one. It *is*, for example, the president's job to uphold the Constitution. Therefore, any president *ought* to uphold it. Or to take an example closer to home, consider the various games you play. The rules of each game tell you how it *is* played. But they also tell you what you *ought* to do when you play it. According to the rules of football, for instance, the game *is* played by eleven players on each side. Therefore, each team *ought* to have eleven players on the field when the ball is in play.

Noncognitivists object that these are not moral *oughts*. What we ought to do according to the rules of football, they say, and what we morally ought to do are two different matters. And, they add, what we ought to do according to the norms of society and what we morally ought to do are also different matters. A large part of my answer to that, of course, is found in this chapter. But one thing should be added here. When noncognitivists say that what we ought to do according to the rules of society and what we morally ought to do are two different matters, they often mean something like this: Even when we accept that our society's rules tell us what we ought to do in a given case, we can still raise the question whether we really ought to do it. That is, we can ask whether any of society's rules is morally correct. And, having asked that, we can answer no. That fact, they claim, shows that there is a real difference between social *oughts* and moral *oughts*.

But does it? I think it shows something else. It shows that we can criticize the norms of a given society, including our own. It shows that we can ask whether a society ought to adopt different rules. And as I argued in the chapter, the acceptance of cultural relativism does not force us to refrain from criticizing the morality of any society, including our own.

whether everyone drives on the right or left side of the road. What matters is that, once the decision is made, everyone adheres to it. But that does not mean that we can rationally adopt *any* rule of the road. We cannot, for example, rationally adopt this rule: If you are wearing dark socks, drive on the right side; if you are wearing light socks, drive on the left. The reason is obvious. The purpose of such rules is to minimize accidents, and this rule will not accomplish that purpose.

Similarly, we cannot rationally adopt *any* moral rule. Suppose we were to adopt this rule: promises ought to be broken whenever it is convenient to break them. As Kant pointed out, if this rule were accepted by all, the institution of promising would become pointless and soon disappear. And, we might add, its disappearance would result in major social breakdowns.

It is interesting to note how many moral disputes turn on this point. Many people argue, for example, that changes in American sexual morality are leading to the breakdown of the family and, consequently, to a breakdown in social stability. Others argue that changes in our attitudes toward those accused or convicted of crimes are leading to a breakdown of society. (Opponents, on the other hand, may argue that society is changing and morality must change with it or become outmoded.) When people argue this way, they are saying that certain moral norms of their culture run counter to the purpose of morality. That is, they are criticizing the morality of their culture by appealing to the social function of morality. And criticisms of this kind are perfectly consistent with the truth of cultural relativism. Once again, even though morality is a social convention, we are free to point out that some conventions work better than others.

The final word?

Once again, the arguments of this chapter suggest that morality is a social convention and that there is no universal moral standard by which we can judge the moralities of different cultures.

Still, the considerations of the two preceding sections suggest that cultural relativism need not disturb us as much as it otherwise might. Although cultural relativism commits us to granting a good deal of latitude when viewing the moralities of different cultures, it does not commit us to the position that anything goes. Just as certain standards of rationality provide limits to what can count as acceptable rules of the road, so do they provide limits to what can count as acceptable moral principles and judgments.

Let us return once more to our hypothetical society that treats some babies as we treat lobsters. We know of no society like that. And that is no accident. It is extremely difficult to imagine a society where such a practice could arise. That is, it is difficult to imagine a society in which such a practice would be consistent with its moral principles, in which the appropriate beliefs about babies would be prevalent, and in which such a practice could have a rational point.

STUDY QUESTIONS

1. Why do claims to moral knowledge seem to be on a different footing from that of other claims to knowledge?
2. What is ethical relativism? Cultural relativism? Why is cultural relativism often believed to be the most reasonable form of ethical relativism?
3. What is a self-evident truth? Why do ethical intuitionists believe that some moral principles are self-evident truths? Why do other philosophers disagree?
4. Why is it easy to distinguish a good race horse from a bad race horse but difficult (if not impossible) to distinguish a good ant from a bad ant? Under what circumstances could you imagine it easy to distinguish a good ant from a bad ant?
5. Why are religion and morality so intimately connected for the religious person? Does this connection provide an answer to the cultural relativist?
6. What does Aristotle mean by *eudaimonia?* Nietzsche by *will to power?* What role do these concepts play in the moral philosophies of these men?
7. Can a scientific study of human beings provide the basis for a universally valid morality? Why or why not?
8. In the beginning of the chapter we raised the following fear about cultural relativism: If the view is true, does that mean that we cannot criticize the norms of a given culture, however repugnant we find them? Why did that fear turn out to be unfounded?
9. What are moral universals? What bearing do they have on the question of cultural relativism?
10. Why have some philosophers (noncognitivists) claimed that moral judgments are neither true nor false? Why have other philosophers disagreed?

GLOSSARY

Cultural relativism. (See *ethical relativism.*)

Emotivism. A form of *noncognitivism.* According to the emotivist, moral judgments are not true or false, but are expressions of the speaker's feelings and commands to the hearer to feel the same way.

Ethical intuitionism. The view that basic moral principles do not require proof or evidence, but are *self-evident truths.*

Ethical naturalism. The view that moral facts are a species of natural facts, where natural facts are those that can be observed or discovered by the methods of science. This view contrasts with *ethical nonnaturalism,* the theory that moral facts cannot be identified with any natural facts.

Ethical relativism. The view that moral judgments are not universally valid, but are true relative to a particular reference point. According to cultural relativism, the reference point is a particular culture, in which case the truth of moral judgments varies from culture to culture. According to individual relativism, the reference point is an individual person, in which case the truth of moral judgments varies from person to person.

Eudaimonia. Greek word usually translated as "happiness" but closer in meaning to "total well-being." According to Aristotle, *eudaimonia* is the goal toward which all people naturally strive and is therefore the highest good.

Flagging. To flag a sentence is to add a phrase that ties the sentence to a particular time, place, group, person, and so forth. For example, the sentence "It is raining" can be place-flagged to read "It is raining in New York City."

Function-words. Words that refer to objects by designating their functions. Examples are "mouse trap," "carving knife," and "surgeon."

Individual relativism. (See *ethical relativism.*)

Moral universals. Moral principles that, according to some philosophers and anthropologists, are found in all cultures.

Noncognitivism. The view that moral judgments are neither true nor false. (See *emotivism* and *prescriptivism.*)

Prescriptivism. A form of *noncognitivism.* According to the prescriptivist, moral judgments are neither true nor false, but are primarily means of guiding actions. That is, moral judgments do not primarily *desc*ribe persons and actions, but *pre*scribe actions.

Self-evident truths. Truths that do not have to be supported by proof or evidence, but are obvious to those who understand the relevant concepts. Certain elementary truths of mathematics and logic are often thought to be self-evident. *Ethical intuitionists* take certain moral principles to be self-evident also.

State of nature. Form of existence outside of society, in which there are no norms governing behavior and everyone acts out of self-interest.

Theological ethics. View that moral principles have their basis in God or a religious conception of humanity's purpose on earth.

Will to power. According to Nietzsche, the fundamental fact of human nature, which drives people to seek power, strength, mastery, and conquest.

Chapter 5

REASON, SELF-INTEREST, AND THE MORAL POINT OF VIEW

We act for any number of reasons. We open the window to let in some fresh air. We set the alarm for seven o'clock to make an eight o'clock class. We buy a drink to quench our thirst. We call a friend because we want some company. We keep a promise because it's the right thing to do.

Our concern in this chapter is with this last reason: because it's the right thing to do. When we act for this reason, when we ask ourselves whether an action is the right thing to do, when we ask ourselves what the right thing to do is, we are taking a particular point of view. The contemporary American philosopher Kurt Baier calls this point of view the *moral point of view*.

There is no one theory of morals we must accept in order to take the moral point of view. Nor are there any particular moral principles we must accept in order to take the moral point of view. Both the utilitarian and the deontologist adopt it. Both the relativist and the intuitionist adopt it. Both the person who believes that lying is always wrong and the person who believes that lying is usually permissible adopt it.

What distinguishes the moral point of view from all others is simply this: When we adopt it on any given occasion, we do so by concerning ourselves with the moral rightness or wrongness of our actions. To care whether our actions are right, to perform an action *because* it is right, to refrain from performing an action because it is wrong—to do these things is to take the moral point of view.

In the preceding chapters, we sought our basic moral principles, and we asked whether their truth depends on the culture in which we live. In this chapter we ask why we should act on moral principles at all. That is, we ask why we should adopt the moral point of view. Or, as the question is usually posed, we ask this: Why should I be moral?

MORALITY AND PRACTICAL REASON

To ask our question is to ask for a *reason* to adopt the moral point of view. It is to ask why it is *more reasonable* to be moral than not to be moral. Most philosophers throughout the history of philosophy have been convinced that it *is* more reasonable than not to be moral. Some have even said that to be moral is nothing other than to listen to the voice of reason before we act.

This is the view of Immanuel Kant, for instance. Kant saw reason as having two aspects—*theoretical* and *practical.* When we engage in the search for knowledge for its own sake, when we engage in pure science, for example, or speculative philosophy, we are using our theoretical reason. When, on the other hand, we ask ourselves what the best course of *action* is, we are using practical reason.

Many philosophers have found this to be a useful distinction. Unlike most of them, however, Kant sees practical reason as having more than just a characteristic *function.* For Kant, it also has a characteristic *content.* The voice of practical reason, he says, issues a specific command: Before we act, we must see that the principle that guides us passes a certain test. We must make sure that our principle is *universalizable.* But to do that is to take the moral point of view. Therefore, to take the moral point of view is simply a matter of listening to the voice of practical reason.

Kant adds that we would *always* take the moral point of view if we were *purely* rational creatures. But we are not. We are guided not only by reason, but by our inclinations as well. These inclinations supply us with alternative principles of action. Sometimes these alternatives will lead us to choose the same action that the voice of practical reason would lead us to choose. But if we choose them because of our inclinations, we are not being moral. We are being moral only if we choose them because the voice of practical reason tells us to. Other times, of course, our inclinations lead us to choose actions not supported by the voice of practical reason. They lead us to choose what is in our own self-interest but not in the interest of the moral point of view.

For Kant, then, the answer to our question is simple. Why should I be moral? Because to be moral is to listen to the voice of reason. The moral point of view is more reasonable than any other because it is dictated by reason, not by inclination. Not to ask what is right is not to listen to reason.

Means and Ends

To accept Kant's answer requires that we accept his psychology. It requires that we view human beings as divided in two. On the one side, we have the voice of reason, which issues a command having one end—morality. On the other side, we have our inclinations, which are the source of other ends—self-preservation, love, pleasure, success, and so forth. In this set-up, practical reason is not a means to achieve some further end. It is an end in itself.

Many philosophers find this difficult to accept. They side with Aristotle instead. According to Aristotle, practical reason is a *mediator* between ends and means. We have a certain end in mind, and the task of practical reason is to supply us with the best means of achieving it. Thus, practical reason tells us to open the window to achieve the end of getting fresh air. It tells us to set an alarm to achieve the end of awakening in time. It tells us to buy a drink to achieve the end of quenching our thirst.

Most of us have moral ends. That is, most of us *want* to be moral. That is why we often use reason to determine what is right. And once we determine what the right thing to do is, we do it *because* it is right. We do not seek a further end. But what about the person who does *not* have moral ends, the person who does *not* take the moral point of view? When such people ask why they should be moral, it is not enough to tell them that being moral is being reasonable. We must give them a *specific* reason. That is, we must show that some further end is achieved by taking the moral point of view. Otherwise, we cannot answer the question to their satisfaction.

MORALITY AND SELF-INTEREST

Aristotle, we saw in the previous chapter, thought that happiness is *the* end of morality, and he articulated a moral system based on that assumption. We will not review his position here. Instead, we will turn to the views of his great teacher, Plato.

Plato had his own important views on the connection between happiness and morality. The truly happy person, he felt, is the moral person. To be moral is to have the inner self in harmony, and that harmony is the essence of true happiness. Why be moral, then? Because it is in our own interest to be moral. Because morality leads to happiness.

Plato based his view on a certain understanding of the human soul. He saw the soul as divided into three parts: reason, appetite, and spirit. Reason, of course, is the part that calculates and decides. It is the controlling function, the executive branch of the soul. "Appetite" refers to our instinctive urges, such as hunger, thirst, and sexual drives. By "spirit," Plato means the quality we refer to when we speak of a spirited horse, for example. It is the quality people have when we call them courageous, or say that they have gumption, moxie, or true grit.

Morality, according to Plato, is the proper ordering of these three parts. When reason controls the appetites, and when spirit is harnessed in the service of reason, a human being is moral. This proper ordering also produces an internal harmony, and it is the source of true happiness because of it. Plato's psychology is rarely taken seriously today. But Plato did consider two independent arguments for the claim that morality leads to happiness.

The first is one that my students often pose. Because we live among others, they say, how others feel about us is very important to our happiness. The respect of others, their trust, their friendship, their help, their concern—we rely on all these things. But if we are not moral, these things will be lacking from our lives. We will be outcasts, scorned, friendless. To be happy, we must get along with others in society. But to get along with others, we must be moral.

Plato rejects this argument, however. He points out two important problems with it. First, the opinions of others are often fickle. They may like us or not, help us or not, for any number of reasons, our morality or lack of morality notwithstanding. The person without morality may have many friends, while the moral person may be friendless. The charming cad may have many women in love with him; the decent introvert, none. The rich and powerful cutthroat may be up to his ears in respect and admiration; the moral nonmanipulator, in scorn.

But even more important, what is crucial to the argument is the *appearance* of morality, not morality itself. As long as others *think* that we are moral, it makes no difference whether we actually *are*. Of course, to keep up the appearance of morality, we will often do what is right. But we need not do it *because* it is right. We need do it only because it will fool the people around us. But that is not to take the moral point of view at all. Moreover, there will be many occasions when we can do the wrong thing without anyone's knowing it. And since it is merely the appearance of morality that matters, we might as well do it. As long as we can be immoral and get away with it, the argument gives us no reason to be moral.

My students sometimes object that such a life of duplicity would be unbearable. Our conscience would bother us, or we'd worry about being found out and punished. Well, if we already are moral, our conscience does bother us when we do something wrong. But we are not asking why *moral* people should be moral. We are asking why someone who does *not* take the moral point of view should be moral. And somebody like that does not experience the twinge of conscience. Similarly, people who feel confident in their cleverness may not worry about being caught and punished.

Although Plato rejects this argument, he offers a second, which he takes to be more powerful. He asks us to imagine a man who does not take the moral point of view, who yields always and only to his appetites. Such a person cannot be happy, he says, because he is never satisfied. As soon as one appetite is satisfied, he turns to another, or he ups the ante on the first. Certainly this strikes us as familiar. We all know people (including ourselves) who are constantly upgrading their stereo systems, trading in their motorcycles for bigger ones, seeking more and more money, better spouses and lovers. Moreover, there is something to be said for someone who can maintain an inner peace and satisfaction through the vicissitudes of life. And this does seem to depend on an inner harmony somewhat like the one sketched by Plato.

Still, this inner harmony, this imperviousness to misfortune, need have nothing to do with morality at all. A prudent person will check her desires from time to time without ever having to take the moral point of view. And someone who takes the moral point of view quite often may still be perpetually dissatisfied— not only with the quality of her sound system, but with the extent of injustice in the world.

The problem with all arguments to the conclusion that morality brings happiness is this—we know full well that life doesn't work that way. Crime goes unpunished, virtue goes unrewarded. The good have as much to fear walking certain streets as the evil. The Mafia hit man may lead a happier life than the decent worker. The embezzler who discovers a foolproof way of diverting company funds can be happier with his expensive cars, his trips to Europe, his steak and lobster, than the honest accountant with her hamburger and morality.

It is, after all, undeniable that to take the moral point of view is to appeal to reasons *other* than those of self-interest. It is to ask what is *right*, not what will make us *happy*. And, as we all know, sometimes the right thing to do is not the thing that is in our self-interest. So, even if it is best to *appear* moral, even if we are more likely to have friends and the happiness they bring if we seem to be moral, if we are really concerned *only* with happiness, we need not worry about *being* moral.

MORAL REASONS AS THE BEST REASONS

If we cannot answer our question by saying that it is in our self-interest to be moral, can we answer it another way? Baier thinks that we can. He offers the following argument, which he adapted from the English philosopher Thomas Hobbes (1588–1679).

What would it be like to live in a situation in which morality did not exist, a situation in which *nobody* took the moral point of view? It would be to live in what Hobbes called a *state of nature*, a condition in which there would be no society whatever. Here's why.

If nobody took the moral point of view, there would be only one reason for acting—self-interest. We would never ask "What is right?" Instead, we would ask "What's in it for me?" But in such a situation, there could be no mutual trust, in which case there could be no cooperation. Any partnership we might form would be dissolved as soon as our partners decided that they would be better off without us. Without a sense of moral obligation, they would turn on us without any notice.

The inevitable result of this situation would be a state of constant fear and war. Knowing that others might stab us in the back as soon as it became in their interest to do so, we would have no choice but to do it to them first. Instead of the golden rule, our motto would be this: Do unto others as they would do unto you, but do it first.

Such a situation would, of course, be intolerable. It would then be in everyone's self-interest to introduce morality. That is, it would be in everyone's interest to introduce reasons for acting that would *override* reasons of self-interest whenever people's interests conflict. If we knew that people would abide by these reasons, fear and distrust would lessen. We could cooperate with one another and be fairly secure that we would not be turned on. By their very nature, then, moral reasons are the *best* reasons for acting. Indeed, they are introduced for just that purpose. That is their function—to override reasons of self-interest.

This should be a familiar point to you. In the first chapter, we saw that being overriding is one of the chief features of moral principles. In ordinary affairs, to say that something is right is to give a decisive reason for doing it. Whenever self-interest and morality conflict, we are to choose in favor of morality. In Baier's terms, moral reasons for acting are better reasons than reasons of self-interest. That is why we have them, and that is why we should follow them.

Why should I be moral, then? The answer is simple. To ask what I should do is to ask what course of action is supported by the best reasons. But moral reasons are, by their very nature, the best reasons. They are introduced for just that purpose. Therefore, we should act on moral reasons. That is, we should take the moral point of view.

Baier's position, you may have noticed, is very similar to Kant's, except that it does not rely on Kant's psychology. Both recognize that moral reasons can and often do conflict with reasons of self-interest. Both claim that we should act on moral reasons because they are the best reasons. But Baier recognizes, as Kant does not, that morality serves some further end. Because morality is a social institution, it serves a social goal. Since it cannot serve that goal unless it overrides self-interest, it must override it.

What Baier does, in effect, is show the connection between two points we made earlier. One, from the first chapter, is that moral principles are overriding. The other, from the second chapter, is that morality is a social phenomenon. This allows him to show *why* moral reasons are the best reasons. Kant could make the same claim only by relying on a suspect psychology.

The Best Reasons for Whom?

Many philosophers accept every step in Baier's argument but the conclusion. What the argument shows, they feel, is that there is a good reason for *society* to have a morality, but not that there is a good reason for *me* to be moral. That is, it answers the question "Why should *we* be moral?" but not the question "Why should *I* be moral?"

Thus, someone who is wondering whether to take the moral point of view might respond this way: "Of course there should be morality. Of course people should take the moral point of view. Of course a world with moral people is better than a world with no moral people. But it would be best for me if everyone *but* me were moral. Then I could count on others yet do whatever is in my own interest. Just because moral reasons are *introduced* to be overriding is no reason for *me* to accept them. Baier tells me why *society* should accept them. He doesn't tell me why *I* should."

My students invariably respond to the above reasoning this way: I should accept moral reasons because it is *unfair* not to. It is wrong for me to take advantage of everyone else. How would I like it if the situation were reversed?

Well, I would not like it if the situation were reversed. But such golden rule arguments miss the point. Since I do not take the moral point of view, I do not act on moral reasons. Since my students' response appeals to moral reasons—fairness and the golden rule—it cannot convince me that I ought to be moral. Moral arguments work only for people who already take the moral point of view. They do not work for people who don't.

CAN THE QUESTION BE ANSWERED?

In discussing Baier's answer to our question, we have unearthed a great difficulty. There seem to be two kinds of reasons we can give for being moral—reasons of self-interest and moral reasons. We can be told to be moral because it will make us happy or because it is right to be moral.

But neither can work. It is clearly not in my self-interest to be moral, and moral reasons are ineffective against someone outside of the circle of morality. Does that mean that our question cannot be answered?

The contemporary American philosopher William Frankena, who fully appreciates the problem, thinks that there is a way out. He asks us to do this. Take a disinterested, objective attitude toward your life, and ask yourself what kind of person you want to be, what kind of life you want to lead. If you do this, he says, you will no doubt include morality in your answer. You will say that you want to be a moral person, that you want to lead a moral life. It is difficult to disagree with Frankena on this point. Few of us are moral monsters. Most of us do take the moral point of view. Since we do, it is not surprising that we would include morality in our descriptions of the good life.

But what about someone who is not moral? In her case, the answer would be different. If she is not moral, if she does not act on moral reasons, if she does not concern herself with what is right, then it is highly unlikely that she would include morality in her description of the good life.

A Helpful Analogy

We seem to have hit an impasse. But our impasse is not unique. It is much like another one. Consider the question "Why should I be rational?" On the face of it, it seems an easy one to answer. To be rational is, in part, to act in

PSYCHOLOGICAL EGOISM

The crucial distinction in this chapter is between two kinds of reasons—moral reasons and reasons of self-interest. Most of us feel that people are capable of acting from both kinds, and that they sometimes act solely from one and at other times solely from the other.

People who always act from reasons of self-interest are often called *egoists.* Some philosophers have felt that *all* people are at bottom egoists. They claim that we always act out of self-interest, that all of our acts are aimed at achieving our own good, that every act, however unselfish it may appear, is really the product of selfish motives.

This view is called *psychological egoism.* It is a factual claim about the actual motivations that guide the behavior of every one of us. Numerous arguments have been advanced in support of this view. We shall consider three closely related ones.

Personal Pleasure

Many philosophers have argued that the sole end of all human action is the agent's own pleasure. Whatever we do, we do because we expect to maximize our own pleasure by doing it. Why do they feel this way? Well, when we act, we do so to achieve some goal. That is, there is something that we want. But why do we want it? We want the goal because we expect to achieve pleasure from getting it. Otherwise, we wouldn't want it. This holds in all cases, even when I want something for somebody else. My true goal is the pleasure *I* will feel when the other person gets it, or the pleasure *I* feel contemplating that outcome. Therefore, my real reason for acting is always a selfish one.

It is easy for the opponent of psychological egoism to accept much of this argument. Certainly, we often do feel pleasure when we get what we want, just as we often anticipate the pleasure that we will feel when we get it. But does that mean that we *always* act for just that reason?

Sometimes we do, of course. When we come into the house on a hot day, for example, and go to the refrigerator for a cold drink, we do so because we expect the cold liquid to feel good going down. This is an obvious case in which we want something because of the pleasure it will give us. But there are other times when the situation is reversed, when we get the pleasure because we get what we want, not the other way around. In these cases, our concern is not our own pleasure. There is something that we want, and once we have gotten it, we derive a certain pleasure from the fact.

Suppose, for example, that I am just sitting down with a beer to watch a ball game on television when the phone rings. It is a friend who needs me to drive her someplace for an important errand. Since I want her to get the errand done, I will turn off the television and drive to her apartment. Afterward, I may very well feel satisfied that I helped her, but my goal at the time was not that feeling of satisfaction. Unlike the case of reaching into the refrigerator for a cold drink, my concern was not my own pleasure, even though I did eventually receive some pleasure from my action. So it seems wrong to say that my motives are always selfish. In some cases at least, my motives do not include any reference to my own pleasure.

Hidden Motives

The psychological egoist has a response to my remarks. Although it *seems* that my motives are not always selfish, this is a case in which appearances are deceptive. If we look deeply enough, we will find that whatever motives I think I am acting on, my real motives, although hidden, are really selfish ones.

Take the example in which I help my friend. Although I think my motive is her well-being, I am really concerned with something else. Perhaps I am trying to make sure that she will do me a similar favor someday. Perhaps I am trying to make her like me more. Perhaps I am trying to reinforce my self-image as a kind, giving person. Perhaps I am seeking praise from her. Perhaps I am a Christian seeking entrance to heaven by helping others. Whatever possibility we may choose here, the psychological egoist's point is that I helped my friend because I believed that there was *something* in it for me. This view reflects, of course, a very cynical turn of mind. If it were true, we would have to alter our opinions of many people. Martin Luther King, Jr., Albert Schweitzer, Mother Teresa, St. Francis—all would become glory-seekers in our eyes.

But is it true? This much is true. It is very difficult to know our real motives in many cases. We are very complicated creatures, and, as psychoanalytic theory has shown, unconscious motivation is a fact of all our lives. But that is a far cry from the claim that all our unconscious motives are selfish. It is also a far cry from the claim that our conscious unselfish motives never control our actions.

The safest thing to say, then, is that this argument is inconclusive. Given the current state of our knowledge, we do know whether to accept it or not. Those who do accept it are motivated more by their own cynicism than by the facts. This is not to say that they are therefore wrong, of course. But it is to say that we remain justified in rejecting it until we are given stronger scientific support for it.

We are so justified because there are cases where it certainly *seems* improbable that the real motivations for the act are selfish. When an atheist gives an anonymous donation to charity, tells nobody about it, does not believe that there is a God to know about it, and is not aware of any conscious motive involving a desire for moral superiority nor of any conscious feeling after the fact of moral superiority, this person seems to provide a counterexample to the psychological egoist's claims.

We All Do What We Want

The psychological egoist might argue that there are no such people as the charitable atheist of the preceding section, or he might argue that a deeper look would uncover some selfish motivation. We shall let these remarks pass, though, and turn to a third argument.

This argument rests on the claim that all of us do what we want to do. Even if we act on somebody else's wants, even if we learn that a friend wants something and then go out to get it for her, we do so because *we* want her to have it. But that is to say that in such cases we are acting just as selfishly as the person who ignores a friend's wants. In both cases, we are doing what we want. Ultimately, it is our own wants that matter. This argument seems to work in a way. That is, *if* we think of selfishness as doing what we want, then I suppose that all of us are selfish. I say this because, as we shall see in Part III, our actions *are* caused by our own wants.

But there is something perverse about thinking of selfishness in such a way. What matters, I think, is not that we *do* what we want, but that we *want* what we want. Some people want things just for themselves. Even if they seem to want something for others, it is only to the extent that it will ultimately bring something back to them. Other people want something for others without any concern for what it will get them.

Although both types of people end up doing what they want, the difference between their wants is very important. And because of that difference, it is perverse to lump both groups together as selfish. People who act on wants that are truly directed toward the interests of others are not acting selfishly. People who act on wants that are directed toward their own interests are.

such a way as to get what you want. Practical reason, as we saw, deals with the relationship between means and ends. We use our reason to achieve our goals. If we don't use our reason, we are far less likely to achieve them.

But notice—this argument appeals only to someone who already is rational. Suppose, however, that someone responds this way. "Why should I care about getting what I want?" You could, I suppose, come up with some kind of answer. "Because it will make you happy," you might say. But then you might hear this. "Why should I care about being happy?" If you were to answer this question, you could very easily be met with another "Why?" Eventually, you would have to throw up your hands in despair. If the other person accepts none of the things you take for granted, there is no way to reason with him.

You could have saved yourself the trouble. If the other person has to ask why he should be rational, no answer will satisfy him. None could. If he is outside the circle of rationality, he accepts no reasons. Therefore, you cannot give him one. You can be rational only when discussing something with another rational person. You can't reason with someone who doesn't listen to reason. At bottom, then, there is only one answer to the question "Why should I be rational?" And it is this: "Because you are."

I think that the same holds true for the question "Why should I be moral?" The only answer we can give is this: "Because you are." If the other person is outside the circle of morality, the answer will not do, of course. But nothing could. That, I think, is the lesson of Frankena's discussion of the question.

THE RATIONALITY OF MORALITY

Having reached the above conclusion, we are now faced with the following questions. If we can't give someone outside the circle of morality a good reason to be moral, does that mean that there *is* no good reason to be moral? Is it ultimately irrational to be moral? The answer is this: no more than the analogous difficulty shows that it is irrational to be rational. Here's why.

Both morality and rationality are *internally* rational. That is, both can be amply justified from *within* their respective circles. Once we agree to be rational, we can always be given and accept good reasons for acting on any particular occasion. Once someone totally ceases to be rational, there is nothing to do but offer that person therapy. Treatment, not reason, is the answer. But that does not show that *we* are being irrational. It shows, rather, that *he* is.

Similarly, once we agree to take the moral point of view, we can always be given and accept moral reasons for *acting* on any particular occasion. And we can always be given and accept moral reasons for *accepting* moral reasons. If we ask why we should be moral on *this* occasion, we can be told that it would be unfair not to. But once someone ceases totally to take the moral point of view, the power of such reasons vanishes. But, once again, that does not show that *we* are being irrational.

On what does the power of reason in general and moral reasons in particular depend? On certain attitudes that we share. Because we have moral sensibilities, because we feel compassion, sympathy, and remorse, moral reasons appeal to us. Because we are the kind of creatures that we are, we are moral. And because we are the kind of creatures that we are, we are rational. Moreover, it is no *accident* that we are that kind of creature. If we were not rational, we would not survive. A species of irrational humans, like a species of water-soluble fish, is an evolutionary impossibility.

Similarly, a society without morality is, if not utterly impossible, utterly unbearable. Certainly, a society such as *ours* would be impossible without morality. Moreover, if the theories of sociobiologist Edward Wilson are correct, or even partly correct, then there is an evolutionary explanation of our being moral as well as rational. Once again, this does not give *me* a reason to be moral, unless I am already within the moral circle. But it does help to explain why *we* are *in fact* moral.

THE FINAL WORD?

Our conclusion is that there is reason to take the moral point of view only if we already take it. If we have consciences capable of bothering us, we can be told to be moral because we will feel guilty if we aren't. If we feel that we ought to treat others as we would have them treat us, we can be told to be moral because it is unfair not to be. Otherwise, such answers will fall on deaf ears.

My students generally greet this conclusion with mixed feelings. On the one hand, they are pleased to see their own answers to the question somewhat vindicated. They like to know that for most of us, appeals to conscience and the golden rule are perfectly adequate answers. On the other hand, they are bothered by the qualification "for most of us." They would like to think that such answers would satisfy everyone, or that some other conclusive answer could be found. When they express these feelings, I tell them two things. First, there is no need to worry that their own answers will lose their force with most people. Due to social and evolutionary causes, most of us share and will continue to share Kant's view of morality. That is, we view and will continue to view moral ends as needing no further justification beyond themselves. Second, it should come as no surprise that we cannot reason with moral monsters. If someone's attitudes put him so far outside the circle of shared human nature that he does not see why he should be moral, we should have expected all along that the reasons that satisfy us would make no difference to him.

STUDY QUESTIONS

1. What is the moral point of view? How does adopting the moral point of view differ from adopting any particular moral principle?
2. What is the difference between theoretical and practical reason? How do Aristotle and Kant differ on the role of practical reason?
3. Is the truly happy person the moral person? Why did Plato think so? What reasons are there for disagreeing with him?
4. Both Kant and Baier believe that moral reasons are the best reasons, although they present different arguments in support of the claim. What are their arguments? Which do you find more persuasive? Why?
5. Why is it important to distinguish the following two questions: (a) Why should I be moral? and (b) Why should there be morality?
6. What are the reasons for concluding that we cannot give someone outside the circle of morality good reason for taking the moral point of view? Why doesn't that show that it is irrational to be moral?
7. What is psychological egoism? What are the arguments in favor of the view? Why do many philosophers remain unconvinced by these arguments?

GLOSSARY

Egoist. Someone who always acts from the motive of self-interest and who considers the interest of another only when it advances his own.

Moral point of view. The point of view from which we ask whether our actions are right before we act, and then act because we believe that they are right. To take the moral point of view, then, is to consider and act on moral reasons.

Practical reason. Reason when it is employed to determine the best course of action. According to Aristotle, practical reason is used to determine the best means to some end, where the ultimate end is the agent's own happiness. According to Kant, practical reason serves no end but morality, which is the voice of practical reason itself.

Psychological egoism. The view that all people always act out of self-interest.

Theoretical reason. Reason when it is employed in the search for knowledge for its own sake.

SELECTIONS

In the following selections, we find John Stuart Mill's defense of utilitarianism against certain objections and W. D. Ross's criticisms of utilitarianism.

The selection by Mill is from Utilitarianism. There he emphasizes that utilitarianism requires us to consider the happiness of all people who will be affected by our actions but does not require us, except on special occasions, to take into account all of society or the entire world. Also, he defends utilitarianism against a variety of charges—that it confuses rightness with expedience, that it neglects too many valuable character traits, and that it is unworkable in practice.

One point worth considering is his claim that utilitarianism and the golden rule are in the same spirit. While some philosophers have agreed, others have not. What do you think?

The second selection is from Ross's The Right and the Good. There Ross argues that it is not the consequences of an action that make it right or wrong, but the kind of action it is.

We have, he argues, a prima facie duty to perform certain kinds of actions. To say that we have a prima facie duty to perform an action is to say that we have a moral reason for doing it. If there are no moral reasons not to do it, then we are morally obligated to do it. (In Ross's words, it becomes our duty sans phrase.) If there are moral reasons not to do it (if our prima facie duties conflict), then we must consider the situation carefully in order to determine what our moral obligation is.

Notice that Ross distinguishes three views that maintain that it is the consequences of our actions that make them right or wrong. First, there is egoism, which claims that it is right to do what is in our own best interest. Second, there is hedonistic utilitarianism, which claims that it is right to do what produces the greatest pleasure for all concerned. That, of course, is Mill's view. Third, there is ideal utilitarianism, which claims that goods other than pleasure must be considered. That is the view of G. E. Moore, against whom Ross directs most of his arguments. Keep in mind, though, that these arguments are intended to refute all forms of utilitarianism, including Mill's.

JOHN STUART MILL

Utilitarianism

The creed which accepts as the foundation of morals Utility, or the Greatest Happiness Principle, holds that actions are right in proportion as they tend to promote happiness, wrong as they tend to produce the reverse of happiness. By happiness is intended pleasure and the absence of pain; by unhappiness, pain and the privation of pleasure. To give a clear view of the moral standard set up by the theory, much more requires to be said, in particular, what things it includes in the ideas of pain and pleasure and to what extent this is left an open question. But these supplementary explanations do not affect the theory of life on which this theory of morality is grounded—namely, that pleasure and freedom from pain are the only things desirable as ends, and that all desirable things (which are as numerous in the utilitarian as in any other scheme) are desirable either for the pleasure inherent in themselves or as means to the promotion of pleasure and the prevention of pain.

Now, such a theory of life excites in many minds, and among them in some of the most estimable in feeling and purpose, inveterate dislike. To suppose that life has (as they express it) no higher end than pleasure—no better and nobler object of desire and pursuit—they designate as utterly mean and groveling, as a doctrine worthy only of swine, to whom the followers of Epicurus were, at a very early period, contemptuously likened; and modern holders of the doctrine are occasionally made the subject of equally polite comparisons by its German, French, and English assailants.

When thus attacked, the Epicureans have always answered that it is not they, but their accusers who represent human nature in a degrading light, since the accusation supposes human beings to be capable of no pleasures except those of which swine are capable. If this supposition were true, the charge could not be gainsaid, but would then be no longer an imputation; for if the sources of pleasure were precisely the same to human beings and to swine, the rule of life which is good enough for the one would be good enough for the other. The comparison of the Epicurean life to that of beasts is felt as degrading precisely because a beast's pleasures do not satisfy a human being's conceptions of happiness. Human beings have faculties more elevated than the animal appetites and, when once made conscious of them, do not regard anything as happiness which does not include their gratification. I do not, indeed, consider the Epicureans to have been by any means faultless in drawing out their scheme of consequences from the utilitarian principle. To do this in any sufficient manner, many Stoic, as well as Christian, elements require to be included. But there is no known Epicurean theory of life which does not assign to the pleasures of the intellect, of the feelings and imagination, and of the moral sentiments a much higher value as pleasures than to those of mere sensation.

It must be admitted, however, that utilitarian writers in general have placed the superiority of mental over bodily pleasures chiefly in the greater permanency, safety, uncostliness, etc., of the former—that is, in their circumstantial advantages rather than in their intrinsic nature. And on all these points, utilitarians have fully proved their case; but they might have taken the other and, as it may be called, higher ground with entire consistency. It is quite compatible with the principle of utility to recognize the fact that some *kinds* of pleasure are more desirable and more valuable than others. It would be absurd that while, in estimating all other things, quality is considered as well as quantity, the estimation of pleasures should be supposed to depend on quantity alone.

If I am asked what I mean by difference of quality in pleasures or what makes one pleasure more valuable than another, merely as a pleasure, except its being greater in amount, there is but one possible answer. Of two pleasures, if there be one to which all or almost all who have experience of both give a decided preference, irrespective of any feeling of moral obligation to prefer it, that is the more desirable pleasure. If one of the two is, by those who are competently acquainted with both, placed so far above the other that they prefer it, even though knowing it to be attended with a greater amount of discontent, and would not resign it for any quantity of the other pleasure of which their nature is capable, we are justified in ascribing to the preferred enjoyment a superiority in quality so far outweighing quantity as to render it, in comparison, of small account.

Now, it is an unquestionable fact that those who are equally acquainted with and equally capable of appreciating and enjoying both do give a most marked preference to the manner of existence which employs their higher faculties. Few human creatures would consent to be changed into any of the lower animals for a promise of the fullest allowance of a beast's pleasures; no intelligent human being would consent to be a fool, no instructed person would be an ignoramus, no person of feeling and conscience would be selfish and base, even though they should be persuaded that the fool, the dunce, or the rascal is better satisfied with his lot than they are with theirs. They would not resign what they possess more than he for the most complete satisfaction of all the desires which they have in common with him.

. . .

According to the Greatest Happiness Principle, as above explained, the ultimate end, with reference to and for the sake of which all other things are desirable (whether we are considering our own good or that of other people), is an existence exempt as far as possible from pain and as rich as possible in enjoyments, both in point of quantity and quality, the test of quality, and the rule for measuring it against quantity, being the preference felt by those who in their opportunities of experience, to which must be added their habits of self-consciousness and self-observation, are best furnished with the means of comparison. This, being, according to the utilitarian opinion, the end of human action, is necessarily also the standard of morality, which may accordingly be defined: the rules and precepts for human conduct by the observance of which an existence such as has been described might be, to the greatest extent possible, secured to all mankind; and not to them only, but, so far as the nature of things admits, to the whole sentient creation.

. . .

I must again repeat what the assailants of utilitarianism seldom have the justice to acknowledge, that the happiness which forms the utilitarian standard of what is right in conduct is not the agent's own happiness, but that of all concerned. As between his own happiness and that of others, utilitarianism requires him to be as strictly impartial as a disinterested and benevolent spectator. In the golden rule of Jesus of Nazareth, we read the complete spirit of the ethics of utility. To do as you would be done by and to love your neighbor as yourself constitute the ideal perfection of utilitarian morality. As the means of making the nearest approach to this ideal, utility would enjoin first that laws and social arrangements should place the happiness, or (as speaking practically it may be called) the interest, of every individual as nearly as possible in harmony with the interest of the whole; and secondly, that education and opinion, which have so vast a power over human character, should so use that power as to establish in the mind of every individual an indissoluble association between his own happiness and the good of the whole—especially between his own happiness and the practice of such modes of conduct, negative and positive, as regard for the universal happiness prescribes, so that not only he may be unable to conceive the possibility of happiness to himself consistently with conduct opposed to the general good, but also that a direct impulse to promote the general good may be in every individual one of the habitual motives of action and the sentiments connected therewith may fill a large and prominent place in every human being's sentient existence. If the impugners of the utilitarian morality represented it to their own minds in this its true character, I know not what recommendation possessed by any other morality they could possibly affirm to be wanting to it, what more beautiful or more exalted developments of human nature any other ethical system can be supposed to foster, or what springs of action, not accessible to the utilitarian, such systems rely on for giving effect to their mandates.

The objectors to utilitarianism cannot always be charged with representing it in a discreditable light. On the contrary, those among them who entertain anything like a just idea of its disinterested character sometimes find fault with its standard as being too high for humanity. They say it is exacting too much to require that people shall always act from the inducement of promoting the general interests of society. But this is to mistake the very meaning of a standard of morals and confound the rule of action with the motive of it. It is the business of ethics to tell us what are our duties or by what test we may know them; but no system of ethics requires that the sole motive of all we do shall be a feeling of duty: on the contrary, ninety-nine hundredths of all our actions are done from other motives, and rightly so done, if the rule of duty does not condemn them. It is the more unjust to utilitarianism that this particular misapprehension should be made a ground of objection to it, inasmuch as utilitarian moralists have gone beyond almost all others in affirming that the motive has nothing to do with the morality of the action, though much with the worth of the agent. He who saves a fellow creature from drowning does what is morally right, whether his motive be duty or the hope of being paid for his trouble; he who betrays the friend that trusts him is guilty of a crime, even if his object be to serve another friend to whom he is under greater obligations. But to speak only of actions done from the motive of duty, and in direct obedience to principle: it is a misapprehension of the utilitarian mode of thought to conceive it as implying that people should fix their minds upon so wide a generality as the world or society at large. The great majority of good actions are intended not for the benefit of the world, but for that of individuals, of which the good of the world is made up; and the thoughts of the most virtuous man need not on these occasions travel beyond the particular persons concerned, except so far as is necessary to assure himself that in benefiting them he is not violating the rights, that is the legitimate and authorized expectations, of anyone else. The multiplication of happiness is, according to the utilitarian ethics, the object of virtue: the occasions on which any person (except one in a thousand) has it in his power to do this on an extended scale, in other words to be a public benefactor, are but exceptional; and on these occasions alone is he called on to consider public utility; in every other case, private utility, the interest or happiness of some few persons, is all he has to attend to. Those alone the influence of whose actions extends to society in general need concern themselves habitually about so large an object. In the case of abstinences, indeed—of things which people forbear to do from moral considerations, though the consequences in the particular case might be beneficial—it would be unworthy of an intelligent agent not to be consciously aware that the action is of a class which, if practiced generally, would be generally injurious, and that this is the ground of the obligation to abstain from it. The amount of regard for the public interest implied in this recognition is no greater than is demanded by every system of morals, for they all enjoin to abstain from whatever is manifestly pernicious to society.

The same considerations dispose of another reproach against the doctrine of utility, founded on a still grosser misconception of the purpose of a standard of morality and of the very meaning of the words right and wrong. It is often affirmed that utilitarianism renders men cold and unsympathizing; that it chills their moral feelings toward individuals; that it makes them regard only the dry and hard consideration of the consequences of actions, not taking into their moral estimate the qualities from which those actions emanate. If the assertion means that they do not allow their judgment respecting the rightness or wrongness of an action to be influenced by their opinion of the qualities of the person who does it, this is a complaint not against utilitarianism, but against having any standard of morality at all; for certainly, no known ethical standard decides an action to be good or bad because it is done by a good or a bad man, still less because done by an amiable, a brave, or a benevolent man, or the contrary. These considerations are relevant not to the estimation of actions, but of persons; and there is nothing in the utilitarian theory inconsistent with the fact that there are other things which interest us in persons besides the rightness and wrongness of their actions.

The Stoics, indeed, with the paradoxical misuse of language which was part of their system, and by which they strove to raise themselves above all concern about anything but virtue, were fond of saying that he who has that has everything, that he, and only he, is rich, is beautiful, is a king. But no claim of this description is made for the virtuous man by the utilitarian doctrine. Utilitarians are quite aware that there are other desirable possessions and qualities besides virtue and are perfectly willing to allow to all of them their full worth. They are also aware that a right action does not necessarily indicate a virtuous character and that actions which are blamable often proceed from qualities entitled to praise. When this is apparent in any particular case, it modifies their estimation not certainly of the act, but of the agent. I grant that they are, notwithstanding, of opinion that in the long run the best proof of a good character is good actions and resolutely refuse to consider any mental disposition as good of which the predominant tendency is to produce bad conduct. This makes them unpopular with many people; but it is an unpopularity which they must share with everyone who regards the distinction between right and wrong in a serious light; and the reproach is not one which a conscientious utilitarian need be anxious to repel.

. . .

Again, Utility is often summarily stigmatized as an immoral doctrine by giving it the name of Expediency and taking advantage of the popular use of that term to contrast it with Principle. But the Expedient, in the sense in which it is opposed to the Right, generally means that which is expedient for the particular interest of the agent himself, as when a minister sacrifices the interests of his country to keep himself in place. When it means anything better than this, it means that which is expedient for some immediate object, some temporary purpose, but which violates a rule whose observance is expedient in a much higher degree. The Expedient, in this sense, instead of being the same thing as the useful, is a branch of the hurtful.

Thus, it would often be expedient, for the purpose of getting over some momentary embarrassment, or attaining some object immediately useful to ourselves or others, to tell a lie. But inasmuch as the cultivation in ourselves of a sensitive feeling on the subject of veracity is one of the most useful, and the enfeeblement of that feeling one of the most hurtful, things to which our conduct can be instrumental; and inasmuch as any, even unintentional, deviation from truth does that much toward weakening the trustworthiness of human assertion, which is not only the principal support of all present social well-being, but the insufficiency of which does more than any one thing that can be named to keep back civilization, virtue, everything on which human happiness on the largest scale depends—we feel that the violation, for a present advantage, of a rule of such transcendent expediency is not expedient and that he, who for the sake of a convenience to himself or to some other individual, does what depends on him to deprive mankind of the good, and inflict upon them the evil, involved in the greater or less reliance which they can place in each other's word, acts the part of one of their worst enemies.

Yet, that even this rule, sacred as it is, admits of possible exceptions is acknowledged by all moralists, the chief of which is when the withholding of some fact (as of information from a malefactor or of bad news from a person dangerously ill) would save an individual (especially an individual other than oneself) from great and unmerited evil, and when the withholding can only be effected by denial. But in order that the exception may not extend itself beyond the need and may have the least possible effect in weakening reliance on veracity, it ought to be recognized and, if possible, its limits defined; and if the principle of utility is good for anything, it must be good for weighing these conflicting utilities against one another and marking out the region within which one or the other preponderates.

Again, defenders of utility often find themselves called upon to reply to such objections as this—that there is not time, previous to action, for calculating and weighing the effects of any line of conduct on the general happiness. This is exactly as if anyone were to say that it is impossible to guide our conduct by Christianity because there is not time, on every occasion on which anything has to be done, to read through the Old and New Testaments. The answer to the objection is that there has been ample time, namely, the whole past duration of the human species. During all that time, mankind have been learning by experience the tendencies of actions, on which experience all the prudence, as well as all the morality of life, are dependent. People talk as if the commencement of this course of experience had hitherto been put off, and as if, at the moment when some man feels tempted to meddle with the property or life of another, he had to begin considering for the first time whether murder and theft are injurious to human happiness. Even then, I do not think that he would find the question very puzzling; but, at all events, the matter is now done to his hand. It is truly a whimsical supposition that if mankind were agreed in considering utility to be the test of morality, they would remain without any agreement as to what *is* useful and would take no measures for having their notions on the subject taught to the young and enforced by law and opinion. There is no difficulty in proving any ethical standard whatever to work ill, if we suppose universal idiocy to be conjoined with it; but on any hypothesis short of that, mankind must by this time have acquired positive beliefs as to the effects of some actions on their happiness; and the beliefs which have thus come down are the rules of morality for the multitude, and for the philosopher until he has succeeded in finding better.

That philosophers might easily do this, even now, on many subjects; that the received code of ethics is by no means of divine right; and that mankind have still much to learn as to the effects of actions on the general happiness—I admit, or, rather, earnestly maintain. The corollaries from the principle of utility, like the precepts of every practical art, admit of indefinite improvement, and, in a progressive state of the human mind, their improvement is perpetually going on. But to consider the rules of morality as improvable is one thing; to pass over the intermediate generalizations entirely, and endeavor to test each individual action directly by the first principle, is another. It is a strange notion that the acknowledgment of a first principle is inconsistent with the admission of secondary ones. To inform a traveler respecting the place of his ultimate destination is not to forbid the use of landmarks and direction-posts on the way. The proposition that happiness is the end and aim of morality does not mean that no road ought to be laid down to that goal or that persons going thither should not be advised to take one direction rather than another. Men really ought to leave off talking a kind of nonsense on this subject, which they would neither talk nor listen to on other matters of practical concernment. Nobody argues that the art of navigation is not founded on astronomy because sailors cannot wait to calculate the Nautical Almanack. Being rational creatures, they go to sea with it ready calculated; and all rational creatures go out upon the sea of life with their minds made up on the common questions of right and wrong, as well as on many of the far more difficult questions of wise and foolish. And this, as long as foresight is a human quality, it is to be presumed they will continue to do. Whatever we adopt as the fundamental principle of morality, we require subordinate principles to apply it by; the impossibility of doing without them, being common to all systems, can afford no argument against any one in particular; but gravely to argue as if no such secondary principles could be had, and as if mankind had remained till now, and always remain, without drawing any general conclusions from the experience of human life, is as high a pitch, I think, as absurdity has ever reached in philosophical controversy.

The remainder of the stock arguments against utilitarianism mostly consist in laying to its charge the common infirmities of human nature and the general difficulties which embarrass conscientious persons in shaping their course through life. We are told that a utilitarian will be apt to make his own particular case an exception to moral rules and, when under temptation, will see a utility in the breach of a rule greater than he will see in its observance. But is utility the only creed which is able to furnish us with excuses for evil-doing and means of cheating our own conscience? They are afforded in abundance by all doctrines which recognize as a fact in morals the existence of conflicting considerations, which all doctrines do that have been believed by sane persons. It is not the fault of any creed, but of the complicated nature of human affairs, that rules of conduct cannot be so framed as to require no exceptions and that hardly any kind of action can safely be laid down as either always obligatory or always condemnable. There is no ethical creed which does not temper the rigidity of its laws by giving a certain latitude, under the moral responsibility of the agent, for accommodation to peculiarities of circumstances; and under every creed, at the opening thus made, self-deception and dishonest casuistry get in. There exists no moral system under which there do not arise unequivocal cases of conflicting obligation. These are the real difficulties, the knotty points both in the theory of ethics and in the conscientious guidance of personal conduct. They are overcome practically with greater or with less success according to the intellect and virtue of the individual; but it can hardly be pretended that anyone will be the less qualified for dealing with them from possessing an ultimate standard to which conflicting rights and duties can be referred. If utility is the ultimate source of moral obligations, utility may be invoked to decide between them when their demands are incompatible. Though the application of the standard may be difficult, it is better than none at all: while in other systems the moral laws all claiming independent authority, there is no common umpire entitled to interfere between them; their claims to precedence one over another rest on little better than sophistry, and unless determined, as they generally are, by the unacknowledged influence of considerations of utility, afford a free scope for the action of personal desires and partialities. We must remember that only in these cases of conflict between secondary principles is it requisite that first principles should be appealed to. There is no case of moral obligation in which some secondary principle is not involved; and, if only one, there can seldom be any real doubt which one it is in the mind of any person by whom the principle itself is recognized.

W. D. ROSS

What Makes Right Acts Right?

The real point at issue between hedonism and utilitarianism on the one hand and their opponents on the other is not whether 'right' means 'productive of so and so'; for it cannot with any plausibility be maintained that it does. The point at issue is that to which we now pass, viz. whether there is any general character which makes right acts right, and if so, what it is. Among the main historical attempts to state a single characteristic of all right actions which is the foundation of their rightness are those made by egoism and utilitarianism. But I do not propose to discuss these, not because the subject is unimportant, but because it has been dealt with so often and so well already, and because there has come to be so much agreement among moral philosophers that neither of these theories is satisfactory. A much more attractive theory has been put forward by Professor Moore: that what makes actions right is that they are productive of more *good* than could have been produced by any other action open to the agent.

   This theory is in fact the culmination of all the attempts to base rightness on productivity of some sort of result. The first form this attempt takes is the attempt to base rightness on conduciveness to the advantage or pleasure of the agent. This theory comes to grief over the fact, which stares us in the face, that a great part of duty consists in an observance of the rights and a furtherance of the interests of others, whatever the cost to ourselves may be. Plato and others may be right in holding that a regard for the rights of others never in the long run involves a loss of happiness for the agent, that 'the just life profits a man.' But this, even if true, is irrelevant to the rightness of the act. As soon as a man does an action *because* he thinks he will promote his own interests thereby, he is acting not from a sense of its rightness but from self-interest.

To the egoistic theory hedonistic utilitarianism supplies a much-needed amendment. It points out correctly that the fact that a certain pleasure will be enjoyed by the agent is no reason why he *ought* to bring it into being rather than an equal or greater pleasure to be enjoyed by another, though, human nature being what it is, it makes it not unlikely that he *will* try to bring it into being. But hedonistic utilitarianism in its turn needs a correction. On reflection it seems clear that pleasure is not the only thing in life that we think good in itself, that for instance we think the possession of a good character, or an intelligent understanding of the world, as good or better. A great advance is made by the substitution of 'productive of the greatest good' for 'productive of the greatest pleasure.'

Not only is this theory more attractive than hedonistic utilitarianism, but its logical relation to that theory is such that the latter could not be true unless *it* were true, while it might be true though hedonistic utilitarianism were not. It is in fact one of the logical bases of hedonistic utilitarianism. For the view that what produces the maximum pleasure is right has for its bases the views (1) that what produces the maximum good is right, and (2) that pleasure is the only thing good in itself. If they were not assuming that what produces the maximum *good* is right, the utilitarians' attempt to show that pleasure is the only thing good in itself, which is in fact the point they take most pains to establish, would have been quite irrelevant to their attempt to prove that only what produces the maximum *pleasure* is right. If, therefore, it can be shown that productivity of the maximum good is not what makes all right actions right, we shall *a fortiori* have refuted hedonistic utilitarianism.

When a plain man fulfills a promise because he thinks he ought to do so, it seems clear that he does so with no thought of its total consequences, still less with any opinion that these are likely to be the best possible. He thinks in fact much more of the past than of the future. What makes him think it right to act in a certain way is the fact that he has promised to do so—that and, usually, nothing more. That his act will produce the best possible consequences is not his reason for calling it right. What lends colour to the theory we are examining, then, is not the actions (which form probably a great majority of our actions) in which some such reflection as 'I have promised' is the only reason we give ourselves for thinking a certain action right, but the exceptional cases in which the consequences of fulfilling a promise (for instance) would be so disastrous to others that we judge it right not to do so. It must of course be admitted that such cases exist. If I have promised to meet a friend at a particular time for some trivial purpose, I should certainly think myself justified in breaking my engagement if by doing so I could prevent a serious accident or bring relief to the victims of one. And the supporters of the view we are examining hold that my thinking so is due to my thinking that I shall bring more good into existence by the one action than by the other. A different account may, however, be given of the matter, an account which will, I believe, show itself to be the true one. It may be said that besides the duty of fulfilling promises I have and recognize a duty of relieving distress, and that when I think it right to do the latter at the cost of not doing the former, it is not because I think I shall produce more good thereby but because I think it the duty which is in the circumstances more of a duty. This account surely corresponds much more closely with what we really think in such a situation. If, so far as I can see, I could bring equal amounts of good into being by fulfilling my promise and by helping some one to whom I had made no promise, I should not hesitate to regard the former as my duty. Yet on the view that what is right is right because it is productive of the most good I should not so regard it.

There are two theories, each in its way simple, that offer a solution of such cases of conscience. One is the view of Kant, that there are certain duties of perfect obligation, such as those of fulfilling promises, of paying debts, of telling the truth, which admit of no exception whatever in favour of duties of imperfect obligation, such as that of relieving distress. The other is the view of, for instance, Professor Moore, that there is only the duty of producing good, and that all 'conflicts of duties' should be resolved by asking 'by which action will most good be produced?' But it is more important that our theory fit the facts than that it be simple, and the account we have given above corresponds (it seems to me) better than either of the simpler theories with what we really think, viz. that normally promise-keeping, for example, should come before benevolence, but that when and only when the good to be produced by the benevolent act is very great and the promise comparatively trivial, the act of benevolence becomes our duty.

In fact the theory of 'ideal utilitarianism,' if I may for brevity refer so to the theory of Professor Moore, seems to simplify unduly our relations to our fellows. It says, in effect, that the only morally significant relation in which my neighbours stand to me is that of being possible beneficiaries by my action.[1] They do stand in this relation to me, and this relation is morally significant. But they may also stand to me in the relation of promisee to promiser, of creditor to debtor, of wife to husband, of child to parent, of friend to friend, of fellow countryman to fellow countryman, and the like; and each of these relations is the foundation of a *prima facie* duty, which is more or less incumbent on me according to the circumstances of the case. When I am in a

---

[1] Some will think it, apart from other considerations, a sufficient refutation of this view to point out that I also stand in that relation to myself, so that for this view the distinction of oneself from others is morally insignificant.

situation, as perhaps I always am, in which more than one of these *prima facie* duties is incumbent on me, what I have to do is to study the situation as fully as I can until I form the considered opinion (it is never more) that in the circumstances one of them is more incumbent than any other; then I am bound to think that to do this *prima facie* duty is my duty *sans phrase* in the situation.

I suggest 'prima facie duty' or 'conditional duty' as a brief way of referring to the characteristic (quite distinct from that of being a duty proper) which an act has, in virtue of being of a certain kind (e.g. the keeping of a promise), of being an act which would be a duty proper if it were not at the same time of another kind which is morally significant. Whether an act is a duty proper or actual duty depends on *all* the morally significant kinds it is an instance of.

. . .

There is nothing arbitrary about these *prima facie* duties. Each rests on a definite circumstance which cannot seriously be held to be without moral significance. Of *prima facie* duties I suggest, without claiming completeness or finality for it, the following division.[2]

(1) Some duties rest on previous acts of my own. These duties seem to include two kinds, (*a*) those resting on a promise or what may fairly be called an implicit promise, such as the implicit undertaking not to tell lies which seems to be implied in the act of entering into conversation (at any rate by civilized men), or of writing books that purport to be history and not fiction. These may be called the duties of fidelity. (*b*) Those resting on a previous wrongful act. These may be called the duties of reparation. (2) Some rest on previous acts of other men, i.e. services done by them to me. These may be loosely described as the duties of gratitude. (3) Some rest on the fact or possibility of a distribution of pleasure or happiness (or of the means thereto) which is not in accordance with the merit of the persons concerned; in such cases there arises a duty to upset or prevent such a distribution. These are the duties of justice. (4) Some rest on the mere fact that there are other beings in the world whose condition we can make better in respect of virtue, or of intelligence, or of pleasure. These are the duties of beneficence. (5) Some rest on the fact that we can improve our own condition in respect of virtue or of intelligence. These are the duties of self-improvement. (6) I think

---

[2] I should make it plain at this stage that I am *assuming* the correctness of some of our main convictions as to *prima facie* duties, or, more strictly, am claiming that we *know* them to be true. To me it seems as self-evident as anything could be, that to make a promise, for instance, is to create a moral claim on us in someone else. Many readers will perhaps say that they do *not* know this to be true. If so, I certainly cannot prove it to them; I can only ask them to reflect again, in the hope that they will ultimately agree that they also know it to be true. The main moral convictions of the plain man seem to me to be, not opinions which it is for philosophy to prove or disprove, but knowledge from the start; and in my own case I seem to find little difficulty in distinguishing these essential convictions from other moral convictions which I also have, which are merely fallible opinions based on an imperfect study of the working for good or evil of certain institutions or types of action.

that we should distinguish from (4) the duties that may be summed up under the title of 'not injuring others.' No doubt to injure others is incidentally to fail to do them good; but it seems to me clear that non-maleficence is apprehended as a duty distinct from that of beneficence, and as a duty of a more stringent character. It will be noticed that this alone among the types of duty has been stated in a negative way. An attempt might no doubt be made to state this duty, like the others, in a positive way. It might be said that it is really the duty to prevent ourselves from acting either from an inclination to harm others or from an inclination to seek our own pleasure, in doing which we should incidentally harm them. But on reflection it seems clear that the primary duty here is the duty not to harm others, this being a duty whether or not we have an inclination that if followed would lead to our harming them; and that when we have such an inclination the primary duty not to harm others gives rise to a consequential duty to resist the inclination. The recognition of this duty of non-maleficence is the first step on the way to the recognition of the duty of beneficence; and that accounts for the prominence of the commands 'thou shalt not kill,' 'thou shalt not commit adultery,' 'thou shalt not steal,' 'thou shalt not bear false witness,' in so early a code as the Decalogue. But even when we have come to recognize the duty of beneficence, it appears to me that the duty of non-maleficence is recognized as a distinct one, and as *prima facie* more binding. We should not in general consider it justifiable to kill one person in order to keep another alive, or to steal from one in order to give alms to another.

The essential defect of the 'ideal utilitarian' theory is that it ignores, or at least does not do full justice to, the highly personal character of duty. If the only duty is to produce the maximum of good, the question who is to have the good—whether it is myself, or my benefactor, or a person to whom I have made a promise to confer that good on him, or a mere fellow man to whom I stand in no such special relation—should make no difference to my having a duty to produce that good. But we are all in fact sure that it makes a vast difference.

FOR FURTHER READING

For the classic statements of utilitarian ethics, see Jeremy Bentham's *Introduction to the Principles of Morals and Legislation*, first published in 1789, and John Stuart Mill's *Utilitarianism*, first published in 1861. Both works are available in a number of editions, and they can be found together in *The English Philosophers from Bacon to Mill*, edited by E. A. Burtt (New York: Random House, 1939). See also Book IV of Henry Sidgwick's *The Methods of Ethics* (New York: Dover, 1966), first published in 1874. In 1903, G. E. Moore published *Principia Ethica* (Cambridge: Cambridge University Press, 1965), which offers the classic statement of ideal utilitarianism.

For a recent and widely discussed defense of utilitarianism, see J. J. C. Smart's "Extreme and Restricted Utilitarianism," *Philosophical Quarterly*, Vol. 6 (1956). Also of interest is John Rawl's "Two Conceptions of Rules," *Philosophical Review*, Vol. 64 (1955), which outlines a form of rule utilitarianism. Both works are widely anthologized and can be found in *Theories of Ethics*, edited by Philippa Foot (Oxford: Oxford University Press, 1967).

All of the above works are somewhat difficult but they can be understood by most introductory students willing to expend the effort. Less difficult expositions can be found in William Frankena's *Ethics* (Englewood Cliffs: Prentice-Hall, 1973) and Gilbert Harman's *The Nature of Morality: An Introduction to Ethics* (New York: Oxford University Press, 1977). The Frankena book is a widely read introductory ethics text and is useful for its discussions of almost all of the topics I have treated in Part I. The Harman is also useful for its discussions of many of these topics. My own discussions of utilitarianism and cultural relativism draw a good deal from his.

For the classic statements of deontological ethics, see Immanuel Kant's *Foundations of the Metaphysics of Morals* (Indianapolis: Liberal Arts Press, 1959), first published in 1785, and W. D. Ross's *The Right and the Good* (Oxford: Oxford University Press, 1973), first published in 1930. Kant's book is notoriously difficult, and the student may wish to consult a commentary such as H. J. Paton's *The Categorical Imperative* (Philadelphia: University of Pennsylvania Press, 1971). An easier exposition of Kant's moral philosophy can be found in S. Körner's *Kant* (Baltimore: Penguin, 1960).

Ethical hedonism is discussed by most of the above works. Bentham, Mill, and Sidgwick favor it; Moore and Ross oppose it. Frankena, once again, provides a useful discussion of the topic. The first important discussions of the relationship among pleasure, happiness, and the good can be found, not surprisingly, in the writings of the ancient Greek philosophers Plato and Aristotle. Plato's arguments against hedonism can be found in his dialogues *Gorgias* and *Philebus*, both available in a number of editions. Aristotle's position is given in his *Nicomachean Ethics* (Indianapolis: Liberal Arts Press, 1962). There Aristotle argues that the good is *eudaimonia*, usually translated as "happiness," but better translated, perhaps, as "total well-being." However translated, *eudaimonia* is not to be equated with pleasure.

A well-known defense of situation ethics is Joseph Fletcher's *Situation Ethics* (Philadelphia: The Westminster Press, 1966). For Sartre's statement of his existentialist ethics, see "Existentialism Is a Humanism," in *Existentialism from Dostoevsky to Sartre*, edited by Walter Kaufmann (New York: The World Publishing Company, 1956).

The most sustained defense of ethical egoism can be found in the writings of novelist-essayist Ayn Rand. See, for example *Atlas Shrugged* (New York: Random House, 1957) and *The Virtue of Selfishness* (New York: Signet, 1964).

R. M. Hare's *Freedom and Reason* (New York: Oxford University Press, 1970) contains the landmark discussion of moral judgments as universalizable and moral principles as overriding all other principles of action. See also Marcus George Singer's *Generalization in Ethics* (New York: Knopf, 1961).

Also, Alasdair MacIntyre's *A Short History of Ethics* (New York: Macmillan, 1973) is a brief but useful history of moral philosophy.

For general overviews of many of the topics discussed in "The Nature of Moral Knowledge," see W. D. Hudson's *Modern Moral Philosophy* (Garden City: Anchor, 1970), G. J. Warnock's *Contemporary Moral Philosophy* (London: Macmillan, 1967) and Mary Warnock's *Ethics Since 1900* (London: Oxford University Press, 1960). Hudson's, the longest of the three, is by far the most detailed. Although it is more difficult than the other two, it is the most helpful in connecting the various positions to the major philosophical movements of the period. Also helpful are Frankena's *Ethics* and Harman's *The Nature of Morality: An Introduction to Ethics.*

A large number of general anthologies cover much of the same ground. Paul W. Taylor's *The Moral Judgment* (Englewood Cliffs: Prentice-Hall, 1963) is devoted exclusively to these topics. Unfortunately, it does not include selections dealing with cultural relativism. Such selections can be found in another anthology edited by Taylor, *Problems of Moral Philosophy* (Belmont, Calif.: Dickenson, 1972). Also recommended is *Readings in Ethical Theory*, ed. by Sellars and Hospers (New York: Appleton-Century-Crofts, 1970).

Harman's book presents a strong argument in favor of cultural relativism. For anthropological defenses of the view, see Ruth Benedict's "Anthropology and the Abnormal," *Journal of General Psychology*, X, 1955, and M. Herskovitz's *Man and His Works* (New York: Knopf, 1948), Chapter 5. For opposing views by other anthropologists, see Clyde Kluckhohn's "Ethical Relativity," *Journal of Philosophy*, 52, 1955, and Ralph Linton's "Universal Ethical Principles," in *Moral Principles of Action: Man's Ethical Imperative*, ed. by Ruth Nanda Anshen (New York: Harper, 1952).

The most well known and widely discussed defense of intuitionism can be found in G. E. Moore's *Principia Ethica*. Other noted intuitionists are Thomas Reid and W. D. Ross. See Reid's *Essays on the Active Powers of Man* (Cambridge, Mass.: MIT Press, 1969), Essay III, first published in 1788, and Ross's *The Right and the Good.*

Aristotle's views on human nature and ethics can be found in his *Nicomachean Ethics*. Nietzsche's views can be found in *Beyond Good and Evil* (New York: Random House, 1966). For Edward Wilson's views, see *On Human Nature* (Cambridge, Mass.: Harvard University Press, 1978) and *Sociobiology: The New Synthesis* (Cambridge, Mass.: Harvard University Press, 1975).

Many philosophers have felt that morality stems from an innate sense of sympathy or compassion, and can thus be seen as precursors of part of Wilson's view. Most important are David Hume and Arthur Schopenhauer. See Hume's *Treatise of Human Nature* (Oxford: Clarendon Press, 1973) Book III, first published in 1739, and *Enquiry Concerning the Principles of Morals* (LaSalle, Ill.: Open Court, 1966), first published in 1751, and Schopenhauer's *On the Basis of Morality* (Indianapolis: Liberal Arts Press, 1965), first published in 1841.

In addition to Aristotle and Nietzsche, many other philosophers have based their ethical views on their views of human nature. Most important in this regard is Baruch Spinoza, whose *Ethics*, first published in 1677, has been very influential. The work can be found in *Spinoza: Selections*, ed. John Wild (New York: Charles Scribner's Sons, 1958). Since it is also a very difficult book, a secondary source is recommended, such as Stuart Hampshire's *Spinoza* (Baltimore: Pelican, 1962).

The most carefully worked-out emotivist theory can be found in C. L. Stevenson's *Ethics and Language* (New Haven: Yale University Press, 1944). Another well-known defense of emotivism can be found in Chapter 6 of A. J. Ayer's *Language, Truth and Logic* (New York: Dover, 1936).

Prescriptivism is most closely identified with R. M. Hare. The theory is worked out in *The Language of Morals* (New York: Oxford University Press, 1964) and *Freedom and Reason*. Another noncognitivist position of interest is J. O. Urmson's. Like Hare, Urmson emphasizes the importance of criteria in value judgments, but he argues that "good" is a grading word. See "On Grading," *Mind*, LIX, 1950. This paper is reprinted in *The Moral Judgment*.

For many of the most important contributions to the debate concerning the relationship between judgments of how things are and judgments of how things ought to be, see *The Is/Ought Question*, ed. by W. D. Hudson (New York: St. Martin's Press, 1969).

Both *Ethics and Language* and *Freedom and Reason* provide extended discussions of moral disputes.

For the best-known denial of the view that human beings have an essential nature that can provide the basis of morals, see Jean-Paul Sartre's "Existentialism Is a Humanism."

Plato's views on morality, happiness, and the divisions of the soul are laid out in his *Republic*, one of the great classics of philosophy. The *Republic* is available in numerous editions. Perhaps the easiest to find is the Penguin Classic edition (Baltimore, 1955).

For Aristotle's views on morality and happiness, as well as on practical reason, see his *Nicomachean Ethics*.

Plato's work is written in the form of a dialogue and is thought by many to have as strong a literary as a philosophical appeal. In addition to his ethical theories, Plato's metaphysics, theory of knowledge, and political philosophy are all considered in detail. Aristotle's work is drier, but not extremely difficult.

For Kant's views, see his *Critique of Practical Reason* (Indianapolis: Liberal Arts Press, 1956), first published in 1788, and his *Foundations of the Metaphysics of Morals*.

Kurt Baier presents his views in *The Moral Point of View* (New York: Random House, 1958). The material I have covered can be found in the final three chapters of the book. For Frankena's views, see the last chapter of *Ethics*. Although Baier's book is written for philosophers, it is highly readable and nontechnical.

For two other contemporary treatments of the issues we have just looked at, see John Hospers' *Human Conduct* (New York: Harcourt, Brace & World, 1961) and Kai Nielsen's "Why Should I Be Moral?" originally printed in *Methodos*, XV (1963), 275–306. The Nielsen paper and the relevant passages from Hospers are reprinted in the Sellars and Hospers anthology, *Readings in Ethical Theory*. Hospers presents a discussion of Baier and a detailed criticism of Plato. Nielsen discusses Hospers' views, as well as those of Baier and Aristotle.

Hobbes's discussion of the state of nature occurs in his *Leviathan* (Indianapolis: Liberal Arts Press, 1958), first published in 1651. Also to be found in the book is his defense of psychological egoism.

An excellent contemporary discussion of psychological egoism is Joel Feinberg's "Psychological Egoism," which appears in his widely used introduction to philosophy anthology, *Freedom and Responsibility* (Belmont, Calif.: Dickenson, 1978). This article was originally written for his own philosophy students. Also valuable is Paul Taylor's introduction to the topic in his anthology *Problems of Moral Philosophy*. This book also contains selections from *Leviathan* and *The Moral Point of View*, Nielsen's paper, and C. D. Broad's

"Egoism as a Theory of Human Values." Broad's article also appears in his *Ethics and the History of Philosophy* (London: Routledge and Kegan Paul, 1952).

The view that pleasure is the goal of all human action is most closely associated with Jeremy Bentham and John Stuart Mill. See Bentham's *Introduction to the Principles of Morals and Legislation* and Mill's *Utilitarianism*.

Part II

POLITICS AND THE INDIVIDUAL

Chapter 6

JUSTICE, RIGHTS, AND THE SOCIAL CONTRACT

The central questions of political philosophy concern the existence and powers of the state. Should there be a state at all? If so, what kind of state? And what are our obligations to it?

It is important to realize that these questions are *moral* ones. They could very easily be asked in the following way. Does the existence of the state have any moral justification? If so, what powers is the state morally justified in exercising? And are we morally obligated to obey all of its laws? To appreciate the force of these questions, let us take a brief look at some of the most important features that any state has.

THE STATE

Most of us take the existence of the state for granted. Although we often argue about the wisdom of certain state policies (such as the building of various missile systems), or the morality of certain state policies (such as the legalization of abortion), or the role that the state ought to play in our daily lives (such as whether various business decisions should be regulated by state agencies), we do not ordinarily ask ourselves whether there ought to *be* a state.

But consider certain fundamental features of the state. For one thing, it holds a monopoly on certain uses of force. It and it alone has the legal right to use force for any reason other than self-defense. Only the state can have a police force or an army. Only the state can imprison us. Only the state can wage war.

For another thing, through its taxation power, the state has the legal right to redistribute wealth. It takes the money that we have earned and spends it, not only for the maintenance of its army and police forces, but for roads, schools, administrative agencies, and for such things as food stamps and welfare payments.

Moreover, the state makes a unique claim to our obedience. It may give me the right to leave its boundaries, but as long as I choose to remain, I must obey its laws on pain of punishment. Whether I agree with its spending policies or not, I must pay taxes. Whether I support a given war or not, if I am a male of the appropriate age, I must register for the draft and, if called, serve. If I am of a certain age, I must attend school. I must refrain from drinking or smoking a variety of substances, if certain laws require it.

No other institution exerts such powers over us. If any other institution were to try, we would erupt in a perfectly justifiable moral outrage. No one else has the *moral right* to wield such power. Why, then, should the state? Why should it be theft for *me* to play Robin Hood, but not the state? Why should it be morally wrong for *racketeers* to sell "protection" to small business owners, but not the state? Why should the state be able to draft me during time of war, but not a neighborhood street gang? How, in short, can we justify the existence of such a coercive monopoly?

THE SOCIAL CONTRACT

Many philosophers—including Thomas Hobbes (1588–1679), John Locke (1632–1704), Jean Jacques Rousseau (1712–1782), and Immanuel Kant (1724–1804)—have attempted to justify the existence of the state by viewing it as the product of a *social contract*. That is, they have thought of the state as an institution created and voluntarily joined by all the individuals who live within its boundaries. Before the contract, these individuals live in a *state of nature*. That is, they live in a condition in which there is no state, and, consequently, no legal limit to their freedom. By entering into the contract, they agree to give up certain freedoms and obey the laws of the state. The notion of such a contract is, of course, a historical fiction. States do not arise that way. Still, it is a *useful* fiction. Here's why.

The notion of a social contract allows us to perform the following thought experiment. Let us imagine a group of individuals who are subject to certain moral constraints but no legal constraints. All of them have a sense of justice, and they are concerned to create a way of living together that will embody that sense of justice. What sort of society would they choose, knowing that they will be bound by the rules of that society? What sort of society would they have the moral right to choose?

The importance of the social-contract conception is this. It shows how the state *could* have come about. And if it shows that the state could have come about in a moral way, it gives the state a moral justification. Moreover, it gives a *particular* kind of state a moral justification—the state that our imagined individuals would choose. So social-contract theory not only justifies the existence of the state, but answers our second question as well—what *kind* of state should we have? As we shall see, this second question admits of different answers, depending on our basic conception of justice. We will focus on two such conceptions, and on the types of state that embody them.

Natural Rights

Let us begin our examination of the social contract with John Locke, whose views had a profound influence on the creation of our own government. (For discussions of the social-contract theories of Hobbes and Rousseau, see Chapter 7.)

Locke viewed the individual in the state of nature this way. All individuals in the state of nature have certain *natural rights.* These rights belong to them because they are human beings, and no one has the right to rob them of these rights. These rights include the right to life and health, and the freedom to act as they choose, and the right to dispose of their property however they see fit—as long as they do not interfere with others' exercise of the same rights. Moreover, all individuals have the right to *protect* these rights. That is, they have the right to defend themselves, punish those who attempt to harm or rob them, and exact compensation from those who succeed in harming or robbing them.

Where do these natural rights come from? Locke thought that there was a moral law of nature embedded in the world by God. We need not buy that claim, though. Instead, we can give Locke a more cautious view—that according to his own sense of justice, a sense of justice that most readers will share, we are morally free to act as we choose as long as we do not harm others by doing so, and we are morally free to protect our lives, health, and property. That is, we can view natural rights as agreed-upon moral rights, rather than rights embedded in the natural order of things.

The important thing to keep in mind is that these moral rights are not granted by the state. They are rights that we believe belong to us whether the state recognizes them or not, whether there even exists a state to recognize them or not.

The Transfer of Rights

Unfortunately, these natural rights are of little value if they are not respected by others. Unless we can *enforce* these rights, our freedom will be hampered and our lives, health, and property will be in jeopardy. That is the situation in which individuals in the state of nature find themselves. Therefore, we can imagine them coming together to ensure that their natural rights will be respected. They will do this by making them enforceable.

How will they proceed? First, they will agree to a system of laws that will

protect their rights, a system of laws that all will adhere to. They will outlaw
stealing, murder, and other acts that interfere with their rights to act and dispose of their property. Second, they will devise a system of applying and en-
forcing these laws. That is, they will create institutions to determine when a law
has been broken, who is to be punished, how that person is to be punished, and
what compensation is to be given to the injured party. They will also create institutions capable of carrying out these decisions. In other words, they will create a state—with legislative, judicial, and police powers.

Locke views such a contract as the *delegation* of rights by individuals to the
community. The individuals who enter into the contract agree to *transfer* certain
natural rights to the community as a whole in order to protect other natural
rights. They give the legislative body the right to pass laws to determine what
actions count as an infringement of their rights. They give the judicial body the
right to determine who has broken these laws and how the legally prescribed
punishments and compensations are to be applied. They give the executive
body the right to enforce these judgments.

Because these delegated rights ultimately belong to the members of the community, the members of the community must maintain effective control over
the people chosen to exercise these rights in their name. That means that the
state must be a *democratic* one. Officials who act in their name must be subject to
majority rule.

Limits on the State

But the majority must have some limits to its powers. The state is not
morally free to do *whatever* the majority wants it to do. Its powers are limited by
the terms of the original contract. And those limits are clear. The state has the
right to protect the natural rights of its members. That is the only right delegated to it by its members. Indeed, it is the only right its members have the *right*
to delegate.

The reason is this. In coming together to form a social contract, the individuals involved are morally free to transfer their own rightful powers. They cannot
transfer any powers they do *not* rightfully have. Since they have the right, subject to the same rights of others, to decide what is necessary for the preservation
of themselves and the rest of humankind, they can transfer that right. Thus,
they can give the state the right to pass laws against murder and theft, for example. Since they have the right to punish others for infringing on their rights,
they can transfer that right. Thus, they can also give the state the right to imprison people who kill or steal.

What about people's right to dispose of their property as they see fit, or the
right to health, or to life? These rights are *not* delegated to the state. Locke gives
two reasons for this. First, to delegate these rights would be to destroy the entire
purpose of the social contract, which is to *protect* these rights. Although there is a
real point to transferring *some* individual rights in order to protect others, there
is no point to transferring *all* of them. In fact, Locke goes so far as to say that the

chief purpose of the social contract is the protection of property rights. Therefore, the state has no right to interfere with them. The state may levy taxes to support its legislative, judicial and police powers—subject to the will of the majority—but it must otherwise respect the property rights of its members. Second, no individual in the state of nature has the right to take his own life, nor can he take the life and property of another, except in defense of his own. Since he does not have these rights, he cannot delegate them. According to Locke, then, no individual *would* delegate his property rights, and no individual *could* delegate his rights to life and freedom, nor could he delegate his *nonexistent* rights to violate those of others.

The Minimal State

Robert Nozick, perhaps the most influential contemporary Lockean, calls the result of such a social contract a *minimal state,* or a *night-watchman state.* Such a state has the right (indeed, the obligation) to protect its citizens from violence, theft, and fraud, and it has the right (and obligation) to enforce contracts between its citizens. It also has the right to levy taxes to finance these functions. And that is it.

What *can't* such a state do? Well, it can't tell its citizens what they can't read, what they can't smoke, what films they can't see, what sexual practices they can't engage in. It can't tell them whom to hire, fire, rent an apartment to, or admit to their places of business. It can't force its citizens to pay for schools or libraries or to contribute to their own retirement through social security taxes. It can't draft them into the army. It can't control prices, wages, or rents. It can't force its citizens to support welfare payments, food stamps, or other programs meant to redistribute wealth for the purpose of financial equality. It can't use tax revenues for disaster relief, for the rebuilding of urban rubble, or for mass transit. It can't use its taxation powers to get its citizens to buy less gasoline.

All of the above policies constitute an infringement of individual rights. In the state of nature, I have the right to read and smoke what I like, and I do not transfer that right to the state. In the state of nature, I have the right to give to the poor or not, and I do not transfer that right to the state. In the state of nature, I have the right to hire whomever I choose, and I do not transfer that right to the state. Even if a majority of the state's citizens decide otherwise, they do not have the moral right to enforce that decision. The terms of the social contract severely limit the majority's right to curtail my freedom.

Moral Side-Constraints

At this point, it is tempting to object to the whole social-contract enterprise. After all, the notion of a social contract is a historical fiction. Why should the majority be bound by the terms of a contract that never took place?

Moreover, why should the majority be bound by Locke's natural rights? If moral rights are merely the agreed-upon moral sentiments of a society, why can't we trust the moral sentiments of the majority to determine what our rights are? Can't we agree that the poor have a right to food, shelter, and medical care? Can't we agree that the state has the right to support public schools and libraries through general tax revenues?

Nozick thinks not. He argues that there are definite moral side-constraints to the will of the majority, that the majority does not have the right to force its will on the minority come what may. His reason is this. From Kant, he borrows this fundamental ethical principle: We have no right to treat another person as a means to our own ends. Every person, by virtue of being a rational being capable of choosing and acting according to her own goals, has a right to pursue those goals. She is not a tool to be used by others for their own ends. She is, in Kant's terms, an end in herself. So even if the majority adopts the noble goal of eradicating poverty, it has no right to use an unwilling person to further that goal. We have the right to pursue this goal through voluntary charities but not to tell the unwilling woman that she must donate so much of her wages to it.

Most of us accept this fundamental principle in our daily lives. We do not think that our schools, employers, friends, or family have the right to force us to contribute to charity. We do not think that others have the right to use us for their own ends, however noble.

The point of Lockean social-contract theory, it might be said, is to show that the same principle applies to the state as well. It is to get us to think of ourselves as Kantian ends in ourselves. It is to remind us of the inherent dignity we think belongs to each individual, and of the freedom that goes with it. It is to remind us that we are the source of the state's moral legitimacy, and that there are moral constraints to what we can legitimize. What we as individuals cannot morally force others to do in a state of nature, we cannot morally empower the state to do.

An alternative approach

Having said all that, we may still be somewhat dissatisfied with the approach of Locke and Nozick. Somehow, the minimal state does not seem *fair*. Consider the late nineteenth and early twentieth centuries, when the American government was far closer to the minimal state than it is today. It was a time when poverty forced young children to quit school and work from dawn to dusk in dangerous work places for paltry wages, when workers who went on strike to improve their lot were quickly replaced by impoverished people willing to work for even lower wages, when workers could be fired for attempting to unionize, and when they had no unemployment compensation to fall back on to feed themselves and their families. Was it fair that millions of people were forced to sacrifice their health and futures while the rich and powerful were permitted to increase their wealth and power at the expense of the poor and powerless? Was it fair that the state protected the factories and mines from striking workers but did not protect the strikers from the ruthless policies of the owners?

Eventually, the American public decided that these things were *not* fair. They decided that all people have a right to decent wages and working conditions, a right to a minimum standard of living, and that the state has an obligation to see that they are not deprived of these rights.

Decades later, we made a similar decision. Faced with continuing poverty of and discrimination against black Americans, we decided that they were not given a fair chance to get their share of America's wealth. We decided that it was unfair that the forces of the state be used to "protect" businesses from prospective black patrons and workers but not to protect blacks from discriminatory practices. We decided that it was unfair that a child of the urban ghetto could not avail himself of the opportunities open to his middle-class white counterpart.

Is there an alternative to the approach of Locke and Nozick that legitimizes such decisions? One recent variation on social-contract theory attempts to provide such an approach. It comes from the contemporary American philosopher John Rawls.

The Veil of Ignorance

Let us suppose that the framers of the social contract wanted to devise the fairest state they could. How would they go about it?

One way of answering this question is to think of an analogous situation—the creation of a new game, for instance. In such a situation, the people involved should adopt rules that everyone is willing to accept. Moreover, if the game is to be fair, the choice of rules must not be determined by one person's knowledge of how the rules will affect her chances of winning. If one person knows in advance which rules will benefit her, and if she has the power to get others to agree to those rules, the result will be unfairly biased in her favor. That is the problem, Rawls feels, with Locke's version of the social contract. Although the people who draw up the social contract are *supposed* to be equal, they are not. Some begin wealthy, others poor. Some have great power, others none. The minimal state is stacked in favor of the rich and powerful and against the poor and weak.

Suppose, however, that they approached the social contract as they would the creation of a fair game. If they did that, they would have to approach it from behind what Rawls calls a *veil of ignorance*. They would have to be ignorant of who would have what goods, who would wield what power, who would have what position in the new state. They would have to devise it in such a way that they would be willing to accept whatever position they would end up with. Only then would the outcome be unbiased. Only then would undue influence be avoided. Only then would the outcome be fair.

Two Principles of Justice

What would the outcome of such a contract be? Rawls claims that the devisers of the contract would agree on the following two principles of justice. The first principle is the *equality principle*. It says that every person has a right to the greatest basic freedom compatible with similar freedom for all. This principle includes two requirements. First, there must be equal freedom for everybody. Second, if the extent of freedom can be increased without violating the first requirement, it must be increased. The other principle is the *difference principle*. It says that all social and economic inequalities must be arranged in accordance with two considerations. First, these inequalities must be to everyone's advantage, including the people on the bottom of the scale. Second, they must be attached to positions that are open to all.

The basic freedoms of the first principle parallel Locke's natural rights, and are roughly the freedoms listed in our own Constitution and Bill of Rights—political freedom, property rights, freedom of speech, thought, religion, assembly, and so forth. What distinguishes Rawls from Locke and Nozick here is not the freedoms, but the way of arriving at them. For Rawls, they arise from mutual agreement. For Locke and Nozick, they are prior constraints on any agreement that might be rightfully reached.

The inequalities of the second principle are the sort that exist between a physician, say, and an unskilled worker. The physician receives greater pay than the unskilled worker, enjoys greater prestige, and reaps the benefits that go along with both. We can justify such inequalities this way. Everyone, including the unskilled worker, benefits if there are enough physicians to serve all. But to ensure that enough people will put up with the long rigors of medical school, some additional benefits must be given them. Therefore, the inequalities are advantageous to all. Moreover, as long as all qualified people are given an equal chance to become physicians, these additional benefits will be available to those who deserve and want them.

But what if the inequalities are *too* great? What if they are larger than required to benefit everyone? In our own society, we try to solve such problems through a progressive tax system and transfer payments to the poor. We tax a higher percentage of the income of the rich, and we attempt to improve the lot of the poor through food stamps and other welfare programs. (Whether these measures are acceptable, inadequate, or too far-reaching is, of course, a matter of national debate.)

What if access to the more heavily rewarded positions is not open to all? What if blacks and women, for example, are excluded from the high-paying professions? In our own society, we try to solve such problems through civil rights legislation. (Once again, whether these measures are acceptable, inadequate, or too far-reaching is a matter of national debate.)

Why would we select such principles from behind the veil of ignorance? The answer is simple. If we did not know whether we would be the ones with limited freedom, and if we did not know whether we would be the ones exploited by the rich, and if we did not know whether we would be the ones denied equal opportunity, we would certainly not accept a system in which such people would exist. It would be like accepting a rigged game without knowing whether it would be rigged in our favor or our opponents'.

TWO CONCEPTIONS OF JUSTICE

Rawls claims that a society built on his two principles is a just society. It is a just society because it is a *fair* one. Thus, he calls his conception of justice *justice as fairness*. Nozick, of course, does not accept this conception of justice. He claims that a society is just only if the state is a minimal state. A minimal state is just because it ensures the natural rights of the individual, because it does not violate crucial moral side-constraints. Individuals, he claims, are *entitled* to the property they have gained by honest means, and they are *entitled* to do with their property as they choose as long as they do not violate the rights of others. Thus, he calls his conception of justice an *entitlement conception of justice*.

Both of these conceptions have played notable roles in the American tradition. The entitlement conception dominated the thinking of the founding fathers. Its influence is evident in the preamble of the Declaration of Independence, for instance, whose author, Thomas Jefferson, was a staunch Lockean. Justice as fairness took a longer time to gain hold, and did not reach its maturity, perhaps, until Franklin Roosevelt's New Deal.

At one time, a good deal of political debate in America could be viewed as a confrontation between these two conceptions. In recent times, many arguments over civil rights legislation fit this model. When Senator Barry Goldwater spoke out against the 1964 Civil Rights Act, for instance, he articulated the entitlement conception. All of us, he argued, have the right to serve or exclude whomever we want in the operation of our business, regardless of the morality of our motives. Against this, the winning side argued that it was unjust to deny black Americans full opportunity to participate in the benefits of the American economy.

As the outcome of that battle indicates, justice as fairness is now in the ascendancy. In the two major political parties, even the most conservative politicians admit that the government has some obligation to help the poor, the distressed, the minorities, and others in need of help. Conservatives are now apt to argue that liberal programs don't work or that they are inefficient, but not that they are unjust. The one exception to this rule appears to be affirmative-action programs. Opponents of these programs do argue that it is unjust to give minorities preference in hiring and school admissions. Otherwise, the entitlement conception of justice is kept alive largely by one small American political party, the Libertarian Party, which you have probably never heard of.

But even if we admit that justice as fairness is the historical winner, we can still ask whether it should have won. Nozick, of course, thinks not. To see why, we can turn to his criticism of Rawls.

Why the Veil of Ignorance?

Suppose that it is the end of the term. You have just completed a course in a subject totally new to you, and you have no idea how you did. Sup-

ANOTHER DEFENSE OF THE MINIMAL STATE

In the main body of this chapter, we discuss a defense of the minimal state based on the concept of natural rights. In what follows, we shall look at another defense of the minimal state, one that does not involve an appeal to natural rights.

Utilitarianism and Democracy

In Chapter 3, we looked at the moral philosophy of John Stuart Mill—utilitarianism. According to the utilitarian view, an action is right if, compared with the alternatives, it results in the greatest balance of happiness over unhappiness when the interests of everyone affected are taken into account.

Obviously, the utilitarian will have little difficulty justifying the existence of *some* sort of state. Without some type of governing body to protect the interests of individuals, it is clear that the balance of happiness over unhappiness (that is, *utility*) will not be maximized. Since the existence of a state increases utility, it is better to have one than not.

But what kind of state? Mill argues that a state in which everyone has a voice in running it is better than one in which only a handful of people run it. That is, the form of state most likely to maximize utility is a democracy.

He gives two reasons for this. First, there is no guarantee that a ruling elite will rule in the best interests of the citizenry. Indeed, there is no guarantee that a ruling elite will even *care* about the best interests of its citizenry. Since most people are more concerned about their own interests than the interests of others, it is more likely that the ruling elite will put itself first. Therefore, it is better if all citizens of the state have the political power to safeguard their own interests. And the state that best ensures that citizens have this power is a democratic state, a state in which every citizen has some say in the running of the government.

Second, it is in the best interests of society as a whole if the individuals within that society are actively and energetically concerned with the problems of that society. But that sort of concern requires a certain sort of character—an active character rather than a passive one, a character willing to seek solutions and act on them. Such a character is not encouraged by a state governed by a small elite. A ruling elite prefers, on the whole, a passive citizenry, one that will not interfere with its own powers. But a democracy does encourage such a character. When citizens have the power to safeguard their own interests in the political sphere, when they can participate in the political decisions that affect their lives, they can be expected to be politically active. And this political activity encourages self-reliance and self-discipline. Therefore, people in a democracy can be expected to turn their energies to improving their own lot and the lot of society as a whole in other spheres as well—medicine, for example, or technology and commerce.

Utilitarianism and the Minimal State

Although democracy is to be preferred to other forms of government on utilitarian grounds, there is no guarantee that majority rule will protect the interests of all citizens. Just as there can be a tyranny of the elite, so can there be a tyranny of the majority. Without some constraints to its power, the majority can stifle the voices of dissenting citizens and interfere with their pursuit of success and happiness. Thus, certain rights must be guaranteed the citizenry. According to Mill, these rights must not be construed as *natural* rights. Rather, their sole justification is to be provided by utility. Thus, the state should grant its citizens those rights that we can reasonably expect to lead to the greatest balance of happiness over unhappiness for everybody concerned.

What are these rights? Among the most important are the freedom of thought and discussion. According to Mill, any idea, no matter how foolish it may seem, must be given its place in the marketplace of ideas. If we do not give every idea a free and open hearing, the search for truth will be seriously hampered. Only by constant challenge to received opinion, only by unfettered inquiry and free debate, can we hope to arrive at the truth. When the majority seeks to protect itself from unpopular ideas by stifling free debate, the pursuit of knowledge and truth is jeopardized. And since it is more reasonable to assume that knowledge will have better consequences for individual lives and society as a whole than prejudice and false belief, we must not jeopardize that pursuit.

But what if we are *certain* that the unpopular ideas are false? Shouldn't we censor them to protect the truth? To these questions, Mill responds that absolute certainty is unattainable. No individual is infallible, nor is the majority infallible. Therefore, the majority cannot hide behind any claims of certainty.

Beyond protecting freedom of thought and expression, the state should grant and protect the right of all citizens to conduct their lives as they see fit as long as their actions do not directly harm others. In this regard, Mill distinguishes between *self-regarding* and *other-regarding* virtues. Self-regarding virtues are the virtues of prudence—protecting one's own health, livelihood, and happiness. Other-regarding virtues include abstaining from violence, theft, fraud, and the like. On utilitarian grounds, the state has the right to enact and enforce laws against violence, theft, and fraud, but does not have the right to enact and enforce laws protecting us from our own lack of prudence.

Why this latter restriction on the powers of the state? Mill was convinced that in the great majority of cases, individuals will be better off if they take care of themselves rather than rely on others to take care of them. Even if there are some cases in which the state can maximize short-run utility by protecting some individuals from themselves, in the long run, utility will best be served if the state does not interfere in such matters. For one thing, the state will more likely than not make bad decisions on some such matters. For another, the citizens will become less self-reliant, and the sort of active and energetic character we want to encourage will be discouraged instead. Thus, such legislation as social security and welfare benefits, as well as laws requiring seat belts in cars and helmets on motorcycle drivers, should not be part of the state's legitimate powers. Nor should the control of private morality. What we are left with, then, is the minimal state.

Does Utilitarianism Lead to the Minimal State?

Is Mill right about the kind of state that utilitarianism justifies? Will the minimal state really maximize utility? Few people today would say *yes.* Whatever flaws our welfare system has, for example, it seems clear that more benefit results from it than harm. It also seems clear that a better welfare system would be more likely to maximize utility than no welfare system at all.

Indeed, it seems that much of the legislation that Rawls would champion in the name of fairness could as easily be championed in the name of utility—civil rights legislation to increase the well-being of minorities, or labor legislation to increase the well-being of workers. In the main body of this chapter, I noted the labor conditions that existed in the late nineteenth and early twentieth centuries, when the United States was closer to the minimal state than it is today. It is unlikely that there was then a greater balance of happiness over unhappiness than there is now.

Moreover, it may be that utility would be maximized by some form of socialism, that is, a society in which the state owned the means of production and controlled the economy in a centralized manner. Mill himself began to wonder along those lines in his later life, although he remained concerned over the future of individual liberty in such a society. The question of socialism, however, is the topic of our next chapter.

pose that everyone else in the course is similarly ignorant. The instructor addresses the class on the final day.

There are ten of you in the course, she says. I have added up the total of your grades in the final exam, and it comes to seven hundred and fifty points. I am willing to divide those points among you according to any pattern you like. That is, I will let *you* pick the final distribution of grades. You can decide that each of you will get a seventy-five, that each of you will get the grade I've already given you, or that the grades will be patterned in any other way. I'll post the grades I've given you on the bulletin board before you make up your minds, but I won't tell you who got which grade. How shall we do it?

Chances are, you and your fellow students would accept the suggestion that the points be distributed equally. (Remember, none of you has any idea how you did.)

Suppose that the instructor asked you not to pick a particular *pattern* of distribution (so many 100s, so many 90s and so forth), but a particular *method* of distribution. In that case, you would still be likely to choose equality. You would probably choose the method (divide the total by ten) that gives the same distribution as the first answer. Why? Because it is doubtful that all of you would be willing to risk being on the bottom.

Of course, you might pick a different distribution. If the instructor told you that she would add more points to the total if you picked some *non*equalizing principle, you might agree on a principle that maximizes the lowest grade. Suppose, for example, that the teacher were willing to add a hundred points to the total if you agreed to allow a spread of at least twenty points between the top grade and the bottom. That is, instead of dividing 750 points among you, she will divide 850 points among you, as long as you are willing to allow some inequalities in the final distribution. In that case, you would probably decide on the following. Give one person a 100, one person an 80, and then divide the remaining points equally among the other eight, giving each a grade of 83.

In other words, you would be acting according to Rawls's difference principle. You would strive for equality, unless the inequalities benefited everyone, even the person at the bottom. By allowing some inequalities in the grade distribution, you have raised the bottom grade from a 75 to an 83.

But you would not agree on the instructor's original distribution. Why not? Because as long as you are behind the veil of ignorance, and as long as you do not accept some moral side-constraints that provide some limits to what *ought* to be chosen, you will pick a principle of distribution that gives you the most desirable pattern of distribution.

But in *this* case, the outcome is *not* a just one. If we assume that the instructor's grading was competent and impartial, then the students involved *deserve* the grades she gave them. That is, they are *entitled* to those grades, and it is unjust to deny an *A* to someone entitled to it. There is no reason, then, to believe that decisions agreed on from behind the veil of ignorance lead to just outcomes. Indeed, there is greater reason to believe that they do not. Here's why.

From behind the veil of ignorance, we are likely to make decisions about the distribution of things according to the pattern that will result. If we do not know how things will turn out for us individually, we are likely to pick a pattern that will minimize our risks. That is what the framers of Rawls's social contract do. That is what you and your fellow students do in our little thought experiment.

But is justice a matter of *pattern*? Isn't justice a matter of how the pattern comes to pass? It certainly seems that way in our thought experiment. We cannot tell the just distribution of grades merely by looking at the alternative patterns. We can tell only by knowing whether the grades on the list were determined by competent and impartial grading and whether they were assigned to the people who received them.

The same thing, Nozick claims, holds for the distribution of goods in a society. Knowing how much of the pie each individual has is not enough. We have to know how that distribution came about. How did the individuals in the society get their share? Are they entitled to it?

The best way to ensure a just distribution, then, is to put some moral limits on what the devisers of the social contract may agree on. That is, there must be some *prior* conception of justice that limits their choices. By making the conception the *result* of bargaining from behind the veil of ignorance, Rawls sacrifices justice. He does not guarantee it.

The Large and the Small

Rawls has a response to this argument. The two principles agreed to from behind the veil of ignorance are basic principles to be applied to the society as a whole. They are meant to determine the basic structure of the society as a whole. They are not meant to be applied to smaller groups within the society.

Let us return to our thought experiment. What we did, in effect, was apply the difference principle to our problem of point distribution. When everyone would not benefit from unequal grades, it was decided that everyone would get the same grade. When everyone would benefit if one person were given a 100, it was decided to allow that inequality. But this conflicted with our belief that the students who *earned* an *A* were *entitled* to an *A*.

But why are they so entitled? The answer is this. If we look at society as a whole, we see that everyone benefits by a system in which people receive the grades they earn. Such a system encourages studying, helps to ensure that people who enter various professions are prepared to do so, and provides a way of determining who is most qualified to enter these professions. That is, by applying the difference principle to the large, we arrive at certain entitlements in the small.

We can put this point another way. In our daily lives, there *are* moral side-constraints to what we may decide. These moral side-constraints are the product of the application of Rawls's two principles to the society at large. The social contract arrived at from behind the veil of ignorance creates certain rights, and the application of these principles in the small can violate these rights. That is what happened in our thought experiment. The people who earned *A*'s have a right to them.

The situation is different, however, when it comes to the creation of the social contract. Our job there is to start from scratch. Our job is to create a society *and* its attendant rights. And our only constraint is to ensure that the outcome not be biased in favor of the rich and strong. That is why we need the veil of ignorance.

Nozick, of course, does not accept this. He claims that the fundamental principles of justice in any society must be applicable in the small as well as the large. He sees no reason why it should be otherwise.

THE FINAL WORD?

We seem to have arrived at a dilemma. On the one hand, we are inclined to think that a just society must put some limits on the inequalities that exist among individuals. On the other, we are reluctant to apply these limits at a level beneath that of society as a whole. Rawls gives us an explanation of this fact and hopes that we will accept it. Nozick does not accept it, preferring instead to trust his intuitions when applied to the small.

How are *we* to decide? My own inclination is to go along with Rawls. Unless we accept Locke's notion of natural rights as coming from God and embedded in the world prior to any society, Rawls's view seems more reasonable.

Recall our discussion of Baier and Hobbes in Chapter 5. In that chapter, I described the state of nature as being without morality as well as without law. Recall also our discussion in Chapter 4, in which I concluded that morality is the product of society. The application of these points to our present discussion is this: If we continue to think in terms of the social contract, moral rights are the *product* of that contract. They are not prior constraints on what may be contracted. The standard against which we measure the justice of our society must itself be a matter of agreement.

That does not mean that we must accept *any* outcome, *however* it comes to be agreed upon. If we believe that the point of the contract is to minimize coercion among individuals, then we must insist on a method that guarantees that the outcome will not itself be the product of such coercion. And if the veil of ignorance guarantees that, it is an acceptable method. And if the product is Rawls's two principles, it is an acceptable product.

STUDY QUESTIONS

1. Many political philosophers believe that it is important to justify the existence of the state. Why?
2. What is social-contract theory? Why do some philosophers believe that it is able to justify the existence of at least some kinds of state?
3. Locke, Nozick, and Rawls agree that we have the rights to life and liberty, but Rawls disagrees with the other two about the source of these rights. How does he disagree? How does the disagreement lead to different views about the rightful powers of the state?
4. What does Rawls mean by the veil of ignorance? Why does he think it crucial to the creation of a just social contract? Why does Nozick disagree? Whom do you think is right? Why?
5. Rawls provides two principles of justice. What are they? According to what conception of justice are they just? Why? How does this conception differ from Nozick's? Which conception do you prefer? Why?
6. According to Rawls, his principles of justice are meant to determine the basic structure of society as a whole, but are not to apply to small groups within society. According to Nozick, Rawls's principles of justice lead to unjust results when applied to small groups. Why does he say that? How does Rawls defend his principles against the charge?
7. How does Mill defend the minimal state? How do his arguments differ from Locke's? Which do you find more effective? Why?

GLOSSARY

Difference principle. Principle of justice advocated by John Rawls. According to this principle, the inequalities permitted by a society must be to everyone's advantage, and they must be attached to positions open to all.

Entitlement conception of justice. Conception of justice advocated by Robert Nozick. According to this conception, individuals are entitled to the property they have gained by honest means, and they are entitled to do with it as they see fit as long as they do not infringe on the rights of others. Thus, justice requires that they be able to keep that property and not be hampered in their use of it unless that use infringes on the rights of others.

Equality principle. Principle of justice advocated by John Rawls. According to this principle, every person in a society has a right to the greatest basic freedom compatible with similar freedom for all.

Minimal state. State advocated by John Locke and Robert Nozick. Such a state has only the following rights and obligations: to protect its citizens from violence, theft, and fraud, to enforce contracts, and to levy taxes to finance these functions.

Natural right. According to such thinkers as John Locke, rights that belong to all human beings by virtue of their being human beings. Natural rights can be recognized by the state, but they exist independently of any state, and they mark the moral limits of state action.

Social contract. Historical fiction used by some political philosophers to justify the existence of the state. According to social-contract theory, the state is the result of an agreement among individuals.

State of nature. In *social-contract* theory, the condition that precedes the existence of the state.

Veil of ignorance. According to John Rawls, the condition under which the devisers of the *social contract* would adopt a just society. Behind the veil of ignorance, none of the devisers would know how the positions in the new society would be distributed. Therefore, they would agree to a society in which they would be willing to live whatever position they would end up having.

Chapter 7

THE MARXIST ALTERNATIVE

It is easy to view the dispute of the previous chapter as a family quarrel. Both Nozick and Rawls can be seen as sons of Locke, more united by their brotherhood than divided by their arguments. Both see the state as a contract among free and equal individuals, as the potential embodiment of some traditional conception of justice. They disagree on what that conception of justice should be, of course, as well as on the proper limitations of the state, and Nozick does come off as the more dutiful son. But when all is said and done, they both fall into their father's camp, which is often called *liberal democracy*.

THREE CONTINUUMS

What is liberal democracy? Well, we can answer that question by distinguishing three continuums. The first continuum refers to the number of independent centers of power a society has. The greater the number of independent centers of power, the more *pluralistic* is the society; the fewer independent centers of power, the more *totalitarian*. So a society in which the press, religion, the family, the institutions of business, and so on are allowed to function independently of each other and the state, the more pluralistic is that society.

The more that one institution controls the others, as when the state censors the press, limits religious practice, or restrains trade, the more totalitarian is that society.

The second continuum concerns the degree of *democratic control* that citizens can exert over their government. The more decisions that the people may participate in, the more often they are able to direct the course of their government and the more power they are able to exert on that course, the more *democratic* is their society. The greater the extent to which these powers are denied them, the more *authoritarian* is their society.

The third continuum concerns the ownership of property. The greater the extent to which the means of production are owned by private individuals, the more *capitalistic* is the society. The greater the extent to which they are publicly owned, the more *socialistic* is the society.

Returning now to liberal democracy, we can say this. A liberal democracy is a society more pluralistic than totalitarian, more democratic than authoritarian, and more capitalistic than socialistic. Since we are dealing with continuums, it is difficult to draw a dividing line that neatly separates liberal democracies from other forms of society. The society advocated by Locke, Thomas Jefferson, and Nozick is clearly a liberal democracy. It is the paradigm of liberal democracy. Rawls strays a bit from that paradigm, as has our own society, but neither Rawls nor the United States has completely left the fold. In this chapter we *will* leave the fold. We will turn to Marxist theory, which turns the assumptions of liberal theory upside down.

IDEOLOGY AND RATIONALIZATION

It is easy to do something in our own self-interest and then rationalize it as the right thing to do. We might selfishly withhold help from others, for instance, and then claim that we did so in order to teach them the virtues of self-reliance.

Let us reconsider Locke's justification of liberal democracy, particularly as it applies to capitalism. Locke says this. We have certain natural rights that the state may not take from us. Most important, we have the right to private property, and the right to use it as we see fit. At first glance, this may seem reasonable enough. You have a right to your toothbrush, bicycle, clothing, radio. But that is *personal* property. What about other types of property? Do landlords have the same right to own rental property? Do individuals have the same right to own factories and mines? Does the same principle that applies to toothbrushes apply in these cases?

It is easy to see that such private, *nonpersonal* property is in the hands of a few. Thus, Locke's natural rights are decidedly in the interest of these few. Insofar as these rights justify private property, they justify the wealth and power of these few individuals. Is Locke's theory of justice a rationalization, then?

According to Karl Marx (1818–1883), it is. It is what he would call *capitalist ideology.* That is, it is the rationalization of the capitalist status quo by the rich and the powerful. It is an instrument for keeping the rest of us in our place. The historical fiction of the social contract is a similar rationalization, Marx would say, as is the notion of free and equal individuals in the state of nature. Both are instruments of oppression by the ruling class—the capitalists, the owners of the means of production. To understand the true nature of the state, we must turn from ideology to history.

Let us turn to history, then. Let us examine Marx's view of history, and then take a Marxist view of the historical development of capitalist society and liberal democracy.

ECONOMICS AND THE STATE

The human being is a social animal. The history of the human race is a history of the societies in which we have lived. Our morals, our religions, our philosophies, our political systems, all are the product of social forces historically developed. According to Marx, the primary forces in this development are economic. The dominant shaping forces of a society center on certain facts about its economic organization. How does production take place? How is labor divided? Who owns what? Who performs what job?

The reason for the dominance of economic organization is this. The divisions of property and labor create separate groups with conflicting interests. That is, it creates *economic classes.* In the earliest societies, tribal societies, class divisions were drawn within the family. Later, the principal dividing lines were drawn between masters and slaves; then, between landowners and serfs; then, between capitalists and workers. At each of these stages, a fitting political organization developed. What makes a political organization fitting is the interest of the most powerful class, the *ruling* class. At any time, the system of political organization is a means for the ruling class to *remain* the ruling class, to maintain its power by *suppressing* the other classes.

In the Middle Ages, for example, economic power was in the hands of the lords of the manor, the holders of large areas of land. The work was done by the serfs, a class of people attached to the land. Whoever held the land on which the serfs worked held their labor as well. This *feudalistic* economy spawned a feudalistic political system, in which the reigning monarch protected the interests of the lords and guaranteed the suppression of the serfs. The famed Magna Carta, which the English barons forced King John to issue in 1215, was essentially the political recognition of the feudal "rights" of the serfs' oppressors.

Locke's liberal democracy grew out of this system. As the towns began to develop, so did the *guild system.* Manufacturing was done in small shops, divided along trade lines. Each shop was run by a master, who trained apprentices and employed journeymen. Gradually, this system was replaced by a more modern manufacturing system, and a new class developed—the middle class, the owners of the new factories. As the middle class grew in economic power, tensions developed between it and the older ruling class, the nobility. Out of this conflict came the middle-class revolution, most dramatically, of course, in France, but no less decisively in England and Germany.

Capitalists took control of political power. A new kind of state was created to protect their interests and strengthen their power. Their private control over their factories and the people who worked there became the cornerstone of this new kind of state. Its job was to protect private property and the exercise of "free trade." An ideology of "natural rights" was devised to justify the capitalists' power.

Meanwhile, workers were oppressed just as the serfs had been in feudalistic societies. Once again, the state was the instrument of oppression by the ruling class. This time, the ruling class was the capitalist class, and the oppressed class was the working class, or the *proletariat.* In England and later in America, this new state took the form of liberal democracy. The capitalists ruled, and the workers were permitted to decide every so often which members of the ruling class would oversee their oppression.

Alienation and Exploitation

According to Marx, capitalist oppression takes two central forms— economic *exploitation* and *alienation.*

Let us begin with economic exploitation. In a capitalistic society, workers are thought of as capital. That is, they are thought of as a means of production, like the machinery in a factory. Wages, then, are a form of production cost, like machine purchases. Since the factory owner's main concern is profit, and since profit is a matter of earnings over expenses, the factory owner will attempt to pay the worker as little as possible, and working hours and conditions will be determined by owner costs and benefits, not by the welfare of the worker.

Such economic exploitation is an easy matter to grasp, and as we saw in the previous chapter, our own society has a history of it. Alienation, however, is more difficult to grasp. What does Marx mean by the term? We can best understand it if we break alienation up into two forms—the alienation of workers from their own *labor,* and their alienation from their own *products.*

We begin with the alienation of workers from their own labor. Marx viewed human beings not only as *social* beings, but as working, acting, *producing* beings. Labor is more to us than a means of earning a living. It is our fundamental activity as human beings. Therefore, it should be our primary means of fulfillment. It should be liberating and humanizing, rather than degrading and dehumanizing. It should be more than drudgery, more than a method of bringing home the bacon. It should be meaningful as well. Workers should not be forced to seek fulfillment in leisure time, after their energies have been drained at the factory.

In capitalist societies, however, labor is a *commodity* like any other. My labor is something I sell, something my employer buys. Even if we forget for the moment the tremendous advantages that the capitalist buyer has in this situation, Marx insists that we must recoil at such a fact. It is as though all workers were forced to become prostitutes, turning what should be an expression of love into an item to be bought and sold. So does capitalism change what should be an expression of individuality into an extension of the machine.

This dehumanization is compounded by capitalist division of labor. Whereas workers were once able to work on a product from beginning to end, they are now consigned to boring, repetitive tasks. They take a spot at the assembly line, where they turn a screw, or set a can upright, or drive a rivet. That is what Marx meant by alienation from our labor, and it leads easily to the second form of alienation, alienation from our products.

When our labor is no longer seen as our own, the products of our labor are no longer seen as our own. Of course, all objects that we make take on an existence independent of us. But in a capitalist system, Marx says, this independence seems to be touched with almost magical properties. Our products end up exerting some strange power over us. They seem to take on a life of their own as they make their way through the capitalist economy, and our relationship to them becomes almost one of worshiper to God.

If this sounds like an odd charge, consider how products are advertised in America. Housewives are told that they can ensure marital bliss by using the right coffee or laundry detergent. Men are told that they can be virile by smoking the right cigarette. We are all told that we can have all the friends, lovers, and good times we want if only we'd drink the right beer or soft drink. In one television commercial for a shaving product, we see a closeup of an attractive couple. The woman stares lovingly at the man as she assures us that "My man got more." In a commercial for a vitamin supplement for women, we again see an attractive couple. This time, the man looks lovingly at the woman while he assures us that "I think I'll keep her." Meanwhile, supermarket and drug-store shelves are stocked with phallus-shaped packages for dishwashing detergents and deodorants, with names like *Joy* and *Tickle.*

Whatever else advertisers may be doing, one can claim that they are exploiting the alienation that Marx saw in the capitalist system. That is, one can claim that they are presenting their wares *not* as products of human labor but as independently existing objects capable of transforming us.

Exploitation and alienation lie at the very heart of capitalism, Marx claimed. And the state, as the instrument of the ruling class, is therefore an instrument of exploitation and alienation.

Revolution and Communism

For Marx, the state is not to be justified, but overthrown. As long as the state is the instrument for the oppression of one class by another—in Marx's time and ours, the proletariat by the capitalists—it must be abolished. What is needed, then, is a revolution by the workers. The final result of the revolution is to be *communism.* After the revolution, private property will be abolished. This is not to say that we will not be able to own toothbrushes and clothing. Rather, it is to say that the means of production will be publicly owned. In the beginning, this means that the means of production will be in the hands of the post-revolutionary state. But with the abolition of private property will come the abolition of economic classes. And when there are no more economic classes, there can be no more class antagonism. When that happens, there will be no more need for the state, since there will be no ruling class that needs it to oppress any other class. So the state will "wither away." Exploitation and alienation will be at an end, and Marx's famous dictum, "From each according to his ability; to each according to his need," will be realized in society.

Marx's goal, then, is a classless, stateless society. But he does justify a transition state, a state that directs the transition to communism. This transition state is needed as an instrument of the workers, to wrest power from the capitalists. The coercive machinery of the state will be used against the capitalists, in the name of the workers. But once its work is done, it will no longer be needed. Only then will true communism appear.

The Dictatorship of the Proletariat

The first communist revolution occurred, of course, in 1917 in Russia, under the leadership of V. I. Lenin (1870–1924). In addition to being a revolutionary and political leader, Lenin was a serious political thinker. He developed and added to the views of Marx, and people now commonly talk of Marxism-Leninism as well as of Marxism.

Of course, Marxism has developed in a variety of ways, many in stark contrast to Marxism-Leninism, but there is an advantage to looking at Lenin's variety first. By doing so, we can look at liberal democracy's principal competitor in today's world—Soviet communism.

The fundamental notion of Lenin's thought, borrowed from Marx, is the *dictatorship of the proletariat*. What does this mean? For one thing, it is meant to describe the character of the transition state between capitalism and communism. Hence, under the dictatorship of the proletariat, the machinery of suppression passes from the hands of the capitalists to the hands of the workers. That is, the coercive powers of the state will be used to strip the capitalists of their power. Most important, the state will assume ownership of the factories, mines, and farms, in order to remove the capitalists' economic power to exploit the workers.

But this step, however important, is not sufficient. Although it strips the capitalists of their economic power, it does not banish capitalist influence altogether. The capitalists will, after all, attempt to regain their economic power. And, given their education, their leftover wealth, and their positions of power in such institutions as the press, schools, and churches, they will be in a position to do so if the state does not stop them. Moreover, they will be able to count on support from other elements in society who benefited under capitalism—small businessmen, for example, and workers in certain privileged trades.

So all institutions of society must be brought into line. The press, for example, must not be permitted to print capitalist ideology. The schools must not be permitted to teach it. The churches must not be permitted to impede the transition to true communism. Thus, the state must exert its power over these institutions as well.

Who will control the machinery of the state? The communist party. It will control the machinery in the name of the workers. It will control this machinery in order to turn the working class into the ruling class, and then to abolish the existence of classes altogether. Although the party will function as the representative of the workers, it will not include all workers in its membership, nor will it be directly controlled by all the workers. Lenin saw the party as the *vanguard* of the proletariat. Its role is to *lead* the workers, to develop a communist doctrine to counter capitalist ideology, to unite the workers through discipline and education, and to prepare them for the final state of true communism.

Under the dictatorship of the proletariat, then, there will be an initial restriction of freedom and democracy. Everyone will work for the state, which Lenin envisioned as a vast syndicate, and the state, under the control of the party, will dictate what is to be produced, how it is produced, who is to work where and under what conditions.

As time passes, however, the workers will gain greater direct control. As they learn more about the operation of the factories, mines, and farms, as they learn to work together in a democratic fashion, as capitalist influence is weeded out, as they become accustomed to working for themselves without capitalist domination, they will no longer need the dictatorship of the proletariat. More and more decisions will pass into their hands, there will be less and less need for coercive machinery, and the state will, as forecast by Marx, wither away.

It is important to emphasize here the extent to which the workers themselves must change during this period of transition. After years of capitalist rule, they have themselves adopted many of the attitudes of their rulers. They have themselves become attached to the "rights" given them by the capitalist state. They have themselves learned to exploit their fellow workers. Thus, they will have to learn to work in harmony. They will have to stop thinking of their labor as a commodity. They will have to learn to commit themselves to the Marxist principle, from each according to his ability, to each according to his need.

The product of these ideas, then, is a state remarkably unlike Locke's. If we return to the three continuums we looked at in the beginning of this chapter, we see that Lenin's dictatorship of the proletariat is at the opposite end of each. Since all institutions are under the control of the state, we find a totalitarian society. Since all means of production are in the hands of the state, we find a socialist one. Since the party controls the machinery of the state, we find an authoritarian one.

Still, Lenin assures us that this situation is temporary. Once the state has withered away, there will be a true democracy, in which the workers have direct control over all aspects of their lives to an extent unheard of in capitalist societies. In this democracy, socialism will not mean state ownership, but true worker ownership. The factories will belong to the people who work there, and the centralization of the transition state will have disappeared.

Transition to What?

Since the Russian revolution, the Soviet state has shown little inclination to wither away. This would come as no surprise to Lenin. He expected international resistance to a large communist state, and he knew that the Soviet Union must keep itself militarily prepared to fight it. But an adequate military requires a state. Therefore, the state could not wither away until the communist revolution achieved worldwide success.

It is doubtful, though, that the state would wither away in any case. Certainly, neither Marx nor Lenin was very specific about how the process would take place, and neither was any more specific about how society would function thereafter. Whatever their private thoughts may have been on these matters, few people today expect that the final stages of communism will appear in the Soviet Union.

Part of the problem, of course, is the complexity of contemporary society, whether capitalist or communist. Another part of the problem, closely related to the first, is the fact of the huge Soviet bureaucracy, as deeply entrenched and self-perpetuating as any.

Still another part of the problem is continued internal resistance to state repression. What Lenin thought of as counter-revolutionary capitalist influence has been difficult to eradicate. Intellectuals such as Andrei Sakharov, for example, continue to oppose the totalitarian nature of the Soviet regime. And as I write this chapter, the workers of Poland, a country with a system much like the Soviet Union's, are engaged in a battle with their government for control of the labor movement.

Thus, it is very difficult to view Lenin's dictatorship of the proletariat as a transition to true communism. It is much easier to view it as a self-perpetuating, undemocratic, totalitarian state. And it seems safe to say that any changes in this situation will come about through internal resistance, as in Poland, rather than through any natural process of withering away.

CAPITALISM AND THE WELFARE STATE

If the predictions of Marx and Lenin concerning the withering away of the proletariat state proved to be overly optimistic, some of their predictions concerning the future of capitalist democracies appear to have fared no better.

If we focus our attention on the United States, for instance, we find little evidence of extreme conflict between workers and capitalists. Nor do we find the extreme forms of exploitation of workers by capitalists that were prevalent in this country a century ago. There are a variety of factors responsible for this development, but most important, perhaps, is the increasing role played by the state in the American economy. Minimum-wage laws, child-labor laws, legislation regulating working conditions, and consumer-protection laws are obvious instances of such state activity. Equally important are government recognition

SOCIAL-CONTRACT THEORY AND THE
TOTALITARIAN STATE

Both the previous chapter and the main body of this chapter may give the impression that the history of social-contract theory is a history firmly in favor of liberal democracy. Although most social-contract theorists were liberal democrats, there were some exceptions. Let us briefly look at two.

The Ruler as Mortal God

Locke and Nozick, we saw, believed that the terms of the social contract are limited by the natural rights of the individual. There are some powers that the "signers" of the contract cannot grant the state.

Thomas Hobbes, on the other hand, believed that the "signers" give away *all* their rights to self-government to the state. According to Hobbes, the state of nature is a state of war, and the only antidote to such a situation is a ruler so powerful that his subjects are in complete awe of him. Notice that Hobbes uses the word "subjects," as opposed to "citizens." In the republican form of government advocated by liberal democrats, all members of the state, whether office holders or not, are citizens. That is, all are granted equal political rights. In the nonrepublican form of government advocated by Hobbes, there is no equality of political rights. The people are subject to the rule of a sovereign, whom Hobbes likens to a mortal god. Thus, they are not citizens, but subjects.

Hobbes lists a dozen features of the ruler's powers. A look at some of these features will give a good picture of the extent of these powers. The first two are closely related. First, his subjects have no right whatever to rebel against him. Second, the ruler is not capable of breaking the social contract. Why does Hobbes say this? According to Hobbes, the contract is formed among the subjects, who agreed to obey the ruler come what may. The ruler, however, makes no promises to his subjects, so there are no promises he can break. Third, even those who did not "sign" the social contract are subject to the ruler's will. Those who refuse can be justly killed. Fourth, the ruler is incapable of acting unjustly. Since the "signers" of the contract grant him all political power, any injuries he inflicts on them cannot be considered unjustly inflicted. Fifth, the ruler cannot be punished by his subjects. Since his power comes from his subjects, anything he does is, in effect, done by them. Therefore, to punish the ruler is to unjustly punish him for what the subjects themselves did. Sixth, it is solely up to the ruler to determine which opinions are beneficial and which are harmful, and to determine whether they may be promulgated, and if so by whom. Seventh, it is solely up to the ruler to legislate all the laws of property. Eighth, the ruler has total judicial power. He and he alone has the right to hear and decide civil disputes among subjects. He and he alone has the right to determine who is to be justly rewarded and punished.

What Hobbes gives us, then, is a ruler whose powers are derived from his subjects but who is not answerable to his subjects in his use of that power. Thus, his power is absolute, and the rights of his subjects are nil. Hobbes justifies a society as authoritarian and totalitarian as any dictatorship of the proletariat.

The General Will

Locke and Nozick are straightforward liberal democrats. Hobbes is equally straightforward in his opposite view. The case of Jean Jacques Rousseau is far more complicated. With his emphasis on liberty, equality, and fraternity, he was as much an inspiration to the French Revolution as Locke was to the American Revolution. Still, his views have been cited with approval by liberal democrats and antiliberal totalitarians alike.

Perhaps the best way to approach Rousseau is to make an important contrast to Locke. Locke saw the social contract as a number of agreements between individuals on the one hand and the government on the other. The result is a highly individualistic society, in which the natural rights of each individual must be respected by the state. Decisions of the state are to be determined by majority will, where that will is the expression of numerous individual voices. If a majority of individuals agrees on a course of action, then that action is taken, as long as it does not infringe on the rights of the minority.

Rousseau, however, saw the contract as an agreement among individuals to form a new kind of society. In this new society, individualism is to be replaced by a new kind of unity, one that embodies what he called the *general will*. The general will is not the voice of the majority, nor is it a compromise among various *individual* interests. Rather, it is the expression of the *common* interest, an interest that emerges as a quality of the society as a whole.

What is agreed to in such a contract? The alienation of all individual rights. As long as some individual rights remain, Rousseau felt, inequality of power will also remain. And with inequality of power, some individuals will have to yield to the power of other individuals. Only with the alienation of all rights can we ensure equal liberty for all members of the society.

By handing over all rights to the community as a whole, no one need worry about handing over any rights to other individuals. No one can be anyone else's slave, and no one can be anyone else's master. Moreover, the result is a community that has, as a whole, perfect freedom. And every individual, as an inseparable part of that whole, shares in that freedom with true equality. The voice of the general will is everybody's will. It is not the will of the majority of individuals.

How is the general will to be determined? Not by general elections. General elections can determine only the preferences of individuals. Rather, it is the legislator's task to determine the general will. Acting on behalf of the community as a whole, the legislator enacts laws for the good of the community as a whole. Through such legislation, true democracy is attained.

Although Rousseau went to great pains to make such an arrangement *sound* liberal and democratic, it is difficult to *hear* it that way. In effect, the legislator is as much a mortal god as Hobbes's ruler. Once again, the result appears to be authoritarian and totalitarian, however much Rousseau professed to be concerned with democracy and liberty.

and protection of workers' right to unionize and strike. Industry-wide labor unions have greatly enhanced the power of the workers to influence the terms of their employment.

Moreover, since Roosevelt's New Deal, the United States has been gradually moving in the direction of a *welfare state.* That is, it has adopted such programs as Social Security, Medicare, Medicaid, food stamps, and various welfare payments in order to increase the economic security of its citizens.

Although it would be foolish to claim that labor has power equal to that of management, or that full economic security belongs to all in America, this much is clear. The conditions that Marx thought would lead to revolution in America and much of western Europe, the conditions that did create a strong Marxist tide here at one time, have greatly diminished. Thus, the welfare state has neutralized class conflicts between capitalists and workers. It has done so by partially reducing the inequalities of Locke's minimal state, and by holding out hope that these inequalities will be reduced even further in the future. In that case, the welfare state provides a genuine alternative to Marxism as means to minimizing economic exploitation.

Marxist humanism

The developments reviewed in the two preceding sections have led many people sympathetic to Marx's views to turn from Marxism-Leninism. These people now doubt that a revolutionary state modeled on Lenin's dictatorship of the proletariat will lead to true communism, and they have come to think that a just, socialist society can evolve through democratic means while maintaining democratic institutions. Such people are often called *Marxist humanists,* or *democratic socialists.* Their goal is a socialist society that guarantees democratic freedoms and a greater degree of pluralism than is to be found in the Soviet Union.

Their criticisms of the capitalist welfare state take four forms. First, they argue that the alienation that Marx found in earlier forms of capitalism is also to be found in the welfare state. Labor is still bought and sold as a commodity, many jobs are still boring and meaningless, and our products maintain their strange hold over us. Although the welfare state is managing to increase economic security for many, it is just as dehumanizing as the minimal state.

This alienation, Marxist humanists claim, has an unacceptable payoff in human relationships. It leads people to treat one another as commodities, to use one another, to exploit one another in everyday affairs—business, social, and sexual. It also leads to competition and friction among various groups within the society, most notably among various ethnic groups. It has even claimed that true love is impossible in a capitalist society, where even love is thought of as a commodity to be bargained for.

Second, it is argued that welfare capitalism continues to neglect various social goods. As long as businesses are governed by the goal of private profit, they will continue to ruin the environment, exhaust natural resources, and use energy unwisely from the standpoint of the public good.

Third, welfare capitalism often amounts to welfare for the rich. Through various forms of tax breaks and even direct handouts, as with the recent massive loans to Chrysler Corporation, inequalities between rich and poor are perpetuated rather than minimized.

Fourth, welfare capitalism continues to leave many segments of society outside the mainstream of the economy. Even in times of economic prosperity, depressed areas such as the South Bronx of New York City maintain high rates of unemployment, and many disadvantaged groups remain disadvantaged whatever happens to the rest of society. Capitalism invariably produces oppressed classes, and in many cases, the best that the welfare state can do is produce a class of permanent welfare recipients.

ANARCHY VERSUS THE INVISIBLE HAND

These four problems, Marxist humanists claim, are not accidental difficulties. They are all caused by fundamental features of the capitalist economy. Most important is the free market.

According to classical capitalist economics, dating back to Adam Smith (1723–1790), if producers, workers, and consumers are left free to make their own choices in the market place, the outcome will be a stable economy. As all seek their own self-interest, producers will produce what is needed, workers will gravitate toward industries where they are needed, and wages and prices will naturally arrive at the optimal levels through the mechanism of supply and demand. It is, Smith said, as though the economy were directed by an "invisible hand." Marx argued not only that such a system leads to alienation and exploitation, but that it is fundamentally anarchistic. In our own time, democratic socialists argue that it leads to the difficulties noted in the previous section.

Consider the problem of social goods. In America today, clean air and water cost money. If the quality of our air and water is to be improved, factories and automobiles must be redesigned; new equipment must be developed and bought. Yet these expenditures do not result in greater income, so it is unlikely that private manufacturing firms will give clean air and water great priority. Similarly, corporate drives for expansion and profit do not naturally lead to conservation of natural resources.

Consider also the problem of large segments of society left out of the mainstream of the economy. With no profit incentive, private industry has no special interest in redeveloping depressed areas. Its natural choices in the market lead it to those areas in which it can best expect to prosper. If the large eastern cities are dying, it can be expected to desert them, rather than selflessly seek to rebuild them.

Thus, a free market economy naturally tends toward the neglect of many serious social problems. Of course, the United States no longer has a totally free market economy. The government intervenes at all stages of production and sales, and through its taxation, spending, and monetary policies, it attempts to control the ups and downs of the economy. But such intervention, democratic socialists argue, will never be sufficient in a capitalist society. Because of the political power wielded by large corporations, banks, and the like, most of the intervention will be to their benefit. That is, we can continue to expect more welfare for the rich and powerful than for the poor and powerless.

The only way to ensure that the means of production are used for the public good, they continue, is to put them in the hands of the public. If the state were to own the factories and mines, if they were all run in accordance with a coherent central policy, if everyone were granted the absolute right to a job, and if all of this were done in a truly democratic way, the result would be a just society in which no segment of the society would be exploited, and in which social goods would not be given short shrift.

Moreover, with the decline of the market economy, we could expect a lessening of alienation. Workers would have a genuine say in the conditions of their employment, their labor would no longer be a commodity to be bought and sold, and their sense of participation and dignity would be increased. And with this lessening of alienation, we could expect an increase in the quality and value of our social relationships with one another.

THE CAPITALIST RESPONSE

Critics of democratic socialism respond in a variety of ways. Some responses boil down to a restatement of the liberal democratic position of Locke and Nozick, with its emphasis on natural rights. Others offer a more direct challenge to the points raised by democratic socialists.

Let us begin with the Marxist attack on the market economy. Defenders of the market economy make two claims. First, they argue that the market is more *efficient* than centralized planning. When there is perfect competition among firms, prices reflect an equilibrium between supply and demand, production responds in a natural way to the needs of consumers, and resources are allocated in the best manner. Central planning interrupts these natural mechanisms, and replaces them with a huge, unresponsive bureaucracy.

Of course, perfect competition is not to be found in today's industrial societies, with their cartels, monopolies, and industries dominated by a few large corporations, so some state intervention is required. Similarly, some state intervention is required to protect the environment, bring those outside the mainstream of the economy into the mainstream, and conserve natural resources. But the most efficient way to achieve these ends is in concert with the market economy, not through extensive centralized planning of the entire economy.

What Marxists call welfare for the rich, it is continued, amounts to just such a program. If we give large corporations tax benefits for expenditures aimed at protecting the environment, or if we provide loans to large corporations to keep them in business in order to protect the jobs of their employees, we are working within the market to achieve the ends that socialists want.

But even more important, defenders of the market economy argue, a free market is more *democratic* than a centralized economy. For one thing, when consumers buy goods and services, they are in effect voting with their dollars. They are voting for those goods and services, and for the firms that offer them. If enough people vote the same way, the goods and services continue to be offered by those firms. If not, appropriate changes are made. For another, the market economy provides the best opportunity for all to advance in society. People have a free choice to pursue the career of their choice, and the best chance to advance in accordance with their capabilities. Centralized planning must end up interfering with these choices, just as it must end up minimizing the effect of consumer votes in the marketplace.

Once again, state intervention is required to ensure that the underprivileged are given a chance to compete in the marketplace, and that minorities are not discriminated against in the marketplace, but such intervention must not destroy the market economy. Thus, the market economy is superior to a centrally controlled economy. And once we allow that, there is no longer any point to preferring socialism to capitalism. We *could* have a market economy in which the means of production were owned by the state, but it would make little or no difference to most of us. Therefore, socialism is to be rejected.

Marxists, as you might expect, are not impressed by these responses. Disregarding questions of efficiency, which are best left to economists, there remain two problems—exploitation and alienation. As long as large corporations continue to hold great economic power, Marxists claim, they will continue to hold great political power. And as long as they hold great political power, they will use it to advance their own ends. To the extent that their ends conflict with the attainment of social goods, to the extent that they are indifferent to the plight of the disadvantaged, it is foolish to expect that economic exploitation will disappear in a capitalist society.

Consider the political situation in America today. Politicians have joined business leaders in calling for less government regulation and for taxation policies more favorable to business. Meanwhile, they have turned their backs on special programs for those segments of society that will not benefit by any economic progress that might result from these measures. Thus, minorities and the poor will continue to be exploited. Moreover, Marxists argue, as long as the market economy persists, so will alienation. And as long as alienation persists, the quality of life of almost all of us will suffer.

THE FINAL WORD?

We have covered a good deal of ground in this chapter. We have touched on a wide variety of issues and looked at a host of arguments. As a result, it is difficult to sort everything out neatly and arrive at comfortable conclusions. But it is now time to try.

Let us begin with Marx's criticisms of capitalist democracy. They are valuable, I think, for a number of reasons. First, they force us to consider how effectively economic power is translated into political power. Second, they lead us to question the extent to which capitalist democracies really are democratic. As long as our places of employment are in private hands, the greater our employers' power to dictate the terms of our employment, and the less our mobility in the job market, the less control we actually have over our lives, regardless of our ability to elect representatives in government. Third, Marx's ideas lead us to question the value of certain "rights" that we ordinarily take for granted. Do private individuals really have the right to the wealth and power that goes with their positions in the economy? Do they even have a right to these positions? Is capitalism flawed because it creates such positions? Fourth, Marx's criticisms lead us to view politics and economics from a particular point of view. Marx viewed them, in part, in connection with his philosophy of the human person. He thought of us as social, productive, working beings whose greatest fulfillment lies in the quality of our work and social relationships. Thus, he forces us to ask whether our own society is organized in such a way as to enhance or limit our possibilities for fulfillment.

As for Marxism-Leninism, there is, I think, less of value to be found. In the end, it does not lead to a classless society, but to a society ordered on new class lines. In this society, the dominant class is the state and party bureaucracy, whose power and potential for oppression exceeds that of the capitalists in a well-ordered welfare state.

The crucial choice facing us, then, is between welfare capitalism and democratic socialism. Is a capitalist society based on Rawls's conception of justice as fairness preferable to a socialist society in which we find both democratic freedoms and central planning? Or is the latter to be preferred?

Two things make this a difficult choice. First, it is more a choice of means than of ends. We are not asked to choose between two conceptions of justice. Nor are we asked to choose between an egalitarian and a nonegalitarian society. Nor are we asked to choose between social goods and private goods. Instead, we are asked to choose between two ways of achieving a just, egalitarian society that does not neglect social goods.

Second, we do not as yet have enough information to make a reliable choice. Will welfare capitalism continue to favor the rich and neglect the underprivileged and members of minority groups? Will it continue to neglect social goods? Can the people reverse these trends through their ballots? Would central planning of the economy lead to great inefficiency? Would it severely limit our economic choices? Would socialism lead to greater or less economic democracy?

Further questions can be asked about the relationship between alienation and capitalism. Would there be less alienation in a socialist society? Would the quality of our relationships really improve? Would we really view our work differently? Would we view others differently?

Our willingness to answer any of these questions is due more to our prejudices, I think, than any strong evidence either way. For example, although there has been much study of alienation by social scientists in recent years, there appear to be no data demonstrating that it would be reduced under socialism. Nor do there appear to be any data indicating that the quality of human relationships would improve under socialism. Similarly, there appears to be no reliable way of forecasting the future of welfare capitalism. Nor can we reliably predict the outcome of centralized social and economic planning. What I recommend, then, is a healthy dose of skepticism toward the arguments of both sides.

STUDY QUESTIONS

1. What is liberal democracy? How does it differ from the alternatives proposed by Marx and later Marxists?
2. Why does Marx oppose social-contract theory? Do you agree with his objections? Why or why not?
3. What is the significance of economic class to Marx's reading of history?
4. What does Marx mean by "alienation"? In what forms does it appear? How do Marxists expect to overcome it?
5. Marx believed that a transition state was necessary to bridge the gap between capitalism and true communism. What was his justification for this transition state? How were his ideas developed by Lenin? What are the reasons for believing that the transition to true communism, at least in the Soviet Union, may not be completed?
6. How does Marxist humanism differ from Marxism-Leninism?
7. What is welfare capitalism? Why do Marxist humanists object to it? To what extent do you agree with their objections?
8. Both Hobbes and Rousseau thought of the social contract as requiring the loss of all individual rights. What were their reasons for thinking so? How do they differ?

GLOSSARY

Alienation. In the philosophy of Karl Marx, a condition that affects workers in a *capitalist* society due to the division of labor and the free market system. In general, to be alienated from something is to be estranged from it. Marx thought that capitalism estranged workers from their true nature as working, producing beings. This shows up, he claimed, in alienation from one's work and from one's products.

Authoritarianism. A nondemocratic form of government.

Capitalism. Economic system in which the means of production are in the hands of private owners.

Communism. In the philosophy of Karl Marx and V. I. Lenin, a form of society in which there is no state and no *economic classes.* In a communist society, the workers will own and operate the means of production themselves, without the need of a state.

Dictatorship of the proletariat. In the philosophy of V. I. Lenin, the transition period between *capitalism* and *communism.* During this period, the state owns the means of production, and the communist party, in the name of the workers,

will use the state machinery to stamp out the remaining vestiges of capitalism.

Economic classes. Interest groups created by divisions of property and labor.

Feudalism. Economic and political system of the Middle Ages in which the land-
holders exchanged services to the monarch for protection by the monarch,
and a group of people known as serfs remained attached to the land.

Ideology. In the philosophy of Karl Marx, the rationalizations used by the ruling
class to justify its power. Such ideologies appear as the dominant philosophy
and religion, among other things, of a particular society.

Invisible hand. In classical *capitalist* economic theory, as espoused by Adam
Smith, a metaphor used to describe how the pursuit of individual interests
results in a stable economy in which resources are most efficiently allocated.

Liberal democracy. System of government that is democratic, *capitalistic,* and *pluralistic.*

Marxist humanism. Form of Marxist philosophy that rejects the excesses of the
dictatorship of the proletariat and advocates a form of *socialism* that maintains
democratic institutions.

Pluralism. Political and social system in which there are many independent centers of power.

Proletariat. The working class.

Socialism. Economic system in which the means of production are owned by the
state.

Totalitarianism. Political and social system in which there is one dominant center
of power having complete control over all other institutions.

Chapter 8

OBEDIENCE
AND REBELLION

Perhaps you have seen this public service spot on television. A highway patrolman is sitting in his car. We ought to obey the fifty-five mile per hour speed limit, he says, because driving at that speed will help to save fuel and lives. Besides, he adds, it's the law. As he says these last words, a speeder races past him. He turns on his siren and begins his chase.

The message is clear. If we don't obey the law, we will be punished, in this case suffer a fine or the loss of our license. But is that the only reason to obey the laws of the state? Do we have a *moral* obligation to obey them as well?

Most of us think that we do. In fact, we often think that if we did not have a moral obligation to obey the law, the state would have no right to enforce it. The state has a moral obligation to *enact* laws, we have a moral obligation to *obey* them, and the state, therefore, has a moral right to *enforce* them. But how far does this moral obligation extend? To all laws? Is it ever right to disobey a law? If so, when? And why? These are the questions we shall examine in this chapter.

THE SUBMISSION OF SOCRATES

The most famous discussion of our obligation to obey the law was inspired by an actual event. Socrates (c. 470–399 B.C.) was tried in ancient

Athens and found guilty of "impiety." His sentence was death. Before the sentence was to be carried out, his students visited him and offered to help him escape. He refused their offer. Why? His reasons are recorded in a dialogue written by Plato.

Socrates argued that he must remain and die because the verdict of the court was the law, and he must obey the law, even though he knew himself to be innocent. Let us look at three of his most important reasons for believing that he must obey the law.

First, he felt that he owed a debt of gratitude to the state. The state, he said, was like a parent. Under its protection, he had been born, nurtured, and educated. Because of that, he owed the same obedience to the state that he did to his parents.

Second, by consenting to live in the state, he had, in effect, consented to obey its laws. By freely choosing to live in Athens and accept the protection of the law, he had entered into a tacit agreement with the state, and part of that agreement required that he obey the law.

Third, he considered what would happen if all citizens of Athens disobeyed the law whenever they disagreed with it. If that were to happen, the result would be anarchy. Therefore, it should not be allowed to happen. But if he expected and relied on other people to obey the law, he should obey the law himself.

Now, we may not agree with Socrates' decision to face death at the hands of the state, but we must note that all three of his reasons are good reasons for obeying the law.

The second reason is particularly interesting, because it relates to our discussion of social-contract theory (see Chapter 6). In that discussion, we looked at the social contract as a historical fiction. But we can also look at it another way, as an ongoing process. Each of us "signs" the contract by accepting the protection of the state. We accept the right of the state to enact and enforce laws, and we obligate ourselves to obey them.

The third reason is also an interesting one, because it embodies a common notion of basic fairness. If there is some goal that I and others want to achieve, and if the achievement of that goal requires general sacrifice, it is unfair of me to reap the benefits of the sacrifice of others without sacrificing my share. If there is a drought, for example, we are all required to do our fair share to conserve water. Similarly, it is only fair that we make certain sacrifices when it comes to obeying the law. If we rely on the obedience of others in order to have a safe, stable, and effective society, we must offer the same obedience ourselves.

Still, we are dissatisfied with Socrates' defense of his decision to remain and die. His reasons for obeying the law are good ones, to be sure, but is he required to act on them in *this* case?

Consider his first reason. If your parents order you to kill yourself (as Athens had ordered Socrates), are you morally obligated to do so? Whatever gratitude you feel toward them, aren't there limits to what they can rightly ask you to do?

Consider his second reason. When we consent to live in a society, do we contract to do *whatever* the state orders us to do? Is that really part of the contract? As we saw in our discussion of Locke, Nozick, and Rawls, the rightful powers of the state are limited by the terms of the social contract. The social contract gives the state the moral right to pass *just* laws. It does not give the state the moral right to take someone's life unjustly.

Consider his third reason. Certainly, if all of us were to disobey *every* law we found disagreeable, anarchy would result. But Socrates' death sentence isn't just *any* law. Isn't this a special case? Suppose we put Socrates' question this way: What would happen if everyone tried to escape being put to death unjustly? Whatever outcome would result, it would not be anarchy. Besides, when we rely on others to obey the law, do we really rely on them to obey *every* law? If not, does fairness still require that *we* obey every law?

My point here is this: Although Socrates gives us good reasons to obey the law, these reasons may not always be decisive. It may be that in particular cases, there are better reasons for *dis*obeying a law. It may also be that there are particular cases in which Socrates' reasons do not even apply.

MORALITY AND THE LAW

Before we pursue the points of the preceding paragraph, let us distinguish three different kinds of laws. First, there are laws that codify the most important shared moral principles of a society, the moral principles that forbid the causing of certain sorts of direct harm to others. Among the obvious laws of this kind are laws against murder, rape, and armed robbery. Actions forbidden by such laws are wrong in any case. It is not merely their illegality that makes them wrong. We would be morally prohibited from committing rape even if rape were not illegal.

Second, there are laws that codify moral principles that do not concern the causing of direct harm to others, and are not, consequently, as widely shared as those that do. Among the most obvious laws of this kind are laws forbidding certain sorts of sexual acts between consenting adults and laws prohibiting the use of drugs like marijuana and cocaine. Whether actions forbidden by these laws would be wrong even if they were not illegal is a matter of dispute. Some people would continue to feel a moral obligation to refrain from certain sexual practices even if they weren't illegal. Others feel no moral obligation to refrain from them even though they are illegal.

Third, there are laws that are enacted because the existence of the state makes them necessary. A state must pay for the services it provides, so it must raise taxes. If the state is a democratic one, it must pass laws governing the procedures to be followed in elections. If it provides services of various types, it must pass laws governing how they are to be provided, who is to receive them, and so forth. These laws, unlike the laws of the first two kinds, have no direct connection with morality. They are not codifications of moral principles, and if there were no such laws, there would be no such duties. They are duties created by the state.

So laws of this kind are laws that *create* moral obligations. How does this come about? First of all, the state creates various institutions and practices. Each of these institutions and practices requires rules and regulations. Because we benefit from these institutions and practices, it is only fair that we follow the associated rules and regulations. Therefore, we are morally obligated to do so. The situation is rather like a game. Before the invention of football, nobody had the obligation to kick an odd-shaped ball between two posts. But now that there is such a game, someone who plays it and is picked as the team's kicker does have such an obligation. He depends on his teammates to do their jobs, and he is therefore obligated to do his.

As we saw in our discussion of Socrates, the same holds for obedience to the law. We depend on others to pay their taxes; therefore we are morally obligated to pay ours. But we also saw that these obligations may not be absolute. What if a particular institution or practice is unjust? Can the state create a moral obligation to obey the laws of such an institution? If so, how?

We can also question the extent of our moral obligation to obey laws of the second type. If a law codifies a moral principle with which I do not agree, and if that moral principle does not concern direct harm to others, am I really obligated to obey it?

UNJUST INSTITUTIONS

No society is perfectly just. Moreover, it is doubtful that any institution is perfectly just. Some people will find legal means of paying less than their fair share of taxes, and some people will be legally required to pay more than their fair share. Some people who do not deserve welfare benefits will receive them, and some who deserve them will not. Some people will escape punishment for their crimes, some will be punished unjustly. Therefore, if we were to say that there is no obligation to follow *any* laws associated with unjust institutions, anarchy would no doubt result. Still, it seems wrong to say that we are morally obligated to obey *all* laws, no matter how unjust.

Our problem, then, is this. According to the social contract, the state has the moral right to enforce only just laws. But, in practice, it is impossible to hold the state to these terms. Some injustices are inevitable. Fortunately, the problem can be solved. There is an important distinction we can make.

To take a particularly obnoxious example, consider the institution of slavery. Certainly, we would not say that a slave has a moral obligation *not* to try to escape. Nor would we say that a free person has a moral obligation to return a runaway slave. Yet, if you will recall the infamous Dred Scott decision of 1857, legal obligations of that sort did exist in this country. In that decision, the Supreme Court ruled that even in a free state, a slave did not have the rights of a citizen, but was to be treated as the property of his owner. When we reflect on our own history, however, the heroes of that period are not the people who returned runaway slaves. Rather, they are the people who worked with the underground railroad, which helped slaves escape to Canada.

The difference between an institution such as slavery and a tax system that allows some injustices is this. Slavery is *fundamentally* unjust. Our indignation over American slavery is not merely due to certain of its features. It is not that slavery would have been acceptable given certain changes, the elimination of beatings, for example. Rather, our indignation is due to the very institution itself. No just society can have such an institution.

On the other hand, most of us agree that our current tax system, despite its injustices, is not *fundamentally* unjust. We agree that taxes must be levied, and we agree that the basic principles underlying our tax system are just. We also agree that our tax money is used in such ways as to give everybody at least some benefit.

Of course, there will be some difficulty in distinguishing institutions and practices that are fundamentally unjust from those that are not, but in many cases, the difficulty will not arise.

Suppose that we adopt the following principle, then: We have no moral obligation to obey the laws of a fundamentally unjust institution or practice. If we do adopt it, we need not worry about justifying widespread disobedience or anarchy.

CIVIL DISOBEDIENCE

The people who worked on the underground railroad did so *secretly.* Their aim in doing so was not to protest the law, nor was it to change it. Rather, their aim was to subvert it. They wanted to help slaves escape. In contrast, people will often disobey the law *publicly,* in order to protest and change it, as well as subvert it. That is, they engage in *civil disobedience.*

What characterizes civil disobedience? Well, as just noted, it is *public* disobedience to the law. It is an act of public protest, meant to draw attention to the unjustness of the law, to gain the support of others in an attempt to change it, and to put pressure on lawmakers to change it.

People who engage in civil disobedience break the law *because* they think it unjust. Still, they show their respect for the rule of law by being willing to accept punishment for breaking it. Although they are willing to break particular laws, their intention is not to undermine the rule of law. Therefore, they are willing to be arrested for their disobedience. Furthermore, it should be emphasized that civil disobedience is indeed *civil.* It is a peaceful form of disobedience, one that does not include violence.

In the 1960s, civil disobedience was quite common in this country. Most of it was prompted by segregation laws and the war in Vietnam. It occurred in two forms—direct and indirect.

Direct civil disobedience is disobedience to the law being protested, exemplified by the sit-ins of the early sixties. In certain areas of the south, segregation laws prohibited blacks from eating at the same lunch counters as whites. In direct violation of these laws, black protestors sat at lunch counters reserved for whites and would not leave until they were physically removed by the police.

Their efforts received nationwide attention, attracted the support of blacks and whites throughout the country, and resulted in the abolition of segregation laws.

Indirect civil disobedience is disobedience to a law other than the one being protested. We can point to a common tactic of antiwar demonstrators as an example of this type. During the 1960s there were a number of legal demonstrations, such as rallies at the Washington Monument and marches to the Pentagon through the streets of Washington. Some demonstrators felt that such activities were insufficient. They felt that they must show the depth of their opposition to the war by exhibiting their willingness to be tear-gassed and arrested. They felt that to protest the war by marching where officials permitted them to march was not to make a sufficiently strong statement. These people broke away from the main demonstrations and held sit-ins, some in government buildings, others in busy intersections of the city. These latter protestors were not breaking any laws directly related to the war. They were breaking city ordinances and disobeying police orders. Thus, their civil disobedience was indirect.

Why resort to indirect civil disobedience? Because direct disobedience is unavailable. In this case, direct disobedience was available to only a few people— men of draft age, for instance, who could burn their draft cards or refuse induction into the military. Thus, for many people, indirect disobedience was the only option.

Objections to Civil Disobedience

Civil disobedience is a controversial tactic, and it has been criticized for a variety of reasons. Let us look at four of the most important ones.

First, many people object that civil disobedience is inappropriate in a democratic society. As long as laws are enacted by elected officials, and as long as we have the right and means to make our feelings known to these officials, there is no need to change the law by breaking it. To resort to civil disobedience in a democratic society, it is argued, is to attempt to coerce the majority through social disruption.

Second, innocent people are often harmed or inconvenienced by civil disobedience. Why should someone who merely wants a ham sandwich and a cup of coffee suffer because demonstrators are disrupting a lunch counter? Why should someone late for an important appointment suffer because demonstrators are blocking an intersection?

Third, what is to count as acceptable civil disobedience? Where are we to draw the line? This is a particularly difficult problem in the case of indirect civil disobedience. Once we concede that it is acceptable to break just laws to protest unjust ones, is there any way to distinguish moral civil disobedience from immoral civil disobedience?

Fourth, civil disobedience, unlike such private disobedience as participation in the underground railroad, *can* lead to anarchy. When people publicly flout the law in large numbers, the result must be a breakdown in respect for the law, regardless of their willingness to be punished. During the sixties, for example, civil disobedience eventually led to violent conflicts between police and demonstrators, damage to public and private buildings, bombings, and even the deaths of innocent people.

Responses to the Objections

The first objection to civil disobedience was that it is not appropriate in a democratic society. Proponents of civil disobedience generally agree that traditional legal means of changing the law should first be tried, unless there is no time to do so. But there are times when these means do not work, when the legislatures and the courts are not responsive to peaceful petitioning and the voters cannot be convinced to change the composition of these bodies. At such times, if the law is fundamentally unjust, civil disobedience is required.

But, the objector asks, isn't that an attempt to achieve by coercion what could not be achieved in a democratic way? The proponent of civil disobedience responds this way. The main point of civil disobedience in a democratic society is not to *coerce* the majority into changing the law. Civil disobedience is a form of moral persuasion. When citizens and lawmakers see that decent people are willing to face jail for their convictions, a strong moral statement has been made. And this statement injects a new dimension into public debate. When millions of people read about ministers and students and ordinary working people being dragged off to jail for the "crime" of sitting at a lunch counter, segregation laws were seen in a new light throughout the country. In that way, attitudes were changed and the way was cleared for passage of civil rights legislation.

Of course, a certain amount of coercion *is* involved in civil disobedience. Part of the point of civil disobedience is to cause some social disruption, so that lawmakers will be willing to change the law in order to restore tranquility. No doubt, the threat of social upheaval did contribute to the passage of civil rights legislation in the sixties. But when the goal is the abolition of a fundamentally unjust institution, in this case segregation, such disruption may be permissible. In other words, proponents of civil disobedience argue, if some mild nonviolent social disruption is required to achieve justice, it is justified by that goal.

This last paragraph can also serve as a response to the second objection to civil disobedience—that it affects innocent people. The inconvenience to white owners and patrons of segregated lunch counters, it is argued, is justified by the goal—the abolition of segregation laws.

But how are we to determine when social disruption and inconvenience are justified? How much disruption and inconvenience are we allowed to create? Where are we to draw the line?

These questions, of course, reflect the third objection to civil disobedience. Proponents of civil disobedience respond this way. When deciding whether to engage in civil disobedience, we must ask ourselves a number of questions. How widespread is the injustice we are protesting? How harmful is the injustice to the people affected by it? What are our chances for success? How widespread will the disruption be? How harmful will it be to those affected by it? What are the options available to us?

In other words, when deciding whether to engage in civil disobedience, we must balance the good we can reasonably expect to achieve by doing so against both the harm we can reasonably expect to cause by engaging in civil disobedience and the injustice that will continue if we do not engage in it.

Such considerations are *utilitarian* ones (see Chapter 3, "The Foundation of Morals"). That is, they involve the consequences of breaking the law as opposed to obeying it. But there are other considerations as well. In a famous essay justifying his own act of civil disobedience, Henry David Thoreau (1817–1862) discussed a *non*utilitarian consideration.

Thoreau had been arrested for refusing to pay his poll tax. This refusal was his way of protesting slavery and the Mexican War. Some passages in his essay describe his refusal as an attempt to stop slavery and the war. If enough people followed his lead, he wrote, slavery and the war would end. The government could not forever continue to put decent men and women into jail.

But he also made another point. His tax dollars were being used to finance a war he considered unjust. They were being used to help prop up the unjust institution of slavery. And whatever usefulness might result from paying his taxes, whatever good these taxes might accomplish in other areas, his conscience would not allow him to contribute to such gross injustices. No state, however democratic, had the right to force him to finance an unjust war.

Thoreau's point may be put this way. There are times when the state requires us to participate in a fundamentally unjust practice or institution. At such times, our choice is not between protesting and looking the other way, but between being a party to the injustice and refusing to be a party to it. And it cannot be immoral to refuse.

But what about our fourth objection—the threat of anarchy? This objection did not bother Thoreau, who had certain predilections in that direction anyway, but it is of concern to most of us, who do not have such predilections.

The proponent of civil disobedience is most likely to deny that this is a real threat. If we confine civil disobedience to cases of fundamental injustice, and if we require either that the civil disobedience have utilitarian justification or that it be a choice of refusal over participation, anarchy will not result. Once again, those who engage in civil disobedience show their respect for the rule of law by allowing themselves to be punished for breaking the law.

But what about the violent incidents that grew out of the civil disobedience of the sixties? Proponents of civil disobedience can respond this way. The violence was not their fault. A good deal of that violence was caused by the police, not the demonstrators. That is, it was a matter of abuse of the law by law enforcers rather than of disrespect for the law of demonstrators. As for violent acts by various individuals and antiwar groups, those cannot be blamed on those who engaged in civil disobedience, but on the violent individuals and groups themselves.

LAWS CODIFYING MORAL PRINCIPLES

Many laws, as we saw earlier, codify moral principles. Some of these are shared moral principles governing actions that cause direct harm to others. Others do not concern moral principles that govern actions causing direct harm to others and are not widely shared. Our obligation to obey the former laws is obvious. What about the latter?

The use of marijuana and cocaine is illegal throughout the United States. In most states, sex between consenting unmarried adults is illegal. So is oral sex between consenting adults, even married ones. Homosexuality is illegal in most states, even between consenting adults. So is prostitution. Many of you have broken at least one of these laws. If you did, then you obviously did something legally wrong. But did you do something morally wrong?

The quick answer is that it depends on your own morality. Some people think that such acts are immoral, and it is because of their feelings on the matter that such acts are illegal. Other people think otherwise. But the point of the question is this. Do these acts *become* immoral when they become illegal? Do we have a moral obligation to refrain from them *because* they are illegal?

Let's return to Socrates' three reasons for obeying the law. First, he said that he owed the state a debt of gratitude. Does that apply here?

Well, we ordinarily show our gratitude to other *people* by doing something in their *interest*. We might help them get out of trouble, for example, or buy them gifts, or take care of their pets when they are away. But is the interest of the state really affected by our private sex lives? Do we harm the state by engaging in oral sex, or help it by refraining? It seems that we do not, in which case Socrates' first reason is irrelevant.

Second, he said that by consenting to live within the state's borders, we consent to obey its laws. But, as we saw, the conditions of this consent are limited. There are limits to what the state can morally require us to do. Can it morally require consenting adults to refrain from certain sexual acts?

Many people think not. A common response to such laws is the claim that the state has no business legislating what consenting adults do in the privacy of their bedrooms. This claim receives support from social-contract theory. Whether we accept the Locke-Nozick theory of the social contract or Rawls's, it does not seem that the contract grants such rights to the state.

Third, Socrates raised the issue of fairness. Since we rely on others to obey the law, it is only fair that we obey the law as well. It is unfair to take advantage of others by benefiting from their sacrifices without making the same sacrifices ourselves.

Does this reason apply here? I think not. This reason applies most obviously

REVOLUTION AND TERRORISM

In the main body of this chapter, the discussion is based on a tacit assumption—that we are dealing with a just society. Thus, our question could be put this way. Is it ever right to disobey unjust laws in an otherwise just society? Our answer, of course, is *yes*.

But what if we are dealing with an unjust society? What if we are dealing with a society that cannot be considered responsive to civil disobedience, a society in which nonviolence and appeals to justice cannot bring about the required changes? Is violence then acceptable? Is outright revolution acceptable? Is terrorism acceptable?

Revolution and the Social Contract

In our own Declaration of Independence, we find a justification of revolution based on Locke's notions of the social contract and natural rights. In the preamble to that document, Jefferson declares that governments are formed by the people to protect their inalienable rights. When the state systematically and repeatedly violates those rights, it is their right and duty to depose the government and replace it with a new one.

Locke put the matter this way. When the state violates our natural rights, it becomes tyrannical. In effect, the rulers put themselves in a state of war with the members of society. Once the members of society have judged that the state of war exists, they are free to revolt against their rulers and substitute a new form of government.

According to this line of thought, then, the revolutionaries do not *initiate* the war. Rather, they find themselves in a state of war and respond in kind. In such cases, armed rebellion is legitimate.

Revolution and Marxism

To Marx and Lenin, you will recall, the state is by nature an instrument of oppression by the ruling class. True justice is to be achieved only when the state has been abolished and true communism reached. Thus, the ultimate justification of revolution is the classless, stateless society.

In that case, revolution is justified against any state but one—the dictatorship of the proletariat. Why that one exception? Because the dictatorship of the proletariat is by nature transitory. It will wither away and leave true communism in its place. Thus, revolution against such a state is a step away from the ideal, not toward it. But you will also recall that it is highly unlikely that any such withering away will occur in a Marxist-Leninist state. How is a Marxist to justify revolution then?

Herbert Marcuse (1898–1979), an influential German-American Marxist theoretician, argues along utilitarian lines. The aim of revolution is to bring about a society with greater freedom and happiness than can be found in the current society. If the revolution succeeds in that goal, it is justified. Otherwise, it is not.

How is one to know in advance that the desired goal will be reached? Marcuse's answer is that we can't. There are no absolute standards of freedom and happiness, he says. Each society attempts to impose its own standards. Consider, for example, the difference between freedom *from* and freedom *to*. On the one hand, we have freedom from fear, want, exploitation, and discrimination. On the other hand, we have freedom to speak, assemble, worship, and dispose of our property as we see fit. Which conception of freedom will be most important depends on the society.

But that means that the success of the revolution will depend in large part on the ability of the new state to convince the people to accept its standards. The best that can be done in advance, then, is to resort to a rough "historical calculus." The would-be revolutionary must examine the social, political, and technological arrangements of society, calculate as nearly as possible how well they serve the interest of human freedom, and compare the result against the potential of the revolutionary program. But the final justification must come from history.

Means and Ends

Revolution will involve some degree of violence. Hence, to justify revolution is to justify violence. In that case, every revolutionary must agree that there is a sense in which the ends justify the means. *Any* means?

Marcuse thinks not. Using the Russian Revolution as his example, he argues that the slave-labor camps of Stalin and the systematic political terror of the communist party were not justified by the ends of the revolution. The ends, he says, must somehow be operative in the means. Although some degree of violence and restriction of freedom is required in any revolution, it is possible to take such measures too far. It is possible to reach the point where the ends can no longer be seen in the means at all. No revolution should be that ruthless.

The question of means and ends brings us to a particularly troubling question—terrorism.

The Terrorist and the Guerilla

The best way to approach terrorism is to distinguish it from another form of contemporary revolutionary violence—guerilla warfare.

Guerilla warfare was the primary tactic used by the Viet Cong and Fidel Castro's Cuban revolutionaries. Rather than engage in conventional military battles, guerillas work in small bands, which operate on a hit-and-run basis. They sneak up on government troops, inflict as much damage as they can in the shortest time, and then retreat into hiding in jungles and mountains. Such tactics are required because of the guerillas' extreme disadvantage in terms of military equipment.

In many respects, terrorists operate like guerillas. They work in small bands, operate on a hit-and-run basis, and retreat into hiding. The difference is that their targets are not military. As various Palestinian and European terrorist organizations show, their targets are primarily civilian—commercial airports, school buses, shops, and restaurants. Their goal is not the defeat of military units. Rather, it is the creation of an atmosphere of terror among the civilian population—hence, the name "terrorism." What is to be gained by such terror? Political capitulation, as opposed to military victory. Terrorists hope that the state will give in to their demands in order to stop their terroristic activities.

The crucial question is this: Is there a significant *moral* difference between the terrorist and the guerilla? If their ends are equally just, is the terrorist's activity justified in the same way as the guerilla's?

I think not. Terrorism cannot be justified, I think, because, unlike guerilla warfare, it is a rebellion against civilization as well as the state. An analogy to conventional warfare should help illustrate my point. Conventional wars among nations are governed by rules of war. Prisoners of war are to be treated according to certain humane standards, for example. They are not to be tortured, they are not to be denied acceptable living conditions, they are to receive proper health care, they are to be permitted to send and receive mail, and so on. Such rules are not always followed, of course, but you will agree, I am sure, that they *ought* to be. Although some people claim to find the notion of rules of war contradictory, they serve an important purpose. Amid all the suffering and destruction of war, they serve, if followed, to maintain at least some semblance of civilization. How important is that? Compare the experience of the American Jew in a Nazi prisoner-of-war camp to the experience of a European Jew in a Nazi death camp.

Similarly, terrorism is a war fought without any rules. The ordinary citizen in a state rocked by terrorism never knows where violence will strike, or how. In such a situation, civilization is in jeopardy. Thus, even just ends cannot justify terrorism. The terrorist risks becoming as bad as or worse than the enemy. That is, in part, what Marcuse meant when he said that the ends must somehow be operative in the means.

to practices and institutions founded by the state. It applies to taxes, for instance, and the various regulations regarding government programs. Sex is not such a practice or institution. It is a private matter that preceded any state and has nothing to do with the operation of the state. Therefore, Socrates' third reason does not seem to apply.

Thus, the reasons we have considered for obeying the law do not require that we obey the laws under discussion. We may conclude, then, that the actions they forbid are a matter of individual conscience.

THE FINAL WORD?

We have seen that, in general, we have a moral obligation to obey the law. That is, there are good moral reasons for obeying the law, and these reasons apply to a good many laws enacted in a just society, even to those laws that are not perfectly just.

However, there are some laws to which these reasons do not apply. They do not apply to fundamentally unjust laws. When a state initiates a fundamentally unjust institution or practice, we are not morally obligated to obey the laws associated with it. We have the moral right to disobey these laws, and we have the moral right to engage in civil disobedience in order to change them if traditional democratic means of changing them have been exhausted. Moreover, when the state intrudes on matters of private conscience in areas where no direct harm to others is involved, we again have the moral right to break the relevant laws.

To come to this conclusion is not to diminish respect for the law. Rather, it is to recognize the limits on what the state can rightfully do, and to recognize the moral claims that the individual has against the state.

STUDY QUESTIONS

1. What were Socrates' reasons for refusing to escape and prevent his own execution? Are these good reasons in general for obeying the law? Which do you think the strongest? The weakest? Why?

2. In this chapter, we distinguished three kinds of law. What are they? Which kind makes the strongest claim to our obedience? Which kind makes the weakest? Why?

3. What is the difference between a fundamentally just institution that nevertheless has unjust features and a fundamentally unjust institution? In what ways is this difference morally important? How many examples of each kind can you think of?

4. What is civil disobedience? What is the difference between direct and indirect civil disobedience? Is there an important moral difference between them? Must they be justified in different ways?

5. Which of the following state policies might lead you to engage in civil disobedience? Would your disobedience be direct or indirect?
   a. Reinstatement of the military draft.
   b. The sending of combat troops to Central America.
   c. The banning of abortion.
   d. The banning of handguns.
   e. The elimination of federal aid to college students.

6. In this chapter, I concluded that the decision to obey or disobey certain laws is a matter of individual conscience. What is the distinguishing feature of such laws? Can you think of any examples of such laws that should not be left to individual conscience?

7. What is Locke's justification for revolution? Marcuse's? Do you agree with either? Both? Why or why not?

8. What is the difference between terrorism and guerilla warfare? What are the moral consequences of this difference? Do you think that it's always easy to distinguish one from the other? Why or why not?

GLOSSARY

Civil disobedience. Nonviolent disobedience to the law aimed at changing laws deemed unjust.

Direct civil disobedience. Form of *civil disobedience* in which the protested laws are broken.

Guerilla warfare. Form of warfare in which small bands attack government troops on a hit-and-run basis and remain in hiding at other times.

Indirect civil disobedience. Form of *civil disobedience* in which laws other than the protested laws are broken.

Terrorism. Violence aimed at civilians in order to create an atmosphere of terror and force the government to capitulate to those committing the violent acts.

SELECTIONS

In the following selections we look at a classic statement of social-contract theory and a classic criticism of it.

The first, from John Locke's Two Treatises of Government, *succinctly lays out the crucial elements of his views—the rights and dangers found in a state of nature, the source of the state's legitimacy, the duties and functions of the state, and the limits on the state's rightful powers.*

The second, from Karl Marx's Economic and Philosophic Manuscripts, *begins with a refusal to engage in social-contract theory. Unlike the "political economist" (Locke, for example) who "puts himself in an imaginary original state of affairs," Marx begins with a "contemporary fact of political economy"—alienation. The kind of political economy he criticizes is, of course, capitalism, in which labor is a commodity subject to the workings of the market.*

JOHN LOCKE

Of the Ends of Political Society and Government

If man in the state of nature be so free, as has been said, if he be absolute lord of his own person and possessions, equal to the greatest, and subject to nobody, why will he part with his freedom, this empire, and subject himself to the dominion and control of any other power? To which, it is obvious to answer, that though in the state of nature he hath such a right, yet the enjoyment of it is very uncertain, and constantly exposed to the invasions of others. For all being kings as much as he, every man his equal, and the greater part no strict observers of equity and justice, the enjoyment of the property he has in this state is very unsafe, very unsecure. This makes him willing to quit this condition, which, however free, is full of fears and continual dangers; and it is not without reason that he seeks out and is willing to join in society with others, who are already united, or have a mind to unite, for the mutual preservation of their lives, liberties, and estates, which I call by the general name, property.

The great and chief end, therefore, of men's uniting into commonwealths, and putting themselves under government, is the preservation of their property; to which in the state of nature there are many things wanting.

First, There wants an established, settled, known law, received and allowed by common consent to be the standard of right and wrong, and the common measure to decide all controversies between them. For though the law of nature be plain and intelligible to all rational creatures; yet men, being biased by their interest, as well as ignorant for want of study of it, are not apt to allow of it as a law binding to them in the application of it to their particular cases.

Secondly, In the state of nature there wants a known and indifferent judge, with authority to determine all differences according to the established law. For everyone in that state, being both judge and executioner of the law of nature, men being partial to themselves, passion and revenge is very apt to carry them too far, and with too much heat in their own cases, as well as negligence and unconcernedness, to make them too remiss in other men's.

Thirdly, In the state of nature there often wants power to back and support the sentence when right, and to give it due execution. They who by any injustice offend, will seldom fail, where they are able by force to make good their injustice; such resistance many times makes the punishment dangerous, and frequently destructive to those who attempt it.

Thus mankind, notwithstanding all the privileges of the state of nature, being but in an ill condition, while they remain in it, are quickly driven into society. Hence it comes to pass that we seldom find any number of men live any time together in this state. The inconveniences that they are therein exposed to by the irregular and uncertain exercise of the power every man has of punishing the transgressions of others, make them take sanctuary under the established laws of government, and therein seek the preservation of their property. It is this makes them so willingly give up everyone his single power of punishing, to be exercised by such alone, as shall be appointed to it amongst them; and by such rules as the community, or those authorized by them to that purpose, shall agree on. And in this we have the original right and rise of both the legislative and executive power, as well as of the governments and societies themselves.

For in the state of nature, to omit the liberty he has of innocent delights, a man has two powers.

The first is to do whatsoever he thinks fit for the preservation of himself, and others within the permission of the law of nature, by which law, common to them all, he and all the rest of mankind are of one community, make up one society, distinct from all other creatures. And were it not for the corruption and viciousness of degenerate men there would be no need of any other, no necessity that men should separate from this great and natural community, and associate into lesser combinations.

The other power a man has in the state of nature is the power to punish the crimes committed against that law. Both these he gives up when he joins in a private, if I may so call it, or particular political society, and incorporates into any commonwealth separate from the rest of mankind.

The first power, viz., of doing whatsoever he thought fit for the preservation of himself and the rest of mankind, he gives up to be regulated by laws made by the society, so far forth as the preservation of himself and the rest of that society shall require; which laws of the society in many things confine the liberty he had by the law of nature.

Secondly, The power of punishing he wholly gives up, and engages his natural force (which he might before employ in the execution of the law of nature, by his own single authority as he thought fit), to assist the executive power of the society, as the law thereof shall require. For being now in a new state, wherein he is to enjoy many conveniences, from the labor, assistance, and society of others in the same community, as well as protection from its whole strength; he has to part also with as much of his natural liberty, in providing for himself, as the good, prosperity and safety of the society shall require; which is not only necessary but just, since the other members of the society do the like.

But though men when they enter into society give up the equality, liberty and executive power they had in the state of nature into the hands of the society, to be so far disposed of by the legislative as the good of the society shall require; yet it being only with an intention in everyone the better to preserve himself, his liberty and property (for no rational creature can be supposed to change his condition with an intention to be worse), the power of the society, or legislative constituted by them, can never be supposed to extend farther than the common good, but is obliged to secure everyone's property by providing against those three defects above-mentioned that made the state of nature so unsafe and uneasy. And so whoever has the legislative or supreme power of any commonwealth is bound to govern by established standing laws, promulgated and known to the people, and not by extemporary decrees; by indifferent and upright judges, who are to decide controversies by those laws; and to employ the force of the community at home only in the execution of such laws, or abroad, to prevent or redress foreign injuries, and secure the community from inroads and invasion. And all this to be directed to no other end but the peace, safety, and public good of the people.

KARL MARX

Alienated Labor

Let us not be like the political economist who, when he wishes to explain something, puts himself in an imaginary original state of affairs. Such an original state of affairs explains nothing. He simply pushes the question back into a grey and nebulous distance. He presupposes as a fact and an event what he ought to be deducing, namely the necessary connection between the two things, for example, between the division of labour and exchange. Similarly, the theologian explains the origin of evil through the fall, i.e. he presupposes as an historical fact what he should be explaining.

We start with a contemporary fact of political economy:

The worker becomes poorer the richer is his production, the more it increases in power and scope. The worker becomes a commodity that is all the cheaper the more commodities he creates. The depreciation of the human world progresses in direct proportion to the increase in value of the world of things. Labour does not only produce commodities; it produces itself and the labourer as a commodity and that to the extent to which it produces commodities in general.

What this fact expresses is merely this: the object that labour produces, its product, confronts it as an alien being, as a power independent of the producer. The product of labour is labour that has solidified itself into an object, made itself into a thing, the objectification of labour. The realization of labour is its objectification. In political economy this realization of labour appears as a loss of reality for the worker, objectification as a loss of the object or slavery to it, and appropriation as alienation, as externalization.

The realization of labour appears as a loss of reality to an extent that the worker loses his reality by dying of starvation. Objectification appears as a loss of the object to such an extent that the worker is robbed not only of the objects necessary for his life but also of the objects of his work. Indeed, labour itself becomes an object he can only have in his power with the greatest of efforts and at irregular intervals. The appropriation of the object appears as alienation to such an extent that the more objects the worker produces, the less he can possess and the more he falls under the domination of his product, capital.

All these consequences follow from the fact that the worker relates to the product of his labour as to an alien object. For it is evident from this presupposition that the more the worker externalizes himself in his work, the more powerful becomes the alien, objective world that he creates opposite himself, the poorer he becomes himself in his inner life and the less he can call his own. It is just the same in religion. The more man puts into God, the less he retains in himself. The worker puts his life into the object and this means that it no longer belongs to him but to the object. So the greater this activity, the more the worker is without an object. What the product of his labour is, that he is not. So the greater this product the less he is himself. The externalization of the worker in his product implies not only that his labour becomes an object, an exterior existence but also that it exists outside him, independent and alien, and becomes a self-sufficient power opposite him, that the life that he has lent to the object affronts him, hostile and alien.

Let us now deal in more detail with objectification, the production of the worker, and the alienation, the loss of the object, his product, which is involved in it.

The worker can create nothing without nature, the sensuous exterior world. It is the matter in which his labour realizes itself, in which it is active, out of which and through which it produces.

But as nature affords the means of life for labour in the sense that labour cannot live without objects on which it exercises itself, so it affords a means of life in the narrower sense, namely the means for the physical subsistence of the worker himself.

Thus the more the worker appropriates the exterior world of sensuous nature by his labour, the more he doubly deprives himself of the means of subsistence, firstly since the exterior sensuous world increasingly ceases to be an object belonging to his work, a means of subsistence for his labour; secondly, since it increasingly ceases to be a means of subsistence in the direct sense, a means for the physical subsistence of the worker.

Thus in these two ways the worker becomes a slave to his object: firstly he receives an object of labour, that is he receives labour, and secondly, he receives the means of subsistence. Thus it is his object that permits him to exist first as a worker and secondly as a physical subject. The climax of this slavery is that only as a worker can he maintain himself as a physical subject and it is only as a physical subject that he is a worker.

(According to the laws of political economy the alienation of the worker in his object is expressed as follows: the more the worker produces the less he has to consume, the more values he creates the more valueless and worthless he becomes, the more formed the product the more deformed the worker, the more civilized the product, the more barbaric the worker, the more powerful the work the more powerless becomes the worker, the more cultured the work the more philistine the worker becomes and more of a slave to nature.)

Political economy hides the alienation in the essence of labour by not considering the immediate relationship between the worker (labour) and production. Labour produces works of wonder for the rich, but nakedness for the worker. It produces palaces, but only hovels for the worker; it produces beauty, but cripples the worker; it replaces labour by machines but throws a part of the workers back to a barbaric labour and turns the other part into machines. It produces culture, but also imbecility and cretinism for the worker. . . .

Up to now we have considered only one aspect of the alienation or externalization of the worker, his relationship to the products of his labour. But alienation shows itself not only in the result, but also in the act of production, inside productive activity itself. How would the worker be able to affront the product of his work as an alien being if he did not alienate himself in the act of production itself? For the product is merely the summary of the activity of production. So if the product of labour is externalization, production itself must be active externalization, the externalization of activity, the activity of externalization. The alienation of the object of labour is only the résumé of the alienation, the externalization in the activity of labour itself.

What does the externalization of labour consist of then?

Firstly, that labour is exterior to the worker, that is, it does not belong to his essence. Therefore he does not confirm himself in his work, he denies himself, feels miserable instead of happy, deploys no free physical and intellectual energy, but mortifies his body and ruins his mind. Thus the worker only feels a stranger. He is at home when he is not working and when he works he is not at home. His labour is therefore not voluntary but compulsory, forced labour. It is therefore not the satisfaction of a need but only a means to satisfy needs outside itself. How alien it really is is very evident from the fact that when there is no physical or other compulsion, labour is avoided like the plague. External labour, labour in which man externalizes himself, is a labour of self-sacrifice and mortification. Finally, the external character of labour for the worker shows itself in the fact that it is not his own but someone else's, that it does not belong to him, that he does not belong to himself in his labour but to someone else. As in religion the human imagination's own activity, the activity of man's head and his heart, reacts independently on the individual as an alien activity of gods or devils, so the activity of the worker is not his own spontaneous activity. It belongs to another and is the loss of himself.

The result we arrive at then is that man (the worker) only feels himself freely active in his animal functions of eating, drinking, and procreating, at most also in his dwelling and dress, and feels himself an animal in his human functions.

Eating, drinking, procreating, etc. are indeed truly human functions. But in the abstraction that separates them from the other round of human activity and makes them into final and exclusive ends they become animal.

We have treated the act of alienation of practical human activity, labour, from two aspects. (1) The relationship of the worker to the product of his labour as an alien object that has power over him. This relationship is at the same time the relationship to the sensuous exterior world and to natural objects as to an alien and hostile world opposed to him. (2) The relationship of labour to the act of production inside labour. This relationship is the relationship of the worker to his own activity as something that is alien and does not belong to him; it is activity that is passivity, power that is weakness, procreation that is castration, the worker's own physical and intellectual energy, his personal life (for what is life except activity?) as an activity directed against himself, independent of him and not belonging to him. It is self-alienation, as above it was the alienation of the object.

FOR FURTHER READING

Locke's major work in political philosophy, in which he develops his theory of the social contract, is *Two Treatises of Civil Government* (New York: Mentor, 1965), edited by Peter Laslett. The work first appeared in 1690. Nozick's theory is developed in his *Anarchy, State, and Utopia* (New York: Basic Books, 1974). Rawls's version of social-contract theory can be found in *A Theory of Justice* (Cambridge: Harvard University Press, 1971). Both the Nozick and Rawls books have appealed to an audience much wider than that of most contemporary philosophy books. Although Nozick's is somewhat more technical in spots than Rawls's, it is written in an engagingly irreverent and witty style.

Hobbes presents his social-contract theory in *Leviathan*, first published in 1651. The relevant sections can be found in *Leviathan: Parts One and Two* (Indianapolis: Bobbs-Merrill, 1958), edited by Herbert W. Schneider. For Rousseau's version, see *The Social Contract* (New York: Dutton, 1976), first published in 1762.

Mill's most important work in political philosophy is *On Liberty* (Indianapolis: Bobbs-Merrill, 1956), first published in 1859. Also important is his *Considerations on Representative Government* (Indianapolis: Bobbs-Merrill, 1958), first published in 1861. Another important utilitarian defense of liberal democracy is Jeremy Bentham's *An Introduction to the Principles of Morals and Legislation* (New York: Macmillan, 1948), first published in 1789.

For the classic account of liberal economic theory, see Adam Smith's *Wealth of Nations*, first published in 1776. The complete work, edited by Edwin Cannan, appears in a University of Chicago Press edition (Chicago, 1977). More useful, perhaps, is *Wealth of Nations: Representative Selections*, edited by Bruce Mazlish (Indianapolis: Bobbs-Merrill, 1961).

The leading contemporary exponent of classical capitalist economic theory is Milton Friedman. His *Free to Choose* (New York: Harcourt Brace Jovanovich, 1980), written with Rose Friedman, is based on the public television series of the same name, and is written for the general reading audience.

For Kant's views on persons as ends in themselves, see his *Foundations of the Metaphysics of Morals*, first published in 1785 (Indianapolis: Bobbs-Merrill, 1959).

For a good general introduction to liberal democratic theory, see Benn and Peters' *The Principles of Political Thought* (New York: The Free Press, 1959).

The best way to approach the writings of Marx, perhaps, is through an anthology. There are many on the market, including *Writings of the Young Marx*, edited by Easton and Guddat (Garden City: Anchor, 1967); *Karl Marx: Selected Writings*, edited by David McLellan (Oxford: Oxford University Press, 1977); *The Marx-Engels Reader*, edited by Robert C. Tucker (New York: Norton, 1978). The Engels of the third work is Friedrich Engels, Marx's friend and collaborator.

Two interesting and helpful works on Marx are Melvin Rader's *Marx's Interpretation of History* (New York: Oxford University Press, 1979) and Adam Schaff's *Marxism and the Human Individual* (New York: McGraw-Hill, 1970). Both books emphasize Marx's humanism.

Lenin's major political work is *State and Revolution* (New York: International Publishers, 1943). The work was first published in 1917.

A good source for Marxist humanism is *Socialist Humanism*, edited by Erich Fromm (Garden City: Doubleday, 1965). This book contains contributions from a wide variety of Marxist thinkers. Perhaps the most influential democratic socialist in America today is Michael Harrington. Two of his more important works are *The Twilight of Capitalism* (New York: Simon and Schuster, 1976) and *The Other America* (Baltimore: Penguin,

1971). The latter book, which shows how certain segments of the population are unaffected by economic upswings in a free market economy, was highly influential in the development of social policy in the Kennedy and Johnson administrations.

Marcuse's views on the moral justification of revolution can be found in his essay "When Revolution Is Morally Justified," in *Ethics and Society*, edited by Richard T. de-George (Garden City: Doubleday, 1966). Also important is his *One Dimensional Man* (New York: Beacon Press, 1964), which was something of a bible to student leftists of the sixties.

Carl Cohen's anthology, *Communism, Fascism and Democracy* (New York: Random House, 1962) is a useful sourcebook, containing selections by major theorists who have influenced communist and democratic thought. Also useful is Robert Heilbroner's *The Worldly Philosophers* (New York: Simon and Schuster, 1953). Almost a modern classic, this book presents short, highly readable treatments of many giants of economic theory, including Marx and Smith.

Socrates' defense of his decision to accept the death penalty appears in Plato's *Crito*, which is available in numerous editions, usually accompanied by three other dialogues: *Euthyphro, Apology, and Phaedo*. Together, the four are known as the "death dialogues" and can be found in editions from Bobbs-Merrill (Indianapolis, 1956) and Penguin (New York, 1954). The Penguin edition is titled *The Last Days of Socrates*.

Thoreau's "On the Duty of Civil Disobedience" is available in many editions, coupled with his famous work *Walden*, including a Holt, Rinehart and Winston edition (New York, 1948). The essay first appeared in 1849. A more recent defense of civil disobedience is Martin Luther King, Jr.'s "Letter from Birmingham Jail," which was directed against criticisms by fellow clergymen of his own civil disobedience. The letter can be found in King's *Why We Can't Wait* (New York: Harper & Row, 1963).

The following anthologies should also be useful: H. A. Bedau's *Civil Disobedience: Theory and Practice* (New York: Pegasus, 1969); Edward Kent's *Revolution and the Rule of Law* (Englewood Cliffs: Prentice-Hall, 1971); J. G. Murphy's *Civil Disobedience and Violence* (Belmont, Calif.: Wadsworth, 1971).

One revolutionary guerilla fighter who had a profound impact both in print and on Latin American politics was Ernesto (Che) Guevara, who fought with Castro in Cuba and was killed fighting in Bolivia. See his *Guerilla Warfare* (New York: Random House, 1968) and *Revolutionary War* (New York: International Publishers, 1968).

Finally, the following books are useful general introductions to political philosophy: George Sabine's *History of Political Theory* (New York: Holt, Rinehart and Winston, 1973); *Social and Political Philosophy*, edited by Somerville and Santoni (Garden City: Doubleday, 1963); and *Society, Law, and Morality*, edited by Frederick A. Olafson (Englewood Cliffs: Prentice-Hall, 1961). The latter two are anthologies of readings from ancient Greece to the twentieth century. An anthology of contemporary essays by leading political philosophers is Anthony Quinton's *Political Philosophy* (New York: Oxford University Press, 1967).

Part III

FREEDOM, ACTION, AND RESPONSIBILITY

Chapter 9

FREE WILL
AND DETERMINISM

We make choices: We walk into an ice cream parlor, read the menu, ponder the alternatives, and finally choose a particular flavor. We open the closet and select a pair of pants. We scan the movie page and settle on a film to see. We decide whether to attend a class or sleep through it, whether to buy a new record album or not. These are very mundane facts about us, which we ordinarily take thoroughly for granted.

We take much else for granted—for example, that many of our decisions are morally important ones. Whether to turn in a classmate for cheating, whether to return the extra change given us by a cashier, whether to lie on a given occasion, whether to keep a promise, whether to avoid a friend to whom we owe money—all of these are morally important. They reflect on our moral characters. We are held morally responsible for them. We can be praised for them, blamed for them, rewarded or punished.

These sets of facts are intimately related. Because we are choosing beings, we are held morally responsible for our actions. Because what we do is up to us, we are fit subjects of moral approval and disapproval. Because we can make our own decisions, we deserve moral praise and blame.

In this chapter and the two that follow it, we shall examine these facts about ourselves and look more closely at their connections.

FREE WILL

When you are deciding whether to order a strawberry or butter pecan ice cream cone, it seems to you that you could very easily make either choice. There are two possible futures, one in which you eat a strawberry cone, one in which you eat a butter pecan cone, and which future will come about seems to be totally unsettled. It is your decision and your decision alone, you feel, that finally settles the matter. And that decision, you feel, is in normal circumstances perfectly free. That is, there is nothing that makes you choose one way or the other. Certainly, there are various influences on you whenever you make a choice, but whether you yield to them or not is up to you. You can choose your favorite flavor, perversely pick a flavor that you don't like, or walk out of the ice cream parlor empty-handed.

What I have been describing here is your sense of your own free will, a free will that you can have under even the most limiting of situations. Your political freedom can be taken from you by a right-wing military coup, but you can choose whether to submit to the new regime or resist it. Your social freedom can be taken from you by your university, but you can choose whether to obey its restrictive rules or disobey them. Your economic freedom can be taken from you by powerful monopolies, but you can choose how to deal with their power. Even in the strict confines of a maximum security prison, your sense of your own free will can remain.

Jean-Paul Sartre (1905–1980) put the matter this way. We are always free to say *no* to anything that comes our way, and therein lies the ultimate expression of our freedom. He said that he himself never felt so free as during the Nazi occupation of France, when he found himself constantly saying *no* to the occupiers by working with the French resistance fighters. This is the freedom Andrei Sakharov exercises when he speaks out against Soviet repression, that James Cagney exercises in countless prison films when he refuses to cooperate with the guards, and that you exercise when you disobey dorm regulations.

Social, political, and economic freedom are granted us by those around us, but freedom of the will, we believe, is ours from birth. Because we are the sort of creatures we are, it is ours until we die, unless it is stolen by something like hypnotism or brainwashing. Short of such aberrations, we believe, our free will remains intact through all manner of adversity. Our futures are unsettled until we decide what they will be.

DETERMINISM

Let us now turn our attention from human freedom to the behavior of inanimate objects. Consider an ordinary pool table, for instance. On it, there are a cue ball and a nine ball. Somebody strikes the cue ball with a cue stick. The cue ball strikes the nine ball, and the nine ball banks off a cushion and stops somewhere in the middle of the table.

Suppose that you knew all of the following before the cue ball was struck: the angle at which the cue ball would be struck, the force with which it would be struck, the distance between the cue ball and nine ball, the exact dimensions and weight of the balls, the quality and texture of their surfaces, the amount of friction created by the surface of the table, its material and irregularities, and the hardness of the cushion. Suppose that you also knew that nothing from the outside was going to interfere with the path of either the cue ball or the nine ball. Suppose that you also knew all the relevant laws governing the motion of physical bodies. In that case, you would be able to calculate with utter certainty exactly where on the table the nine ball would end up.

In fact, whenever you play pool you make rough calculations of just that sort. You know approximately how hard you must strike the cue ball in order to hit the nine ball with enough force to get it to reach the pocket, at what angle you have to hit it, and so forth. Better pool players are better, in part, because their knowledge of such matters is better. They also know how to get the cue ball to end up where they want it, in order to set themselves up for their next shot. Part of learning to be a good pool player is learning such things.

Why can we predict the action of pool balls so well? Because they are completely *determined* events. That is, they are the only outcomes that are physically compatible with everything that came before them. Given certain conditions that obtain at the time the cue ball is struck, and given certain laws of nature, there is one and only one possibility. Therefore, if we know all of these conditions and the relevant laws of nature, we can predict with utter certainty where any ball will end up.

Many events are similarly determined—changes in the weather, for example. That weather forecasters make mistakes in their predictions is due to ignorance on their part, not to any inherent unpredictability of the weather. There are too many things going on in the skies to take fully into account. But if the weather forecasters did know all of these things, their predictions would not misfire.

To say that an event is determined, then, is not to say that we *can* predict it. It is to say that we *could* predict it if we knew all the relevant conditions and laws. Think of an object falling to the ground. Whether we can predict how long it will take to hit the ground depends on a number of factors. If we hold a piece of chalk so many feet from the ground and then let go, it is a simple matter to calculate the duration of its fall. The calculation of the duration of a leaf's fall from a tree is far more complicated. Because the leaf is so light, because its edges are so irregular, because the shifts of the wind are so frequent and subtle, we could never have sufficient information for our calculations. But its fall is no less determined than the chalk's.

Both are determined because both are governed by causal laws. A causal law says that events of a certain type are invariably followed by events of another type provided that certain conditions obtain. Take the striking of a match. Striking a match causes it to light. That is, the match's lighting is a determined event. Of course, not every struck match lights. The match may be wet, there may be impurities in it, there may be insufficient oxygen in the atmosphere, the striking surface may be damaged, and so forth. So striking doesn't always cause lighting. But if a match is struck in optimum conditions, it will light. And if we know that these conditions obtain, we can predict with certainty that it will light. We can do this because its lighting is the only outcome causally compatible with these conditions.

DETERMINISM AND HUMAN CHOICES

Despite what was said earlier about your sense of your own free will, many philosophers and behavioral scientists believe that human behavior is determined. That is, they believe that all human behavior is governed by causal laws, far more complicated than those governing the striking of a match, perhaps, but in principle the same. So when you order a strawberry cone, that is the only outcome compatible with everything leading up to it, just as the actual stopping place of the nine ball is the only outcome compatible with everything leading up to it. And if we knew all the laws governing human behavior, and all the conditions that obtained immediately before the decision was made, we could predict with utter certainty that you would order strawberry.

People who feel this way are called *determinists.* Notice, the determinist does not believe that we do not make choices. Such a view would be absurd, since it is obvious to us that we make choices all the time. Nor does the determinist believe that our choices make no difference. Just as the path of the cue ball makes a difference to what happens to the nine ball, so do our choices make a difference to what we do. All the determinist says, in effect, is that our choices are caused. Our actions are the result of a long causal process, and one crucial part of that process is the decision to perform that action.

Thus, the determinist agrees with much of what was said earlier in this chapter. What the determinist does not believe is this: that the two alternative futures—the one in which we eat strawberry ice cream and the one in which we eat butter pecan—are equally possible. Only one is causally compatible with the conditions leading up to our decision.

The Argument from Predictability

Throughout the years, a variety of arguments in favor of determinism have been advanced. Some have relied on common-sense observations, others have been supported by sophisticated scientific theories. Let us first consider a common-sense argument, the *argument from predictability.*

When I walk into a classroom to meet my students for the first time, most of them know nothing about me except that I am a philosophy professor. Yet with that small bit of information, they can predict many things about me—that I will assign readings, grade them, lecture on philosophy, hold office hours, for instance, and that I will not remove my clothes, go to the corner, and recite the

Gettysburg Address in Italian. As the term progresses, they can predict much more—that I will begin each class with a few jokes, look for certain things on exams, become annoyed by certain comments and appreciate others, dress in certain ways, return to certain examples, and so on.

Indeed, it is that way with everyone we know. The better you know someone, the better you can predict her behavior. Think of your best friend or your parents. You know that you can count on them for certain things, that you can tell them certain things safely but not other things, that you will enjoy doing certain things with them but not other things, that they will let you get away with certain things but not other things, that they will laugh at certain jokes but not others, and so on.

To get to know someone is to get to know her character—her strengths and weaknesses, likes and dislikes, hopes and fears, wants, habits, peeves, moods, and ways of reacting to different situations. And because of that, our ability to predict increases as our knowledge increases.

It seems, then, that what stands in the way of perfect prediction is our own ignorance. If we knew the other person's character completely, we could predict what she would do in any situation. But if we could do that, determinism must be true.

In fact, it could be said that we are all determinists in our daily lives. If we weren't, it is doubtful that we'd have the courage to wake up each morning. If we couldn't safely predict that motorists would at least slow down when they reach a stop sign, we wouldn't take our chances on the roads. If we didn't believe that knowledge of someone's character allowed us to predict what life would be like with her, we wouldn't marry. If we didn't believe that someone's character provided a reliable indication of future behavior, we wouldn't trust our friends or vote for the candidates of our choice.

Of course, our predictions are often wrong. But when they are, we do not chalk up our mistakes to the free will of the other person. Rather, we reason in the same way that the weather forecaster does when he makes a mistake. We look for some explanation, some cause of the unexpected behavior, some factor that was unknown to us when we made the prediction. John promises Mary to meet her at ten. She knows him to be a reliable person. At ten-thirty, he has yet to arrive. Does she shrug her shoulders and say that it's a case of free will in action? No. She thinks that something must have happened to him, or that something unexpected came up to delay him. She looks for a cause of his lateness. That is, she behaves like a determinist.

Behavioral Conditioning

The argument from predictability shows that determinism is a reasonable view, but it is not conclusive. Determinism will not be conclusively proved until scientists can devise laws governing human behavior. Probably the most famous and ambitious attempt to do just that comes from the school of psychology associated with the contemporary American B. F. Skinner—*behaviorism.* According to the behaviorist, human behavior can be explained without any reference to desires, beliefs, intentions, or decisions. It can be fully explained by laws that treat human persons as a certain sort of machine—a *stimulus-response* machine, the behavior of which is governed by the laws of *operant conditioning.*

We can illustrate this view by the example of a rat in a contraption known as a *Skinner box.* In the box are a lever that can be pressed for food and a light that flashes on and off. The light flashes on. If the rat moves toward the lever it is given a food pellet; otherwise, not. When the light flashes on again, the process is repeated. Eventually, the rat will move toward the lever whenever the light flashes on. Then it will get food only when it moves all the way to the lever. Eventually, it will move all the way to the lever whenever the light flashes on. Then it will get food only when it presses the lever. Eventually it will press the lever whenever the light flashes on.

What has happened here? The rat has been *conditioned* to press the lever for food. It has learned to give a conditioned *response* (pressing the lever) whenever it is given a certain *stimulus* (the flashing on of the light). The key to the process is the food pellet, which, in Skinner's terminology, *reinforces* the response. First, the movement toward the lever is reinforced by the food pellet. Then, movement that ends at the lever. Then, pressing the lever. When the process is completed, the rat presses the lever whenever the light flashes on, because the response to the stimulus has been sufficiently reinforced.

According to Skinner, that is how all learning takes place, not only for rats in a box, but for human beings in the outside world. Certain behaviors are reinforced in certain conditions, and when these conditions continue to arise, we behave in the reinforced ways. Free will has no part to play in the process at all.

There are, as we shall see, controversies surrounding Skinner's views, but this much is clear—human beings *can* be conditioned. Skinner's theories have led to therapies for a variety of behavioral problems—speech defects, phobias, and sexual problems, to name but three—and these therapies have often achieved notable success.

Moreover, it does seem that much of our ordinary behavior is the product of conditioning. When introducing Skinner to my students, I ask the following questions. How many believe that American democracy is preferable to Soviet communism? How many believe that rape is wrong? How many believe that Robert Redford is more handsome than I am? How many believe that vanilla tastes better than chocolate?

There is invariably unanimous agreement over the first three questions, and close to an even split over the fourth. It is hard to escape the belief that the responses to the first three are the products of conditioning. They concern values that lie at the heart of our culture, and their acceptance is constantly reinforced by our homes, schools, churches, films, and television screens. Since our society has no interest in our choice of ice cream flavors, this bit of behavior is not subject to such massive conditioning.

Psychological Mechanism

Although Skinner's theories have been very helpful in behavioral therapies, many psychologists and philosophers have doubted their usefulness in the explanation of human behavior. The problem, they claim, is that human beings are too complicated to be thought of as stimulus-response machines. To explain their behavior, we must take into account the person's beliefs about the stimulus as well as the stimulus, and we have to take into account the person's beliefs about his own behavior as well as the behavior itself. In short, if we are to think of human beings as machines, we must look inside to understand their behavior. We must answer such questions as these: How do they translate light patterns on the retina into beliefs about their environment? How do they store their memories? How do beliefs, memories and desires result in actions? How are rational decisions made? How is information of different sorts processed? How is the machine built so that it can learn the things that it does? How is intelligence possible?

Questions such as these form the agenda of *cognitive psychologists*—psychologists who attempt to map out the functions within the brain that govern our behavior. They also form the agenda of researchers in a new field called *artificial intelligence*, who attempt to design computer programs that can simulate the workings of the human mind. They also form the agenda of philosophers seeking a unified view of persons in keeping with the results of cognitive science.

These thinkers look at us as *information-processing* machines, as very complicated computers, made of organic matter rather than electronic circuitry. We shall examine this way of looking at persons in Chapter 12 and discuss some of the results gained from it in Chapter 20. For now, we can concentrate on a few relevant points.

According to this view, psychological processes are *mechanistic*. That is, they are processes that we could program a machine to perform. This holds not only for mathematical computations, but for all thinking processes, including learning and decision-making. Thus, to deliberate or make inferences or choose to do something is to run a certain sort of program, as a computer does when it performs certain calculations.

Moreover, most of these processes are *unconscious*. Although the results of *some* of our programs (a decision to order strawberry ice cream, for instance) come to our conscious attention, the processes themselves and many of their results are often unknown to us. Far from being under our conscious control, they are automatic and hidden from our introspection.

Where do these programs come from? Many of them are part of our genetic heritage, the product of the evolutionary history of the human race. The most important of these are our learning programs, which lead not only to new information but to new programs as well. Unlike your pocket calculator, we are self-designing machines, capable of altering old programs and adding new ones. But these processes are themselves, it is felt, mechanistic. With sufficient ingenuity we could design a computer to do the same thing.

If this view, which we may call *psychological mechanism*, is correct, it is difficult to maintain that we have free will. If our behavior is the product of mechanistic processes, it is governed by physical laws. And if it is governed by physical laws, it is determined.

ARGUMENTS IN FAVOR OF FREE WILL

Despite what has been said above, some philosophers continue to hold that human behavior is not determined. These philosophers are often called *libertarians*, and they make the following arguments.

First, they offer their own common-sense argument. Why do we believe that we have free will? Because it *seems* to us that we do. We are conscious of our choices, and we are not conscious of anything causing them. We feel no inner compulsion or necessity forcing us to go one way or another.

Moreover, it is impossible to think otherwise when it comes time to act. We cannot just sit back and wait for our actions to happen. Without choices, we will not act at all. So we must choose. Moreover, we cannot sit back and wait for our *choices* to happen. We must make them. We must deliberate, weigh the pros and cons of the alternatives, and come to a reasoned decision. So even if we act like determinists with respect to the actions of others, constantly predicting and explaining away wrong predictions, we must be libertarians with respect to our own actions. How, then, can we deny that we have free will?

In addition to this common-sense argument, libertarians criticize the arguments in favor of determinism. Thus, they respond to the argument from predictability this way. The predictability of human behavior does not show that it is determined. All it shows is that most people are *rational*. Why can we safely predict that people will stop or at least slow down when approaching a stop sign at a busy intersection? Because as long as they don't want to injure themselves, which most people don't, it is irrational not to. Why can I safely predict that a friend will not order peas and carrots in a restaurant? Because he hates peas and carrots, and it is irrational to order food that one hates without good reason to do so, and my friend has no such reason.

Libertarians, the defense continues, do not claim that free human actions are arbitrary or inexplicable or totally unpredictable. Of course if we know what a person likes and doesn't like we can predict what he will do on many occasions. We can do that because it is rational to be guided in our actions by our likes and dislikes, and because it is a safe assumption that people will usually behave rationally.

But we can grant all of that without being forced into accepting determinism. To say that we *often* act rationally is not to say that we *must* act rationally. Nor is it to say that rational thought and action are determined. If there is more than one rational course of action in any given situation, as there most assuredly is in most if not all cases, then there is no reason why I cannot freely choose either.

And there is no reason why this element of freedom cannot account for incorrect predictions, rather than the ignorance of the person making the predictions.

This line of defense can be used against Skinner as well. It is possible to view behavioral conditioning this way. People tend to repeat actions that have rewarded them in the past. If they are always rewarded for a certain action in certain circumstances, it is likely that they will act in the same way when those circumstances arise again. Why? Because they aren't stupid. They know that if the act was rewarded in the past, it will probably be rewarded in the future. But to grant that is not to grant that they are machines of a certain sort. It is only to point out the obvious fact that they often act rationally.

Furthermore, the fact that scientists find it fruitful to think of us as machines does not mean that we *are* machines. Suppose, for example, that the scientist is attempting to understand how we learn about our environment through our senses. If we stick to vision, our problem is this: How does the brain translate light patterns on the retina into a vast number of beliefs about the causes of those patterns? One way of answering this question is to devise a computer program to perform the same task. Since such a program is beyond current capabilities, the scientist breaks the process down into simpler tasks. How can a computer be programmed to recognize faces from different angles? How can it be programmed to recognize a variety of different shapes as the letter *A?* These programs, it is hoped, give us some clue as to how we perform the same tasks. Since these tasks are performed by us automatically, it is no threat to our free will that they are mechanistic.

But then the scientist broadens her scope. She designs chess-playing programs, music-composing programs, poetry-writing programs, and other programs simulating creative, rational human activity. These programs are also helpful in the understanding of human performance of these activities. They can help us see what steps are involved, what order they take, and so on.

These programs are *models* of human activity, then. That is, they are items that represent certain features of human activity, the way that an arrangement of plastic balls can represent certain features of our solar system. But just as not all features of the solar system are modeled by the plastic balls, and just as some features of the plastic balls do not belong to the solar system, so are certain features of human cognitive processes not modeled by the programs, and so do certain features of the programs not belong to human cognitive processes. Perhaps our free will is not modeled by them. Perhaps the mechanism of the model does not belong to our cognitive processes.

We can put this point another way. Suppose we knew every step a chess player went through in deciding to make a certain move. We could then program a computer to go through exactly those steps. Suppose we could do this for every possible situation that could arise in a game of chess. In that case, we could design a computer program to model this player's chess playing. But there might be one important difference between the model and the chess player. Whereas the model might go through exactly the same steps every time it came to the same situation, the chess player might not. Some feature has been left out of the model, then—free will.

THE DETERMINIST'S RESPONSE

How does the determinist respond to these arguments? Let us begin with the first libertarian argument, that it seems to us that we have free will.

Determinists have not been impressed by this argument. Just because it *seems* to us that we have free will is no guarantee that we really do. After all, the determinist does not claim that there is some irresistible force inside of us *compelling* us to behave as we do. The determinist's claim is merely that human choice and behavior are the products of natural, causal processes, not that there is some inner necessity that we could introspect, that we could feel the way we do a pain.

Let's see what happens when we deliberate. Suppose that you are trying to decide between ravioli and broiled fish in a restaurant. You like the taste of both, although you prefer the taste of ravioli. Still, the ravioli has many more calories, and you are trying to watch your weight. On the other hand, the fish is more expensive, and you are trying to keep within a budget. Then again, you ate fish the night before. Matters are further complicated by the fact that you are with a date and you don't want your breath to smell of spicy sauce. You ponder these considerations, and finally choose the fish. Now as you go through this process, it certainly seems to you that your choice is undetermined. You decide what you want, and then you order it.

But are you freely choosing what you want? Is what you want really the result of a free choice? Many would say that it is not. What you are really doing, it might be said, is weighing the pros and cons of each alternative until you *discover* what you want. Figuratively, you are loading a scale—placing so many weights on the ravioli side, so many on the fish side, until the scale decisively tips in one direction. When that happens, the decision is made.

In that case, what you are doing is running through a decision-making program, just as a computer does. The program automatically rejects items on the menu you don't like or can't afford, and then leads you to deliberate consciously over the remaining two items. Each step in the deliberation is a step in the program. Some steps involve listing the pros and cons of each alternative, some involve the weighting of each, and the final one involves the totaling and comparing. Although the move from one step to the next is a determined event, it does not feel forced on you, because it is perfectly natural. It is the way your mind naturally works.

But isn't your decision to watch your weight a matter of free choice? Or your decision to live within a budget? Not at all, the determinist responds. Such decisions are made in the same way that the decision to order fish is made—by a deterministic process of weighting, totaling, and comparing. Thus, our failure to introspect some inner compulsion or necessity does not damage the determinist's position.

What about the other libertarian arguments? These are a bit stronger. Indeed, many determinists agree with most of the points these arguments raise. For example, take the claim that our predictions of the behavior of others are based on our assumption that others are rational, rather than on any deterministic assumption. This is obviously true. Similarly, many determinists believe that Skinner's theories do presuppose rationality when applied to human behavior. Take a familiar case: Your phone rings at an inconvenient time. Suppose you answer it anyway. Skinner would explain that by saying that you had been reinforced in the past for answering a ringing phone and that's why you answered it this time. If you don't answer it, he would explain *that* by saying that you'd been reinforced in the past for *not* answering it at such times.

But could he have predicted which you would do in advance? Perhaps, but he would have to know a few things. Do you know who is calling? Are you expecting an important call? How inconvenient is the call? But once he starts taking these things into account, he's no longer thinking of you as a stimulus-response machine. Rather, he's thinking of you as a rational agent.

Similarly, let's think of what makes something a reinforcement. Let's say that the previous times you've answered the phone, you've had pleasant conversations, good news, calls from people you've not heard from in years, and important messages. These count as reinforcements for you because you value such things. But someone else might not care about them, and would never put down a book or stop watching a ball game on television or interrupt a conversation to answer a phone. So your own likes and dislikes have to be taken into account. But other things have to be taken into account as well. For example, your *beliefs* have to be taken into account. How you interpret a conversation makes a big difference as to whether it is pleasant, and how you interpret a message makes a big difference as to whether it is important to you. So even the characterization of something as a reinforcement depends on our taking people as rational agents.

So whatever success Skinner's theories may have in therapies, we cannot think of human beings as mere stimulus-response machines. We must think of them as rational agents. So the crucial difference between the libertarian and the determinist is this—are rational processes in the human mind mechanistic or not?

The libertarian argues that the success of cognitive psychology and artificial intelligence does not show that rational processes are mechanistic. And, once again, most determinists would agree with that. The success of these fields shows that rational processes *can* be mechanistic, and by doing that it undermines important objections to mechanism, but it does not show that rational human processes *are* mechanistic. What *would* show it? Some larger theory about the human mind. What sort of theory? A theory that holds that mental processes are either causally dependent on brain processes in a certain way or are identical with brain processes of a certain kind. Since the brain is a physical object, it must obey laws of nature. Therefore, if mental processes are either dependent on brain processes in the required way, or identical with brain processes, they must obey laws of nature. And these laws are most probably deterministic.

Of course, determinism may be true even if such a theory of the human mind is not, but most determinists hold such a theory. Is there anything else that would show determinism to be true? Yes, something noted earlier in this chapter. If scientists could give a physical explanation of human behavior, if they could explain our behavior with causal laws referring to the workings of our nervous system, say, then the dispute would be settled in favor of the determinist.

THE FINAL WORD?

It may seem that we have left the determinist and libertarian at a stalemate. And, for the time being, we have. Still, there are a couple of important points we can make about the dispute.

First, determinism is a very *plausible* thesis. Although the arguments we have considered are not decisive, they are powerful. Not only do they give good reasons for believing that determinism is true. They also show why our feeling that we have free will is not a good reason to accept libertarianism.

Second, determinism will receive additional support in Part IV. In Chapter 12, we shall examine various theories of the human mind. There we shall find that the most reasonable theory is just the sort of theory that is most hospitable to determinism.

Therefore, whether we are inclined (as I am) to accept determinism or not, we cannot easily dismiss it. What we must do, then, is see whether the acceptance of determinism would undermine our understanding of ourselves as morally responsible agents. That is the topic that will occupy our attention in the next two chapters.

STUDY QUESTIONS

1. Why is it natural for us to believe that we have free will? Do the reasons that come to mind strike you as good reasons? Why or why not?

2. What is determinism? Why do determinists believe that the predictability of human behavior supports their case? Why do defenders of human free will believe otherwise? What do you think?

3. What is behavioral conditioning? How is a rat in a laboratory conditioned? Why does Skinner believe that the success of behavioral conditioning shows that human beings do not have free will? How do libertarians respond? Do you agree with their response? Why or why not?

4. What is psychological mechanism? What are the similarities between this view and the views of Skinner? What are the differences? Which seems more reasonable to you? Why?

5. Some determinists claim that to decide what we want to do is really to discover what we want to do. What do they mean by that? Can you think of any of your own decisions that seem to refute the claim?

6. Sometimes it seems to us that it doesn't matter which of two alternatives we take, as when you must choose between two courses to fulfill a university requirement and you really don't care which one you will take. Still, you make your choice anyway. Some people believe that this is a genuine case of free will. Do you think such cases prove that you have free will, or do you think that the determinist can explain why they don't?

7. Psychological mechanists claim that the successful modeling of certain processes of the human mind lends support to the claim that the mental processes of human beings are also mechanistic. Libertarians disagree. What are their reasons for disagreeing?

8. Libertarians attempt to answer most arguments in favor of determinism by referring to human rationality. How powerful do you think these responses are?

GLOSSARY

Argument from predictability. Argument claiming that the predictability of human behavior shows that human behavior is *determined.*

Behaviorism. School of psychology associated with B. F. Skinner. Behaviorists believe that the learned behavior of all animals (including humans) is better understood as the product of *operant conditioning* than as the product of wants, purposes, and beliefs.

Causal law. A law of the natural or social sciences that says that under the right conditions an event of one kind will invariably be followed by an event of another kind.

Determinism. The view that human behavior is *determined.* To say that an event is determined is to say that it is the only outcome causally compatible with everything that came before it. Events that are determined are governed by *causal laws.*

Libertarianism. The view that human behavior is not *determined.*

Model. An object or system that has certain features representing the features of some other object or system.

Operant conditioning. A method of changing an animal's behavior. When operant conditioning is applied, the animal is given some reinforcement for giving a certain response to a certain stimulus. After a time, the animal will perform that response whenever it is presented with the stimulus. According to *behaviorists,* learned human behavior is the product of operant conditioning.

Psychological mechanism. The view that machines can be programmed to perform any psychological process that the human mind performs.

Simulation. The imitation of the behavior of one system by another system.

Chapter 10

DETERMINISM AND HUMAN ACTION

Perhaps you have seen the bumper sticker that reads "Guns Don't Kill. People Do." The people who display this message do so to fight gun-control legislation. Whether you agree with the political aspect of their message or not, there is a sense in which the message is true. Guns, like other tools used by human beings, are not *agents.* They do not *act.* They do not *choose* to fire. They merely *respond* to the pressure of a human finger on the trigger.

Let us think of all physical motion as *behavior.* If we do, we can speak of the behavior of the planets, clouds, stereo systems, automobiles, guns, plants, insects, electrons, and human beings. That is, we can say that any physical object is capable of behaving. In that case, *actions* form a very small part of the behavior we find in the world.

Indeed, actions form only a small part of the behavior of the human body. When you toss and turn in your sleep, for instance, you are not acting. If a sudden tic causes your arm to move, you are not acting. If your leg responds to the tap of a physician's hammer on your knee, you are not acting. Similarly, the beating of your heart is not an action of yours. Neither are the growth of your hair and fingernails, the activity of your digestive system, the workings of your liver and kidneys.

So if a human action is a body movement, it is not *just* a body movement. If it is a bit of behavior, it is not *just* behavior. What is the difference, then, between an action and a mere body movement? What happens when you wave to a friend that does not happen when your arm suddenly twitches? Why can *we* act but not plants?

BEHAVIOR AND RESPONSIBILITY

The above questions are important ones, because the distinction between actions and other types of behavior is crucial to our assignment of moral responsibility. Although we hold the weather responsible for crop failures, rock slides responsible for damage to automobiles, bacteria responsible for various diseases, we do not hold them *morally* responsible. We do not think of them as deserving punishment for what they cause. We do not think of bacteria as being evil creatures. Similarly, we do not hold human beings morally responsible for all of their behavior. If you slap someone because you don't like his looks, you deserve moral blame. If, on the other hand, a sudden twitch sends your hand into another's face, you do not deserve moral blame. In the first case you acted. In the second you did not.

How do we distinguish the two cases? Intuitively, our answer is this. In the first case, the movement of your arm is the product of your own free choice. In the second case, it is the product of purely causal processes. Thus, the difference between actions and other types of behavior seems to boil down to a matter of free choice. If the behavior is the product of a free choice, it is an action. Otherwise, it is not. Bacteria do not act, because they are not capable of free choice. Human beings do act, because they are.

Or are they? In the preceding chapter, we saw that there is good reason to believe that human behavior is governed by causal laws. Suppose that this claim is true. Does that mean that we really do not act? That we merely behave? If so, does that mean that we cannot hold one another morally responsible for our behavior?

Many determinists have answered yes to these questions. B. F. Skinner, whose views we looked at in the preceding chapter, dismisses all talk of freedom, responsibility, action, and creativity. According to Skinner, we do not act at all. He even goes so far as to compare the writing of a poem to a hen's laying of an egg. We do not *create* poems, he says. Rather, we *have* them. We shall examine Skinner's and other arguments below. But first, let us look a bit more closely at the notion of human action.

REASONS AND ACTIONS

Is there a way of distinguishing a mere body movement from an action that does not depend on the notion of free will?

It certainly seems that there is. After all, whether determinism is true or not, we can still distinguish a twitch of the arm from a wave to a friend. How do we do so? Most obviously, when my arm twitches, it does not move because I have a *reason* to move it. When I wave to a friend, I do so for a reason—to attract his attention, say. So an action is the product of a person's reason for acting. A mere body movement is not.

But what is a reason? What is it to act for a reason?

One widely accepted answer to these questions comes from the contemporary American philosopher Donald Davidson. According to Davidson, a reason to act is a combination of a want and a belief. When I act for a reason, I do so because I want to accomplish some goal and believe that a certain body movement will accomplish that goal. So an action is the product of a want and a belief.

Take the example of waving to a friend. The goal I want to achieve is the attracting of his attention, and I believe that I can achieve it by moving my arm. When my arm twitches, however, it does not move because I want to achieve any goal and believe that a movement of my arm will achieve it.

Waving to a friend is a very simple case. Matters are often more complicated, and a number of wants and beliefs may be involved. In a game of chess, for example, I move my arm in order to checkmate my opponent's king. That is, I want to checkmate my opponent's king and believe that I can do so by moving my knight. So my goal then is to move my knight, and I believe that I can achieve it by moving my arm.

We can complicate matters still further. In the above cases, I *wanted* to attract my friend's attention and to move my knight. But sometimes we perform actions that we *don't* want to do. We let mosquitoes into the house, hurt people's feelings, break things, and so on. We don't do these things on purpose. We don't have a reason to do them. But they are actions of ours just the same. Suppose I walk into a table, knocking over and breaking an expensive vase. Knocking over the vase is an action of mine, for which I can be held responsible. Yet I did not knock it over because I believed that I could achieve a desired goal by doing so.

Still, the action was the product of a want and a belief. Here's how. Anything we do can be described in a variety of ways. At this moment, for instance, I am moving my fingers. But we can also describe what I am doing in these ways. I am typing, pressing keys, writing a book, earning a living, making a series of clicking noises, putting my thoughts on paper, depositing ink marks on paper, and numerous other things. All of these are different ways of describing the same action. Or, you might say, they are all different actions performed by the same body movement. Philosophers are divided on this point. Fortunately, for our purposes it doesn't matter which side is right. So let us say, for the sake of simplicity, that they are different ways of describing the same action.

To return to the broken vase, what am I doing as I knock it over? I am walking across the room. And I *do* have a reason for that—to answer the phone, say. So my knocking over of the vase was the product of a reason. I wanted to answer the phone and believed that I must walk across the room to do so. Since my knocking over of the vase is the same action as my walking (or an action performed by the same body movement by which my walking is performed), it is the product of the same reason. Of course, a reason for walking across the room is not a reason for knocking over a vase, but that is not important here.

What is an action then? It is a body movement that can be described in such a way that we can say that the person did it because he wanted to achieve a goal and believed that doing what he did would help him achieve it. In other words, it is a body movement that is the product of an appropriate belief and an appropriate want.

REASONS AND CHOICES

It may seem to you that something has been left out of the above account—choice. Has it?

That depends. If you think of a choice as a certain sort of inner act, the conscious recitation inside your head of a sentence like "Now I will walk across the room," then the element of choice *has* been left out. But it should be. After all, many of your actions are not the product of such a conscious inner recitation. As you read this book, do you consciously tell yourself when you come to the end of a page that you will now turn to the next one? When you play basketball, do you consciously tell yourself that you will fake left? When you drive a car, do you consciously tell yourself that you will brake? When you climb steps, do you consciously tell yourself to lift your foot at each step? When you are conversing with a friend, do you consciously rehearse each sentence before you say it? More often than not, the answer to these questions is no.

But if we think of choice in another way, then the element of choice has *not* been left out. In the previous chapter, we looked at the decision-making process. This process, we saw, is a way of arriving at a particular want on a particular occasion. In one of our examples, it was the desire to order broiled fish. Once you arrived at that want, your choice was made.

Thus, the element of choice enters our account of action this way. You enter any situation with an intricate complex of wants, preferences, and beliefs. When you begin a game of chess, for instance, you begin with a desire to win, preferences for certain sorts of strategies, and many beliefs about how to play the game. Every time your opponent moves a piece, you are presented with a new situation. You then calculate the best move to make. Since you come into the game with a desire to make the best move in every situation, you then arrive at the desire to make the calculated move. At that point the choice is made—when the appropriate belief and desire have been arrived at. This may happen consciously, as it usually does when you play chess, or unconsciously, as it usually does when you play ball. Either way, the outcome is your choice.

If we think of choices in this way, we can see how unimportant the inner recitation of a sentence like 'Now I will walk across the room' is. To say that consciously to yourself is not to *make* a choice. It is a product of the choice, just as your walking across the room is. Whether you recite it to yourself or not, the choice is still made.

Do reasons cause behavior?

We now have a way of distinguishing actions from other types of behavior. Actions are caused by appropriate wants and beliefs. Other forms of behavior, such as the twitch of an arm, are caused in other ways. Another way of making our point is this. Actions are explained in terms of reasons. They are a form of *rational* behavior. A bit of behavior is an action if it is the product of an agent's design, if it fits into a network of goals and purposes. Because plants, planets, electrons, and the like do not have reasons, they cannot act. Because we do, and because our reasons cause us to behave, we can. Now that we have reached this conclusion, it might seem that we have finished the work of the chapter. But we have not. Our conclusion is acceptable only if some of our behavior is caused by reasons.

B. F. Skinner thinks that it is not. According to Skinner, our explanations of human behavior in terms of reasons are pseudo-explanations—the vestiges of a prescientific attitude. Wants and beliefs, purposes and goals, do not cause our behavior. Our behavior is the result of operant conditioning. We are not rational agents. We are stimulus-response machines. We behave the way we do because we have been conditioned to do so. We do not act, then. We merely behave.

Our situation is this. We are faced with two theories of human behavior. If we accept one, we explain some human behavior in terms of an agent's reasons. If we accept the other, we explain the same behavior in terms of operant conditioning. Skinner says that the two theories are competitors. Only one can be true. And the true theory is the second one.

Behaviorism and Rational Agents

But matters are not so simple, as we shall now see. Let us return to our friend from the previous chapter, the rat in the Skinner box, and its conditioned behavior, the pressing of the lever. Skinner explains this behavior as follows. Because a certain behavior (pressing the lever) that follows a certain stimulus (the flashing of a light) has been reinforced in the past (by a food pellet), the rat will press the lever whenever the light flashes. Someone else might explain the behavior this way. The rat knows that it will get food if it presses the lever after seeing the light flash. Since it wants to eat, it will press the lever the next time it sees the light flash.

The second explanation refers to the wants and beliefs of the rat. The first refers instead to a stimulus, a response, and a reinforcement. It does not refer to anything going on inside the rat's mind. Since he can explain the rat's behavior without referring to anything going on in its mind, Skinner believes that it is foolish to look for causes there. And since we can do the same thing with human behavior, he thinks that it is foolish to look for causes in *our* minds.

But can we? As we saw in the last chapter, Skinner cannot explain human behavior without trading on the assumption that beliefs and wants influence our behavior. He does not need this assumption when dealing with the rat in the Skinner box because he has constructed an artificially simple situation. There is only *one* food stimulus, the light, and it serves *only* as a food stimulus. There is only *one* food response, the pressing of the lever, and it serves *only* as a food response. And there is only *one* reinforcement, the food pellet, and it serves *only* as a reinforcement.

In the life of a human being, however, things are much more complex. Someone raises an arm. Is he waving to me? To someone else? Is he threatening me? Someone else? Is he stretching a sore muscle? Reaching for something? Testing the tightness of his jacket? He can be doing any one of those things. But whichever one he is doing, what counts in the explanation of my behavior is what I *think* he is doing. That is, whether the raising of the arm counts as a friendly stimulus or a threat stimulus or no stimulus at all depends on my *beliefs* about it. Similarly, as we saw in the previous chapter, whether something is a *reinforcement* for me depends on my beliefs about it.

Even certain facts about my *response* depend on my beliefs about it. Suppose I respond to the arm movement by clapping my hands. If I believe that hand clapping frightens people, then I am trying to ward off a threat. If I believe that it is a friendly gesture, I am returning a greeting. So the nature of my response is a function of what I think I am doing.

Thus, Skinner's theories do not allow us to explain human behavior without reference to what goes on in the human mind. They do not erase the need to view human beings as rational agents. So we can continue to distinguish human actions from other behaviors in terms of reasons.

Mechanism and Action

The victory over Skinner may seem a hollow one to you. If determinism is true anyway, what have we gained by saving the influence of goals and beliefs from Skinner's assault? What good is it to be told that we are not stimulus-response machines, if we are then told that we are another kind of machine? Is it any better to be like a computer than a rat in a Skinner box? Is an information-processing machine any more capable of acting than a stimulus-response machine?

Beneath these questions lurks the following argument. We call some human body movements actions because we explain them in terms of rational processes. But suppose these processes are mechanistic. In that case, we could, in principle, program a computer to do the same thing. And we could, if we wanted, explain the computer's behavior by saying it "wants" to achieve a certain goal and "believes" that the behavior in question is the best way to achieve it, but we would only be talking picturesquely. The computer is *really* behaving that way because it has been programmed to do so. Or, even more tellingly, it is *really* behaving that way because it is a physical machine obeying causal laws. So if we *really* want to explain its behavior, we should do so in terms of circuits and electricity, not in terms of wants and beliefs.

But the same holds for *human* behavior as well, the argument continues. If our rational processes are mechanistic, then we obey the same kinds of laws. But in that case, if we *really* want to know why we behave as we do, we must explain our behavior in terms of firing neurons in our nervous system, not in terms of wants and beliefs. But that is how we explain twitches and heartbeats. Therefore, what we call actions are not actions at all. They are just body movements. So if psychological mechanism is true, we don't act.

Crucial to this argument is the belief that physical explanations take precedence over any other kind of explanation. If we can explain something physically, there is no need to explain it in any other way. Physical explanations are the *real* ones. All others are merely temporary measures, to be replaced by physical ones when they come along. Of course, if something can*not* be explained physically, that is another matter. But if mechanism is true, then human behavior *can* be explained physically.

Three Stances Toward Behavior

The above argument has been discussed by the contemporary American philosopher Daniel Dennett. His discussion turns on three ways of explaining the behavior of a machine. We can illustrate these ways by using one of his own examples, a chess-playing computer.

The first way we can view the behavior of the computer is from what Dennett calls the *physical stance.* That is, we can view it as a mere machine and try to explain and predict its behavior by referring to the workings of its electronic circuitry. This is the stance that the engineer and mechanic take toward the computer. This way of looking at it will not be very useful in most cases, however, because of the machine's enormous physical complexity. Of course, this stance is most useful if we want to correct a malfunction in the machine, but it is practically worthless if we are watching a game and trying to predict its next move.

For these purposes, the *design stance* is a bit more useful. This is the stance that the programmer takes toward the computer. To take this stance is to concentrate on the program, or instructions, that the machine follows. If we know the computer's program, we can try to predict its moves by checking to see how it is programmed to play. But this stance is almost as limited as the physical stance. In many cases, the machine's program is so complex that even the programmer cannot predict its moves from the design stance.

Fortunately, a third stance is open to us, what Dennett calls the *intentional stance*. To take this stance is to assume that the computer is a rational agent. It is to attribute to it goals, beliefs, and reasoning powers. Be sure to note that when we do this, we are not attributing the *programmer's* beliefs to the machine. As the machine plays, we are attributing to it beliefs about the game in progress. When the programmer designed the machine, she had no such beliefs. This is the stance that people naturally take when they play against the chess-playing computer.

The intentional stance will often be the most useful of the three. That is, if we think of the machine as a rational agent and ask ourselves what moves a rational agent would make in various circumstances, we can predict the machine's behavior better than we could from the other stances.

Which stance we take, Dennett emphasizes, is a matter of choice. Depending on our purposes, we may take any one. If the machine begins to behave erratically, for example, we will take the physical stance toward it. That is, we will assume that there is a physical malfunction and try to correct it. If we notice that the computer makes an illegal move in certain circumstances, we will take the design stance. That is, we will assume that a mistake has been made in the program and try to correct it. But if we are trying to beat the computer in a game of chess, we will most likely take the intentional stance. That is, we will view it as we do any other opponent.

The same thing, he adds, is true of human beings. If, for example, a human being is suffering from severe depression, it is often best to take the physical stance. That is, we explain his behavior as the product of a chemical problem in the brain—as a malfunction analogous to a short circuit in a computer—and prescribe appropriate drugs to correct it.

At other times, it is more useful to take the design stance. Suppose that someone is the victim of a phobia, an irrational fear of dogs, for example. Through behavioral conditioning, say, or hypnosis, the person can often be cured. What we are doing in such cases is reprogramming the phobic person. That is, we are assuming that there is some flaw in the person's design and correcting it.

There is an interesting connection between the above examples. In each case, we take the physical or design stance because there is a *breakdown* in rationality, which we attribute to either the person's physical makeup or design. That is, we resort to those stances because of a problem from the point of view of the intentional stance. But these breakdowns are rare. Ordinarily, the intentional stance suits our purposes fine. We can predict what people will do from this stance, and, by reasoning with them, we can change what they will do. The other stances, on the other hand, do not suit our ordinary purposes. Indeed, our physical makeups and designs are so complex, the ranges of our behavior are so broad, and the situations in which we find ourselves are so varied that it is highly doubtful that the physical and design stances will ever suit our ordinary purposes as well as the intentional stance. The intentional stance, then, is a practical necessity.

MECHANISM AND ACTION REVISITED

We turned to Dennett's views in order to evaluate a particular argument. According to that argument, if mechanism is true, human beings do not act. They just behave.

Why? If we use Dennett's terms, we can put the reason this way. If mechanism is true, then human behavior can, in principle, be explained from the design and physical stances. But in that case, explanations from the intentional stance are not to be taken seriously. They do not *really* explain anything. They should be replaced by the others, particularly explanations from the physical stance. But from that stance, we do not act. Therefore, human beings do not *really* act at all. Their bodies just move.

But why must intentional explanations be replaced by physical ones? Why are they not real explanations? After all, they do work very well—not only for ordinary purposes, but for the purposes of the social sciences. Sociologists, anthropologists, historians, political scientists, economists—all take the intentional stance toward human behavior. Must they be replaced by physics? Indeed, how could they be?

If we must take the intentional stance to predict ordinary human behavior, we must also take it to predict ordinary economic and political behavior. Even if economists and political scientists couch their explanations in terms that make no explicit reference to the rationality of human beings—which they rarely do—that does not mean that they have sidestepped the intentional stance. Just as Skinner must rely on the rationality of human beings to apply his theory, so must economists and political scientists rely on it to apply theirs. Many physical objects can serve as money, just as many body movements can be a threat stimulus. What is important in both cases are our *beliefs* about the objects and movements.

Given the importance of the intentional stance, then, why is it not to be taken seriously? One possible answer, considered by Dennett, is this. When we explain extremely depressed behavior from the physical stance, we are in effect showing that an explanation from the intentional stance is inappropriate. The depressed behavior is *not* to be explained by the depressed person's goals and beliefs, but by a chemical problem. That suggests that whenever we can give a physical explanation of behavior, an intentional explanation is inappropriate.

But, as Dennett says, it shows no such thing. Just because intentional explanations are inappropriate when there is a physical breakdown, that does not mean that they are inappropriate at all other times. If a computer short-circuits, we do not explain its behavior from the design stance. That does not mean that it is inappropriate to explain its normal behavior from the design stance. Both the design stance and the intentional stance are appropriate in some situations and inappropriate in others. To think that their inappropriateness in some cases shows that they are always inappropriate is simply a mistake.

THE FINAL WORD?

Our conclusion, then, is this. Even if human behavior is determined, we can continue to think of ourselves as rational agents, as creatures with goals and beliefs who act *because* of these goals and beliefs. Therefore, we can say not only that we behave, but that we perform actions as well.

Once again, the difference between actions and other forms of behavior is not merely terminological. If we did not act, if we merely behaved, we could not be held morally responsible for our actions.

But it is not enough to say that we act. After all, we are not held morally responsible for *all* of our actions. We are held morally responsible only for those actions that we perform of our own free will. But if determinism is true, that means that we do *nothing* of our own free will. And that means that we can never be held morally responsible for our actions.

Or does it? That is the question to be considered in the next chapter.

STUDY QUESTIONS

1. Which of the following behaviors are also actions?
   a. Kicking a football.
   b. Kicking in response to a sharp tap on the kneecap.
   c. Scratching an itchy nose.
   d. Wincing in pain.
   e. Sneezing.
   f. Clearing the throat with a cough.
   Are any of the above difficult to decide? Why?
2. What is it to do something for a reason? How is it that some actions can be considered the products of reasons even if they are not done on purpose?
3. Sometimes we are conscious of making decisions, at other times we aren't. Is there an important difference between the two? Explain.
4. According to Skinner, we don't act. We merely behave. What are his reasons for saying that? How can he be challenged?
5. When we are hungry, we eat. Using Dennett's three stances toward human behavior, can you provide three different explanations of that fact? (Here's a hint: try thinking of instinctual behavior, like a cat's chasing a mouse, as the result of programs that the animal is born with.)
6. Suppose we someday are able to give a completely physical explanation of all human behavior. Would we then be forced to conclude that psychological explanations were no longer applicable? Give reasons for your answers.

GLOSSARY

Design stance. One point of view from which we can explain the behavior of certain systems. When we explain behavior from the design stance, we explain it as the product of the system's program.

Intentional stance. One point of view from which we can explain the behavior of certain systems. When we explain behavior from the intentional stance, we explain it as the product of the system's wants and beliefs.

Physical stance. One point of view from which we can explain the behavior of certain systems. When we explain behavior from the physical stance, we explain it as the product of physical laws.

Chapter 11

DETERMINISM
AND MORAL
RESPONSIBILITY

In Chapter 9 we asked whether human actions are determined. Although we could not provide a decisive answer to the question, we did conclude this much: Determinism is a reasonable view that must be taken seriously. Part of taking determinism seriously involves pursuing its consequences. If the view should turn out to be true, how drastically would that change our understanding of ourselves?

In Chapter 10 we saw that one important aspect of our self-understanding would not be threatened by the truth of determinism. Even if determinism is true, we can continue to think of ourselves as rational agents who act according to our own goals and purposes. In this chapter we take a look at another important aspect of our self-understanding—our view of ourselves as morally responsible agents. How would the truth of determinism affect our judgments of moral responsibility?

MORAL RESPONSIBILITY

What is it to be held morally responsible for an action? It is to be held fit for punishment, blame, praise, or reward. It is to *deserve* these things. It is to deserve moral censure if you have done something wrong, moral commendation if you have done something right.

That human beings can be held morally responsible for their actions, that we are morally responsible agents, is a fundamental assumption of human society. It underlies the network of rights and duties that makes society as we know it possible. A society, among other things, is a moral community. Its members share certain norms of behavior, are expected to act in accordance with them, and are held accountable if they do not act in accordance with them.

Moreover, moral responsibility is an important component of our conception of ourselves as *persons*. Whatever else may distinguish us from dogs and cats, there is this: We are held *morally* responsible for what we do; they are not. Although we *expect* a housebroken dog not to soil a rug, although we *punish* it if it does soil a rug, we do not think of it as having a *duty* not to soil a rug. We do not think of it as *immoral* if it soils a rug. Nor do we think that we are giving a dog *moral education* when we housebreak it.

But human beings are given moral educations. We are taught what our duties are. And depending on how we respond to our moral educations, we are judged good or evil, moral or immoral. That is a large part of what makes us persons.

But what if determinism is true? What if we have no more free will than a dog? Could we still be held morally responsible for our actions?

INCOMPATIBILISM

Many philosophers have felt that determinism is incompatible with moral responsibility, and are called, accordingly, *incompatibilists*. The reasons for being an incompatibilist are fairly straightforward. First, there is the matter of the excuses we normally accept for relieving someone of responsibility for an action. If I am blamed for something, and I can show that I did not do it of my own free will, I am off the hook. If, for example, my action is the result of brainwashing, hypnotism, or insanity, I am not held morally responsible for it. In the first two cases, the person who brainwashed me or hypnotized me is. I am innocent, because my action was not the product of my own free choice. In the third case, the question of moral responsibility does not even arise.

Similarly, if a bank teller empties his till because a gunman is holding his family hostage, he is not held morally responsible for robbing the bank. He did not act of his own free will. He was forced to do what he did.

But if determinism is true, nobody ever does anything of his own free will. In that case, the excuse is open to us in all situations. So we can never be held morally responsible for our actions.

The second argument goes like this. We are only morally blameworthy for things that are our fault. But to be at fault is more than to be the cause of something bad. If John shoots Mary with a pistol, the pistol caused her death, but the murder is not the pistol's fault. The pistol is not to blame. John is.

What makes John blameworthy but not the pistol? He could have done otherwise. Whether the gun fired was up to him and nobody but him. The gun could not have done otherwise. Once he decided to pull the trigger, the matter was settled. Before he decided to pull the trigger, nothing was settled.

But if determinism is true, John could *not* have done otherwise. His decision to pull the trigger was also settled before he made it. It was the only outcome physically compatible with what came before, just as the firing of the pistol was. Therefore, he cannot be held morally responsible for his action.

Third, if determinism is true, my actions are the product of my character. They are the product of various computations, and the variables of these computations are my likes and dislikes, fears, hopes, desires, and so forth. That is, I act the way I do because I am the sort of person I am, because of the sort of character I have.

But if determinism is true, my character is the product of forces beyond my control. It is the product of my heredity and environment. Thus, I am not responsible for my character. But if I am not responsible for my character, I am not responsible for my actions. It is merely a matter of *luck* that I have the character I have, and therefore a matter of luck that I do good or evil. My character is not my fault, and neither are my actions.

John Hospers, a contemporary American philosopher, put the above point this way. Suppose we discovered that eating a certain combination of foods always resulted in the committing of a crime. Suppose, for example, that every time people eat liver, mashed potatoes, and peas and carrots, they kill someone. If someone were to eat such a meal without knowing the inevitable result, we would not hold that person morally responsible for murder. But if determinism is true, we are in an analogous situation all the time. A certain combination of genes and environment will inevitably result in a certain sort of character, and that sort of character will inevitably result in certain sorts of actions in certain situations. So we cannot be held morally responsible for them.

COMPATIBILISM

The above are all powerful arguments. Still, there are many philosophers who believe that determinism and moral responsibility are *not* incompatible, and are accordingly called *compatibilists*. Let us now turn to their arguments.

First, let us take a closer look at our acceptance of the ordinary claim that an act was not done of the agent's free will. Does it really have anything to do with determinism? Compatibilists think that it does not. Here's why.

When I say that I did not act of my own free will in such cases, I am not saying that my action was a determined event. I am saying that my action was *coerced*, either by some outside force, such as the gun pointed at my family, or by some inner interference with my normal decision-making processes, such as mental illness. I am saying that the action was not the product of the normal play of my wants and beliefs, but of something else. I am saying that I was forced, compelled, made to do it, that I had no real choice in the matter.

Similarly, when I say that I *did* do something of my own free will, I am not saying that my action was an *un*determined event. I am saying that my action was *not* coerced. I am saying that no outside force or internal aberration interfered with the normal play of my wants and beliefs. I am saying that I did have a real choice, and that I did what I did because I wanted to do it.

This distinction, between doing something because you want to do it and doing it because you are coerced into doing it, remains whether or not determinism is true. There is a real and important difference between the professional bank robber and the teller who empties the till to save his family's lives. The first awakens in the morning as you and I do, showers, shaves, straps his holster on as he dresses, and goes to work. He is not insane, nor is he hypnotized or brainwashed. Nobody is forcing him to rob banks. He is just pursuing his career. The poor teller is doing no such thing. It is this difference that is marked by the phrase "of one's own free will"—not the difference between determined and undetermined events.

But, the incompatibilist asks, is it really the professional bank robber's *fault* that he robs banks for a living? After all, if determinism is true he could not do otherwise. Even if his acts are the product of his own choices, even if he robs banks for a living because he wants to, if determinism is true, he robs banks because he has to. Every time he robs a bank, his actions are the only ones causally compatible with what came before. He cannot do otherwise. How can we hold him morally responsible?

The compatibilist responds this way. Of course he could do otherwise. He could do otherwise if he *wanted* to. If he wanted to change professions, he could. Because he doesn't, he won't. That is what makes him deserving of moral blame and punishment. The teller, on the other hand, does *not* want to rob the bank, but he is made to anyway. His emptying of the till does not reflect badly on his character. The professional's robberies *do* reflect badly on his character. He wants to rob banks so he does. And that is why we hold him responsible for his robberies.

But, the incompatibilist counters, is that *fair?* Does he really *deserve* to be held responsible? Does he really deserve moral censure? After all, even though his actions are the product of his character, if determinism is true, he did not *make* his character. That the teller's character is decent and the bank robber's not is merely a matter of luck. It is not the bank robber's fault that he wants to rob banks. His character is the product of heredity and environment. But if it is not his fault that he wants to rob banks, he cannot be held morally responsible for robbing them.

The compatibilist's response to this point is a complicated one. In part, it deals with our notions of fairness. In part, it deals with the roles of morality, responsibility, and punishment in our lives, and the importance of various attitudes we can and do take toward others. The best way to approach it is to ask the question, "Why do we hold one another responsible for our actions?"

PUNISHMENT AND RESPONSIBILITY

To ask why we hold one another *responsible* for our actions is, in part, to ask why we *punish* one another for our actions. Why, for instance, do we put armed robbers in prison?

One reason that comes readily to mind is this. We put armed robbers in prison to keep them off the streets. If we did not keep them off the streets, the rest of us would live in constant danger and fear. We also put them in prison to deter other people from committing armed robbery. Without the threat of punishment, we feel, many people would act in ways that would harm the rest of us. Another reason for putting armed robbers in prison is rehabilitation. Although it doesn't always work out that way, we hope that once they have done their time, convicts will become useful members of society. Thus, prisons are often called correctional institutions.

What ties these three reasons together is this. All three hinge on the *usefulness* of prisons, and of punishment in general. We punish people, hold them morally responsible for their actions, because it is socially useful to do so. This does not hold merely for *legal* punishment and responsibility. When we punish children for misbehaving, morally rebuke someone for breaking a promise, or morally criticize someone for being deliberately rude, similar considerations of social usefulness justify our doing so.

Moreover, when we *refrain* from punishing someone, it is because these considerations do *not* apply. Why don't we put the coerced bank teller in prison for emptying the till? Because we do not want to keep him off the streets. Nor do we want to deter others from doing what he did in the same circumstance. Nor do we think he needs rehabilitation. Why don't we put the dangerously insane in prison? Because the behavior of the insane—at least in theory—can best be changed in mental hospitals. Because they need treatment, not rehabilitation. And because the insane are not, it is thought, deterred by prison sentences.

When we speak of the fairness of punishment, then, it must be against this setting. People *deserve* punishment if they are *fit* subjects for punishment. And we determine whether they are fit subjects for punishment in accordance with the socially useful practices we have devised.

Of course, to say this is not to say that in every case we *ask* whether it is useful to punish someone. What we do instead is ask about the circumstances surrounding the action. Was the agent coerced? Was she insane? Was the harm she caused an unavoidable accident? Was it the product of excusable ignorance? If we can answer *no* to these and similar questions, we can hold her responsible. We can say that she deserves punishment. We come to this conclusion by deciding that she acted of her own free will, in the sense discussed above—*not* by deciding that it is useful to punish her. But we can *justify* punishing people who do wrong of their own free will by the social usefulness of doing so.

REASON AND RESPONSIBILITY

It is difficult to disagree with the above response of the compatibilist. Still, it is, as it stands, most unsettling. The problem is this. It seems to treat the punishment of human beings exactly as we treat the punishment of dogs. Why do we punish a dog for soiling the rug? Because it is useful to do so.

But what does that have to do with *moral responsibility?* Just because we find it useful to punish dogs, that does not mean that we hold them morally responsible for what they do. Similarly, just because we find it useful to punish human beings, that does not mean that punishing them for what they do is all there is to holding them morally responsible. The incompatibilist does not say that if determinism is true we should not punish people. Rather, the incompatibilist says that if determinism is true we should not hold them morally responsible. We should not think of them as deserving *moral* blame. We should not think of them as getting their *just deserts.* We should not, that is, attach any *moral stigma* to them. This is the point that the compatibilist response misses. But we can add to the compatibilist response so that it does *not* miss this point. Here's how.

First, we grant that moral responsibility *does* involve more than being held fit for punishment. What else is necessary? Well, in the beginning of this chapter, we noted two of those things. Morally responsible agents have *duties,* I said. They also receive a *moral education.* The importance of these facts is this. Our conception of ourselves as being morally responsible goes hand in hand with our conception of ourselves as being capable of *moral reasoning.* We can think about what is right and wrong, try to ascertain what our duties are in particular circumstances, and act accordingly because it is our duty as we see it.

In other words, we know the difference between right and wrong, and our knowledge of that difference makes a difference in how we act. Why do we obey the fifty-five mile-per-hour speed limit? Perhaps we do it to avoid a speeding ticket. But perhaps we do it because it is right—because we want to do our share in conserving energy. Sometimes we act as we do to avoid punishment, but sometimes we act as we do out of a sense of duty.

Because moral reasoning guides our behavior, we engage in *moral discussions* and *moral arguments.* We try to convince one another to behave in various ways by appealing to moral principles, and to our sense of right and wrong. But to do this is to treat one another as morally responsible agents, just as to reason morally is to treat ourselves as morally responsible agents.

Suppose we were not to treat ourselves and others in this way. Then we *would* be viewing ourselves and others like dogs. Training would replace education, and manipulation would replace moral persuasion. In effect, we would be retreating from the intentional stance to the design stance, both of which we discussed in the previous chapter. We would be thinking of morally wrong acts as undesirable behavior—as a problem requiring reconditioning rather than moral persuasion.

Perhaps we could do this, and perhaps it would be as socially useful as our current system, which rests on moral responsibility. But would we *want* to, even if determinism turns out to be true? Very few of us would, I believe, although B. F. Skinner, for one, recommends such a course.

At any rate, whether we would want to or not, the compatibilist does not believe that this course would be *forced* on us by the truth of determinism. The usefulness of viewing ourselves as morally responsible agents, and the importance of that view to our conception of ourselves as persons, provide warrant enough for maintaining it.

But if we do maintain it, we cannot stop thinking of some people as deserving *moral* blame. We cannot stop thinking of some people as being *evil*, of getting their *just deserts* when they are punished for their acts. Such notions, and the moral stigma that goes with them, are crucial to our conceptions of a moral community.

HUMAN ATTITUDES AND RESPONSIBILITY

The above remarks show that the assignment of moral responsibility to people is not merely a matter of social usefulness, but the result of a certain attitude toward them. If we view one another as reasonable agents, then we view one another as capable of moral reasoning. And if we view one another as capable of moral reasoning, we view one another as morally responsible agents.

The connection between moral responsibility and human attitudes has been most forcefully stressed, perhaps, by the contemporary British philosopher P. F. Strawson. Strawson pursues the connection this way. Human nature being what it is, and because we live in human communities, we place great importance on the attitudes and intentions others have toward us. In fact, many actions that offend us do so just because of the attitudes they express. Think, for example, about your reactions to being laughed at, rudely interrupted, or stood up by a date. Incidents such as these cause you to form various negative attitudes toward the people who offend you—resentment, for instance. And actions that express more favorable attitudes cause you to form more favorable attitudes—gratitude, for instance.

Resentment and gratitude are what Strawson calls *personal reactive attitudes*, because they arise as reactions to attitudes that people display toward *us*. But there are also attitudes that arise as reactions to attitudes that people display toward *others*. Strawson calls attitudes of this kind *vicarious* reactive attitudes. Indignation is such an attitude. When we see somebody treat another person disrespectfully, we often feel something similar to what we feel when *we* are treated disrespectfully. When the treatment is directed toward ourselves, the feeling is called resentment. When it is directed toward others, it is called indignation. Thus, Strawson calls indignation a vicarious analog to resentment. There are vicarious analogs to many personal reactive attitudes. When we see somebody do a favor for another person, for instance, what we feel cannot be called gratitude, unless we consider it a favor to ourselves as well. But the feeling is often very close to gratitude.

These attitudes represent certain expectations we have of others, as well as certain demands we feel justified in making of them. The personal attitudes represent expectations and demands concerning attitudes and intentions toward *us*. The vicarious ones represent *generalized* expectations and demands, expectations and demands concerning attitudes and intentions toward *everyone*.

Because we have these attitudes, we are capable of, and naturally have, another set of attitudes. We feel *obliged* to act in certain ways toward others, and we feel *remorse* and *guilt* if we don't. Moreover, we think of others as being similarly obliged, and as being appropriate subjects of remorse and guilt. That is, we develop a moral sense and expect others to develop it as well.

So moral responsibility is closely tied to our view of persons as having intentions and attitudes, of having reasons for acting and acting on those reasons. It is also tied to our reactions to people when we view them that way. And as long as determinism does not lead us to believe that this view of human beings is inappropriate—that is, as long as it does not force us to give up the intentional stance—it is not incompatible with moral responsibility.

UNDERSTANDING AND RESPONSIBILITY

The compatibilist's case can be summed up this way. A morally responsible agent is first of all a *rational* agent, someone who acts for her own reasons, according to her own purposes and beliefs. Second, a morally responsible agent is someone capable of acting for *moral* reasons, someone who has a sense of right and wrong. Third, a morally responsible agent is someone whose behavior can be *affected* by the reasoning of others, someone who can be influenced by moral argument. Even if determinism is true, we are such agents. Therefore, if determinism is true, we can still be held morally responsible for our actions.

In particular circumstances, of course, we are sometimes let off the hook. But the excuses we give and others accept do not give support to incompatibilism.

Most philosophers are convinced by this line of argument, and by the considerations in its support that we have examined in this chapter. Still, there is a final argument for incompatibilism that is difficult to ignore. It was often advanced by famed trial lawyer Clarence Darrow (1857–1938) in defense of his clients, as well as such philosophers as John Hospers. It reflects a deep-seated human attitude that we express in such phrases as "There but for the grace of God go I" and "To understand is to forgive."

Let us approach this argument by recalling the classic film *Angels with Dirty Faces*, which often appears on late night television. Two young boys in an impoverished New York City neighborhood are running from the police after having committed a petty crime. One is caught and sent to reform school, where he comes under the irreversible influence of hardened young criminals. He grows up to become a hardened criminal himself, played by James Cagney. The other escapes, and through a series of lucky breaks grows up to be a priest, played by Pat O'Brien, dedicated to helping boys in danger of turning out like Cagney.

Much of the film is a duel between Cagney and O'Brien, each seeking to influence the boys after his own image. At the end of the film, Cagney is executed for murder. O'Brien tells the boys that they should all say a prayer for a boy who couldn't run as fast as he could.

The point of the film, like that of many films of the same era, is this. Certain conditions are breeding grounds for crime. Some people are trapped by these conditions; others manage to escape. What makes the difference is luck. Had O'Brien been caught, he would have ended up the murderer. Had Cagney escaped, he would have ended up the priest.

In giving voice to this feeling, O'Brien was not suggesting that Cagney should not have been punished for his crimes. He was suggesting, though, that there is a deeper sense in which Cagney was not responsible for what he did. He was merely unlucky. Our attitude toward him should be one of pity, not a complacent holier-than-thou attitude. And this attitude should lead us to change the conditions that made him a criminal, to prevent the same thing from happening to the next generation.

Speaking more generally, we often feel the way that O'Brien felt about Cagney. Despite the reasons we give for our actions, despite our ability to explain what we do in terms of purposes, wants and beliefs, we often trace the causes of our behavior to circumstances beyond our control. And the more completely we can do this, the more the action in question seems inevitable—and the more likely we are to forgive the person if the action was wrong. This is a normal human attitude, as normal as Strawson's personal reactive attitudes.

But if determinism is true, Hospers argues, we should take this attitude toward everyone. This is not exactly to say that we should retreat from the intentional stance. Nor is it to say that we should stop viewing one another as people capable of moral reasoning, influence, and decision. Rather, it is to say that we should adopt a fourth stance toward one another, from which we can see one another as both agents and victims. From this stance, we are not responsible for our actions.

To adopt this view is to adopt a very *weak* form of incompatibilism. It is to say, in effect, that for ordinary purposes the truth of determinism would not force us to give up our beliefs about moral responsibility. But it is also to say that, these ordinary purposes notwithstanding, there is a deep sense in which no one is responsible for his actions.

RESPONSIBILITY AND MORAL PERSPECTIVES

Is Hospers right? Would the truth of determinism force us to say that we are not, ultimately, responsible for our actions?

Well, he does seem to be right about this much. If determinism is true, *some* change in attitude is required. People we think of as evil would deserve some degree of sympathy and compassion. But is that the same as relieving them of ultimate moral responsibility for their actions?

Another way of viewing the matter is suggested by the contemporary American philosopher Elizabeth Lane Beardsley, who argues as follows. When we pass moral judgment on people, we can do so from a variety of moral perspectives. From one perspective, we judge only the rightness or wrongness of a particular *act,* and we make no judgment of praise or blame. That is, we criticize the act, but not the agent.

From a second perspective, we criticize the agent as well. We blame or praise her. That is, we make a judgment of her *moral worth.* We say that she is either a good or bad person.

From a third perspective, we make a judgment concerning the amount of *moral credit* due the agent. That is, we view her action in light of various circumstances in order to see what we might have expected her to do. Was her background such that it was unlikely that she would have done something so praiseworthy? Do most people from a similar background fail to do what she did? If so, then she deserves more moral credit for her action than people from another background.

This third perspective is the one suggested by *Angels with Dirty Faces.* Because of the events of Cagney's youth, we are inclined to give him less moral *dis*credit for his crimes than we would be to someone who grew up in more advantageous circumstances. Notice, however, that this judgment does not interfere with our judgment of his moral worth. We cannot deny that he is a morally bad person. What we can do, though, is view his badness in a certain context.

Hospers seems to be saying that if determinism is true, nobody deserves any moral credit or discredit, that moral responsibility and determinism are incompatible from Beardsley's third perspective. He also seems to be saying that this should have some effect on our judgments of moral worth, that it should lead us to judge people as lucky or unlucky, rather than good or evil.

Beardsley denies these claims. She believes that if determinism is true, there is a *fourth* moral perspective that we can take. From this perspective, she says, we can view everyone as *ultimately* morally equal. Even though some people are morally superior to others, even though some are more deserving of moral credit than others, we can still stand back and admit that there is a point of view from which nobody deserves more praise or blame than anyone else.

There are two important points to make about this fourth perspective. First, it does not interfere with judgments made from the other three. It does not keep us from making the full range of moral judgments we ordinarily make. We can continue to speak of people as being good or wicked, and we can continue to think of them as getting their just deserts.

Second, it is a legitimate *moral* perspective. To say that there is a sense in which we are all, ultimately, moral equals, is not to say that none of us is, ultimately, a morally responsible agent. To say that would be to adopt an incompatibilist position. And Beardsley is not an incompatibilist. Rather, she believes that there are a number of moral facts about us. We are morally responsible

A SURPRISING FORM OF INCOMPATIBILISM

While asking whether determinism is compatible with moral responsibility, we took something for granted. We assumed without argument that *inde-terminism* is compatible with moral responsibility. That is, we assumed that if our behavior is *not* determined, there is no reason to deny that we are morally responsible for our actions.

There is nothing surprising about this assumption, of course. As I have often pointed out in these past three chapters, we ordinarily assume that we are morally responsible agents just *because* we have free will. And it is not until we begin to take determinism seriously that we begin to doubt that we are morally responsible agents.

Still, some philosophers have attempted to turn our ordinary beliefs on their head. They have not been content to argue that determinism is *compatible* with moral responsibility. They have gone on to claim that determinism is *required* by moral responsibility. That is, they have claimed that we cannot be held morally responsible for our actions if determinism is false.

Two Arguments

Such philosophers have offered two related arguments for this surprising claim.

First, they have argued this way. We are held morally responsible for our actions only if they are the products of our character. To return to our earlier example, the professional thief is blamed for robbing banks because his robberies are the product of his normal wants. The teller who empties his till to save his family is not held morally responsible because his action is not. The thief's actions reflect badly on his character. The teller's action does not.

But that means that our actions *must* be caused by our character if we are to be held responsible for them. Suppose that our actions were not caused by our character. In that case, they would give no evidence at all as to the nature of our character. But that means that we couldn't judge what kind of person the agent is by her acts. And if we couldn't do that, we couldn't say that an action shows her to be a good or wicked person. That is, we couldn't praise or blame her because of her actions. But if we couldn't do that, we couldn't hold her *morally* responsible for them.

The second argument goes like this. Either an event is caused by some other event or it isn't. If it is, it is determined. If it isn't, then it is purely random and arbitrary. That is, it cannot be explained at all. Therefore, either our actions are determined or inexplicable and arbitrary. But certainly we cannot be held responsible for actions that are inexplicable and arbitrary. If there is no *reason* for my doing something, how can I be held responsible for it? Isn't it more like a twitch or a knee jerk than a real action? Haven't we already seen that we can be held responsible for something only if it is done for some reason?

The Arguments Evaluated

These arguments are related by a common assumption. They both assume that the only form of explanation is a *causal* one. The first assumes that if my character does not cause my actions, it cannot explain them. The second assumes that if my actions are not caused, they cannot be explained. But such assumptions are very suspicious. Certainly, no libertarian has ever said that actions are arbitrary or inexplicable. Instead, the libertarian says this: Actions can be given a unique kind of explanation—*rational* explanations. As long as we can show that our actions are *reasonable,* as long as we can show that they are done for *reasons,* as long as we can explain them in terms of our goals and beliefs, then they are neither arbitrary nor inexplicable.

This point was made most forcefully, perhaps, by the American philosopher William James (1842–1910). To reject determinism, James said, is to allow for an element of chance in the world. It is to say that human actions are not *necessitated* by the past. But that does not mean that they are totally *unrelated* to the past. Nor does it mean that they are irrational, the products of absolute accident.

James asks us to consider what many of you would take to be an ordinary exercise of your free will. Suppose that you are deciding which route to take to class. Your choice is between two perfectly natural and rational possibilities. After you have made your choice, it is very easy to look back and explain why you made it. To the determinist, he says, that means that your choice was necessitated by what came before. But, James argues, we could just as easily have given an explanation of your choice if you had chosen the other route. Either choice can be easily connected to your wants and beliefs. Either one can be given a rational explanation. Why, then, must we say that the outcome was necessitated by the past? And why must we say that if it was *not* necessitated by the past, it was purely arbitrary? As long as the chosen outcome is rationally related to the past, as long as you have a reason to choose it, it is a product of your character whether it is determined or not.

So it will not do to say that determinism must be true if we are to be held morally responsible for our actions.

agents, and therefore we may be good or evil, praiseworthy or blameworthy, deserving of moral credit or not. But our actions are determined, and therefore we are ultimately moral equals. These two sets of facts do not conflict with each other. Rather, they combine to make up the complete moral picture.

The final word?

The topic examined in this chapter is a complex one. It touches on a variety of factors, and the arguments on both sides appeal not only to our reason and moral sense, but to a number of deeply entrenched (and often conflicting) emotions and attitudes. Because of this complexity, it is difficult to arrive at a firm conclusion. But we can, I think, say this much. Most philosophers today find the considerations in favor of compatibilism more forceful than those in favor of incompatibilism. And I think that the arguments I have presented here show this to be a reasonable stand.

Still, there is a pull to the weak incompatibilist position advanced by

Hospers. Given a predilection on our part to show compassion and forgiveness toward people in certain sorts of situations, if determinism is true, it is difficult to see how its truth could fail to affect our attitudes toward all wrong-doers. Hospers thinks it should change our attitudes in a fundamental way. Beardsley, on the other hand, thinks it should add a new dimension to them.

I am inclined to agree with Beardsley. Her view seems to be more in keeping with those of Strawson, considered in this chapter, and Dennett, considered in the previous one. Moreover, it seems to capture much of what is attractive in Hospers's view.

I do not think, though, that our present inclinations on this matter are at all conclusive. Finally, the matter depends on a moral decision on our part. And this decision will not and cannot be made until most of us accept determinism, discuss its ramifications among ourselves, and see how it actually does affect the full range of our attitudes. Our present inclinations, I think, are reasoned predictions as to what we will finally decide.

STUDY QUESTIONS

1. What is incompatibilism? What arguments have philosophers offered in favor of the view?
2. According to compatibilists, when we excuse someone from moral responsibility for an action because it was not done of that person's own free will, what we mean by "free will" has nothing to do with the free will versus determinism controversy. Why do they say that? Do you agree?
3. Both compatibilists and incompatibilists agree that we can continue to punish people for certain actions even if determinism is true. What are their reasons for believing that? And what do incompatibilists mean when they say that we should not hold the people we punish morally responsible?
4. In this chapter, I made the following claim: If we were to stop viewing one another as morally responsible agents, we would in effect be giving up the intentional stance for the design stance. What were my reasons? Do you agree? Why or why not?
5. What does Strawson mean by personal reactive attitudes and vicarious reactive attitudes? How does he connect the two notions to the question of moral responsibility?
6. According to Hospers, if determinism is true we should view one another as lucky or unlucky, not good or evil. Why?
7. What are Beardsley's four moral perspectives? How do they relate to the arguments of Hospers? With whom do you agree—Beardsley or Hospers? Why?
8. Why have some philosophers argued that we cannot hold one another morally responsible for our actions if determinism is not true? Why have others disagreed?

GLOSSARY

Compatibilism. The view that determinism and moral responsibility are compatible. According to this view, we can continue to hold people morally responsible for their actions even if determinism is true.

Incompatibilism. The view that determinism and moral responsibility are incompatible. According to this view, we cannot hold people responsible for their actions if determinism is true.

Personal reactive attitudes. Attitudes such as resentment, which we feel in response to the attitudes that others display towards us.

Vicarious reactive attitudes. Attitudes such as indignation, which we feel in response to the attitudes that people display toward others.

SELECTIONS

The following selections provide dramatically different positions on human freedom and responsibility.

The first is from Jean-Paul Sartre's Being and Nothingness. *Sartre takes the extreme position that we are responsible for everything that happens to us, even our own births. According to Sartre, human existence is a constant series of free choices. These choices make us who we are and they make the events around us what they are. By choosing what we will be, we choose what our world will be. (For a discussion of Sartre's views, see Chapter 14.)*

Sartre uses many technical terms, which require a bit of explanation. First, there is for-itself. *This is Sartre's term for an individual human being as a free, choosing agent. Second, there is* facticity. *This is Sartre's term for the facts of our lives that cannot be altered—birth, for instance, or race. Third, there is* projects. *This is Sartre's term for our choices. He uses it to emphasize the creative nature of our choices. They create us and they create our world. Thus, when he says that my birth appears to me "across a projective reconstruction of my for-itself," he means that it cannot be separated from the choices that make me who I am.*

The second selection is from B. F. Skinner's Beyond Freedom and Dignity. *Skinner claims that modern science has shown that human beings do not have free will. Our behavior, he says, is the product of our environment. Therefore, it is our environment, not ourselves, that is responsible for what we do. We deserve neither credit nor blame.*

Notice, though, that Sartre and Skinner agree on one point— the connection between free will and responsibility. For Sartre it is our freedom that makes us responsible for what we do. For Skinner, it is our lack of freedom that makes us not responsible.

JEAN-PAUL SARTRE

Freedom and Responsibility

Although the considerations which are about to follow are of interest primarily to the ethicist, it may nevertheless be worthwhile after these descriptions and arguments to return to the freedom of the for-itself and to try to understand what the fact of this freedom represents for human destiny.

The essential consequence of our earlier remarks is that man being condemned to be free carries the weight of the whole world on his shoulders; he is responsible for the world and for himself as a way of being. We are taking the word "responsibility" in its ordinary sense as "consciousness (of) being the incontestable author of an event or of an object." In this sense the responsibility of the for-itself is overwhelming since he is the one by whom it happens that *there is* a world; since he is also the one who makes himself be, then whatever may be the situation in which he finds himself, the for-itself must wholly assume this situation with its peculiar coefficient of adversity, even though it be insupportable. He must assume the situation with the proud consciousness of being the author of it, for the very worst disadvantages or the worst threats which can endanger my person have meaning only in and through my project; and it is on the ground of the engagement which I am that they appear. It is therefore senseless to think of complaining since nothing foreign has decided what we feel, what we live, or what we are.

Furthermore this absolute responsibility is not resignation; it is simply the logical requirement of the consequences of our freedom. What happens to me happens through me, and I can neither affect myself with it nor revolt against it nor resign myself to it. Moreover everything which happens to me is *mine*. By this we must understand first of all that I am always equal to what happens to me qua man, for what happens to a man through other men and through himself can be only human. The most terrible situations of war, the worst tortures do not create a non-human state of things; there is no non-human situation. It is only through fear, flight, and recourse to magical types of conduct that I shall decide on the non-human, but this decision is human, and I shall carry the entire responsibility for it. But in addition the situation is *mine* because it is the image of my free choice of myself, and everything which it presents to me is *mine* in that this represents me and symbolizes me. Is it not I who decide the coefficient of adversity in things and even their unpredictability by deciding myself?

Thus there are no *accidents* in a life; a community event which suddenly bursts forth and involves me in it does not come from the outside. If I am mobilized in a war, this war is *my* war; it is in my image and I deserve it. I deserve it first because I could always get out of it by suicide or by desertion; these ultimate possibles are those which must always be present for us when there is a question of envisaging a situation. For lack of getting out of it, I have *chosen* it. This can be due to inertia, to cowardice in the face of public opinion, or because I prefer certain other values to the value of the refusal to join in the war (the good opinion of my relatives, the honor of my family, etc.). Anyway you look at it, it is a matter of a choice. This choice will be repeated later on again and again without a break until the end of the war. Therefore we must agree with the statement by J. Romains, "In war there are no innocent victims." If therefore I have preferred war to death or to dishonor, everything takes place as if I bore the entire responsibility for this war. Of course others have declared it, and one might be tempted perhaps to consider me as a simple accomplice. But this notion of complicity has only a juridical sense, and it does not hold here. For it depended on me that for me and by me this war should not exist, and I have decided that it does exist. There was no compulsion here, for the compulsion could have got no hold on a freedom. I did not have any excuse; for as we have said repeatedly in this book, the peculiar character of human reality is that it is without excuse. Therefore it remains for me only to lay claim to this war.

But in addition the war is *mine* because by the sole fact that it arises in a situation which I cause to be and that I can discover it there only by engaging myself for or against it, I can no longer distinguish at present the choice which I make of myself from the choice which I make of the war. To live this war is to choose myself through it and to choose it through my choice of myself. There can be no question of considering it as "four years of vacation" or as a "reprieve," as a "recess," the essential part of my responsibilities being elsewhere in my married, family, or professional life. In this war which I have chosen I choose myself from day to day, and I make it mine by making myself. If it is going to be four empty years, then it is I who bear the responsibility for this.

Finally, as we pointed out earlier, each person is an absolute choice of self from the standpoint of a world of knowledges and of techniques which this choice both assumes and illumines; each person is an absolute upsurge at an absolute date and is perfectly unthinkable at another date. It is therefore a waste of time to ask what I should have been if this war had not broken out, for I have chosen myself as one of the possible meanings of the epoch which imperceptibly led to war. I am not distinct from this same epoch; I could not be transported to another epoch without contradiction. Thus *I am* this war which restricts and limits and makes comprehensible the period which preceded it. In this sense we may define more precisely the responsibility of the for-itself if to the earlier quoted statement, "There are no innocent victims," we add the words, "We have the war we deserve." Thus, totally free, undistinguishable from the period for which I have chosen to be the meaning, as profoundly responsible for the war as if I had myself declared it, unable to live without integrating it in *my* situation, engaging myself in it wholly and stamping it with my seal, I must be without remorse or regrets as I am without excuse; for from the instant of my upsurge into being, I carry the weight of the world by myself alone without anything or any person being able to lighten it.

Yet this responsibility is of a very particular type. Someone will say, "I did not ask to be born." This is a naive way of throwing greater emphasis on our facticity. I am responsible for everything, in fact, except for my very responsibility, for I am not the foundation of my being. Therefore everything takes place as if I were compelled to be responsible. I am *abandoned* in the world, not in the sense that I might remain abandoned and passive in a hostile universe like a board floating on the water, but rather in the sense that I find myself suddenly alone and without help, engaged in a world for which I bear the whole responsibility without being able, whatever I do, to tear myself away from this responsibility for an instant. For I am responsible for my very desire of fleeing responsibilities. To make myself passive in the world, to refuse to act upon things and upon Others is still to choose myself, and suicide is one mode among others of being-in-the-world. Yet I find an absolute responsibility for the fact that my facticity (here the fact of my birth) is directly inapprehensible and even inconceivable, for this fact of my birth never appears as a brute fact but always across a projective reconstruction of my for-itself. I am ashamed of being born or I am astonished at it or I rejoice over it, or in attempting to get rid of my life I affirm that I live and I assume this life as bad. Thus in a certain sense I *choose* being born. This choice itself is integrally affected with facticity since I am not able not to choose, but this facticity in turn will appear only in so far as I surpass it toward my ends. Thus facticity is everywhere but inapprehensible; I never encounter anything except my responsibility. That is why I can not ask, "*Why* was I born?" or curse the day of my birth or declare that I did not ask to be born, for these various attitudes toward my birth—i.e., toward the *fact* that I realize a presence in the world—are absolutely nothing else but ways of assuming this birth in full responsibility and of making it *mine*. Here again I encounter only myself and my projects so that finally my abandonment—i.e., my facticity—consists simply in the fact that I am condemned to be wholly responsible for myself. . . . The one who realizes in anguish his condition as *being* thrown into a responsibility which extends to his very abandonment has no longer either remorse or regret or excuse; he is no longer anything but a freedom which perfectly reveals itself and whose being resides in this very revelation.

B. F. SKINNER

Beyond Freedom and Dignity

Unable to understand how or why the person we see behaves as he does, we attribute his behavior to a person we cannot see, whose behavior we cannot explain either but about whom we are not inclined to ask questions. We probably adopt this strategy not so much because of any lack of interest or power but because of a longstanding conviction that for much of human behavior there *are* no relevant antecedents. The function of the inner man is to provide an explanation which will not be explained in turn. Explanation stops with him. He is not a mediator between past history and current behavior, he is a *center* from which behavior emanates. He initiates, originates, and creates, and in doing so he remains, as he was for the Greeks, divine. We say that he is autonomous—and, so far as a science of behavior is concerned, that means miraculous.

The position is, of course, vulnerable. Autonomous man serves to explain only the things we are not yet able to explain in other ways. His existence depends upon our ignorance, and he naturally loses status as we come to know more about behavior. The task of a scientific analysis is to explain how the behavior of a person as a physical system is related to the conditions under which the human species evolved and the conditions under which the individual lives. Unless there is indeed some capricious or creative intervention, these events must be related, and no intervention is in fact needed. The contingencies of survival responsible for man's genetic endowment would produce tendencies to *act* aggressively, not feelings of aggression. The punishment of sexual behavior changes sexual *behavior,* and any feelings which may arise are at best by-products. Our age is not suffering from anxiety but from the accidents, crimes, wars, and other dangerous and painful things to which people are so often exposed. Young people drop out of school, refuse to get jobs, and associate only with others of their own age not because they feel alienated but because of defective social environments in homes, schools, factories, and elsewhere.

We can follow the path taken by physics and biology by turning directly to the relation between behavior and the environment and neglecting supposed mediating states of mind. Physics did not advance by looking more closely at the jubilance of a falling body, or biology by looking at the nature of vital spirits, and we do not need to try to discover what personalities, states of mind, feelings, traits of character, plans, purposes, intentions, or the other perquisites of autonomous man really are in order to get on with a scientific analysis of behavior.

There are reasons why it has taken us so long to reach this point. The things studied by physics and biology do not behave very much like people, and it eventually seems rather ridiculous to speak of the jubilance of a falling body or the impetuosity of a projectile; but people do behave like people, and the outer man whose behavior is to be explained could be very much like the inner man whose behavior is said to explain it. The inner man has been created in the image of the outer.

A more important reason is that the inner man seems at times to be directly observed. We must infer the jubilance of a falling body, but can we not *feel* our own jubilance? We do, indeed, feel things inside our own skin, but we do not feel the things which have been invented to explain behavior. The possessed man does not feel the possessing *demon* and may even deny that one exists. The juvenile delinquent does not feel his *disturbed personality.* The intelligent man does not feel his *intelligence* or the introvert his *introversion.* (In fact, these dimensions of mind or character are said to be observable only through complex statistical procedures.) The speaker does not feel the *grammatical rules* he is said to apply in composing sentences, and men spoke grammatically for thousands of years before anyone knew there were rules. The respondent to a questionnaire does not feel the *attitudes* or *opinions* which lead him to check items in particular ways. We do feel certain states of our bodies associated with behavior, but as Freud pointed out, we behave in the same way when we do not feel them; they are by-products and not to be mistaken for causes.

There is a much more important reason why we have been so slow in discarding mentalistic explanations: it has been hard to find alternatives. Presumably we must look for them in the external environment, but the role of the environment is by no means clear. The history of the theory of evolution illustrates the problem. Before the nineteenth century, the environment was thought of simply as a passive setting in which many different kinds of organisms were born, reproduced themselves, and died. No one saw that the environment was responsible for the fact that there *were* many different kinds (and that fact, significantly enough, was attributed to a creative Mind). The trouble was that the environment acts in an inconspicuous way: it does not push or pull, it *selects*. For thousands of years in the history of human thought the process of natural selection went unseen in spite of its extraordinary importance. When it was eventually discovered, it became, of course, the key to evolutionary theory.

The effect of the environment on behavior remained obscure for an even longer time. We can see what organisms do to the world around them, as they take from it what they need and ward off its dangers, but it is much harder to see what the world does to them. It was Descartes who first suggested that the environment might play an active role in the determination of behavior, and he was apparently able to do so only because he was given a strong hint. He knew about certain automata in the Royal Gardens of France which were operated hydraulically by concealed valves. As Descartes described it, people entering the gardens "necessarily tread on certain tiles or plates, which are so disposed that if they approach a bathing Diana, they cause her to hide in the rosebushes, and if they try to follow her, they cause a Neptune to come forward to meet them, threatening them with his trident." The figures were entertaining just because they behaved like people, and it appeared, therefore, that something very much like human behavior could be explained mechanically. Descartes took the hint: living organisms might move for similar reasons. (He excluded the human organism, presumably to avoid religious controversy.)

The triggering action of the environment came to be called a "stimulus"—the Latin for goad—and the effect on an organism a "response," and together they were said to compose a "reflex." Reflexes were first demonstrated in small decapitated animals, such as salamanders, and it is significant that the principle was challenged throughout the nineteenth century because it seemed to deny the existence of an autonomous agent—the "soul of the spinal cord"—to which movement of a decapitated body had been attributed. When Pavlov showed how new reflexes could be built up through conditioning, a full-fledged stimulus-response psychology was born, in which all behavior was regarded as reactions to stimuli. One writer put it this way: "We are prodded or lashed through life." The stimulus-response model was never very convincing, however, and it did not solve the basic problem, because something like an inner man had to be invented to convert a stimulus into a response. Information theory ran into the same problem when an inner "processer" had to be invented to convert input into output.

The effect of an eliciting stimulus is relatively easy to see, and it is not surprising that Descartes' hypothesis held a dominant position in behavior theory for a long time, but it was a false scent from which a scientific analysis is only now recovering. The environment not only prods or lashes, it *selects*. Its role is similar to that in natural selection, though on a very different time scale, and was overlooked for the same reason. It is now clear that we must take into account what the environment does to an organism not only before but after it responds. Behavior is shaped and maintained by its consequences. Once this fact is recognized, we can formulate the interaction between organism and environment in a much more comprehensive way.

There are two important results. One concerns the basic analysis. Behavior which operates upon the environment to produce consequences ("operant" behavior) can be studied by arranging environments in which specific consequences are contingent upon it. The contingencies under investigation have become steadily more complex, and one by one they are taking over the explanatory functions previously assigned to personalities, states of mind, feelings, traits of character, purposes, and intentions. The second result is practical: the environment can be manipulated. It is true that man's genetic endowment can be changed only very slowly, but changes in the environment of the individual have quick and dramatic effects. A technology of operant behavior is, as we shall see, already well advanced, and it may prove to be commensurate with our problems.

That possibility raises another problem, however, which must be solved if we are to take advantage of our gains. We have moved forward by dispossessing autonomous man, but he has not departed gracefully. He is conducting a sort of rear-guard action in which, unfortunately, he can marshal formidable support. He is still an important figure in political science, law, religion, economics, anthropology, sociology, psychotherapy, philosophy, ethics, history, education, child care, linguistics, architecture, city planning, and family life. These fields have their specialists, and every specialist has a theory, and in almost every theory the autonomy of the individual is unquestioned. The inner man is not seriously threatened by data obtained through casual observation or from studies of the structure of behavior, and many of these fields deal only with groups of people, where statistical or actuarial data impose few restraints upon the individual. The result is a tremendous weight of traditional "knowledge," which must be corrected or displaced by a scientific analysis.

Two features of autonomous man are particularly troublesome. In the traditional view, a person is free. He is autonomous in the sense that his behavior is uncaused. He can therefore be held responsible for what he does and justly punished if he offends. That view, together with its associated practices, must be re-examined when a scientific analysis reveals unsuspected controlling relations between behavior and environment. A certain amount of external control can be tolerated. Theologians have accepted the fact that man must be predestined to do what an omniscient God knows he will do, and the Greek dramatist took inexorable fate as his favorite theme. Soothsayers and astrologers often claim to predict what men will do, and they have always been in demand. Biographers and historians have searched for "influences" in the lives of individuals and peoples. Folk wisdom and the insights of essayists like Montaigne and Bacon imply some kind of predictability in human conduct, and the statistical and actuarial evidences of the social sciences point in the same direction.

Autonomous man survives in the face of all this because he is the happy exception. Theologians have reconciled predestination with free will, and the Greek audience, moved by the portrayal of an inescapable destiny, walked out of the theater free men. The course of history has been turned by the death of a leader or a storm at sea, as a life has been changed by a teacher or a love affair, but these things do not happen to everyone, and they do not affect everyone in the same way. Some historians have made a virtue of the unpredictability of history. Actuarial evidence is easily ignored; we read that hundreds of people will be killed in traffic accidents on a holiday weekend and take to the road as if personally exempt. Very little behavioral science raises "the specter of predictable man." On the contrary, many anthropologists, sociologists, and psychologists have used their expert knowledge to prove that man is free, purposeful, and responsible. Freud was a determinist—on faith, if not on the evidence—but many Freudians have no hesitation in assuring their patients that they are free to choose among different courses of action and are in the long run the architects of their own destinies.

This escape route is slowly closed as new evidences of the predictability of human behavior are discovered. Personal exemption from a complete determinism is revoked as a scientific analysis progresses, particularly in accounting for the behavior of the individual. Joseph Wood Krutch has acknowledged the actuarial facts while insisting on personal freedom: "We can predict with a considerable degree of accuracy how many people will go to the seashore on a day when the temperature reaches a certain point, even how many will jump off a bridge . . . although I am not, nor are you, compelled to do either." But he can scarcely mean that those who go to the seashore do not go for good reason, or that circumstances in the life of a suicide do not have some bearing on the fact that he jumps off a bridge. The distinction is tenable only so long as a word like "compel" suggests a particularly conspicuous and forcible mode of control. A scientific analysis naturally moves in the direction of clarifying all kinds of controlling relations.

By questioning the control exercised by autonomous man and demonstrating the control exercised by the environment, a science of behavior also seems to question dignity or worth. A person is responsible for his behavior, not only in the sense that he may be justly blamed or punished when he behaves badly, but also in the sense that he is to be given credit and admired for his achievements. A scientific analysis shifts the credit as well as the blame to the environment, and traditional practices can then no longer be justified. These are sweeping changes, and those who are committed to traditional theories and practices naturally resist them.

FOR FURTHER READING

Historically, among the most important determinists are Thomas Hobbes, Baruch Spinoza, and John Stuart Mill. Hobbes may be thought of as the first modern mechanist. In *Leviathan* (Indianapolis: Bobbs-Merrill, 1958), first published in 1651, Hobbes argued that persons are purely physical beings and that their behavior could therefore be completely explained in the same way as any machine, according to physical laws. Spinoza's view is far more complicated. In his *Ethics,* first published in 1677, he argued that there is only one substance, which can be called either God or Nature, and that this substance has two aspects, physical and mental. Persons, who are part of this substance, also have these two aspects. Their behavior is determined because all of nature is determined. The work is available in *Spinoza: Selections,* edited by John Wild (New York: Scribner's, 1958). Mill, in *An Examination of Sir William Hamilton's Philosophy* (Buffalo: University of Toronto Press, 1979), first published in 1872, gives a classic statement of the argument from predictability.

Two important philosophers who have tried to reconcile free will and determinism are Gottfried Wilhelm Leibniz and Immanuel Kant. Their reasoning is highly complex and depends on their respective metaphysics, that is, their views on the ultimate nature of reality. For Leibniz's views, consult *Leibniz: Selections,* edited by Philip P. Wiener (New York: Scribner's, 1951); for Kant's, the third section of *Foundations of the Metaphysics of Morals* (Indianapolis: Bobbs-Merrill, 1959), which first appeared in 1785.

Skinner's views can be found in *Beyond Freedom and Dignity* (New York: Knopf, 1971); *Walden Two* (New York: Macmillan, 1960); *Science and Human Behavior* (New York: The Free Press, 1953). The first is a popular exposition of his views; the second is a fictional account of a utopian society based on behavioral conditioning.

Skinner's views are criticized by Daniel Dennett in "Skinner Skinned," which can be found in Daniel Dennett's *Brainstorms* (Montgomery, Vt.: Bradford, 1978). My own criticisms of Skinner owe much to Dennett. The book also contains a number of excellent essays dealing with mechanism, artificial intelligence, cognitive psychology, and moral responsibility. The views mentioned in my discussion of Dennett can also be found in this book. *Minds and Machines,* edited by Alan Ross Anderson, contains some important papers on mechanism, including A. M. Turing's landmark essay, "Computers, Machinery and Intelligence," which first appeared in *Mind,* volume 59 (1950).

Two well-known criticisms of psychological mechanism are Hubert Dreyfus' *What Machines Can't Do* (New York: Harper & Row, 1972) and Joseph Weizenbaum's *Computer Power and Human Reason* (San Francisco: W. H. Freeman and Company, 1976). Weizenbaum is a computer scientist at MIT, and his book is a somewhat impassioned warning to the lay reader. It is also a good introduction to computers and artificial intelligence. So is Margaret Boden's *Artificial Intelligence and Natural Man* (New York: Basic Books, 1977), which discusses some of the most intriguing artificial-intelligence programs.

An excellent collection of readings in cognitive psychology is *Thinking,* edited by P. N. Johnson-Laird and P. C. Wason (Cambridge: Cambridge University Press, 1977). The readings are fairly technical for the most part, but the book offers a good indication of the scope of cognitive psychology. An easier introduction is the text by Lyle Bourne, Roger Dominowski, and Elizabeth Loftus, *Cognitive Processes* (Englewood Cliffs, N.J.: Prentice-Hall, 1979).

The most forceful defender of free will is Jean-Paul Sartre, whose *Being and Nothingness* (New York: Citadel, 1956) is a modern, if difficult, classic. Sartre's views are discussed in Chapter 14. Other important defenders in the history of philosophy include René Descartes and William James. See Descartes' *Meditations on First Philosophy*, first published in 1641, and *The Principles of Philosophy*, first published in 1644. Both are available in *The Philosophical Works of Descartes* (Cambridge: Cambridge University Press, 1970), translated by Haldare and Ross. See James's "The Dilemma of Determinism," in *The Will to Believe and Other Essays* (New York: Dover, 1956), first published in 1897.

More recently, A. I. Melden criticized the basis of some deterministic theories in his *Free Action* (London: Routledge & Kegan Paul, 1961).

Among recent attempts to reconcile free will and determinism, two important ones are C. J. Ducasse's *Nature, Mind and Death* (LaSalle, Ill.: Open Court, 1951) and R. E. Hobart's "Free Will as Involving Determinism and Inconceivable Without It," published in the journal *Mind*, volume 43 (1934).

There are many anthologies in print containing essays on free will and determinism. Many of the essays deal with the relationship between determinism and moral responsibility. One important collection is Sidney Hook's *Determinism and Freedom in the Age of Modern Science* (New York: Collier, 1961), which contains the papers read at a symposium conducted in 1957. Included is Hospers' "What Means This Freedom?" The views expressed in that paper are those mentioned in my discussion of Hospers. Also included is Paul Edwards' "Hard and Soft Determinism," a very influential statement of incompatibilism, and criticisms of Hospers and Edwards by Elizabeth Lane Beardsley. For Beardsley's most detailed account of her positions, see "Determinism and Moral Perspectives," in *Readings in Ethical Theory* (New York: Appleton-Century-Crofts, 1970), edited by Sellars and Hospers. My discussion of Beardsley was based on that essay, which first appeared in *Philosophy and Phenomenological Research*, XXI, 1960. Sellars and Hospers contains other papers on determinism and moral responsibility, including sections of John Hospers' "Meaning and Free Will," which first appeared in *Philosophy and Phenomenological Research*, X, 1950.

Another useful collection is Bernard Berofsky's *Free Will and Determinism* (New York: Harper & Row, 1966). Included are both the Hospers paper and the Hobart paper. Also included are the following: a portion of libertarian C. A. Campbell's "Is 'Free Will' a Pseudo-problem?," in which he argues that determinism and moral responsibility are not compatible; a portion of Moritz Schlick's "When Is a Man Responsible?," in which he argues that free will and moral responsibility are compatible; a selection from Sartre's *Being and Nothingness*; and Donald Davidson's "Actions, Reasons, and Causes," which contains the views mentioned in my discussion of Davidson. Campbell's paper first appeared in *Mind*, volume 60 (1951); Schlick's, in *Problems of Ethics* (New York: Prentice-Hall, 1939); Davidson's, in *The Journal of Philosophy*, volume 60 (1963).

Other anthologies include *Freedom and the Will* (New York: St. Martin's, 1963), edited by David Pears, and *Freedom and Determinism* (New York: Random House, 1966), edited by Keith Lehrer.

For Strawson's defense of compatibilism, see "Freedom and Resentment," in *Studies in the Philosophy of Thought and Action*, edited by Strawson (London: Oxford University Press, 1968).

In recent years, many books and papers have appeared in what has come to be known as the theory of action. These works discuss such issues as the nature of human action, explanation of human action, the relation between actions and body movements, as well as the free will issue. In addition to Melden's book, there are L. E. M. Ansombe's *Intention* (Ithaca: Cornell University Press, 1963); Jerry Fodor's *Psychological Explanation* (New York: Random House, 1968); Arthur Danto's *Analytical Philosophy of Action* (Cambridge: Cambridge University Press, 1973); Alvin Goldman's *A Theory of Human Action* (Englewood Cliffs: Prentice-Hall, 1970); Richard Taylor's *Action and Purpose* (Englewood Cliffs: Prentice-Hall, 1966); Judith Jarvis Thomson's *Acts and Other Events* (Ithaca: Cornell University Press, 1977).

Two useful anthologies are Care and Landesman's *Readings in the Theory of Action* (Bloomington: Indiana University Press, 1968) and Alan White's *The Philosophy of Action* (London: Oxford University Press, 1968). A useful introduction to action theory is Lawrence H. Dalis' *Theory of Action* (Englewood Cliffs: Prentice-Hall, 1979).

Part IV

THE NATURE OF PERSONS

Chapter 12

BODIES AND MINDS

We describe human beings in many different ways. Some of these descriptions are not significantly different from our descriptions of the rest of the world. Since we all have bodies, we can be given purely physical descriptions. We can be described as having a certain weight, size, shape, and so forth. But there are other ways of describing human beings that do not seem to apply to the rest of the world. We love, contemplate, write and read poetry, for example, and are held morally responsible for our actions. Thus, we seem on the one hand to be part of nature, and on the other hand to be somehow separate from it. We make this separation not only between ourselves and inanimate objects, but between ourselves and other animals as well. A beaver's dam is generally considered to be part of nature. Hoover Dam is not. Through their activity, other animals contribute to nature. Through our activity, we alter it.

Why do we distinguish ourselves from beavers—or any other animals—in this way? In part, because our products are products of the *human mind*. Even if we allow that animals can think and feel, the human mind is taken to be different. Because of its sophistication, because of its ability to set itself apart from nature through contemplation, planning, and choice, we do not think of its operations as being controlled by natural laws. Human actions are not blind. They are governed by *reason*.

So we are subject to mental descriptions and physical descriptions, have mental qualities and physical qualities, minds and bodies. But what is a mind? What are these mental qualities? How are they related to the physical world? Are we *really* set apart from nature?

MIND-BODY DUALISM

It is a common view that minds and bodies are radically different *sorts* of things, that minds and bodies are made up of two radically different stuffs—mental stuff and physical stuff. This view is called *mind-body dualism.* We are naturally led to dualism by our ordinary beliefs about mental and physical objects. Think of the qualities that physical objects such as tables and chairs have. They have size, shape, mass. They obey the causal laws of nature. They can be given an exact location in a shared, public space. And they are publicly knowable.

To say that they are publicly knowable is to say that all of us who are not perceptually impaired can know of them in the same ways. We can see the same physical objects, smell them, feel them, hear them, and taste them. Even those physical objects that cannot be perceived are public. It is the physicist's training that allows him to learn about electrons, and that training is available to all of us.

But what about mental objects, such as thoughts, fears, and mental images? How tall is a thought? Are most fears round or square? How much does a mental image of an orange weigh? How many wishes can we pack into a cubic inch? Are hopes generally behind beliefs, next to them, or in front of them? Such questions do not seem to be answerable. The problem is not that we haven't gotten around to weighing or measuring mental objects. Rather, such questions seem somehow misguided, perhaps even nonsensical. Mental objects, it is felt, are not the *sort* of thing that *can* have size, shape or weight. Nor can they have exact spatial location. We can, of course, give them an *approximate* location. My thoughts, we say, are where I am. Moreover, they are in my head. But beyond that, we are at a loss.

These beliefs about mental objects are closely connected to another belief about them—that they are not publicly knowable. The contents of my own mind are private. Only I can know for certain what I am thinking and feeling. Only I can know for certain how the world looks to me, what my pains feel like, what mental images I am having, and so forth. The rest of you can only infer these things about me, on the basis of my behavior. But you can be wrong.

Suppose that I am dreaming of a dog chasing a cat. I can see and hear the dog and cat in my mind. You cannot. While I am sleeping you can only infer that I am dreaming by my rapid eye movements. After I awake, I can tell you that I was dreaming of a dog chasing a cat, and you will no doubt believe me. But your knowledge of the dream is still different from mine. Only I saw and heard the dog and cat. Only I *could* have seen and heard them. They are completely private to me. The privacy of my dreams is not due to the fact that they are in my head. My brain is in my head, but any scientist could poke around in my brain to see what is going on in there. But could she see the dog and cat of my dream? Would she be able to see them with a large enough microscope? Hardly.

Mental objects thus seem to exist in a private space, accessible only to the person having them. It is this feature of mental objects that inclines us to deny that they have size, shape, weight, and so forth. If they did have such qualities, then anyone could observe them. The privacy of mental objects also inclines most people to accept dualism. If my mind is part of my body, then anything in my mind must be in my body. But anything in my body must be public, because my body is public. But thoughts and images and pains are not public. Therefore, they cannot be in my body. Hence, my mind must be distinct from my body.

René Descartes (1596–1650) characterized the difference between mind and body this way. The body, like all physical objects, is essentially an *extended* substance. That is, its defining qualities are size and shape. The mind is essentially a *thinking* substance. That is, it is defined by its ability to think, choose, feel, imagine and so forth. Neither can have the essential quality of the other. The body cannot think, and the mind cannot have size and shape. If it were otherwise, the distinction between the two would disappear. If we begin by accepting the distinction between mind and body, we are then faced with the following question: What is the *relation* between mind and body?

Interactionism

The common-sense answer to our question is that the mind and body are in *causal interaction* with each other. The mind causes things to happen in the body, and the body causes things to happen in the mind. This is the form of dualism associated with Descartes, and is often called *Cartesian interactionism,* or *Cartesian dualism.*

How does the body act on the mind? Most important, events in our body cause us to perceive the external world. Light hits our eyes, causing activity in our brains, and we become visually aware of the external world. Sound waves strike our ears, causing different activity in our brains, and we hear external sounds. But there are many other ways in which the body acts on the mind. If we do not eat, we *feel* hunger. If we do not drink, we *feel* thirst. If something goes wrong in our bodies, we often *feel* pain.

How does the mind act on the body? Most significantly, by its decisions, and by its beliefs and desires. We decide to open the window, and our bodies carry out the decision. We see a car coming at us, want to avoid being hit, believe that the best way to avoid it is by getting out of the way, and our body gets out of the way. We may say, then, that the body is both the mind's agent in the world and the mind's way of learning about the world. The body tells the mind what is going on, and the mind tells the body what to do about it. Although interactionism is the common-sense view, many philosophers have found it inadequate.

First, there is something mysterious about this causal interaction. If the body is in public space, but the mind is not, how can the mind act on the body? How can it connect with something in another space altogether?

Think about ordinary cases of causal activity. How do you move a book? Usually, you place your hand against it and push it. Or you place your hand against something else, say a yardstick, and then push it against the book. Between affecting object and affected object, some contact must be made, whether direct or indirect. But how can contact be made if the two objects do not share the same space?

To further illustrate the problem, let us think of another nonphysical object—the square root of two. Can the square root of two push a book? Of course not—because it does not occupy physical space, because it cannot get up against a book to push it. But neither can a mental object, such as a wish or a desire. So how can it cause anything to happen in the body?

A second difficulty involves a physical law—the conservation of energy. According to current physical theory, the level of energy in the world is constant. But if mental objects can act on the physical world, new energy is brought into the world every time the mind causes the body to do something.

Third, as scientists come to understand how the nervous system works, the possibility of explaining human behavior in purely physical terms grows greater. If we can give a completely physical explanation of behavior, as many scientists and philosophers think likely, there is no reason to believe that any nonphysical substance causes the body to do anything. In that case, belief in one half of the interaction should be rejected.

None of these difficulties is insurmountable. Curt Ducasse, a contemporary American defender of Cartesian interactionism, argues this way. Against the first difficulty, he argues that there is no mystery at all to Descartes' view. Philosophers who demand an explanation of how mental states can affect the physical world are making an illegitimate demand. The only time we can legitimately ask how one event causes another is when there are intervening steps between the two. How, for example, does pressing the keys of my typewriter cause letters to appear on paper? The answer is that the keys are connected to letter-shaped pieces of metal. When I press the keys, the letter-shaped pieces strike the ribbon and press it against the paper. And because the ribbon has ink on it, it leaves an impression on the paper.

But suppose we ask how pressing a key can cause the key to move. In that case, all we can say is this. According to certain laws of nature, that is the way the world works. Similarly, when the critic of Descartes asks how a mental state can cause a brain state, the only response we can give is this. According to the laws that govern mental states and brain states, that is how the world works. If the answer to our previous question is not mysterious, Ducasse says, neither is the answer to this one.

Against the second difficulty, Ducasse makes this point. The energy conservation principle applies only to closed systems. That is, it applies only to systems that have no outside forces working on them. Some scientists may believe that the physical world is a closed system, but that is just an assumption on their part. If their assumption is false, then the principle does not apply to the physical world as a whole. And interactionists believe that the assumption *is* false. They believe that mental events have effects on the physical world.

What about the third difficulty—the likelihood of a complete physical explanation of human behavior? Interactionists have a response to this as well. They argue that the physical explanations of behavior are *not* complete. When scientists describe the physical processes that cause behavior, they leave out the mental processes that also play a role. One physical process does not directly cause the next. First it must cause something to happen in the mind, which then causes something to happen in the brain.

None of these responses can be rejected out of hand. Still, many philosophers have turned to another form of dualism, which does not have these difficulties.

Epiphenomenalism

The most commonly accepted form of dualism among philosophers and scientists is *epiphenomenalism.* According to this view, mental states are mere by-products (or *epiphenomena*) of the brain. That is, certain types of activity in the brain create certain types of mental activity, but this mental activity has no effects whatever. Decisions, beliefs, desires, pains, and so forth have no effect on our behavior at all. Even without them, we would behave as we do now. We would continue to talk, argue, write poetry, avoid oncoming traffic, and the like, even if we had no internal life. Although we have minds, they are purposeless. The causes of our behavior are entirely physical.

To illustrate this view, we can think of a factory. In the factory, there are raw materials that move along an assembly line. The line is powered by a furnace, fueled by coal. Along the line are various machines that work on the raw materials. At the end of the line we have the finished product. Everything mentioned plays some role in the production of the finished product. One thing left out, though, is the smoke leaving the chimney. The smoke plays no role in the process. It makes no contribution to the finished product whatever. It is a mere by-product of the process. According to the epiphenomenalist, the situation is the same with thoughts. Just as the factory would operate the same way with smokeless fuel, so would we behave the same way with brains that did not create thoughts. Our mental life is like the smoke escaping the chimney.

Suppose that you are sitting at your desk and someone throws a piece of chalk at you. Let us describe what happens next, first according to the interactionist, then the epiphenomenalist.

The interactionist story: Light from the chalk strikes your eye, causing a chain of neural firings in your brain. This chain of firings causes you to have a mental image of the chalk. This image causes other firings, which in turn causes you to

have the thought that the chalk is going to hit you. This thought causes you to
want to avoid the chalk, causing further firings, causing in turn the decision to
duck. This decision causes still further firings, and you duck.

If we label the neural firings BS (for brain state) and the thoughts, images and
so forth MS (for mental state), and if we represent causal connections by means
of arrows, we can diagram the above as follows:

Chalk MS_1 $MS_2 \rightarrow MS_3$ MS_4

$\nearrow$ — $BS_1 \rightarrow BS_2 \rightarrow BS_3$ BS_4 $BS_5 \rightarrow BS_6$ $BS_7 \rightarrow BS_8 \rightarrow$ Ducking

Light

Notice that in the above diagram, brain states cause mental states, and mental
states cause brain states. Both are needed to produce the behavior of ducking.

Now the epiphenomenalist story: Light strikes the eye, causing a chain of
neural firings. Some of these firings create various mental states. One firing
causes an image of the chalk, one causes the belief that the chalk is coming, one
causes the desire to avoid it, one causes a decision to duck. None of these mental states causes anything else. The brain states that cause them have two kinds
of effects. They cause a mental state, but they also cause another brain state. At
the end of the chain of firings comes your ducking.

We can diagram the epiphenomenalist's story as follows:

Chalk MS_1 MS_2 MS_3 MS_4

$\nearrow$ — $BS_1 \rightarrow BS_2 \rightarrow BS_3 \rightarrow BS_4 \rightarrow BS_5 \rightarrow BS_6 \rightarrow BS_7 \rightarrow BS_8 \rightarrow$ Ducking

Light

Notice that the arrows go only one way. Brain states cause mental states, but
mental states cause nothing, not even other mental states. This view is, of
course, highly counterintuitive. After all, it seems perfectly obvious that our
decisions affect our behavior. Don't we notice this every time we make a decision and then act on it?

But the epiphenomenalist has an answer. Whenever we see one kind of event
invariably follow another, we are inclined to think that the first causes the second. But it is not always true that the first causes the second. Sometimes the two
are caused by some third event. Such is the case with our decisions and actions.
A certain type of brain state causes us to make a certain type of decision, and
also causes us to act in a certain way. When we wave to a friend, for instance, it
is not our decision to wave that causes us to wave. Rather, activity in our brain
causes both the decision and the wave. Because we are not aware of the brain
state, but only of the decision and the action, we assume that the decision

PARALLELISM

In addition to interactionism and epiphenomenalism, there is another form of dualism that some philosophers have adopted. This view is known as parallelism, and its most well known advocate is Gottfried Wilhelm Leibniz (1646–1716).

According to the parallelist, mental states and brain states have no causal connection between them. Mental states do not cause brain states and brain states do not cause mental states. Instead, there are two distinct causal series, the mental and the physical, which do not interact with each other. Using the same symbols that we used to diagram interactionism and epiphenomenalism, we can diagram this view as follows:

$$MS_1 \rightarrow MS_2 \rightarrow MS_3 \rightarrow MS_4$$

$$BS_1 \rightarrow BS_2 \rightarrow BS_3 \rightarrow BS_4$$

How does it happen, then, that when someone pinches me I feel pain, or that when I choose to raise my arm I do so? How is it that the mental and physical worlds parallel each other as they do?

The possibilities are as follows: First, the parallel is merely a coincidence. Second, the two causal series are like two clocks, each set (most likely by God) to tick away in a pre-established harmony. This was Leibniz's view. Third, there is some force (most likely God) constantly intervening to make things work out right. Since none of these answers is very plausible, parallelism is not widely accepted today.

causes the action. But we are mistaken. We are like the person who sees that rain always follows the falling of the barometer and then assumes that the barometer pulls the rain out of the sky.

Thus, our "awareness" that decisions cause behavior does not defeat epiphenomenalism. Still, there is something very suspicious about the view. To see why, let us compare the epiphenomenalist view of mental states to the smoke emitted from a factory. True, the smoke plays no role in the production process, but it does have *some* effects. It can be seen and smelled, for instance. Also, it can cause your eyes to sting. It can harm plant and animal life, interact with moisture in the air to form smog, darken buildings, make car windshields dirty, and so on. But thoughts, according to the epiphenomenalist, can do nothing of the sort. They quite literally do nothing at all. If that is true, they are like nothing else in the universe. They are absolutely useless.

This does trouble some philosophers. If everything else in the universe plays some role in its workings, why should mental states be different? Why should we have evolved with minds at all if they serve no purpose? If minds have no survival value, why should natural selection have favored creatures with minds over creatures without minds?

MATERIALISM

At this point, many philosophers have made the following argument. Human beings obviously think, feel, decide, and so forth. Since it is the mind that is responsible for such things, we obviously have minds. If there are minds, they must have some effects. It is reasonable to suppose that they have the effects we ordinarily believe them to have. That is, it is reasonable to believe that they cause us to behave in certain ways. But it is the brain that causes us to behave the way we do. Therefore, the mind must be the brain. That is, the mind is a physical object.

To say that the mind is physical is to adopt a *materialist* theory of mind. Materialists, unlike dualists, believe that human beings are purely physical beings, and that any mental state must be some state of the physical body. Materialism has none of the problems of interactionism or epiphenomenalism. Unlike interactionism, it does not make the mind's effects on behavior at all mysterious, nor does it violate the law of conservation of energy. Unlike epiphenomenalism, it does not rob the mind of its functions. If materialism is true, then the mind does have a place in the world's causal story.

Mind-Brain Identity

One form of materialism is the view that mental states are *identical* with *brain states*. To have a certain kind of mental state is the same thing as having a certain type of brain state. To think a certain sort of thought is to have a certain sort of thing happen in the brain. To feel pain is to have another sort of thing happen in the brain. To wish for good weather is to have another sort of thing happen in the brain. This theory is called the *mind-brain identity theory*. Although it has been accepted by many contemporary philosophers, it is most closely associated with the Australians D. M. Armstrong and J. J. C. Smart.

Once we reject interactionism and epiphenomenalism, it seems natural to accept the identity theory. But before we embrace it, we should remember why we were inclined to accept dualism in the first place. There were two reasons. First, there was the privacy of mental objects. Only I can see the dogs and cats in my dreams. Only I can know what I'm thinking. Second, we said that mental objects cannot have the qualities that physical objects have. Thoughts and wishes and fears cannot have weight or size or shape or definite spatial location. But according to the identity theory, a mental state is identical with a brain state. In that case, how can a mental state be private? How can we deny that it has shape or size?

The identity theorist's response to these questions is a tricky one. It goes like this: Nobody else can see the dogs and cats in my dreams because there are no dogs and cats in my dreams. They simply do not exist. Neither do thoughts and wishes and fears. That is why they cannot have size or shape: because they do not exist.

At first glance, this answer seems as preposterous as the claim that decisions do not affect behavior. If there are no such things as thoughts and wishes and mental images, then what can mental states possibly be? If thoughts are not identical with brain states, what are the mental states that are identical with brain states?

The identity theorist's response is this: Mental states are not *objects*, like tables or chairs. They are *events*, like the kicking of a football. *Thinking* is a mental state. So are *wishing* and *hoping* and *dreaming*. These are all mental events, things that we do. But there are no such objects as *thoughts, wishes, hopes,,* or *images*.

What is the difference between an event and an object? An event is a happening, an occurrence. It is what objects do, what happens to objects. Take, for example, the event of kicking a football. If I kick a football, there are only two objects involved—me and the ball. There is also the event of my kicking the ball, but that event is *not* a third object. True, we sometimes talk as though there were such objects as kicks. We say that someone made a good kick, or that a kick saved a game, or that a field-goal kicker made five kicks during a game. But that is just a manner of speaking. There are no such objects as kicks.

Similarly, there are no such objects as handshakes. If I shake a friend's hand, the only objects involved are my hand and my friend's hand. We can talk as though there were a third thing. We can say, for example, that I gave my friend a firm handshake, but that is not at all like giving someone a firm container. To give a firm handshake is to shake hands firmly. That is, there is only the event of shaking hands, but no such object as a handshake. Shaking hands is something we do.

So it is with mental states, the identity theorist says. We can think that today is Monday. That is something that we do. It is an event. Even though we can talk about our thought that today is Monday, that does not mean that there is an object in our mind that is the thought that today is Monday. It is merely a manner of speaking, like talking about a firm handshake or a good kick. Similarly, we can dream that a dog is chasing a cat. That is also something we do. It is also an event. Even though we can talk about dream dogs and dream cats, that does not mean that there are mental dogs and cats running around in our minds. It is merely a manner of speaking.

So of course a scientist cannot poke around in our brains and find the sentence that today is Monday, or a little dog chasing a little cat. But the scientist can observe the thinking process or the dreaming process. These processes or events do exist, and they are as public as any other event. Since the thoughts, dogs, and cats do not exist, they cannot be seen.

Thus, the alleged privacy of the mind is an illusion. Mental objects are not private. They simply do not exist. Only mental events exist, and they are identical with brain processes.

Moreover, we can now see why mental states cannot have certain qualities, such as weight. Thoughts are weightless for the same reason that handshakes and kicks are. Only objects can have weight. Events cannot. Thus, the major objection to materialism can be answered. But, apart from the difficulties we found with dualism, is there any reason to think the identity theory true?

LOGICAL BEHAVIORISM

The identity theorist denies that there are mental objects, but claims that there are mental events. Another kind of materialist, the *logical behaviorist*, goes one step further, refusing to accept mental objects *and* mental events. But if there are neither mental objects nor mental events, what are we talking about when we talk about beliefs and wishes and pains?

The logical behaviorist's answer is that we are talking about behavior and certain *dispositions* to behave. A disposition is a tendency, an inclination. Some ordinary dispositions are fragility and elasticity. To say that something is elastic is to say that it will stretch if pulled. To say that something is fragile is to say that it will break if treated roughly. More generally, then, to say that something has a certain disposition is to say that certain things will happen to it under certain conditions.

What kind of dispositions are beliefs and pains? To believe that something is true is to be disposed to assent to it, for one thing. If I believe that it is raining I am disposed to say that it is. But I am also disposed to stay indoors, carry an umbrella if I go outside, and so forth. Similarly, if my arm hurts, I am disposed to rub the sore part of my arm, wince, say "ouch," and so forth.

Although logical behaviorism drew a good deal of acceptance earlier in the century, it has few supporters today. It has been rejected for quite a few reasons. Two important ones are the following:

First, any mental state is compatible with any kind of behavior. People in pain can cover it up, people with certain beliefs can refuse to act as though they have these beliefs, etc. Also, people might be disposed toward pain behavior and belief behavior even though they are not in pain and do not have the relevant belief. In that case, even though certain dispositions often *accompany* certain mental states, it seems misguided to say that these states *are* these dispositions.

Second, logical behaviorism seems to deny the obvious. When we get into the dentist's chair, we are not afraid of the disposition to say "ouch." There is a very real feeling, called *pain*, and it is that feeling that we fear. Pains most certainly seem to be something that *happen* in us, and any theory that denies this is not very plausible.

Identity and Correspondence

Many philosophers have felt that the identity theory can be proved by the scientist. To show how, let us look at how another identity theory was proved.

As some of you may have learned in high-school science, temperature is the same thing as mean kinetic molecular energy (the average energy of a substance's molecules due to their motion). How did the scientist learn this?

Scientists found that whenever a bowl of water has a certain temperature, it also has a certain mean kinetic molecular energy (MKE), and that whenever it has a certain MKE, it also has a certain temperature. That is, a *one-to-one correspondence* was discovered between temperature and MKE. Once this correspondence was discovered, it was possible to replace the laws of temperature with certain laws about the motion of molecules. Why should this be so? Why should temperature and MKE correspond so perfectly? Why should the laws of temperature be replaceable by laws of the motion of molecules? The simplest answer is that temperature is *identical* with MKE. And that is the answer that scientists accept.

Suppose that the same kind of correspondence can be found between mental states and brain states? Suppose that whenever I have a certain sensation, it can be shown that exactly the same type of brain state occurs. Let's say that whenever I feel a particular sort of pain, there is a particular sort of firing in my brain. Wouldn't the simplest explanation of this correspondence be that the pain is *identical* with the firing? Wouldn't this explanation be preferable to saying that the sensation is some useless by-product of the brain state? Why suppose that there is some mysterious private entity that does nothing at all?

Let us illustrate this way of thinking by imagining a story that parallels what we have said so far.

Some people who have never seen a watch find one alongside a road. They pick it up and examine it, noticing that the second hand makes a regular sweep around the watch's face. After some discussion, they conclude that the watch is run by a gremlin inside. They remove the back of the watch but cannot find the gremlin. After further discussion, they decide that it must be invisible. They also decide that it makes the hands go by running along the gears inside the watch. They replace the watch's back and take it home.

The next day the watch stops. Someone suggests that the gremlin is dead. Someone else suggests that it's probably sleeping. They shake the watch to awaken the gremlin, but the watch remains stopped. Someone finally turns the stem. The second hand begins to move. The person who said that the gremlin was asleep smiles triumphantly. The winding has awakened it.

After some months, someone claims that the watch can work without a gremlin. He takes apart the watch and explains the movements inside to the others. The others claim that he is leaving out what really makes the watch run. Of course, the winding contributes to the turning of the gears. But only because it wakes up the gremlin, which then resumes its running. Finally, a number of people begin to agree. The gremlin is not needed to run the watch. But because they are so used to believing in gremlins, they do not say that there is no such gremlin inside. Instead, they say that it is there, but only as a resident. It does not contribute to the watch's working.

But the man who figured out that the watch worked without the intervention of a gremlin is dissatisfied. If we do not need the gremlin to explain how the watch works, why continue to believe that it exists? Isn't it simpler to say that it does not?

Think of the watch as the human body, and the gremlin as some nonphysical substance called the mind. In the beginning, the people that discovered the watch were interactionists. When it was claimed that the watch worked without the intervention of the gremlin, some people agreed but some did not. They

split between interactionism and epiphenomenalism. Gradually, epiphenomenalism won out—not because interactionism was decisively proved wrong, but
because it no longer seemed as reasonable as epiphenomenalism. If they could
explain how the watch ran without the gremlin, it seemed foolish to say that it
could not work without the gremlin. But once it was accepted that the gremlin
served no purpose, it was no longer reasonable to assume that it was still there.
Of course, no one could prove for certain that it did not exist, but it seemed
foolish to believe otherwise.

The identity theorist claims that it is equally unreasonable to accept mind-
body dualism. A nonphysical mind is just as suspect as the gremlin. The only
difference between the two cases is this: whereas there is no gremlin at all, there
is a mind. The mistake is in thinking that it is anything over and above the
brain.

Functionalism

What if the scientist does not find the needed correspondences between mental states and brain states? What if the same kind of brain state does
not always accompany the same kind of pain or thought? In that case, we could
not say that a certain type of mental state is identical with a certain type of brain
state. The mind-brain identity theory would be proved false. Does that mean
that we would have to reject materialism and accept some form of dualism?
This question is a crucial one, because it seems that scientists will *not* discover a
one-to-one correspondence between brain states and mental states. For one
thing, many different kinds of creatures have mental states—not only humans
and other primates, but dogs and cats, birds, various forms of marine life, perhaps even creatures from other planets. It is thought to be unlikely that they all
have brains so similar to ours that whenever they are in pain they have the same
kind of brain state that we do. Second, it is not even certain that the required
correspondences exist in humans.

Consequently, if materialism is to survive, we must look for an alternative to
the identity theory. The alternative accepted by most philosophers of mind
today is *functionalism*. We can best explain this theory by turning away from
minds and brains and examining something a bit less complicated. Think, for
example, of the game of chess. Let us imagine a chess board with a variety of
chess pieces on it. We can describe this situation in two ways.

First, we can give a *physical* description of it. We can say that there is a
wooden board of such and such a size and weight, having sixty-four squares of
equal size, alternating in color between red and black. We can then number the
squares and describe the block of wood on each square in terms of its size,
shape, weight, and color.

Second, we can give an *abstract* description of the situation. Rather than describe it in physical terms, we can describe it in terms of the rules of chess. We
can say, for example, that white's king has been placed in check by black's
bishop. This description is an abstract one because it says nothing about the

physical facts of the case. The board can be wood, plastic, or cardboard. The pieces can be dominoes, checkers, or paper clips. None of this matters at all. We can use the same description regardless of the physical makeup of the board and pieces. In fact, a game of chess does not even need a board and pieces. It can be played through the mail, for instance.

Thus, the abstract description is independent of the physical one. The same game of chess may be played with different physical objects, and the same physical objects may be used to play another game, such as checkers. One way of expressing this point is to say that a game of chess can be *embodied* in many different ways, and that the same physical system can embody many different abstract systems. In other words, it is not just the physical facts that make something a game of chess. A knight is not a knight because it is shaped like a horse. It is a knight because it moves according to certain rules. Anything can be a knight, as long as it functions the way a knight is supposed to function.

Similar remarks apply to computers. There are two ways to describe the workings of a computer. A physical description will describe the workings of the circuits, the flow of electricity, and so forth. But that is not how we usually describe the workings of a computer. More often than not, we give an abstract description of it. To give an abstract description of a computer's workings is to talk about the *program* it is following. It is to describe it as performing certain computations.

A computer program is like a game of chess. Its description is totally abstract. Any number of physical machines can embody a particular program. And the same physical machine can embody any number of different programs. Suppose, then, that a computer is adding two and two. In that case, certain things are happening in the machine in accordance with a certain program. What makes those physical happenings the addition of two and two is the program. Just as any physical object can be a knight if it functions according to the proper rules, so can any machine activity be the addition of two and two if it functions according to the proper rules.

According to the functionalist, the brain is like the chess pieces and the physical computer. We can describe its workings in two ways. If we describe its workings in neurophysiological terms, we are giving a physical description of it. If we describe its workings in mental terms, we are giving an abstract description of it.

Moreover, these descriptions are related to each other in the same way that physical and abstract descriptions are related in the cases of the chess pieces and the computer. What makes a particular brain state an act of thinking is not the *kind* of brain state it is. It is an act of thinking because it performs the appropriate *function* in the brain's "program."

More precisely, a creature has a mind if its brain embodies an appropriate abstract description. This abstract description can be called a *psychology*. The brain embodies a psychology if it has states that correspond to the abstract states of the psychology. What are these abstract states? Psychological states, such as

CAN MACHINES THINK?

According to functionalism, to have a mind is to embody an abstract psychology. Suppose that technology were so advanced that we could build a computer that embodied a human psychology. Suppose, that is, that we could build a computer that worked exactly like the human brain. Would that computer think, fear, believe, love, or feel pain?

The immediate temptation is to say no, but before succumbing to it, consider two humanlike machines portrayed in films. Think first of R2D2 in the film *Star Wars*. Think also of HAL in *2001: A Space Odyssey*. Many people, including me, were convinced as we watched these films that R2D2 really *wanted* to save the princess from her abductors and that HAL was really *afraid* when one of the astronauts was dismantling him with a screwdriver.

Many reasons have been advanced for denying that a computer or robot that behaved like us and had an electronic brain that worked like our protein brains would really have a mind. Machines cannot be original, it is said. They have no free will. They can only do what they are programmed to do. They are not alive. They are just collections of circuits, wires, and pieces of metal. They cannot be conscious.

Are these objections compelling? Many philosophers think not. Take the first group of objections, dealing with originality and free will. Are free will and creativity really necessary features of minds? How creative is a dog? Do horses have free will? Are pigs very original?

Then again, as shown in Part III of this book, it is not clear that *we* have a free will. But whether we do or not, we still think and feel. Also, a good case can be made that we, like computers, are also programmed. How is this programming carried out? In two ways. First, we are born partially programmed by our genes. Second, the programming is continued by our conditioning. If it is objected that we can learn in ways other than conditioning, it can be responded that there are machines that can learn as well.

Furthermore, there is a sense in which our most sophisticated machines *are* creative and original. Some can write poetry and music, for example. Some are so complex that even their programmers cannot predict what they will do. If the degree of such creativity and originality is relatively limited as yet, there is every reason to believe that these limits will be surpassed in the coming years.

What about the other objections? Does it matter that machines are not alive? That they are made of metal and synthetic materials instead of protein? That they cannot be conscious?

We can rule out the last question as being *question-begging*. To say that it is question-begging is to say that it assumes what it should be proving. That is, in trying to decide whether a machine can think, feel, hope, and so forth, we are in effect trying to decide whether it can have conscious states. We cannot assume at the outset that it cannot.

Concerning the other questions, there are two considerations we might note. First, it is not clear whether the materials out of which something is made should matter. Why is it that only things made of protein can think? Isn't such a view similar to racism or sexism or speciesism (that is, discrimination against other species)? Many philosophers are far from convinced that only things made of protein can think.

Still (and this is the second consideration), many philosophers believe that there is a great difference between thoughts and beliefs, on the one hand, and pains and itches, on the other. The latter are often called *raw feels*. Whereas there is no particular *sensation* associated with most intellectual operations or most emotions, that is not the case with pains. To be in pain, these philosophers feel, is more than embodying a certain program. Whereas beliefs can be programmed, the raw feels cannot. Only something made of the proper materials can experience raw feels.

The debate over whether a computer can be programmed to feel pain is far from settled. Even if it is decided that computers cannot feel pain, however, that does not mean that they cannot think. There is no reason to believe that the ability to feel pain is necessary for the ability to think. We certainly have no difficulty imagining a totally desensitized human being thinking.

For my own part, I am strongly inclined to think that it is in principle possible for computers to think and fear and want, but doubt that they can feel pain. But the jury is still out on both matters. It is my guess that it will remain out until we have built machines like R2D2 and HAL. It is also my guess that once we have built them, it will be very hard to deny that they think, fear, and want, just as it is very hard to deny these things of the machines in the movies. It may also be hard to deny that they feel pain.

---

thoughts, beliefs, fears, hopes, and wishes. How does a brain state correspond to a psychological state? By performing the appropriate functions. A piece of wood corresponds to a knight by moving in certain ways. The flipping of a switch inside a computer corresponds to a certain computation by following the rules of a computer program. The firing of certain neurons corresponds to a sudden fear in an analogous way. A psychology is like a program. Psychological states are like steps in a program. If the neural firing follows the appropriate steps in the "program," it is a sudden fear.

How, then, does a functionalist differ from an identity theorist? The identity theorist says that two creatures are in the same mental state only if their brain states are the same according to some physical description. The functionalist, on the other hand, says that two creatures are in the same mental state only if their brain states are the same according to an abstract description. That is, the identity theorist requires a similarity in how the brains are *built*. The functionalist requires a similarity in how the brains *work*. So even if there are Martians that feel pain, functionalism will not be proved false if their brains are built differently from ours. All that matters is that their brains embody a psychology similar to ours.

It may seem that this difference is a trivial one. After all, both views are materialistic. Both deny that the mind is a nonphysical substance. Isn't that what really counts? Well, what really counts depends on one's interests. And as we shall see in the next chapter, functionalism and the identity theory may have radically different payoffs when it comes to a matter that many people are interested in—life after death.

THE FINAL WORD?

We began this chapter by noting that human beings consider themselves somehow distinct from the rest of nature. The basis of this distinction, we said, is the human mind.

It is now time to re-examine this common belief. If functionalism or any other form of materialism is true, do we lose our uniqueness? Are we somehow less special because we are purely physical?

On the one hand, we do seem less special. If we are purely physical, then our behavior is governed by physical laws. In that case, there is a sense in which everything we do is as natural as the behavior of the beaver when it builds its dam. But that is not the end of the matter. Physical descriptions and explanations of human behavior do not tell the whole story. We do not *just* move our hands. We also caress the cheek of someone we love, write music and poetry, design buildings with an eye toward beauty as well as function. We do not *just* move our bodies. We play and work and love and sacrifice, at times even knowingly lay down our lives for a good we will not live to see.

Physical descriptions can describe only the movements of our bodies. Physical explanations can explain only the movements of our bodies. In order to capture the full richness of human life we need other types of description, other forms of explanation. We must refer to emotions, thoughts, feelings, goals, and choices. We must allow that the physical processes in our brains are not *just* physical processes, but embody such abstract processes as contemplation and rational decision-making.

Whether these processes are carried out by physical stuff or nonphysical stuff should be of little importance. Whatever the stuff of our makeup, whatever natural laws our body movements obey, this much remains true. We still fall in love, create works of great beauty, pursue knowledge for its own sake, and perform actions of true nobility and self-sacrifice. To be part of nature is not to be indistinguishable from the rest of it.

STUDY QUESTIONS

1. What is mind-body dualism? What ordinary beliefs about such mental objects as thoughts and images have led many people to accept the view?
2. What is Cartesian interactionism? What objections can be raised against it? How can these objections be answered? Do you find these answers satisfactory? Why or why not?
3. What is epiphenomenalism? How does the view avoid the objections raised against interactionism? What new objections does it face?
4. According to supporters of the mind-brain identity theory, there are mental

states but no mental objects. What do they mean by the claim? What objections is it meant to avoid?

5. What evidence does the mind-brain identity theorist expect to find in favor of his view? Why does he think this evidence will clinch his case?

6. What is functionalism? How does it differ from the identity theory?

7. What is the difference between a physical description and an abstract description? According to functionalism, how do these different kinds of description apply to the human brain?

8. Suppose that you spent an evening talking to what you took to be a human being but was really a robot. Suppose also that you came to various conclusions about what it thought and believed and how it felt about many things. After learning of your mistake, would you then conclude that it didn't really think or believe or feel anything? Why or why not?

GLOSSARY

Abstract description. A description of an object, state, or event that is independent of any physical description of that object, state, or event. An example of an abstract description is the description of a game of chess in a newspaper. There, every move of the game is described without reference to the physical qualities of the board and pieces actually used. The same game can be reproduced by anybody, using any number of things for the board and chess pieces.

Begging the question. Assuming the conclusion of an argument that one is attempting to prove. Suppose I were to say that John is an honest man. You ask me how I know that and I reply that I know it because he told me so. You then ask me how I know that I can believe him, and I answer that I can believe him because he is an honest man. In this example, I have assumed the conclusion of my argument—that John is an honest man.

Cartesian interactionism. (Also called "Cartesian dualism.") A form of *mind-body dualism.* According to Cartesian interactionism, events in the physical body cause events in the nonphysical mind, and events in the mind cause events in the body.

Dispositions. Inclinations or tendencies. Something has a particular disposition if it behaves in certain ways under certain circumstances. A brittle object, for example, is one that has a tendency to break. That is, it will shatter if struck.

Embodiment. The physical realization of an *abstract description.* The arrangement of wooden pieces on a board, for example, can be the embodiment of a certain situation in the game of chess.

Epiphenomenalism. A form of *mind-body dualism.* According to this view, mental states are mere by-products (epiphenomena) of the brain, having no influence on behavior or other mental states.

Functionalism. The view that the human brain is analogous to a computer. On this view, a given brain state is also a given mental state because it performs the appropriate function in the appropriate "program." That is, the human brain *embodies* certain *abstract descriptions.*

Logical behaviorism. The view that mental states are neither events nor objects, but *dispositions* to behave. On this view, to have a toothache is to be disposed to wince, say "ouch," rub one's jaw, go to the dentist, and so on.

Materialism. In philosophy of mind, the view that human beings are purely physical, and that mental states are states of the physical body.

Mind-body dualism. The view that the mind is nonphysical and the body physical. (See *Cartesian interactionism, epiphenomenalism,* and *parallelism.*)

Mind-brain identity theory. The theory that mental states are identical with brain states. According to this view, to be in pain is to have a certain sort of event occur in the brain.

One-to-one correspondence. A relationship between two groups of things, such that each member of one group is matched with one and only one member of the other.

Parallelism. A form of *mind-body dualism.* According to parallelism, events in the mind and events in the brain do not influence one another.

Raw feels. Mental states characterized by a certain sort of sensation. Raw feels include pains, tickles, and itches, but do not include beliefs, thoughts, and desires.

Chapter 13

PERSONAL IDENTITY
AND LIFE
AFTER DEATH

It is Sunday night. After a long night of hard drinking, John Badger puts on his pajamas, lowers the heat in his Wisconsin home to fifty-five degrees and climbs into bed beneath two heavy blankets. Meanwhile, in Florida, Joe Everglade kisses his wife goodnight and goes to sleep.

The next morning, two very confused men wake up. One wakes up in Wisconsin, wondering where he is and why he is wearing pajamas, lying under two heavy blankets, yet shivering from the cold. He looks out the window and sees nothing but pine trees and snow. The room is totally unfamiliar. Where is his wife? How did he get to this cold, strange place? Why does he have such a terrible hangover? He tries to spring out of bed with his usual verve but feels an unaccustomed aching in his joints. Arthritis? He wanders unsurely through the house until he finds the bathroom. What he sees in the mirror causes him to spin around in sudden fear. But there is nobody behind him. Then the fear intensifies as he realizes that it was his reflection that had stared back at him. But it was the reflection of a man thirty years older than himself, with coarser features and a weather-beaten face.

In Florida, a man awakens with a young woman's arm around him. When she too awakens, she snuggles against him and wishes him good morning. "Who are you?" he asks. "What am I doing in your bed?" She just laughs, then tells him that he will have to hurry if he is going to get in his ten miles of jog-ging. From the bathroom she asks him about his coming day. None of the names or places she mentions connect with anything he can remember. He climbs out of bed, marveling at the ease with which he does so, and looks first out the window and then into the mirror over the dresser. The sun and swim-ming pool confound him. The handsome young man's reflection terrifies him.

Then the phone rings. The woman answers it. It is the man from Wisconsin. "What happened last night, Mary? How did I get here? How did I get to look this way?"

"Who is this?" she asks.

"Don't you recognize my voice, Mary?" But he knew that the voice was not his own. "It's Joe."

"Joe who?"

"Your husband."

She hangs up, believing it to be a crank call. When she returns to the bed-room, the man in her husband's robe asks how he got there from Wisconsin, and why he looks as he does.

PERSONAL IDENTITY

What happened in the above story? Who woke up in Joe Everglade's bed? Who woke up in John Badger's? Which one is Mary's husband? Has Bad-ger awakened with Everglade's memories and Everglade with Badger's? Or have Badger and Everglade somehow switched bodies? How are we to decide? What considerations are relevant?

To ask such questions is to raise the problem of *personal identity*. It is to ask what makes a person the same person he was the day before. It is to ask how we determine that we are dealing with the same person that we have dealt with in the past. It is to ask what constitutes personal identity over time. It is also to ask what we mean by the *same person*. And to answer this question, we must ask what we mean by the word "person."

Persons

In the previous chapter, we asked what a human being is. We asked what human beings are made of, what the nature of the human mind is, and whether human beings are part of nature or distinct from it.

To ask what a *person* is, however, is to ask a different question. Although we often use the terms "person" and "human being" interchangeably, they do not mean the same thing. If we do use them interchangeably, it is only because all the persons we know of are human beings, and because, as far as we know, whenever we are confronted with the same human being we are confronted with the same person.

But the notion of a human being is a *biological* notion. To identify something as a human being is to identify it as a member of *Homo sapiens,* a particular species of animal. It is a type of organism defined by certain physical characteristics.

The notion of a person, on the other hand, is *not* a biological one. Suppose, for instance, that we find life on another planet, and that this life is remarkably like our own. The creatures we discover communicate through a language as rich as our own, act according to moral principles, have a legal system, and engage in science and art. Suppose also that despite these cultural similarities, this form of life is biologically different from human life. In that case, these creatures would be persons, but not humans. Think, for example, of the alien in *E.T.* Since he is biologically different from us, he is not human. He is, however, a person.

What, then, is a person? Although philosophers disagree on this point, the following features are relatively noncontroversial.

First, a person is an intelligent, rational creature. Second, it is a creature capable of a peculiar sort of consciousness—self-consciousness. Third, it not only has beliefs, desires, and so forth, but it has beliefs *about* its beliefs, desires, and so forth. Fourth, it is a creature to which we ascribe moral responsibility. Persons are responsible for their actions in a way that other things are not. They are subject to moral praise and moral blame. Fifth, a person is a creature that we treat in certain ways. To treat something as a person is to treat it as a member of our own moral community. It is to grant it certain rights, both moral and legal. Sixth, a person is a creature capable of reciprocity. It is capable of treating us as members of the same moral community. Finally, a person is capable of verbal communication. It can communicate by means of a *language,* not just by barks, howls, and tail-wagging.

Since, as far as we know, only human beings meet the above conditions, only human beings are considered to be persons. But once we recognize that to be a person is not precisely the same thing that it is to be a human being, we also recognize that other creatures, such as the alien in *E.T.* is also a person. We also recognize that perhaps not all human beings are persons—human fetuses, for example, as some have argued. Certainly, in the American South before the end of the Civil War, slaves were not considered to be persons. We might also mention a remark of D'Artagnan, in Richard Lester's film version of *The Three Musketeers.* Posing as a French nobleman, he attempted to cross the English Channel with a companion. When a French official remarked that his pass was only for one person, D'Artagnan replied that he was only one person—his companion was a servant.

Moreover, once we recognize the distinction between human beings and persons, certain questions arise. Can one human being embody more than one person, either at the same time or successive times? In the example we introduced at the beginning of this chapter, has Badger's body become Everglade's and Everglade's Badger's? Can the person survive the death of the human being? Is there personal survival after the death of the body?

The Memory Criterion and the Bodily Criterion

Concerning identity through time in general, two issues must be distinguished. First, we want to know how we can *tell* that something is the same thing we encountered previously. That is, we want to know what the *criteria* are for establishing identity through time. Second, we want to know what *makes* something the same thing it was previously. That is, we want to know what *constitutes* identity through time.

Although these issues are related, they are not the same, as the following example illustrates. We can *tell* that someone has a case of the flu by checking for certain symptoms, such as fever, lack of energy, and sore muscles. But having these symptoms does not *constitute* having a case of the flu. It is the presence of a flu virus—not the symptoms—that makes an illness a case of the flu.

We commonly use two criteria for establishing personal identity. The first is the *bodily criterion*, the second the *memory criterion*. How do we apply them?

We apply the bodily criterion in two ways. First, we go by physical resemblance. If I meet someone on the street who looks, walks, and sounds just like Mary, I assume that it is Mary. Since the body I see resembles Mary's body exactly, I assume that the person I see is Mary. But that method can sometimes fail us, as in the case of identical twins. In such cases, we can apply the bodily criterion in another way. If I can discover that there is a continuous line from one place and time to another that connects Mary's body to the body I now see, I can assume that I now see Mary. Suppose, for example, that Mary and I went to the beach together, and have been together all afternoon. In that case, I can say that the person I am now with is the person I began the day with.

There are, however, times when the bodily criterion is not available. If Mary and Jane are identical twins, and I run across one of them on the street, I may have to ask who it is. That is, I may have to rely on Mary's memory of who she is. And, if I want to make sure that I am not being fooled, I may ask a few questions. If Mary remembers things that I believe only Mary can remember, and if she remembers them as happening to *her*, and not to somebody else, then I can safely say that it really is Mary.

Generally, the bodily criterion and the memory criterion do not conflict, so we use whichever is more convenient. But what happens if they do conflict? That is what happened in our imagined story. According to the bodily criterion, each person awoke in his own bed, but with the memories of someone else. According to the memory criterion, each person awoke in the other's bed with the body of someone else. Which criterion should we take as decisive? Which is fundamental, the memory criterion or the bodily criterion?

The Constitution of Personal Identity

To ask the above questions is to ask what *constitutes* personal identity. What is it that makes me the same person I was yesterday? What makes the author of this book the same person as the baby born to Sam and Belle Olen in

1946? Answers to these questions will allow us to say which criterion is fundamental.

Perhaps the most widely discussed answer to our question comes from John Locke (1632–1704), whose discussion of the topic set the stage for all future discussions. According to Locke, the bodily criterion cannot be fundamental. Since the concept of a person is most importantly the concept of a conscious being who can be held morally and legally responsible for past actions, it is *continuity of consciousness* that constitutes personal identity. The bodily criterion is fundamental for establishing sameness of *animal*, but not sameness of *person.*

Suppose, for instance, that John Badger had been a professional thief. If the person who awoke in Badger's bed could never remember any of Badger's life as his own, but had only Everglade's memories and personality traits, while the man who awoke in Everglade's bed remembered all of Badger's crimes as his own, would we be justified in jailing the man who awoke in Badger's bed while letting the man who awoke in Everglade's go free? Locke would say no. The person who awoke in Badger's bed was not Badger.

If we agree that it is sameness of consciousness that constitutes personal identity, we must then ask what constitutes sameness of consciousness. Some philosophers have felt that it is sameness of *mind,* where the mind is thought of as a continuing nonphysical substance. Although Locke did not deny that minds are nonphysical, he did not believe that sameness of nonphysical substance is the same thing as sameness of consciousness. If we can conceive of persons switching *physical* bodies, we can also conceive of persons switching *nonphysical* ones.

Then what does Locke take to be crucial for personal identity? *Memory.* It is my memory of the events of Jeffrey Olen's life as happening to *me* that makes me the person those events happened to. It is my memory of his experiences as *mine* that makes them mine.

Although Locke's answer seems at first glance a reasonable one, many philosophers have considered it inadequate. One reason for rejecting Locke's answer is that we don't remember everything that happened to us. If I don't remember anything that happened to me during a certain period, does that mean that whoever existed "in" my body then was not me? Hardly.

Another reason for rejecting Locke's answer is that memory is not always accurate. We often sincerely claim to remember things that never happened. There is a difference, then, between *genuine* memory and *apparent* memory. What marks this difference is the *truth* of the memory claim. If what I claim to remember is not true, it cannot be a case of genuine memory.

But that means that memory cannot constitute personal identity. If I claim to remember certain experiences as being my experiences, that does not make them mine, because my claim may be a case of apparent memory. If it is a case of genuine memory, that is because it is true that the remembered experiences are mine. But the memory does not *make* them mine. Rather, the fact that they *are* mine makes it a case of genuine memory. So Locke has the situation backward. But if memory does not constitute personal identity, what does?

Some philosophers have claimed that, regardless of Locke's views, it *must* be sameness of mind, where the mind is thought of as a continuing nonphysical entity. This entity can be thought of as the self. It is what makes us who we are. As long as the same self continues to exist, the same person continues to exist. The major problem with this answer is that it assumes the truth of mind-body dualism, a position we found good reason to reject in the previous chapter. But apart from that, there is another problem.

In one of the most famous passages in the history of philosophy, David Hume (1711–1776) argued that there is no such self—for reasons that have nothing to do with the rejection of dualism. No matter how hard we try, Hume said, we cannot discover such a self. Turning inward and examining our own consciousness, we find only individual experiences—thoughts, recollections, images, and the like. Try as we might, we cannot find a continuing self. In that case, we are justified in believing only that there are *experiences*—not that there is a continuing *experiencer*. Put another way, we have no reason to believe that there is anything persisting through time that underlies or unifies these experiences. There are just the experiences themselves.

But if we accept this view, and still require a continuing nonphysical entity for personal identity, we are forced to the conclusion that there is no such thing as personal identity. We are left, that is, with the position that the idea of a person existing through time is a mere fiction, however useful in daily life. And that is the position that Hume took. Instead of persons, he said, there are merely "bundles of ideas."

Thus, the view that personal identity requires sameness of mind can easily lead to the view that there is no personal identity. Since this conclusion seems manifestly false, we shall have to look elsewhere. But where?

The Primacy of the Bodily Criterion

If neither memory nor sameness of mind constitutes personal identity, perhaps we should accept the view that sameness of *body* does. Perhaps it is really the bodily criterion that is fundamental.

If we reflect on the problem faced by Locke's theory because of the distinction between genuine and apparent memory, it is tempting to accept the primacy of the bodily criterion. Once again, a sincere memory claim may be either genuine memory or apparent memory. How can we tell whether the claim that a previous experience was mine is genuine memory? By determining whether I was in the right place in the right time to have it. And how can we determine that? By the bodily criterion. If my *body* was there, then *I* was there. But that means that the memory criterion must rest on the bodily criterion. Also, accepting the primacy of the bodily criterion gets us around Hume's problem. The self that persists through and has the experiences I call mine is my physical body.

This answer also has the advantage of being in keeping with materialism, a view accepted in the previous chapter. If human beings are purely physical, then persons must also be purely physical, whatever differences there may be between the notion of a person and the notion of a human being. But if persons are purely physical, what makes me the same person I was yesterday is no different in kind from what makes my typewriter the same typewriter it was yesterday. In both cases, we are dealing with a physical object existing through time. In the latter case, as long as we have the same physical materials (allowing for change of ribbon, change of keys, and the like) arranged in the same way, we have the same typewriter. So it is with persons. As long as we have the same physical materials (allowing for such changes as the replacement of cells) arranged in the same way, we have the same person.

Although this answer is a tempting one, it is not entirely satisfactory. Suppose that we could manage a brain transplant from one body to another. If we switched two brains, so that all the memories and personality traits of the persons involved were also switched, wouldn't we conclude that the persons, as well as their brains, had switched bodies? When such operations are performed in science-fiction stories, they are described this way.

But this possibility does not defeat the view that the bodily criterion is fundamental. It just forces us to hold that the bodily criterion must be applied to the brain, rather than the entire body. Personal identity then becomes a matter of brain identity. Same brain, same person. Unfortunately, even with this change, our answer does not seem satisfactory. Locke still seems somehow right. Let us see why.

Badger and Everglade Reconsidered

Returning to our tale of Badger and Everglade, we find that some troubling questions remain. If Mrs. Everglade continues to live with the man who awoke in her bed, might she not be committing adultery? Shouldn't she take in the man who awoke in Badger's bed? And, once again assuming that Badger was a professional thief, would justice really be served by jailing the man who awoke in his bed? However we answer these questions, one thing is certain—the two men would always feel that they had switched bodies. So, probably, would the people who knew them. Furthermore, whenever we read science-fiction stories describing such matters, we invariably accept them as stories of switched bodies. But if we accept the bodily criterion as fundamental, we are accepting the impossible, and the two men in our story, Mrs. Everglade, and their friends are mistaken in their beliefs. How, then, are we to answer our questions?

If we are unsure, it is because such questions become very tricky at this point. Their trickiness seems to rest on two points. First, cases like the Badger-Everglade case do not happen in this world. Although we are prepared to accept them in science-fiction tales, we are totally unprepared to deal with them in real life.

Second, and this is a related point, we need some way of *explaining* such extraordinary occurrences. Unless we know how the memories of Badger and Ev-

MULTIPLE PERSONALITY

In recent years there have been two well-known books, both made into films, each about a woman having several radically distinct personalities— *The Three Faces of Eve* and *Sybil*. Based on actual cases, the books give detailed and fascinating accounts of the lives of the two women.

Each personality had its own memories, its own values, its own behavior patterns, even its own name. At any given time, Eve or Sybil would assume one of these personalities. Whatever happened to her during that time would be remembered as happening only to that personality. When Eve or Sybil assumed another personality, she would either claim not to know of these experiences or claim that they had happened to someone else. The other personalities were thought of and spoken of in the third person.

Unlike science fiction and fantasy cases, the multiple-personality phenomenon is something that happens in the real world. What are we to say about it? On the one hand, we are tempted to say that each woman embodied several persons. Very often their psychiatrists spoke as though that were true. On the other hand, there is an equally strong temptation to say that each woman embodied only one person, somehow split into different personalities. Thus, we sometimes call such cases instances of *split* personality, rather than of *multiple* personality.

The first temptation is due to the fact that each woman seems to embody several distinct streams of consciousness. That is, we are led to view each woman as consisting of several persons by the *memory criterion*. The second temptation is due to the fact that each woman has only one body. That is, we are led to view each woman as one person by the *bodily criterion*. Which criterion should we accept? If there is one body but several streams of consciousness, how many persons are there? When discussing the Badger-Everglade case, we said that our answer must depend on our explanation of what happened. I think that the same thing holds for the Eve and Sybil cases.

How are such cases explained? At present, they are generally given psychoanalytic explanations. A typical psychoanalytic explanation might go like this. All of us have various aspects to our personalities. Sometimes we are forced to repress some of these aspects for one reason or another. Perhaps one of them arouses deep feelings of guilt in us; perhaps we feel we must repress it to win the love of our parents. If the repressed aspect is strong enough, and if we are unwilling to recognize it as being ours, it can cause an inner conflict resulting in a case of split or multiple personality.

This type of explanation seems to require that there is one person managing the various aspects of his or her personality. It makes the phenomenon of multiple personality seem like a strategy unconsciously adopted by *one* person to resolve inner conflict. Thus, if we accept this type of explanation, it seems that we should accept the view that the phenomenon involves one badly fractured person, rather than several persons "in" one body. So when dealing with Eve and Sybil, we should rely on the bodily criterion, not the memory criterion.

erglade came to be reversed, we will be unable to decide the answers to our questions. In the movies, it is assumed that some nonphysical substance travels from one body to another, or that there has been a brain transplant of some sort. On these assumptions, we are of course willing to describe what happens as a change of body. This description seems to follow naturally from such explanations.

What explains what happened to Badger and Everglade? We can rule out change of nonphysical substance, because of what was said in the previous chapter and earlier in this chapter. If we explain what happened as the product of a brain switch, then the bodily criterion applied to the brain allows us to say that Badger and Everglade did awaken in each other's bed, and that Mrs. Everglade would be committing adultery should she live with the man who awoke in her bed.

Are there any other possible explanations? One that comes readily to mind is hypnotism. Suppose, then, that someone had hypnotized Badger and Everglade into believing that each was the other person. In that case, we should not say that there had been a body switch. Badger and Everglade awoke in their own beds, and a wave of the hypnotist's hand could demonstrate that to everyone concerned. Their memory claims are not genuine memories, but apparent ones.

But suppose it was not a case of hypnotism? What then? At this point, many people are stumped. What else could it be? The strong temptation is to say nothing. Without a brain transplant or hypnotism or something of the sort, the case is impossible.

Suppose that we accept this conclusion. If we do, we may say the following: The memory criterion and the bodily criterion cannot really conflict. If the memories are genuine, and not apparent, then whenever I remember certain experiences as being mine, it is possible to establish that the same brain is involved in the original experiences and the memory of them. Consequently, the memory criterion and the bodily criterion are equally fundamental. The memory criterion is fundamental in the sense that consciousness determines what part of the body is central to personal identity. Because sameness of consciousness requires sameness of brain, we ultimately must apply the bodily criterion to the brain. But the bodily criterion is also fundamental, because we assume that some physical object—the brain—must remain the same if the person is to remain the same.

The Memory Criterion Revisited

Although the answer given above is a tidy one, it may still seem unsatisfactory. Perhaps it is a cheap trick just to dismiss the Badger-Everglade case as mere fantasy and then ignore it. After all, if we can meaningfully describe such cases in books and films, don't we have to pay some attention to them? As long as we can imagine situations in which two persons can switch bodies without a brain transplant, don't we need a theory of personal identity to cover them?

Philosophers are divided on this point. Some think that a theory of personal identity has to account only for what can happen in this world, while others think it must account for whatever can happen in any conceivable world. Then again, some do not believe that there is any conceivable world in which two persons could change bodies without a brain switch, while there are others who are not sure that such things are impossible in the actual world.

Without trying to decide the matter, I can make the following suggestion for those who demand a theory of personal identity that does not rely on the assumption that genuine memory is tied to a particular brain.

In the previous chapter, I concluded that functionalism is the theory of mind most likely to be true. To have a mind, I said, is to embody a psychology. I also said that we don't merely move our bodies, but write poetry, caress the cheek of someone we love, and perform all sorts of human actions. I might have expressed this point by saying that we are not just human beings, but persons as well. What makes a human being a person? We are persons because we embody a psychology.

If that is true, then it may also be true that we are the persons we are because of the psychologies we embody. If it is a psychology that makes a human being a person, then it is a particular psychology that makes a particular human being a particular person. Sameness of psychology constitutes sameness of person. In that case, we can agree with this much of Locke's theory—it is continuity of consciousness that constitutes personal identity. But what is continuity of consciousness, if not memory?

An answer to this question is provided by the contemporary British philosopher Anthony Quinton. At any moment, we can isolate a number of mental states belonging to the same momentary consciousness. Right now, for instance, I am simultaneously aware of the sound and sight and feel of my typewriter, plus the feel and taste of my pipe, plus a variety of other things. Such *momentary* consciousnesses belong to a continuous *series.* Each one is linked to the one before it and the one following it by certain similarities and recollections. This series is my own *continuity* of consciousness, my own *stream* of consciousness. It is this stream of consciousness that makes me the same person I was yesterday.

If we accept Quinton's theory, we can then say that the memory criterion, not the bodily criterion, is fundamental. We can also say that, even if in this world continuity of consciousness requires sameness of brain, we can conceive of worlds in which it does not. To show this, let us offer another possible explanation of the Badger-Everglade situation.

Suppose a mad computer scientist has discovered a way to reprogram human beings. Suppose that he has found a way to make us the embodiment of any psychology he likes. Suppose further that he decided to experiment on Badger and Everglade, giving Badger Everglade's psychology and Everglade Badger's and that is why the events of our story occurred. With this explanation and the considerations of the previous paragraphs, we can conclude that Badger and Everglade did change bodies. By performing his experiment, the mad scientist has made it possible for a continuing stream of consciousness to pass from one body to another. He has, in effect, performed a body transplant.

THE SPLIT BRAIN

The human brain is divided into two hemispheres, often referred to as the right brain and the left brain. In right-handed people, the left hemisphere is the dominant one. It bears primary responsibility for the movement of the body. Also, as recent scientific investigation has discovered, it bears primary responsibility for language use as well as analytic and intellectual thought. The right hemisphere, on the other hand, is thought to be the nonverbal, nonanalytic, intuitive or artistic side.

Of course, it would be misguided to make too much of this. For one thing, it has been shown that under certain circumstances each hemisphere can take over the functioning of the other. For another thing, the distinction between the analytic and the artistic is not always easy to draw. If we think, for example, of music with a good deal of formal elegance and precision, such as a Bach fugue, or of the analytic cubism of Picasso and Braque, the distinction seems to break down.

Still, the two hemispheres do engage in a division of mental labor, as numerous experiments have shown. These experiments were performed on people who had undergone a type of surgery for the control of epileptic seizures. In this surgery, the main nerve connections between the two hemispheres (the cerebral commissures) were severed. After surgery, the patients continued to lead normal lives, although in the beginning some found that the right hand occasionally didn't know what the left hand was doing. One man, for example, would push away his dinner plate with one hand while drawing it closer with the other.

But the most interesting effects of the severing of the commissures were found through scientific studies on these patients. For example, it was found that if an object was placed on the left side of the visual field, it could not be identified by name, even if it was a common object. Indeed, the subjects would claim not to have seen it. Still, they were able to pick out the object nonverbally, by pointing, for instance.

Similarly, if shown a dollar sign on the left hand of the visual field and a question mark on the right, the subjects would say that they saw a question mark but draw a dollar sign when asked to draw what they saw. If simultaneously asked to perform one task by a voice from the left and another task by a voice from the right, the subjects would perform both but were unable to say why they had performed the task they had been asked to do from the left side.

What explains such findings? The right brain is connected to the left side of the body, and the left brain to the right. Information from the left eye and ear is carried to the right brain, and information from the right eye and ear is carried to the left brain. Also, the right brain controls the movement of the left side of the body, and the left brain controls the movements of the right side.

Apparently, in normal people the two hemispheres work together so well by passing along information via the cerebral commissures. When the commissures are severed, this cooperation ends. So if an object is on the left side of the visual field, the left brain, responsible for language use, does not have the necessary information about it, and the subject cannot say what was seen. But the right brain, having the information, can cause the subject to identify it nonverbally. As some people have put it, only the right brain sees the object. Therefore, the left brain cannot say what it is, but the right brain can point it out anyway. However we describe the phenomenon, the evidence shows that there is a definite split in both the memory-storage system and in the motor-control center.

Roland Puccetti has argued that the evidence shows much more. These patients have literally two distinct minds, he claims, and if there are two minds, there must be two persons. Further, if each patient is really a combination of two persons, then we must say that even normal people are combinations of two persons. Why? For two reasons.

First, it is unreasonable to assume that the operation *created* two persons where there had been only one. It is more reasonable to assume that the operation breaks off the communication between two persons who existed prior to the operation. Second, each hemisphere is capable of operating without the other. In operations removing one hemisphere, we find that a complete person remains. This suggests that in normal cases we have two persons in constant communication with each other, acting *as if* they were a single unit.

Against this view, it could be said that in the patients studied, it is *as if* there were two different minds, whereas there is really only one. Or, it could be said, the operation divides one mind into two, in which case there is one person having two different minds. The first response assumes that the disconnecting of the hemispheres neither creates two minds nor separates two previously existing ones. The second answer assumes that one person can have two minds.

Puccetti, of course, denies both assumptions. Should we? I think not. I think that we should disagree with Puccetti for two reasons.

First, even in the abnormal cases, the patients generally act as one person. Apart from infrequent early difficulties, such as pushing away and pulling in the dinner plate, there are few if any conflicts between the hemispheres. Similarly, the patients are not aware of dual visual experiences, dual memory systems, or dual motor control systems. Hunger, thirst, feelings, and emotions are shared by both sides. No personality differences are exhibited, as in cases of multiple personality. In short, there is no sense of things happening to, or being controlled by, or being experienced by, one person rather than another. Thus, it seems misleading to talk about two minds, let alone two persons. If this is true in the split-brain cases, it is most certainly wrongheaded to talk of two persons in the same body in normal cases.

Second, to accept Puccetti's view is to raise all sorts of puzzles. Who am I—the right person or the left person? Who is to be praised, blamed, rewarded, or punished? How do we avoid punishing the left person for the right one's crimes? Since none of these questions seems to have a satisfactory answer, it seems best to reject the view that forces them on us.

Before ending this discussion, let me consider one possibility not considered by Puccetti. Suppose that the hemispheres of my brain were transplanted into two different bodies. In that case, do we have one person with two bodies, or two persons? And if we have two, which one is me? Would my parents suddenly have two sons? If I were married, who would be my wife's husband? If I'd committed a crime, who should be jailed?

It seems that we would have to say that there were two persons. Even though they would begin with precisely the same memories, each would from then on acquire new ones. Since there would be two distinct lives, two distinct sets of experiences, two distinct sets of actions, it would be difficult to accept that there would be only one person. As for the other questions, I am at a total loss.

Should we accept Quinton's theory? There seems to be no good reason not to. In fact, there are at least two good reasons for accepting it. First, it seems consistent with a functionalist theory of the mind. Second, it allows us to make sense of science-fiction stories while we continue to believe that in the real world to be the same person we were yesterday is to have the same brain.

LIFE AFTER DEATH

Is it possible for the person to survive the death of the body? Is there a sense in which *we* can continue to live after our bodies have died? Can there be a personal life after death?

According to one popular conception of life after death, at the death of the body the soul leaves the body and travels to a realm known as heaven. Of course, this story must be taken as metaphorical. Does the soul literally leave the body? How? Out of the mouth? Ears? And how does it get to heaven? By turning left at Mars? Moreover, if the soul remains disembodied, how can it perceive anything? What does it use as sense organs? And if all souls remain disembodied, how can one soul recognize another? What is there to recognize?

As these questions might suggest, much of this popular story trades on a confusion. The soul is thought of as a translucent physical substance, much like Casper the ghost, through which other objects can pass as they do through air or water. But if the soul is *really* nonphysical, it can be nothing like that.

If this story is not to be taken literally, is there some version of it that we can admit as a possibility? Is there also the possibility of personal survival through reincarnation as it is often understood—the re-embodiment of the person without memory of the former embodiment?

Materialism and the Disembodied Soul

So far, we have considered both the mind and the body as they relate to personal identity. Have we neglected the soul? It may seem that we have, but philosophers who discuss the mind-body question and personal identity generally use the terms "mind" and "soul" interchangeably. Is the practice legitimate, or is it a confusion?

The practice seems to be thoroughly legitimate. If the soul is thought to be the crucial element of the person, it is difficult to see how it could be anything but the mind. If it is our character traits, personality, thoughts, likes and dislikes, memories, and continuity of experience that makes us the persons we are, then they must belong to the soul. If they are taken to be crucial for one's personal identity, then it seems impossible to separate them from one's soul.

Moreover, people who accept some version of the popular conception of life after death noted above believe in certain continuities between earthly experiences and heavenly ones. In heaven, it is believed, we remember our earthly lives, we recognize friends and relatives, our personalities are like our earthly personalities, and we are judged by God for our actions on earth. But if we believe any of this, we must also believe that the soul cannot be separated from the mind.

If that is the case, it is difficult to accept the continued existence of a disembodied soul. Once we accept some form of materialism, we seem compelled to believe that the soul must be embodied. Does that rule out the possibility of any version of the popular story being true?

Some philosophers think that it does. Suppose, for instance, that the mind-brain identity theory is true. In that case, when the brain dies, so does the mind. Since the mind is the repository of memory and personality traits, it is identical with the soul. So when the brain dies, so does the soul.

This is a powerful argument, and it has convinced a number of people. On the other hand, it has also kept a number of people from accepting materialism of any sort. If it is felt that materialism and life after death are incompatible, and if one is firmly committed to the belief in life after death, then it is natural for one to reject materialism.

Is there a way of reconciling materialism and life after death? I think so.

Although it seems necessary that persons must be embodied, it does not seem necessary that the same person must be embodied by the same body. In our discussion of personal identity, we allowed that Badger and Everglade might have changed bodies, depending on our explanation of the story. Let us try a similar story.

Mary Brown is old and sick. She knows she will die within a couple of weeks. One morning she does die. At the same time, in some other world, a woman wakes up believing herself to be Mary. She looks around to find herself in a totally unfamiliar place. Someone is sitting next to her. This other woman looks exactly like Mary's mother, who died years earlier, and believes herself to be Mary's mother. Certainly, she knows everything about Mary that Mary's mother would know.

Before the woman believing herself to be Mary can speak, she notices some surprising things about herself. She no longer feels old or sick. Her pains are gone, and her mind is as sharp as ever. When she asks where she is, she is told heaven. She is also told that her husband, father, and numerous old friends are waiting to see her. All of them are indistinguishable from the persons they claim to be. Meanwhile, back on earth, Mary Brown is pronounced dead. Is this woman in "heaven" really Mary Brown? How could we possibly explain the phenomenon?

Suppose we put the story in a religious context. Earlier, we saw that one possible explanation of the Badger-Everglade case is that some mad computer scientist had reprogrammed the two so that each embodied the psychology of the other. Suppose we replace the mad scientist with God, and say that God had kept a body in heaven for the purpose of embodying Mary's psychology when she died, and that the person believing herself to be Mary is the new embodiment of Mary's psychology. Would this count as a genuine case of life after death?

If we accept the Badger-Everglade story, appropriately explained, as a case of two persons switching bodies, there seems no reason to deny that Mary has continued to live "in" another body. But even if we are unsure of the Badger-Everglade case, we can approach Mary Brown's this way. What is it that we want to survive after death? Isn't it our memories, our consciousness of self, our personalities, our relations with others? What does it matter whether there is some nonphysical substance that survives? If that substance has no memories of a prior life, does not recognize the soul of others who were important in that earlier life, what comfort could such a continuing existence bring? In what sense would it be the survival of the *person?* How would it be significantly different from the return of the lifeless body to the soil?

If we assume that our story is a genuine case of personal survival of the death of the body, we may wonder about another point. Is it compatible with Christian belief? According to John Hick, a contemporary British philosopher who imagined a similar story, the answer is yes. In I Corinthians 15, Paul writes of the resurrection of the body—not of the physical body, but of some spiritual body. Although one *can* think of this spiritual body as a translucent ghostlike body that leaves the physical body at death, Hick offers another interpretation.

The human being, Hick says, becomes extinct at death. It is only through God's intervention that the spiritual body comes into existence. By the resurrection of this spiritual body, we are to understand a *recreation* or *reconstitution* of the person's body in heaven. But that is precisely what happened in our story.

Thus, a materialist view of the nature of human beings is not incompatible with the Christian view of life after death. Nor, for that matter, is it incompatible with the belief that the spiritual body is nonphysical. If we can make sense of the claim that there might be such things as nonphysical bodies, then there is no reason why a nonphysical body could not embody a psychology. Remember—according to functionalism, an abstract description such as a psychology is independent of any physical description. Just as we can play chess using almost anything as chess pieces, so can a psychology be embodied by almost anything, assuming that it is complex enough. So if there can be nonphysical bodies, there can be nonphysical persons. Of course, nothing said so far assures us that the Christian story—or any other story of life after death—is true. That is another matter, to be considered in Part VII.

Reincarnation

Much of what has been said so far does, however, rule out the possibility of reincarnation as commonly understood. If human beings are purely physical, then there is no nonphysical substance that is the person that can be reincarnated in another earthly body. Moreover, even if there were such a substance, it is difficult to see how its continued existence in another body could count as the reincarnation of a particular person, *if* there is no other continuity between the old life and the new one. Once again, personal survival requires some continuity of consciousness. It is not sameness of *stuff* that constitutes personal identity, but sameness of consciousness. This requirement is often overlooked by believers in reincarnation.

But suppose that there is some continuity of consciousness in reincarnation. Suppose that memories and the rest do continue in the next incarnation, but that they are not easily accessible. Suppose, that is, that the slate is not wiped completely clean, but that what is written on it is hard to recover. In that case, the passage of the soul into a new incarnation would count as personal survival *if* there were such a soul to begin with.

Assuming, again, that there is not, what can we say about the possibility of reincarnation? To conceive of such a possibility, we must conceive of some very complicated reprogramming by God or some mad scientist or whatever. I shall leave it to you to come up with such a story, but I shall say this much. There does not seem to be any good reason to think that any such story is remotely plausible, least of all true.

THE FINAL WORD?

In this chapter we looked at two closely related questions: What constitutes personal identity? And is it possible for a person to survive the death of her own body?

The answer to the second question depended on the first. If we had concluded that the basis of personal identity is sameness of body, then we would have been forced to conclude that life after death is impossible. And there did seem to be good reason to come to these conclusions. How, we asked, could we assure that any memory claim is a case of genuine memory? Our answer was this. In the cases likely to confront us in our daily lives, we must establish some physical continuity between the person who had the original experience and the person who claims to remember it.

But the problem with this answer is that it is too limited. Because we can imagine cases like the Everglade-Badger example, and because our science-fiction tales and religious traditions offer stories of personal continuity without bodily continuity, we can say the following. Regardless of what happens in our daily lives, our concept of a person is a concept of something that does not seem tied to a particular body. Rather, our concept of a person seems to be tied to a particular stream of consciousness. If there is one continuing stream of consciousness over time, then there is one continuing person. Our question, then, was whether we can give a coherent account of continuity of consciousness from one body to another.

The answer was yes. Using the computer analogy of the functionalist, we can explain such continuity in terms of programming. If it is possible to "program" another brain to have the same psychology as the brain I now have, then it is possible for me to change bodies. And if it is possible for me to change bodies, then it is also possible for me to survive the death of my body.

STUDY QUESTIONS

1. What is a person? Why is the concept of a person different from the concept of a human being?
2. What is the memory criterion of personal identity? The body criterion? Which criterion did Locke think to be the decisive one? Why?
3. What is the difference between genuine memory and apparent memory? Why does this distinction create problems for Locke's view of personal identity?
4. Why did Hume deny that there is such a thing as a self? Why did that lead him to say that there is no such thing as personal identity?
5. Some philosophers have claimed that the memory criterion and the bodily criterion cannot conflict. What are their reasons for saying so?
6. How does Quinton explain personal identity? How is his view similar to Locke's? How is it different? Does it avoid the objections that face Locke's view? Why or why not?
7. When discussing life after death, I presented a story in which somebody named Mary Brown awoke in heaven just as somebody named Mary Brown died on earth. Did the same person who died on earth awake in heaven? Give reasons for your answer.
8. Some people have said that multiple personality cases show that there can be more than one person in the same body. Others have claimed that split-brain cases show that all of us have two persons in our bodies. How do you evaluate these claims?

GLOSSARY

Apparent memory. Cases in which a person seems to remember something but does not actually remember it, either because it did not happen or happened in a way significantly different from the way the person remembers it as happening.

Bodily criterion. Method of establishing personal identity. To use the bodily criterion is to determine whether we are dealing with the same person at different times by determining whether we are dealing with the same body at different times.

Continuity of consciousness. Sameness of consciousness from one moment to the next. Two *momentary consciousnesses* are continuous if they are connected in the appropriate way. According to Locke, the appropriate connection is memory. According to Quinton, the connection is supplied by a series of momentary consciousnesses united by similarities and recollection.

Memory criterion. Method of establishing *personal identity.* To use the memory criterion is to determine whether we are dealing with the same person at different times by determining whether the later person remembers the experiences of the earlier person as his own.

Momentary consciousness. A collection of awarenesses occurring at the same time and united in a single awareness. For example, as you eat an orange, your awareness of the taste, smell, looks, and feel of the orange forms a momentary consciousness.

Multiple personality. Psychological disorder in which the patient appears to split into several distinct personalities, as though there were several persons in the same body.

Personal identity. Sameness of the person through time.

Chapter 14

EXISTENTIALIST CONCEPTIONS OF THE PERSON

In the preceding two chapters, we examined the nature of persons from a particular perspective. Our starting point was the human mind and its relation to nature. After settling on a tentative resolution of the issue, we then discussed the nature of the person and its relation to mind and body. Although this perspective has been dominant in Western philosophy from Plato's time to the present, there is another perspective that has been prevalent in the philosophy of continental Europe during much of this century. This perspective is the *existentialist* perspective.

Existentialism is a philosophical movement that is usually dated back to the Danish theologian Søren Kierkegaard (1813–1855). Its roots extend back much further, however. Existentialist themes can be found in the Bible—in the book of Ecclesiastes, for example—and in the writings of St. Augustine (A.D. 354–430) and Blaise Pascal (1623–1662), two noted Catholic thinkers. Although the movement has not exerted great influence on American philosophy, its influence on other aspects of American culture has been enormous. Existentialism has, for example, spawned schools of clinical psychology and psychoanalysis. It has also provided new directions for American theology, both Christian and Jewish, and has colored much of American literature, drama, and art.

It is easy enough to name the most important figures in the movement, but it is difficult to talk about existentialism as a unified philosophy. There is, indeed, much disagreement among the philosophers lumped together as existentialists. Still, there are some things that may be said, guardedly perhaps, about the movement as a whole.

First, existentialist conceptions of the person begin with a phenomenological approach to their subject. That is, they begin with human reality as experienced directly by the human being. Although their writings are highly theoretical, as we shall see, they begin with a sense of what it is *like* to be a human being. Each starts with some aspect of human experience that he takes to be crucial to human reality and develops his theory from there. Thus, there is something decidedly subjective about the existentialist approach. For example, regardless of what the scientist may say about the causes of human behavior, an existentialist like Jean-Paul Sartre will insist on emphasizing human freedom—because we cannot help but experience ourselves as freely choosing beings, fully responsible for our choices. If that is human reality as we must experience it, then a philosophy of human reality cannot deny it.

Second, existentialists view what they do as *ontology*. What is ontology? As existentialists use the word, it means something different from what it does to American philosophers. Outside of existentialist circles, to do ontology is to ask what sorts of entities exist. Are there physical objects and nonphysical ones? Individual objects, like tables and chairs, and abstract objects, like numbers and colors? Actual entities, such as my sister, and possible entities, such as the sister I might have had? Both objects and events?

For an existentialist, ontology is not so much a matter of existence as it is a matter of *being*. Rather than ask what kinds of entities exist, they ask more abstract questions: What is being? What *ways* of being are there? To ask such questions is not to ask whether certain kinds of entities exist. Rather, it is to ask in the first instance what the fundamental ways of being human are: What are the fundamental ways in which I relate to the world? Each of these fundamental ways is taken to be a form of being, where "being" does not mean behaving, but something much deeper than that, a basic structure of human reality. So in giving their ontologies, existentialists are not so much concerned with whether we are physical or nonphysical entities or both, but with what the fundamental structures of human reality are.

Third, existentialist conceptions of the person cannot be divorced from ethics. To talk about fundamental ways of being is to talk about fundamental ways of being with others, and to do that is to raise all sorts of ethical questions.

The above is, unfortunately, highly abstract. It will become clearer, I hope, as we look at particular existentialist conceptions. Since there is no one existentialist view of persons, but just a way of proceeding, in the rest of the chapter I will set two different existentialist conceptions against each other—the first belonging to Martin Buber (1878–1965), the second to Sartre.

BUBER: I AND THOU

When we reflect on our relationships with others, we often think such things as this: He doesn't really love me; he's just using me. She doesn't allow me any freedom; it's as though she thinks she owns me. I always feel as though he's comparing me with others. It seems that I do all the work; I keep giving, and she keeps taking. Sometimes he treats me like an object. She's always trying to change me.

On the other hand, we also think such things as this: When I'm with her, I feel like the only man in the world. He makes me feel as though he loves me for *me*, and not for my body or my money. She loves me just the way I am. He loves me and doesn't demand anything from me. When she says she understands, she really does, as though it were her problem as well as mine.

We are all familiar with such thoughts, and with the relationships that engender them. For Buber, the two types of relationships characterized by these thoughts are the fundamental facts of human reality. To be a person is, in the first place, to relate to the world in one of the above ways. The first way is what Buber calls the *I-It* relationship. The second is what he calls the *I-Thou* relationship.

The difference is marked by whether we treat the other person as an object. If we think of the other as being another object in the world, to be studied, compared with other things, used, we are in the realm of I-It. If, on the other hand, we approach the other as unique, as beyond comparison, as someone who engages us in a fully reciprocal relationship, we are in the realm of I-Thou. As Buber has put it, an It is in the world, while the world is in a Thou. He also says that an It is something we talk *about*, whereas a Thou is something we talk *to*. An It is named, categorized, described, a thing to be experienced. A Thou is addressed, someone who shares a spiritual space Buber calls the *Between*. Is my love as pretty as Sophia Loren? To ask such a question is to be in the realm of I-It. If my love is a Thou to me, such a question cannot arise.

A number of points must be made about this distinction. First, no one can remain in the realm of I-Thou forever. Even with someone we deeply love, there must be alternations between I-Thou and I-It. Second, there is nothing intrinsically wrong with that. We cannot have an I-Thou relationship with everyone we meet, nor can we expect never to think about a loved one in an ordinary sort of way.

Third, it is a mistake to think of the I-Thou relationship as being something extraordinary, that can happen only between lovers and good friends. It can happen at the bank, if we stop thinking of the teller as someone there just to cash a check. It can happen in the classroom, if the teacher fully relates to you, rather than just lectures. It can even happen between you and a sunset or a painting. The important thing is what Buber calls *exclusiveness*. A Thou excludes everything but the Thou. It fills the world, so to speak—it is not an It alongside other Its.

Finally, both I-Thou and I-It *precede* the I. That is, the I grows out of the I-

Thou and I-It relationships. Without these relationships, there is no I. Moreover, the I is different in each case. In the I-Thou relationship, the I is one sort of person. In the I-It, the I is another sort of person. Persons, Buber says, appear only in relationships, and the persons we are depend on the relationships we grow out of.

I can illustrate the passage from I-It to I-Thou with a personal story. When I was an undergraduate, I had a most uncomfortable relationship with a psychology professor. More often than not our interchanges were unfriendly and sarcastic. On the last day of class, he did not present a standard lecture, but instead read selections from a wide variety of people—poets, scientists, artists, and philosophers—all trying to describe the sense of self that had been omitted from the course.

I was very moved by his reading, and after class I approached him at the front of the lecture hall. His glance as I approached was for the first time friendly. I returned his friendly look and said, "I want to thank you for the best hour I've ever spent in this university." He said nothing, but nodded and grasped my shoulder. I grasped his in return, and then left for my next class.

What, then, is Buber's conception of the person? A being that grows out of the I-Thou relationship. It is impossible to place too much stress on the word *grows.* We are not static beings, but beings constantly in a state of *becoming,* insofar as we are in the realm of I-Thou. Although I-It is unavoidable, although it too is a fundamental way of being in the world, true growth comes out of the I-Thou. To paraphrase Buber, we need a Thou to become.

SARTRE: HELL IS OTHER PEOPLE

Whereas Buber's starting point is the sort of encounter that I had with my teacher, Sartre's is a radically different type of experience—the sense of shame before another person's look.

Imagine yourself returning to your dorm late one night. As you walk past the window of your room, you notice your roommate inside, with a boyfriend or girlfriend. Your curiosity gets the better of your decency, so you stop and stare at the two inside. As you do so, you lose yourself in the spectacle inside. All that you are aware of is the scene before your eyes. Suddenly you hear a footstep, and you turn to see someone staring at you. You are no longer master of the situation. You are trapped by the other's look. You have suddenly become aware of being a peeping Tom in the other's eyes, and you are ashamed.

What has happened? Sartre's explanation of being caught in the act is a complex one, requiring a very important distinction. That is the distinction between what he calls *being in-itself* and *being for-itself.* How is this distinction drawn?

Being in-itself is the form of being characterizing *nonhuman* reality. The world out there is, for Sartre, brute matter. Apart from human choices, it is just there. It has no purpose, no independent pattern or meaning, no possibilities whatever. It is my consciousness of this typewriter as a typewriter that makes it a tool for a certain purpose. Otherwise, it is just what it is—a hunk of matter. Its purposes are my purposes. Its possibilities are the possibilities that I give it.

Being for-itself, on the other hand, characterizes a crucial aspect of *human* reality. What I am is always up to me. Unlike being in-itself, I *choose* what I am. I am a philosophy professor by choice. At any moment I can choose to be something else. You are a student by choice. At any moment you can choose to be something else.

In that case, I am not *really* a philosophy professor, in the way that this typewriter is *really* a hunk of matter. The philosophy professor is just a current choice of mine. What I *really* am is my freedom to choose whatever I will be. Unlike the typewriter, I *am* my possibilities. I have no essential nature apart from my freedom.

But aren't some things beyond my choice? Take my past, for instance. I can't choose not to have been born in the United States. I can't choose not to have had the parents who bore me and reared me. Sartre does not deny this, of course, but denies that such things are limitations of my freedom. If I can't choose who my parents will be, I must still choose the *kind* of son I will be to them. If I can't choose not to be thirty-three years old, I must still choose *how* I will be thirty-three. In that sense, my freedom is absolute. Even in prison, my freedom cannot be taken away. I must constantly choose how I will be a prisoner, what my cell and jailer will be to me. What I am still remains up to me.

Thus, as being for-itself, as freedom, I am pure possibility. And it is because this is true that I can imbue the world of the in-itself with possibility. In choosing to write this book, I give this hunk of matter the possibility of typing letters on a page. In choosing myself, I choose the world I will have. There are not really two choices at all, just one. I and my world are chosen together.

Now let us return to your dorm window. As you stare at the people inside, they are objects in your world. They are a spectacle, there only for you. You are pure freedom, they are pure object. But then things are turned around on you. You are suddenly an object in someone else's world. The person staring at you has turned you into a peeping Tom. Your world has been replaced by the other's. Your freedom has vanished. You have experienced what Sartre calls the death of your possibilities. You are a peeping Tom the way my typewriter is a typewriter.

In Sartre's terminology, you have moved from the for-itself to the *for-others*. To be caught by another's look is to experience another aspect of human reality—being for-others. It is to experience yourself as a thing, rather than as freedom. The only way to change this is to reverse the direction of the look. If you can trap the other in your look, you can regain your possibilities. But that is to rob the other of his.

Thus, for Sartre, human relationships are necessarily like the children's game of laying hand above hand, each player trying to get a hand on top and keep it there. Human relations are perpetual conflicts.

In his play *No Exit,* Sartre illustrates this conflict by imagining hell as a living room shared by three people. In this room there is perpetual light. The people

inside can never escape the look of the others. For Sartre, this is the perfect metaphor for death. Death is the ending of all choice, of all possibility. So is the
look.

In one scene, two of the characters attempt to "climb out of hell together" by
making love. One is Garcin, a revolutionary who had fled his country at the first
sign of danger. The other is Estelle, who had killed her child. The third character, Inez, stymies them by her look. She constantly reminds them that she is
watching, constantly asks aloud whether *coward* Garcin can take *baby killer* Estelle. Of course, under those circumstances he cannot. Hell, he concludes at the
end of the play, is other people.

BUBER VERSUS SARTRE

The two fundamental dimensions of human reality according to
Sartre, then, are being for-itself and being for-others. But if we look at this view
from Buber's vantage point, we discover that for-itself and for-others are two
aspects of the I-It relationship. As being for-itself, I experience others as an It.
As being for-others, I experience myself as the other's It. In neither case is there
the true reciprocity of the I-Thou relationship. Instead, there is a constant battle
to be on the dominant side of the look.

Is there any possibility of an I-Thou relationship for Sartre? No. We certainly
seek such a relationship, he realizes, but it is forever beyond us.

Our quest for an I-Thou relationship manifests itself in love. To love, Sartre
says, is to want to be the whole world for the one we love. In other words, the
goal of love is to be the object of a completely different kind of look, which will
not peg us, say, as a peeping Tom, a look that does not view us as an object of
study or comparison. In love, we want to be viewed by another freedom that
does not overwhelm our own. We want a relationship of two for-itselfs. But this
is impossible. My lover cannot help viewing me as an object. Ultimately, my
lover remains the look, always endangering my own freedom. My only recourse
is to trap her in my look. Thus, love must degenerate into conflict. The initial
project of love is shown to be a deception.

Is Sartre right on this point? If we think about it, we are forced to admit that
his view raises many disturbing points of recognition. The feeling that we are
locked in a duel for dominance seems to arise in even the best of relationships.
The feeling that we are loved for ourselves, just as we are, seems difficult if not
impossible to maintain for any length of time.

We enter a party, for example, and find ourselves jealous as we feel ourselves
compared with others who are better looking, wittier, more intelligent, or more
athletic. Or we make love and try to keep our lover so excited that he or she
cannot just watch us. But what are we to make of these feelings? Do they represent a decline from I-Thou to I-It, or do they show that I-Thou is a sham? Has
Sartre missed something crucial?

It seems that he has. Buber's view raises as many points of recognition as

Sartre's. We do seem to enter into I-Thou relationships, and if we are lucky, we seem to enter into them often. There are times when we experience great joy in the gaze of a lover, and that joy does not appear to be based on a deception.

If that joy is not based on a deception, then there is something wrong with Sartre's starting point. That is, there must be something terribly misguided about taking the look as revealing our fundamental ways of being in the world. It must be a mistake to view ourselves as fundamentally for-itselfs and for-others.

The mistake, I think, is this. A for-itself is not a *person,* whereas the I of the I-Thou relationship is. I will support this claim in the following section.

Persons and the For-itself

What is a person? In the previous chapter, I listed six characteristics of persons. Among them were self-consciousness, language, beliefs about one's own psychological states, and an awareness of belonging to a moral community. As Sartre describes the for-itself, it has none of these characteristics. All of them belong to the realm of the for-others.

To see why, let us imagine what a pure for-itself might be like. I say "imagine" because, as Sartre realizes, none of us is a pure for-itself. All of us have been looked at, and to be looked at even once is to be forever "contaminated" by being for-others.

To begin, a pure for-itself could not objectify itself, that is, it could not think about itself, or be capable of self-consciousness. It is only under the look that we can first experience ourselves as objects of thought. But in that case, a pure for-itself could not meet our first condition for being a person.

Further, without self-consciousness, the other conditions cannot be met. If I cannot objectify myself, I cannot, for example, think of my actions as *my* actions. I can be aware of the objects I am acting on, but I cannot be aware that *I* am acting. When I introduced the peeping Tom example, for instance, I said that the peeping Tom was aware only of the spectacle on the other side of the window. It took the look to make the peeping Tom self-aware. But that is to say that self-awareness, including the awareness of oneself as an agent in the world, belongs to the for-others.

Suppose, then, that I cannot view myself as an agent in the world. In that case, I cannot view myself as a member of a moral community. I cannot view myself as responsible for my actions. I cannot view myself as having rights and duties. I cannot even recognize my past actions as *mine.* Indeed, I can think of *nothing* as mine, not even my own body. As a pure for-itself, my body is not mine. My body is not an object for me any more than I am an object for myself. My body is not an instrument of the for-itself; it *is* the for-itself.

This point can be easily illustrated. Take an experienced bowler, for example. As she concentrates on the pins before her, approaches the foul line, and releases the ball, her world is made up solely of the pins and alley markings. She is not aware of her concentration, nor is she aware of her steps or arm movements. Nothing exists for her but the objects of her concentration. It is only later that she thinks of what she did. It is only later that she thinks of her body as being an instrument for bowling, like the ball. (To see what would result if she did think of her body while bowling, try this experiment. The next time you go bowling with someone, ask her what she does with her left arm as she bowls.)

But to think of oneself and one's body that way is to be in the dimension of the for-others. It is to make oneself a thing. So to be a pure for-itself is to be without self-consciousness of any sort, which not only rules out viewing oneself as a member of a moral community, but also rules out having beliefs about one's own beliefs. As a pure for-itself, I could not even recognize my feelings or beliefs as mine, any more than I could recognize my acts or body as mine.

Furthermore, a pure for-itself would be without language. To be a member of a linguistic community is, Sartre says, to resign ourselves to seeing ourselves through eyes other than our own. Language and self-consciousness cannot be separated.

The upshot of the above remarks, then, is this. None of us is or could be a pure for-itself. And if we were, we would not be persons. Thus, the for-itself is only an abstraction, and a very limited one at that. To speak of the for-itself as human reality is to speak of a strangely limited, even ghostlike, reality.

What about the for-others? For Sartre, the for-others is almost a fall from a state of grace. To be aware of my body as an object, to recognize my actions and beliefs as mine, to speak a shared language—all that is to be alienated from myself.

But, as we have seen, it is in the realm of the for-others that we meet the conditions for being a person. That is, we are persons, beings capable of living the rich and shared lives that we do, precisely because of the for-others. But in that case, it is not clear what the for-others alienates us from.

Persons and the I-Thou Relationship

In contrast to what we have just seen about Sartre's views, there is nothing abstract, ghostlike, or limited about the I in the I-Thou relationship. The I who enters into this relationship is not an abstraction, but a full-blooded person.

What accounts for this difference? This: Buber recognizes, as Sartre does not, that we cannot divorce human freedom from our freedom as persons. To share a common way of life, to view ourselves as members of a linguistic and moral community, to reflect on our own inner and active lives as well as the lives of others, is not to fall from a prior state of pure freedom. Rather, it is to be capable of precisely the sort of freedom that is distinctive to persons.

Buber would agree with Sartre that these aspects of human life are due to our interactions with others, but would strongly disagree that they necessitate an alienation of our possibilities. On the contrary, they constitute the starting point of our possibilities. What is characteristic of all that we call human life begins with our relationships with others. To define human reality and freedom apart from these relationships, and then introduce them as if something foreign, is, in this view, thoroughly wrongheaded. Prior to our distinctively human way of life, prior to our lives as persons, there are others.

Perhaps the best way to make this point is to say that persons are essentially *cultural* beings—beings that emerge only within a shared way of life. It is this point that Buber recognizes when he says that the I-Thou precedes the I. If we hang on to this insight, we see that what is fundamental is not being for-itself or being for-others, but what may be called (in keeping with Sartre's way of talking) *being-as-a-person.* We also see that this fundamental way of being is not the source of conflict between ourselves and others, but something made possible by others. In that case, the I-Thou relationship is neither an impossibility nor a deception. Because I am a Thou, I can be an I. Because I am an I, I can be a Thou.

THE FINAL WORD?

In the debate between Buber and Sartre, we have come down on the side of Buber. Does that make Sartre totally wrong?

I think that Sartre provides a useful description of the realm of the I-It. The conflicts he describes, the shame we feel at being caught in the act, our resistance to being pegged or categorized, our attempts to use others to affirm our own power—all of this is recognizable, and all of it is amenable to an analysis in terms of being for-others and being for-itself.

Sartre's error, though, is to take the terms of this analysis as final. To do so is to miss all the enrichment offered by the I-Thou. It is to fail to see that the dynamics of the for-itself and for-others come into play only when we have lapsed from the I-Thou. To find ourselves in the presence of another free being is not a fall. To assert ourselves over such a being is. It is a fall from the I-Thou.

STUDY QUESTIONS
1. What does Buber mean by I-Thou? I-It? Can you think of examples from your own life of each kind of relationship?
2. Buber and Sartre take different kinds of ordinary experiences as their starting points. How do these experiences differ? How do these differences lead to different conceptions of the human being?
3. What does Sartre mean by being in-itself? Being for-itself? Being for-others? Can you think of examples from your own life when you shifted from being for-itself to being for-others? From being for-others to being for-itself?
4. Why does Sartre believe that the I-Thou relationship is impossible? Do you agree? Why or why not?
5. A pure for-itself, I said, would not be a person. How did I support that claim? How did the claim affect my evaluation of Sartre's views? How do you think Sartre would respond?

6. Buber would say that Sartre's descriptions of the for-itself and for-others apply only to the I that emerges from the I-It, not to the I that emerges from the I-Thou. Do you agree that there is a real difference here? Why or why not?

GLOSSARY

Being for-itself. In the philosophy of Sartre, a crucial aspect of human reality. As being for-itself, I am nothing but my freedom to choose what I will be. However others may characterize me, these characterizations at best reflect certain choices of mine, not my real nature. I am not, for example, *really* a philosophy professor. Although I now choose to be one, I can always choose otherwise. Because I can choose otherwise, I am *really* my freedom to do so.

Being for-others. In the philosophy of Sartre, the aspect of human reality we experience when we feel ourselves stripped of our freedom. Other people view me as an object in their world, not as a pure freedom (a *being for-itself*). To them, I am *really*, say, a philosophy professor, and not my freedom to choose otherwise. When I am aware of myself as such an object in their world, I am aware of myself as a being for-others.

Being in-itself. In the philosophy of Sartre, the way of being characteristic of nonhuman reality. Nonhuman objects in the world cannot choose what they will be. They have no possibilities other than those given them by the choices of human beings.

Exclusiveness. In the philosophy of Buber, a characteristic feature of the *I-Thou* relationship. When we are in the realm of I-Thou, we relate to the other (the Thou) as though the other were the whole world to us, not a mere object in the world.

Existentialism. An important movement in European thought, which emphasizes fundamental aspects of human reality based on conceptions of what it is *like* to be a human being.

I-It Relationship. In the philosophy of Buber, one of the two basic ways of being related to the world. In the I-It, we view the other (the It) as a thing to be used, experienced, described, categorized, and so forth.

I-Thou Relationship. In the philosophy of Buber, one of the two basic ways of being related to the world. In the I-Thou, we view the other (the Thou) not as an object, but as a free being. (See *exclusiveness*.)

SELECTIONS

In the following selections, two contemporary philosophers argue on opposite sides of the mind-body issue.

In the first, from the essay "The Nature of Mind," D. M. Armstrong argues in favor of the mind-brain identity theory. What is perhaps most striking about his argument is that he bases his rejection of dualism on what he takes to be the findings of modern science. Science is well on its way to giving a complete physical account of human beings, he claims. Therefore, dualism must be rejected. Also striking is his defense of appealing to science for a solution rather than such fields as religion and literature.

Thus, when Armstrong defends the identity theory, he defends it against another form of materialism rather than against dualism. This other form of materialism is behaviorism—the view that mental states are not events that occur inside of us, but dispositions to behave in certain ways. Armstrong's major argument against that view is that it conflicts with our own experiences. When we have a thought or feel a pain, we are very much aware of something going on inside of us.

In his essay "In Defense of Dualism," Curt Ducasse argues in favor of Descartes' views. What is most striking about this selection are Ducasse's responses to various objections to Descartes' views. Notice how he rejects the claim that there is something mysterious about the alleged interaction between mind and body, and how he argues that this interaction need not violate the principle of conservation of energy.

Notice also how he rejects other forms of dualism—epiphenomenalism, parallelism, and the double-aspect theory. (The double-aspect theory maintains that mental states and physical states are two different aspects of the same substance. According to this view, there is a dualism of mental and physical characteristics, but not of mental and physical substances. The view is most closely associated with the seventeenth-century philosopher Baruch Spinoza.)

D. M. ARMSTRONG

The Nature of Mind

Men have minds, that is to say, they perceive, they have sensations, emotions, beliefs, thoughts, purposes, and desires. What is it to have a mind? What is it to perceive, to feel emotion, to hold a belief, or to have a purpose? In common with many other modern philosophers, I think that the best clue we have to the nature of mind is furnished by the discoveries and hypotheses of modern science concerning the nature of man.

What does modern science have to say about the nature of man? There are, of course, all sorts of disagreements and divergencies in the views of individual scientists. But I think it is true to say that one view is steadily gaining ground, so that it bids fair to become established scientific doctrine. This is the view that we can give a complete account of man *in purely physico-chemical terms*. This view has received a tremendous impetus in the last decade from the new subject of molecular biology, a subject which promises to unravel the physical and chemical mechanisms which lie at the basis of life. Before that time, it received great encouragement from pioneering work in neurophysiology pointing to the likelihood of a purely electro-chemical account of the working of the brain. I think it is fair to say that those scientists who still reject the physico-chemical account of man do so primarily for philosophical, or moral, or religious reasons, and only secondarily, and half-heartedly, for reasons of scientific detail. This is not to say that in the future new evidence and new problems may not come to light which will force science to reconsider the physico-chemical view of man. But at present the drift of scientific thought is clearly set towards the physico-chemical hypothesis. And we have nothing better to go on than the present.

For me, then, and for many philosophers who think like me, the moral is clear. We must try to work out an account of the nature of mind which is compatible with the view that man is nothing but a physico-chemical mechanism.

And in this paper I shall be concerned to do just this: to sketch (in barest outline) what may be called a Materialist or Physicalist account of the mind.

But before doing this I should like to go back and consider a criticism of my position which must inevitably occur to some. What reason have I, it may be asked, for taking my stand on science? Even granting that I am right about what is the currently dominant scientific view of man, why should we concede science a special authority to decide questions about the nature of man? What of the authority of philosophy, or religion, of morality, or even of literature and art? Why do I set the authority of science above all these? Why this 'scientism'?

It seems to me that the answer to this question is very simple. If we consider the search for truth, in all its fields, we find that it is only in science that men versed in their subject can, after investigation that is more or less prolonged, and which may in some cases extend beyond a single human life-time, reach substantial agreement about what is the case. It is only as a result of scientific investigation that we ever seem to reach an intellectual consensus about controversial matters.

In the Epistle Dedicatory to his *De Corpore* Hobbes wrote of William Harvey, the discoverer of the circulation of the blood, that he was 'the only man I know, that conquering envy, hath established a new doctrine in his lifetime'. Before Copernicus, Galileo and Harvey, Hobbes remarks, 'there was nothing certain in natural philosophy.' And, we might add, with the exception of mathematics, there was nothing certain in any other learned discipline.

These remarks of Hobbes are incredibly revealing. They show us what a watershed in the intellectual history of the human race the seventeenth century was. Before that time inquiry proceeded, as it were, in the dark. Men could not hope to see their doctrine *established*, that is to say, accepted by the vast majority of those properly versed in the subject under discussion. There was no intellectual consensus. Since that time, it has become a commonplace to see new doctrines, sometimes of the most far-reaching kind, established to the satisfaction of the learned, often within the lifetime of their first proponents. Science has provided us with a method of deciding disputed questions. This is not to say, of course, that the consensus of those who are learned and competent in a subject cannot be mistaken. Of course such a consensus can be mistaken. Sometimes it has been mistaken. But, granting fallibility, what better authority have we than such a consensus?

Now this is of the utmost importance. For in philosophy, in religion, in such disciplines as literary criticism, in moral questions in so far as they are thought to be matters of truth and falsity, there has been a notable failure to achieve an intellectual consensus about disputed questions among the learned. Must we not then attach a peculiar authority to the discipline that can achieve a consensus? And if it presents us with a certain vision of the nature of man, is this not a powerful reason for accepting that vision?

I will not take up here the deeper question *why* it is that the methods of science have enabled us to achieve an intellectual consensus about so many disputed matters. That question, I think, could receive no brief or uncontroversial answer. I am resting my argument on the simple and uncontroversial fact that, as a result of scientific investigation, such a consensus has been achieved.

It may be replied—it often is replied—that while science is all very well in its own sphere—the sphere of the physical, perhaps—there are matters of fact on which it is not competent to pronounce. And among such matters, it may be claimed, is the question what is the whole nature of man. But I cannot see that this reply has much force. Science has provided us with an island of truths, or, perhaps one should say, a raft of truths, to bear us up on the sea of our disputatious ignorance. There may have to be revisions and refinements, new results may set old findings in a new perspective, but what science has given us will not be altogether superseded. Must we not therefore appeal to these relative certainties for guidance when we come to consider uncertainties elsewhere? Perhaps science cannot help us to decide whether or not there is a God, whether or not human beings have immortal souls, or whether or not the will is free. But if science cannot assist us, what can? I conclude that it is the scientific vision of man, and not the philosophical or religious or artistic or moral vision of man, that is the best clue we have to the nature of man. And it is rational to argue from the best evidence we have.

Having in this way attempted to justify my procedure, I turn back to my subject: the attempt to work out an account of mind, or, if you prefer, of mental process, within the framework of the physico-chemical, or, as we may call it, the Materialist view of man.

Now there is one account of mental process that is at once attractive to any philosopher sympathetic to a Materialist view of man: this is Behaviourism. Formulated originally by a psychologist, J. B. Watson, it attracted widespread interest and considerable support from scientifically oriented philosophers. Traditional philosophy had tended to think of the mind as a rather mysterious inward arena that lay behind, and was responsible for, the outward or physical behaviour of our bodies. Descartes thought of this inner arena as a *spiritual substance,* and it was this conception of the mind as spiritual object that Gilbert Ryle attacked, apparently in the interest of Behaviourism, in his important book *The Concept of Mind.* He ridiculed the Cartesian view as the dogma of 'the ghost in the machine'. The mind was not something behind the behaviour of the body, it was simply part of that physical behaviour. My anger with you is not some modification of a spiritual substance which somehow brings about aggressive behaviour; rather it is the aggressive behaviour itself; my addressing strong words to you, striking you, turning my back on you, and so on. Thought is not an inner process that lies behind, and brings about, the words I speak and write: it is my speaking and writing. The mind is not an inner arena, it is outward act.

It is clear that such a view of mind fits in very well with a completely Materialistic or Physicalist view of man. If there is no need to draw a distinction between mental processes and their expression in physical behaviour, but if instead the mental processes are identified with their so-called 'expressions', then the existence of mind stands in no conflict with the view that man is nothing but a physico-chemical mechanism.

However, the version of Behaviourism that I have just sketched is a very crude version, and its crudity lays it open to obvious objections. One obvious difficulty is that it is our common experience that there can be mental processes going on although there is no behaviour occurring that could possibly be treated as expressions of these processes. A man may be angry, but give no bodily sign; he may think, but say or do nothing at all.

In my view, the most plausible attempt to refine Behaviourism with a view to meeting this objection was made by introducing the notion of *a disposition to behave.* (Dispositions to behave play a particularly important part in Ryle's account of the mind.) Let us consider the general notion of disposition first. Brittleness is a disposition, a disposition possessed by materials like glass. Brittle materials are those which, when subjected to relatively small forces, break or shatter easily. But breaking and shattering easily is not brittleness, rather it is the *manifestation* of brittleness. Brittleness itself is the tendency or liability of the material to break or shatter easily. A piece of glass may never shatter or break throughout its whole history, but it is still the case that it is brittle: it is liable to shatter or break if dropped quite a small way or hit quite lightly. Now a disposition to *behave* is simply a tendency or liability of a person to behave in a certain way under certain circumstances. The brittleness of glass is a disposition that the glass retains throughout its history, but clearly there could also be dispositions that come and go. The dispositions to behave that are of interest to the Behaviourist are for the most part, of this temporary character.

Now how did Ryle and others use the notion of a disposition to behave to meet the obvious objection to Behaviourism that there can be mental processes going on although the subject is engaging in no relevant behaviour? Their strategy was to argue that in such cases, although the subject was not behaving in any relevant way, he or she was *disposed* to behave in some relevant way. The glass does not shatter, but it is still brittle. The man does not behave, but he does have a disposition to behave. We can say he thinks although he does not speak or act because at that time he was disposed to speak or act in a certain way. *If* he had been asked, perhaps, he would have spoken or acted. We can say he is angry although he does not behave angrily, because he is disposed so to behave. *If* only one more word had been addressed to him, he would have burst out. And so on. In this way it was hoped that Behaviourism could be squared with the obvious facts. . . .

But although in this way the Behaviourists did something to deal with the objection that mental processes can occur in the absence of behaviour, it seems clear, now that the shouting and the dust have died, that they did not do enough. When I think, but my thoughts do not issue in any action, it seems as obvious as anything is obvious that there is something actually going on in me which constitutes my thought. It is not simply that I would speak or act if some conditions that are unfulfilled were to be fulfilled. Something is currently going on, in the strongest and most literal sense of 'going on', and this something is my thought. Rylean Behaviourism denies this, and so it is unsatisfactory as a theory of mind. Yet I know of no version of Behaviourism that is more satisfactory. The moral for those of us who wish to take a purely physicalistic view of man is that we must look for some other account of the nature of mind and of mental processes.

But perhaps we need not grieve too deeply about the failure of Behaviourism to produce a satisfactory theory of mind. Behaviourism is a profoundly unnatural account of mental processes. If somebody speaks and acts in certain ways it is natural to speak of this speech and action as the *expression* of his thought. It is not at all natural to speak of his speech and action as identical with his thought. We naturally think of the thought as something quite distinct from the speech and action which, under suitable circumstances, brings the speech and action about. Thoughts are not to be identified with behaviour, we think, they lie behind behaviour. A man's behaviour constitutes the *reason* we have for attributing certain mental processes to him, but the behaviour cannot be identified with the mental processes.

This suggests a very interesting line of thought about the mind. Behaviourism is certainly wrong, but perhaps it is not altogether wrong. Perhaps the Behaviourists are wrong in identifying the mind and mental occurrences with behaviour, but perhaps they are right in thinking that our notion of a mind and of individual mental states is *logically tied to behaviour*. For perhaps what we mean by a mental state is some state of the person which, under suitable circumstances, *brings about* a certain range of behaviour. Perhaps mind can be defined not as behaviour, but rather as the inner *cause* of certain behaviour. Thought is not speech under suitable circumstances, rather it is something within the person which, in suitable circumstances, brings about speech. And, in fact, I believe that this is the true account, or, at any rate, a true first account, of what we mean by a mental state.

How does this line of thought link up with a purely physicalist view of man? The position is, I think, that while it does not make such a physicalist view inevitable, it does make it *possible*. It does not entail, but it is compatible with, a purely physicalist view of man. For if our notion of the mind and mental states is nothing but that of a cause within the person of certain ranges of behaviour, then it becomes a scientific question, and not a question of logical analysis, what in fact the intrinsic nature of that cause is. The cause might be, as Descartes thought it was, a spiritual substance working through the pineal gland to produce the complex bodily behaviour of which men are capable. It might be breath, or specially smooth and mobile atoms dispersed throughout the body; it might be many other things. But in fact the verdict of modern science seems to be that the sole cause of mind-betokening behaviour in man and in the higher animals is the physico-chemical workings of the central nervous system. And so, assuming we have correctly characterised our concept of a mental state as nothing but the cause of certain sorts of behaviour, then we can identify these mental states with purely physical states of the central nervous system.

CURT DUCASSE

In Defense of Dualism

The first point to which attention must be called is that, beyond question, there are things—events, substances, processes, relations, etc.—denominated "material," or "physical," that there are also certain others denominated instead "mental," or "'psychical," and that no thing is denominated both "physical" and "psychical," or both "material" and "mental." Rocks, trees, water, air, animal and human bodies, and the processes occurring among them or within them, are examples of the things called "material" or "physical"; emotions, desires, moods, sensations, cravings, images, thoughts, etc., are examples of the things called "mental" or "psychical."

To question whether the first *really* are physical or the second *really* are psychical would be absurd, as it would be absurd to question whether a certain boy whom his parents named "George" really was George. For just as "George" is a name, so "physical" or "material," and "psychical" or "mental," are names; and a name is essentially a *pointer*, which does point at—designates, indicates, denotes, directs attention to—whatever it actually is employed to point at.

It is necessary, however, to ask what characteristic shared by all the things called "physical" or "material" determined their being all designated by one and the same name; and the same question arises with regard to those denominated instead "psychical" or "mental." Evidently, the characteristic concerned had to be an obvious, not a recondite one, since investigation of the recondite characteristics respectively of physical and of psychical things could begin only *after* one knew which things were the physical and which the psychical ones.

In the case of the things called "physical," the patent characteristic common to and peculiar to them, which determined their being all denoted by one and the same name, was simply that all of them were, or were capable of being, *perceptually public*—the same tree, the same thunderclap, the same wind, the same dog, the same man, etc., can be perceived by every member of a human public suitably located in space and in time. To be material or physical, then, *basically* means to be, or to be capable of being, perceptually public. And the unperceivable, recondite things physicists discover—electrons, protons, etc., and the processes that occur among them—only have title at all to be also called physical *derivatively*—in virtue, namely, (and *only* in virtue) of their being *constituents* of the things that are perceptually public.

On the other hand, the patent characteristic which functioned as a basis for the application of one identical name to all the things called "psychical" or "mental" was their *inherently private* character, attention to them, as distinguished from attention to what they may signify, being accordingly termed "introspection," not "perception."

The events called "psychical," it must be emphasized, are private in a sense radically different from that in which the events occurring inside the body are private. The latter are private only in the sense that visual, tactual, or other exteroceptive perception of them is *difficult*—indeed, even more difficult for the person whose body is concerned than for other persons—such perception of those events being possible, perhaps, only by means of special instruments, or perhaps only by anatomical "introspection"(!), i.e., by opening up the body surgically and looking at the processes going on inside it. The "privacy" of intra-somatic stimuli, including so-called "covert behavior," is thus purely adventitious. The privacy of psychical events, on the other hand, is *inherent and ultimate*.

It is sometimes alleged, of course, that their privacy too is only adventitious. But this allegation rests only on failure to distinguish between being *public* and being *published.* Psychical events can be more or less adequately published. That is, perceptually public forms of behavior correlated with occurrence of them can function as *signs* that they are occurring—but *only* as signs, for correlation is not identity. Indeed, correlation presupposes non-identity.

Psychical events *themselves* are never *public* and never can be made so. That, for example, I *now remember* having dreamed of a Siamese cat last night is something which I can *publish* by means of perceptually public words, spoken or written. Other persons are then *informed of it.* But to be informed *that I remember* having so dreamed is one thing, and to *remember* having so dreamed is altogether another thing, and one *inherently private.* The dreaming itself was not, and the remembering itself is not, a *public* event at all and cannot possibly be made so in the way in which my *statement* that I remember that I so dreamed is or can be made public.

How then does it happen that we have names understood by all for events of inherently private kinds? The answer is, of course, that we heard those names—e.g., "anger," "desire," "remembering," etc.,—uttered by other persons when they perceived us behaving in certain more or less stereotyped manners. But the point crucial here is that although each of us acquires his vocabulary for mental events in this way, the words of it, at the times when they are applied by others to *his* behavior, denote *from him* not primarily or perhaps at all his behavior, but the particular kind of inherently private event, i.e., of physical state, which *he* is experiencing at the time. It is only in "behaviorese," i.e., in the language of dogmatic behaviorism, that for example the word "anger," and the words "anger-behavior," both denote the same event, to wit, the event which ordinary language terms "behaving angrily."

There are several varieties of behaviorism, but they agree in that they attempt to account for the behavior of organisms wholly without invoking a psychical cause for any behavior—that is, wholly by reference to physical, perceptually public causes, present and/or past.

Dogmatic behaviorism is the pious belief that the causes of the behavior of organisms, including human organisms, *are never other than physical.* Nothing but this dogma dictates that even when no physical occurrences are actually found that would account for a given behavior, physical occurrences nevertheless *must* be assumed to have taken place.

Empirical or methodological behaviorism, on the other hand, is not thus fideistic. It is simply *a research program,* perfectly legitimate and often fruitful—the program, namely, of *seeking,* for all behavior, causes consisting of physical, i.e., of perceptually public stimulus events, present and past. Evidently, the fact that one undertakes to search for causes of this kind for all behavior leaves entirely open the possibility that, in many of the innumerable cases where no physical causes adequate to account for the given behavior can in fact be observed, the behavior had a psychical not a physical cause.

For, contrary to what is sometimes alleged, causation of a physical by a psychical event, or of a psychical event by stimulation of a physical sense organ, is not in the least paradoxical. The causality relation—whether defined in terms of regularity of succession, or (preferably) in terms of single antecedent difference—does not presuppose at all that its cause-term and its effect-term both belong to the same ontological category, but only that both of them be *events.*

Moreover, the objection that we cannot understand how a psychical event could cause a physical one (or vice versa) has no basis other than blindness to the fact that the "how" of causation is capable at all of being either mysterious or understood only in cases of *remote* causation, never in cases of *proximate* causation. For the question as to the "how" of causation of a given event by a given other event never has any other sense than *through what intermediary causal steps* does the one cause the other. . . .

Again, the objection to interactionism that causation, in either direction, as between psychical and physical events is precluded by the principle of the conservation of energy (or of energy-matter) is invalid for several reasons.

(A) One reason is that the conservation which that principle asserts is not something known to be true without exception, but is . . . only a defining-postulate of the notion of a *wholly closed* physical world, so that the question whether psycho-physical or physico-psychical causation ever occurs is (but in different words) the question whether the physical world *is* wholly closed. And that question is not answered by dignifying as a "principle" the assumption that the physical world is wholly closed.

(B) Anyway, as C. D. Broad has pointed out, it might be the case that whenever a given amount of energy vanishes from, or emerges in, the physical world at one place, then an equal amount of energy respectively emerges in, or vanishes from, that world at another place.

(C) And thirdly, if "energy" is meant to designate something experimentally measurable, then "energy" is defined in terms of causality, *not* "causality" in terms of transfer of energy. That is, it is not known that *all* causation, or, in particular, causation as between psychical and physical events, involves transfer of energy.

These various objections to interactionism—which, let it be noted, would automatically be objections also to epiphenomenalism—are thus wholly without force.

Epiphenomenalism, however, is open to the charge of being *arbitrary* in asserting that psychical events are always effects of physical events but never themselves cause other psychical events nor cause any physical events. For the experimental evidence we have—that, for instance, decision to raise one's arm causes it to rise under normal circumstances—is of exactly the same form as the experimental evidence we have that, under normal circumstances, burning one's skin causes occurrence of pain.

Psychophysical "parallelism" has widely been adopted as supposedly an alternative escaping the difficulties which—mistakenly, as we have now seen—are alleged to stand in the way of interactionism. "Parallelism," however, is really the name not of a solution but of a problem. For the parallelism itself remains to be accounted for. And the "double-aspect" explanation, or would-be explanation, of it is but an empty figure of speech unless and until the "substance," of which mind and brain are alleged to be two "aspects," has first been shown to exist. And this never yet has been done.

Interactionism, then, as presented in what precedes, though not as presented by Descartes, is a perfectly tenable conception of the relation between some mental events and some brain events, allowing as it does also that some brain events have bodily causes, and that some mental events directly cause some other mental events.

FOR FURTHER READING

There are many anthologies on the market that contain important contributions to the mind-body problem. Two that contain both classical and contemporary readings are Anthony Flew's *Body, Mind, and Death* (New York: Macmillan, 1964) and David M. Rosenthal's *Materialism and the Mind-Body Problem* (Englewood Cliffs: Prentice-Hall, 1971). The emphasis in the Rosenthal volume is on contemporary sources; in the Flew volume, the emphasis is on the classical.

Sidney Hook's *Dimensions of Mind* (New York: Collier, 1961), contains original papers delivered at a 1959 symposium at New York University. Contributors include psychologists and natural scientists, in addition to philosophers. C. V. Borst's *Mind/Brain Identity Theory* (New York: St. Martin's, 1970) brings together many of the most important recent papers on the mind-body problem.

For a short general overview of many of the issues discussed in "Bodies and Minds," see Jerome A. Shaffer's *Philosophy of Mind* (Englewood Cliffs: Prentice-Hall, 1968).

Descartes' central works are *Discourse on the Method*, first published in 1637, and *Meditations on First Philosophy*, first published in 1641. These works are available in a number of editions, including a two-volume collection of Descartes' writings translated by Elizabeth Haldane and G. R. T. Ross, *The Philosophical Works of Descartes* (Cambridge: Cambridge University Press, 1970). This edition includes a series of objections to *Meditations* by many of Descartes' contemporaries, and Descartes' *Replies to the Objections.*

A well-known criticism of Descartes' view, in which his theory is called "the ghost in the machine," can be found in the first chapter ("Descartes' Myth") of Gilbert Ryle's *The Concept of Mind* (New York: Barnes and Noble, 1949).

For a contemporary defense of dualism, see *Moore and Ryle: Two Ontologists* (Iowa City: University of Iowa Press, 1965), by Laird Addis and Douglas Lewis. See also C. J. Ducasse, "Minds, Matter and Bodies," in *Brain and Mind*, edited by J. R. Smythies (New York: Humanities Press, 1965). Ducasse's paper is followed by critical comments by others and by his replies.

The classical account of parallelism is given by Gottfried Wilhelm Leibniz, who claimed that the parallelism of mind and body is due to a pre-established harmony. See *Discourse in Metaphysics* (1686), *The Monadology* (1714) and "Considerations on the Principle of Life, and on Elastic Natures, by the Author of the Pre-established Harmony" (1705). All can be found in *Leibniz: Selections*, edited by Philip D. Weiner (New York: Charles Scribner's Sons, 1951).

Epiphenomenalism is defended by biologist T. H. Huxley in his 1874 essay, "On the Hypothesis That Animals Are Automata and Its History," available in *Collected Essays* (Westport, Conn.: Greenwood Press, 1969), and widely anthologized. See also George Santayana's *The Realm of Essence* (Westport, Conn.: Greenwood Press, 1974), first published in 1928; also C. D. Broad's *The Mind and Its Place in Nature* (New York: Humanities Press, 1925).

A classical materialist account of mind is provided by Thomas Hobbes, a contemporary of Descartes. See his *Leviathan* (Indianapolis and New York: Bobbs-Merrill, 1958), first published in 1651, and his objections to Descartes' *Meditations* in Haldane and Ross, vol. 2.

The mind-brain identity theory has been most vigorously advanced by Australian philosophers D. M. Armstrong and J. J. C. Smart. See Armstrong's *A Materialist Theory of Mind* (New York: Humanities Press, 1968) and Smart's "Sensations and Brain Processes," *Philosophical Review*, LXVIII (1959). Smart's paper is widely anthologized, and can be found in Rosenthal and in Borst.

The principal defenders of functionalism are Jerry A. Fodor and Hilary Putnam. Putnam's papers on the topic can be found in the second volume of his *Philosophical Papers*, titled *Mind, Language and Reality* (New York: Cambridge University Press, 1975). Individual papers can be found in Flew, Hook, Rosenthal, and Borst. See also Chapter 5 of Fodor's *Psychological Explanation* (New York: Random House, 1968). This chapter can also be found in Rosenthal. For a theory of mind similar in many respects to functionalism, see Daniel Dennett's *Brainstorms* (Montgomery, Vt.: Bradford, 1978). Dennett's book is remarkably readable and nontechnical for contemporary philosophy.

Discussions of whether machines can think can be found in Putnam, Dennett, and Hook. Also recommended is an anthology by Alan Ross Anderson, *Minds and Machines* (Englewood Cliffs: Prentice-Hall, 1968). *The Modeling of Mind*, edited by Kenneth Sayre and Frederick Crosson (New York: Clarion, 1968) includes a wide variety of articles on computers and artificial intelligence, written by philosophers and scientists. Although many of the selections are highly technical, they offer interesting accounts of attempts to program computers to perform various functions of the human mind. Keith Gunderson's *Mentality and Machines* (Garden City: Anchor, 1971) is a widely discussed treatment of important topics concerning minds and machines. Some philosophers believe that Aristotle's theory of mind is a precursor to functionalism. His theory can be found in *De Anima*, available in *Introduction to Aristotle*, edited by Richard McKeon (New York: Modern Library, 1947).

Probably the most discussed defense of behaviorism is Ryle's *The Concept of Mind*, which offers a somewhat weak form of behaviorism. Important criticisms of Ryle's view can be found in Putnam and the first two chapters of Fodor. A more thoroughgoing and uncompromising form of behaviorism is defended by Rudolf Carnap in his 1931 essay, "Psychology in Physical Language," which can be found in *Logical Positivism*, edited by A. J. Ayer (New York: The Free Press, 1959). Although rough reading, Carnap's paper is extremely important. A more recent defense of behaviorism can be found in George Pitcher's *A Theory of Perception* (Princeton: Princeton University Press, 1971).

In addition to the theories of Ryle, Carnap, and Pitcher, which are distinctively philosophical forms of behaviorism, we might mention the *psychological* behaviorism associated with such psychologists as B. F. Skinner. Psychological behaviorists attempt to explain behavior without the use of any mentalistic language. Thus, all references to thoughts, feelings, purposes, and the like, are avoided, in favor of publicly observable phenomena. See Skinner's *Science and Human Behavior* (New York: The Free Press, 1953) and *Beyond Freedom and Dignity* (New York: Knopf, 1971). The latter book, written for the popular market, is both readable and provocative. For an entertaining criticism of Skinner, see "Skinner Skinned" in *Brainstorms*.

Locke's views on personal identity are expressed in his *Essay Concerning Human Understanding*, Book II, Chapter 27. First published in 1690 and repeatedly revised by Locke for later editions, it is now available in a number of editions, including one by Dover, published in New York in 1959. Important classical criticisms of Locke can be found in Thomas Reid's *Essays on the Intellectual Powers of Man* (Cambridge: MIT Press, 1969), first published in 1785, and Joseph Butler's "Of Personal Identity," first published in 1736 and available in *The Works of Joseph Butler*, ed. by W. F. Gladstone (London: Oxford University Press, 1896). For a contemporary criticism, see Anthony Flew's "Locke and the Problem of Personal Identity," *Philosophy* 26 (1951).

Hume's views can be found in Book I, Part 4 of *A Treatise of Human Nature* (Oxford:

Clarendon Press, 1973), first published in 1739. Hume is criticized by Terence Penelhum in "Hume on Personal Identity," *Philosophical Review* 64 (1955).

For Quinton's views, see "The Soul," *Journal of Philosophy* 59 (1962).

Recent books of interest include Sydney Shoemaker's *Self-Knowledge and Self-Identity* (Ithaca: Cornell University Press, 1962), P. F. Strawson's *Individuals* (Garden City: Anchor, 1963), Bernard Williams' *Problems of the Self* (Cambridge: Cambridge University Press, 1973) and Joseph Margolis' *Persons and Minds* (Dordrecht, Holland: Reidel, 1978). Both Shoemaker and Williams take the bodily criterion to be fundamental, and Williams claims that the person is identical with its body. Strawson does not deal directly with the problem of personal identity, but presents an influential theory of persons. Margolis views persons and their bodies as distinct entities, the former being embodied by the latter, and criticizes the views of Williams and Strawson. Also, the concluding chapter of Dennett's *Brainstorms* presents a fascinating science-fiction case that explores many puzzles concerning personal identity.

Puccetti's views can be found in "Brain Bisection and Personal Identity," *British Journal for Philosophy of Science* 24 (1973). For criticisms, see Chapter 6 of Margolis.

Both Puccetti and Margolis list extensive bibliographies concerning split-brain patients. Included are Michael Gazzaniga's *The Bisected Brain* (New York: Appleton-Century-Crofts, 1970); a series of papers by J. E. Bogen et al., "The Other Side of the Brain," which appeared in four issues of *Bulletin of the Los Angeles Neurological Society*, from 1969 to 1972; and the following by R. W. Sperry: "Brain Bisection and Consciousness," in *Brain and Conscious Experience* (New York: Springer-Verlag, 1966), edited by J. C. Eccles, and "Hemisphere Deconnection and Unity of Conscious Awareness," *American Psychologist* 23 (1968). For a popular treatment of the differences between the two hemispheres, see Maya Pines' "We Are Left-Brained or Right-Brained," in the magazine section of the New York *Times*, September 9, 1973.

The Eve and Sybil cases can be found in *The Three Faces of Eve* (New York: Popular Library, 1974) by Corbett Thigpen and Henry Cleckley, and *Sybil* (New York: Warner Books, 1974), by Flora R. Schrieber.

Hick's account of life after death appears in "Theology and Verification," *Theology Today* 17 (1960). For another interesting discussion, see C. B. Martin's *Religious Belief* (Ithaca: Cornell University Press, 1959).

A portion of Hick's paper can be found in Flew's *Body, Mind, and Death*. Flew's volume also contains relevant selections by Locke, Hume, and Butler, in addition to other classical philosophers, beginning with Plato, who held that the person is identical with the nonphysical soul. Two other useful anthologies are John Perry's *Personal Identity* (Berkeley: University of California Press, 1970) and Amelie Rorty's *The Identities of Persons* (Berkeley: University of California Press, 1976).

Søren Kierkegaard, the father of existentialism, was an unusually prolific writer. Perhaps the best place to start is *A Kierkegaard Anthology* (New York: Modern Library, 1946), edited by Robert Bretall. This volume contains generous selections from Kierkegaard's most important works. Among these works are *Fear and Trembling*, first published in 1843, and *The Sickness unto Death*, first published in 1849, both of which are available in one volume (Princeton: Princeton University Press, 1954); *Concluding Unscientific Postscript* (Princeton: Princeton University Press, 1941), first published in 1846; *The Concept of Dread* (Princeton: Princeton University Press, 1957), first published in 1844. Of these, only *The Concept of Dread* is not included in the Bretall anthology.

Sartre's major work is *Being and Nothingness* (New York: Citadel, 1956), first published in 1943. This book is extremely difficult. Much more accessible are his plays and novels, which exemplify his philosophy to a remarkable extent. Most important is his play *No Exit*, available in *No Exit and Three Other Plays* (New York: Vintage, 1955). His two best-known novels are *Nausea* (New York: New Directions, 1959) and *The Age of Reason* (New York: Modern Library, 1947). See also *The Philosophy of Jean-Paul Sartre* (New York: Vintage, 1972), an anthology of his works edited by Robert D. Cummings.

Martin Buber's major work is *I and Thou* (New York: Scribner's, 1970), first published in 1922. Also important is *Between Man and Man* (New York: Macmillan, 1965), which brings together shorter writings of Buber's from 1929 to 1938. Included is an extended criticism of Kierkegaard.

Besides Kierkegaard, Sartre, and Buber, there are three other important existentialist philosophers who should not be neglected. Most important is Martin Heidegger, whose *Being and Time* (New York: Harper & Row, 1962) is probably the most influential (and difficult) work of any twentieth-century Continental philosopher. First published in 1927, it left an indelible mark on European philosophy, theology, and, for that matter, the entire European intellectual climate. See also his *Basic Writings* (New York: Harper & Row, 1977), edited by David Farrell Krell.

Karl Jaspers' major work is his three-volume *Philosophy* (Chicago: Chicago University Press, 1969, 1970, 1971), first published in 1932. *Philosophy of Existence* (Philadelphia: University of Pennsylvania Press, 1971), first published in 1938, is shorter and easier to read. Still easier is his *Man in the Modern Age* (Garden City: Doubleday, 1957), first published in 1931. This book is highly nontechnical and presents Jaspers' criticism of twentieth-century society.

Gabriel Marcel's major work is the two-volume *Mystery of Being* (Chicago: Gateway, 1960), first published in 1950. Also important is his *Philosophy of Existentialism* (New York: Citadel Press, 1961), which contains papers written between 1933 and 1946, including a criticism of Sartre's philosophy. Like Sartre, Marcel wrote plays illustrating his philosophy. See *Three Plays* (New York: Hill and Wang, 1965).

Whereas the existentialism of Sartre is vigorously atheistic, that of Marcel, who converted to Catholicism, is decidedly religious. In many respects, his views are similar to those of Buber, who was a Jewish theologian. The philosophies of Heidegger and Jaspers, while not atheistic, are secular, although Jaspers' views are closer to the views of Kierkegaard, a theologian, than are the views of the others.

Other important existentialist theologians include Rudolf Bultmann—deeply influenced by Heidegger—Paul Tillich, and Nicolas Berdyaev. See Bultmann's *Kerygma and Myth* (New York: Harper & Row, 1961), which presents his "demythologized" version of traditional Christian theology and includes essays by five of his critics; Tillich's *Systematic Theology* (Chicago: Chicago University Press, 1967), his major work, and his shorter but equally influential *The Courage to Be* (New Haven: Yale University Press, 1952); and Berdyaev's *The Destiny of Man* (New York: Harper & Row, 1960).

In addition to Kierkegaard, two great nineteenth-century writers are important forerunners of twentieth-century existentialism. Fyodor Dostoevsky, the Russian novelist, deals with existentialist themes in most of his works—most importantly in *Notes from Underground*, contained in *Three Short Novels of Dostoevsky* (Garden City: Doubleday, 1960), and *The Brothers Karamazov* (New York: Modern Library, 1950), considered by many people to be the greatest novel ever written. The German philosopher Friedrich Nietzsche is often considered an atheistic Kierkegaard, although his thought is far more wide-ranging. A passionate and poetic writer who often expressed his views in aphorisms, Nietzsche was a highly readable and quotable thinker and one of the greatest German stylists. Many of his important works, including the towering *Thus Spake*

Zarathustra, can be found in *The Portable Nietzsche* (New York: Viking, 1954) edited by Walter Kaufmann. See also his *Beyond Good and Evil* (New York: Vintage, 1966) and *On the Genealogy of Morals* (New York: Vintage, 1969).

Albert Camus, a twentieth-century novelist, playwright, and essayist, is often thought of as an important existentialist thinker, largely because of his novel *The Stranger* (New York: Vintage, 1946), and his essay *The Myth of Sisyphus* (New York: Vintage, 1955).

Useful anthologies include Walter Kaufmann's *Existentialism from Dostoevsky to Sartre* (Cleveland and New York: World, 1956) and *Four Existentialist Theologians* (Garden City: Anchor, 1958), edited by Will Herberg.

William Barrett's *Irrational Man* (Garden City: Anchor, 1962) is an excellent introduction to existentialism. H. J. Blackham's *Six Existentialist Thinkers* (New York: Harper & Row, 1959) provides short essays on Kierkegaard, Nietzsche, Heidegger, Jaspers, Marcel, and Sartre.

Part V

KNOWLEDGE AND SCIENCE

Chapter 15

WHAT CAN
WE KNOW?

"I know *where* my book is."

"I know *who* rang the bell."

"I know *why* you are angry."

"I know *what* you said to Mary."

"I know *how* to swim."

"I know *John* very well."

"I know *that* twice two is four."

Sentences of the above kind are among the many ways in which we express what we know. Although philosophers have been interested in all of them, their major concern is *knowing-that*.

Why? Primarily because knowing-that is taken to be the most basic sort of knowledge. That is, all of the others are either forms of knowing-that or have knowing-that as a component.

To know *where* my book is, for example, is to know *that* it is on my desk, say. To know *who* rang the bell is to know *that* it was Jane. To know *why* you are angry is to know *that* you are angry because I offended you. To know *what* you said to Mary is to know *that* you said you would cut your philosophy class.

The situation is a bit more complicated with knowing *John* and knowing *how*. The former, called *knowledge by acquaintance*, involves knowing *that* John is witty, generous, or whatever, but it involves something else. To know John is also to be acquainted with him. That is, it is to have met him as well as to know various things about him.

Similarly, knowing *how* to swim involves a certain ability as well as knowing *that* swimming involves certain sorts of movements. Someone who knows that a swimmer is supposed to move his arms and legs in certain ways does not really know how to swim unless he is able to swim. So knowing how is a combination of knowing-that and having a certain skill.

Since knowing-that is the basic form of knowledge, we shall restrict our attention in what follows to it, with the understanding that what is said will apply to the other forms as well.

WHAT IS KNOWLEDGE?

Philosophers represent knowing-that with the formula "*S* knows that *p*," where *S* stands for any person and *p* stands for any statement. Thus, "*S* knows that *p*" represents any such sentence as "John knows that twice two is four," "Mary knows that today is Monday," and "Jane knows that Columbus sailed to America in 1492."

And when they ask what knowledge is, philosophers ask what conditions have to be met whenever it is true to say "*S* knows that *p*." The idea is to find a set of *necessary and sufficient conditions* for knowing-that. To say that the conditions are *necessary* is to say that all of them must be met if someone is to have knowledge. To say that they are *sufficient* is to say that anyone who meets all of them must have knowledge. If all conditions are met, we have knowledge; if any one of them is not met, we don't.

The necessary and sufficient conditions for "*S* is a bachelor," for instance, are the following: *S* is a man, and *S* is not married. The conditions are *necessary* because anyone who either is married or is not a man cannot be a bachelor. A married man, a woman, or a child is not a bachelor. The conditions are *sufficient* because anyone who is a man and is not married is therefore a bachelor.

What, then, are the necessary and sufficient conditions for "*S* knows that *p*"? What, that is, is knowledge?

Justified True Belief

Philosophers have been concerned with giving a definition of knowledge at least as far back as the time of Plato, in the fourth and fifth centuries B.C. Indeed, the definition most accepted today is one that Plato considered at some length in his dialogue *Theaetetus*. What is this definition?

First, to know that *p* is to *believe* that *p*. If I have no conviction at all that *p*, if I have no inclination to accept *p* as true, then I cannot know *p*.

But certainly not *all* of our beliefs count as knowledge. For example, since my name is Jeff, no one can know that my name is Mary, regardless of how strongly one might believe it. Nor can anyone know that Columbus sailed to America in 1066. We can know only what is *true*. Only our true beliefs can count as knowledge.

It is important to emphasize here that truth is a purely *public* and *objective* matter. As we use the term here, there is no such thing as "true for me" and "true for you." Truth is for everybody, and it holds for everybody regardless of whether any one person believes it or not. No matter how many people once believed that the earth was flat, it was never true that the earth *was* flat. Although some people have a tendency to say that it was true for the people before the time of Columbus that the world was flat, and true for us that it is round, such talk is not to be taken literally. Before the time of Columbus, most people believed that the world was flat, but they believed *falsely*. Although they *thought* it true that the world was flat, it was *not* true. The belief that *p* is true does not make *p* true, not even for those who have the belief. If *p* is true, it is true for everybody. If it is false, it is true for no one.

Second, truth is *independent* of anybody's beliefs. A statement may be false even if everyone believes it to be true, and it may be true even if nobody believes it to be true. Indeed, there may be true statements that we will never know to be true. For instance, it may be true that there is life on some far distant planet that we will never reach. Whether we ever find that out does not affect the statement's truth.

Third, even though the world is always changing, there is a sense in which truth is *eternal*. That is, we can always understand a true statement in such a way that it always *was* true and always *will* be true. Take the statement that it is not raining in Stevens Point, Wisconsin. Although it has rained here in the past and will rain here in the future, if we take the statement to be "It is not raining in Stevens Point, Wisconsin, at 11:30 A.M., July 16, 1979," then the statement is eternally true. Thus, true statements cannot become false, nor can false statements become true. And in that case, knowledge cannot become false belief, and false belief cannot become knowledge.

Are *all* of our true beliefs knowledge? It may seem so at first glance, but further thought assures us otherwise. Suppose that I claim to know that Paul Newman is now taking a nap. You would no doubt ask me *how* I know that. If I respond that he looks just like my old college roommate, and my old college roommate always took a nap at this time, you would not take my claim seriously. Even if it were to turn out to be true that Paul Newman is now taking a nap, you would still not grant that I knew it. Why not? Because my reasoning was not *reliable*. Because it was a mere *coincidence* that I was right. Because my true belief was just a *lucky guess*. If, on the other hand, you were in Newman's house and Joanne Woodward were to come from their room where she had seen him napping, the situation would be different. Joanne Woodward's true belief would not be a matter of luck. She would know that her husband was napping.

WHAT IS TRUTH?

In this chapter, I note three important *characteristics* of truth—that it is public, independent of our beliefs, and eternal. What I did not do, however, is say what truth *is*. I did not, that is, say what *makes* a statement true.

Historically, there have been three major answers to this question. All have attracted, and continue to attract, many supporters, even though each has serious problems. Below, I shall discuss each of the three—the correspondence theory of truth, the coherence theory of truth, and the pragmatist theory of truth. But first, a warning: Although philosophers talk of *the* correspondence theory, and *the* coherence theory and *the* pragmatist theory, each phrase covers a number of related theories. So my remarks should be taken as relating to *types* of theories, rather than *individual* theories.

The Correspondence Theory

The *correspondence theory of truth* is generally considered the most intuitive of the three. Certainly, it comes closest to capturing our common-sense conception of truth.

What is it that makes a statement true? The *facts*, we often say. A statement is true if it fits, or agrees with, or *corresponds* to the facts. Otherwise, it is false. Although this answer *seems* right, and although it remains the most favored of the three, nobody has been able to state it in a satisfactory way. Basically, there are two problems.

First, although we talk about facts all the time, nobody is quite clear about what a fact is. We know what it is to see objects and events, but what is it to see a fact? Are there really facts out there in the world, in addition to objects and events? When we see a red ball, do we also see the *fact* that the ball is red? When we face the facts, what are we facing?

That there is a genuine difficulty about the nature of facts can be seen by considering the problems we have in trying to count them. Certainly, we have no difficulty in counting ordinary things in the world, such as tables and chairs, books and pencils, people and dogs, hairs and blades of grass. Unfortunately, matters are not so easy when it comes to facts.

If, for example, John is a bachelor, then he's an unmarried man. How many facts do we have here? One? Or is the fact that he's a bachelor distinct from the fact that he's an unmarried man? Similarly, if he's a bachelor, then it's true that he's either a bachelor or an elephant, a bachelor or a kangaroo, a bachelor or the Wizard of Oz, a bachelor or the square root of two, and so on indefinitely. How many facts is that? One, or an infinite number?

What about *negative* facts? It is true that I'm not an elephant, not a kangaroo, not the Wizard of Oz, and not the square root of two. Are all these things negative facts about me? If so, then we are off on another infinite list. Even if we are not bothered by that, do we really want to accept the existence of negative facts? Isn't there something suspicious about such entities?

Faced with these problems some philosophers, myself included, are inclined to think of facts as being nothing other than true statements. Many of the things we say about facts support this view. When we say that a book contains many facts, for example, we seem to mean that it contains many true statements. But if this view is correct, then facts cannot *make* statements true—they *are* the true statements in themselves.

The second difficulty with the correspondence theory concerns the nature of correspondence. How *does* a statement correspond to the facts? The best-known answer comes from Ludwig Wittgenstein (1889–1951), who thought of statements as *pictures* of facts. According to Wittgenstein, there is a perfect language into which all statements can be translated. Each word in the perfect language corresponds to a basic element in the world, and the arrangement of the words in any true statement corresponds to the arrangements of the elements that make up the fact corresponding to the statement. In that way, a statement pictures a fact the way a portrait pictures a person. A word stands to an element the way an area of a portrait stands to a part of the body. And just as the appropriate areas of a portrait are arranged in the same way that the person's eyes, nose, and mouth are arranged, so are the words arranged in the same way that the elements of the fact are.

Few philosophers still accept this account of correspondence, however. Apart from the difficulties surrounding the notion of a fact, philosophers are suspicious of the notion of a perfect language that can picture reality.

The Coherence Theory

According to the correspondence theory, statements are made true by something other than statements—facts. According to the *coherence theory*, statements are made true by *other statements*.

How does this work? The statements we believe form a vast, interrelated system. What makes a statement true is the way it fits into that system. If it fits into the system in the appropriate way, if it *coheres* with the entire system, it is true. If not, it is false.

Although this theory has little initial plausibility, there is at least one good reason why some philosophers have been drawn to it. As we shall see in the next chapter, coherence is our only way of determining whether a statement is true. That is, coherence is our ultimate test of truth. Why, for example, do I consider it true that I am sitting at this typewriter? Because this belief fits in with my other beliefs better than any of the alternatives—that I am now hallucinating, for instance. So if coherence is my test for truth, the argument goes, then it is reasonable to suppose that it is what makes for truth.

The chief difficulty with the coherence theory is that it cannot rule out the possibility that the same statement may be both true and false. Suppose that there are two entirely different belief systems, both completely coherent. According to the coherence theory, we then have two systems of true statements. But suppose the systems conflict. Suppose, that is, that each system denies what belongs to the other. In that case, all truth will be relative. We will have to distinguish "true for me" and "true for you." Since that is unacceptable, the coherence theory is also unacceptable.

The Pragmatist Theory

The *pragmatist theory of truth* is similar to the coherence theory, but manages to avoid the fatal objection noted above. Let us see how.

According to Charles Sanders Peirce (1839–1914), the founder of the American philosophical movement known as *pragmatism*, the purpose of our beliefs is to predict future experience. If our beliefs lead us to unwelcome surprises, they are rejected. If they prevent unwelcome surprises, they are kept. Suppose, for example, that I believe the door to my office is open. If I attempt to walk through the door and get a pain in my nose, I reject the belief. If I manage to get through the door without such an unwelcome surprise, I keep the belief.

Once we think of beliefs in this way, we can view the search for knowledge as a process aiming toward an ideal end point, where we will reach the best belief system for predicting experience. All and only those statements that belong to this final system are true. What makes a statement true, then, is that it belongs to this final system.

Thus, coherence plays an important role in the pragmatist theory. Ultimately, a statement is true because it coheres with a certain system of beliefs. But not just any system will do. For Peirce, there is only one best system, and from the beginning of our search for knowledge we have been approaching it. Thus, there is no possibility of there being two incompatible but true systems. Truth remains objective.

Although Peirce's view has recently been attracting much attention among American philosophers, many remain dissatisfied with it. I will mention two reasons for this dissatisfaction.

First, Peirce's theory assumes that the history of science moves in a straight line, with each successive theory taking us a step closer to the truth. Some philosophers have argued that this is mistaken. They claim that theories replace one another, but do not get us any closer to any final truth. Although I think that Peirce is right on this point, the issue is too complicated to pursue here. We will, however, pursue it in Chapter 17.

The second objection may be decisive, however. Many philosophers think that it is possible that even our final theories about the world may be mistaken. No matter how useful our final theories may be, no matter how well our final system of beliefs may cohere, it is still possible that the world is not the way we believe it is. If the world is independent of us, then it is possible that even our best theories may not be true.

This objection, of course, appeals to the correspondence theory. It assumes that there is something about the world that makes statements true, even if we can never be certain what it is. That is a powerful part of our ordinary conception of truth, and it remains to be seen whether the pragmatist theory can debunk it.

The point of this example is that a true belief cannot be knowledge unless we have good *grounds*, or *evidence*, or strong *reasons* for believing it. That is, our belief must be *justified* enough to *warrant* our holding it. Put another way, there are certain *ways* that we can come to have knowledge, and if we arrive at our beliefs in some other way, we do not come to have knowledge. True beliefs due to superstition, hunches, guesses, faulty reasoning, and the like, do not count as knowledge.

Thus, we must introduce a third condition for knowledge. Knowledge must be *justified* true belief. To say that S knows that p, then, is to say that the following conditions hold:

1. *S* believes that *p*.
2. *p* is true.
3. *S* is completely justified in believing that *p*.

Knowledge and Certainty

To say that knowledge is justified true belief is not yet enough to tell us what we know and what we don't know. Two of our conditions are somewhat vague.

Take the belief condition. How strong must our beliefs be? How *confident* must we be that we are right? If you are taking an exam and have strong doubts about your answers, do these doubts rule out your answers as instances of knowledge?

Consider also the justification condition. How *justified* must you be before you are completely justified? How strong must your reasons be? How good must your evidence be? Must it be so good that it rules out *any* possibility of error? Or only any *reasonable* possibility of error? If the latter, what counts as a reasonable possibility of error? If you have never seen your birth certificate, how do you know that your name is really what you think it is? Couldn't your parents have changed their minds after the birth certificate was signed? That is what happened to my father, for example, who did not know his real name until he began school and the teacher called him "Samuel." Perhaps you still do not know yours. Is the possibility I just raised a reasonable one? Must you check your birth certificate before you can know your name?

The questions of the preceding two paragraphs involve the relationship between knowledge and *certainty*. But it is important to notice that two distinct types of certainty are involved—*psychological* certainty and *epistemic* (after the Greek word *episteme*, meaning "knowledge") certainty. The questions regarding the belief condition involve *psychological* certainty. The degree of psychological certainty a belief has is a fact about the *believer*, not the statement believed. It is a matter of how confident the believer is, of how much the believer is willing to risk or bet on the basis of the belief. The questions regarding the justification condition involve *epistemic* certainty. The degree of epistemic certainty a belief has is a fact about the *statement* believed. It is a matter of how probable the statement is, given the evidence. Although the degree of psychological certainty would always match the degree of epistemic certainty in the case of a perfectly rational being, the two types of certainty often differ—which should come as no surprise, given that none of us is a perfectly rational being. To show how they can differ, let us consider two examples.

Consider first the statement that twice two is four. No statement seems more epistemically certain. Many people think it impossible that the statement could be false. Indeed, in standard systems of probability, the statement is given the probability of 1. (A probability of 1 means that the statement cannot be false; a probability of 0, that it cannot be true; a probability of .5, that it has an equal chance of being true or false; a probability of .25, that it has a one out of four chance of being true; and so on). Still, there are children, for example, who have very little psychological certainty about this statement. Having just learned arithmetic, they may hem and haw before answering the question if put by their teacher. They may even withdraw their answer if the teacher sternly asks if they are sure. The *statement* is certain, but *they* are not.

Or consider any statement to the effect that a particular team will win the World Series. The degree of epistemic certainty of such statements will change as the baseball season progresses. In the beginning of the season, the probability is fairly low even for the best teams, since injuries, bad trades, unexpected slumps, and so forth, can keep them from even getting into the Series. Still, there are people who feel absolutely certain, even before the season has begun, that their team will win the World Series, and are willing to risk a good deal of money on that belief.

Having distinguished the two types of certainty, we can now ask two questions. How much psychological certainty is required for knowledge? How much epistemic certainty is required?

Strong and Weak Knowledge

Some philosophers have felt that the word "know" has two senses— a *strong* sense and a *weak* sense. The difference between the two is marked by the degree of psychological and epistemic certainty required. To have knowledge in the strong sense is to be absolutely confident that you are right, so confident that you believe that nothing can turn up to prove you wrong. Not only that, but your justification must be so strong that you are completely justified in being so confident. To have knowledge in the weak sense, on the other hand, is to have less justification. Although you are fairly confident that you are right, your evidence is such that you are not justified in ruling out the possibility of further evidence that might prove you wrong.

Suppose, for example, that a friend asks you if you know where your car is. If you had left it in the parking lot an hour or so ago, you would no doubt say that you know that it is in the parking lot. But suppose that the friend asks you if you *really* know where it is. At that point, you would probably consider a number of possibilities, that it might have been stolen, for instance, and then admit that perhaps you don't *really* know that it's in the lot. Indeed, the fact that your friend asked if you *really* know might get you to think that your friend knows something that you don't. You might even stop whatever you're doing and go outside to check.

What happened in the above story, some think, is this. The word "really" signaled a shift from the weak to the strong sense of "know." Given your memory of parking the car in the lot and the absence of any reason to believe that it had been moved, you were willing to claim that you knew that it was in the lot. But when asked if you *really* knew that, you were no longer willing to make the claim. Although your evidence was good enough for knowledge in the weak sense, it was not good enough for knowledge in the strong sense. Thus, if it turns out after checking that your car is where you left it, you had a justified true belief that it was there, and you did have knowledge in the weak sense. But, given the limited strength of your justification, you did not have it in the strong sense.

If we accept the distinction between strong and weak knowledge, we can easily see that most of the things we ordinarily claim to know cannot count as knowledge in the strong sense. Consider most of the things you have learned in school. In history, for example, you learned that Columbus sailed to America in 1492. Are you completely justified in believing that *nothing* can turn up to prove that false? Hardly. Although it is admittedly unlikely, it is possible that the man who commanded the Nina, Pinta, and Santa Maria was not Columbus, but some other man who claimed to be Columbus. It is also possible that some documents may someday be discovered that will prove that to us. Since nothing that you now know rules out these possibilities, you cannot know in the strong sense that Columbus sailed to America in 1492.

Similarly, you may have learned that the speed of light is constant, approximately 186,000 miles per second. Are you completely justified in believing that nothing can turn up to prove that false? Once again, you are not. Just as the theories of Isaac Newton were overturned by those of Albert Einstein, so may Einstein's theories, including the claim that the speed of light is constant, be overturned by future theories.

Furthermore, we have already seen that you may not have strong knowledge of your own name, or of the location of your car, bicycle, or motorcycle. Similar considerations would also show that you do not know the following in the strong sense: that what you read in today's newspaper is true, that you were eating real meat the last time you thought you were, that your body has all the internal organs you think it has, and that oranges are a kind of fruit.

At this point, you may well be wondering how far we may extend this list. Is there *anything* we can know in the strong sense, or is all our knowledge of the weak variety? Can you know in the strong sense that you are now reading this book? That you have a nose? That you are now in the city you think you're in? That twice two is four? Or is there, for each statement, some evidence that could conceivably turn up to cause you to change your mind? We will begin discussing this issue in the next section. But first, there is another matter that we should briefly consider.

Some philosophers disagree with the claim that there are two senses of "knowledge." They would interpret the conversation about the location of your car this way. When you first said that you knew where your car was, you were speaking *loosely*, as when you say, for example, that the state of Kansas is flat. The state of Kansas is not *really* flat, of course. It does have some slopes, and you would admit that if someone were to press you on the point. Similarly, when your friend asked you if you *really* knew where your car was, you admitted that you didn't. Just as Kansas is not literally flat, so you did not literally know. There is, then, no weak sense of "know." Rather, we just use the word loosely from time to time, just as we use the word "flat" loosely.

Does the word "know" have both a strong and weak sense? It seems to me that it is impossible to decide the question. Whether or not our ordinary use of the word is a matter of loose speaking cannot be settled. The facts seem to support both sides of the controversy equally. Moreover, I don't think that the dispute is an important one. What *is* important is this: What can we *really* know? Whether we take this question to mean "What can we know in the strong sense?" or "What can we know, period?" is secondary. Put another way, our major concern should be what we can *know for certain*. It is to this question that we now turn.

A GENEROUS VIEW OF KNOWLEDGE

The terms "strong knowledge" and "weak knowledge" were introduced by the contemporary American philosopher Norman Malcolm. According to Malcolm, we can know all sorts of things for certain. We know, for instance, the simple truths of arithmetic, such as twice two is four. But we can also know for certain a number of other things. Suppose that, after considering the possibility that your car might have been stolen, you go outside to check. You see a car that looks exactly like yours in the parking space in which you left your car. You are satisfied, but your friend is not. "Suppose it's another car that looks like yours," he says. To satisfy him, you unlock the door with your key, show him your owner's card in the glove compartment and even check the car's serial number. Once you have done all that, you have done everything you can do to prove that it's your car. You have, in effect, made *sure* that it is yours. You now, according to Malcolm, know it for certain. It no longer makes sense to ask for further assurance.

Or suppose that you are looking for a ten-dollar bill you believe you left in a dresser drawer. You open the drawer, and it appears to be empty. You run your hand around it, remove it from the dresser, and turn it upside down. Nothing falls out. At that point you are perfectly justified in believing that nothing can turn up to prove that the bill is in the drawer. You know for certain that it is not. You also know for certain that you have teeth, that you are reading this book, that you feel pains, that you feel a chair beneath you, that you are now bored or interested, that you had breakfast this morning, and so on. There is such a thing as making sure, and once you *have* made sure, your knowledge is certain.

SKEPTICISM

Other philosophers have argued that we know little or nothing for certain, because we are rarely, if ever, justified in believing that nothing can turn up to prove us wrong. This view is called *skepticism*. A skeptic with regard to any statement is someone who denies that it is or can be known. A total skeptic denies that we can know anything.

One famous skeptical argument comes from René Descartes (1596–1650). My senses have often deceived me, the argument goes. Sometimes what I thought was one thing was really something else. Sometimes I have even believed that I saw or heard something when there was nothing there to see or hear. Sometimes I have thought all sorts of things were happening to me only to awake to find that I had been dreaming.

If my senses *sometimes* deceive me, then I can never be totally sure that they are not deceiving me now. Even if I do everything that Malcolm counts as making sure, it is still possible that I am dreaming. Indeed, it is even possible that there is no external world at all. Perhaps everything I take to exist out there is really in my own mind. Suppose, for example, that there is no God, but some evil genius instead, who does nothing but give me false beliefs. Suppose that this deceiver even deceives me when I do simple arithmetic, and that twice two is not really four.

All of this is no doubt unlikely, but we cannot rule out the possibility, however slight, that it is true. Nor, to update Descartes' tale of the evil genius, can we totally rule out this possibility. Suppose that one night in my sleep I was kidnapped by a mad scientist, who inserted electrodes in my brain and is now causing all the experiences I am now having in my mind. Although I think I am sitting at my typewriter, I am really lying unconscious on some laboratory table. Unlikely, but not impossible.

Let us also consider a contemporary skeptical argument. According to this argument, any beliefs we now have may be overturned by the advance of science—from the "truths" of arithmetic to our beliefs about the existence of tables, chairs, and pains.

We shall begin with mathematics. In high school, you no doubt learned a system of geometry known as Euclidean geometry, after its founder, Euclid (c. 300 B.C.). According to Euclidean geometry, parallel lines can never meet. Until the nineteenth century, it was believed that this principle could not be denied without involving geometry in all sorts of contradictions. It would have been generally accepted that it was known for certain that parallel lines could never meet. This was a truth of mathematics as undeniable as twice two is four. Even now, most of you reading this continue to believe that.

Still, in the nineteenth century, alternative systems of geometry were devised. Although no one believed that they applied to actual space—only Euclidean geometry described the world in which we live, it was thought—these systems were perfectly consistent. Then, when Einstein introduced the general theory of relativity in 1916, matters changed. According to Einstein, real space does not conform to Euclidean geometry. Instead, it conforms to one of the geometries devised in the nineteenth century—Riemannian geometry, after its deviser, Georg Riemann (1826–1866). One of the most startling aspects of Einstein's theory is the claim that parallel lines will eventually meet if extended far enough. Since the theory was introduced, it has been supported by a good deal of evidence, and scientists now believe that Euclidean geometry does not give a true description of actual space.

There are many ways of interpreting this development. One way is this. Mathematics is part of natural science. No matter how certain any "truth" of mathematics may be, new scientific theories can overturn it, just as they may overturn any other part of natural science. In that case, we cannot be completely justified in believing that nothing will turn up to prove it wrong. No matter how high our psychological certainty, the required epistemic certainty is lacking.

What about such beliefs as the belief that this is my car, after I have done everything that Malcolm calls making sure? Can science ever overturn that belief?

Contemporary skeptics think that it can. As we shall see in Chapter 19, the world as described by the physicist is a world far different from the world as we experience it. The physicist's world is made up of *microtheoretical* entities, such as electrons and quarks, which are entirely unlike tables and chairs and cars. Saving the details of the physicist's world for later, I will say for now that this world lacks many of the qualities we experience as a matter of course. Whereas the experienced world has *sensed qualities*, such as color and taste and smell, the physicist's world has only *physical magnitudes*, such as energy and wavelength. Our world is a world of experience; theirs, a world of equations.

Some philosophers have claimed that the physicist's world is thoroughly incompatible with our own. If there are tables and chairs and cars, there cannot be electrons and quarks. If there are electrons and quarks, there cannot be tables and chairs and cars. Some have even gone further and claimed that there is better reason to believe that there are electrons than there is to believe that there are cars. Therefore, there are no cars. If there are no cars, it is false to say of anything that it is my car—because there are none. It is like saying of something that it is a witch, or a ghost, or a gremlin.

I am not concerned at this point to decide whether this view is right. That will come later. The point, for now, is this. A skeptic could very well argue that the fact that we can even discuss this issue says something about knowledge. As we learn more about the world through scientific investigation, any belief we now have may be discarded. Certainly, any belief can at least be *considered* for discarding. Scientific revolutions such as Einstein's show us that no concepts are fixed. They can be widened, narrowed, shown to apply in ways we never thought possible, or even shown to have no application whatever. Any concept may go the way of *parallel line* or, like *witch*, be discarded. But in that case, we can never be completely justified in believing that any belief cannot be disproved. So certain knowledge is impossible.

Evaluating Skeptical Arguments

Many of the skeptic's arguments turn on issues that we will discuss in later chapters. Whether mathematics is a part of natural science or whether it is a form of knowledge different from scientific knowledge is a question to which we'll return in the next chapter. Similarly, whether scientific theories provide knowledge of the world that can overturn all of our ordinary beliefs will also be discussed.

Let us suppose for the moment, however, that the skeptic is right about these matters. Let us suppose, that is, that any belief we now hold is revisable. Does that mean that we cannot have certain knowledge of anything? Many philosophers have argued that the skeptic places unreasonable demands on what is to count as knowledge. According to these critics, the skeptic requires an *absolute* certainty that is *in principle* impossible, and to require such certainty is to severely distort our ordinary conceptions of knowledge and certainty.

According to these ordinary conceptions, the argument goes, I *can* make certain that my drawer is empty, for example. When I have done everything that is reasonably required to make sure that it is, when I have run my hand around it and turned it upside down, then I am certain enough. That is what we *mean* by "certain." And once we have achieved that level of certainty, we are justified in believing that nothing can count as evidence against the belief. To raise the absurd possibility of some evil genius, or to invoke some remote possibility in the far reaches of science misses the point. Certain knowledge does not require that it is *absolutely impossible* that I am mistaken.

The force of this argument can be illustrated by the following anecdote. In the early 1960s, the comic Mel Brooks appeared on the old Steve Allen television show. He dialed a phone booth and the phone was answered by a man who'd obviously had too much to drink. Brooks told the man that he had left a suit of clothes in the booth and asked the man to look for it. There followed the sound of shuffling about for a few minutes, after which the man reported that he couldn't find it. Brooks replied that he was sure the suit was there. The man said he'd look again. There followed more shuffling about. When the man reported once again that the suit was not there, Brooks told him that the suit was blue. Armed with this new information, the man searched the phone booth again. The next time he picked up the receiver, Brooks told him that the suit had a red cape. Again the man looked, and again he reported no success. Finally, Brooks added the information that the suit had a big *S* on the front. And for the last time, the man searched the phone booth for the suit. The studio audience, of course, laughed uproariously throughout the entire business. Although much of the humor came from the fact that the man did not realize that he was searching for Superman's suit, the greater part came from the fact that you can only spend so much time searching a phone booth for something as large as a suit of clothes. Eventually you reach a point at which no new information about the color justifies further checking. The butt of Brooks's prank had made certain that the suit was not in the phone booth long before he stopped looking. Clearly, the possibility of an evil genius did not warrant further searching.

The antiskeptic's point can also be illustrated by another example. Suppose you call a friend to borrow a book you need for an assignment due tomorrow. Suppose further that he tells you that he doesn't know for certain where the book is. You ask him to look for it and then call a number of other friends, none of whom has a copy. An hour later, almost in a state of panic, you call your friend back. Once again he tells you he's not certain where it is. You run to the library to see if there's a copy on the shelves, but the library is closed. Finally, you decide to search your friend's apartment yourself, although you fear it may be too late to complete the assignment in time. When you arrive at your friend's apartment you see the book on the desk at which he is sitting.

"You found it!" you exclaim in relief.

"Not really," he says. "I thought I was seeing it all along, but I wasn't certain. After all, my senses have deceived me in the past. Besides, can we ever *really* know that books exist?"

At this point, you would no doubt be tempted to burn all of Descartes' books—which is precisely the point of the antiskeptic's argument. The possibilities entertained by the skeptic are entirely unworthy of consideration. To take them seriously would be to distort our ordinary conceptions of knowledge and certainty beyond recognition.

Is the antiskeptic right? I think he is clearly right about this much: The possibilities considered by the skeptic are not the possibilities we consider in our ordinary life, in which case your hypothetical friend was certainly misleading you in our illustration. Put another way, your friend had all the certainty you required, and it was perverse of him to tell you he didn't know for certain where the book was.

That does not mean that the skeptic is wrong, though. Nor does it mean that skeptics distort our ordinary conceptions when they deny that we can know anything for certain. It just means, I think, that skepticism is a highly unusual attitude to adopt in ordinary life—so unusual that unless we know in advance that someone is a skeptic, we tend to interpret his remarks in a nonskeptical way. Whatever doubts your friend had about the location of his book are not the doubts you expected him to have. Since he was well aware of that, he was being perverse. But his perverseness is rather like that of the person who denies that there is any juice in the ice box because the house has a refrigerator instead of an ice box. Such people are exasperating, but not necessarily wrong.

THE FINAL WORD?

Are the skeptic's doubts unreasonable? The answer to this question is a complicated one, because reasonable doubts in one context may be thoroughly unreasonable in another. The matter depends on one's purposes, and what is at stake.

In the ordinary affairs of everyday life, it does seem unreasonable to worry about evil geniuses and the far reaches of science. The ordinary methods of making sure, emphasized by Malcolm, have proved to be highly reliable guides to our actions. When I believe myself to be looking at a book, holding a book, turning its pages, and reading it, I have every reason to claim to know that I am doing so, and no reason to believe that some evil genius is deceiving me. More-over, whatever havoc science may someday play with our ordinary under-standing of reality, it will not affect our daily lives before then.

On the other hand, we are not merely practical creatures. The scientist and philosopher will continue to seek deeper theoretical understandings of our world, and many nonscientists and nonphilosophers will continue to reflect on these understandings and where they might lead us. In this frame of mind, it is valuable to remember that any belief we now hold may someday be up for grabs. Although it is no doubt wise to put the bogeyman of the evil deceiver behind us, since there appears to be no good reason to think that such a de-ceiver exists, it is equally wise to give our theoretical imagination a free rein, since absolute certainty may be as much a bogeyman as Descartes' evil genius.

According to Hindu thought, the world of ordinary experience is *maya*, or il-lusion. Although we can and must distinguish between "illusion" and "reality" within the world of maya, mystical insight reveals to us that there is a deeper division between all of maya and ultimate reality. The contemporary skeptic's view is similar in one respect—it tells us to act on the certainty that is available to us, while it cautions us that however practical our relatively certain beliefs may be, a deeper understanding of reality may show them to be false. This is not to say that they *are* false; rather, it is to remind us that a certain humility is in order.

My cautious conclusion, then, is this. A *minimal* skepticism should be the re-sult of the arguments we have looked at. It is perfectly acceptable to claim to know all sorts of things, as long as such claims do not entice us to believe that what we claim to know cannot be given up, come what may. If Einstein has shown us that we do not know *everything* we think we do, he has not shown us that we do not know *anything* we think we do.

This point can be illustrated by comparing our beliefs to road maps. As long as they guide us through the world in a useful way, it is foolish to discard them because it is conceivable that a better map *may* come along. On the other hand, it is equally foolish to be so certain about our current maps that we refuse to recognize a better map if it *does* come along.

STUDY QUESTIONS

1. What does it mean to say that knowledge is justified true belief? What are the reasons for characterizing knowledge that way?
2. What is the difference between psychological certainty and epistemic cer-tainty? Does your degree of psychological certainty always match the degree of epistemic certainty of what you believe? Can you think of cases in which it doesn't?
3. Which of the following statements would Malcolm say you know in the weak sense? The strong sense? Do you agree with Malcolm in all of these cases? Why or why not?
   a. All men are mortal.
   b. Whales are mammals.

   c. Water is wet.

   d. You are now reading a book.

   e. No bachelor is married.

   f. Paris is the capital of France.

   g. Pain hurts.

   h. Thomas Jefferson wrote the Declaration of Independence.

4. What is skepticism? What arguments did we consider in support of skepticism? How persuasive do you find them? Why?

5. According to Malcolm, we can know things for certain even though it is not absolutely impossible that we are wrong. Why does he say that? Do you agree? Why or why not?

6. What is the correspondence theory of truth? Why does it appeal to many philosophers? What problems have other philosophers found with it?

7. What is the coherence theory of truth? The pragmatist theory? How are they similar? How does the pragmatist theory avoid the major objection to the coherence theory?

GLOSSARY

Coherence theory of truth. Theory that holds that the truth of a statement depends on the entire system of beliefs to which it belongs. According to this theory, an entire system of beliefs is true if it coheres, or fits together, in the appropriate way, and an individual member of the system is true because it belongs to that system.

Correspondence theory of truth. Theory that holds that a statement is true if it fits, or agrees with, or corresponds to the facts, and false if it does not.

Epistemic certainty. The degree of support a statement has. The greater the likelihood, given the evidence, that a statement is true, the greater its epistemic certainty.

Justified true belief theory of knowledge. Theory that holds that someone knows a statement if and only if three conditions are met: (1) the statement must be true; (2) the person must believe that the statement is true; and (3) the person must be completely justified in believing that it is true.

Knowing-how. Type of knowledge that depends, in part, on a particular skill or ability. To know how to swim, for example, is both to know certain things about swimming and to be able to swim.

Knowing-that. Knowledge that a statement is true. Examples of knowing-that are knowing that dogs are mammals, knowing that there are seven days in a week, and knowing that twice two is four.

Knowledge by acquaintance. Form of knowledge exemplified by knowing a person or city. This form of knowledge includes knowing certain things *about* the person or city, but also includes having *met* the person or having *been in* the city. I know my father, for example, but only know about George Washington. Similarly, I know Stevens Point, Wisconsin, but only know about Tokyo.

Maya. According to Hindu thought, the world of ordinary experience, which is really a world of illusion, beyond which lies true reality

Necessary and sufficient conditions. A list of conditions that something must meet if it is to be a certain sort of thing, and that, taken together, guarantee that something that meets them is that sort of thing. For example, the necessary and sufficient conditions for something's being a vixen are that it is a fox and that it is a female. Anything not a fox or not a female is not a vixen. Anything that is a fox and is a female is a vixen.

Physical magnitude. Any physical characteristic that can be described numerically, such as size, mass, force and energy.

Pragmatism. American philosophical movement beginning with Charles Sanders Peirce (1839–1914) and including, most notably, William James (1842–1910), John Dewey (1859–1952), C. I. Lewis (1883–1964), and W. V. Quine (b. 1908). Although there is considerable disagreement among pragmatists on various issues, they share the same emphasis on the usefulness of beliefs and theories in predicting experience.

Pragmatist theory of truth. Theory that holds that truth is determined by an ideal end point toward which all human investigation is converging. This end point is a total system of beliefs that is the most useful system for predicting experience.

Psychological certainty. The degree of confidence a person has that a given statement is true. The more confident the person, the higher the degree of psychological certainty.

Sensed qualities. Physical characteristics that we identify by how they look, sound, feel, smell, or taste. Examples are redness, loudness, warmth, and sweetness.

Skepticism. The denial that a statement or group of statements is or can be known. A total skeptic is someone who denies that we can know anything at all.

Strong knowledge. Knowledge with a high degree of *psychological* and *epistemic* certainty. If I know something in this strong sense, I am completely confident that nothing can turn up to prove me wrong, and I am completely justified in feeling that way.

Weak knowledge. Knowledge that allows for a degree of doubt. If I know something in this weak sense, my justification is strong enough to warrant my belief, but not strong enough to warrant the belief that nothing can turn up to prove me wrong.

Chapter 16

THE JUSTIFICATION
OF OUR BELIEFS

Knowledge, we saw, is *justified* true belief. A true belief can count as knowledge only if we have good grounds for accepting it. Otherwise, it is merely a lucky guess or an accident that we are right, and not knowledge. In this chapter, we will look at how we justify our beliefs. But first, we must make an important distinction—between our *reasons* for holding a belief, and the *causes* of our doing so.

Reasons and causes

To give our justification for a particular belief is to answer the questions "Why do you believe that?" and "How do you know that?" If our justification is a good one, it shows that our belief is a rational one, and that it is more likely true than not. But notice—not all answers to the question "Why do you believe that?" are relevant to our justification. Some answers do nothing to show that the belief is more likely true than not. Suppose, for instance, that you are asked why you believe that Western-style liberal democracy is a better system of government than Soviet-style communism. Two types of answers, both true, can be given. First, you might say that you believe it because you grew up in America and were conditioned to believe it. Second, you might say that you believe it because you believe that the system of government that guarantees the greatest amount of freedom for all is the best system, and Western-style liberal democracy guarantees greater freedom than Soviet-style communism.

The first answer provides a *cause* of your belief, but it does not provide a *reason*. Although it mentions an undeniable factor in your coming to hold your belief, it does nothing to show that your belief is rational or correct, nor does it provide anyone else with a reason for agreeing with you. Certainly, if we were debating the question, your first answer would do nothing to convince me that you are right. The second answer, however, does provide a reason. It attempts to show that it is more reasonable to believe that liberal democracy is better than communism, that it is true that liberal democracy is the better system. It is precisely the sort of answer that you would give in a debate.

The difference between a cause and a reason is this: Although both answer the question "Why do you believe it?," only the second answers the question "Why is it rational for someone to believe it?" or "What considerations *support* your belief?" or "What other beliefs show that your belief is more likely true than not?"

In other words, to give your reasons for holding a belief is to offer an *argument*. It is to say "I believe *p* because I believe *q*, *r*, and *s*; and if *q*, *r*, and *s* are true, then *p* is true also." For example, I believe that it is now 11:30 because I believe that my watch says it is 11:30 and that my watch is correct; and if it is true that my watch says 11:30 and is correct, then it is true that it is 11:30. Similarly, I believe that it didn't rain last night because I believe that the grass is not wet but would be wet if it had rained; and if it is true that the grass is not wet but would be wet if it had rained, then it is true that it did not rain. Thus, our interest in what follows will be in reasons rather than causes.

JUSTIFICATION CHAINS

In the ordinary course of events, the question "How do you know?" is usually given a short answer. How do I know the time? By my watch. How do I know that my sister is planning to visit me? She told me so. How do I know that Japan is in Asia? I learned it in school. Although these answers are usually sufficient in daily life, they do not really mark the end of the matter. Take the first answer—that I know the time by my watch. How do I know my watch is correct? Similarly, how do I know my sister told me the truth? How do I know that my teachers were right about Japan?

Each of these further questions has an answer, of course, but their answers raise still further questions. Suppose I say that I know my watch is correct because I checked it against the school clock. How do I know the school clock is correct? How do I know that I read my watch and the clock accurately when I compared them?

As we continue to spin out answers and questions, it becomes obvious that our justifications for believing what we do are far more complicated than we immediately realize. To give some idea of this complexity, let us take my belief that I had orange juice this morning. How do I know that?

Well, most obviously, I remember drinking it. But how did I know it was orange juice when I drank it? Well, it looked, tasted and smelled like orange juice. Also, it came from a can marked "orange juice." But how did I know it looked, tasted and smelled like orange juice? Because I have seen, tasted, and smelled orange juice before, and the stuff I drank this morning looked, tasted, and smelled the same way. But how do I know that I remembered the look, taste, and smell accurately? And how do I know that all the other stuff I thought was orange juice really was orange juice? Moreover, how do I know the label on the can was honest?

At this point, my justification begins branching out in all sorts of directions. No doubt, I will mention various federal and state regulations, the reputation of the supermarket in which I bought the juice and of the company that produced it, other instances in which my memory of look, smell, and taste were accurate, the corroboration of my beliefs by other people, and so on—and all of these considerations will lead to still further ones.

Thus, even the simplest belief is justified in a number of complicated ways, involving a wide variety of beliefs about current and past experiences, all of them admitting of further justification. We can think of this series of questions and answers as a *justification chain,* or, more accurately, as a set of individual justification chains leading to the same belief. One chain runs through my beliefs about the look, taste, and smell of what I drank this morning and of the other things I thought to be orange juice, another through my beliefs about the label on the can and the reliability of the supermarket and producer. In turn, each of these chains breaks up into further chains, which will themselves break up into still further chains.

A few points about justification chains warrant immediate mention. First, every link in these chains is a *belief.* We justify the initial belief by appealing to other beliefs, and then justify these other beliefs by appealing to still other ones. That is why the chains can continue as they do. All beliefs are capable of justification, but the only way we can justify them is by appealing to other beliefs.

Second, the vast majority of beliefs in the chain are *not consciously entertained* when we accept the initial belief. While drinking my orange juice this morning, I gave no conscious thought whatever to the can it came in, federal regulations, or the smell of any other orange juice I'd had. Such beliefs came to the fore only when I began thinking in earnest about my justification.

Third, my own *observations* play a crucial role in such chains. Even if I must depend on the testimony of others in many cases for part of the justification of my beliefs, their testimony is still something that I hear or see, and my judgment about the reliability of any bit of testimony must depend on other observations of mine. If I believe what I learned in school, it is because my own observations have confirmed many of the other things I learned in school. If I believe my sister when she tells me she's planning on visiting me, it is because my own observations have shown me that she can be trusted.

Fourth, the search for *explanations* also plays a crucial role in justification chains. That is, each link is connected to the next one by an *explanatory statement*. Take my beliefs that what I drank this morning was orange juice and that what I drank this morning tasted like orange juice. These two links are connected by the explanatory statement "What I drank this morning tasted like orange *because* it was orange juice." Likewise, the belief that what I drank was orange juice is connected to the belief that the label on the can said it was orange juice by the explanatory statement "The label said it was orange juice *because* it was orange juice."

This is no accident. If one belief serves as a reason for another, there must be some connection between the two beliefs that allows the one to serve as a reason for the other. Suppose, for example, I told you that my reason for believing that the Phillies beat the Cubs last night is that I slept until nine this morning. You would no doubt be very confused by that remark. But suppose I added this: I have a friend who is a Cubs fan and knows that I am a Phillies fan. If the Cubs had won she would have awakened me at six this morning to rub it in. In that case, you would no longer be confused. Why not? Because the Cubs' loss *explains* why I was not awakened at six.

Fifth, *generalizations* form an important part of justification chains. At each step along the way, we depend on statements beginning with such words as "all," "every," or "most." Why can I say that this liquid is orange juice because it looks, tastes, and smells like orange juice? Because I believe that anything (or almost anything) that looks, tastes, and smells like orange juice is orange juice. Why can I say that I slept until nine this morning because the Phillies beat the Cubs? Because I believe that whenever the Cubs beat the Phillies, my friend will call me at six the next morning.

THE WEB OF BELIEF

When we reflect on the large number of varied beliefs that belongs to any justification chain, it begins to look as though almost any belief can be involved in the justification of any other belief. It begins to seem that if we are asked how we know any one statement, we may eventually have to appeal to all of our other beliefs.

On the face of it, this seems absurd. After all, whenever we are asked how we know a particular thing, we can give a relatively short answer that will satisfy the asker. Also, it is difficult to see how all of my beliefs can be suitably connected. My belief that there is peanut butter in the house, for instance, seems totally unrelated to my belief that there is only one president of the United States. How could one be part of the other's justification?

I can explain how with an example I often use with my students. At some
point in class, I will "accidentally" bump into the table at the front of the room.
I then write the following statements on the blackboard:

"I was fifteen feet away from the table."
"I can take no step longer than a yard."
"The table did not move."
"I took two steps."
"I bumped into the table."

Notice that the above statements are inconsistent. That is, not all of them can
be true. At least one must be false. Either the table moved, or I took more than
two steps, or I was closer than fifteen feet from the table, or I can take eight-foot
steps, or I didn't bump into it.

Which is it?

Since my students saw that I was only about three feet from the table, they all
say that the first statement is the false one. If I agree with them, I can justify my
belief as follows: Obviously, I was closer to the table that I'd thought, because I
bumped into it after taking two steps, and I can take no step longer than a yard,
and the table didn't move.

But why should I agree with them? I could do otherwise. I could say, for example, that I didn't really bump into the table—because I was fifteen feet away,
took two steps, the table didn't move, and I can't take a step longer than a yard.
Or I could say that the table must have moved—because I took two steps, am
unable to take a step longer than a yard, was fifteen feet away from the table
and bumped into it. Or I could say that I obviously can take a step over seven
feet, or that I obviously took five steps. Why say that I was closer to the table
than I'd thought?

No doubt, you are tempted to say that I *know* that the table didn't move, and
that I *know* that I can't take eight-foot steps, and that I *know* that I only took two
steps, and that I *know* that I bumped into the table. The problem with that answer is that I also thought I *knew* that I was fifteen feet away from it. Obviously, I
have to admit that one of the things I thought I knew is false, but why the distance to the table? Because it is most *rational* to say that I was wrong about the
distance. But why is that?

The question asks, in effect, what our standards of rationality are. When our
beliefs conflict, how are we rationally to choose which one to reject? Our answer to this question will tell us something very important about the justification of our beliefs.

Why is it most rational to say I misjudged the distance to the table? Because it
is more *likely* that I misjudged it than that I was wrong about the other beliefs.
After all, people often misjudge distances, especially when their mind is on
something else. So the hypothesis that I misjudged the distance has an *initial
plausibility* compared with the other hypotheses.

What else? Well, my students saw what happened, and they say that I was less than fifteen feet away from the table. So this belief is corroborated by the testimony of others. If I were to disagree, I would need an explanation of their being wrong. Are they lying? If so, why all of them? Am I the victim of a conspiracy? Are they victims of a mass hallucination? Did someone drug the water supply? These questions demonstrate that the hypothesis that I misjudged the distance is the *simplest* one to accept. If I accept it, no further explanation is needed. If I reject it, a whole bundle of further explanations is required. So *simplicity* is an important factor.

Anything else? Well, suppose that I were to say that the table moved. But how? As I walked toward it, I could see everyone else in the room, and nobody was even close to the table. Did they move it by a concentration of mental energy? Or did the table move itself? But I don't believe that there is any such thing as mental energy that can move tables. If my students have such a power, how could they have acquired it? Do I have it? Does everyone? Why have I never seen it displayed? If there is such a thing, don't all my beliefs about the laws of nature have to be changed?

And if the table moved itself, why haven't I seen any other table move itself? What about chairs, typewriters, books, glasses of beer? Can they move themselves as well? Must all my beliefs about the difference between animate and "inanimate" objects be thrown out the window?

The point is this. If I agree that I misjudged the distance to the table, I need change few, if any, of my other beliefs. But if I choose another alternative, the number of other beliefs that must be changed grows considerably. Indeed, if I were to say that the table moved itself, it would be difficult to find an end to the process. Who knows how many beliefs I would have to change before I removed all the inconsistencies? Therefore, *conservatism* is an important factor. We choose the hypothesis that requires the fewest changes in our other beliefs.

We are now in a position to see how it is that any belief can enter into the justification of any other belief. My beliefs form one huge network. Some are *particular* statements, that is, statements about individual things; others are *general* statements, that is, statements about entire groups of things. The particular statements serve as *evidence* for the general ones. If I believe that this emerald is green and that emerald is green, and so on for every emerald I have seen, these particular beliefs provide evidence for the general belief that all emeralds are green. Moreover, the general statements serve to *explain* the particular ones. If I believe that all emeralds are green, that belief explains why this thing is green. It is green because it's an emerald, and all emeralds are green.

Furthermore, general beliefs serve as evidence and explanations for other general beliefs. If all gins make me drunk and all bourbons make me drunk and all vodkas make me drunk, that is evidence for the general statement that all liquors make me drunk. And the general statement that all liquors make me drunk explains why all gins make me drunk.

Let us think of this network of beliefs as a map. The particular beliefs are country roads and city streets. The general beliefs are major highways connecting the smaller streets, and the most general beliefs are the interstate highways connecting the other highways. In this way, the smallest dirt road in Oregon is connected to the narrowest back alley in New York. So, eventually, is my belief about the peanut butter in my house connected to my belief about there being only one president of the United States at a time.

Take my general belief that inanimate objects cannot move themselves. Think of all the objects in the world that are connected by that belief. Think also of the other beliefs I have about these objects that are connected to the belief that they are inanimate. How many of those must be changed if I decide that the table moved itself? How many other general beliefs will I have to give up if I change those particular beliefs? Then how many other particular beliefs? Where will the process end?

Of course, we don't think about such matters when we unexpectedly bump into a table. We just automatically conclude that the table was closer than we'd thought. But these matters explain why we automatically come to that decision. We do so because the experience of bumping into a table puts our entire network of beliefs on the line, and rather than create havoc in that network, we choose the simplest, most conservative hypothesis. That is how the entire network enters into our justification for every belief in that network. It is also why we give such short answers to the question "How do you know that?" Since the entire network is taken for granted, there is no reason to go too deeply into it. A short "by my watch" will suffice when asked how I know the time, just as a short "because I bumped into it" will suffice when asked how I know the table was closer than I'd thought.

Once we recognize all of this, we can see that the metaphor of the justification chain is a bit misleading. It makes the justification of beliefs seem like single lines, proceeding independently of one another in a single direction. Instead, the lines cross and merge and move every which way, as all of our beliefs help to justify one another.

Thus, a more apt metaphor, borrowed from the contemporary American philosopher W. V. Quine, is that of a vast *web* of belief. This metaphor emphasizes that justification is a matter of *explanatory coherence*. To say that is to say that a belief is justified if it fits well into the entire network. If it is consistent with our other beliefs, provides evidence for other beliefs in the network, and is explained by other beliefs in the network, then we are justified in believing it. And when it comes to choosing between rival hypotheses, we are justified in believing the one that fits in the best. Since the hypothesis that I misjudged the distance to the table fits in better than any other hypothesis, that is the hypothesis I am justified in accepting. Indeed, it is because it fits better than the others that it has the initial plausibility it does.

A PRIORI KNOWLEDGE

According to Quine's metaphor of the web, all of our beliefs justify and are justified by all of our other beliefs. They are all connected by an explanatory network, and changes in one place can require changes elsewhere. Thus, all of our beliefs are connected to our observations of the world. What we observe can lead us to change any of our beliefs, no matter how certain we may have been that they were true. As our example of bumping into the table shows, we try to change as few beliefs as possible, but we cannot rule out the possibility that some observations will require sweeping changes in the web.

Such sweeping changes do not occur often. When they do occur, they are usually heralded as scientific revolutions, such as when Albert Einstein (1879–1955) replaced Isaac Newton's (1642–1727) world view with his special and general theories of relativity, and when Charles Darwin (1809–1882) presented his theory of evolution, and when Sigmund Freud (1856–1939) revealed the powers of unconscious motivation. Similar sweeping changes may also occur in our personal lives, as when we embrace a new religion with great fervor or decide that atheism is the correct attitude and reject all religion.

Are any beliefs *immune* from this process? Many philosophers believe so. They hold that some beliefs do not depend on observation for their justification, and that no observations whatever could show them to be wrong. Beliefs of this type are said to count as *a priori* knowledge, meaning that their justification is independent of experience. A priori knowledge is contrasted with *empirical* knowledge, which does depend on observation for its justification.

Thus, these philosophers give certain beliefs a privileged place in the web. They are protected by something like a one-way glass. The beliefs behind the glass, our a priori knowledge, provide justification for the beliefs in front of it, our empirical beliefs, but nothing that happens in front of the glass can change what goes on behind it.

A variety of beliefs have been held to be a priori. Among them are the truths of logic and mathematics, the belief that everything has a cause, and the belief that nothing can be red all over and green all over at the same time.

Unfortunately, some alleged a priori knowledge has been given up. Modern physics, for example, tells us that events occurring at the level of such basic particles as the electron cannot be given causal explanations. This has led many philosophers to restrict their claims about the a priori to logic and mathematics, to which we now turn.

LOGIC AND MATHEMATICS

Logic and mathematics are called *formal systems*. That is, they begin with certain statements called *axioms*, from which are derived a number of other statements called *theorems*.

An *axiom* is a statement that is accepted without proof. According to many philosophers, the axioms of logic and mathematics are *self-evident*. To say that a statement is self-evident is to say that its truth can be recognized by anyone who understands the statement and reflects upon it with sufficient care. It is also to say that the statement requires no observational support or evidence. In the chapter on moral knowledge (Chapter 4), we looked at two statements of this type—the law of identity in logic (everything is identical with itself) and Euclid's axiom in geometry that equals added to equals are equal.

Someone could, of course, run around with a yardstick to find observational evidence for Euclid's axiom, but that is something of a fool's errand. Try, if you will, to imagine a case where it would fail to hold. Indeed, if you were to measure two lines and find that they are equal, and then measured two other lines and found that they were equal, and then joined one from the first pair to one of the second and then joined the other two, you would refuse to accept any measurement that showed the resultant lines unequal. You would say, instead, that you mismeasured, or that something is wrong with your yardstick, or that you were the victim of a hallucination. That is, you would let nothing count as evidence against the statement.

A *theorem* is a statement that is derived from a set of axioms. To say that it is *derived* from axioms is to say that it follows necessarily from the axioms. That is, certain operations are performed that guarantee that the results (the theorems) are true. The theorems are not self-evident, but since the axioms are, the truth of the theorems is guaranteed.

For example, take the statement that 5,492 times 24 equals 131,808. Although the truth of the statement is not self-evident to you, you can assure yourself of its truth by performing the computation yourself, where the truth of each step in the computation is self-evident. We can say, then, that the statement follows necessarily from such self-evident truths as "4 times 2 equals 8."

When we view logic and mathematics in this way, we can easily see why they are held to be a priori. Starting with self-evident axioms, we can continue to spin out theorems indefinitely without ever having to seek observational evidence. Certainly, you do not feel it necessary to find 5,492 barrels, each containing 24 apples, and then count them all, and then repeat the process for oranges, paper clips, puppies, and so on, before accepting that 5,492 times 24 equals 131,808. Still, some philosophers have grown suspicious of the special place afforded mathematics and logic. Let us see why.

Russell's Paradox

There is a barber who shaves all and only those people who do not shave themselves. Does he shave himself? Suppose we say that he does. If he does shave himself, that means that he does not, because he only shaves people who do not shave themselves. So let us say that he does not. But in that case, he does shave himself, because he shaves all people who do not shave themselves.

We have arrived at a contradiction. If he shaves himself he doesn't; if he doesn't shave himself, he does. Although this may seem a harmless paradox, the British philosopher Bertrand Russell (1872–1970) showed that it has far-reaching implications for a branch of mathematics known as *set theory*.

A *set* is a collection that is defined by its members. That is, set *A* is identical with set *B* if *A* and *B* have precisely the same members. Otherwise, they are different. So every time we add or subtract anything from the collection, we have a different set.

There are two ways of identifying a set. One way is to pick out every member by name. Another way is to pick out a certain characteristic and speak of the set of all things having that characteristic. Thus, we can identify the same set as the set consisting of the first three presidents of the United States or as the set consisting of George Washington, John Adams, and Thomas Jefferson.

Until Russell's discussion of his paradox, it was a basic assumption of set theory that we can name a set by naming any characteristic. Russell's paradox showed this basic assumption to be false. There is no set consisting of the people shaved by Russell's barber. There cannot be, because such a set would be self-contradictory. If it includes the barber it doesn't; if it doesn't include him, it does. Thus, Russell's paradox teaches us to be wary of claims to self-evidence. Even in mathematics, what may seem self-evident one day may be shown false the next. Still, Russell's paradox does not show that mathematics is empirical rather than a priori. The basic assumption was not shown false by *observation*. It was rejected because it led to contradictory theorems. Let us now turn to a recent development that has led some philosophers to claim that mathematics *is* empirical.

EINSTEIN AND EUCLID

In the previous chapter, I said that according to Einstein's general theory of relativity, parallel lines eventually meet in space if extended far enough. It is time to take a closer look at that claim.

In the diagram below, we have three lines, *A*, *B*, and *C*. Both *A* and *B* are perpendicular to *C*. In that case, *A* and *B* are parallel to one another, and, according to Euclidean geometry, they will never meet, no matter how far they are extended.

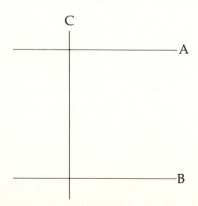

Until the nineteenth century, this was taken to be self-evident. To deny it, people believed, would lead to contradictory theorems. But in the nineteenth century, geometries were devised that did deny it, and these geometries proved to be perfectly consistent. No contradictions could be derived from them. Although this was taken as a landmark result, no one thought that these geometries could replace Euclidean geometry. They were interesting formal systems, but only Euclid's, it was thought, could describe the real world.

There were two good reasons for believing this. First, Euclid's *parallel postulate* (as the claim about parallel lines is called) seemed to be a necessary truth about the world. It was considered inconceivable that space could be such that parallel lines could ever meet. In fact, the philosopher Immanuel Kant (1724–1804) had argued quite persuasively that space had to be Euclidean.

Second, Euclidean geometry lay at the foundation of physics. According to the physics of the time, light traveled through a vacuum in straight lines, and light rays traveling along paths *A* and *B* of our diagram could never meet. So Euclid's parallel postulate held a special place both in ordinary experience and science. The discovery of non-Euclidean geometries, it was thought, could do nothing to change that.

Then came Einstein's general theory of relativity. According to Einstein, two light rays traveling along paths *A* and *B* will eventually meet. How can that happen? Here is another diagram.

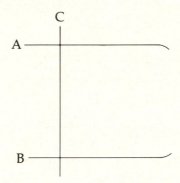

When we look at this diagram, our immediate inclination is to deny that the paths are straight. Isn't it obvious that the lines have begun to curve?

Well, the lines on our *diagram* have certainly curved, but the point of Einstein's theory is that the paths of the light rays are straight—it is *space* that is curved. Euclidean geometry assumes that space is *not* curved. The geometry Einstein used, as noted in the previous chapter, is Riemannian geometry, which assumes that space *is* curved.

Why make the assumption that space, rather than the light ray, is curved? Well, how do we determine that a line is straight? One way is by determining that it is the shortest distance between two points. That, indeed, is the classic definition of a straight line—the shortest distance between two points. And how do we determine that? By taking a measuring stick and laying it down end over end from one point to another. The path that requires us to lay it down the fewest number of times is the shortest one, and therefore the straight one. Well, according to Einstein, the paths *A* and *B* of our second diagram are, in the appropriate conditions, straight by that test.

Another way of determining that something is straight is by lining it up to the eye. Hold the end of a pencil up to one eye. As you gaze along the pencil and move it around, holding the end in the same place, it will reach a position at which you can only see the end of the pencil. At that position, you can say that it is straight. Were it bent, you would always be able to see another part of the pencil. This test is used both by carpenters testing for warps in wooden planks and pool players testing for warps in pool cues. But it also works, under the appropriate conditions, for paths *A* and *B* of our second diagram. That is, anyone traveling one of those paths would have no way of telling that it is curved, and it would appear perfectly straight when lined up to the eye.

So there are at least three good reasons for accepting Einstein's claim that paths *A* and *B* in our second diagram are straight. First, they pass our common tests for straight lines. Second, they are paths followed by light rays in a vacuum, and such paths have always been considered perfectly straight. Third, there is a consistent geometry that preceded Einstein's theory that also considers them straight. Are there any other reasons?

Choosing the Better Theory

There are two ways of interpreting our second diagram, each belonging to a different theory. According to one, paths *A* and *B* are parallel straight lines traveling through curved space. According to the other, paths *A* and *B* begin as parallel straight lines and then curve.

We have already looked at three reasons for accepting the first theory. But we can easily think of two good reasons for accepting the second. One is that Euclidean geometry has played an important and reliable role in science and our ordinary lives for as long as it has been around. We use it every time we shoot pool, build shelves, draw diagrams and maps, or survey property. Engineers use it, as do architects, tailors, and people who mark out football fields and tennis courts. The second is that it is highly counterintuitive to think of *space* as being curved. How can space, of all things, be curved?

How, then, are we to choose? How did the physicists choose? Suppose we accept Einstein's account. If we do, we have two things to explain: how space can be curved and why Euclidean geometry works so well. The curvature of space is explained this way. The nature of space is determined by the matter that is in it. It is a mistake to think of empty space as having certain characteristics that are unaffected by what is in that space. There is no universe without matter. So the space in our universe has the characteristics it does because of the matter in our universe. How does matter determine the characteristics of space? By its gravity. Paths *A* and *B* of our second diagram are the paths that light rays follow when they approach a large body, the sun, for instance, from opposite sides. The gravitational field of the body creates a curvature in space. The success of Euclidean geometry is explained this way. Euclidean geometry works "in the small" because the curvature of space is not a factor to be reckoned with "in the small." It is only at great distances that it begins to affect our calculations.

Suppose, on the other hand, we reject Einstein's account and insist that paths *A* and *B* curve. If we do, we must explain two things: how light rays in a vacuum bend, and why the paths pass our tests for straight lines. The curvature of light in a vacuum is explained this way: Gravity bends the light rays. Just as light is bent when it passes through water, so is it bent when passing through a gravitational field. That the paths pass our tests for straight lines has two explanations, one for each test. The paths seem to be the shortest distance between two points because gravity changes the size of measuring sticks. Just as temperature changes affect the size of objects, so does gravity. The paths pass the second test because the light is bent. Just as a straight stick appears bent when half submerged in water, so does a bent path appear straight when passing through a gravitational field. In other words, our ordinary tests for straightness are unreliable "in the large." Adjustments have to be made due to highly unusual forces.

So we seem to have a standoff. Either theory seems to "fit the facts" equally well. Each can explain away the difficulties.

Such apparent standoffs are not unusual in the history of science. Although we like to think that one theory can be proved by a series of experiments, matters are far more complicated than that. The complications arise because of the resiliency of the web of belief. Let us see how.

THE CENTER OF THE WEB

The web of belief is set up in such a way that it is always possible to hold any belief, come what may. To return to the example of bumping into the table, I could have refused to believe that the table did not move. Instead, I could have said that the table really moved itself. Of course, I would then have to change all sorts of other beliefs in my web, but if I were willing to do so, I could continue to believe that I was really fifteen feet away. Of course, that would be highly unusual behavior. To be willing to give up all my beliefs about inanimate objects on the basis of one experience is most odd. Why is that?

Think of our beliefs as being spread throughout our web. Some beliefs are in the center, some on the edges, and the rest scattered in between. The beliefs on the edges are those we are most willing to give up in the face of unexpected observations. The ones in the center are those we are least willing to give up, those we are most likely to hold, come what may. For most of us, the belief that tables do not move themselves is much closer to the center than the belief that we have not misjudged the distance to the table. A great number of unexpected observations would have to occur before we would begin to believe that tables move themselves. As we get closer and closer to the center, our beliefs seem to be totally protected from unexpected observations, so protected that we cannot

SELF-JUSTIFYING BELIEFS

In the discussion of justification, I concluded that all of our beliefs form a vast web held together by explanatory coherence, that each member of the web is ultimately justified by every other member of the web, and that observations are relevant to the justification of every member.

Although this view has many adherents among contemporary philosophers, many others disagree with it. In the main body of this chapter, we considered the major source of disagreement—mathematical knowledge. In what follows, we will look at another.

To give our justification for holding a belief is to give our reasons for holding it. And to give our reasons is to offer an *argument*. It is to say that we believe *p* because we believe *q, r,* and *s,* and if *q, r,* and *s* are true, so is *p*. Suppose we are then asked to justify our beliefs that *q, r,* and *s* are true. We then give another argument. But suppose that our argument goes like this. We believe *q, r,* and *s* because we believe *p,* and if *p* is true, so are *q, r,* and *s*. Our reasoning has come full circle. We justified one belief by appealing to three others, and then justified the three others by appealing to the first belief. Clearly, this is unacceptable, as the following example shows.

Suppose that you ask Mary why she trusts John, and she answers that she trusts him because he's honest. Suppose that you then ask her how she knows he's honest, and she answers that he told her so, and she can trust whatever he says. How does she know she can trust him? Because he's honest. How does she know he's honest? Because she can trust him. The circle is obvious. But in that case, it is also obvious that she has not really justified her belief that he is honest or the belief that she can trust him. Unless she can break out of the circle, her justification is illusory. She must find some other belief to justify the beliefs in the circle—that he has never lied to her before, for instance.

This point is an important one. If every belief in the web justifies and is justified by every other belief, all justification eventually comes full circle. But if that is true, then it seems that we are not really justified in believing anything.

Thus, many philosophers have claimed that there must be some *self-justifying beliefs,* beliefs that do not depend on the rest of the web for their justification, but contribute to the justification of all beliefs in the rest of the web. If there are such beliefs, the circle is broken, and we are justified in believing anything that is justified by them. If not, we are justified in believing nothing. Are there any such beliefs?

Beliefs About Current Sense Experience

The most frequently mentioned candidates for self-justifying beliefs are beliefs about *current sense experience*. Beliefs of this type are beliefs about how things now *seem* to us, beliefs about how things look, sound, feel, taste, and smell, right now. An example of such a belief is this: I now seem to see something that looks like a typewriter, and I now seem to be touching something that feels like a typewriter, and I now seem to be hearing something that sounds like a typewriter.

Why are such beliefs the most frequently mentioned? For two reasons. First, these beliefs do contribute to the justification of our other beliefs. All of our beliefs are justified by observation, I said earlier. But what is our justification for believing that we observe what we think we do? What, for example, is my justification for believing that I *do* see and hear and feel a typewriter? That I *seem* to. That is, I believe I see, hear, and feel a typewriter because it seems to me that I see, hear, and feel something that looks, sounds, and feels like a typewriter. So if observation is relevant to the justification of all beliefs, so must beliefs about current sense experience be relevant.

Second, such beliefs do not at first seem to depend on any other beliefs. How do I know that things seem a certain way to me? Because they do. Period. How things seem to me is a fact about my own mind, and such facts are purely transparent. If I believe that things seem a certain way to me, then I am completely justified in that belief. Nothing else is relevant to my justification.

Suppose, for example, that I should suddenly hear my alarm clock go off and then awaken to find myself in bed. That would show that I wasn't really seeing a typewriter at all. I was dreaming. But it would not show that it did not seem to me that I saw something that looked like a typewriter.

Why the difference? My belief that I am really seeing a typewriter depends on a number of beliefs, including the belief that I am awake. So finding that I was asleep and dreaming destroys my justification for believing I am actually seeing a typewriter. Since my belief that it now seems to me that I see something that looks like a typewriter does not depend on any other beliefs, no further observations can destroy my justification for believing it.

Although the above remarks are persuasive, they do conceal a problem. Beliefs about how things seem *do* depend on other beliefs for their justification. Take even the simple belief that I seem to see something that looks red and round. This belief depends on many other beliefs for its justification— that I can distinguish red from maroon, for example, and that I can distinguish a round shape from an oval one. And these beliefs also admit of justification. Indeed, all of my beliefs about having seen red and round things are relevant, as are my beliefs about the proper conditions for distinguishing red from maroon and round from oval. Therefore, we must conclude that beliefs about current sense experience are not self-justifying.

Empiricism versus Rationalism

The view that all beliefs find their ultimate justification in self-justifying beliefs about current sense experience is the most extreme form of *empiricism*. More generally, an empiricist is someone who believes that all knowledge, often excepting knowledge of logic and mathematics, is empirical. But the great empiricist tradition, beginning with John Locke (1632–1704), George Berkeley (1685–1753), and David Hume (1711–1776), and running through John Stuart Mill (1806–1873), Bertrand Russell (1872–1970), and the German-American philosopher Rudolf Carnap (b. 1891), has included the claim that all justification of empirical beliefs ends in beliefs about sense experience, which are self-justifying.

Another great tradition in philosophy is the *rationalist* tradition, beginning with René Descartes (1596–1650), Baruch Spinoza (1632–1677), and Gottfried Wilhelm Leibniz (1646–1716), and running through Immanuel Kant (1724–1804), who is often said to have reconciled rationalism and empiricism, and the American philosopher Brand Blanshard (b. 1892). Rationalists, to a varying degree, hold that much of our knowledge beyond mathematics and logic is a priori.

Perhaps the most extreme rationalist was Spinoza, whose great philosophical system encompassed virtually every aspect of human knowledge, from ethics and religion to physics and psychology. Spinoza presented his system on the model of geometry, beginning with axioms and definitions and then offering formal proofs of a great number and variety of theorems.

Thus, rationalists agree with empiricists that justification chains end in self-justifying beliefs; but, in opposition to empiricists, they claim that many of these beliefs are a priori.

But we have already seen that there is good reason to believe that observation is relevant to the justification of all beliefs. In that case, there is good reason to reject rationalism.

Circles and Webs—Pragmatism

We began our search for self-justifying beliefs because of the following argument: If justification is a matter of explanatory coherence, then all justification eventually comes full circle. But if all justification comes full circle, all justification is illusory. Therefore, unless there are some self-justifying beliefs that get us out of the circle, we are not justified in believing anything. Since I have rejected the leading candidates for self-justifying beliefs, must I also conclude that we are not justified in believing anything? I think not.

It is a mistake, I think, to compare our webs of belief to the kind of circular reasoning exhibited by Mary when she answers our questions about John's trustworthiness. Our webs are not constructed like big circles. They are, rather, vast and intricate criss-crossing networks, which are designed to accommodate the fullest range of experience in the best possible way. If our webs succeed in this task, it is no fatal flaw that there are no self-justifying beliefs.

To accept this conclusion is to adopt the alternative to empiricism and rationalism known as *pragmatism*. When discussing theories of truth in the previous chapter, I noted that one classical theory is the pragmatist theory. The theory of justification defended in this chapter may be called the pragmatist theory of justification. Like the pragmatist theory of truth, the pragmatist theory of justification emphasizes the coherence of our entire web of belief and the usefulness of that web in both the practical and theoretical aspects of life. Unlike the empiricist and rationalist theories of justification, it does not require that any of our beliefs be certain or self-justifying. All beliefs are justified by their place in the web, and any belief may be discarded in our pursuit of the best web.

imagine changing them. The belief that twice two is four, for example, seems entirely immune from revision.

Although most of us put the same beliefs in the center, it is possible to put anything there. Think of the paranoid, for instance. A paranoid is convinced that there is a plot against him, and nobody can convince him otherwise. That belief is in the center of his web, and he will go to the most outlandish extremes to maintain it, come what may.

The point of these remarks is that no observation or series of observations forces any particular beliefs on us. Depending on the geography of our web, we can believe whatever we like. That is not to say that all beliefs are equally rational. Far from it. The paranoid is not as rational as the rest of us. Nor is the person who decides that the table moved itself.

Why not? For the reasons already offered. The most rational geography of our web of belief is the one that allows for the greatest simplicity and conservatism. The paranoid must always explain why the plots against him never succeed, how various people were enlisted into the conspiracy, why the conspiracy began in the first place, why nobody else is aware of it, and so on. The belief that the paranoid places in the center demands constant adjustment in the rest of the web. Were he to drop that belief, after the initial adjustments life would go much more smoothly for him.

The same considerations are involved in choosing among rival scientific theories. Observations alone do not settle the issue. When Galileo (1564–1642), for example, explored the heavens with his telescope, his observations did not by themselves prove that the earth and other planets revolved around the sun. Those who believed that the earth was at the center of the universe responded by saying that their theory was basically right but needed certain minor adjustments. It was only when these "minor" adjustments grew more and more complicated that the far simpler theory of Galileo gained general acceptance. Why did it take the others longer than Galileo to come around? Because their belief that the earth was at the center of the universe was close to the center of their web.

Returning to Einstein and Euclid, we find this situation. Euclidean geometry was at the center of science's web. So were a number of other beliefs—that light travels in a straight path, for instance, and that there are no forces acting on measuring sticks in the way required by the alternative to Einstein's theory. Clearly, some very basic beliefs had to give. Since Einstein's theory left us with a smoother, less complicated, more useful web, just as Galileo's did centuries earlier, it was adopted. Thus, we say that parallel lines do eventually meet.

THE FINAL WORD?

Our excursion into physics has been a long but fruitful one. It has shown us how a belief thought to be an example of a priori knowledge can be overturned by the advance of science. It has shown us that the combination of observation and theory can influence any part of our web, including the basic assumptions of mathematics. It has shown us that the axioms of mathematics and logic are not self-evident truths, but hypotheses about the world, which may be close to the center of our web, but are not unrevisable.

The moral, then, is this. It is a mistake to draw a firm line between empirical knowledge and a priori knowledge. Observation is relevant to the justification of all of our beliefs. Although scientists *could* have held on to Euclidean geometry come what may, although they *could* have kept it immune from revision, they did not. Instead, they took the more rational course of accepting the best total theory. Ultimately, the demand for explanatory coherence, the first principle of justification, led them to reject their commitment to Euclidean geometry.

That does not mean, however, that there is *no* difference between mathematical beliefs and others. Our beliefs about mathematics are at the very center of our web. They are protected from revision by the other beliefs surrounding them. They are to be given up only when it would lead to intolerable strain to give them up.

The difference between empirical beliefs and so-called a priori beliefs is a difference of degree, then, not of kind. The closer a belief is to the center of the web, the greater our dependence on it. As we get closer to the center, any changes require greater and greater changes in the rest of the web.

My belief that a certain book is on the shelf in this room, for example, is on the edge of the web. If I don't find the book, I will believe it is someplace else, and that is the end of the matter. My belief that twice two is four, however, is in the center. To give it up would be to change so many other beliefs that I cannot even imagine doing so. Therefore, it seems to be totally protected from unexpected observations. But if continued observations, however unimaginable, should show that even greater havoc would result by keeping the belief, or if it could be shown that the rejection of the belief would not lead to such havoc as we now imagine, it is then up for grabs.

That is what Einstein and Riemann showed concerning Euclidean geometry. The parallel postulate could be given up without undue strain, and the result is a better theory.

STUDY QUESTIONS

1. What is the difference between our reasons for holding a belief and the causes of our holding a belief?
2. In this chapter I used two metaphors for the way that we justify our beliefs. First I talked of justification chains, then of the web of belief. Why is each metaphor appropriate? Why is the web metaphor more appropriate?
3. What role do generalizations play in the justification of our beliefs? What role do explanatory statements play?
4. What makes one hypothesis simpler than another? More conservative? What roles do simplicity and conservatism play in the justification of our beliefs?
5. Some philosophers have contrasted a priori and empirical knowledge.

What is the difference between the two types of knowledge? What candidates for a priori knowledge have been offered by philosophers?

6. What is a formal system? Why have some philosophers believed that the theorems and axioms of formal systems are known a priori?

7. What does Einstein's general theory of relativity show about the way we justify mathematical knowledge?

8. What does it mean to say that some beliefs are in the center of our web? Which of your beliefs are in the center of your web? What would it take to get you to change them?

9. Why have some philosophers believed that some of our beliefs must be self-justifying? What beliefs have they taken to be self-justifying? Why do other philosophers think that these beliefs are not self-justifying?

10. What is empiricism? Rationalism? How are they similar? Different? How do they compare with pragmatism?

GLOSSARY

A priori knowledge. Knowledge that does not depend on observation for its justification.

Argument. Process of reasoning in which certain statements (the reasons) are used to show that another statement (the conclusion) is true or most likely true.

Axiom. In *formal systems,* a statement that is used to *derive* other statements, but is not derived from any other statement.

Circular reasoning. An *argument* in which the same statement appears as both the conclusion and one of the reasons supporting the conclusion. For example: Everything in the Bible is true. Why? Because it's the word of God. How do I know? Because it says so in the Bible, and everything in the Bible is true.

Derive. To derive one statement from another is to show that if the second statement is true, the first one must also be true.

Empirical knowledge. Knowledge that depends on observation for its justification.

Empiricism. The view that all knowledge, or all knowledge apart from mathematics and logic, is *empirical.* Empiricists characteristically hold that empirical knowledge has its ultimate justification in *self-justifying beliefs* about current *sense experience.*

Explanatory coherence. A feature attributed to belief systems by many philosophers in order to explain how we justify our beliefs. Roughly, a system has explanatory coherence if its members are connected by *explanatory statements.*

Explanatory statement. A statement of the form "Such and such is true or happened because of so and so." For example: "The grass is wet because it rained last night."

Formal system. A system of statements in which some statements (the *theorems*) are *derived* from other statements (the *axioms*). Examples are mathematics and logic.

General statement. A statement about all members of a particular group. For example: "All swans are white," and "Nobody likes peas and carrots."

Hypothesis. An *explanatory statement* provisionally adopted in order to test if it is true. For example, if my car does not start on a cold morning, I may adopt the hypothesis that the battery is dead. I will then test the hypothesis by attempting to start the car with the help of jumper cables.

Justification chain. A series of statements, each one justified by the statements following it.

Parallel postulate. A postulate of Euclidean geometry, according to which we can draw through a given point one and only one line that is parallel to a second line and will never meet that second line.

Particular statement. A statement about individual members of a group. For example: "John doesn't like peas and carrots," and "Some people like peas and carrots."

Rationalism. The view that we have a priori knowledge extending beyond our knowledge of mathematics and logic.

Russell's paradox. Named after Bertrand Russell, a paradox that shows that certain *sets* are impossible, because if something belongs to the set it does not, and if it does not it does. For example, take the statement, "This sentence is false." If it is true, then it is false. (If it belongs to the set of true statements, it doesn't.) If it is false, it is true. (If it doesn't belong to the set of true statements, it does.)

Self-justifying beliefs. Beliefs that do not depend on other beliefs for their justification. To hold such a belief is automatically to be justified in holding it.

Sense experience. Experiences that accompany all observations. Our sense experiences are the ways in which things look, sound, feel, smell, and taste to us. That is, they are the ways things seem to us when we observe them.

Set theory. Branch of mathematics dealing with sets. A set is a collection defined by its members. Whenever a member is added or dropped, a new set is formed.

Chapter 17

SCIENTIFIC
EXPLANATION

In Chapters 15 and 16, I have been assuming that scientific theories have as much of a claim to be considered cases of knowledge as do our ordinary beliefs. Indeed, I have gone so far as to say that scientific theories can even overthrow our ordinary beliefs about the world, even those that, like the belief that parallel lines never meet, seem to be self-evident. In this chapter, we will examine some reasons for doubting this assumption.

Two attitudes toward science

When I introduce my students to the theory of knowledge, I often ask them to name some statements they think they know. After writing the statements on the blackboard, I then ask them to rank the statements in order of certainty. Once, a student insisted that the statement "There are electrons" is more certain than any of the following: "I am sitting in a classroom," "It seems to me that I am sitting in a classroom," "This wall is yellow," and "This wall looks yellow to me." Expressing some surprise, I asked her why she felt that way. Her answer was that science tells us the facts, whereas the rest is just our own opinions.

This answer reflects one commonly held attitude toward science. According to this attitude, currently accepted scientific theories are more certain than even our own observations. Science, as my student said, deals with fact; the rest of us deal only with opinion.

But there is a second commonly held attitude toward science, reflected by the following anecdote.

As our class discussions of the theory of knowledge continue, I tell my students about the physicist's view of the world, stressing that the elementary particles, such as electrons and quarks, are colorless. "How do you know that?" a student once asked. "That's what the physicists say," I answered. "But that's just their opinion," he responded. "Why take their word for it?"

According to this attitude, the word of the scientist carries no more authority than that of the common person, even when it comes to matters generally considered part of the scientist's expertise. We often come across this attitude in conflicts between scientific theories and religious beliefs, as when fundamentalist Christians say that the theory of evolution is just that—a theory—and therefore holds no greater claim to our acceptance than the creation account given in Genesis. In both cases we are dealing with mere opinion.

Both of these attitudes are, of course, extreme ones. The first ignores two crucial points. First, the observations of the scientist are used to provide evidence for scientific theories. If their observations are mere opinion, how can their theories be anything else but mere opinion? If, that is, theories are accepted on the basis of certain observations, we cannot relegate those observations to the realm of mere opinion while maintaining that the theories are pure fact.

This is not to say that theories don't lead us to discount observations. To the contrary, they sometimes do. When we see a stick half submerged in water and the stick appears bent, we often discount the observation because of our theory of light refraction. The stick isn't really bent, we say. It just looks bent because the water refracts the light. But even in this case, the observation that the stick appears bent is taken as evidence for the theory of light refraction.

Moreover, the first attitude ignores another crucial point. Scientific theories change. Any currently accepted theory may be modified because of further observations or even replaced by another theory. Once it was thought that the sun revolved around the earth; now it is believed that the earth revolves around the sun. Once it was thought that the atom was the smallest particle; now it is believed that electrons and quarks are basic. Once it was thought that the passage of time was absolute; now it is believed to be relative to speed and gravitational pull.

The second attitude ignores the expertise of the scientist. Granted, theories do change and scientists often admit that they were wrong, but that does not mean that their beliefs about the nature of elementary particles are mere opinions, on a par with our own opinions about the ultimate nature of matter. By way of comparison, think of the physician. Physicians often err, but we do not on that account put our health in the hands of anybody who has an opinion on the matter. However fallible individual physicians may be, and however imperfect the current state of medical knowledge may be, it is far more reasonable to trust a physician's diagnosis of a medical problem than, say, a plumber's, just as it is far more reasonable to call a plumber when installing new bathroom fixtures than it is to call a physician. Similarly, given their training, scientists are best able to tell us about the elementary particles. If they are wrong, it is far more likely that their mistakes will be discovered by other scientists—not by me and my students during a class discussion.

So there is a middle ground, somewhere between these two attitudes, that is most reasonable. Scientific theories may be overturned, so it is a mistake to take them as gospel. But they provide the best explanation we have to date, and they are not to be relegated to the realm of mere opinion. This middle ground is a bit wider than it might first appear. Within it, there are two opposing attitudes, each a less extreme version of the two attitudes noted above.

SCIENCE AND TRUTH

Can we reasonably expect science to lead us to the truth? When we have arrived at the best scientific theories we can develop, will we have arrived at the truth? Is there such a thing as scientific advance? If so, does science advance toward the truth?

The middle ground that we claimed in the previous section leaves room for conflicting answers to these questions. The first answer, which we may call the *Peircean view*, after Charles Sanders Peirce (1839–1914), is a positive one. According to this view, science proceeds in an orderly way, with each adjustment to accepted theories and each replacement of one theory by another taking us closer to the truth. That is, science progresses toward an ideal theory, which is the one true theory about the world, and each step in this progression is a step more nearly approximating that true theory. At any point in this progression, we can say that currently accepted theories are more nearly true than earlier ones.

The second, *non-Peircean* answer is a negative one. According to this view, science does progress, but it is mistaken to view the progression of science as a march toward the truth. The non-Peircean attitude has two forms. The first, called *instrumentalism*, views scientific theories as instruments or tools for the prediction of future observations. Just as some saws are better than others for cutting wood, so are some theories better than others for predicting future observations. But just as we do not call the better saw the true or more nearly true one, so should we not call the better theory the true or more nearly true one.

The other non-Peircean attitude may be called the *Kuhnian view*, after the contemporary American historian of science Thomas Kuhn. According to Kuhn, the characteristic activity of science is puzzle-solving. The puzzles to be solved and the procedures for solving them are supplied by what he calls a *paradigm*. What is a paradigm? It is a body of accepted theory shared by the members of a scientific community that determines the research objectives of the members of that community. Newtonian physics, for example, was such a paradigm for three centuries. In its place we now have relativity theory and quantum mechanics as the paradigms of physics.

When a body of theory becomes the paradigm of a particular science, it presents many puzzles to the scientists. Chiefly, these puzzles involve the refinement of the theory in areas in which it has had some success and the extension of the theory to areas in which it has not yet been applied. Scientists working in evolutionary theory, for example, deal with such puzzles as these: Why should particular traits become dominant in certain species? What is the most important unit in evolution—the species, the group, the individual, or the gene pool? Are social behavior and institutions the product of the same mechanisms as physical traits?

In the normal course of scientific activity, science progresses by solving these puzzles and generating new ones. In extraordinary times, as when Newton's paradigm was replaced by Einstein's, it advances by changing paradigms. But neither sort of advance is an advance toward the truth.

Why not? Because different paradigms are different ways of looking at the world—different ways of seeing it, describing it, examining it and attempting to understand it. Although there are various reasons for preferring one paradigm to another, these reasons should not lead us to declare the preferred one more nearly true than the other.

We will have more to say about the Peircean and non-Peircean attitudes later in this chapter. But first, let us take a look at scientific reasoning.

INDUCTION AND DEDUCTION

Philosophers distinguish two types of reasoning—*deduction* and *induction*. Good deductive reasoning, called a *valid deductive argument*, is said to be *truth-preserving*. The best way to see what this means is to look at an example. Consider the following:

1. Either today is Saturday or I'm a monkey's uncle.
2. I'm not a monkey's uncle.
3. Therefore, today is Saturday.

The first two statements of the above argument are called *premises*. The third is the *conclusion*. Notice—if the premises are true, there is no way that the conclusion can be false. That is, the above argument follows a certain rule of reasoning that guarantees that if the premises are true, so is the conclusion. That is what we mean when we say that deductive reasoning is truth-preserving. It is also why we can say the following: A valid deductive argument is one that follows a rule of reasoning that guarantees that if the premises are true, so is the conclusion.

Inductive reasoning, on the other hand, is *not* truth-preserving. Good inductive reasoning, called *warranted inference*, is reasoning that shows that the conclusion is *acceptable* given certain other statements, called the *evidence, grounds,* or *reasons.* That is, the reasons in a warranted inference, unlike the premises of a valid argument, confer only a high degree of likelihood on the conclusion. They do not guarantee that the conclusion is true.

Most of our everyday reasoning is inductive. If I look at my watch and say that the time is such and such, I am reasoning inductively. If a friend tells me something and I believe what I am told, I am reasoning inductively. If I hear a loud bang and conclude that a car backfired, I am reasoning inductively. If I taste a brand of peanut butter, like the taste and then decide to continue buying that brand, I am reasoning inductively. In each case, I conclude that the most likely explanation of the evidence is a certain conclusion. That is, I accept the hypothesis that I take to be most likely.

The notion of explanation is crucial here. Hypotheses, the conclusions of inductive inferences, are, as we saw in the previous chapter, justified by explanatory statements. My watch says twelve o'clock *because* it is twelve o'clock. My friend said what she did *because* she believes what she said, and she believes it *because* she has good reason to believe it, and she has good reason *because* it is true. I heard a bang *because* a car backfired. This peanut butter tastes the way it does *because* it was prepared a certain way, and other jars of this brand will taste the same *because* they are made the same way.

Scientific reasoning is also inductive, but it is inductive reasoning of a special kind. Let us see what this kind is.

Theoretical Induction

Ordinarily, inductive inferences proceed like this. We observe certain kinds of regularities and infer that these regularities will continue. I have observed, for example, that backfiring cars make a loud noise, so when I hear a similar noise I infer that it was caused by a backfiring car. Similarly, we observe white and only white swans and conclude that all swans are white.

Of course, we cannot always make a warranted inference to the conclusion that observed regularities will continue. Such an inference is warranted only if we are warranted in believing that something explains these observed regularities and will continue to explain future regularities. That is, we cannot infer that observed regularities will continue if they were purely coincidental. The inference that all swans are white, for example, is warranted by the belief that there is something about the genetic make-up of swans that makes them white. The inference that my friend is now telling the truth is warranted by the belief that she is a reliable person, and that this aspect of her character explains the fact that she has told the truth before and will continue to tell the truth.

Thus, warranted induction requires more than observed regularities. It also requires a certain theory explaining these regularities, or at least the justified belief that such a theory can be devised. Suppose, for example, that you toss a coin five times and each time it comes up tails. Is the conclusion that it will come up tails the next time warranted? That depends. If you have additional reason to believe that the coin is not a fair one, the fact that it came up tails five times in a row might warrant that conclusion, if the additional evidence is strong enough. Otherwise, the conclusion that the next toss will come up tails is not warranted. In the former case, the assumption that the coin is not a fair one provides an explanation of the five tosses, and that explanation will explain why the next toss will be tails. In the latter case, there is no such explanation. The five tosses came up tails by pure coincidence.

Thus, a suitable theory (in this case about the coin) is required for an inference that observed regularities will continue. How can we test the theory? In the case of the coin, we can run two sorts of tests. For one thing, we can continue tossing it. If it continues to come up tails, even after a thousand tosses, that is good evidence that it is not a fair coin. If it begins coming up heads with the same regularity as it does tails, that is good evidence that it is a fair coin. Second, we can examine the coin. If, for example, we find that both sides are tails, we have observed that it is not a fair coin. Or, if we notice that the coin is weighted on one side, causing it to come up tails, we have in that way observed that it is not a fair coin.

The second sort of test provides *direct* evidence for the hypothesis that the coin is not a fair one. The evidence is direct because it is a matter of simple *observation* of what makes the coin unfair. The first sort of test, on the other hand, provides *indirect* evidence. It is indirect because we observe only the *consequences* of the hypothesis. That is, we reason this way. *If* the coin is not a fair one, it will continue to turn up tails. Since it does continue to turn up tails, no matter how often we toss it, it is reasonable to conclude that it is unfair.

In our ordinary lives, we make use of both direct and indirect evidence. In the testing of scientific theories, however, direct evidence is generally unavailable. This is because scientists often attempt to explain what they observe by appealing to something that they do not observe and often cannot observe. Thus, their inferences are somewhat different from many ordinary ones. They do not infer that certain observed regularities explain other observed ones. Let us call this form of induction *theoretical induction.*

Famous examples of this sort of induction are the genetic theory of Gregor Mendel (1822–1884) and Sigmund Freud's (1856–1939) theory of unconscious motivation. Why is it that certain traits are passed on from generation to generation with a certain distribution? Mendel's answer was that there is some hidden factor (now called a *gene*) that transmits these traits, and that some are *dominant* and some *recessive*. Take the example of blue and brown eyes. If I inherited blue-eye genes from my mother and brown-eye genes from my father, I will be brown-eyed, because brown eyes are a dominant trait and blue eyes recessive. If my wife also inherited both blue- and brown-eye genes, she will also have brown eyes. But there is one chance out of four that our child will have blue eyes, because there is one chance out of four that the child will inherit my blue-eye genes and its mother's. Thus, this theory explains why a certain percentage of children of brown-eyed parents will have blue eyes.

Similarly, why is it that we behave in certain ways, even when we claim to want to behave in other ways? Freud's answer was that our motivation for such behavior is unconscious. Whatever we consciously want, believe, fear, and so forth, there are unconscious wants, beliefs, and fears that govern our behavior. Moreover, these unconscious motivations even govern our behavior that we think is done for conscious reasons.

Likewise, contemporary physicists explain all sorts of laboratory phenomena by appealing to such entities as electrons and quarks. There is, for example, a bit of apparatus known as a Wilson cloud chamber. Under certain conditions, a line of condensed vapor will appear in the chamber. What is the explanation of the line? An electron is passing through the chamber, leaving a vapor trail.

Notice that Mendel didn't observe the genes. Nor did Freud observe unconscious motivations, nor do physicists observe electrons or quarks. Rather, such things are *posited* by the scientist. They are not observed entities or events, but *posits*. Scientists accept their existence on the basis of observation and theory, but they are not themselves observed.

Theory selection and confirmation

Two questions appear at this point. First, why choose one theory over any other? Why choose to explain behavior in terms of unconscious motivation? Why not say, for example, that the behavior is purely arbitrary, or that it is controlled by some outside force, the devil, for instance? There are any number of possible explanations. Why pick that one?

Well, the reasons were given in the previous chapter. There, I noted simplicity, conservatism, and usefulness in predicting future observations. All of these considerations favor the positing of unconscious motivation over the positing of satanic possession.

But how do we test these theories? We test them by seeking indirect evidence. Because usefulness in predicting future observations is an important feature of theories, scientists test them by seeing whether predicted observations occur. If Mendel's theory is correct, we can expect to observe a certain distribution of inherited traits in successive generations. If Freud's is correct, we can expect to observe certain behavior in certain circumstances. If a predicted observation occurs, the observation is said to be a *confirming instance* of the theory, and the theory is said to be *confirmed*. If the predicted observation does not occur, the observation that occurs instead is said to be a *disconfirming instance*, and the theory is said to be *disconfirmed*.

Notice that I said "confirmed" and "disconfirmed," not "proved" and "disproved." One expected observation does not *prove* that a theory is true, nor does one unexpected observation *disprove* it. In general, scientists avoid talk of proof and disproof. Instead, they talk of confirmation and disconfirmation. And theories that have many confirming instances and few or no disconfirming ones are called highly confirmed—not proved.

Thus, to speak of theory versus fact is misleading in science. There is no sharp distinction, just a continuum. At the one end, there are highly confirmed theories currently accepted by scientists; at the other, highly disconfirmed theories rejected by scientists. In between, there are theories of lesser and greater *degrees of confirmation.*

Theory Revision and Theory Rejection

One remark in the above section may seem somewhat puzzling. A highly confirmed theory, I said, has many confirming instances and few, if any, disconfirming ones. This means that scientists accept theories with disconfirming instances. Why don't they reject a theory when disconfirming instances are found? What do they do when they come across one?

Well, there is no *one* thing that they do in such cases. Sometimes they will make certain revisions in the theory so that the revised theory is one that would have made the proper prediction. Once a theory is developed, it does not remain static, but is constantly refined and revised. To continue the metaphor of the previous chapter, a theory is like a web. At the center may be something like the statement that the speed of light is constant, or that unconscious motivation determines behavior, or that genes transmit inherited traits, or that species change through natural selection. But the theory includes much more—certain details regarding how natural selection works, for example, or the ways in which unconscious motivations are formed. If the predicted observations don't occur, changes will be made in these less central points, but not at the center.

Sometimes scientists will treat disconfirming instances as outstanding puzzles, which they will either proceed to tackle immediately or put off for a time, depending on how pressing they are compared with other puzzles. Sometimes they may even ignore an unexpected result, attributing the failure to experimental error.

For an example of theory revision, consider the following well-known chapter in the history of science. Early in the nineteenth century, the theory of the solar system included the following: Seven planets orbit the sun, and their orbits obey the law of gravity. On the basis of this theory, certain predictions were made concerning the orbit of Uranus. When these predictions turned out to be wrong, two astronomers working independently, John C. Adams (1819–1892) in England and Urbain Leverrier (1811–1877) in France, predicted that there must be an eighth planet, and in 1846, Neptune was discovered. The important point here is that scientists did not reject the belief that the planets orbit the sun, nor did they reject the law of gravity as accepted. Instead, they assumed that there was an unknown planet. The unexpected orbit of Uranus was seen as a puzzle for astronomical theory, not as a reason for rejecting it.

Of course, the proliferation of puzzles can get out of hand, and attempts to solve them can introduce greater and greater strain on the troubled theory. That is what happened to the theory of the ancient astronomer Ptolemy, according to which the earth remains stationary in the center of the universe and the other bodies orbit the earth. As unpredicted observations multiplied, so did the revisions. The earth was moved slightly off center, the other planets were said to move in odd, inexplicable ways, and there seemed to be no underlying principles or laws providing any systematic unity to the hodgepodge of calculations.

These adjustments to Ptolemaic theory are perfect examples of what philosophers call *ad hoc assumptions.* That is, they were introduced to patch up particular failings of the theory, but had no applications beyond those particular failings. They were thrown in after the fact but did not prevent the need for further patching up. Contrast such adjustments to the adjustment of Adams and Leverrier. In this case, the positing of Neptune's existence made possible the prediction of many future observations beyond the quirks in Uranus's orbit.

But the strain on Ptolemaic theory was not itself enough to bring about the rejection of the theory. An entire theory is not scrapped unless there is another theory to take its place. In this case, the replacing theory was provided by Copernicus (1473–1543), who placed the sun at the center instead of the earth. The result was a simpler theory, unified by certain principles of motion, and unhampered by the huge number of ad hoc assumptions that plagued Ptolemaic theory. Still, Ptolemy's views were not immediately replaced by Copernicus's. Further and more precise observations followed, providing greater confirmation of the Copernican view. But even more importantly, there came the work of Galileo (1564–1642) and Johannes Kepler (1571–1630), which vastly improved on Copernicus's theory and provided the first truly modern view of the heavens.

At that point, a scientific revolution occurred. In Kuhn's terms, one paradigm was replaced by another, as theories were changed and the direction of scientific research radically altered.

AN ADVANCE TOWARD TRUTH?

All of the above is fairly uncontroversial. But a question arises: Why say that successive theories bring us closer to the truth? Why not say instead that successive theories are more useful, or simple, or whatever, and leave it at that?

To ask these questions is to return to the debate between the Peirceans and non-Peirceans. The Peirceans, once again, believe that science aims toward a final, true theory of the world, and that the history of science is a succession of theories bringing us ever closer to that goal. Non-Peirceans do not deny that science progresses, but deny that we can rightly speak of this progress as a series of closer approximations of truth.

Thus, one kind of non-Peircean, the instrumentalist, claims that scientific theories are mere tools for predicting observations, and that we can rightfully speak of them as being better or worse tools, but not as being more or less true.

THE PROBLEM OF INDUCTION

Most everyday and scientific reasoning, we saw, is inductive reasoning. In fact, we use induction so often that we take its reliability for granted. But is our faith in induction justified? Some philosophers have answered no.

The so-called problem of induction was first introduced by David Hume (1711–1776). His presentation of the problem proceeded as follows. Nature, as we have all noticed, has conformed to certain regularities in the past. Objects thrown into the air have fallen to the ground, water has frozen at thirty-two degrees Fahrenheit, ducks have not suddenly turned into chickens, and so forth. Noticing this, we naturally assume that these regularities will continue. It is because of this assumption that we rely on inductive inference. If we did not believe that these regularities would continue, there would be no reason to believe induction reliable.

But what is our reason for believing that these regularities *will* continue? Certainly, we do not involve ourselves in any contradictions by entertaining the possibility that all regularities might suddenly be upset. The world would become a very strange place, of course, but there is nothing logically impossible about such strangeness.

It seems that we can justify induction only by resorting to past experience. Since the world has conformed to certain regularities in the past, it is reasonable to believe that it will continue to do so. The problem with this line of reasoning is that it assumes what it aims to prove. That is, it resorts to induction in order to justify induction. Such circular reasoning, Hume argued, provides no justification at all.

Science Without Induction

Hume took his argument to be decisive, and accepted its skeptical consequences. Some contemporary philosophers, led by Karl Popper, also accept Hume's argument as decisive, but, unlike Hume, argue that science does not rest on induction at all. These *anti-inductivists*, as we shall call them, claim that the task of science is not to show that theories are *true*, but to show that they are false. Scientists do not seek to *verify* theories; rather, they seek to *falsify* them.

According to this view, a scientific hypothesis is a *conjecture*, which can be tested by a number of *crucial experiments*. These experiments are said to be crucial because, if the predicted observations do not occur, the conjecture has been shown to be false. If the predicted observations do occur, however, that is no reason to think the conjecture true. All that we are entitled to say is that it has not been shown to be false.

Thus, crucial experiments do not support conjectures, in the sense of giving evidence for their truth. If they do not refute a conjecture, the job of the scientist is to run another crucial experiment that might refute it. Even if the conjecture is never refuted, the best that we can say is that it has not been shown to be false. We are never justified in claiming that it is true.

This view has two serious problems, though. First, it does not seem consistent with the practice of actual scientists. As we saw in the main body of this chapter, scientists do *not* submit all statements in a theory to crucial tests. Theories are tested, of course, but disconfirming instances do not immediately lead to their rejection. Disconfirming instances are often taken as puzzles, not refutations.

Second, it seems to neglect the *practical* use to which scientific theories are put. We depend on scientific theories in all sorts of practical matters, and we do so because we believe that there is good reason to think them true, not because they have not been proved false. Many things have not been proved false, but that by itself is no reason to act on them.

Thus, most philosophers have been more inclined to seek a justification of induction than to do without induction. Let us look at two much-discussed attempts.

A Linguistic Argument and a Pragmatic Argument

Hume assumed that the only way to justify induction is to show that induction must lead to true predictions. Some philosophers, however, have claimed that induction can be justified in other ways.

Consider, for example, the following *linguistic* argument. To justify a belief is to show that it is reasonable. To justify the belief that we can rely on induction, then, is to show that it is reasonable to do so.

But what do we mean by the word "reasonable"? According to the argument under consideration, part of what we mean is something like "in accordance with the principles of induction." That is, it belongs to the meaning of "reasonable" that induction is reasonable. And in that case, induction needs no further justification. It is reasonable to rely on it because that is what we mean by "reasonable."

Consider also the following *pragmatic* argument. Although we cannot be certain that induction will lead to successful predictions, we can be certain of this much—if anything can, induction can. If induction is ultimately unreliable, then so is any other method.

Suppose that nature conforms to certain regularities. In that case, induction will eventually lead to their discovery and therefore to successful predictions. If nature does not conform to any regularities, then induction will not lead to successful predictions, but neither will any other method.

Therefore, we cannot lose by relying on induction. We are like a dying patient deciding whether to undergo surgery, where the patient does not know whether the surgery will be successful but does know that nothing else can save his life. He has nothing to lose by having the operation, but everything to gain.

Do these arguments provide acceptable solutions to Hume's problem? Most philosophers think not. Hume's problem is not that there is no reason whatever to rely on induction. It is, rather, that there is no reason to believe that it will lead to the truth. And no examination of the meanings of words can assure us that it will lead to truth, nor will arguments turning on safe betting strategies.

But there is another, more important objection to these arguments. There is no *one* method called induction. Rather, there are infinitely many possible inductive methods. Even if the two arguments considered show that it is reasonable to rely on induction, they do not show that it is more reasonable to rely on the methods we now use than on any other inductive methods.

A Circular Justification

Hume claimed that any attempt to justify induction by appealing to past experience is circular, and therefore unacceptable. Must we agree with him? Perhaps not. In the previous chapter, we saw that there is a sense in which the justification of *all* beliefs is circular. Since justification is a matter of explanatory coherence, every belief helps to justify every other belief, in which case all justification must come full circle. But that does not mean that we are not justified in believing anything, I said. Our webs are not constructed like big circles. Instead, they are constructed like vast, intricate, crisscrossing networks. In other words, justification is not a matter of proceeding in one direction along a closed circle, but of establishing the coherence of the entire network.

Our belief that the inductive methods we use will lead to truth is the glue that holds the network together, but it is also part of the network itself. In that case, its justification must proceed like the justification of any other belief. That is, it is justified by its place in the network and the usefulness of the entire network in predicting experience.

If such a justification is circular, as Hume claims, perhaps the circle is not a *vicious* one. Perhaps, that is, it does not prevent us from being justified in believing that induction will lead to truth.

The chief reason for adopting this position is the nature of theoretical induction. If we cannot achieve direct evidence for our theories, if, for example, we can never observe electrons or quarks, if our decision to accept electron theory is based on its usefulness in predicting observations, then why say that electron theory is true? Why say that there *are* electrons?

Whenever we devise and accept a scientific theory, the selection of that particular theory is in no way *forced* on us. We have certain standards of selection, of course, but what is there to guarantee that these standards lead to *truth?* The theory that combines conservatism and simplicity with the ability to predict observations without reliance on ad hoc assumptions is certainly the most *useful* theory, but why should the most useful one be the true one?

Implicit in this argument is the following view of science: The major task of science is the discovery of observable regularities. Scientific theories lead to success in this task by acting as a middleman. By positing various entities and forces, they allow us to predict that certain regularities will occur. But we can accept them as useful middlemen without committing ourselves to their truth.

Also implicit in this argument is a certain view of scientific explanation: To explain a certain phenomenon is to be able to predict future occurrences of the same phenomenon. To explain *compulsive behavior,* such as excessive hand washing or overeating, in terms of unconscious motivation is to adopt a way of predicting such behavior in the future. To explain the distribution of different eye colors in a generation in terms of dominant and recessive genes is to adopt a way of predicting future distributions. Thus, scientific explanations are merely tools for prediction, and we need not concern ourselves with questions of truth and falsity.

But both of these implicit assumptions are suspect. Science does not merely seek to discover and predict observable regularities. It also seeks to *understand* them. It seeks to discover *why* they occur and *how* they occur. If theories are merely tools for prediction, then science does not really help us understand the world at all, and these regularities will forever remain a mystery to us.

Likewise, to explain something is not merely to learn how to predict future occurrences of it. It is also to understand why our predictions are successful. Suppose, for example, that every time your philosophy instructor comes into class needing a shave he gives you a surprise quiz. Once you notice this, you will be able to predict when he will give you a quiz and when he will not. But you do not know *why* he gives you a quiz on those and only those days. Your ability to predict a quiz does not mean that you can explain its occurrence. Only when you have learned *why* the regularity exists will you know its explanation. If, for example, you learn that he comes into class unshaven because he has been out all night, you might adopt the hypothesis that he gives you a quiz because he has not had time to prepare a lecture. If your hypothesis is *true*, you have explained the quizzes. Otherwise, you have not.

Therefore, to accept instrumentalism is either to distort the aim of science or to convict science of failing to achieve its aim. But to say this is not to say that instrumentalism is wrong. Perhaps, that is, science does not really provide explanations. Perhaps our best scientific theories are not close approximations of the truth.

Against these claims, we can say the following. The methods of science are highly refined variations of our ordinary methods for getting at the truth. They have evolved out of centuries of trial and error. They have been put to the test in our ordinary lives and in scientific enterprises of ever-increasing theoretical sophistication. No doubt, it is mistaken to claim that they are absolutely certain to arrive at the truth some day. Still, the arguments considered in this section are not enough to make it unreasonable to believe that they will.

If the methods of science constitute the best way we have of investigating certain sorts of problems, and if the acceptance of scientific theories is governed by these methods, then it is reasonable to believe that progress from one theory to the next is an advance toward truth.

ARE COMPETING THEORIES INCOMMENSURABLE?

Our response to the instrumentalist assumes that there are fairly well defined ways of choosing among competing theories, that supporters of competing theories share at least rough agreement on these methods, and that after a sufficient period of reasoned debate these methods will support the theory coming closest to the truth.

What if these assumptions are overly optimistic? What if observation and reasoned debate can take disagreeing scientists only so far, after which the choice of one theory among two or more must be made on some other basis?

These are the questions posed by Kuhn, who argues that rival paradigms are *incommensurable*. By that he means that they cannot be compared in a totally objective and rational manner. When some scientists want to introduce a new paradigm at the same time that others remain faithful to the existing one, there is a clash between two radically different ways of looking at the world, and there is no neutral ground from which a decisive solution can be found. Let us look at two reasons for adopting this view.

First, Kuhn claims, adherents of rival theories quite literally do not see the same things, so observations cannot provide a suitable neutral ground. What we see when we look at the world depends on our beliefs about what we are seeing. Prior beliefs create expectations, and these expectations help to form our observations. The beliefs belonging to rival theories are often so different that they make it impossible for disputing scientists to have the same observations. One scientist cannot observe what a disputant observes until the conversion process has already begun.

The situation is in many ways analogous to a religious conversion or a mystical experience. The born-again Christian and the Zen disciple who achieves *satori* (or enlightenment) do not first observe evidence for their new world views and then have their experiences. The experiences and evidence and world views are brought about together. The born-again Christian has to be brought to see the world as a continuing miracle. The Zen disciple has to be brought to see that the distinctions of ordinary thought are not ultimate. And more than reasoned debate is required to bring them to that point. Something fundamentally *nonrational* is required.

To make this analogy is not to convict scientists of being *irrational*. Kuhn does not say that they fly in the face of reason. Rather, his claim is that something is needed *in addition* to reason. A commonly cited example of how expectations help to form observations is the duck-rabbit drawing.

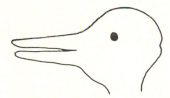

Some of you looking at this figure immediately see a duck. Others immediately see a rabbit. In order for you to change your perception, you have to think of the figure differently. You have to tell yourself that certain lines depict a duck's bill, not rabbit ears. You have to think of the figure as facing to the left, not to the right. If you first see it as a rabbit, that is, you have to *think* of it as a duck before you can *see* it as a duck. According to Kuhn, the same thing applies to scientists in times of paradigm disputes. Where one scientist sees a duck, the other sees a rabbit. Where one sees compelling evidence for the new theory, the other sees a mere puzzle for the old.

Second, supporters of rival theories cannot always agree on *what* needs to be explained, let alone *how* it is to be explained. If different theories take different things as basic and not in need of explanation, how can there be an objective way of deciding which provides the best explanation?

According to the physics of Aristotle (384–322 B.C.), for example, the natural state of matter is rest. Whereas motion always has to be explained, rest never has to be explained. If an object stops moving, we need not ask why. If it continues to move, we must ask why.

According to the physics of Isaac Newton (1642–1727), however, it is not motion that requires explanation, but *change* of motion. If a moving object stops, explanation is needed. If it slows down or speeds up, explanation is needed. If it changes direction, explanation is needed. If an object at rest begins to move, explanation is needed. But if a moving object does not change direction or speed, explanation is no more required than if an object at rest remains at rest.

The difference between Aristotle and Newton here is not merely a matter of disagreement concerning the law of *inertia* (as Newton's principle is called). Instead, Kuhn says, the difference concerns a fundamental way of looking at the world. Thus, when a Newtonian looks at a freely swinging object tied to a rope attached to the ceiling, he sees a *pendulum*. When an Aristotelian looks in the same direction, he sees an object trying to achieve its natural state of rest at the bottom. The difference is not *how* to explain the motion of a pendulum, but *what* is to be explained.

Thus, the argument goes, the Newtonian and Aristotelian paradigms are incommensurable. Each takes a different phenomenon as basic, and each is supported by different observations requiring different types of explanations. Ultimately, a conversion is needed to end the dispute. One side must come to see the world differently.

The Peircean Response

Kuhn's arguments have attracted many philosophers to the Kuhnian view, but many others remain unconvinced. For one thing, even if we grant that disputing scientists see things differently, that does not mean that we must grant that they literally see different things. Even if the Aristotelian does not describe what he sees as a pendulum, even if he cannot think of it or see it as a pendulum, that does not mean that he is not seeing a pendulum. If two people receive similar light patterns from the same source, they are seeing the same thing, whatever they think it is.

Moreover, there is always some neutral way of describing what is seen. If describing it as a pendulum unfairly slants the observation in favor of the Newtonian, we can always describe it as a ball on a string. And if all else fails, we can fall back on the light patterns on the observers' retinas. The point here is that even if different theories involve radically different beliefs about what is observed, there is always some body of shared beliefs that allows for a neutral description. Consequently, we can say that the disputants see the same thing, and we can describe what they see in such a way that they would both agree.

Also, that different theories take different phenomena as basic does not show that these theories cannot be compared and evaluated. Whether we take rest or change of motion as basic has numerous consequences for the resultant theories, and we can compare the theories accordingly. Once again, considerations of simplicity, predictive power, conservatism, and lack of reliance on ad hoc assumptions come into play here. It may take time before these considerations allow us to pick out the best theory, and something like a conversion experience may accompany the acceptance of that theory by some scientists, but that does not mean that the rival theories are incommensurable. Nor does it mean that the new theory does not lead us closer to the truth.

The final word?

Our conclusion, then, is a Peircean one: Science leads to truth. But before leaving the topic, let me introduce two further considerations in support of that view.

The first comes from the contemporary American philosopher Hilary Putnam, perhaps the most energetic of today's Peirceans. We can put this point in the form of a question: If scientific theories are neither true nor approximately true, why do they work so well? Why is talk of electrons and quarks so successful? Why is the positing of unconscious motivation so powerful in our understanding of one another? The best answer is that science works so well because its theories are true or nearly true. Indeed, there is no other good explanation for its success. If its theories are not even approximately true, their success is nothing but a miracle.

It is important to note here that the success of science is not limited to the prediction of laboratory phenomena. Televisions, computers, and so forth, are a large part of the success of science. So, for better or worse, are nuclear power plants and weapons.

Second, although science does sometimes progress through radical shifts, the advance of science is more continuous than the Kuhnian view might make it appear. Successive theories often replace previous ones with radically different conceptions of the world, but there is a sense in which they contain the earlier theories in themselves. However radical the break may at first seem, important continuities can be found.

Let us think of the extraordinary success that Newton's theories had and still have. The physics and geometry we learn in high school are those of Newtonian physics, and engineers and others continue to use the Newtonian framework with great success. But this success is explained by Einstein's theories. Newton's laws can be taken as special cases of Einstein's. When we apply Einstein's "in the small," we come up with measurements much like Newton's. That is, Einstein's cover the situations in which Newton's are applicable plus those in which Newton's are inapplicable.

This does give us a picture of progress toward the truth.

STUDY QUESTIONS

1. What is the Peircean view of science? How does it differ from instrumentalism and the Kuhnian view?
2. What is deductive reasoning? Inductive reasoning? How does a valid argument differ from a warranted inference?
3. What is theoretical induction? When scientists reason by theoretical induction, how do they select their hypotheses? How do they test them?
4. What is a confirming instance of a theory? A disconfirming instance? What options are open to scientists when they come upon a disconfirming instance of their theory?
5. According to the instrumentalist, scientific theories should be thought of as tools for prediction. Why do they say that? Why have other philosophers disagreed?
6. What does Kuhn mean by the claim that rival theories are incommensurable? How does he support the claim? How do Peirceans respond?
7. What is an ad hoc assumption? What role does the notion play in the acceptance and rejection of scientific theories?
8. Why did Hume believe that induction is in need of justification? Why did he believe that induction could not be justified? Why did Popper believe that science does not rest on induction?
9. What three attempts at justifying induction did we consider? How well do they succeed?

GLOSSARY

Ad hoc assumption. An assumption that is (1) made to save a theory from a particular *disconfirming instance,* but that (2) has no application beyond that instance. In other words, an ad hoc assumption explains why a particular experiment does not come off but provides no help in predicting the outcome of future experiments.

Anti-inductivism. The view that science does not attempt to verify hypotheses by *induction,* but instead tries to falsify them by exposing them to crucial experiments.

Confirmation. The successful outcome of an observational test of a hypothesis. To confirm a hypothesis is to show that an observation predicted by the hypothesis occurs. If it does, the hypothesis is confirmed, and the predicted observation is said to be a confirming instance of the hypothesis. If it does not, the hypothesis is *disconfirmed,* and the unpredicted observation is said to be a disconfirming instance.

Deduction. A form of reasoning governed by rules that are *truth-preserving.* To say that the rules are truth-preserving is to say that they guarantee that, if the *premises* are true, so is the conclusion. A deductive argument that conforms to these rules is a *valid* one.

Direct evidence. To acquire direct evidence for a hypothesis is to observe directly that the hypothesis is true. Direct evidence is contrasted with indirect evidence. To acquire *indirect evidence* for a hypothesis is to observe that some consequence of the hypothesis is true. Take, for example, the hypothesis that it is raining outside. If people come into my office and tell me that it is raining, and they are carrying wet umbrellas and wearing wet clothes, I have indirect evidence for the hypothesis. If I go outside and observe the rain myself, I have direct evidence.

Disconfirmation. (See *confirmation.*)

Incommensurability of theories. A feature ascribed to scientific theories by some philosophers. To say that two theories are incommensurable is to say that they cannot be compared in a totally objective way.

Indirect evidence. (See *direct evidence.*)

Induction. Form of reasoning that is not *truth-preserving*. In a good (that is, *warranted*) inductive inference, true evidence statements do not guarantee that the conclusion is true, but show that the conclusion is acceptable, or likely to be true.

Instrumentalism. The view that scientific theories are neither true nor false, but better or worse instruments for predicting observations.

Paradigm. A body of theory accepted by a scientific community and determining the research objectives of that community.

Posit. To accept the existence of something (an object or force, for instance) on the basis of indirect evidence and its ability to explain observed phenomena. Anything so posited is called a *posit.*

Premise. A statement in a deductive argument from which the argument's conclusion is drawn.

Theoretical induction. Form of induction in which only *indirect evidence* can be acquired. In theoretical induction, one *posits* the existence of an entity, force, or whatever, and seeks to *confirm* its existence by observing whether predicted observations occur.

Truth-preserving. (See *deduction.*)

Validity. (See *deduction.*)

Warranted inference. (See *induction.*)

SELECTIONS

The following two selections exemplify opposing views of our ability to have certain knowledge. In the first, from Meditations on First Philosophy, René Descartes takes a skeptical view. In the second, from the essay "Knowledge and Belief," Norman Malcolm argues that we can know many things for certain.

Notice the extent to which Descartes' argument hinges on the unreliability of the senses. Our senses can deceive us when we are awake. Can we be certain on any particular occasion that they are reliable? And even if they seem totally reliable on a given occasion, how can we know that we are not dreaming? How can we know that we have not always been dreaming? Perhaps there is no external world at all. Perhaps my perceptions are the result of some evil genius intent on deceiving me.

Notice the extent to which Malcolm is unimpressed by such "what if I'm dreaming?" arguments. True, we can imagine that we are dreaming or hallucinating, but that doesn't mean that we can't be sure that we're not. Notice also how he considers different types of cases, and how he uses them to appeal to our ordinary conceptions of what it is to make sure that something is true.

RENÉ DESCARTES

The Skeptical Attitude

It is now some years since I detected how many were the false beliefs that I had from my earliest youth admitted as true, and how doubtful was everything I had since constructed on this basis; and from that time I was convinced that I must once for all seriously undertake to rid myself of all the opinions which I had formerly accepted, and commence to build anew from the foundation, if I wanted to establish any firm and permanent structure in the sciences. But as this enterprise appeared to be a very great one, I waited until I had attained an age so mature that I could not hope that at any later date I should be better fitted to execute my design. This reason caused me to delay so long that I should feel that I was doing wrong were I to occupy in deliberation the time that yet remains to me for action. To-day, then, since very opportunely for the plan I have in view I have delivered my mind from every care [and am happily agitated by no passions] and since I have procured for myself an assured leisure in a peaceable retirement, I shall at last seriously and freely address myself to the general upheaval of all my former opinions.

Now for this object it is not necessary that I should show that all of these are false—I shall perhaps never arrive at this end. But inasmuch as reason already persuades me that I ought no less carefully to withhold my assent from matters which are not entirely certain and indubitable than from those which appear to me manifestly to be false, if I am able to find in each one some reason to doubt, this will suffice to justify my rejecting the whole. And for that end it will not be requisite that I should examine each in particular, which would be an endless undertaking; for owing to the fact that the destruction of the foundations of necessity brings with it the downfall of the rest of the edifice, I shall only in the first place attack those principles upon which all my former opinions rested.

All that up to the present time I have accepted as most true and certain I have learned either from the senses or through the senses; but it is sometimes proved to me that these senses are deceptive, and it is wiser not to trust entirely to anything by which we have once been deceived.

But it may be that although the senses sometimes deceive us concerning things which are hardly perceptible, or very far away, there are yet many others to be met with as to which we cannot reasonably have any doubt, although we recognise them by their means. For example, there is the fact that I am here, seated by the fire, attired in a dressing gown, having this paper in my hands and other similar matters. And how could I deny that these hands and this body are mine, were it not perhaps that I compare myself to certain persons, devoid of sense, whose cerebella are so troubled and clouded by the violent vapours of black bile, that they constantly assure us that they think they are kings when they are really quite poor, or that they are clothed in purple when they are really without covering, or who imagine that they have an earthenware head or are nothing but pumpkins or are made of glass. But they are mad, and I should not be any the less insane were I to follow examples so extravagant.

At the same time I must remember that I am a man, and that consequently I am in the habit of sleeping, and in my dreams representing to myself the same things or sometimes even less probable things, than do those who are insane in their waking moments. How often has it happened to me that in the night I dreamt that I found myself in this particular place, that I was dressed and seated near the fire, whilst in reality I was lying undressed in bed! At this moment it does indeed seem to me that it is with eyes awake that I am looking at this paper; that this head which I move is not asleep, that it is deliberately and of set purpose that I extend my hand and perceive it; what happens in sleep does not appear so clear nor so distinct as does all this. But in thinking over this I remind myself that on many occasions I have in sleep been deceived by similar illusions, and in dwelling carefully on this reflection I see so manifestly that there are no certain indications by which we may clearly distinguish wakefulness from sleep that I am lost in astonishment. And my astonishment is such that it is almost capable of persuading me that I now dream.

Now let us assume that we are asleep and that all these particulars, e.g. that we open our eyes, shake our head, extend our hands, and so on, are but false delusions; and let us reflect that possibly neither our hands nor our whole body are such as they appear to us to be. At the same time we must at least confess that the things which are represented to us in sleep are like painted representations which can only have been formed as the counterparts of something real and true, and that in this way those general things at least, i.e. eyes, a head, hands, and a whole body, are not imaginary things, but things really existent. For, as a matter of fact, painters, even when they study with the greatest skill to represent sirens and satyrs by forms the most strange and extraordinary, cannot give them natures which are entirely new, but merely make a certain medley of the members of different animals; or if their imagination is extravagant enough to invent something so novel that nothing similar has ever before been seen, and that then their work represents a thing purely fictitious and absolutely false, it is certain all the same that the colours of which this is composed are necessarily real. And for the same reason, although these general things, to wit, [a body], eyes, a head, hands, and such like, may be imaginary, we are bound at the same time to confess that there are at least some other objects yet more simple and more universal, which are real and true; and of these just in the same way as with certain real colours, all these images of things which dwell in our thoughts, whether true and real or false and fantastic, are formed.

To such a class of things pertains corporeal nature in general, and its extension, the figure of extended things, their quantity or magnitude and number, as also the place in which they are, the time which measures their duration, and so on.

That is possibly why our reasoning is not unjust when we conclude from this that Physics, Astronomy, Medicine and all other sciences which have as their end the consideration of composite things, are very dubious and uncertain; but that Arithmetic, Geometry and other sciences of that kind which only treat of things that are very simple and very general, without taking great trouble to ascertain whether they are actually existent or not, contain some measure of certainty and an element of the indubitable. For whether I am awake or asleep, two and three together always form five, and the square can never have more than four sides, and it does not seem possible that truths so clear and apparent can be suspected of any falsity [or uncertainty].

Nevertheless I have long had fixed in my mind the belief that an all-powerful God existed by whom I have been created such as I am. But how do I know that He has not brought it to pass that there is no earth, no heaven, no extended body, no magnitude, no place, and that nevertheless [I possess the perceptions of all these things and that] they seem to me to exist just exactly as I now see them? And, besides, as I sometimes imagine that others deceive themselves in the things which they think they know best, how do I know that I am not deceived every time that I add two and three, or count the sides of a square, or judge of things yet simpler, if anything simpler can be imagined? But possibly God has not desired that I should be thus deceived, for He is said to be supremely good. If, however, it is contrary to His goodness to have made me such that I constantly deceive myself, it would also appear to be contrary to His goodness to permit me to be sometimes deceived, and nevertheless I cannot doubt that He does permit this.

There may indeed be those who would prefer to deny the existence of a God so powerful, rather than believe that all other things are uncertain. But let us not oppose them for the present, and grant that all that is here said of a God is a fable; nevertheless in whatever way they suppose that I have arrived at the state of being that I have reached—whether they attribute it to fate or to accident, or make out that it is by a continual succession of antecedents, or by some other method—since to err and deceive oneself is a defect, it is clear that the greater will be the probability of my being so imperfect as to deceive myself ever, as is the Author to whom they assign my origin the less powerful. To these reasons I have certainly nothing to reply, but at the end I feel constrained to confess that there is nothing in all that I formerly believed to be true, of which I cannot in some measure doubt, and that not merely through want of thought or through levity, but for reasons which are very powerful and maturely considered; so that henceforth I ought not the less carefully to refrain from giving credence to these opinions than to that which is manifestly false, if I desire to arrive at any certainty [in the sciences].

But it is not sufficient to have made these remarks, we must also be careful to keep them in mind. For these ancient and commonly held opinions still revert frequently to my mind, long and familiar custom having given them the right to occupy my mind against my inclination and rendered them almost masters of my belief; nor will I ever lose the habit of deferring to them or of placing my confidence in them, so long as I consider them as they really are, i.e. opinions in some measure doubtful, as I have just shown, and at the same time highly probable, so that there is much more reason to believe in than to deny them. That is why I consider that I shall not be acting amiss, if, taking of set purpose a contrary belief, I allow myself to be deceived, and for a certain time pretend that all these opinions are entirely false and imaginary, until at last, having thus balanced my former prejudices with my latter [so that they cannot divert my opinions more to one side than to the other], my judgment will no longer be dominated by bad usage or turned away from the right knowledge of the truth. For I am assured that there can be neither peril nor error in this course, and that I cannot at present yield too much to distrust, since I am not considering the question of action, but only of knowledge.

I shall then suppose, not that God who is supremely good and the fountain of truth, but some evil genius not less powerful than deceitful, has employed his whole energies in deceiving me; I shall consider that the heavens, the earth, colours, figures, sound, and all other external things are nought but the illusions and dreams of which this genius has availed himself in order to lay traps for my credulity; I shall consider myself as having no hands, no eyes, no flesh, no blood, nor any senses, yet falsely believing myself to possess all these things; I shall remain obstinately attached to this idea, and if by this means it is not in my power to arrive at the knowledge of any truth,

I may at least do what is in my power [i.e. suspend my judgment], and with firm purpose avoid giving credence to any false thing, or being imposed upon by this arch deceiver, however powerful and deceptive he may be. But this task is a laborious one, and insensibly a certain lassitude leads me into the course of my ordinary life. And just as a captive who in sleep enjoys an imaginary liberty, when he begins to suspect that his liberty is but a dream, fears to awaken, and conspires with these agreeable illusions that the deception may be prolonged, so insensibly of my own accord I fall back into my former opinions, and I dread awakening from this slumber, lest the laborious wakefulness which would follow the tranquillity of this repose should have to be spent not in daylight, but in the excessive darkness of the difficulties which have just been discussed.

NORMAN MALCOLM

A Generous View of Knowledge

Some philosophers have held that when we make judgments of perception such as that there are peonies in the garden, cows in the field, or dishes in the cupboard, we are "taking for granted" that the peonies, cows, and dishes exist, but not knowing it in the "strict" sense. Others have held that all empirical propositions, including judgments of perception, are merely hypotheses. The thought behind this exaggerated mode of expression is that any empirical proposition whatever *could* be refuted by future experience—that is, it *could* turn out to be false. Are these philosophers right?

Consider the following propositions:

(i) The sun is about ninety million miles from the earth.
(ii) There is a heart in my body.
(iii) Here is an ink-bottle.

In various circumstances I should be willing to assert of each of these propositions that I know it to be true. Yet they differ strikingly. This I see when, with each, I try to imagine the possibility that it is false.

(i) If in ordinary conversation someone said to me "The sun is about twenty million miles from the earth, isn't it?" I should reply "No, it is about ninety million miles from us." If he said "I think that you are confusing the sun with Polaris," I should reply, "I *know* that ninety million miles is roughly the sun's distance from the earth." I might invite him to verify the figure in an encyclopedia. A third person who overheard our conversation could quite correctly report that I knew the distance to the sun, whereas the other man did not. But this knowledge of mine is little better than hearsay. I have seen that figure mentioned in a few books. I know nothing about the observations and calculations that led astronomers to accept it. If tomorrow a group of eminent astronomers announced that a great error had been made and that the correct figure is twenty million miles, I should not insist that they were wrong. It would surprise me that such an enormous mistake could have been made. But I should no longer be willing to say that I *know* that ninety million is the correct figure. Although I should *now* claim that I know the distance to be about ninety million miles, it is easy for me to envisage the possibility that some future investigation will prove this to be false.

(ii) Suppose that after a routine medical examination the excited doctor reports to me that the X-ray photographs show that I have no heart. I should tell him to get a new machine. I should be inclined to say that the fact that I have a heart is one of the few things that I can count on as absolutely certain. I can feel it beat. I know it's there. Furthermore, how could my blood circulate if I didn't have one? Suppose that later on I suffer a chest injury and undergo a surgical operation. Afterwards the astonished surgeons solemnly declare that they searched my chest cavity and found no heart, and that they made incisions and looked about in other likely places but found it not. They are convinced that I am without a heart. They are unable to understand how circulation can occur or what accounts for the thumping in my chest. But they are in agreement and obviously sincere, and they have clear photographs of my interior spaces. What would be my attitude? Would it be to insist that they were all mistaken? I think not. I believe that I should eventually accept their testimony and the evidence of the photographs. I should consider to be false what I now regard as an absolute certainty.

(iii) Suppose that as I write this paper someone in the next room were to call out to me "I can't find an ink-bottle; is there one in the house?" I should reply "Here is an ink-bottle." If he said in a doubtful tone "Are you sure? I looked there before," I should reply, "Yes, I know there is; come and get it."

Now could it turn out to be false that there is an ink-bottle directly in front of me on this desk? Many philosophers have thought so. They would say that many things could happen of such a nature that if they did happen it would be proved that I am deceived. I agree that many extraordinary things could happen, in the sense that there is no logical absurdity in the supposition. It could happen that when I next reach for this ink-bottle my hand should seem to pass *through* it and I should not feel the contact of any object. It could happen that in the next moment the ink-bottle will suddenly vanish from sight; or that I should find myself under a tree in the garden with no ink-bottle about; or that one or more persons should enter this room and declare with apparent sincerity that they see no ink-bottle on this desk; or that a photograph taken now of the top of the desk should clearly show all of the objects on it except the ink-bottle. Having admitted that these things *could happen,* am I compelled to admit that if they did happen then it would be proved that there is no ink-bottle here *now?* Not at all! I could say that when my hand seemed to pass through the ink-bottle I should *then* be suffering from hallucination; that if the ink-bottle suddenly vanished it would have miraculously ceased to exist; that the other persons were conspiring to drive me mad, or were themselves victims of remarkable concurrent hallucinations; that the camera possessed some strange flaw or that there was trickery in developing the negative. I admit that in the next moment I could find myself under a tree or in the bathtub. But this is not to admit that it could be revealed in the next moment that I am now dreaming. For what I admit is that I might be instantaneously transported to the garden, but not that in the next moment I might *wake up* in the garden. There is nothing that could happen to me in the next moment that I should call "waking up"; and therefore nothing that could happen to me in the next moment would be accepted by me now as proof that I now dream.

Not only do I not *have* to admit that those extraordinary occurrences would be evidence that there is no ink-bottle here; the fact is that I *do not* admit it. There is nothing whatever that could happen in the next moment or the next year that would by me be called *evidence* that there is not an ink-bottle here now. No future experience or investigation could prove to me that I am mistaken. Therefore, if I were to say "I know that there is an ink-bottle here," I should be using "know" in the strong sense.

It will appear to some that I have adopted an *unreasonable* attitude toward that statement. There is, however, nothing unreasonable about it. It seems so because one thinks that the statement that here is an ink-bottle *must* have the same status as the statements that the sun is ninety million miles away and that I have a heart and that there will be water in the gorge this afternoon. But this is a *prejudice*.

In saying that I should regard nothing as evidence that there is no ink-bottle here now, I am not *predicting* what I should do if various astonishing things happened. If other members of my family entered this room and, while looking at the top of this desk, declared with apparent sincerity that they see no ink-bottle, I might fall into a swoon or become mad. I *might* even come to believe that there is not and has not been an ink-bottle here. I cannot foretell with certainty how I should react. But if it is *not* a prediction, what is the meaning of my assertion that I should regard nothing as evidence that there is no ink-bottle here?

That assertion describes my *present* attitude towards the statement that here is an ink-bottle. It does not prophesy what my attitude *would* be if various things happened. My present attitude toward that statement is radically different from my present attitude toward those other statements (e.g., that I have a heart). I do *now* admit that certain future occurrences would disprove the latter. Whereas no imaginable future occurrence would be considered by me *now* as proving that there is not an ink-bottle here.

These remarks are not meant to be autobiographical. They are meant to throw light on the common concepts of evidence, proof, and disproof. Every one of us upon innumerable occasions of daily life takes this same attitude towards various statements about physical things, e.g., that here is a torn page, that this dish is broken, that the thermometer reads 70, that no rug is on the floor. Furthermore, the concepts of proof, disproof, doubt, and conjecture *require* us to take this attitude. In order for it to be possible that any statements about physical things should *turn out to be false* it is necessary that some statements about physical things *cannot* turn out to be false.

This will be made clear if we ask ourselves the question, When do we *say* that something turned out to be false? When do we use those words? Someone asks you for a dollar. You say "There is one in this drawer." You open the drawer and look, but it is perfectly empty. Your statement turned out to be false. This can be said because you *discovered* an empty drawer. It could not be said if it were only probable that the drawer is empty or were still open to question. Would it make sense to say "I had better make sure that it is empty; perhaps there is a dollar in it after all?" Sometimes; but not always. Not if the drawer lies open before your eyes. That remark is the prelude to a search. What search can there be when the emptiness of the drawer confronts you? In certain circumstances there is nothing that you would call "making sure" that the drawer is empty; and likewise nothing that you would call "its turning out to be false" that the drawer is empty. You *made* sure that the drawer is empty. One statement about physical things *turned out to be false* only because you *made sure* of another statement about physical things. The two concepts cannot exist apart. Therefore it is impossible that *every* statement about physical things *could* turn out to be false.

FOR FURTHER READING

There are many relatively easy books available that deal with knowledge, doubt, certainty, and skepticism. Two that have achieved the status of classics are Bertrand Russell's *The Problems of Philosophy* (New York: Oxford University Press, 1972), originally published in 1912, and A. J. Ayer's *The Problem of Knowledge* (Baltimore: Penguin, 1956). Three books specifically intended as introductions to the theory of knowledge are, in ascending order of difficulty, Adam Morton's *A Guide Through the Theory of Knowledge* (Encino, Calif.: Dickenson, 1977), D. W. Hamlyn's *The Theory of Knowledge* (Garden City: Doubleday, 1970) and Roderick Chisholm's *Theory of Knowledge* (Englewood Cliffs: Prentice-Hall, 1977).

For a comprehensive anthology bringing together a wide variety of sources, classical to contemporary, see *Belief, Knowledge, and Truth*, edited by Robert R. Ammerman and Marcus G. Singer (New York: Charles Scribner's Sons, 1970).

More specialized anthologies include *Knowing*, edited by Michael D. Roth and Leon Galis (New York: Random House, 1970); *Essays on Knowledge and Justification*, edited by George S. Pappas and Marshall Swain (Ithaca: Cornell University Press, 1978); *Empirical Knowledge*, edited by Chisholm and Robert J. Swartz (Englewood Cliffs: Prentice-Hall, 1973); and *Truth*, edited by George Pitcher (Englewood Cliffs: Prentice-Hall, 1964). The papers in Roth and Galis are concerned primarily with the justified true belief theory of knowledge. Additional selections on these topics, along with recent discussions of skepticism, can be found in Pappas and Swain. This anthology also brings together important contemporary papers on the debate on whether justification proceeds from self-justifying beliefs or is a matter of coherence. So does Chisholm and Swartz, which contains further readings on skepticism. Pitcher contains a series of related papers on contemporary theories of truth. The difficulty of the papers included in these anthologies varies widely. The most technical are in Pappas and Swain. The papers in Roth and Galis, on the other hand, were selected for reading by undergraduate students being introduced to the theory of knowledge, so they are relatively easy to read.

Chapter 5 in Russell's *The Problems of Philosophy* and the final chapter of his *Mysticism and Logic* (Garden City: Doubleday, 1917) concern knowledge by acquaintance. The latter reading can be found in Ammerman and Singer. Also to be found there is Gilbert Ryle's well-known paper "Knowing How and Knowing That," from *Proceedings of the Aristotelian Society*, 46 (1945–46).

Plato's discussion of the justified true belief theory can be found in his *Theaetetus* (Indianapolis and New York: Bobbs-Merrill, 1949). Extended discussions can also be found in Ayer and Chisholm, in addition to the anthologies noted above. Norman Malcolm's "Knowledge and Belief," in which he develops a justified true belief theory and distinguishes strong and weak knowledge, can be found in Roth and Galis and in Ammerman and Singer. It can also be found in Malcolm's *Knowledge and Certainty* (Englewood Cliffs: Prentice-Hall, 1963).

For Descartes' skeptical arguments, see his *Meditations on First Philosophy*, contained in *The Philosophical Works of Descartes*, translated by Haldane and Ross (Cambridge: Cambridge University Press, 1970). Norman Malcolm's short book, *Dreaming* (New York: Humanities Press, 1962), is a famous and controversial rebuttal to Descartes.

The most discussed contemporary skeptic is Peter Unger. See his "A Defense of Skepticism," *The Philosophical Review*, 80 (1971). This paper, which is in Pappas and Swain, contains Unger's argument that there is no weak sense of "knowledge." See also his *Ignorance* (London: Oxford University Press, 1975). Also important are two papers by

Keith Lehrer—"Why Not Skepticism?," *The Philosophical Forum*, 2 (1971), and "Skepticism and Conceptual Change," in Chisholm and Swartz. "Why Not Skepticism?" also appears in Pappas and Swain. The contemporary skeptical arguments I have presented owe a great deal to Lehrer's arguments. See also Lehrer's *Knowledge* (London: Oxford University Press, 1974), which deals with theories of truth as well as skepticism.

Also, no bibliography on skepticism would be complete without including David Hume's *An Enquiry Concerning Human Understanding* (LaSalle, Ill.: Open Court, 1966), first published in 1751. There, Hume argues that most of our beliefs depend on our belief that the future will resemble the past, which we are not completely justified in believing.

In addition to Pitcher's anthology, Ammerman and Singer contains a large and varied section on theories of truth. Also valuable is Alan White's slim volume, *Truth* (Garden City: Doubleday, 1970).

Wittgenstein's picture theory is presented in his notoriously difficult *Tractatus Logico-Philosophicus* (New York: Humanities Press, 1961). For an easy and readable introduction to Wittgenstein's views, see David Pears' *Ludwig Wittgenstein* (New York: Viking, 1970). For a more recent version of the correspondence theory, see J. L. Austin's "Truth," in his *Philosophical Papers*, edited by J. O. Urmson and G. J. Warnock (New York: Oxford University Press, 1970). This paper is in Pitcher's anthology, which also contains important criticisms of Austin's theory.

Coherence theories of truth are presented by Brand Blanshard in *The Nature of Thought* (Atlantic Highlands, N.J.: Humanities Press, 1964), and F. H. Bradley in *Essays on Truth and Reality* (Fair Lawn, N.J.: Oxford University Press, 1914).

Peirce's views on truth can be found in *Peirce: Selected Writings*, edited by Philip Wiener (New York: Dover, 1966), and *Essays in the Philosophy of Science*, edited by Vincent Tomas (Indianapolis and New York: Bobbs-Merrill, 1957). See also "Truth, Thought, and Reality," in Ammerman and Singer. This selection comes from a longer piece, "How to Make Our Ideas Clear," which first appeared in *Popular Science Monthly*, 1878, and is reprinted in Tomas and in Wiener. John Dewey's pragmatist theory can be found in *Reconstruction in Philosophy* (Boston: Beacon Press, 1957), part of which appears in Ammerman and Singer under the title "The Instrumentalist Account of Truth." William James's theory appears in *Pragmatism* (New York: Washington Square Press, 1963). Excerpts can be found in Ammerman and Singer, under the title "The Pragmatic Theory of Truth." For a famous criticism of James, see Bertrand Russell's 1908 essay, "William James's Conception of Truth," in *Philosophical Essays* (New York: Simon and Schuster, 1966).

The arguments in Chapter 16 reflect the profound influence of W. V. Quine and Hilary Putnam on contemporary philosophy in general and me in particular. For an excellent and readable account of Quine's views on the matters discussed in this chapter, see the book he wrote with J. S. Ullian, *The Web of Belief* (New York: Random House, 1978). For a more sophisticated account, see his "Two Dogmas of Empiricism," in *From a Logical Point of View* (New York: Harper & Row, 1963), and "Epistemology Naturalized," in *Ontological Relativity and Other Essays* (New York: Columbia University Press, 1969).

Putnam's views can be found in his *Philosophical Papers*, vol. 1—*Mathematics, Matter and Method* (New York: Cambridge University Press, 1979). The papers included are highly technical, but Putnam is a surprisingly clear and graceful writer, and his papers on science and its relationship to mathematics and logic are informative and compelling.

For an excellent introduction to the philosophy of mathematics, see Stephen F. Barker's *Philosophy of Mathematics* (Englewood Cliffs: Prentice-Hall, 1964). A large portion of the book is devoted to geometry, both Euclidean and non-Euclidean.

Two recent books of interest on the justification of our beliefs are Keith Lehrer's *Knowledge* (London: Oxford University Press, 1974) and Gilbert Harman's *Thought* (Princeton: Princeton University Press, 1973). Harman's theory of justification relies on explanatory coherence. Lehrer also offers a coherence theory of justification, although not explanatory coherence. Although neither book can be considered an introduction to its subject, they are less difficult than most contemporary philosophy books. Chisholm's book offers a theory of justification based on the view that beliefs about current sense experience are self-justifying and help to justify all empirical knowledge.

For the great classics of empiricism, see John Locke's *An Essay Concerning Human Understanding* (New York: Dover, 1959), first published in 1690; George Berkeley's *A Treatise Concerning the Principle of Human Knowledge*, first published in 1710, and his *Three Dialogues Between Hylas and Philonous*, first published in 1713, both available in *Berkeley's Philosophical Writings*, edited by David M. Armstrong (New York: Collier, 1965); and David Hume's *A Treatise of Human Nature* (Oxford: Clarendon Press, 1973), first published in 1739, and *An Enquiry Concerning Human Understanding*. For an introduction to Locke, Berkeley, and Hume, see *The Empiricists* (Garden City: Doubleday, 1961), which includes generous selections from their writings.

For the great classics of rationalism, see *The Philosophical Works of Descartes*; Spinoza's *Ethics*, first published in 1677, which can be found in *Spinoza: Selections*, edited by John Wild (New York: Scribner's, 1958); and *Leibniz: Selections*, edited by Philip Weiner (New York: Scribner's, 1951). Generous selections from Descartes, Spinoza, and Leibniz can be found in *The Rationalists* (Garden City: Doubleday, 1960).

For important continuations of the empiricist tradition, see John Stuart Mill's *A System of Logic* (Buffalo: University of Toronto Press, 1974), first published in 1843; Bertrand Russell's *The Philosophy of Logical Atomism*, first published in 1918 and available in *Logic and Knowledge*, edited by Robert C. Marsh (New York: Putnam, 1971); Rudolf Carnap's *The Logical Structure of the World* (Berkeley: University of California Press, 1967), first published in 1928; and A. J. Ayer's *The Foundations of Empirical Knowledge* (New York: St. Martin's, 1969), first published in 1940. Russell's book and Carnap's are far more difficult than the others. Fortunately, Russell also wrote *The Problems of Philosophy*, which is far easier than the other, and is often used in introductory courses.

Although the classical rationalist tradition did not fare as well in later years as did the empiricist tradition, one later book remains a towering achievement in the history of philosophy—Immanuel Kant's *A Critique of Pure Reason* (New York: St. Martin's, 1965), first published in 1781. This work is often said to reconcile empiricism and rationalism, because it grants that there is a good deal of a priori knowledge (the rationalist side), but restricts the application of such knowledge to objects that can be observed (the empiricist side). That is, although he allows for more a priori knowledge than empiricists do, he also attempts to put a limit on unbridled speculative thought. Although Kant's influence on later philosophy is inestimable, the *Critique* is extremely difficult reading for even the most sophisticated reader. He attempted a more popular exposition of his views in *Prolegomena to Any Future Metaphysics* in 1783 (Indianapolis and New York: Bobbs-Merrill, 1950), but most people find it just as difficult as the *Critique*. The introductory student's best bet is to consult a secondary source, such as S. Korner's *Kant* (Baltimore: Penguin, 1960).

A more recent rationalist work is Brand Blanshard's *Reason and Analysis* (LaSalle, Ill.: Open Court, 1973), which is interesting for its criticism of contemporary British and American philosophy.

For examples of pragmatist writings, see the works of Peirce, Dewey, James, and Quine cited above.

There are many introductions to Einstein's theories of relativity. Bertrand Russell's *The ABC of Relativity* (New York: Signet, 1959), is short, clear, and demands no background in science or advanced mathematics. A. d'Abro's *The Evolution of Scientific Thought from Newton to Einstein* (New York: Dover, 1950), is longer, dryer, and more sophisticated—but it also gives a far more detailed account of Einstein's theories. More recently, Nigel Calder's *Einstein's Universe* (New York: Viking, 1979), offers a readable and well-illustrated presentation of Einstein's theories for the general public.

There is a wide variety of available books dealing with the philosophy of science, extending from short and readable general introductions to highly technical works on specific topics. Among the most useful introductions are Norwood Russell Hanson's *Observation and Explanation* (New York: Harper & Row, 1971), Carl Hempel's *Philosophy of Natural Science* (Englewood Cliffs: Prentice-Hall, 1966), and *An Introduction to the Philosophy of Science*, by Karel Lambert and Gordon G. Brittan, Jr. (Englewood Cliffs: Prentice-Hall, 1970). Both Hanson and Hempel are important figures in contemporary philosophy, and their introductory books provide excellent introductions to their own views as well as to the philosophy of science. Hempel's views dominated the philosophy of science from the 1930s to the 1960s, and they continue to set the stage for many discussions of science. Hanson, who died in 1967, was one of the crucial figures in the emergence of new directions in the philosophy of science during the 1950s and 1960s. Hempel's most notable work can be found in his *Aspects of Scientific Explanation* (New York: The Free Press, 1965). Hanson's major work is *Patterns of Discovery* (Cambridge: Cambridge University Press, 1958).

Also useful are Israel Scheffler's *Science and Subjectivity* (New York: Bobbs-Merrill, 1967), and Stephen Toulmin's *Foresight and Understanding* (New York: Harper & Row, 1961). Although less general and somewhat more difficult than the introductory books noted above, they will reward careful reading by the introductory student. Scheffler's book is a sustained criticism of the Kuhnian view of science, and Toulmin's is a criticism of the view that to explain is to predict.

Peirce's writings on science can be found in *Essays in the Philosophy of Science*, and *Peirce: Selected Writings*. For the most influential contemporary defense of what I have called the Peircean view, see both volumes of Hilary Putnam's *Philosophical Papers—Mathematics, Matter and Method* and *Mind, Language and Reality* (New York: Cambridge University Press, 1975). Many of the arguments I have presented in favor of the Peircean view are adaptations of Putnam's.

Kuhn's views appear in his *The Structure of Scientific Revolutions* (Chicago: University of Chicago Press, 1970). This book is highly readable and should present few if any difficulties to the introductory student. It is also to be recommended for its presentation of numerous episodes in the history of science.

Another influential work expounding the incommensurability of scientific theories is Paul Feyerabend's *Against Method* (Atlantic Highlands, N.J.: Humanities Press, 1975), which draws even more radical conclusions than Kuhn's book.

For Popper's anti-inductivist views, see *The Logic of Scientific Discovery* (New York: Harper & Row, 1965) and *Objective Knowledge* (Oxford: Oxford University Press, 1972). The earlier book has been the more influential of the two, but the later includes essays that the introductory student will find far more accessible.

Important criticisms of Kuhn, Feyerabend, and Popper can be found in Putnam. Important criticisms of Kuhn and Feyerabend can be found in Scheffler. Also, *Criticism and the Growth of Knowledge,* edited by Imre Lakatos and Alan Musgrave (New York: Cambridge University Press, 1974), contains papers delivered at a symposium on the views of Kuhn and Popper.

For Hume's presentation of the problem of induction, see his *Enquiry Concerning Human Understanding.* For a readable introduction to the problem, see Brian Skyrms' *Choice and Chance* (Belmont, Calif.: Dickenson, 1966).

A number of papers dealing with the problem, including discussions of the linguistic and pragmatic justifications of induction, can be found in *The Justification of Induction,* edited by Richard Swinburne (New York: Oxford University Press, 1974). See also P. F. Strawson's *Introduction to Logical Theory* (London: Methuen, 1952) and Hans Reichenbach's *Experience and Prediction* (Chicago: Chicago University Press, 1938).

Finally, the market is flooded with introductory logic books dealing with deduction and induction. The most widely used is Irving Copi's *Introduction to Logic* (New York: Macmillan, 1972), but almost any of the others will do equally well.

Part VI

THE SENSES AND REALITY

Chapter 18

ARE WE DIRECTLY IN TOUCH WITH AN EXTERNAL WORLD?

As we saw in Part V, the senses are our primary source of knowledge. We learn about the world by *perceiving* it. We see objects and events in the world, hear them, smell them, taste them, and feel them, and in that way come to know about them.

Because of the primary role played by the senses in giving us knowledge, philosophers have always been interested in perception. How do we perceive objects? How do we come to know of them through the senses? What is the relationship between the way the world appears and the way it really is? Questions such as these will occupy us in the next three chapters.

DIRECT AND INDIRECT PERCEPTION

All of us have seen and heard many people on television and in films—Johnny Carson delivering a monologue, perhaps, or Humphrey Bogart and Peter Lorre hunting the Maltese Falcon, Robert Shaw being eaten by a great white shark, and so forth. As we have seen and heard these things, we have also seen and heard people sitting on the couch beside us or in the theater seats in front of us. Although we use the words "see" and "hear" in both cases, it is clear that we do not see Robert Shaw and the shark in the same way that we see the person in front of us. The latter person is directly in front of our eyes. Robert Shaw is not. Indeed, Shaw, like Bogart and Lorre, is no longer alive. What *is* directly in front of our eyes is his image on the screen.

Are we *really* perceiving Robert Shaw, then, or merely his image on the screen? Rather than give this question a simple yes or no answer, philosophers distinguish two kinds of perception—*direct* and *indirect.* To perceive something *directly* is to perceive it without the mediation of any representation of that thing. To perceive it *indirectly* is to perceive it via some representation. Since Robert Shaw is not directly in our visual field, we are seeing him indirectly. We see him via his image on the screen.

Visual images are not the only kind of representation mediating our perception of the world. Just as we see Shaw indirectly via the image on the screen, so do we hear him indirectly via the film soundtrack. Likewise, we feel something indirectly by touching it while we are wearing gloves, and taste and smell it indirectly by experiencing an aftertaste or the lingering scent in a room long after the object is gone. In all such cases, the object itself is not directly and immediately present to the senses, but something else is. Thus, the object is perceived indirectly.

SENSE DATA

To see Johnny Carson on television is to see him indirectly, I said. Do the people in the studio audience see him directly? Do we see the people on the couch next to us directly? Are they directly present to our visual field, or do we directly see representations of them? Many philosophers have felt that we do *not* perceive the physical world directly. They have claimed that even when something is directly before our eyes, we are still perceiving it via some representation.

To appreciate one of the reasons for feeling this way, try the following experiment. Stare at this page for a moment, and then close your eyes. What happened when you did so?

When I ask my own students to try this experiment, they usually report that the book went away. But did it really? Of course not. Closing your eyes cannot make the *book* go away. Still, we are most surely tempted to say that *something* vanishes when we close our eyes. If not the actual book, then what? At this point, my students answer that their *image* of the book vanishes.

I then ask them to watch me as I walk about the room. First I cross the front of the room and then walk to the back, where I turn around and return to the front. I then ask the students in the last row to draw what they saw when I was in front of the room and what they saw when I was in the back. In the first drawing, the area representing my head to my waist is not as tall as the area representing the blackboard behind me. In the second, the area representing my head alone is taller than the area representing the blackboard. Something changes size as I walk about the room, they all agree. To those in the back, it grows larger as I walk in their direction. To those in the front, it grows smaller. But whatever changes size cannot be me. I am five foot eleven wherever I happen to be standing. Besides, how can I both grow and shrink at the same time? But whatever is directly in the visual field of my students does change size, they all say. Don't their drawings demonstrate that? Once again, it is their image that changes size, they say.

Philosophers who agree with my students call such an image a *sense datum*. A *visual* sense datum is a two-dimensional array of color, a visual image. These philosophers claim that there are also nonvisual sense data, which belong to the other four senses. An *auditory* sense datum, for example, is a sound. If you hear a motorcycle coming toward you, the sound gets louder. But the motorcycle itself is not making any more noise as it approaches you. What gets louder, then? Your auditory sense datum.

Similar considerations lead to the belief in tactile sense data. Place one hand in the refrigerator and the other in the oven, and then place both in the same pail of water. The temperature will feel different to each hand. Yet the actual temperature of the water is uniform throughout the pail. What are you directly feeling, then? The tactile sense datum. We also have *smell* and *taste* sense data, it has been claimed. If you have ever tasted orange juice after brushing your teeth, you know how radically the apparent taste of an object can change. Since the actual taste cannot change, it must be a sense datum that you are directly tasting.

In all of the above cases, we are led to believe that we are directly perceiving sense data for the same reason—the way that we perceive something is different from the way it really is. That is, appearance and reality differ. Given this difference, we conclude that we must be directly perceiving something other than the physical object, which we are only indirectly perceiving. That is, the sense datum *mediates* our perception of the object. Through it we perceive the object, just as we perceive Johnny Carson through his image on the television screen.

The Argument from Physics

The considerations we have just discussed are often referred to as the *argument from illusion*. Although this argument has historically been the most influential of all arguments for the existence of sense data, there is another that has received much attention in recent years. We may call this argument the *argument from physics*. It proceeds as follows.

The world as we see it has a number of qualities—size, shape, motion, and color, to name the most obvious ones. Although the world as described by the physicist has the first three of these qualities, it does not have color. The wall that I am now looking at appears to me as a flat expanse of yellow. According to the physicist, however, it is a cloud of colorless molecules. And if the individual molecules are colorless, the entire cloud must be colorless. A cloud of colorless things cannot add up to a yellow thing. Therefore, that flat expanse of yellow cannot be out there on the surface of the wall. But whatever I am directly seeing is that flat expanse of yellow. So I cannot be directly seeing the wall. Instead, I must be directly seeing my sense datum of the wall.

When my students first hear this argument, their inclination is to say that the flat expanse of yellow really *is* out there on the surface of the wall. It is provided, they say, by the light that strikes it.

There are, however, two problems with this reply. First, it gives the impression that the light provides something like a yellow coat of paint over the wall. That is, they seem to think that the light covers the colorless cloud of molecules with a coat of yellow light. But how could the light color the entire cloud without coloring any of the individual molecules that make up the cloud? How, that is, can light make the wall yellow without making any of its parts yellow?

Second, according to physicists, light is no more colored than the molecules that make up the wall. Light is a form of *electromagnetic radiation,* as are x-rays and radio waves. Like all forms of electromagnetic radiation, it consists of the emission of colorless packets of energy called *photons.* These photons travel in waves of greater or lesser frequency. At certain frequencies, the radiation will not be light, but another form of radiation, such as radio waves. Moreover, the difference between what is called, say, white light and what is called red light is also a matter of frequency. So when physicists call some light white and other light red, they do not mean that it is white or red the way my visual experience of a sheet or an apple is white or red. They mean instead that it travels with a certain frequency.

But why call light waves of a certain frequency red? The answer is that certain light frequencies are *correlated* with certain visual experiences of color. When light of a certain frequency bounces off a wall, I will have the visual experience of whiteness. When light of another frequency bounces off the same wall, I will have a visual experience of redness. To say that light of a certain frequency is red, then, is to say that it is correlated with the visual experience of redness. Similarly, to say that the wall is yellow is to say that a normal observer looking at it in normal light will have a visual experience of yellow.

Thus, physical objects and light are colored in a different sense than our visual experiences are colored. Physical objects and light are colored in a *dispositional* sense—that is, in the sense that they have a tendency to cause visual experiences of color. An apple is red in the sense that in normal light it causes a normal observer to have a visual experience of redness. Similarly, light is red in the sense that it causes a normal observer to have a visual experience of redness. But neither the apple nor the light is red in the way that the visual experience is.

The situation here is similar to the situation with the word "healthy." We speak of both healthy people and healthy food, but food and people are not healthy in the same sense. Some foods are healthy in the sense that they contribute to the health of people who eat them. That is, they are healthy in a dispositional sense. Similarly, we speak of both happy people and happy coincidences, but people and coincidences are not happy in the same way. A coincidence is happy in the sense that it has the tendency to make people happy. That is, it is happy in the dispositional sense.

A disposition, then, or a *dispositional quality*, is a tendency to do certain things, or to have certain effects. Just as being healthy is a dispositional quality of certain foods, so is being red a dispositional quality of certain light frequencies and certain physical objects. It is their tendency to cause certain visual experiences in people.

So the apple's surface does not have a red expanse across it, and the light does not cover it with a red expanse. Therefore, the argument concludes, the red expanse must belong to our sense datum of the apple.

What Is a Sense Datum?

Whether there really are such things as sense data is a matter of controversy among philosophers. For the present, however, let us accept the conclusion of the arguments we have considered and assume that sense data do exist. What are they?

So far, we have said this much about them. They are the things we directly perceive whenever we perceive a physical object. That is, they are representations of physical objects. When someone is standing before my open eyes, I directly see an image of that person, and through that image become aware that she is before my eyes. When she talks, I directly hear an auditory sense datum, and through that sense datum become aware that she is talking. But what *sort* of entity is the image of the person in front of me? *Where* is it?

At first, many of my students think that the images they are directly aware of are the images on their retinas. What vanishes when they close their eyes, they say, what changes size and shape as I walk about the room, is the image cast by light on the back of their eyes. But visual sense data cannot be retinal images for the following reasons.

First, most of us have two eyes, and hence two retinal images. But when we look at a physical object we usually have only one sense datum of it. Moreover, the image on each retina is slightly different from the other. Since the eyes are spatially separated, the image on each has a different perspective. Thus, the two images cannot even be superimposed to make a perfect fit.

Second, the images on the retina are upside down, while our sense data are right-side up.

Third, as you stare at this page, your sense datum is a stable image. That is, if you move neither the book nor your position, there is no change in the image. But retinal images are *not* stable. Your eyes are in constant motion, so there is a rapid succession of different images.

Fourth, your sense data have different proportions from the proportions of the retinal image. As you move the book closer to or farther away from your eyes, the size of your sense datum does not vary as much as the size of the images on your retina. This phenomenon is known as *size constancy*. Our brains make certain adjustments in the size of the retinal image. They also make adjustments in the *shape* of the retinal image. If you hold up a coin and rotate it around an axis, the coin will appear rounder to you than the images on your retinas. This phenomenon is known as *shape constancy.*

Fifth, we have visual sense data even where there is no retinal image, as when we dream while asleep.

Therefore, the retinal images may provide certain information, which is used by the brain to form sense data, but they cannot be the sense data themselves. The sense data are the outcome of a complicated process, of which the retinal images are just the beginning.

What *are* visual sense data, then, if not retinal images? The standard answer is that they are *mental* images. That is, they are images in our minds of the physical objects in the external world. Similarly, *all* sense data are said to be mental entities. Auditory sense data are mental entities created in the mind after sound waves strike the ear, tactile sense data are mental entities created in the mind after something presses up against the skin, and so forth. Sense data are the mental products of complex physical processes involving the sense organs and the nervous system.

THE CAUSAL THEORY OF PERCEPTION

Although the term "sense data" is a new one to you, my guess is that you have always believed in their existence. My own students, for example, invariably enter my course with the following conception of how vision works. Light bounces off an object and hits us in the eye, causing all sorts of activity in the brain. At the end of the process, we get a mental image of the object, and we know that the object is there because of that mental image.

This view seems to be the common-sense view of perception, and is the theory espoused by John Locke (1632–1704) and many philosophers since. It is called the *causal theory of perception,* because it is often expressed in the following way: To perceive a physical object is to have a sense datum of that object which is caused by the object in the appropriate way.

It is important to stress the phrase "in the appropriate way." Not every case of having a sense datum of an object caused by that object is a case of perceiving it. Suppose, for example, that I have a fight with a friend, and that I have a dream about the fight that night. Although the images of my friend in the dream are sense data of her, and although she caused the dream and hence the sense data by having the fight with me, I am not really seeing her. Nor am I hearing her, even though I have auditory sense data in the dream that are caused by what she said in the fight.

Each sense involves a certain causal process. To perceive something through one of these senses is to have a sense datum that is the product of that process. Vision must involve light coming from the seen object, hearing must involve sound waves coming from the heard object, touch must involve something pressing against me, and so forth. Thus, the phrase "in the appropriate way" is meant to indicate that the sense datum is the result of the causal process required by the form of perception specified.

Locke's theory is also called a *representational* theory of perception, because it holds that we cannot perceive physical objects directly. In order to see, hear, feel, or otherwise perceive a physical object, I must directly see, hear, feel, or otherwise perceive a sense datum of that object. And this sense datum is a representation of that object. Thus, according to Locke's theory, we are never directly in touch with the physical world, but are directly in touch only with our mental representations of it.

OBJECTIONS TO SENSE DATA

Although Locke's theory is very much like the common-sense theory of perception, many philosophers have questioned whether we really do perceive sense data. Three of the more important objections to the existence of sense data are as follows.

First, sense data are taken to be mental entities. But, as we saw in Chapter 12, many philosophers deny that there is any such thing as a mental entity. That is, to accept the existence of sense data is to accept a form of mind/body dualism, according to which the human mind and its contents are private and distinct from the human brain and its activity. But this view is incompatible with the various forms of materialism currently in favor among philosophers, according to which human beings are purely physical and the mind is considered to be nothing over and above the activity of the brain.

Second, if we accept the view that we are directly aware of sense data but not of the physical world, we can easily be led to a form of skepticism about the existence of the physical world. If I never directly perceive anything but the contents of my own mind, how can I know that there is anything physical out there? Even if I suppose that there must be something out there causing my sense data, what reason do I have to think that the causes of my sense data are anything like the things we think they are?

Third, many philosophers have begun to think that sense data are entirely unnecessary. According to Locke's theory, we first see the image of the apple and then acquire all sorts of beliefs—that there is an apple in front of us, that it is red, of a certain shape, size, and so forth. But is the image really necessary? Isn't it simpler to say something like this? Light bounces off the apple, strikes us in the eye, causes all sorts of brain activity, and at the end of the process we come to have all sorts of beliefs about the apple.

Such a theory of perception is, like Locke's, a causal theory, but it is not a representational theory. That is, it views perception as a causal process, but denies that one of the links in the causal chain is a sense datum that represents the perceived object. According to this theory, then, we are not first directly aware of a sense datum and then indirectly aware of the perceived object. We are directly aware of the perceived physical object itself.

DIRECT REALISM

The theory I have just sketched is called *direct realism*. Direct realism is accepted by many contemporary philosophers. Among its most forceful defenders is the contemporary American philosopher George Pitcher. According to Pitcher, to perceive a physical object is to come to have a very rich and varied collection of beliefs about that object which are caused by the object in the appropriate way. To see an apple, for instance, is to come to have a number of beliefs about the color, size, shape, texture, position, etc., of the apple. But it is more than just the acquisition of such beliefs. The beliefs have to be acquired in a certain way. They have to be acquired via the reception of information about the object which we receive as a light pattern on the retina. This information is processed by the brain, and the result is our beliefs about the object.

The immediate difficulty faced by this theory, of course, comes from the two arguments we looked at for the existence of sense data. What do my students draw if not their image of me? What gets bigger and smaller if not their image of me? Where is the flat expanse of yellow if not in my sense datum of the wall? Where is the color I see, or the sound that I hear, if not in my sense data? How, that is, can we explain the difference between appearance and reality, if not by positing the existence of sense data?

Let us begin to answer these questions by reconsidering the argument from illusion. In general, the argument works like this. Things don't always appear as they are. They appear to change size and shape, for instance, even though the real size and shape remain the same. Therefore, we must be seeing an appearance that does change size and shape, and this appearance is a sense datum.

Is there an alternative explanation of the difference between appearance and reality? The direct realist offers the following. To see a physical object is to acquire beliefs about the object from certain information received by a particular causal process. But this information is carried by a medium of some sort—light waves in the case of seeing, sound waves in the case of hearing, and so forth. For various reasons, something might interfere with the way the medium carries this information.

Take the example, much discussed by philosophers of perception, of a straight stick half submerged in water. Such a stick will appear to be bent. Why? Because the light reflected by the stick is refracted as it passes from the water to the air. In that case, the light carries the same information it would be carrying if it had been reflected by a bent stick not submerged in water. This causes the belief that the stick is bent rather than straight. So a mistaken appearance of an object is not a sense datum, but a complex of false beliefs.

But this is not quite right. After all, we *know* that the stick is straight. How can we say that we *believe* otherwise? Perhaps, then, we should say something like this. The information carried by the light is processed by the brain. Some of the processes involved are automatic and unconscious, while other processes are not. When light from the submerged stick strikes the retina, the automatic processes result in the following processed (mis)information—that the stick is bent. The *non*automatic processes then correct this misinformation, resulting in the belief that the stick is really straight. But the automatic processes continue to produce the same processed misinformation. The results of the automatic processes are not really beliefs, then, but steps on the way to beliefs. If the nonautomatic processes do not correct them—as in the case in which the stick is *not* submerged in water—the results do become beliefs. If the nonautomatic processes *do* correct them, they do not become beliefs. So let us call them tendencies to believe, rather than beliefs.

What are my students drawing, then, when they draw what they see as I walk about the room? According to the direct realist, they are drawing me, and not their mental images of me. There are no such mental images to draw. Why do the areas that represent me vary in size? Because the automatic processes in their brains result in the tendency to believe that I am changing size. Not because there are mental images that vary in size. There are no such images. Thus, the direct realist denies that there are such things as mental appearances. Just because I *appear* to change size, that does not mean that there is an actual *appearance* of me that *does* change size.

Thus, we can characterize the difference between the believer in sense data and the direct realist by the way they construe the difference between the way something appears and the way it really is. According to the believer in sense data, if something appears to me in a certain way, then I am having an appearance of it that is that way. If a straight stick appears bent, for instance, I am really seeing a bent appearance. According to the direct realist, if something appears a certain way, I am not having an appearance of it, but am receiving certain information about it that I process in a certain way. If a straight stick appears bent, I am really seeing the stick, but I am receiving the misinformation that it is bent. To see a physical object is to receive information about it, and the way it is seen is a matter of how the information is processed, not of any image of it.

Similarly, what happens when I close my eyes? What goes away? Not my image of what I was seeing. What happens is that I stop receiving certain information. But what about dreams? If I dream about my friend, am I not having mental images of her? The direct realist says no. When I dream, I am having the same sort of beliefs that I would have if I were really perceiving my friend. So when I awake, I remember the dream as a visual experience. That is, I remember the dream as though I had really been seeing something. But I was not seeing anything at all in my dreams. I just believed that I was.

Emergent Qualities

What about the argument from physics? If the wall is not really yellow, and if light does not cover it with a yellow veneer, and if I have no yellow image of it in my mind, where is the flat expanse of yellow I claim to see? Even if the direct realist can explain dreams and the difference between appearance and reality, how can the direct realist explain color?

The direct realist's answer is this. There are many cases in which a collection of things can have certain qualities that no individual member of the collection can have. The molecules that make up the water in a bowl, for example, are not wet, but the water is. The molecules that make up a dog cannot be happy or sad, smart or stupid, nor can they be in pain. But the dog can be all of those things.

Such qualities as wetness and happiness are what philosophers call *emergent qualities.* That is, they are qualities that a collection of things can have, but that the members of that collection cannot have. If wetness and happiness can be emergent qualities, why can't color? If a cloud of molecules can be wet even if none of the individual molecules in the cloud are wet, why can't a cloud of colorless molecules be yellow? Thus, the direct realist's answer to the argument from physics is to say that color is an emergent quality. Therefore, we need not posit the existence of sense data to explain color, any more than we must posit sense data to explain wetness or happiness.

THE FINAL WORD?

Has the direct realist successfully answered the arguments for the existence of sense data? Most contemporary philosophers think so. However, there are some who believe that the answer to the argument from physics is not adequate. That is, they do not think that color can be an emergent quality like wetness. What is the difference between the two qualities?

It is easy to see how wetness can emerge. If a substance's molecules have a certain sort of motion, they will cling together to form a solid. As the motion of the molecules increases with heat, the substance will cease to have a definite shape. That is, it will turn to liquid. It will become wet. So it is easy to understand wetness as being nothing over and above the organization of a substance's molecules.

But matters seem different with color. If the molecules on the surface of the wall are organized in a certain way, how can that make the surface of the wall yellow? The answer seems to be this. The wall will now reflect light of a certain frequency, and the reflected light will cause in us a visual experience of yellowness. But, once again, that just means that the wall is yellow in a dispositional sense. It does not mean that there is a flat expanse of yellow on the wall.

The problem, then, is this. A flat expanse of yellow does not seem to be merely a matter of the organization of molecules, the way wetness is. Unlike wetness, it seems to be something produced in us by the organization of molecules. But if that is true, it becomes difficult to deny that there are visual sense data.

It seems to me that the question of color remains an unsettled issue for philosophers, in which case the question of sense data must also remain an unsettled issue. Hence, it is impossible to say whether the direct realist has successfully answered the arguments for the existence of sense data. Until we are clearer on how color can emerge, we cannot settle the dispute.

Still, I think that this much can be said. If philosophers do eventually decide that we must posit the existence of sense data, they will probably decide that sense data are not mental entities, but physical ones. Given the predominant view that persons are purely physical beings, it is doubtful that philosophers will give this view up because of the problem of color. Instead, they will more likely decide that sense data are theoretical *physical* entities, like electrons and quarks. This view has already been adopted by one influential contemporary philosopher, Wilfrid Sellars, and it has been gaining acceptance among others in recent years. But, once again, the safest thing to say at this point is that the jury is still out.

STUDY QUESTIONS

1. According to some philosophers, we perceive physical objects indirectly and sense data directly. What do they mean by this?
2. What is the argument from illusion? The argument from physics? How do these arguments support the claim that sense data are the direct objects of perception?
3. What reasons do philosophers give to support the claim that visual sense data cannot be images on the retina?
4. Locke's theory of perception is both a causal theory and a representational theory. What is the causal aspect of his theory? The representational aspect?
5. What is direct realism? How does it differ from Locke's theory of perception?
6. How do direct realists respond to the argument from illusion and the argument from physics?
7. What is an emergent quality? Why do some philosophers believe that color is an emergent quality? Why do others disagree?

GLOSSARY

Argument from illusion. An attempt to prove the existence of *sense data* from the difference between appearance and reality. Since things do not always appear the way they are, the argument goes, I must be *directly perceiving* an appearance (a sense datum) rather than the actual thing.

Argument from physics. An attempt to prove the existence of *sense data*. Since the objects we *directly perceive* have color, the argument goes, but physical objects, being clouds of colorless molecules, do not, we must be directly perceiving something (sense data) other than physical objects.

Causal theory of perception. The view that perception is a causal process in which the perceived object plays a characteristic causal role. A causal theory of perception may be either a *representational* theory or a *direct realist* theory. According to the former, to perceive a physical object is to have a *sense datum* of the object caused in the appropriate way. (To see an apple, for example, is to have a red round visual sense datum caused, in part, by light reflecting from the apple and striking the retina.) According to the latter, to perceive a physical object is to acquire certain beliefs about the object caused in the appropriate way. (To see an apple, for example, is to acquire many beliefs about its color, shape, size, and so forth, caused, in part, by light reflecting from the apple and striking the retina.)

Direct perception. The perception of something without the mediation of a representation of that thing. To perceive something directly is to have no copy, image, reproduction, or the like, between the perceiver and the perceived thing. (See *indirect perception.*)

Direct realism. The view that we *directly perceive* physical objects and not *sense data.*

Dispositional quality. A tendency, or propensity, to behave in certain ways or cause certain things to happen. According to some philosophers, certain qualities (such as color) that we ordinarily perceive are dispositional qualities of the perceived object. To say that something is red is, in this view, to say that it causes a normal perceiver to experience redness in normal lighting.

Electromagnetic radiation. The movement of energy through space in waves of differing length. Depending on the wavelength, radiation will be in various forms, including light, x-rays and gamma rays (both shorter in wavelength than light), and radio waves (longer than light waves). A physical object's perceived color depends on the wavelength of the light emitted or reflected from it.

Emergent quality. A quality possessed by an entire system but not possessed by any of the entities of which it is composed. Wetness, for example, is an emergent quality, because a puddle of water is wet but none of the molecules composing it is wet.

Indirect perception. Perception of something that is mediated by a representation of that thing. To perceive something indirectly is to perceive it via some image, copy, reproduction, or the like. To see somebody on a television screen, for example, is to see that person indirectly.

Photon. An elemental packet of radiant energy. *Electromagnetic radiation* travels in waves of photons.

Representational theory of perception. The view that we *indirectly perceive* physical objects by *directly perceiving* representations of them.

Sense datum. Internal representations of external physical objects. According to most believers in the existence of sense data, they are mental images, sensations, sounds, tastes, and smells. According to others, they are theoretical physical particles, on the order of such particles as electrons. According to sense-data theorists, whenever we perceive a physical object we are *directly perceiving* a sense datum.

Shape constancy. The tendency of the brain to compensate for changes in shape of the retinal image caused by changes in the angle of vision. For example, if an observed coin is partially rotated, the apparent shape of the coin will be rounder than the retinal image caused by the coin.

Size constancy. The tendency of the brain to compensate for changes in size of the retinal image caused by changes in the distance of the observed object. If, for example, an object recedes from the observer, the apparent size of the object does not grow smaller in proportion to the retinal image caused by the object.

Chapter 19

THE MANIFEST IMAGE
AND THE
SCIENTIFIC IMAGE

In the previous chapter, we touched on the difference between the world as we experience it and the world as the physicist describes it. The contemporary American philosopher Wilfrid Sellars has characterized these two ways of viewing the world as the *manifest image* and the *scientific image*. In this chapter, we will take a closer look at these two images. Are they compatible? Can the world really be both as we experience it and as the physicist describes it? Can the same object be both a red apple and a cloud of colorless molecules? If so, how can the two images be joined? If not, which of the two should we reject?

THE MANIFEST IMAGE

The manifest image is the world of ordinary experience. It is the world of such familiar objects as tables and chairs. It is the world that contains all the qualities we experience these objects as having: color, taste, smell, warmth, cold, hardness, softness, sound, size, shape, motion, and so on. Whether or not we directly perceive sense data, these qualities are experienced as *out there* in the external, physical world. Unlike tickles, itches, pains, and so forth, which we also experience, color, size, warmth, and the rest seem to belong to the objects we perceive, not to ourselves. A knife blade may induce in us experiences of color, coldness, and pain, but we do not experience the color and coldness as belonging to us. The pain is *our* pain; the color and coldness are the *knife's*.

Put another way, we can distinguish our *experience* of the color from the *color* itself. We can distinguish our *experience* of the coldness from the *coldness* itself. We do not distinguish our experience of the pain from the pain. The knife *causes* all these experiences in us, but it does not *have* all the qualities we experience. Color and coldness, like size and shape, are believed to be *in* the knife. Pain is not. What is in the knife is the capacity, or *disposition,* to cause pain.

Second, we experience the qualities we take to be out there in different ways. Some we experience *quantitatively,* others *qualitatively.* That is, some we experience as measurable quantities; others, not. Size, for example, is experienced quantitatively. It lends itself quite easily to measurement. Different objects, however unlike, are readily seen as fitting a numerical scale with respect to size. One *looks* twice as long as the other, three times as wide, half as big around, or whatever, and our judgments can be confirmed by yardsticks or tape measures.

Color, on the other hand, is experienced *qualitatively.* We do speak of one shade as being brighter than another, or darker than another, or perhaps even redder or bluer than another, but we do not naturally experience these relationships as fitting a numerical scale, as we do size relationships. Certainly, we have no natural vocabulary for units of redness, the way we have for units of length. Similarly, we speak of a lemon as being more sour than a grapefruit, but we have no natural vocabulary for units of sourness or sweetness. Size is naturally experienced as a matter of measurable units; color and sweetness are not.

Of course, we can measure the light frequencies reflected by various objects and get numerical relationships in that way, but that is not a measure of color *as experienced,* the way that placing a yardstick against an object is a measure of length as experienced. We experience color as a quality, as a flat expanse of red or blue. We do not experience it as light frequency.

THE SCIENTIFIC IMAGE

The manifest image is the world of ordinary observable objects—tables, chairs, apples, animals, trees, and so forth. The scientific image is a world of *microtheoretical entities*—objects that cannot be observed, but are posited by the physicist. It is a world of molecules and their components—atoms, electrons, protons, quarks. In the scientific image, then, tables and chairs are viewed as clouds of unobservable particles. Thus, as described by the physicist, they are far different from the way we experience them. Most important, they are described *quantitatively.* The qualities they have are measurable ones: size, shape, mass, velocity, energy, force, and so on.

If we look at this list, we see that many of the qualities of the manifest image survive in the scientific one. Others, however, do not survive. Color, warmth, taste, and smell, for example, do not survive. These qualities do have *replacements* in the scientific image, though. Color is replaced by frequency of light waves, for instance. Instead of saying that an object is blue, the physicist says that it reflects light waves of a certain frequency in certain conditions. Similarly, warmth is replaced by mean kinetic molecular energy, a quantity that objects have due to the motion of their molecules.

Of course, it can be said that warmth *is* mean kinetic molecular energy, but warmth as mean kinetic molecular energy is not the same thing as warmth as experienced by us. Our *experience* of warmth is dependent on the peculiarities of the human nervous system. Different creatures might be built differently and have no such sensations, or they might have our sensation of warmth when touching something cold and our sensation of cold when touching something warm. It is our makeup, then, that provides the *qualitative* aspect of warmth. But mean kinetic molecular energy is independent of our makeup. Creatures with no sensations of warmth could still discover it and study it.

The same situation holds for color. The *qualitative* aspect of redness is provided by us. Different creatures might not be sensitive to the spectrum in the way that we are. Qualitative redness might not even be in their world. But they could still discover and study light frequencies.

Thus, we can emphasize two aspects of the attributes belonging to the scientific image. First, they are attributes that can be measured quantitatively. Second, they are attributes independent of the human mind.

THE RELATION OF THE IMAGES

How can we relate the manifest and scientific images? How is the apple we see, smell, and taste related to the cloud of molecules in the scientific image?

There are three possibilities here. One view, the view of John Locke, is that the two images can be very neatly joined. According to Locke, the red apple and the colorless cloud of molecules are one and the same thing. Some philosophers, however, have disagreed with Locke on this point. Bishop George Berkeley (1685–1753), an early critic of Locke, argued that Locke's view is literally nonsensical. His solution to our questions was to dismiss the scientific image altogether. According to Berkeley, there is a red apple but no colorless cloud of molecules. (I should note here that neither Locke nor Berkeley used the word "molecule." According to the physics of their time, matter was composed of fundamental particles often called "corpuscles.") Sellars, a contemporary critic of Locke, takes a third approach, and dismisses the manifest image. According to Sellars, there is a colorless cloud of molecules but no apple. Let us look first at Locke, then at his critics.

Primary and Secondary Qualities

Locke, it will be recalled from the previous chapter, saw the world as consisting of both physical objects, which we experience indirectly, and sense data, which we experience directly. According to Locke, our sense data are caused by physical objects and represent them to us, rather as Johnny Carson's image on the television screen is caused by Carson and represents him to us.

What is the difference between sense data and physical objects? For one thing, sense data are *mental* entities, that is, objects existing in our minds. Physical objects, on the other hand, are *material* objects, that is, objects made of matter and existing out there in the external world.

There are other important differences as well. Most important, sense data have all the qualities of the world as experienced, but physical objects have only the qualities of the world as described by the physicist. The qualities of physical objects are the qualities that are independent of the human mind and can be measured quantitatively. They are the qualities Locke called *primary qualities*— size, shape, motion, mass. These are the qualities, he said, that are *really in* the physical object.

Warmth, color, smell, taste, and sound, however, belong only to sense data—not to physical objects. They do not exist in the objects themselves. They are not, Locke says, really in them. What does really exist in physical objects is the *power to cause our experience* of these qualities. Thus, we can speak of physical objects as having warmth, color, and so forth only in a *dispositional* sense—not in the sense that our sense data have them. A physical object is red in the sense that it causes us to have red sense data, and it is warm in the sense that it causes us to have warm sense data.

If we want to learn about the qualities that are *really in* the object and are responsible for these dispositions, we must turn to the scientist. The scientist will tell us that these dispositions are due to the primary qualities of the particles that make up the object. We will learn, for example, that the disposition to cause the sensation of warmth is due to the motion of the molecules in the object. We will also learn that the disposition to cause our experience of color is due to the organization of the molecules in the object. Thus, the dispositions are really in the object. The actual warmth and redness as *experienced* by us, however, are not.

Locke calls these dispositions that depend on the primary qualities of the molecules *secondary qualities*. He also calls color, warmth, taste, and smell secondary qualities. Therefore, if we were to ask whether secondary qualities are really in the object, we would have to answer yes and no—yes, if we mean secondary qualities as dispositions; no, if we mean secondary qualities as expanses of color and so forth. The latter belongs only to sense data.

There is no similar ambiguity regarding the primary qualities. Shape, size, motion, and mass are really in the object. These qualities do not have dispositional senses. When we say that something is square, we are not talking about a mere disposition to cause square sense data. We are talking about squareness as we experience it.

According to Locke, then, there is no problem in describing the same object as both a red apple and a cloud of colorless molecules. His theory of secondary qualities provides a bridge between the manifest and scientific images. It connects the world of experience to the world of the scientist in such a way that we can still talk of redness and warmth as being out there in the physical world. Of course, we have to be careful when we talk that way. We must be sure that we do not confuse warmth as the motion of molecules with warmth as an experienced quality. But as long as we do not so confuse them, we can join the two images.

Berkeley's Criticisms

The first criticisms of Locke's attempt to join the two images came from Bishop George Berkeley. Berkeley aimed a barrage of criticisms against Locke, but we shall examine the two most important ones.

First, Berkeley claimed that Locke's theory leads to skepticism about the existence of physical objects. If tables and chairs are the causes of our sense data, he said, then we can never know that they exist. Why not? All knowledge, Locke and Berkeley agreed, comes from experience. But all we can ever directly experience are our sense data. But in that case, we can never directly experience material objects. We can never directly experience tables and chairs, apples and oranges. Then why should we think that they are out there?

Locke assumes that whatever is out there causing our sense data must resemble our sense data. If my sense data represent a world of individual objects having size, shape, and motion, then the causes of my sense data must be individual objects having size, shape, and motion. But how can we ever know that?

To appreciate the force of this objection, think of a normal situation in which you infer the existence of a cause from observing the effect. If you see a lit match, for example, you infer that someone struck it. Why? Because you have often observed that the striking of a match causes it to light, and because you assume that this case is no different. But you have never seen an apple cause your sense data of an apple. All you have ever seen are your sense data. So you have no justification for believing that your sense data are caused by physical objects, rather than by something else. Thus, if we divide the world up as Locke does, into the world of experience (sense data), on the one hand, and the world of everyday physical objects (matter), on the other, we can never know that these physical objects exist.

Second, Berkeley charges that Locke's theory is literally nonsense. Locke's conception of physical objects, Berkeley claims, is incoherent—as meaningless as the notion of a square circle. Let us see why he says this.

All of our meaningful ideas, Berkeley claimed, come from experience. Since we cannot experience matter, the notion of matter must be meaningless. We think otherwise, because we have been using the word for so long that we take it for granted. But if we really tried to imagine the physical world as described by Locke, we would fail. We cannot imagine a world having size, shape, mass, and motion, yet not having color, taste, smell, sound, or warmth.

We can appreciate the force of this objection by imagining that there are people who have never heard of matter. These people, let us suppose, believe that there are only minds and sense data. That is, they think of themselves as disembodied souls inhabiting a world of experience, but not of matter. Now let us imagine the following conversation between two such people.

John: Have you ever wondered where our sense data come from?
Mary: A few times, but I could never figure out the answer.
John: Well, I think I figured it out. They come from physical objects.
Mary: Really? What are physical objects?
John: Well, they're kind of like sense data, except they're made of matter.
Mary: Matter? What's matter?
John: It's a kind of stuff that isn't a mind.
Mary: Is it *in* somebody's mind, the way that sense data are?
John: No, it's someplace else—in physical space.
Mary: What kind of thing is that?
John: Well, physical space isn't a thing, exactly. It's what physical things are in.
Mary: You mean it's a nothing?
John: Well, sort of.
Mary: How can a something be in a nothing?
John: I know it sounds strange, but that's how it is.
Mary: Tell me some more about these physical objects.
John: Well, they're a lot like our sense data.
Mary: You mean they have size and shape and color and taste and . . .
John: Well, not color and taste. But they do have size and shape.
Mary: Let me get this straight. There's a something in a nothing that's made up of something called matter, and it's just like sense data except it has no color— and that's where my sense data come from.

If you sympathize with poor Mary as she tries to understand what John is talking about, then you can appreciate Berkeley's objection.

Idealism

Let us suppose that Berkeley's criticisms of Locke are sound. Let us suppose, that is, that Locke's notion of physical objects makes no sense, and that even if it did, we could never know whether such things really exist. What are we left with, then? We are left with the world of our imagined Mary and John: a world of minds and their sense data; a world that is entirely mental.

Some philosophers, including Berkeley, have claimed that that's all there is. Such philosophers are called *idealists.* According to idealists, the ultimate nature of reality is mental. Nothing exists but ideas (including sense data) and the minds that have them. But what happens to tables and chairs, mountains, planets, our own bodies? Don't such things exist?

According to Berkeley, tables and chairs and our bodies *do* exist. But they are not, as Locke supposed, made of matter. Nor do they exist independently of minds. Rather, they are mental objects. They are nothing but collections of sense data.

What, for example, *is* an apple? It is what I see, feel, taste, and smell. But what do I see, feel, taste, and smell? My sense data. Then what is the apple? It is the collection of the sense data I experience as I have the experience of eating it. Apart from these sense data, there is no apple. It is only a collection of tastes, smells, colors, and so forth—that is, of sense data.

This view raises, of course, some serious questions. First, we ordinarily distinguish between reality and illusion. According to Locke's theory, the difference is marked by the presence of a material object. If there is a material object out there causing our sense data, what we see is really there. Otherwise, we are dreaming, hallucinating, or imagining. How can Berkeley mark the difference? If material objects are nothing but collections of sense data, the difference seems to collapse.

Second, apples and tables and chairs are *public* objects. You and I, for example, can see and touch and taste the same apple. But sense data are not public. I see mine, but not yours. You see yours, but not mine. How, then, can we see the same apple if Berkeley is right? It seems that the apple you see is a collection of your sense data, while the apple I see is a collection of mine.

Third, apples and tables and chairs exist even when nobody is perceiving them. Nobody is in my refrigerator right now, so nobody is perceiving any of the food inside it. Yet the eggs and orange juice and meat I saw this morning continue to exist just the same. But if these things are just collections of sense data, and nobody is now having any sense data of them, they can't exist. How can Berkeley account for the existence of objects no human being is perceiving?

Berkeley does have answers to these questions. In fact, he has one answer that he applies to all three questions: God. According to Berkeley, it is God who causes most of our sense data, and because of that we can appeal to God in order to explain the difference between illusion and reality, how apples can be public, and how objects can exist when no human perceives them. Locke can explain such things by appealing to matter; Berkeley, by appealing to God. Here's how.

What is the difference between illusion and reality? When are my sense data of real objects and when are they not? If they come from God, Berkeley says, they are of real objects. If they are products of my own mind, then they are dreams, hallucinations, or imaginings. Similarly, the reason we can say that all of us can see and taste the same apple is that we are getting our sense data of it from the same source—God. Because God sends us the same sense data, we are seeing the same physical object. Finally, we can say that the food in my refrigerator now exists even though no human is perceiving it, because God is perceiving it. God, according to Berkeley, perceives everything, and therefore nothing goes out of existence when human beings are not perceiving it.

Berkeley's answer to these questions raises a further question, though. If, as he says, we cannot accept Locke's answer because we have no reason to believe that there is matter out there causing our sense data, why should we accept Berkeley's? Do we have any better reason to believe that God is out there causing them?

Berkeley thinks that we do. After all, we know that minds exist from our own case. You know that your mind exists by direct acquaintance, and I know that mine exists in the same way. Further, you know that your own mind can conjure up sense data just as I know that mine can. Close your eyes and picture anything you'd like, and you have a case of your own mind conjuring up a sense datum. So we know from our own experience that minds cause sense data. We have no such experience of matter causing sense data, because we can never experience matter.

But some sense data are *not* caused by our own minds. They seem to come from another source. What is that source like? Well, says Berkeley, it must be another mind. But it must be a mind capable of giving us all the same sense data, and it must be a mind capable of perceiving everything that exists. What else could such a super-mind be but God?

Berkeley's view, then, is very much like heaven on earth. All of us are just minds, or souls, without material bodies. But just as we expect to perceive things in heaven just the same, so do we perceive things here. How? By God's intervention. He causes us to have sense data of things that would not otherwise exist.

Does Matter Exist?

Has Berkeley refuted Locke? Has he shown that it is foolish to believe in the existence of matter? Most philosophers think not. For one thing, they do not believe that Berkeley has shown that the notion of matter is meaningless. It may be that we would not be able to understand the notion of matter if we were like the Mary of my story—that is, *if* we had grown to maturity believing only in the existence of minds and sense data. But we are not like Mary. We learned about physical objects in physical space long before we had any conception of sense data. When we grew accustomed to our world, when we first started to learn our way in it, we grew accustomed to a physical world that we took to be out there. Indeed, for most of us, it is far easier to understand Locke's view than it is for us to understand Berkeley's.

Besides, it is not clear that such people as the Mary of my story *could* exist. Could we learn to communicate with each other if we believed that we didn't share the same physical space? Could we talk to each other about what we see and hear if we didn't believe that what we see and hear is out there in physical space? Many philosophers think not.

So Locke's theory does not seem nonsensical. But that does not answer Berkeley's second criticism, namely, that we can never know that it is true. If we can never directly experience matter, why should we believe that it is out there causing our sense data? This question has troubled philosophers for centuries. Perhaps it has crossed your own mind on occasion. Maybe this is all a dream, you may have thought. Maybe there is no external world.

The best answer that philosophers have found to this question may be a disappointment to you, since it is no better (or worse) than any common-sense answer you may have come up with yourself. The answer is this: It is silly to believe otherwise. There is no reason to take any other possibility seriously.

For as long as the human race has been on earth, we have believed that there is an external world. This belief has been fundamental to our entire way of thinking, so fundamental that we take it thoroughly for granted. Except in the most uncommon of reflective moments, we do not ask whether there is an external world at all. We may ask whether particular things (like the Loch Ness monster) or types of things (like creatures on Mars) exist, but we do not seriously entertain the possibility that there is no matter at all out there. The altogether natural assumption that there is matter out there is not merely a simple belief alongside other beliefs. It is the basis of all other beliefs.

To give it up, then, would be to call everything else into question. Of course, as we have seen in Part V, such basic beliefs may be called into question and ultimately rejected. But we need *good reason* for doing so. And neither Berkeley nor anyone else has provided such a reason for giving up our belief in the existence of matter. So we remain justified in believing that the external physical world exists.

Tables, Chairs, and Clouds of Molecules

Locke, then, seems to have a decisive edge over Berkeley. But there is another, more recent challenge to Locke's view, which is just as bold and radical as Berkeley's. Once again, Locke unites the scientific and manifest images as follows. There are primary and secondary qualities. Both exist in the manifest image. The world as we experience it has both size and color. In the scientific image, however, the secondary qualities exist only as dispositions, which objects have because of the primary qualities of the molecules that make them up. Physical objects are not really colored, in the way that color is experienced by us. Instead, they are colored in a dispositional sense, in the sense that they cause us to have experiences of color. So we can say that apples are red, lemons are yellow, grass is green, and so forth, but we mean something different by that from what we mean when we say that our sense data of apples are red, that our sense data of lemons are yellow, or that our sense data of grass are green.

Wilfrid Sellars finds this as unacceptable as Berkeley did. But while Berkeley responded by sweeping away the scientific image, leaving us with a world of experience but not matter, Sellars responds by sweeping away the manifest image. While Berkeley said that there are tables, chairs, and apples, but not matter, Sellars says that there is matter but not tables, chairs, or apples. For Sellars, what is out there are clouds of molecules. And clouds of molecules cannot be tables, chairs, or apples.

A VARIATION ON IDEALISM

According to the idealism of Berkeley, physical objects are not material causes of sense data, but collections of sense data that are caused by God. Many philosophers have been attracted to some aspects of this view, but they have not been happy about Berkeley's reliance on God. The claim that God causes our sense data, they feel, is no more knowable than the claim that material objects do.

What they found attractive about Berkeley's view is this. It provides a way of talking about physical objects that does not depend on any assumptions about the ultimate nature of reality. In other words, it suggests that we can say everything we want to say about tables and chairs without committing ourselves to the existence of anything other than sense data.

Two questions naturally arise here. First, why should anybody find this attractive? Second, how can it be done? We will deal with these questions in order.

Objects and Experience

What meaning do physical objects have for you? What difference does it make to you that there is a chair under you now? That there is a clock on the wall? That there is an apple in the refrigerator?

One answer to these questions is this. The meaning of physical objects to you is their *payoff* in your own *experience*. The difference between there being an apple in the refrigerator and the refrigerator being empty is the experiences you have when you open the refrigerator door. If there is an apple, you will have the visual *experience* of one, and, if you like, the experience of touching it, lifting it from the shelf, and eating it.

But what are these experiences? What is it to have the visual experience of an apple? It is, many philosophers have said, to have a certain kind of visual sense datum. If we grant that, then we can conclude the following—the meaning of physical objects to us is the sense data we have of them under various conditions.

And that, many philosophers have felt, is Berkeley's great insight. What is required, then, is a way of translating all our talk about physical objects into talk about sense data. If it can be found, we will have vindicated Berkeley. We will have shown that all our talk about tables and chairs really comes down to talk about sense data.

Phenomenalism

The view that physical-object talk can be translated into sense-datum talk is called *phenomenalism*. According to this view, a statement about physical objects means the same thing as some other statement about sense data.

For example, the statement "There is a brown table in front of me" means something like this: "I am now having a brown visual sense datum of such and such a shape, and if I were to have the sensations associated with moving my arm, I would have a tactile sense datum of hardness and an auditory sense datum of a thumping sound . . . ," and so forth, for all the possible sense data I could have of the table. More generally, *any* statement about a physical object I am now perceiving means the same thing as an infinitely long statement about the sense data I am now having and would have under all possible circumstances.

What about physical objects I am not perceiving? Since I am not now having any sense data of these objects, statements about them cannot be about my current sense data. Instead, they must be about sense data I could have. Therefore, they must mean the same thing as infinitely long statements about the sense data I would have under all possible circumstances.

For instance, the statement "There is an orange in the refrigerator" means something like this: "If I were to have a visual sense datum of a white rectangle, and the sensation of moving my arm, I would then have a tactile sense datum of coldness and hardness, and if I were to have a sensation of pulling, I would then have a round orange visual sense datum, and if I were to have the sensation of moving my arm again, I would have a tactile sense datum of something round, soft, and cold . . . ," and so forth, for all the possible sense data of the orange. The phenomenalist position can be summed up this way, then: Talk about physical objects is really talk about actual and possible sense data.

Notice that nothing is said about the causes of my sense data in these translations. Do my sense data come from matter? God? My own mind? These questions, the phenomenalist says, have no answer. Indeed, there is no point to asking them. Since we can never *experience* the causes of our sense data, what they are makes no difference whatever. All that matters is our own experience.

But what happens to the distinction between illusion and reality? What is the difference between seeing an orange and hallucinating one? What is the difference between seeing an oasis and seeing a mirage? According to the phenomenalist, the difference is in our sense data. If, after the experience of diving in, I get the experience of wetness, I saw a real oasis. If I get the experience of a mouthful of sand instead, I saw a mirage. The difference, then, is in further sense data. If further sense data are the kind I would have expected, I was perceiving the real thing. If not, I was perceiving an illusion.

Phenomenalism Evaluated

Although phenomenalism enjoyed a good deal of popularity earlier in the century, it is now generally considered to be a historical relic. Two factors in particular contributed to its demise.

First, the same criticisms we leveled against Berkeley apply equally well to the phenomenalist. Once again, we can ask why we should give up our commitment to the existence of an external material world. The phenomenalist can reply, like Berkeley, that his view shows how talk about physical objects can be meaningful, and that it protects us from skepticism about the existence of physical objects, but we have already argued that Locke's view is not meaningless, and that it need not lead to skepticism.

But even more important, philosophers have by and large despaired of providing the translations required by phenomenalism. The problem is that it seems impossible to provide translations that make no reference to physical objects at all.

The reason is this. The sense data we have are dependent on all sorts of things, not just the objects we are perceiving. They depend, for example, on a variety of perceptual conditions—such as lighting—plus certain facts about ourselves.

Suppose that I have the experience of opening the refrigerator door but the refrigerator light isn't working. In that case, I will not have an orange round visual sense datum—even if there is an orange in the refrigerator. Or suppose my hand goes numb when I reach for the orange. In that case, I will not have a tactile sense datum of something round, cold, and soft—even if I touch the orange.

So we cannot translate physical-object talk into talk about only sense data. We can, at best, translate it into talk about the sense data we would have when the lighting is just so, when our bodies are working in a certain way, and so forth. But to grant that is to grant that phenomenalism cannot succeed. It is to grant that the meaning that physical objects have for us goes beyond the sense data we have of them.

We think that we see tables and chairs, Sellars says, but we are wrong. What we really see are clouds of molecules. No, that is not quite right. *We* don't really exist either, if we think of ourselves as we do in the manifest image. Rather than say that *we see* clouds of molecules, we should say this. Light of a certain frequency bounces off a cloud of molecules and strikes another cloud of molecules, causing a great deal of activity in the second cloud, and that activity terminates in the production of a small colored particle (a sense datum). In other words, according to Sellars, if we really want to describe the world accurately, we should make no reference to the objects of the manifest image. Such objects do not exist.

Why say such a thing? Sellars' arguments are very complicated, but his basic strategy is fairly straightforward. Like Berkeley, he believes that it is wrong-headed (perhaps even nonsensical) to talk of the objects of the manifest image (tables and chairs and apples and so forth) as having secondary qualities only in a dispositional sense. Tables and chairs and apples cannot be colored in that way only. If there really are such things as apples, they must be red in the sense that they have a patch of red on their surfaces. If there is nothing out there that does have a patch of red on the surface, then there is nothing out there that is an apple. Instead, there are only colorless clouds of molecules organized in a certain way. We thought they were apples, but we were wrong.

We can put Sellars' point another way. We ordinarily think of science as explaining certain things about apples—why they are red, why they taste and smell the way they do, and so forth. Part of the explanation, we feel, is that they are composed of molecules of a certain sort, and that these molecules are arranged in a certain way. Sellars, however, finds this ordinary view misguided. Science has not shown us why apples look, smell, and taste a certain way. Instead, it has shown us that there are no apples at all, but only clouds of molecules that we took to be apples.

An analogy will help here. We used to think that there were witches. One of the qualities we thought that witches had was that of being in league with the devil. As it turned out, the people we thought to be witches were not in league with the devil. Rather, they were victims of psychological disorders. What did we then say? That witches were not in league with the devil? No. We said that there are no witches. The quality of being in league with the devil was such an important part of our conception of witches that we had to say that there are no witches. It would have been foolish to say that there are witches, but that they are just the victims of psychological disorders.

The same situation holds for the objects of the manifest image, Sellars claims. If the objects of the external world are not really colored, not really sweet or sour, but are these things only in a dispositional sense, then they are no more apples than people with psychological disorders are witches.

Of course, Sellars isn't suggesting that we stop calling certain clouds of molecules "apples." After all, even though we know that the earth revolves around the sun instead of the other way around, we can still say that the sun rises and sets. What he is saying is that we should realize that such ways of talking are not really accurate. If we want to talk with complete accuracy, we should talk about clouds of molecules instead of tables and chairs and apples.

Do Tables and Chairs Exist?

Although Sellars has provoked a good deal of discussion in recent years, his position has not, in its extreme form, been widely accepted. That is, most philosophers have not been convinced that the manifest image is incompatible with the scientific image. They have not accepted the claim that the same thing cannot be both a table and a cloud of molecules.

What is wrong with Sellars' argument, then? Well, let us return to the witch analogy. It does not seem that certain beliefs about color are crucial to our conception of tables and chairs, the way that being in league with the devil is crucial to our conception of witches. In other words, Sellars has not convinced most philosophers that the objects of the manifest image cannot be colored in a dispositional sense only. Why not? Well, the reason is much like the reason for our response to Berkeley. Why should we think otherwise? Why should we think that having color patches on their surfaces is a defining quality of the objects of the manifest image, the way that being in league with the devil is a defining quality of witches?

After all, it is not as though there were *nothing* in the scientific image corresponding to the manifest image. Color has its counterpart, warmth has its counterpart, taste and smell have theirs. As long as we can match the qualities of the manifest image to their counterparts in the scientific image, there seems no reason to deny that the objects of the manifest image are as real as the objects of the scientific image. That is, there seems no reason to deny that the findings of science teach us *why* we can say that apples are red and lemons yellow, rather than teach us that we *cannot* say such things about anything out there.

We can make this point another way. In the case of witches, our concern was to protect ourselves from the devil's influence. When we found that the people we called "witches" were irrelevant to that concern, that their actual qualities did not provide any useful connection to our original conception of witches, we declared that there were none.

The situation is different, though, when we compare the objects of the scientific and manifest images. The objects of the manifest image fit into our lives in countless ways, and nothing we have learned about the objects in the scientific image has seriously upset that. If anything, what we have learned has enriched the ways they fit into our lives. The counterparts we have found in the scientific image have enabled us to exploit and enjoy the qualities of the manifest image to an extraordinary degree. Just think of such mundane examples as color television sets and stereo equipment. The point here is that the connections we have discovered between the two images are highly useful—so useful, in fact, that the two images seem to merge very nicely.

Natural Kinds and Cultural Kinds

Still, there is an important lesson to be learned from Sellars. Although the scientific image has counterparts to this chair and this table, although it has counterparts to red things and warm things, it does not have counterparts to chairs in general and tables in general. The counterpart to this chair is this cloud of molecules. The counterpart to red things are the things that reflect light of a certain frequency. But there is no group of things distinguished by science that corresponds to chairs.

Part of the lesson, then, is that the scientific image divides the world up in a very different way from the way the manifest image does. We can express this by saying that the scientific image divides the world up into *natural kinds*. What is a natural kind? Well, the best way to define it is to contrast it with *cultural kinds*. But before we can do that, we must explain what a kind is.

Languages contain a number of general terms—for instance, "apple," "spice," "water," "tiger," and "chair"—that refer to some things but not to others. Each of these words, then, refers to a kind of thing. To be a spice is to be a certain kind of thing. To be an apple is to be a certain kind of thing. Thus, language divides the world up into kinds. These kinds reflect our own interests, our own social practices. The kind *spice*, for instance, reflects certain eating practices. Certain things play a particular role in our preparation of food, and we mark that role by the word "spice." The same holds true for the kind *apple*.

But there is an important difference between the kind *spice* and the kind *apple*. The only relevant thing that spices have in common is that they are used in certain ways, that they play a certain role in certain practices. Apples, on the other hand, have something else in common, which can be discovered by the scientist. That is, the kind *apples* exists independently of our eating practices; the kind *spice* does not.

Similarly, what chairs have in common is the role they play in our lives. They are for sitting. But all the bits of stuff we call water have more in common than the fact that we can drink them, wash in them and so forth. They are all H_2O. The difference, then, is that *water* and *apple* are *natural* kinds; *spice* and *chair* are not. The latter are what we can call *cultural* kinds. What, finally, is the difference? Cultural kinds reflect only human interests and practices. Natural kinds reflect more. They reflect underlying similarities to be discovered by the scientist. That is why the scientific image contains no counterpart to chairs in general, or tables in general. Because chairs and tables are not natural kinds. And once we grasp this, we can see that there is a sense in which Sellars is right.

The world of the manifest image, compared with the world of the scientific image, is a subjective one. The qualities we note, the kinds we distinguish, depend on the peculiarities of the human nervous system and human culture. The manifest image, that is, is distinctively human. The scientific image, on the other hand, gets us beyond the distinctively human. Put another way, it explains the world of appearance by showing us what underlies it. It reveals a world we could share with creatures radically different from ourselves. This does not mean that the objects of the manifest image are not real, while the objects of the scientific image are. It does suggest, though, that the divisions of the manifest image are on a different footing from the divisions of the scientific image. The divisions of the manifest image are concerned mainly with the relationships between things in the world and ourselves. The divisions of the scientific image are concerned mainly with the relationships the things in the world have to one another.

THE FINAL WORD?

We have answered "yes" to the questions posed at the beginning of this chapter. The manifest and scientific images are compatible. The same thing can be both a red apple and a cloud of colorless molecules. There is no need to reject the scientific image, nor is there a need to say that the scientific image shows that the objects of the manifest image do not exist.

What is the relationship between the two images, then? It is this. The world as described in the manifest image is *our* world. It is the world as it appears to us, the world as it presents itself to us in experience, that we make our way in. The world as described in the scientific image is the objective correlate of that world.

To call something a brown chair is to place it in relationship to our own lives and our own perceptual experiences. To call it a cloud of colorless molecules that reflects light of a certain frequency is to sever that relationship. The two images, then, reflect two different attitudes: one involved and practical, the other detached and theoretical.

Sellars agrees with these remarks. But he takes an additional step. The latter attitude results in true descriptions of the world, he says. We should view the results of the former attitude as something other than true descriptions. Instead of taking this last step, we have concluded that the descriptions of the manifest image *can* be true—*if* they are understood in the context of the scientific image.

STUDY QUESTIONS

1. What is the difference between the manifest image and the scientific image?
2. Explain Locke's distinction between primary and secondary qualities. How does the distinction allow Locke to reconcile the manifest and scientific images?
3. What objections did Berkeley raise against Locke's joining of the manifest and scientific images? How can the supporter of Locke respond to these objections? Which do you find more persuasive—the objections or the response? Why?
4. What is idealism? According to Berkeley's version of idealism, what is the difference between reality and illusion?
5. According to Berkeley, it is more reasonable to believe that God, not matter, is the cause of our sense data. Why?
6. What is phenomenalism? How is it similar to idealism? Different from it? What objections have been raised against phenomenalism?
7. Why does Sellars claim that the objects of the manifest image do not really exist? Why do many philosophers disagree?
8. What is a natural kind? A cultural kind? How is the distinction between natural and cultural kinds related to the distinction between the manifest and scientific images?

GLOSSARY

Cultural kinds. Kinds that reflect human interests and practices but do not reflect underlying similarities to be found by the scientist. Spices, for example, form a cultural kind, in that they play a certain role in human eating practices, but, unlike such *natural kinds* as apples, they do not form a distinct biological division.

Idealism. The view that reality is fundamentally mental. According to the idealist, even so-called external physical objects are collections of mental objects, that is, sense data.

Manifest image. The world of ordinary experience, which includes such everyday middle-sized objects as tables and chairs, plus all the qualities we perceive as belonging to these objects, including color, smell, and taste.

Natural kinds. Kinds that reflect underlying similarities to be found by the scientist, and that therefore form a distinct scientific division. Water, for example, is a natural kind, because all bits of water are composed of H_2O molecules. Gold is also a natural kind, because all bits of gold have an atomic number of 79. (See *cultural kinds*.)

Phenomenalism. The view that all talk about physical objects derives its meaning from talk about sense experience. According to the phenomenalist, it is possible to translate all sentences about physical objects into sentences about the sense experience one is currently having and the sense experience one would have under certain conditions.

Primary qualities. Perceived qualities of physical objects that are independent of the human mind and can be measured quantitatively. These qualities, including size, shape, motion, and mass, are said to be really in the perceived object, unlike the object's *secondary qualities.*

Scientific image. The world as described by the physicist, which includes such theoretical entities as electrons and quarks, but does not include such ordinary objects of experience as tables and chairs, which belong only to the manifest image. Although the objects of the scientific image share some qualities with those of the manifest image—motion and mass, for instance—they do not share others—color and taste, for instance.

Secondary qualities. Perceived qualities of physical objects that are dependent on the human mind and cannot be measured quantitatively. These qualities, including color, taste, smell, warmth, and sound, are said to be in the object only in a dispositional sense. For example, an apple is said to be red only in the sense that it causes a human perceiver to have a visual experience of red when they see it. (See *primary qualities.*)

Chapter 20

THE PSYCHOLOGY
OF PERCEPTION

Observation, we saw in Part V, is relevant to all our beliefs. All knowledge ultimately depends on perception. Still, the connection between observation and belief is closer in some cases than in others. In some cases, the connection is so close that we can affirm the old saying, "Seeing is believing." Why do you believe you are now holding a book? Because you see it. Why do I believe the walls in my study are yellow? Because I see that they are.

In other cases, the connection is not so close. Take the belief that all crows are black. No one observation assures us of that. Indeed, quite a few observations are needed before we are even justified in believing it. But no matter how many times we see black and only black crows, more is needed before we can justifiably claim that all crows are black. We can never *see* that all crows are black. Hence, we must consciously appeal to a number of *other* beliefs and then *infer* that all crows are black.

When we come to mathematical beliefs, the connection becomes even more remote. No one observation or group of observations can prove *or* disprove them. Still, as we saw in Part V, the combination of observation and theoretical considerations can overturn them.

In this chapter, we will be concerned with beliefs of the first kind, where the connection between observation and belief is closest.

PERCEPTUAL BELIEFS

Cases of the first kind are called cases of *perceptual beliefs*. What is a perceptual belief? It is a belief directly prompted by an observation. It is a belief you hold because it seems to you that you *see* that it is true, *hear* that it is true, and so forth, for all five senses.

What counts as a perceptual belief varies from person to person. Suppose that you and some friends see a car parked across the street. All of you, presumably, can see that it is a car, and that it is, say, blue. Similarly, you can all see that it has tires, bumpers, and a hood. But only some of you will see that it is a Ford, say, and even fewer of you that it is a 1976 Granada. If one of you knows whose car it is, that person will also be able to see that so-and-so's car is parked across the street. For all of you, then, the beliefs that there is a car across the street, that it is blue, that it has tires, bumpers, and a hood are perceptual beliefs. For some of you, the belief that there is a Ford across the street is a perceptual belief. For some, the belief that there is a 1976 Granada across the street is a perceptual belief. For only one of you, the belief that so-and-so's car is across the street is a perceptual belief.

Simple Perceptual Beliefs

Many philosophers distinguish a certain kind of perceptual belief, and label beliefs of that kind *simple* perceptual beliefs. Simple perceptual beliefs are those that do not consciously depend on any background information. Returning to the car example, we can illustrate the difference as follows. Suppose that you immediately recognize the car as a 1976 Granada. Suppose that one of your friends does not, but begins to wonder what year and make it is. She looks at the car carefully, compares it in her mind with other cars she's seen, and finally comes to the same conclusion that you automatically came to. Although both of you see that there is a 1976 Granada across the street, for you the belief is a simple perceptual one, while for her it is merely a perceptual one. You did not need to make conscious comparisons; she did. We can call your friend's belief an *inferential* perceptual belief, to show that her belief was the product of both perception and conscious inference. She did not *just* see that there was a 1976 Granada across the street. She saw that it was a car of a certain style and then consciously inferred that it was a 1976 Granada.

It is also possible to divide simple perceptual beliefs. Some are about how things *are*; others, about how things *look*. Suppose, for example, that you see a straight stick half submerged in water, and that, without any conscious thought, you come to believe that there is a straight stick that looks bent. In that case, you have two simple perceptual beliefs—that there *is* a straight stick, and that it *looks* bent.

The Importance of Background Information

What distinguishes a simple perceptual belief from other perceptual beliefs, I said, was the lack of conscious appeal to background information. The word "conscious" is crucial here, because even simple perceptual beliefs involve appeals to background information, although unconscious.

Returning to our car example, we can see that the same background information is relevant to your belief that there is a 1976 Granada across the street and your friend's, although she had to appeal to the information consciously, while you did not.

Consider, in this regard, another example. You and the same friend are walking in the woods and an animal quickly scoots past you. Both of you catch the same glimpse of it, but your friend instantly sees that it is a boxer dog, while you do not. You can tell only that it is a middle-sized brown animal. You ask her how she could tell what kind of animal it was, and she responds that it is a neighborhood dog that often plays in this part of the woods.

But the relevance of background information is far more pervasive than these examples suggest. Take the simple case of looking at a red ball. Your belief that there is a red ball in front of you depends on a number of other beliefs—that the lighting is normal, that you are not wearing glasses with tinted lenses, that you are not looking into a mirror, that you have not suddenly turned color blind, that you are not hallucinating, that there are no objects around that look just like red balls but are something else, and so on. If you were not to believe that these things were true, if, for example, you were to believe that you were wearing glasses with red-tinted lenses and that someone had left some cheese in the room, your simple perceptual belief would be far different.

The point of these remarks is this. Simple perceptual beliefs are prompted by *sensory stimulation*—light striking the eye in the case of vision, sound waves striking the ear in the case of hearing, and so forth for all the senses. But a wide variety of perceptual beliefs can be prompted by such stimulation. Many incompatible beliefs are compatible with the same stimulation. The same pattern of light on the retina can be caused by a number of physical objects, and, purely on the basis of the light pattern, we cannot tell which object is out there. Thus, we must make use of a good deal of background information to make our judgment.

INFERENCE AND PERCEPTION

The considerations of the preceding section lead to the following question: By what process do sensory stimulation and background beliefs lead to simple perceptual beliefs? Alternatively, what goes on in the human brain between stimulation of the senses and the acquisition of simple perceptual beliefs? This question has been of interest to both philosophers and *cognitive psy-*

chologists, that is, psychologists interested in such *cognitive processes* as thought, perception, recognition, and the like.

One answer that has been receiving the bulk of recent attention is *unconscious inference.* Although it *seems* to us that we can tell that a red ball is in front of us without any inference whatever, the facts of the matter are otherwise. What goes on is something like (but, as we shall see, much more complicated than) this: We infer that there is a red ball in front of us because we see something that looks like a red ball and because we believe that the conditions are such that the thing that looks like a red ball is a red ball.

That is, we take into account how the thing looks to us, our beliefs about the perceptual conditions that in part determine how it looks to us, various beliefs about the way things look under different perceptual conditions and about what sorts of things we might run into at this time and place, and then infer certain conclusions about what we are now seeing. All of this happens very quickly, of course, and at the unconscious level. Thus, they are automatic processes, rather like habits we begin to acquire as infants when we began to learn how to see.

We can compare the situation to driving a car. When you first learned how to drive, there was a lot you had to keep in mind. You had to orchestrate the workings of the clutch pedal and accelerator as you kept an eye on your speed and traffic conditions and tried to remember which way to move the gearshift to get to the next gear, and so forth. At the time, the task of juggling all of these matters probably struck you as a most difficult one, but after a while, your thinking became automatic. Now you can drive without giving many of these factors any conscious attention at all. Indeed, if you are driving along a very familiar route, you may find yourself at the end of it without any memory of most of the drive.

Perception, it seems, is much the same. We learn how to recognize objects and then use what we learn in an automatic manner. Sometimes, however, our inferences are not so automatic, as when we awaken in a strange room and find ourselves totally disoriented. But usually we go about acquiring simple perceptual beliefs without any conscious effort.

How Things Look

The previous section's description of our unconscious perceptual inferences was highly simplified. It gave the impression that we have noninferential beliefs about how things look, from which we infer other beliefs about how things are. Some fascinating studies by cognitive psychologists, however, suggest that even our beliefs about how things look are the products of inference. According to these studies, we do not only make unconscious inferences from our beliefs about how things *look* to beliefs about how things *are;* we also make inferences from beliefs about how things *are* to beliefs about how things *look.*

In the following sections, we shall look at three kinds of perceptual phenomena that suggest this: shape and size constancy, optical illusions, and ambiguous figures.

Shape and Size Constancy

One aspect of the visual process should be familiar to you. Whenever you see a physical object, light bounces off the object, passes through the lens of the eye, and casts an image on the retina. The size and shape of that image are determined by a number of things, including the distance of the object from the eye and the angle from which you see it. Variations in the size and shape of these images occur in accordance with the laws of optics. As the object moves farther away, the image grows proportionately smaller. As a flat round object is rotated on its axis, the image grows more and more elliptical until it turns into a straight line. The process is much like the photographic process, in which light passes through the lens of the camera and casts an image on film. Both processes occur in accordance with the same laws of optics.

Knowing this, we might expect that the *apparent* size and shape of an object (the way the size and shape appear to us) would vary in the same proportion as they do in photography. That is, we might expect the following: If a camera takes a picture of two coins, one of which is farther from the camera than the other, the relative sizes of their images on the film would be in the same proportion as the relative apparent sizes of the coins if we saw them from the same distance. Similarly, we might expect this: If a camera takes a picture of a coin partially rotated on its axis, the shape of the image on the film would be the same as the apparent shape of the coin if we saw it from the same angle.

Yet in normal circumstances, these expectations would be mistaken. In the first case, the apparent sizes of the coins would be closer to each other than the sizes of the film images. In the second, the apparent shape of the coin would not be as elliptical as the film image. Since we *know* that the two coins are really the same size, the brain makes certain *adjustments* in the retinal images to bring the apparent sizes closer together. Since we also *know* that the coin is really round, the brain makes certain *adjustments* in the retinal image to bring the apparent shape closer to the shape we know the coin to be. These adjustments are called, respectively, *size constancy* and *shape constancy*.

Perhaps you have noticed these phenomena yourselves without realizing it. Perhaps, for example, you have seen television commercials in which someone holds the product close to the camera and the product looks disproportionately large to you. Or you may have seen a close-up photograph of someone in which the nose seems disproportionately large. In many cases, these images are not the result of a distorting camera lens. The images on the film stand in the same proportion as the images on the retina. The reason the former images seem distorted is that the camera does not make the adjustments that the brain does. That is, there is no counterpart in the photographic process to size constancy.

Two interesting characteristics of constancy are worth noting. First, it is much more marked in adult perceivers than in children. In children, apparent size and shape are closer to the size and shape of the retinal image. In adults, they are closer to actual size and shape. This suggests that shape and size constancy are *learned* processes. Second, constancy depends on the viewers' knowledge of the

real size and shape of the seen object, and on their knowledge of the actual distance of the seen object.

Both of these characteristics suggest the same thing—that even simple perceptual beliefs about how things look to us depend on background information.
And this conclusion suggests that the unconscious inferences we make whenever we perceive something are more complicated than we first thought. Earlier,
I said that our beliefs about how things are are the product of inferences based
on how they look and background information. It now seems that our beliefs
about how things look are themselves the product of inferences that appeal to
background information and beliefs about perceptual conditions. If we believe,
for example, that we are seeing a car at a certain distance, we unconsciously
infer that the car looks a certain size in relation to other things in our visual
field.

Hypothesis and Perception

How do these unconscious inferences work? One answer that is
gaining increasing acceptance among psychologists and philosophers is this:
When light casts an image on the retina, it causes certain *provisional hypotheses* in
the perceiver. These provisional hypotheses are *tentative beliefs* about the size,
shape, color, and distance from the perceiver of the objects seen. These hypotheses are then tested in a variety of ways. They are tested against various
background beliefs, for example. Are they consistent with what I expect to see?
If not, where is my mistake? Am I wrong about what I *expected* to see or what I
believe I *do* see? They are also tested against further hypotheses. As I continue
to look, new hypotheses are caused by the light striking my eye. Are the hypotheses consistent? If not, which ones should I reject? Which ones fit in most
easily with background beliefs and other hypotheses?

This process of hypothesis creation and hypothesis testing occurs almost instantaneously, so quickly and automatically that it is unconscious. The goal of
the process is to arrive at a coherent set of beliefs about how things are and how
things look. The beliefs in this set must cohere not only among themselves, but
also with the beliefs held before the process began.

In Part V we saw that we justify our beliefs about the world by appealing to
explanatory coherence. Our beliefs belong to one vast network, and as new hypotheses are considered we test them against other beliefs in the network.
Sometimes we accept the new hypothesis without having to make any changes
in the network. Sometimes we reject the new hypothesis because it does not fit
in with the network. Sometimes we accept the new hypothesis and make
changes in the network to create a good fit. Our decision is determined by our
judgment as to which of the three possibilities leaves us with the best total network.

It seems that this process governs perception as well. To perceive something
is, in part, to acquire new beliefs. And the acquisition of these beliefs involves
unconscious inference. This unconscious inference is a matter of testing and

accepting new hypotheses, allowing us to enrich our beliefs about the world and maintain a coherent network at the same time.

Optical Illusions

Shape and size constancy show that how things look to us is determined not only by the retinal image, but by background beliefs as well. Another phenomenon that shows the same thing is our perception of optical illusions. Consider two well-known illusions, the Muller-Lyer illusion and the Ponzo illusion.

In both illusions, two lines of equal length do not look equal, even if the perceiver knows that they are. In the Muller-Lyer illusion, each line has an arrowhead at each end. At the ends of one line, the arrowheads point *away* from the line. At the ends of the other, they point *into* the line. The former line looks much longer than the latter.

In the Ponzo illusion, the two lines are set parallel to each other between two converging lines, so that one of the two parallel lines is closer to the converging lines than the other. Although the parallel lines are equal in length, the former looks longer than the latter.

Since both lines in each illusion are the same length, and since they are also seen at the same distance from the eye, they cast images of equal length on the retina. Why, then, do they appear to be unequal?

Psychologist R. L. Gregory provides the following answer. Both illusions, he says, are examples of misplaced size constancy. In both cases, we apply the same automatic adjustments to the retinal images that we ordinarily apply in normal cases. Let us see how.

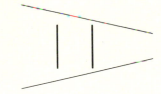

Fig. 20-1a. The Ponzo Illusion

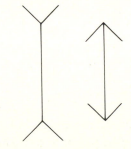

Fig. 20-1b.   The Muller-Lyer Illusion

If we look at the Muller-Lyer illusion, we can see that the arrowheads look like corners. When the arrowheads point *into* the line, we seem to be looking at a corner from the *inside,* with the walls coming *toward* us. When the arrowheads point *away* from the line, we seem to be looking at the corner from the *outside,* with the walls going *away* from us. This gives the impression that the first line is farther away from us than the second. But if the first line is farther away, but still casts an image of the same size as the second line, it must, we think, really be bigger. Thus, the brain makes certain adjustments to make it look bigger. That is exactly what we ordinarily do when we are looking at real corners at different distances from us.

Similarly, the converging lines of the Ponzo illusion suggest two railroad tracks receding into the distance. The narrower the gap between them, the farther away they appear. Therefore, the parallel lines between them suggest two railroad ties at different distances from us. When we look at real railroad ties receding from us, we know that they are the same size and make appropriate adjustments to bring their apparent sizes closer together. So, when looking at the Ponzo illusion, we make similar adjustments. But since the two lines are really the same size, when we increase the size of one, it looks larger to us.

Ambiguous Figures

Constancy and optical illusions show us that unconscious inference plays a major role in perception. Certain other phenomena show us that this inference is a matter of hypothesis-testing. An example of such a phenomenon is the *ambiguous figure*—a figure that can be seen in more than one way.

Consider, for example, the Necker cube (Fig. 20-2). It is possible to see this figure in two ways. First, we may see the face with the circle in the center as the front of the cube. Second, we may see the same face as the back of the cube. Most people who look at it tend to alternate between the two ways of seeing it,

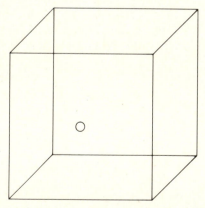

Fig. 20-2.   The Necker Cube

so that it seems to reverse in depth by sudden jumps. Consider also the duck-rabbit drawing (Fig. 20–3), which can be seen as either a duck's head or a rabbit's head.

Fig. 20-3.   The Duck-Rabbit

What happens when the Necker cube reverses depth, or the duck-rabbit drawing changes from a duck's head to a rabbit's? Suppose that you first saw the latter as a duck's head. In order to see it as a rabbit's head, you have to *think* of it differently. You have to think of it as a rabbit's head and then look for something that confirms the belief. The first confirming evidence will probably be the lines to the left, which you can take to be a rabbit's ears instead of a duck's bill. Then you can see the eye as looking to the right instead of the left, and the small notch on the right as a rabbit's mouth. That is, you entertain certain hypotheses about what you are looking at, and when enough of these hypotheses are confirmed you suddenly see it as a rabbit's head.

The process is similar with the Necker cube. If you see the face with the circle in the center as the front of the cube, the cube will recede from you in an *upward* direction. When it reverses depth, it seems to recede in a *downward* direction. Thus, the way the cube recedes from you confirms or disconfirms your hypothesis about which face is in front. What you are in effect doing when you reverse the cube is mentally rearranging it—not by shifting the actual lines, but by shifting your beliefs about them. At first these beliefs are untested hypotheses, and the cube will not reverse. But once the hypotheses are confirmed, the cube suddenly reverses depth.

This process of hypothesis creation and testing occurs in all cases of visual perception. What distinguishes perception of the Necker cube is that two conflicting hypotheses receive the same degree of confirmation resulting in sudden reversals of the figure. In normal cases, one best set of hypotheses is reached. Normally, these final conclusions are accurate. When they are not, as in the Muller-Lyer figure, we have cases of optical illusions.

PERCEPTION AND RATIONALITY

In the preceding two chapters, we treated perception as a *causal* process. To perceive a physical object, we saw, is, in part, to acquire certain beliefs about the object that are caused by the object in the appropriate way. In the present chapter, we have seen that perception is also a *rational* process. To perceive a physical object is, in part, to infer certain beliefs about the object. It is, we might say, to arrive at a highly confirmed theory about the object after a complex process of hypothesis testing.

Thus, *perceptual knowledge* is much like all other knowledge. In Part V, it was said that knowledge is justified true belief. To know that something is true, we must believe that it is true, it must be true, and we must have good reason for thinking it true.

Although many philosophers have applied the justified true belief model of knowledge to perceptual knowledge, they have often applied it somewhat differently to simple perceptual knowledge. Such philosophers have said something like this: Whereas most beliefs are the product of reasoning, simple perceptual beliefs are not. They are the product of a causal process that does not involve reasoning. Therefore, the justification of such beliefs cannot appeal to a reasoning process that *leads* to these beliefs, the way that the justification of other beliefs can and does. Simple perceptual beliefs, in this view, can be justified only by appealing to reasons that we *might* have used or *could* have used *if we had* done any reasoning.

But if the view presented in this chapter is correct, the above view is mistaken. When we perceive something, all of our final beliefs about what we see are the product of reasoning, most of it unconscious. And this reasoning provides justification for these beliefs in the same way that conscious reasoning provides justification for other beliefs.

OBJECTIONS TO UNCONSCIOUS INFERENCE

The notion of unconscious inference is a controversial one, and many philosophers have not accepted it. Inference, they have claimed, must be a conscious, *deliberate* process. It must be a process that we are aware of, that we can have some control over. It cannot be an automatic process of the brain. An important reason for feeling this way is that reasoning is taken to be something that *we do*, not something that *happens to us*. The processes I have been describing, it might be argued, are *not* things that we do.

An analogy may be helpful here. When you raise your arm to wave to a friend, that is quite a different matter from an involuntary twitch of your arm. The former movement is an *action* of yours. It is something that *you* do. The latter, however, is something that your *arm* does. It is something that *happens* to you. If your arm were to twitch involuntarily and someone were to ask you why you were waving it, you would reply that you had not waved it at all. Your arm just moved by itself, you would say. Inference, an objector might claim, is more like waving than it is like twitching. The processes I have been describing are more like twitching.

An objector might also appeal to another analogy. The brain is always working. It controls our leg and arm movements as we walk, just as it controls the beating of our heart. Both the walking and beating serve some purpose, but of very different kinds. When I walk, I walk because I want to go someplace, get some fresh air, or whatever. I walk *because* of some purpose of *mine*. Walking, then, is a deliberate, purposeful activity of mine. The beating of my heart, however, is a different matter. Even though I want to live, and even though the beating of my heart is crucial to my continued life, my heart does not beat *because* I want to live. *I* am not beating my heart for some purpose, although it may be said that my *brain* is causing my heart to beat for some purpose.

Similarly, the objector would say, we may say that the brain is processing information when I see something, but not that I am making any unconscious inferences.

The objection may be put still another way. In Part V, I distinguished reasons and causes. Although it is true that I prefer American-style democracy to Soviet communism both because I grew up in America and because I believe that American-style democracy affords greater freedom, only the latter answer gives a *reason* for my preference. The former gives merely a *cause*. Whereas the latter provides some reason for believing that I am right in my preference, the former does not. Whereas the latter justifies my preference, the former does not. The processes I have been describing, the objector could claim, are merely causal processes. They cannot provide reasons for my perceptual beliefs.

The Objections Considered

Our objector does not deny the findings of the cognitive psychologist. He readily agrees that the beliefs we bring into a perceptual situation affect how we perceive something, just as he agrees that they do so through automatic brain processes. Where the objector and I disagree is on the interpretation of these findings. Should these processes be interpreted as inferences? The objector thinks not, because of certain longstanding beliefs about what inferences must be like.

What are my reasons for thinking otherwise? For one thing, since the pioneering work of psychologist Herman von Helmholtz (1821–1894), cognitive psychologists have interpreted these processes as inferences. Of course, we are not *bound* to agree with them, but we should not disagree without good reason. And I do not think there is good reason to disagree in this case.

Let us consider what an inference is. First, it is a way of acquiring beliefs. Second, it is a way of reaching these new beliefs on the basis of old beliefs. Third, it is a process that ideally conforms to standards of rationality. When we infer a belief, we arrive at it because it coheres with our other beliefs, because it seems more plausible than the alternatives given our other beliefs, because it seems most likely to be true given our other beliefs. And the processes that occur during perception fit this pattern.

But what about the objector's claim that inference must be conscious and deliberate? The best response to this claim is this: Psychologists have shown us that this view is mistaken. They have learned something new about inference. It can be unconscious and automatic.

It is not, after all, unusual for science to overturn conventional wisdom. Consider Freud's striking discoveries concerning unconscious beliefs, desires, and motivations. Before Freud's work, it was felt that such things *must* be conscious. Now references to the unconscious are commonplace. If we can accept unconscious *beliefs* due to Freud's theories, there seems no reason to reject unconscious *inferences*.

THE FINAL WORD?

We are left, then, with the following view of perception. Perception is the acquisition of beliefs in certain ways that involve both causal processes and reasoning. In visual perception, the causal process begins with light bouncing off the perceived object, includes images on the retina, and ends with certain hypotheses about the object. These hypotheses are then tested against a wide variety of background beliefs, against further hypotheses, against new information carried by light, and are either accepted or rejected. All of this activity occurs very quickly, and unconsciously, but it is thoroughly rational. As the brain interprets, accepts and rejects, its goal is the most coherent picture of the perceived situation, a picture that coheres within itself and that fits in most comfortably with as many background beliefs as possible. Thus, we may say that the brain infers the best picture of the world that it can, using the same principles of reasoning that we use in conscious, deliberate inferences.

This view of perception explains how background beliefs affect even our simplest perceptual beliefs, both about how things are and how they appear. It explains why these beliefs are usually correct and why, as in the case of illusions, they are sometimes mistaken. It explains size and shape constancy, and why both kinds of constancy are to some extent learned skills.

Although I have emphasized the rational aspect of perception in this chapter, I will close this section by emphasizing the causal aspect. If the rational aspect shows the degree to which perceptual knowledge is like all other knowledge, the causal aspect shows why perceptual knowledge is so important to us. The light which strikes us in the eye, the sound waves that strike our ears, and so forth, provide the information that enables us to learn about the world. Perception is where knowledge begins, and the touchstone against which knowledge is tested.

STUDY QUESTIONS

1. What is a perceptual belief? How do simple perceptual beliefs differ from inferential perceptual beliefs? Why is background information relevant to both kinds?

2. What are shape and size constancy? Why do these phenomena show that background information is relevant even to simple perceptual beliefs about how things look to us?
3. What does it mean to say that perception is a process of hypothesis creation and hypothesis testing? How does the perception of ambiguous figures show the importance of hypotheses in perception?
4. In what respects is perceptual knowledge like other knowledge?
5. Some philosophers claim that unconscious inference plays a major role in perception. Why? Why do others object to the notion of unconscious inference? How can these objections be answered?

GLOSSARY

Ambiguous figure. A figure capable of being seen in more than one way, for example, the duck-rabbit drawing, which can be seen as either a duck or a rabbit.

Apparent size and shape. The size and shape an object appears to be to someone observing that object.

Cognitive processes. Psychological processes that involve the reception, storage, and treatment of information. Such processes include perception, recognition, thinking, reasoning, and image-forming.

Cognitive psychology. The scientific study of *cognitive processes.*

Inferential perceptual beliefs. Beliefs that are prompted by observation but that involve conscious appeal to background information. If, for instance, you see a photograph of someone and must consciously think about the picture before you are able to recognize the person, your belief that you are seeing a photograph of that person is an inferential perceptual belief.

Optics. The study of the properties of light, including the principles of perspective and the influences exerted by reflecting surfaces and refractive media on the path of light through space.

Perceptual beliefs. Beliefs that are prompted by observation.

Shape and size constancy. The tendency of the brain to compensate for changes in shape and size of the retinal image caused, respectively, by changes in the angle of vision and distance of the observed object. If, for example, an object recedes from the observer, the *apparent size* of the object does not grow smaller in proportion to the retinal image caused by the object. Similarly, if an observed coin is partially rotated, the *apparent shape* of the coin will be rounder than the retinal image caused by the coin.

Simple perceptual beliefs. Beliefs prompted by observation that do not involve conscious appeals to background information. If, for example, you see a dog and immediately recognize that it is a dog, your belief that it is a dog is a simple perceptual belief.

SELECTIONS

In the following selections, we find arguments for two views we have discussed—idealism and direct realism.

The first is from George Berkeley's The Principles of Human Knowledge. *Although he never mentions John Locke by name, Locke is obviously the target of his arguments. Thus, he criticizes the view that our sense data resemble the physical objects that cause them and the distinction between primary and secondary qualities.*

Here are three terminological points to keep in mind. First, Berkeley uses the term "idea" instead of "sense datum." Second, when he says of physical objects that their "esse is percipi," he means that for physical objects, to be is to be perceived. Third, by materia prima, *he means bare matter, matter having no qualities whatever. (Aristotle's views on the subject are discussed in our introductory chapter on ancient Greek philosophy.)*

The second selection is from George Pitcher's A Theory of Perception. *Notice that his theory is a causal one, like Locke's, but does not involve sense data. When we see an object, we acquire beliefs about it, but we do not acquire sense data of it.*

GEORGE BERKELEY

Idealism

1. It is evident to any one who takes a survey of the *objects of human knowledge,* that they are either *ideas* actually imprinted on the senses; or else such as are perceived by attending to the passions and operations of the mind; or lastly, *ideas* formed by help of memory and imagination—either compounding, dividing, or barely representing those originally perceived in the aforesaid ways. By sight I have the ideas of light and colours, with their several degrees and variations. By touch I perceive hard and soft, heat and cold, motion and resistance; and of all these more and less either as to quantity or degree. Smelling furnishes me with odours; the palate with tastes; and hearing conveys sounds to the mind in all their variety of tone and composition.

And as several of these are observed to accompany each other, they come to be marked by one name, and so to be reputed as one *thing.* Thus, for example, a certain colour, taste, smell, figure and consistence having been observed to go together, are accounted one distinct thing, signified by the name apple; other collections of ideas constitute a stone, a tree, a book, and the like sensible things; which as they are pleasing or disagreeable excite the passions of love, hatred, joy, grief, and so forth.

2. But, besides all that endless variety of ideas or objects of knowledge, there is likewise Something which knows or perceives them; and exercises divers operations, as willing, imagining, remembering, about them. This per-

ceiving, active being is what I call *mind, spirit, soul,* or *myself.* By which words I do not denote any one of my ideas, but a thing entirely distinct from them, wherein they exist, or, which is the same thing, whereby they are perceived; for the existence of an idea consists in being perceived.

3. That neither our thoughts, nor passions, nor ideas formed by the imagination, exist without the mind is what everybody will allow. And to me it seems no less evident that the various sensations or ideas imprinted on the Sense, however blended or combined together (that is, whatever objects they compose), cannot exist otherwise than in a mind perceiving them. I think an intuitive knowledge may be obtained of this, by any one that shall attend to what is meant by the term *exist* when applied to sensible things. The table I write on I say exists; that is, I see and feel it: and if I were out of my study I should say it existed; meaning thereby that if I was in my study I might perceive it, or that some other spirit actually does perceive it. There was an odour, that is, it was smelt; there was a sound, that is, it was heard; a colour or figure, and it was perceived by sight or touch. This is all that I can understand by these and the like expressions. For as to what is said of the *absolute* existence of unthinking things, without any relation to their being perceived, that is to me perfectly unintelligible. Their *esse* is *percipi;* nor is it possible they should have any existence out of the minds or thinking things which perceive them.

4. It is indeed an opinion strangely prevailing amongst men, that houses, mountains, rivers, and in a word all sensible objects, have an existence, natural or real, distinct from their being perceived by the understanding. But, with how great an assurance and acquiescence soever this Principle may be entertained in the world, yet whoever shall find in his heart to call it in question may, if I mistake not, perceive it to involve a manifest contradiction. For, what are the forementioned objects but the things we perceive by sense? and what do we perceive besides our own ideas or sensations? and is it not plainly repugnant that any one of these, or any combination of them, should exist unperceived?

5. If we thoroughly examine this tenet it will, perhaps, be found at bottom to depend on the doctrine of *abstract ideas.* For can there be a nicer strain of abstraction than to distinguish the existence of sensible objects from their being perceived, so as to conceive them existing unperceived? Light and colours, heat and cold, extension and figures—in a word the things we see and feel—what are they but so many sensations, notions, ideas, or impressions on the sense? and is it possible to separate, even in thought, any of these from perception? For my part, I might as easily divide a thing from itself. I may, indeed, divide in my thoughts, or conceive apart from each other, those things which perhaps I never perceived by sense so divided. Thus, I imagine the trunk of a human body without the limbs, or conceive the smell of a rose without thinking on the rose itself. So far, I will not deny, I can abstract; if that may properly be called *abstraction* which extends only to the conceiving separately such objects as it is possible may really exist or be actually perceived asunder. But my conceiving or imagining power does not extend

beyond the possibility of real existence or perception. Hence, as it is impossible for me to see or feel anything without an actual sensation of that thing, so is it impossible for me to conceive in my thoughts any sensible thing or object distinct from the sensation or perception of it.

6. Some truths there are so near and obvious to the mind that a man need only open his eyes to see them. Such I take this important one to be, viz. that all the choir of heaven and furniture of the earth, in a word all those bodies which compose the mighty frame of the world, have not any subsistence without a mind; that their *being* is to be perceived or known; that consequently so long as they are not actually perceived by me, or do not exist in my mind, or that of any other created spirit, they must either have no existence at all, or else subsist in the mind of some Eternal Spirit: it being perfectly unintelligible, and involving all the absurdity of abstraction, to attribute to any single part of them an existence independent of a spirit. To be convinced of which, the reader need only reflect, and try to separate in his own thoughts the *being* of a sensible thing from its *being perceived.*

7. From what has been said it is evident there is not any other Substance than *Spirit,* or that which perceives. But, for the fuller proof of this point, let it be considered the sensible qualities are colour, figure, motion, smell, taste, and such like, that is, the ideas perceived by sense. Now, for an idea to exist in an unperceiving thing is a manifest contradiction; for to have an idea is all one as to perceive: that therefore wherein colour, figure, and the like qualities exist must perceive them. Hence it is clear there can be no unthinking substance or *substratum* of those ideas.

8. But, say you, though the ideas themselves do not exist without the mind, yet there may be things like them, whereof they are copies or resemblances; which things exist without the mind, in an unthinking substance. I answer, an idea can be like nothing but an idea; a colour or figure can be like nothing but another colour or figure. If we look but never so little into our thoughts, we shall find it impossible for us to conceive a likeness except only between our ideas. Again, I ask whether those supposed *originals,* or external things, of which our ideas are the pictures or representations, be themselves perceivable or no? If they are, then *they* are ideas, and we have gained our point: but if you say they are not, I appeal to any one whether it be sense to assert a colour is like something which is invisible; hard or soft, like something which is intangible; and so of the rest.

9. Some there are who make a distinction betwixt *primary* and *secondary* qualities. By the former they mean extension, figure, motion, rest, solidity or impenetrability, and number; by the latter they denote all other sensible qualities, as colours, sounds, tastes, and so forth. The ideas we have of these last they acknowledge not to be the resemblances of anything existing without the mind, or unperceived; but they will have our ideas of the *primary qualities* to be patterns or images of things which exist without the mind, in an unthinking substance which they call Matter. By Matter, therefore, we are to understand an inert, senseless substance, in which extension, figure, and motion do actually subsist. But it is evident, from what we have already

shewn, that extension, figure and motion are only ideas existing in the mind, and that an idea can be like nothing but another idea; and that consequently neither they nor their archetypes can exist in an unperceiving substance. Hence, it is plain that the very notion of what is called *Matter* or *corporeal substance*, involves a contradiction in it.

10. They who assert that figure, motion, and the rest of the primary or original qualities do exist without the mind, in unthinking substances, do at the same time acknowledge that colours, sounds, heat, cold, and such-like secondary qualities, do not; which they tell us are sensations, existing in the mind alone, that depend on and are occasioned by the different size, texture, and motion of the minute particles of matter. This they take for an undoubted truth, which they can demonstrate beyond all exception. Now, if it be certain that those *original* qualities are inseparably united with the other sensible qualities, and not, even in thought, capable of being abstracted from them, it plainly follows that *they* exist only in the mind. But I desire any one to reflect, and try whether he can, by any abstraction of thought, conceive the extension and motion of a body without all other sensible qualities. For my own part, I see evidently that it is not in my power to frame an idea of a body extended and moving, but I must withal give it some colour or other sensible quality, which is acknowledged to exist only in the mind. In short, extension, figure, and motion, abstracted from all other qualities, are inconceivable. Where therefore the other sensible qualities are, there must these be also, to wit, in the mind and nowhere else.

11. Again, *great* and *small*, *swift* and *slow*, are allowed to exist nowhere without the mind; being entirely relative, and changing as the frame or position of the organs of sense varies. The extension therefore which exists without the mind is neither great nor small, the motion neither swift nor slow; that is, they are nothing at all. But, say you, they are extension in general, and motion in general. Thus we see how much the tenet of extended moveable substances existing without the mind depends on that strange doctrine of *abstract ideas*. And here I cannot but remark how nearly the vague and indeterminate description of Matter, or corporeal substance, which the modern philosophers are run into by their own principles, resembles that antiquated and so much ridiculed notion of *materia prima*, to be met with in Aristotle and his followers. Without extension solidity cannot be conceived: since therefore it has been shewn that extension exists not in an unthinking substance, the same must also be true of solidity.

GEORGE PITCHER

Direct Realism

It does not seem possible to deny that the physiologist's causal account of perception, as far as it goes and in its main lines, is correct. It cannot be denied that in the case of vision, for example, light rays reflected or emitted from objects enter the eyes of the perceiver and form images on his retinas, that electro-chemical signals are sent along the nerve fibres making up his optic nerves, and that the visual centers in his brain are thus stimulated. There is, of course, a tremendous amount that we do not yet know about what goes on in the eye, the optic nerve, and especially in the brain, when a person sees something; but the broad outlines of the story are surely beyond dispute. . . . There is no reason whatever to suppose and good reason not to suppose, that the stimulation of the visual centers in the brain gives rise to visual sense-data, or to the awareness of visual sense-data. What are we to say *does* happen, then, as a result of the brain stimulation? One right answer might be: The person sees the object(s) from which the light was reflected or emitted. This is true but not helpful, since what we as philosophers are after is precisely an account of what it *is* to see something.

One traditional answer is: The person then acquires some knowledge about the object(s) from which the light was reflected or emitted. But since knowledge can presumably be analyzed in terms of true belief (plus, of course, some other notions), it might be better to phrase this traditional answer as follows: The person acquires certain true beliefs about the object(s) from which the light was reflected or emitted. From this, the following rudimentary theory of perception could be derived: sense perception is the acquiring of true beliefs concerning particular facts about one's environment, by means of or by the use of, one's sense organs. Thus, for example, to see something is just to acquire certain true beliefs about it by the use of one's eyes. If this analysis—or rather this first rough approximation of an analysis—could be modified and elaborated so as to meet several more or less obvious objections, it would be, I think, a highly tempting one.

Suppose there is an insect crawling across a white piece of paper which is lying in front of someone on his desk. If he sees that the insect is crawling across the piece of paper, almost everyone would agree that this necessarily involves his acquiring, by the use of his eyes, the belief that the insect is crawling across the paper. But to see *that such-and-such is the case* is to see something in what some philosophers have called the propositional sense of 'see'; and it might be maintained that this kind of seeing is entirely dependent on a more basic kind—viz., on seeing in the non-propositional sense of the term—and that to see something in this more basic sense does not necessarily involve the acquiring of any beliefs. Thus, in our present example, in order for the person to see that the insect is crawling across the paper, he must see the insect and he must see the piece of paper; and—so the claim would go—neither of these "acts" of (non-propositional) seeing can plausibly be said to be constituted by the acquiring of any beliefs about the insect or the paper. But is this contention correct?

There can be no doubt that one's first reaction to the thesis that seeing something consists of nothing but acquiring certain true beliefs about it by using one's eyes is to dismiss it as obviously false. But I think, on the contrary, that one can go a long way towards defending the thesis; it is not nearly so outrageous as it appears to be at first glance. If, for example, our man with the insect on his paper comes, as the result of using his eyes in a certain way—I mean, by looking at the insect and the paper—to believe, truly, and in fact to know, such things as that there is a piece of paper lying before him, that it is white and rectangular, approximately so big, and that there is an insect crawling over it that is grey, is about half an inch long, has several legs, is now near the upper right hand corner of the piece of paper, and so on—then is this not enough to constitute his actually seeing the insect and the piece of paper? What more could possibly be required? It will doubtless be objected that what is left out of this account is the very essence of seeing—namely, the sensuous visual presentation or manifold. But the answer to this might well be that to be aware of, or to have, that visual presentation or manifold just *is* to know, by means of using one's eyes, that there is a piece of paper lying before one, that it is white and rectangular, and so on. And this reply could be dismissed out of hand as being obviously inadequate only if the having of beliefs and knowledge were to be construed—wrongly—as necessarily involving the making of judgments, or the conscious entertaining of thoughts. So there is something to be said for the thesis.

Indeed, I think the thesis is very nearly correct. At least this much, anyway, seems to me to be true: an adequate theory of sense perception can be formulated which employs as its central notion that of acquiring certain kinds of beliefs. In this chapter I propose to present and defend just such a theory; but first it would be well to attend to a preliminary matter.

Many will be put off at the outset by the very idea of a theory of sense perception that is couched in terms of acquiring beliefs. "It seems wholly unnatural," they might object, "to suppose that we all go around, for most of our waking life, acquiring *beliefs* about things in our environment. If the circumstances are perfectly ordinary, then when the man in your earlier example looks down and just happens to see an insect crawling across a piece of paper, are we really supposed to imagine that he thereby acquires a new set of *beliefs?* Surely the whole idea sounds very fishy indeed." This objection speaks out not only against the *identification* of perception with the acquiring of (true) beliefs, but also against the far weaker thesis that in normal, everyday cases of perception, one regularly acquires beliefs as an adjunct of, or as the *result* of, seeing something, hearing something, or whatever. It objects, in short, to any sort of intimate connection between the concepts of sense perception and belief.

The objection does not, nor does it pretend to, take the form of an argument; rather, it merely voices an intuitive feeling of dissatisfaction with the idea that the acquiring of beliefs has anything very essential to do with sense perception. Whatever psychological force this feeling may have derives, I think, solely from the fact that one does not usually *speak* of the acquisition of beliefs in connection with seeing, hearing, and the rest. We would not, for example, ordinarily say of someone who sees an insect crawling across a piece of paper that he thereby acquires the belief that there is an insect be-

fore him, that it is crawling on a piece of white paper, and so on; it is far easier and more natural, if we bother to take note of the fact at all, to say simply
that he sees an insect crawling across a piece of paper. By using the 'see'-lo-
cution, we can efficiently sum up the relevant information acquired by the
perceiver and indicate, moreover, the means by which he acquired it. But
precisely *because* of these facts, it is positively to be expected that when one
tries to give a philosophical theory of sense perception, i.e., to say what it *is*,
he will be forced to bring in notions that "sound odd" in just the way
pointed out by the objection. Therefore, if one is to indulge in philosophical
theories of perception at all, he must be prepared to treat lightly such objections as the one now under discussion. I realize that the issue between me
and the propounder of the objection could only be settled, if at all, by a full
scale discussion of such matters as the nature and point of certain kinds of
philosophical theories and the importance of ordinary language in philosophy. But there is here no possibility of going into those matters in the necessary detail, and so I must content myself with the bare assertion that since I
am determined to offer something that I take to be a philosophical theory of
sense perception, I cannot and do not consider the objection to be of much
weight.

It might, however, look unduly brash to leave it at that. Therefore, I shall
venture a few more words in an effort to allay the possible misgivings of
readers who feel the psychological force of the objection. I want to urge that
although we do not always, or even ordinarily, speak of beliefs in connection
with sense perception, nevertheless we sometimes do, and furthermore we
always might or could so speak, without excessive oddity. Thus, leaving
aside for the moment the precise nature of the connection between perception and belief, I want to argue that it is entirely reasonable to think that in
perceptual situations somethings that can aptly be called beliefs enter in in
an important way.

Let us consider one or two examples. Suppose that someone, spying a
chair in the corner, walks across the room with the intention of sitting down
in it, but that when he does so, the thing dissolves at the first touch, to his
utter consternation, into fragments—for it is made of very thin, very fragile
glass and painted to look like an ordinary chair. How can it be denied that
before he attempted to sit down in the object he had the belief that the
thing was a chair, and that it was sturdy enough to support his weight? Certainly as he sits or lies there dumbfounded among the debris, it would be
correct to say of him that he had thought (assumed, believed) that the thing
was a chair and was substantial enough to carry his weight. And this way of
speaking would be entirely unexceptionable even if his misinformation had
been gleaned solely from his own perceptual sources.

The foregoing example was perhaps a bit spectacular, but it is easy to
think of innumerable humdrum ones. If I see a teapot and some cups on a
table in a house I am visiting, then although I should no doubt be puzzled if
someone were to ask me whether I thought, or believed, there was a teapot

on the table, whether I thought, or believed, there were some cups on the table, whether I thought, or believed, the teapot and cups were white (they were!), and so on, then I should have to confess that yes, I did believe those things, despite the fact that those thoughts had not entered my head before the questions were raised. My believing those things, what is more, stems pretty directly from my seeing the teapot and the cups.

Whether or not, then, we go on to *identify* perception with the acquiring of beliefs, there seems to be no persuasive reason to deny that one always, or nearly always, acquires certain beliefs at least as the *result* of seeing something, hearing something, and so on. The concepts of perception and belief, in other words, are not nearly so alien to one another as the objection we have been considering claims they are.

Indeed, I think we can go further: I think reasons can be given for *identifying* certain perceptual states of a person—e.g., the state of *x*'s looking *F* (or *F-er*) to him—with his being in a certain kind of belief-state. Consider, for example, the moon illusion: the moon standardly looks larger when it is near the horizon than it does when near the zenith. The best explanation we have of this phenomenon at present seems to be this. When the moon is near the horizon, it looks farther away, because of the intervening terrain over which it is seen; and since the angle it subtends in our visual field is the same near the zenith and near the horizon, it looks larger near the horizon—for normally if two objects, *x* and *y*, subtend the same visual angle, but we know, or think, that *x* is farther away than *y*, *x* will look larger to us than *y*.

The question I now want to raise is: What can the moon's looking larger to us when it is near the horizon than when it is near the zenith *consist in?* What is the nature of that perceptual state? It cannot consist in the moon's subtending a larger angle in our visual field, because it demonstrably doesn't. The only answer that I can think of is that it consists in our automatically *believing*, or assuming, or having an immediate impulse or inclination to believe, as we look at the moon near the horizon, that it really *is* larger than it normally is—i.e., when it is higher in the sky. If this is in fact the nature of that perceptual state—and I cannot think of anything else that it might be—then there is reason for thinking that perceiving and believing may be very intimately bound up with one another in all cases.

I shall call any belief like those concerning the teapot and cups—any belief, namely, that is acquired by using one's sense organs in standard ways—a *perceptual belief*. This is not the time to attempt a full-scale account of the nature of belief; but I want to indicate very briefly what general sort of view I hold about the nature of perceptual beliefs, so that the reader will know what thesis it is that I shall be defending in these pages.

Philosophers have sometimes distinguished two main kinds of beliefs: conscious and nonconscious. A conscious belief, it is held, is one that the believer is currently aware of having, in that he is actually entertaining a certain proposition and assenting to it, either overtly or covertly. There can be little doubt that the having of any belief entails much more than just entertaining and assenting to a proposition; but anyway if a conscious belief is one that requires at least the performance of those two acts, perceptual beliefs are not conscious beliefs. I shall not be defending the absurd thesis that sense perception consists, either wholly or in part, of entertaining propositions and assenting to them, of making (conscious) judgments, or anything of that sort.

A nonconscious belief is one that the believer is not at the moment consciously considering. The usual view is that to have a belief of this kind is to have a complex disposition to act (or behave) in certain ways under certain specifiable conditions. I shall hold that perceptual beliefs are one and all nonconscious. Furthermore, I would wish to defend the usual—i.e., dispositional—view as to the nature of such beliefs. There are well-known formidable-looking objections to the dispositional view of belief but I think, and in any case shall here simply have to assume, that they can be met.

FOR FURTHER READING

Locke's philosophy of perception can be found in his *Essay Concerning Human Understanding* (New York: Dover, 1961). The *Essay* was published by Locke in five editions, the first in 1690 and the fifth in 1706. It includes Locke's presentation of the argument from illusion and his defense of the causal theory and representational theory of perception, as well as his discussion of primary and secondary qualities.

Berkeley's views, including his own classic presentation of the argument from illusion and his criticisms of Locke, can be found in his *Treatise Concerning the Principles of Human Knowledge*, first published in 1710, and *Three Dialogues Between Hylas and Philonous*, first published in 1713. Both are available in *Berkeley's Philosophical Writings*, edited by David M. Armstrong (New York: Collier, 1965). They can also be found, along with sections of Locke's *Essay*, in *The Empiricists* (Garden City: Doubleday, 1961). The *Dialogues* was intended as a popular statement of the views of the earlier book, and it is generally more readable and entertaining.

The most discussed contemporary presentation of the argument from illusion is in A. J. Ayer's *The Foundations of Empirical Knowledge* (New York: St. Martin's, 1964), first published in 1940. See also his *The Problem of Knowledge* (Baltimore: Penguin, 1956). Both books also provide classic discussions of phenomenalism. The former is a defense of phenomenalism. The latter is sympathetic to the view, but somewhat critical of it. A famous criticism of Ayer's account and of his presentation of the argument from illusion can be found in J. L. Austin's *Sense and Sensibilia*, reconstructed from manuscript notes by G. J. Warnock (New York: Oxford University Press, 1964). Austin is justifiably admired for his highly readable and witty writing style, which is nowhere more evident than in this book. A similar criticism of the argument from illusion is given by A. M. Quinton in "The Problem of Perception," *Mind*, LXIV (1955).

What I have called the argument from physics can be found in Wilfrid Sellars' *Science, Perception and Reality* (New York: Humanities Press, 1963). This book also contains his criticisms of phenomenalism and his account of the scientific and manifest images. Although most of the essays in this work are extraordinarily difficult, his account of the two images in one essay, "Philosophy and the Scientific Image of Man," is a notable exception and well worth reading.

George Pitcher's *A Theory of Perception* (Princeton: Princeton University Press, 1971) offers a sustained attack on the existence of sense data and a sustained defense of a *non*representational causal theory. My account of direct realism owes a great deal to his.

The most discussed contemporary defense of a representational causal theory is H. P. Grice's "The Causal Theory of Perception," *Proceedings of the Aristotelian Society*, XXV (1961). A more recent defense of a representational theory is Frank Jackson's *Perception* (New York: Cambridge University Press, 1977).

Although Locke's account of the distinction between primary and secondary qualities has been the most widely discussed, it was not the first. Earlier treatments can be found in the following: Galileo's "The Assayer," first published in 1623 and available in *Discoveries and Opinions of Galileo*, translated by Stillman Drake (Garden City: Doubleday, 1969); Descartes' *Principles of Philosophy*, first published in 1644 and available in Haldane and Ross; Robert Boyle's *The Origin of Forms and Qualities* (Manhattan Beach, Calif.: Sheffield Press, 1979), first published in 1966. Another important early treatment is Isaac Newton's, in his *Opticks* (New York: Dover, 1952), first published in 1704, fourteen years after Locke's *Essay*.

For more recent discussions of primary and secondary qualities, see C. D. Broad's *The*

Mind and Its Place in Nature (New York: Humanities Press, 1976), first published in 1925; Roderick Chisholm's *Perceiving* (Ithaca: Cornell University Press, 1959); D. M. Armstrong's *Perception and the Physical World* (London: Routledge and Kegan Paul, 1961); R. J. Hirst's *The Problems of Perception* (New York: Humanities Press, 1978); and Jonathan Bennett's *Locke, Berkeley, Hume* (Oxford: Oxford University Press, 1971).

All of the above are fairly sophisticated for the introductory student. More accessible is Keith Campbell's discussion in *Metaphysics: An Introduction* (Encino and Belmont, Calif.: Dickenson, 1976).

For a nineteenth-century ancestor of phenomenalism (and descendant of Berkeley's idealism), see John Stuart Mill's *An Examination of Sir William Hamilton's Philosophy* (Buffalo: University of Toronto Press, 1979), which first appeared in 1872. Mill's view lies halfway between Berkeley's and Ayer's. Important twentieth-century statements of phenomenalism include Bertrand Russell's *Our Knowledge of the External World* (New York: Humanities Press, 1972), first published in 1914, and C. I. Lewis' *Analysis of Knowledge and Valuation* (LaSalle, Ill.: Open Court, 1971), first published in 1940.

Perhaps the best introduction to the psychology of perception is R. L. Gregory's *Eye and Brain* (New York: McGraw-Hill, 1973), which was a major influence on many of the positions developed in my own discussion. Gregory's book is thorough, readable, and heavily illustrated.

For details of many important studies in the psychology of perception, see *Experiments in Visual Perception* (Baltimore: Penguin, 1966), edited by M. D. Vernon, and *Perceptual Learning and Adaptation* (Baltimore: Penguin, 1970), edited by P. C. Dodwell. Both are collections of scientific papers written by the leading researchers in the field. The Vernon book includes some important experiments on constancy, and the Dodwell includes a generous selection from H. von Helmholtz's *Physiological Optics*, first published in 1866.

For a fascinating philosophical treatment of many psychological experiments in perception, see Pitcher's *A Theory of Perception*. For an influential philosophical treatment of unconscious inference, see Gilbert Harman's *Thought* (Princeton: Princeton University Press, 1973). Also interesting is Jerry Fodor's *The Language of Thought* (New York: Crowell, 1975). Harman's concern is to develop a unified theory of reasoning and knowledge, while Fodor's is to develop a theory of mind heavily informed by current theories in cognitive psychology.

A landmark treatment of the duck-rabbit figure can be found in Ludwig Wittgenstein's *Philosophical Investigations* (New York: Macmillan, 1953), one of the most influential philosophy books of the century. Norwood Russell Hanson expands on Wittgenstein's views in *Patterns of Discovery* (Cambridge: Cambridge University Press, 1972). Unlike Pitcher and Harman and Fodor, Hanson rejects the notion of unconscious inference in perception. Other influential rejections of unconscious inference in perception can be found in Austin's *Sense and Sensibilia* and Quinton's "The Problem of Perception."

Much of my chapter on psychology of perception was adapted from my paper "Perception, Inference and Aesthetic Qualities," which appeared in *The Monist*, 62 (1979). This paper deals with the connections between the psychology of perception and our perception of works of art. Two interesting works on this subject, both of which influenced my paper and, consequently, this chapter, are E. H. Gombrich's *Art and Illusion* (Princeton: Princeton University Press, 1956) and Julian Hochberg's "The Representation of Things and People," in Maurice Handelbaum, ed., *Art, Perception, and Reality* (Baltimore: Johns Hopkins, 1972). Gombrich is an art historian, and Hochberg a psychologist.

Finally, the following anthologies are useful: *Locke and Berkeley: A Collection of Essays,* edited by D. M. Armstrong and C. B. Martin (Notre Dame: University of Notre Dame Press, 1968); *Perceiving, Sensing and Knowing* (Berkeley and Los Angeles: University of California Press, 1976), edited by Robert J. Swartz; *Perception: Selected Readings in Science and Phenomenology*, edited by Paul Tibbetts (New York: Quadrangle, 1969); *The Philosophy of Perception* (New York: Oxford University Press, 1967), edited by G. J. Warnock. The first contains many excellent essays on Locke and Berkeley. The Swartz is especially useful with respect to sense data and the causal theory. The papers by Grice and Quinton appear in both the Swartz and the Warnock.

Part VII

RELIGIOUS BELIEF

Chapter 21

DOES GOD EXIST?

Is it reasonable to believe in the existence of God? This question has concerned not only philosophers, but religious thinkers as well. Some religious thinkers, such as St. Thomas Aquinas (1224–1274), thought that the existence of God could be proved beyond a reasonable doubt. Others, such as Søren Kierkegaard (1813–1855), thought that belief in God was an offense to reason. According to this line of thought, belief in the existence of God requires a leap of faith. That is, to believe in the existence of God, one must leap beyond the evidence, beyond the dictates of reason.

In this chapter, we shall look at the reasonableness of belief in God's existence. In doing so, we shall treat the statement "God exists" as a hypothesis, which we call the *theistic hypothesis*. That is, we shall ask whether the existence of God provides the best explanation of the existence of the world as we know it, or of any features of the world as we know it. Is the statement "God exists" likely to be true? We shall also ask another question. Even if the hypothesis is not likely to be true, are there other reasonable grounds for accepting it?

To treat the existence of God as a hypothesis is to take a decidedly philosophical attitude toward the matter. It is to approach it from the point of view of the agnostic and to focus on available evidence and alternative explanations. In adopting this attitude, we deliberately ignore a variety of considerations.

For one thing, we ignore any claims of revelation. Whether the Bible, say, is the word of God is something to be considered only after we have decided to accept the hypothesis. For another thing, we ignore personal religious experiences. Although people have reported various sorts of personal encounters with God's presence, such reports may be given a host of psychological explanations. Our decision to treat them as accurate reports of God's work on earth must await a prior decision to accept the existence of God. In effect, what we must do when we take a philosophical attitude toward our question is suspend the influence of faith.

Is this a fair way of proceeding? From one perspective, it may appear that it is not. The deeply religious person most assuredly does not treat the existence of God as a hypothesis. To the deeply religious person, God is a constant presence, the cornerstone of an entire way of life, rather than a being whose existence is accepted as the best explanation of available evidence. In other words, to the deeply religious person, God is the central fact of a life of faith. To suspend the influence of faith, then, to treat God's existence as a hypothesis like any other, is in some sense to distort what we are talking about.

That much is undeniable. However, religious thinkers such as Aquinas have offered various arguments for the existence of God, and they have expected these arguments to be evaluated on their own merits. In that case, as long as we confine our attention to the arguments themselves, as long as we do not confuse the life of faith with the power of individual arguments, we remain on safe ground.

Besides, to suspend the influence of faith is not to ignore it. Indeed, after we evaluate Aquinas's arguments for God's existence, we shall turn to another justification for belief in God, which refuses to divorce God from the life of faith.

ANSELM'S GOD

What do we mean by "God" in our question? Certainly, there are many conceptions of God that people have accepted and continue to accept. The conception that will concern us here is one that has historically been shared by important segments of the three great Western religions—Judaism, Christianity, and Islam.

This conception has been captured best, perhaps, by the medieval theologian St. Anselm (1033–1109). According to Anselm, God is the being so great that we cannot conceive of any greater being. That is, God is so great that he has every conceivable perfection.

Five perfections are particularly important. First, God is *perfectly good*, in the sense that he does no evil. Second, God is *omniscient* (knows all there is to be known), and third, he is *omnipotent* (has infinite power). Fourth, God is a *personal* God. That is, he is a being capable of acting in the world, of coming into personal relations with human beings, and of loving us and being loved by us. Fifth, God is a *necessary* being. He is the one being in the universe that must exist. Although it is conceivable that there might have been a universe without human beings, trees, the earth, our sun, and so forth, according to Anselm's conception of God, it is inconceivable that there might have been a universe without God. God's nonexistence, according to Anselm, is impossible. God is the one necessarily existing thing.

THE FIRST CAUSE

The first argument for the existence of God we shall consider is a common one, which has no doubt occurred to you. Philosophers call it the *cosmological* argument, and its most famous formulations come from Aquinas. Aquinas stated the argument in a number of ways. The most-discussed version proceeds as follows.

Everything in nature must have a cause. My existence, for example, was caused by my parents. But every cause must itself have had a cause. My parents' existence, for example, was caused by my grandparents, and their existence by my great-grandparents. What we have, then, is a series of causes, in which every event is the cause of some later event and the effect of some earlier event. But this series of causes cannot reach back forever. It cannot be an infinite series. There must have been some first cause. For if there had been no first cause, there could have been no second cause. And if there had been no second cause, there could have been no third cause. And if there had been no third cause, there could have been no fourth, and so on. In other words, without a first cause, there would be nothing at all. But there most obviously is something—an entire universe. Therefore, there is a first cause.

This first cause must, of course, be something the existence of which needed no cause. That is, it must be something that exists necessarily—something that could not have failed to exist. Such a thing could only be God. Therefore, God exists.

Although this argument undoubtedly has great intuitive appeal, it also has serious problems. Although my own students have been swayed by it long before taking their first philosophy course, they are often concerned by the following. First, assuming that the argument does prove the existence of a first cause, why does it have to be God? Second, even if the first cause is properly called God, what guarantee do we have that it is anything like Anselm's God?

These points are well taken. At best, the argument gives us a first cause, some unique event or being that needed no cause itself. But it is a far step from such an event or being to a God worthy of our worship.

Blaise Pascal (1623–1662), whom we shall discuss later in this chapter, put the matter this way. Such arguments at best give us what he called a philosopher's God. They do not give us the God of Abraham, Isaac, and Jacob. That is, they

THE ONTOLOGICAL ARGUMENT

Most arguments for the existence of God share a common feature—God's existence is inferred in order to explain the existence of the world. Anselm, on the other hand, thought that God's existence could be proved another way. According to Anselm, God's existence follows necessarily from our conception of him. As long as we can think of God as a being so great that we can conceive of no greater being, we cannot deny that God exists without involving ourself in a hopeless contradiction. This argument is called the *ontological argument,* and has been used by a number of important philosophers since Anselm, including René Descartes (1596–1650), Baruch Spinoza (1632–1677), and Gottfried Wilhelm Leibniz (1646–1716).

In its most discussed form, the argument goes like this: God is the being so great that we can conceive of no greater being. Suppose that we conceive of something that has all conceivable perfections yet does not exist. That cannot be God, because we can conceive of a being alike in all respects that does exist, and that which exists is greater than that which doesn't. Therefore, existence is a perfection which must belong to God. That is, God must exist.

Is Existence a Perfection?

Although the logic of Anselm's argument appears, on the face of it, to be impeccable, the argument also appears, on the face of it, to be a cheap trick, as though Anselm simply defined God into existence. This was pointed out by a contemporary of Anselm, a monk named Gaunilo, who objected that he could just as easily define a perfect island into existence. Imagine an island called The Lost Island, which is so great we can conceive of no greater island. Now conceive of an island that has every conceivable perfection yet does not exist. This cannot be The Lost Island, because we can imagine an island alike in all respects that does exist. Therefore, The Lost Island exists.

What, then, is wrong with Anselm's argument? In his famous criticism of the argument, Immanuel Kant (1724–1804) argued that it is wrong to think of existence as a perfection, or, indeed, as any sort of property at all. This point can be illustrated as follows. Think of your bedroom, and as you do, describe it to yourself. That is, list as many of its properties as you can. No doubt, you will list the color of its walls, the furniture inside, its size, and so forth. One thing you would ordinarily not list is its existence. Or try this. Imagine describing your ideal lover. No doubt, you will think of looks, character, personality, intelligence, wealth, sexual tastes, and who knows what else. What you will not ordinarily think of is existence.

Why do we leave existence out in such cases? Because it adds nothing to our conception. Once you have listed all the qualities you want your ideal lover to have, it is understood that anybody who has them must exist. Existence is not a property, but a necessary condition of having any properties at all.

So of course, when we conceive of God, we conceive of him as existing. That does not mean, however, that God *really* exists, any more than our conception of The Lost Island guarantees that it exists.

A Second Version of the Argument

Kant's criticism has generally been accepted as decisive against the onto-logical argument as presented above. In recent years, however, attention has been focused on another version of the argument, also found in Anselm. According to this version, it is not simply existence that is taken to be one of God's perfections, but *necessary* existence. Our conception of God is of a being that could not have failed to exist, of a being whose nonexistence is impossible, of a being who always was, always will be, and of whom it could not have been otherwise. And certainly, to say that about God is to ascribe a property to him.

Many philosophers have denied that there is any such property as neces-sary existence. Anything that exists, they claim, might not have existed. But to say that is to beg the question against Anselm. That is, it is to assume from the outset that Anselm's God cannot exist.

Does God's existence follow from our conception of him as necessarily existing? The commonly accepted answer is no. To say that it belongs to our conception of God that he necessarily exists is to say that anything that does not necessarily exist is not God. Necessary existence is like any other of God's perfections. Anything that is not perfectly good is not God. Anything that is not omnipotent is not God. And anything that does not exist necessarily is not God. In other words, the best that this argument can claim is that *if* God exists, he exists necessarily, just as it is true that *if* he exists, he is perfectly good and omnipotent.

Necessity and Possible Worlds

The statement "If God exists, he exists necessarily," probably sounds strange to you. After all, when we say *"If* such and such is true," we seem to be say-ing that it is possible that it is *not* true. But if it belongs to our conception of God that he exists necessarily, how can we say, without contradiction, that it is possible that he does not exist? Isn't that the point of Anselm's argument? That is the point, of course, but it is not well taken. The following example from mathematics will show why.

All mathematical truths are taken to be necessary truths. One way of ex-pressing this is to say that mathematical truths are true in all possible worlds. What is a possible world?

The terminology comes from Leibniz, and has been brought back to philo-sophical discussions by the contemporary American philosopher Saul Kripke. The world in which we live might very well have been different. My parents might have never met, in which case I would never have been born. Hitler might have decided to invade England rather than Russia, in which case Ger-many might have won World War II. You might have decided not to go to college, in which case you might now be holding down a full-time job or traveling around the country. In saying what might have been, I am stipulat-ing different possible worlds. That is, I am conceiving of worlds that do not exist but might have, rather as a novelist does, or a playwright, or a liar, for that matter. To say that a mathematical truth, "twice two is four," for in-stance, is a necessary truth, then, is to say that there is no possible world in which twice two does not equal four.

There is in mathematics a claim called Goldbach's conjecture, which says that every even number above two is the sum of two prime numbers. (A prime number is a number divisible only by itself and one.) This is called a conjecture, because nobody knows whether it is true. If it *is* true, then, being a mathematical truth, it is necessarily true. But if it is *false*, then, being a mathematical falsehood, it is necessarily false. That is, if an even number above two that is not the sum of two primes exists in this world, then that number exists in all possible worlds. If it does not exist in this world, then it does not exist in any possible world.

The same can be said of Anselm's God. If he exists in this world, then he exists in all possible worlds. But if he does not exist in this world, then he does not exist in any possible world. So if, along with Anselm, we think of God as necessarily existing, then we must think of him as existing in all possible worlds or no possible worlds. That is the proper conclusion of Anselm's argument. God's existence, on the other hand, is not.

do not prove the existence of a loving God who intervenes for the good in human affairs. And that is the God in whom we are interested. A distant first cause with no personal attributes is of no interest to the religious concerns of humankind.

But there is a more fundamental problem with the cosmological argument—the premise that there could not have been an infinite series of causes. Aquinas's support for this premise seems to be based on a misconception. He assumes that anyone who denies that there was a first cause is somehow removing some event or being from the universe, thereby removing everything else. That is, he seems to have in mind something like a house of cards. If we remove the bottom cards, the entire house comes crashing down. Similarly, if we remove the first cause, the entire history of the universe comes crashing down. But when we deny that there was a *first* cause, we are not *removing* any causes from the universe. Rather, we are saying that for any cause you might pick out, no matter how far back, it in turn is the effect of some earlier cause. It is like saying that the house of cards has no bottom, that for any row of cards you might pick, there is some row beneath it. It is to say that the history of the universe is infinite.

The Big Bang

But is the history of the universe infinite? If scientists are right, it is not. According to current science, the universe did have a beginning—the big bang. In the beginning, all matter was concentrated in one large mass. This mass exploded, creating the present universe.

Where did this mass come from? Perhaps it was always there. Or perhaps there was a universe before ours, which collapsed in on itself and then exploded to create ours. Perhaps there was an infinite series of universes, each one collapsing in on itself and then exploding into a new one.

Such questions are difficult to answer, and scientists are divided on the point. Some think that there is so much matter in the universe that gravity will cause the universe to collapse in on itself. Others think that there is not enough matter to cause that to happen. If the first group is right, then it is reasonable to believe that the huge mass that exploded into our universe was the result of a previously collapsed one. If the second group is right, then it is probably more reasonable to believe that the huge mass was always there.

But surely, one is tempted to say, *something* must have created this mass of matter. *Something* must have caused a *first* big bang or the *unique* big bang that created our universe. This temptation arises because of the difficulty we have in grasping the notion of anything stretching backward for an infinite duration. It also arises because of a fundamental limitation of scientific explanation. Science cannot explain everything. It must always leave off at some point taken to be basic. Explanation must stop somewhere. And the force of Aquinas's argument comes from our dissatisfaction with science's stopping point. Can't we explain the unexplainable by appealing to God?

We can, of course, but if we do so, we must face the following rejoinders. First, appeals to God in this case succeed only in pushing our problem back a step. If God's existence cannot be explained, how have we improved our understanding of anything? And if we cannot grasp the notion of matter stretching backward for an infinite duration, how can we grasp the notion of God doing so? Moreover, there is a further problem. Suppose that God did cause the first big bang or the one unique big bang. Either he created the mass of matter out of nothing or there was something that, along with God, always existed. Either way, the theistic hypothesis leaves more unexplained that the atheistic one. The first answer, which is accepted by much Christian theology, leaves us with two mysteries—God's existence and creation out of nothing. The second, which is implied by the creation story in Genesis, also leaves us with two mysteries—God's existence and the existence of something else. The atheistic hypothesis, on the other hand, only leaves us with one mystery—the existence of the mass of matter. Thus, the appeal to God not only pushes the mystery back a step, but seems to multiply mysteries as well.

THE ARGUMENT FROM DESIGN

The cosmological argument, we have seen, is far from conclusive. It does not show that there must have been a first cause, nor does it show that if there was a first cause, it must be God. Still, there is another argument, also advanced by Aquinas, which is believed by some people to provide additional support for the theistic hypothesis. This argument is known as the *argument from design*.

The argument goes like this. Just look around. It is impossible not to be struck by the order of the universe. Consider, for example, such ordinary events as the migration of birds. Every autumn they travel south; in the spring, they return. Or think of the water that falls as rain, allowing plant and animal life to flourish, and then returns to the atmosphere to fall as rain once again.

Think also of the seemingly miraculous interdependence of all living things. Modern ecology has taught us to think of the world in terms of *ecosystems* contained within ecosystems. A lake is an ecosystem, for example—a delicately balanced system of living things, in which distinct species of fish and plant contribute to the health of the whole. But the health of the lake depends also on the health of the larger ecosystem in which it is to be found, the entire forest, and the brooks that feed the lake. Ultimately, we can look at the earth itself as an ecosystem, in which every species has a role to play, as do wind patterns, rock formations, sand dunes, and so forth.

Think also of the remarkable organization of any individual living thing, of the nervous system of human beings, for instance, or of such organs as kidneys and livers, and the functions they play in our lives. Think of how well various creatures fit into their environments, of the variety of instinctual behaviors and colors and sensory abilities exhibited in different parts of the world.

Everything, it seems, has a purpose. Obviously, there is some design exhibited here. And where there is design, there must be a designer. And what must this designer be like? Well, given the enormous size and complexity of the universe, the knowledge and power of the designer must be infinite. And given the benign nature of the universe, we cannot deny the ultimate goodness of the designer. Therefore, the universe cannot have been created by blind causal processes. It must have been created by God. Nothing else can account for the orderliness and purposiveness of nature.

Hume's Criticisms

The most famous discussion of the argument from design comes from David Hume (1711–1776), who provided many powerful criticisms of it.

First, assuming that the world is the product of design, does that mean that there must have been one designer? Given the immensity of the task (designing and building an entire universe), might we not assume that it was performed by a committee? Take a relatively small task, like the design and construction of a building. The architect usually does not select the furniture or artwork, and neither the architect nor the interior designer creates the artwork or furniture, and neither the architect nor the interior designer nor the artists nor the furniture designer erects the building. The larger and more complex the artifact, the more hands and minds involved. Why should it be otherwise with the universe itself?

Second, granting that there is but one designer, what evidence do we have of perfect goodness? Or any goodness at all? I once read (I forget where) a variation of the argument from design: the world is such a colossal muckup that it must have been designed by a grand practical joker. We shall discuss in the next chapter certain problems concerning God's goodness, but for the time being, just think whether you could suggest any improvements in the world.

Perhaps you might make cancer less painful, for instance, or do away with it altogether.

The point here is that if we look at the world without any preconceptions of the designer, we would not conclude that he or she was perfectly good. But even if we did, given the evidence found on the small part of the universe we inhabit, what guarantee do we have that the rest of the universe is so perfect? Might not the rest of the universe be an utter mess? What would we think of the designer, for example, if we'd been born on the moon?

Furthermore, the argument rests on the idea that the world is analogous to a human artifact—a building, say, or a watch. Perhaps that is the wrong way to look at it. Perhaps it is more accurate to think of it as an organic whole, like a plant. Although individual buildings and watches are products of designers, individual plants are not. Where does a plant come from? Another plant. Perhaps the world came from another world, in like manner. In that case, wouldn't God be more correctly likened to an oak tree than an architect?

Although Hume apparently meant this last point to be taken somewhat humorously, there are many human cultures that do not take it in that way. The biblical creation story is far different from those of many other religions. According to some ancient creation stories of Japan, the Middle East, and Australia, for example, the world is the product of a sexual union between a god and goddess. Adherents to this point of view see the world as an organic whole, an animal, and assume that it was created like any other animal. Who is to say that the artifact analogy is any more appropriate, given the evidence before us?

The answer we are most tempted to fall back on is this—purpose. Everything seems to be put here for a purpose, and that means that there must be some designer whose purpose that is. But does it?

Purposiveness Without Purpose

There is good reason to answer our question negatively. Things can seem to have been put someplace for a purpose even though there was no guiding hand involved. According to Darwin's theory of evolution, for example, that is the case with dominant traits of species.

Evolutionary theory seems to deal with purpose, in that it explains why different species have different traits in terms of the purposes of these traits. Why do giraffes have long necks? To eat the leaves from tall trees. Why do fish have gills? To take in oxygen without having to surface. Why do tigers have sharp teeth? To tear apart raw meat. But according to Darwin, these traits did not come about through the influence of some guiding hand. Rather, they came about by blind causal mechanisms. Traits are carried by genes. For various reasons, mutation and the like, genes are changed, producing new traits. If these traits have survival value, if they help the individuals who have them adapt better to their environment, these individuals will live to reproduce. Eventually, these traits will become dominant throughout the species. Otherwise, they will probably die out or continue in a minority of the members of the species.

Consider evolution in action today. A newly discovered poison is used to protect crops from insects. The first year, most of the insects are killed. But some survive because of some genetic variation that made them immune to the poison. The survivors reproduce and before long the insects are capable of doing the same damage they did earlier, the new poison notwithstanding.

So apparent purpose need not lead us to believe in a designer. Of course, if we already believe in God, we can say that the evolutionary process just described (called *natural selection*) is the way that God achieves his purpose. But if we are starting from scratch, if, that is, we begin as agnostics, there is no pressure to say so.

RATIONAL DECISION

The argument from design, then, like the cosmological argument, is at best inconclusive. Does that mean that we should reject the theistic hypothesis, or at least remain agnostic toward it? If our decision here turned only on the likelihood that the hypothesis is or is not true, we would have to answer yes to this question. But, it might be argued, our decision turns on much more. In fact, Pascal argued just that.

Theism, Pascal pointed out, is more than just the acceptance of the statement "God exists." It includes the acceptance of a number of other statements, as well as the adoption of an entire way of life. Belief in God appears in the context of an entire religious story and of a religious way of life. For Pascal, to believe in God is also to believe that the Christian story is true. And to believe in that story is to adopt a whole way of life—including participation in religious rituals and adoption of certain moral principles—if for no other reason than to gain entrance to heaven. Once we realize that, we must see that the probability of a single hypothesis is only one consideration in a complex decision. To see why, consider the following example.

The weather report says that there is a 40 percent chance of rain this afternoon. Is it more rational to adopt the hypothesis that it will rain, or that it will not rain? If only probability were concerned, it would be more rational to adopt the hypothesis that it will not rain. But it is not. Suppose, for example, that you will go swimming if you work on the hypothesis that it will not rain, bowling if you work on the hypothesis that it will. In that case, your problem is really to decide whether to go to the beach or the bowling alley. You'd prefer to swim, all other things being equal, but all other things are not equal. It may rain. And if you go to the beach and it does rain, your afternoon will be ruined. If you go bowling, on the other hand, you run no such risk. So what do you do? If you are rational, you balance the likelihood of rain against the comparative values to you of swimming versus bowling and the displeasure it would cause you if your afternoon were to be ruined. If swimming is much more fun to you than bowling, and if having your afternoon ruined is not such a dire prospect, you will probably decide to go to the beach. That is, you will work on the hypothesis that it will not rain. If, on the other hand, you prefer swimming to bowling only marginally, and if you would hate to be stuck at the beach on a rainy day, you will probably choose to go bowling. That is, even though the probability of rain is only 40 percent, you will work on the hypothesis that it will rain.

What you are doing when you deliberate in such a way is calculating the *expected utility* of the alternatives. That is, you think of the possible consequences of the alternative decisions, decide how much you like or dislike these consequences, and then take into account the likelihood that these consequences will occur. The result is the expected utility of each alternative, and if you are rational, you choose the alternative with the highest expected utility.

In the example we just looked at, there are two alternatives—to go to the beach or to bowl. Each alternative has two relevant possible consequences. On the first alternative, you will either end up swimming or being stuck at the beach in the rain. Assign to each possible consequence the appropriate positive or negative value. Then multiply the first by 60 percent (the probability that it will not rain) and the second by 40 percent (the probability that it will rain). The sum of these two figures gives you the expected utility of going to the beach. Similar computations will give you the expected utility of going bowling. You can then select the alternative with the highest result.

Two factors are relevant, then: the value placed on the possible consequences of your decision, and the likelihood that these consequences will occur. The more you prefer swimming to bowling, the more rational it is for you to go to the beach. But the more likely that it will rain, the more rational it is for you to go to the bowling alley instead.

Pascal's Wager

Pascal treated the question of God's existence as a problem of rational decision. Let us suppose that we choose not to believe in God. Certain advantageous consequences will come to us whether or not God exists. We can avoid boring church services, for instance, and we can drink and smoke to our heart's content, as well as lead any sort of sex life we like. These may be great advantages. Of course, if there really is a God, we end up paying for these advantages by spending eternity in hell. Spending eternity in hell, it seems, is infinitely awful. And if we are right? If God does not exist? Well, in that case, there seems to be nothing extra gained. After all, we won't be around after we die to gloat to our believing friends.

Suppose, on the other hand, that we choose to believe in God. If so, certain disadvantages will come to us whether or not God exists. We're stuck with the boring church services, for one thing, and personal habits and our sex lives will be severely hampered. But if we're right, and there is a God, we get to spend eternity in heaven, which amounts to something infinitely wonderful. Of course, we could be wrong. But being wrong in this case is much better than being wrong if we choose atheism.

Thus, as long as there is some probability, however small, that God exists, the expected utility of theism is infinitely wonderful, while the expected utility of atheism is infinitely awful. So the rational decision-maker will bet on theism.

Criticisms of Pascal's Wager

There are two standard criticisms of Pascal's wager. The first is that a person can't *choose* to believe whatever he'd like, regardless of the evidence. Stare at this book, for example, and try to believe that it isn't there. Obviously, you can't. Or stare at your watch and try to believe that it's run by an invisible gremlin. Once again, you can't. Similarly, if you believe that there is very little likelihood that God exists, you cannot choose to believe that he does.

But this objection misses Pascal's point. To return to our initial example, if I choose to work under the hypothesis that it will rain (that is, if I choose to go bowling), I don't really *believe* that it will rain. I adopt the hypothesis as a working assumption, not as a belief. That is what Pascal advises us to do regarding God's existence—adopt it as a working assumption.

But is that enough to convince God, should he exist, that we should be admitted into heaven? Well, maybe yes, maybe no. But Pascal did not believe that this was a real problem. If we act on the theistic hypothesis, if we truly behave as Christians, if we really live the life of faith, what was once a best bet will turn into a genuine belief, either through force of habit or, perhaps, God's intervention.

The second objection is a bit trickier. Pascal imagines only two alternatives—atheism and Christianity. But there are other religions, with their own dogmas and rituals and ways of life. Assuming that we cannot practice all of them, and assuming also that the wrong choice bars us from the positive consequences of the true religion, doesn't Pascal's wager become unworkable?

Not really. As the objection stands, we can respond as follows. The existence of many religions merely complicates our deliberations. Now we must calculate the expected utility of all religions. We must now decide not only between swimming and bowling, but also among playing pool or poker, seeing a movie, reading, visiting a friend, or whatever. Or, to use a different analogy, we are now at a horse race, having to balance the betting odds on each horse against our judgment that it will win, rather than having to do the same for two teams in the Stanley Cup finals.

Will this rejoinder to our second objection do the trick? Not quite. There is a problem in choosing among religions that does not arise in choosing among horses. Many religions promise an eternal reward if accepted, and warn of an eternal misery if not. Buddhism, for example, teaches that all life is suffering, and that we are doomed to an eternal cycle of death and rebirth unless we achieve *Nirvana*, a state of infinite peace that frees us from that cycle. In that case, the expected utility of accepting Buddhism is infinitely positive, while the expected utility of rejecting it is infinitely negative. But that is the same pair of expected utilities offered by accepting or rejecting Christianity. How can one rationally choose, then?

If we restrict ourselves to mathematics, we can't choose. Mathematically, the positive expected utility of accepting Buddhism equals that of accepting Christianity, and the negative expected utility of rejecting Buddhism equals that of rejecting Christianity. Still, we can make a choice following the spirit of Pascal's wager. Does an eternity in hell *seem* more awful to you than an eternity of death and rebirth? Does the Christian story seem less improbable than the Buddhist one? If so, choose Christianity. If the nod goes the other way, choose Buddhism.

A Live Hypothesis?

What can be said about Pascal's wager? I think that as long as we believe that there is some probability, however small, that the Christian story (or some other story promising eternal reward and threatening eternal misery) is true, the force of his argument is inescapable.

If, on the other hand, we think that the Christian story (or any other story promising eternal reward and threatening eternal misery) is utterly impossible, the force of the argument evaporates. Although the product of an infinite magnitude and any number other than zero is infinite, the product of zero and any other number is zero.

But notice, the conclusion of Pascal's argument is that it is rational to *behave* as though God exists, not that it is rational to *believe* that God exists. Recall our first example of rational decision-making: should we go to the beach or go bowling? The point of the example was that it may be rational to *act* on the assumption that it will rain even though it may not be rational to *believe* that it will. The same point holds for Pascal's wager. If we believe that the Christian story is not utterly impossible, then it may be rational to *act* on the assumption that it is true. But if we also believe that the story is highly improbable, it is not rational to *believe* that it is true.

What must be added to Pascal's argument to make belief in God rational? The American philosopher William James (1842–1910), in an argument similar to Pascal's, required that the existence of God be a *live* hypothesis. What is a live hypothesis? One with enough likelihood that it can be taken as a serious competitor to its rivals.

Suppose, for example, that we are midway through the major-league baseball season, and that the Yankees lead the American League East and the Phillies lead the National League East. Suppose also that I believe that these two teams will meet each other in the World Series. A friend of mine believes that the Astros, who lead the National League West, will appear in the Series against the Yankees. Another friend believes that the Expos, who trail the Phillies by only two games, will meet the Brewers, who trail the Yankees by a game and a half. All of these would be live hypotheses. However, if we suppose that the Cubs have the worst record in the National League and that the Mariners have the worst record in the American League, then the hypothesis that these two teams will meet in the Series would not be a live one. Of course, if someone were to bet me $2 million against fifty cents that such a meeting would occur, I would take the bet. That is, for purposes of the wager, I would act as though the Cubs and the Mariners would meet in the World Series. That would be rational. But to *believe* that they would meet would not be.

What we must ask, then, is whether the existence of God is a live hypothesis.

Naturalism versus Theism

To ask whether the theistic hypothesis is a live one is to ask, in effect, whether it is worthy of serious consideration. Recalling our discussion of Aquinas's arguments for God's existence, we can ask this: although these arguments do not *prove* that God exists, do they at least show that God's existence is a hypothesis worthy of serious consideration? Here, opinion varies. It seems, though, that the worth of the hypothesis stands or falls on the strength of its chief rival—*naturalism*.

Naturalism is the view that all natural phenomena have natural explanations. According to the naturalist, science can provide explanations of everything that happens in the world. That is not to say that current science, restricted to current theories and laws, can do the job. Rather, it is to say that as long as science can grow, change its theories, posit new forces and particles and laws, we can expect it to explain all natural phenomena.

The naturalist tends to see God as a placeholder in the history of humankind's search for understanding. Whenever we could not understand something, we explained it by referring to the will of God. But as we acquired greater understanding, God as a hypothesis was given less work to do. Changes in the weather were no longer seen as reflections of God's moods, such natural catastrophes as earthquakes were no longer seen as acts of God, and the vicissitudes of history were no longer seen as God's balancing of the moral scales. Now when we cannot otherwise explain some event, we do not fall back on God as an explanation. Instead, we marshal the forces of science. But that is to say that we no longer treat God as a serious hypothesis.

What can be said against the naturalist? This. As William James pointed out, whether a hypothesis is live depends on who is entertaining it. To the naturalist, the existence of God is not a live hypothesis. But it is possible to accept science as a powerful tool of human understanding yet continue to entertain the possibility that the world was created by God. Although naturalism is a view *justified* by the history of human learning, it is not *forced* on us by that history. The question of the origin of the universe is such a unique one that it is not at all unreasonable to think that some unique answer is required. This uniqueness makes the theistic hypothesis a live one, and that, combined with Pascal's wager, makes it reasonable not only to act as though the hypothesis is true, but to believe that it is true.

THE FINAL WORD?

It is useful, I think, to frame the debate between the theist and the naturalist in the context of the imaginary debate presented in Part IV of this book. In Chapter 12, I compared belief in a nonphysical mind to belief in a nonphysical gremlin running a watch. In the beginning, the gremlin was put forth as a hypothesis to explain the workings of the watch. As the real workings of the watch became understood, there was no longer any reason to believe in the gremlin. According to the naturalist, God has gone the way of the gremlin.

According to the theist, there remains at least one unexplained phenomenon—the existence of a universe—allowing us to keep the hypothesis of God's existence alive. The naturalist disagrees. Rational belief in Anselm's God depends on much more than ignorance of the origins of the universe. Anselm's God was part of a larger view of the cosmos, a view that saw the constant influence of God in human and natural history. In Part V, we saw that justification is a matter of explanatory coherence. A belief is justified because it fits into our network of beliefs better than its competitors. The naturalist claims that Anselm's God has lost its network, that he does not belong in the same network that contains modern physics and astronomy and evolutionary theory. Naturalism belongs there instead.

If we continue to believe that the existence of God is a live hypothesis, then, it is not because this belief is justified by the other beliefs in the modern network. Rather, it is because of a nonrational religious impulse—a need to find purpose in a world of blind causal mechanisms, perhaps, or a passionate desire for eternal life, or a drive to express our wonder and awe through worship of something perfectly good and powerful.

In his discussion of religious belief, James stressed the influence of our nonrational side—what he called our passional natures. If we assimilate this side to the life of faith, then it seems that we must agree with Kierkegaard, whose view we contrasted with Aquinas's at the beginning of this chapter—theistic belief requires a leap of faith.

STUDY QUESTIONS

1. Explain Anselm's conception of God.
2. What are the two versions of Anselm's ontological argument? Why does Kant's criticism of the first version not apply to the second? What other criticism can be raised against the second?
3. Why did Pascal charge that the cosmological argument could only prove the existence of a philosopher's God, not the God of Abraham, Isaac, and Jacob?
4. Why did Aquinas believe that there must be a first cause? What flaw in his reasoning have philosophers claimed to find?
5. In my discussion of the cosmological argument, I claimed the following: The atheistic hypothesis leaves us with one mystery, while the theistic hypothesis leaves us with two. What were my reasons for making the claim? Do you agree? Why or why not?
6. What is the argument from design? How did Hume criticize the argument? Do you agree with his criticisms? Why or why not?
7. How does evolutionary theory show purposiveness can arise without the need of some guiding hand?
8. How did Pascal turn the question of religious belief into a problem of rational decision-making?

9. What two objections are often raised against Pascal's wager? How can these objections be answered? Do you agree with these answers? Why or why not?

10. What is a live hypothesis? Is God's existence a live hypothesis? How would the naturalist answer this question? Do you agree or disagree? Why?

GLOSSARY

Argument from design. An argument for the existence of God. According to this argument, the order exhibited by the universe must be due to some designer, and that designer must be God.

Cosmological argument. An argument for the existence of God. According to one of the most-discussed formulations of the argument, every natural event must have a cause. But the sequence of causes cannot extend infinitely into the past. Therefore, there must be some first cause, and that first cause must be God.

Ecosystem. A system of interrelated parts consisting of a community of organisms and its environment.

Expected utility. A measure of the desirability of a contemplated course of action. We calculate expected utility by determining the possible consequences of the action, their desirability or undesirability, and the probability that each consequence will occur.

Live hypothesis. A hypothesis considered worthy of consideration.

Naturalism. The view that every natural event has some natural explanation.

Natural selection. In evolutionary theory, the process by which certain traits survive through biological reproduction and other traits do not. Roughly, the process goes like this: Certain traits are introduced by genetic variation. If enough members of a given species survive to reproduce the trait, it becomes a dominant trait of the species. Otherwise, it does not.

Ontological argument. An argument for the existence of God. According to this argument, given an adequate conception of God, we cannot deny that he exists without involving ourselves in a contradiction.

Theistic hypothesis. The hypothesis that God exists.

Chapter 22

THE PROBLEM
OF EVIL

In the preceding chapter, we looked at Anselm's conception of God. According to Anselm, God is the being so great that we can conceive of no greater being. He is, among other things, all-knowing, all-powerful, and perfectly good.

We also asked whether there is good reason to believe that such a God exists. And when discussing one proposed reason, the argument from design, we asked whether, looking at the world with no preconceptions, we would infer that the designer is perfectly good. In this chapter, we will push this question a bit further. Rather than ask whether the world as it is provides adequate evidence for the existence of Anselm's God, we will ask the following: Is the existence of Anselm's God compatible with the world as we know it?

THE PROBLEM OF EVIL

People suffer. In hospitals today, there are human beings dying of bone cancer. Their pain is so intense that no amount of medication can relieve it. Their families, their friends, their doctors can do nothing but watch them die in agony. If God knows how these people suffer, and if he is able to stop their suffering, why doesn't he? If their doctors were able to stop it but did not, we would not think them the least bit good. Why should it be otherwise with God?

Six million Jews died at the hands of the Nazis. Many were herded so tightly into boxcars that they were crushed to death. Those that survived the journey were deposited in work camps or death camps. In the work camps they slept many to a bed, were starved beyond recognition, and used in heinous medical experiments. In the death camps they were crowded into "showers" in which poison gas came from the shower heads. They were tortured, raped, otherwise brutalized—and they prayed. If God heard their prayers, why did he let the holocaust continue?

As I write this paragraph, the population of Cambodia is being destroyed. Hundreds of thousands of children are starving to death. Their bellies are distended, their eyes stare blankly from wretchedly gaunt faces, they are in constant pain, and they are too weak to swat the flies from their faces. Because of political squabbles between the Vietnamese and Cambodians, emergency supplies, including food, are not permitted to reach them. Why must these innocent children suffer? If even the hardest of human beings do not deny food to a starving child, how can God?

What these events illustrate is the problem of evil: If God knows everything that happens to us (if he is omniscient), and if he can do whatever he wants to stop it (if he is omnipotent), and if he is perfectly good, why is there suffering?

More formally, the problem is this. The following four statements appear to be inconsistent:

1. God is perfectly good.
2. God is omnipotent.
3. God is omniscient.
4. There is suffering.

The problem for the believer in Anselm's God is to show that they are *not* inconsistent.

There have been many attempts to deal with this problem, extending back at least as far as the Book of Job. Job, a man of great righteousness, lost all—his wealth, his children, his health. His friends, far less righteous than he, came to his house and hounded him to admit his sins. Job protested his integrity throughout their insults, and finally raised his voice to heaven and demanded that God explain to him why he must be allowed to suffer. When God did respond to Job, it was to give him no explanation at all. Speaking out of a whirlwind, he boasted of his knowledge and power, and then he reprimanded Job for calling to account one so powerful. Job, in turn, repented for questioning what he could not understand.

The upshot of the story, then, is that God has some reason for allowing us to suffer, although it is beyond our comprehension. Still, many thinkers have attempted to comprehend it, for such a reason may erase the appearance of inconsistency in our four statements. These statements are inconsistent only if a perfectly good God both aware of and capable of stopping great suffering *would* stop it. But perhaps he would not.

THE BEST OF ALL POSSIBLE WORLDS

Our judgments about suffering are the products of our limited point of view. Certainly, my own suffering and the suffering of those close to me are of paramount importance to me. But perhaps from the point of view of the entire universe, from a God's-eye point of view, our own suffering is not that important. Given this possibility, it may very well be that once *everything* is taken into account, including those things not known to us, it would be apparent that our world, whatever its flaws, is the best of all possible worlds, and that any lessening of human suffering would have a disastrous effect someplace else. This was the view of Gottfried Wilhelm Leibniz (1646–1716), who argued as follows. Before God created the world, he was able to imagine every possible world. That is, he could foresee what would happen if he created the world one way, what would happen if he created it another, what would happen if he created it still a third way, and so on, until all possible ways of creating it were exhausted. Knowing what would happen in all possible worlds, God chose the best one, and brought it into existence.

On the face of it, this seems absurd. Indeed, Voltaire (1694–1778) satirized Leibniz's view mercilessly in his novel *Candide*. Candide, the novel's hero, suffered every sort of indignity and cruelty as he traveled the world, while a Leibniz-like philosopher assured him that this was the best of all possible worlds.

It is not difficult to sympathize with Voltaire. Would something terrible really happen if cancer pain were not so awful? If a polio vaccine had been discovered years before Salk gave us his vaccine in the 1950s? If Hitler had never come to power? In fact, as we pointed out in the previous chapter, it is not hard for us to imagine any number of improvements in the world. If this is really the best that God could do, it is tempting to say, then it seems doubtful that he is omnipotent.

Still, Leibniz's claim can be beefed up a bit. Let us see how.

Some First Stabs at an Answer

When I present the problem of evil to my students, they are quick to provide a variety of answers. When I describe a scene of a woman painfully dying of cancer, for instance, they invariably say that pain is needed to let us know that something is wrong with our bodies. If disease and injury did not cause pain, we would be unaware of them and their damage would increase.

The problem with this response, though, is that the poor woman already knows that something is wrong. She has gone to the doctor and been given the best of medical care. The pain serves no purpose any more. Her suffering is pointless. Why doesn't God intervene? Or why didn't he build us in such a way that the pain would naturally stop once we reach that point? Besides, as Joseph Heller pointed out in his novel *Catch-22*, God could have devised another method for letting us know that something is wrong with us—a light in our forehead that flashes red, for instance, rather like the light that informs us that the oil pressure in our car is low. If Detroit could think of such a thing, why not God?

Another answer involves an appeal to contrast. We could not, my students say, appreciate pleasure unless we knew pain as well. I am not sure that this is true, nor am I sure that Anselm's God could not have made us in such a way that we could appreciate pleasure without knowing pain, but even if we grant this point, there remains this problem. Why do we need as *much* pain and suffering as we have? Do people have to die in Hitler's death camps to appreciate freedom and dignity? And what about the children in Cambodia, who die knowing *only* pain? What good does their suffering do them? Or anyone else?

My students are also quick to try the following. Since humans sin, justice demands that we be punished. Pain is God's way of punishing us. When I respond that there seems to be no correlation between the amount of suffering any individual endures and that individual's sins, they resort to the notion of original sin. Since Adam ate the apple, we are all worthy of punishment. This seems hard to buy, though. Whether the biblical story of the fall is true or false, it is difficult to justify the suffering of innocent children on that score. Would a human being who tortured a child for the sins of some distant ancestor be thought perfectly good? Hardly.

Suffering and Higher Good

The above answers have not played a major role in most discussions of the problem of evil. I mentioned them only to clear the way for two other answers, which have attracted the most attention in the literature. The first of these answers goes like this.

There is something unseemly, many have thought, about confining our discussion to *physical* suffering and pleasure. Many of the things we value in this world cannot be brought down to this level. Think, for example, of such human qualities as courage, loyalty, kindness, compassion, charity, forgiveness, and so forth. Surely, a world that has these qualities is better than a world that does not.

Think also of our admiration of such people as Jonas Salk, who gave us the first polio vaccine, or of Martin Luther King, Jr., who dedicated his life to the attainment of social justice. Surely, a world with people such as these is better than a world without them. Think also of such scientists as Marie Curie and Albert Einstein, and of the patient search for knowledge exhibited by them and a host of other, lesser-known researchers and theorists, and of the joy and pride we take in new discoveries and understanding. Once again, a world with such people and gains is better than a world without them.

But could we have such a world without human pain? Could we act courageously if there were nothing to fear? Feel compassion if confronted only by happy people? Forgive those who have not hurt us? Could there be a Jonas Salk without disease? A Martin Luther King, Jr., without injustice?

And if God were constantly to intervene in human affairs in order to prevent suffering, could science arise or continue? With constant intervention, how could there be any regularities in the world? And with no regularities, how could there be science? And with no science, how could there be a Curie? An Einstein?

Pain is necessary, then, for the higher goods we so value. A world without pain would be a world without courage or charity, a world without heroes and knowledge. Such a world would be vapid, shallow, uninteresting. Human beings could not attain the heights they have attained.

Although this line of reasoning certainly has its force, it also has its problems.

First, is it worth it? Is the courage displayed in war worth the death, disease, starvation, rape, and terror produced by war? Is the suffering of children justified by Salk's discovery of a polio vaccine? Is a world with slavery, discrimination, and poverty, and Martin Luther King, Jr.'s struggle against them better than a world without any of them? Is it really better to create a world with suffering so that it can, little by little, be diminished (but not eradicated) than to create a world without suffering? It is most difficult to answer such questions affirmatively.

Second, are disease, war, and the grosser forms of injustice really necessary for these higher goods? Can't we exhibit courage, loyalty, kindness, dedication, and the like, in the face of far lesser hurts? And would science really be made impossible if there were far less suffering? Certainly, if suffering were to be severely diminished in *this* world, a good deal of intervention on God's part would be required, but if he had made the world differently, perhaps it would not be.

Third, suffering leads not only to higher *goods*. It leads to additional *evils* as well. Just as we can display courage, loyalty, and kindness in the face of suffering, so can we display cowardice, treachery, and cruelty. Just as human suffering produces people dedicated to eradicating it, so does it produce people who will exploit it. So even if (as is improbable) we say that these higher goods do make human suffering worthwhile, we can still ask why God permits these additional evils. Even if there must be pain, why must there be deliberate cruelty? Why must it be possible for one evil person, such as Hitler, to cause far more suffering than can be alleviated by one such as King?

THE FREE-WILL SOLUTION

This last question leads us to perhaps the most important attempt to solve the problem of evil. These additional evils are all due to human beings. Indeed, most suffering, it might be said, is due to the actions of human beings. And what makes such cruel actions possible is human free will. More than that, such actions *must* happen if human beings have free will. To have free will is to be capable of doing both good and evil. And as long as we are capable of doing evil, we will sometimes do evil.

Now, if evil is the inevitable outcome of free will, and if a world with free creatures is a better world than one in which there are no free creatures, if there is far more value to creatures who act on their own free will than to creatures who do good out of necessity, then a good part of the problem of evil is solved. God created us with free will in order to create a better world, and a good deal of unnecessary human suffering is our responsibility.

But what about human suffering not the product of human actions? We are not responsible for diseases, droughts, earthquakes, hurricanes, or floods. How can the free-will solution deal with them?

The contemporary American philosopher Alvin Plantinga responds this way. According to the Christian story, human beings are not the only free creatures created by God. Before creating us, God created the angels. And one angel, Satan, chose to rebel against him. Many natural disasters, so-called acts of God, can thus be understood as acts of Satan. Just as the creation of free human beings leads to the infliction of suffering, so does the creation of free angels.

Philosophers have leveled three sorts of criticisms against the free-will solution. First, they have questioned the relative value of free will as opposed to the negative value of the suffering that has resulted from it. Second, they have asked whether it is true that free will must result in great evil. Third, they have questioned whether the theist is entitled to the solution at all. We shall look at these three criticisms in turn.

The Value of Free Will

In Part III, we asked whether we actually have free will. No doubt, many of you believed (and continue to believe) that we do, in large part because you *wanted* to believe it. This obviously shows that you value free will very highly. Still, do you value it so highly that you think it worth the suffering that has resulted from it? Is your free will worth the Nazi death camps? The destruction of Cambodia? The rapes and murders in high-crime areas and the fears of people who are forced for economic and racial reasons to live in them?

Those of us who do not believe in free will do not feel particularly demeaned by our belief, nor do we feel that life has lost any value. We still have our loves and our joys, and we continue to find a degree of beauty and goodness in the world. It is hard for us to imagine anyone thinking that free will is so valuable that it justifies all the suffering that humankind has known. Would a perfectly good God really create us (and the Devil) with free will if he knew what would result? What would you be more horrified to learn—that you do not have free will, or that your entire family has been killed by a sniper? That you do not have free will, or that the Soviet Union has launched nuclear missiles aimed at the United States?

Surely, when we discussed determinism in Part III, it could not have seemed so horrible that you would prefer having free will to having your family. Indeed, if determinism boils down to the position that our voluntary acts are caused by our wants and beliefs, and that our wants and beliefs are caused by the interaction between our characters and the rest of the world, it seems to be a fairly benign sort of view. How can it be worse than the vast amount of human suffering the world has known?

Must Free Will Result in Great Evil?

An important part of the free-will solution is the claim that to have free will is to be capable of doing evil, and that as long as we are *capable* of doing evil, we *will* do evil. Let us examine this claim.

If we look at it closely, we see that it is true only on the assumption that God does not intervene to stop us from doing evil. But why should a perfectly good, omniscient, omnipotent God *not* intervene in that way? Of course, if God were to intervene *every* time someone chose to do evil, the world would be utterly chaotic. But it does not seem that chaos would result if he chose to intervene only in times of massive suffering. If the Bible is to be believed, he did so in ancient times. If he could rescue the Jews from Pharaoh, who enslaved them, why not from Hitler, who almost exterminated them? If he could send manna from heaven during the Jews' wanderings in the desert, why not to the starving children of Cambodia?

A human being who does not intervene when possible to stop great suffering is not considered perfectly good. If it is true that God always can, but rarely (if ever) does, how can *he* be considered perfectly good?

Consider, also, this problem. If God is omniscient, then he knows what will happen in the future. He knew, for example, that Hitler would launch World War II and the death camps, and he knew that various people would end up as mass murderers. Knowing these things, why did he allow them to be born?

We can put this last point another way. It is a fact of nature that some kinds of fetuses are naturally aborted before the nine-month term of pregnancy is completed. These fetuses are often physical monsters, so badly deformed that they could not survive outside of the mother's womb. Such natural abortions can be seen as genuine blessings to the mother. Perhaps God could have made it a fact of nature that all fetuses destined to become moral monsters, such as Hitler, suffer the same fate. Would this not be a genuine blessing to all of humanity?

Finally, consider this. Perhaps it's not true that creatures with free will *must* be capable of doing evil. Think of the limitations you already have. You cannot choose to become a duck, to retract your fingernails the way a cat retracts its claws, to shrink or grow taller at will. Perhaps there could have been similar natural laws preventing certain sorts of choices.

Suppose, for example, that we were incapable of feeling certain kinds of emotions—hatred, jealousy, and resentment. Then we would be incapable of acting vindictively and spitefully. Or suppose that the natural feeling of sympathy were so strong in us that we could not choose to be deliberately cruel. Or suppose that it were a law of nature that every time someone wished to commit a particularly heinous crime, genocide, for instance, he went into instant paralysis. Surely, such possibilities are not beyond the power of an omnipotent God.

Omniscience and Free Will

In the preceding two sections, we asked whether the free-will solution really is a solution to the problem of evil. In this section, we ask an even deeper question: Is the believer in Anselm's God *entitled* to the free-will solution? Put another way, the question is this: If Anselm's God really exists, can human beings (or any other creatures) have free will?

Many philosophers have thought not. Here's why. Anselm's God is omniscient. If he is omniscient, then he knows not only the past and the present, but the future, too. And if he knows the future, he knows what you and I and any other person will do. But if he really *knows* what we will do, that means that our actions are determined. If they were not, they would not be knowable in advance. But if our actions are determined, we do not have free will. Therefore, the free-will solution is not open to the believer in Anselm's God.

The key step in this argument, of course, is the claim that if God knows what we will do, our actions must be determined. The claim is defended as follows.

Knowledge, we saw in Part V, is justified true belief. That is, if I know that something is true, I must think it true, be right, and I must have good reason for thinking it true. Now, if God knows what I will do before I do it, that means that he has a true belief that at some future date I will perform a particular action. But this true belief cannot be a lucky guess. If it were, it would not be knowledge. How, then, does God know?

Two possibilities come readily to mind. First, he has a God's-eye view of the universe. That is, he sees everything that is happening now, and knows every law of nature. And, knowing all of this, he can deduce with absolute certainty what will happen at any future time. But that, you will recall, is exactly what determinism is—the view that any event can be deduced from the conditions that came before it plus relevant laws of nature.

Second, some religious thinkers have said that God does not *deduce* that future events will occur. Rather, he *sees* that they will, in the same way he sees that present events are occurring. According to this point of view, all of history is present to God. That is, from God's point of view, our distinction between past, present, and future does not exist. He sees everything at once.

Many philosophers find this most puzzling. Some even go so far as to say it makes no sense. But whether it does or does not make sense, it does not seem to make his omniscience and our free will compatible.

Perception, we saw in Part VI, is a *causal* process. If I see something occur, my visual experience of it is caused by that occurrence. So if God sees that I will eat an anchovy pizza next Friday at exactly eight o'clock in the evening, my eating of that pizza must be causing his visual experience of my eating it.

But remember—one way of describing determinism is this. If at any given time, one and only one action is causally compatible with everything that came before, that action is determined. But certainly, if God now sees what I will do before I do it, then only that action is causally compatible with whatever comes before it. Therefore, my act is determined.

Indeed, no matter how God comes to know my actions before they occur, the answer is still the same—my actions are determined. We can see this by approaching the point from another direction.

If God is omniscient, then he has beliefs about everything that has occurred and will occur, and none of those beliefs can be wrong. But if none of his beliefs about the future can be wrong, then the future is already settled. The point is not that God *makes* the future happen in such a way as to fit his beliefs about it. Rather, it is that the present is such that there is only one future compatible with it, and that is the future that God believes will occur. If God cannot be wrong, then no other future can happen.

The upshot of our discussion is this, then. If human beings have free will, God is not omniscient. But if he is omniscient, we do not have free will.

A GREAT BUT IMPERFECT GOD?

If we look at the various proposed solutions to the problem of evil, we find that they all have something in common. Each one claims that suffering is a necessary precondition or outcome of some greater good. But in the responses to these solutions, we find either that suffering is not necessary for that good, or that the world would be better without the suffering and the alleged greater good.

Therefore, we seem forced to say this. If God exists, then either (1) he is doing the best he can, in which case he is not omnipotent; (2) he can do better but doesn't, in which case he is not perfectly good; or (3) he would do better if he knew what was happening here on earth, but he doesn't, in which case he is not omniscient. That is, each solution can solve the problem only by denying one of the attributes of Anselm's God.

Thus, our conclusion seems to be this: If God exists, he is not Anselm's God. Anselm's God is incompatible with the fact of human suffering. But if we accept this conclusion, the following question arises. Is a God other than Anselm's God, a lesser God compared with Anselm's, worthy of worship? Many people have thought that an imperfect God is not worthy of worship. Need a theist buy that claim?

I think not. Indeed, if we look at the Old Testament, we find ample evidence that the biblical writers did *not* think of God as Anselm did. Although their God was undeniably a great God, he was not perfect. Although they probably saw him as omnipotent, and although they certainly saw him as being extraordinarily good and knowing, they do not seem to have seen him as perfectly good and omniscient.

Consider, for example, chapter 18 of Genesis, verses 20 to 33. There God tells Abraham that he has heard of great evil in Sodom, and that "I will go down to see whether they have done altogether according to the outcry which has come to me; and if not, I will know" (from the Revised Standard Version). Thus, God tells Abraham that he does *not* know whether Sodom is as evil as he has heard. Further in the chapter, Abraham and God argue about the fate of Sodom. Interestingly enough, Abraham wins the argument. He even says to God, "Wilt thou indeed destroy the righteous with the wicked? . . . Far be it from thee! Shall not the Judge of all the earth do right?" This strongly suggests that God's goodness is great, but not infinitely so.

Consider also the Ten Commandments, Exodus 20. There God says that he is a jealous God, even though he forbids covetousness among the Jews. "I The Lord your God am a jealous God, visiting the iniquity of the fathers upon the children to the third and fourth generation of those who hate me." Thus, he claims to punish the innocent for the sins of their ancestors, not out of justice, but out of jealousy.

Moreover, in Genesis 3, when Adam hides from God after eating the forbidden fruit, God calls to Adam, asking where he is, and does not seem to know that Adam ate the fruit until Adam admits to being ashamed of his nakedness.

The point here is that Anselm's conception of God is a comparatively late one in the Judeo-Christian tradition, coming in the wake of a good deal of Christian theology. Of course, one could read these passages with Anselm's God in mind and interpret them accordingly, but if one reads them without preconceptions, it is hard to avoid the conclusion that the biblical writers thought of God as being something less than perfect. It was enough for them, it appears, that God be good, powerful, and knowing. Such a God was still considered eminently worthy of worship.

THE FINAL WORD?

In the preceding chapter, it was concluded that reason does not lead to belief in Anselm's God; in this chapter, that reason cannot reconcile his existence with the fact of human suffering. This conclusion can be avoided, of course. The believer in Anselm's God can, perhaps, take comfort in God's voice from the whirlwind, and, with Job, accept what cannot be understood. Or he can deny that human suffering is an evil, which a perfectly good God must eradicate if he could.

Believers in Anselm's God have done both. To those who take the first approach, the philosopher can say nothing. After pointing out the intractability of the problem of evil, her task is done. To those who take the second approach, the philosopher can only note that it is a perverse one. Both our feelings and our morals tell us that needless suffering is an evil to be prevented and stopped. To deny this point is to turn our backs on the cornerstone of human decency.

STUDY QUESTIONS

1. What is the problem of evil?
2. According to Leibniz, ours is the best of all possible worlds. What did he mean by that?
3. According to one answer to the problem of evil, physical suffering is required for the existence of goods that are higher than physical pleasure. How can that claim be supported? Why have many people considered the claim an inadequate answer? What are your views on the matter?
4. According to the free-will solution to the problem of evil, the following claims are true:
   a. If human beings have free will, then great evil will sometimes result.
   b. A world with free will and the great evil that results from it is better than a world without free will and its resultant evil.

   What can be said for and against these claims? Which side seems more reasonable to you? Why?
5. Why have many philosophers claimed that, if God knows the future, we cannot have free will?

Chapter 23

THE MEANING
OF LIFE

In Chapter 21, I concluded that religious belief is a matter of faith, not reason. In the words of Søren Kierkegaard, we must take a "leap of faith" beyond our evidence in order to believe in God. Why take that leap?

There are numerous ways of answering that question. Anthropologists and sociologists, for example, talk about the importance of religious institutions to their societies and about the ways that various societies condition us to become a part of these institutions. Psychoanalysts, on the other hand, talk about the role of unconscious conflicts in our adoption of religious faith.

In this chapter, we will look at another answer. This answer was briefly noted at the conclusion of Chapter 21. There I spoke of a common desire to know that the events of our world are not merely the product of blind causal processes, but also of some *purpose*. That is, many people long to know that there is some larger *meaning* to what happens, and that our existence here on earth has some ultimate significance.

WHY AM I HERE?

This longing has been expressed most poignantly, perhaps, by Pascal. Looking up at the stars, he thought of the inconceivable infinities of time and space, and he asked himself these questions: Why am I *here*, rather than *there*? Why *now*, rather than *then*?

A quick answer to these questions is this: Everybody has to be someplace. But such an answer will not, of course, do. Neither will the following answer: His parents lived in a certain place at a certain time, and that is why he was born when and where he was born. This latter answer will not do because Pascal was not looking for a *cause* of his existence. He was looking for a *reason*. He wanted to know what *purpose* his being there and then served.

But this longing for meaning extends beyond our own individual lives. When a loved one dies, we want to know why, and our question cannot be answered by the mention of a disease. When an earthquake kills thousands of people, we want to know why, and our question cannot be answered by the mention of moving plates beneath the surface of the earth. When six million Jews died in the Nazi holocaust, we wanted to know why, and that question could not be answered by the mention of Hitler's evil and his demagogic power. Such answers give *causal* explanations, while the questions are seeking purpose. For what purpose did these people die? If there was no such purpose, if their deaths were just blind happenings, they are that much harder to bear.

The Religious Promise

Religion holds out the promise of an answer to such questions. In the preceding chapter, we discussed the problem of evil as a problem for the theist. If God is perfectly good, all-knowing, and all-powerful, why is there human suffering? That is a *logical* problem, a problem of reconciling what appear to be inconsistent statements. But there is another problem of evil. This second one is not a logical problem, but a more *personal* one. It is this: What is the meaning of human suffering? Unlike the first, it is not *caused* by our conception of God. Rather, it is a problem that many hope can be *answered* by God. God, many feel, has purposes that we cannot understand. There is a purpose for everything, even though it eludes us. Whether we ever understand those purposes or not, at least we can take some comfort in our faith that they exist.

The above remarks suggest that religion holds only a promise of meaning. We can't understand the why of things, but from a God's-eye point of view, it is possible to understand it. The problem is not that there is no meaning, but that we cannot have a God's-eye point of view. Therefore, we are reduced to faith.

But there is more to the matter than that. Religion can give us a sense that there is a definite, knowable purpose to our lives. Consider, in this regard, standard Christian teachings. From these we can learn that our job is to love and serve God. How are we to do that? The answer is to be found in various places in the Bible, such as the Sermon on the Mount. We can also learn that our job is to get to heaven. That is, we can learn to think of this world as an anteroom to the next, and of our lives here as a pilgrimage to the next world.

In more recent times, many Christian thinkers have emphasized another role for the Christian—to make Jesus incarnate in this world through social justice. According to these teachings, our purpose is to make this world a better one.

Now, there are many atheists who assign themselves many of the same purposes—to live according to the moral principles embodied in the words of
Jesus, or to press for greater social justice in the world. In light of our current
concern, though, there is an important difference. The Christian's purpose is
God's. It fits into a larger plan. It ensures some wider meaning and significance
to the individual Christian life. We are not here as the result of blind causal
happenings. We are here for a definite purpose. If we accept that purpose, there
is no danger of our lives being meaningless.

In the Bible, this danger of meaninglessness comes through most strongly in
Ecclesiastes. There, the writer questions whether there is reason to do anything,
given the futility of life. The wise and the foolish, the good and the evil—all
have the same fate, death. And while they await that fate, there is no hope for
true novelty or gain: "there is nothing new under the sun," and "there was
nothing to be gained under the sun." Moreover, the writer notes that life is
filled with oppression and injustice, and that the wicked often prosper while
righteous suffer. "All is vanity," he concludes.

Yet that is not his final conclusion. His final conclusion is this: "Fear God, and
keep his commandments; for this is the whole duty of man." Thus, after all his
words on the futility of life, he finds, in his religious belief, some purpose to life.

Absurdity and Human Existence

The principal theme of Ecclesiastes is that life without God would be
meaningless. This theme has persisted up to the present age, and it has received
much attention in our own century—not only from religious thinkers, but from
atheistic thinkers as well.

Perhaps the best-known and most compelling proponent of this view is the
atheistic writer Albert Camus (1913–1960). In a famous essay, Camus compared
human life to the plight of Sisyphus, a figure from Greek mythology. Sisyphus
was sentenced by the gods to spend eternity rolling a rock up a mountain. Every
time he succeeded in his task, the rock would roll back down to the bottom.
Then, Sisyphus would follow it down and begin pushing it back up again.

Why make this comparison? According to Camus, the fundamental fact of
human existence is absurdity. Life is absurd because we are all strangers in an
alien universe. We seek to understand, to unify the various elements of the
world. We seek a unified whole, in which everything has a purpose. But the universe is not like that. Without God, there is no larger plan in which everything,
including our own lives, fits. It is this lack of fit between the universe and our
own aspirations that Camus calls the Absurd. Thus, our actions here on earth
are as futile and pointless as the eternal task assigned to Sisyphus.

On the face of it, this view seems blatantly false. Think of Jonas Salk, who
gave us the polio vaccine. Most of you take his achievement for granted, but I
was born in the mid-1940s and grew up in a period when polio was an ever-
present threat, when parents were afraid to let their children swim in public
pools, and when we were constantly confronted with images of children in leg

braces, crippled for life. Because of Salk's achievement, there are millions of healthy children who would otherwise have been like the children of the posters. Because of Salk's achievement, a great fear has been lifted. Surely his life was not pointless!

Think also of great leaders who changed the course of history—Napoleon, for instance, or Lenin, or America's founding fathers. Or think of such creative artists as Beethoven, Michelangelo, or Shakespeare, whose works have endured for centuries and given great joy to millions of people. How could their lives have been meaningless? What difference does it make that there is no God?

Well, from one point of view, of course, it makes no difference. We are convinced that the world is a better place for the likes of Salk and Beethoven, and we value them for that. And we can value them whether there is a God or not. But there is a deeper sense, Camus might insist, in which it does make a difference if there is no God.

The polio vaccine and a Beethoven symphony matter to us. To us they are important. Because of our own desires, they have a certain point. But what do they matter to the universe? What importance do they *ultimately* have? What point do they have from any perspective external to us?

Let us put this point another way. From the point of view of the universe as a whole, human history and human concerns are supremely unimportant. The history of human life, not to mention that of any individual human life, is almost infinitesimal compared with that of the universe, or even our own planet. Moreover, our planet is almost infinitesimally small compared with the entire universe. Had humankind never existed, the universe would be none the worse off. As a whole, then, we do not matter. But if humankind does not matter, why should an individual's contribution to humankind matter?

If there is a God, and if God has a plan in which humankind figures, things are different. There is a larger purpose, which human history and individual contributions to that history serve. Even after human history comes to an end, that history will have mattered, because it served its purpose. Without some such larger plan, it will not have mattered at all.

Most of us think such thoughts rarely, if at all. Perhaps they occur to us when, like Pascal, we stare at the stars on a clear night. Perhaps they occur to us during periods of profound depression, when there seems to be no good reason to get out of bed in the morning. To thinkers like Camus, however, such thoughts focus on the central fact of the human condition—that we are strangers in an absurd, meaningless world.

An Uncommon Fallacy

To Camus, questions concerning the meaning of life were central. This feeling was shared by many other thinkers of twentieth-century continental Europe. It was also shared by many twentieth-century theologians in America. Among contemporary secular philosophers in the English-speaking world, however, there has been a certain discomfort in entertaining questions about the meaning of life. These philosophers have felt that there is something defective about such questions. Some have held that these questions are pathological. Some have gone so far as to consider them meaningless, nonsensical.

The English philosopher J. L. Austin (1911–1960) expressed his discomfort this way. It is perfectly natural to ask the following questions: What is the point of going to school? What is the point of brushing my teeth? What is the point of watching my weight? All of these questions have straightforward answers: To gain knowledge, to avoid tooth decay, to be healthy and attractive.

But consider this question: What is the point of doing anything at all? This question does not admit of a straightforward answer. Why not? According to Austin, the "question" is a pseudo-question, not a real question at all. When we phrase it, we commit what he calls the fallacy of asking about nothing-in-particular.

We can best grasp Austin's idea by looking at other examples of the fallacy. What is the sum of five and five? Ten. Three and one? Four. These answers are easy to supply. But what is the sum of any two numbers? Or try this one. What is my typewriter on? My desk. What is my kettle on? My stove. Once again, the answers are easy to supply. But what is anything on?

The point of the fallacy is this. There are many questions that we can significantly ask of particular things, but we cannot ask of anything in general. When we try to ask them anyway, we commit the fallacy of asking about nothing-in-particular.

Usually, we do not try to ask them, of course. The absurdity of doing so is obvious. But there is one such question that does not strike us as obviously absurd: What is the point of doing anything at all? This question, Austin wryly notes, leads us either to commit suicide or to join the church.

Why? Because we *want* it to have an answer. And when we discover that it does not, it leads to the sense of meaninglessness described by Camus and the writer of Ecclesiastes. What do we do when that sense hits us? Some decide that life is not worth living. Others seek to find meaning in religious belief. But if Austin is right, such extreme measures are uncalled for. Rather than worry about the meaninglessness of life, we should redirect our attention to particular actions. Rather than worry about the point of doing anything at all, we should remember the point of doing all the little ordinary things we do every day. If we can't do that, therapy is in order.

Therapy? Well, consider this. One of the marks of clinical depression is the inability of the patient to think of a reason for doing anything. To the clinically depressed, no reason will do. There is not even any point to getting out of bed in the morning. In such cases, dialogues such as this are not uncommon:

"You have to get out of bed."

"Why?"

"So you can go to work."

"Why?"

"So you can support yourself and your family."

"Why?"

"So none of you will starve."

"Why?"

"So you can live."

"Why?"

Such people are looking for the point of doing anything. When dealing with them, we cannot help them by giving them the point of doing any particular thing. No answer will help. Suppose that we were to say that they should live because God wants them to. They can still respond by asking why they should do what God wants.

Our conclusion is this. If we come to ask about the meaning of life via the pseudo-question "What's the point of doing anything at all?" we can get no answer. Even appeals to God's plan cannot answer a pseudo-question. Pseudo-questions have at best pseudo-answers.

Silence and the Mystical

There is, however, another way to approach the question of the meaning of life. To ask for the point of any action is to ask for some context into which it fits. This context is provided by some purpose that the action serves. Suppose, then, that someone asks for some wider context into which some particular actions will fit, some larger purpose that some particular actions will serve. That is not to commit Austin's fallacy.

Why seek some larger purpose? People who seek one would answer as follows. If our actions do not serve some larger purpose, then our lives serve no larger purpose, and if our lives serve no larger purpose, they have no meaning.

Some people can find this larger purpose in purely earthly pursuits. Think once again of Salk, Beethoven, and Napoleon. Each made some contribution to the history of mankind. Through medicine, art, and political history, they served some wider purpose of humanity.

But then we run up against the theme of Ecclesiastes and Camus. Does human history serve some larger purpose? Is there some wider context into which human history fits? If not, then serving human history is ultimately meaningless. Thus, Ecclesiastes appeals to God for life's meaning, and Camus denies that life is ultimately meaningful.

Some philosophers, though, are as skeptical of this type of reasoning as Austin was of the sort of reasoning we examined in the previous section. Ludwig Wittgenstein (1889–1951), for example, felt that questions of ultimate meaning could neither be asked nor answered. We have the sense, he said, of the world as a limited whole. Therefore, we want to place it in some wider context, to give it some ultimate meaning. But that is just what we cannot do. There is nothing outside the world that can reveal itself in the world. The world is composed of all the facts that there are. These facts are learned through science. Once we have described them all, we have described all there is to be described. We have learned all that there is to learn, namely, *how* the world is. There are no further questions to ask, no further answers to be had. At that point, we are reduced to silence.

It should be stressed that Wittgenstein was not unsympathetic to what he called the problem of life. Rather, he felt that there are just some things that we cannot talk about. They belong to the realm of the mystical, and they must be passed over in silence. The trick to dealing with the problem, he felt, was not to find an answer—since there is none—but to realize that the solution to the problem is the vanishing of the problem.

The Absurd Hero

It would be nice if we could end on this last note. Unfortunately, we cannot. There remains one of Austin's points—that questions regarding the meaning of life lead people to commit suicide or join the church. Put another way, the point is this. Some people demand that life have some ultimate meaning. If they find it in religion, all is well. If they don't, they conclude that life is not worth living.

Camus felt that the question of suicide was the central philosophical question. For him, the question of suicide was this. A world without God is a world without hope—for either an afterlife or a life in this world with ultimate meaning. Can life be worth living in such an absurd world?

His answer was *yes*. Life, as Camus saw it, was a series of experiences. Although we cannot say that some experiences are more meaningful than others, and hence more worthwhile, we can say this: Since experiences are all we have, let us have as many as we can. Let us also live them heroically. That is, let us live them without any hope or regret, without any illusions about their ultimate significance. Let us live them with the sense that we, and not any God, are the masters of our fate, and let us live them in revolt against false answers to the problem of life.

Thus, he mentions five absurd heroes. The first four are the conqueror, the Don Juan, the actor, and the creator. All live lives of diversity. And if they realize the ultimate futility of their lives, they can live them in freedom and revolt. The fifth absurd hero is Sisyphus himself. According to the myth, his sentence was the result of his own revolt against the gods. Already in the underworld, he had been permitted to return to earth in order to settle a score with his wife. But he loved life too much to return. So the gods forced him back to the underworld, and the rock was his punishment.

That Sisyphus is an absurd hero to Camus is not surprising. What is surprising is this. Camus imagines Sisyphus happy as he walks down the mountain to begin pushing the rock back up. Why? Because he has made his own fate. And because he can scorn the gods and his own situation. And because he can continue to experience all that is around him. And because he can go on without hope and regret. In short, because he fully understands his situation yet goes on. Thus, Camus sees nothing disturbing about likening human life to the plight of Sisyphus. If he can be happy, so can we.

Is LIFE WORTH LIVING?

Is Sisyphus happy? I doubt it. I also doubt that most of you think he is. If I am right, then Camus does not help us escape Austin's dilemma—commit suicide or join the church. Does that mean that without God life is meaningless and not worth living?

I think not. Although, like Wittgenstein, I have a certain sympathy for concern with what he calls the mystical, I also have a certain skepticism for concern with the point of view of the universe. Put another way, although I have given much thought to questions of ultimate meaning, and although I have read and loved the great works of literature that have grappled with these questions, I think there is something terribly misguided about letting these questions affect our feelings about life's worth. Regardless of their ultimate meaning, the lives of young polio victims mattered to them and their families. And because they mattered, Jonas Salk's life had meaning and value enough. As for the rest of us, although we may not be able to hope for the impact of a Jonas Salk, we do affect the lives of those we meet. And if we affect them in a positive way, our lives too have meaning and value enough.

Most of my students are religious. Of those that are, many question whether life would be worth living without religious belief. Often, I respond something like this: Pizza would taste just as good whether or not there is a God. Although the remark is meant to be humorous, it is not meant to be facetious. There is, I think, an important, if rather ordinary, point buried in it.

It is a biological, psychological, and cultural fact about us that we like and want certain things—not only such things as pizza and beer, but such things as love, recognition, success, and friends. Whatever our likes and wants, there is one interesting fact about them—they propel us into the future. Because it pleases us to get what we like and want, we go after it if we can. If it is the sort of thing we can't go after, we eagerly await or hope for it. Either way, our likes and our wants give us good reason to stick around.

I can mention my grandmother to illustrate this point. My grandmother is about ninety years old. All her friends and relations of her generation have died, as have many relations of the next generation. She often complains about having lived too long and just as often gives the impression of waiting to die. Because she lives a thousand miles away, I rarely get to see her, but I do call a couple of times a month. In the autumn, I promise to see her during the Christmas holidays. In winter, I tell her I'll try to see her during the summer. She gets similar promises from my sister.

Like too many people her age, she has few desires left but for visits from her grandchildren. But that desire is enough to propel her into the future. When I make my promises, she says that she hopes she will see me, meaning that she hopes to live that much longer. When I do see her, her desire is satisfied. And when I leave, it is replaced by another one—to see me and her other grandchildren again. Thus, even to one tired of living, there is a future worth waiting for.

My rather banal point here is that as long as we want something, life is worth living. And as long as we are engaged in going after it or waiting for it, the question of the meaning of life is unlikely to arise. We are too busy ·going through the business of living. That is, our wants provide us with many individual purposes for many individual acts, so we just do them. That we are all going to die someday, or that human history has no ultimate significance from the point of view of the universe, is irrelevant.

My point can be put another way. Although it is natural to wonder about the ultimate meaning of life from time to time, we should not lose sight of the meanings of individual hours and days. Although it is natural to wonder about our purpose here on earth from time to time, we should not lose sight of the purposes of individual actions.

The pessimism of Ecclesiastes, then, is unwarranted. And as for Pascal's musings about his own insignificance as he looked up at the stars, we can turn them on their head. I recall looking at a cartoon (*Peanuts*, I think) in which two characters looked at those stars and one said something like this. When she looked up at so many stars so very far away, she couldn't help thinking how insignificant *they* all are. The moral? Insignificance is a matter of where we focus our concerns.

As for Sisyphus, it should not matter whether he really is happy as he walks down the mountain. What should matter is whether he was happy during his return to earth. That the gods had to force him back to the underworld suggests that he was.

THE FINAL WORD?

Questions about the meaning and worth of life can arise in at least three contexts. They can arise as the result of fallacious reasoning. They can arise as the result of great depression. They can arise as the result of a commonly felt human need. When they arise in the first two contexts, therapy is in order—whether philosophical or psychological. When they arise in the third, we must look elsewhere. Religion is the most obvious place to look, and from Ecclesiastes through Pascal to the present, it has provided a satisfactory answer to many of us.

For those who cannot take Kierkegaard's leap of faith, Camus provides another answer—a heroic attitude. Although I quibbled with Camus about the happiness of Sisyphus, there is a genuine appeal to his suggestion. Indeed, Camus would agree with much of what I said in the preceding section. In one of his novels, *The Stranger*, he presents an absurd heroine much like my grandmother. The novel begins with the announcement of the death of the narrator's mother. The old woman died in a home for the aged. Although she knew that death was near, she became engaged to a man in the same home. Regardless of the ultimate significance of her life, she managed to find meaning in her last days.

What makes Camus' answer so appealing, then, is that it embodies a rather trite (but right) old adage—life is what you make it.

Wittgenstein suggests another attitude—silence. The riddle of life can neither be asked nor answered, so we must say nothing. Yet to be silent about it is not to ignore it. The proper silent attitude can bring about some sort of resolution, and that resolution, although it cannot be described, can bring about a feeling for the sense of life. That resolution involves a vanishing of the problem, but that is all that can be said.

In a way, Wittgenstein's suggestion is reminiscent of Zen Buddhism. Zen Buddhists seek to achieve enlightenment by puzzling over riddles (called *koans*) that have no solution. Here is a famous example: We know the sound of two hands clapping. But what is the sound of one hand clapping? Once enlightenment is reached, all that can be said is this. Before enlightenment, I saw mountains and trees. Now I see mountains and trees.

STUDY QUESTIONS

1. Why have some thinkers felt that life without God is (or would be) meaningless?
2. What is Austin's fallacy of asking about nothing-in-particular? How does it relate to questions about the meaning of life?
3. Why did Wittgenstein recommend silence in the face of questions about the meaning of life? How does his recommendation differ from Austin's? Which recommendation do you find more appealing? Why?
4. What does Camus mean by the Absurd? How is the Absurd exemplified by the plight of Sisyphus? Why does Camus call Sisyphus an absurd hero?
5. Is Sisyphus happy?
6. As long as we have wants, I said, life is worth living. Do you agree? Why or why not?

SELECTIONS

The following selections present classic discussions of the problem of evil.

The first is from David Hume's Concerning Natural Religion. *There, Hume isolates four conditions that he takes to be responsible for human suffering and claims that all four could have been avoided by God.*

Although Hume strongly suggests that the existence of these conditions is incompatible with the existence of a perfectly good, all-knowing and all-powerful God, he does not actually make that claim. In fact, he allows that it might be possible to reconcile the existence of the two. His major concern in this passage is to criticize the argument from design. His arguments are meant to show that, even if we assume that the world must have had a designer, the suffering we find in the world forces us to conclude that the designer is indifferent to human suffering.

The second selection is from Gottfried Wilhelm Leibniz's Theodicy. *There, Leibniz responds to four arguments. The first concludes that God lacks power, knowledge, or goodness. The second, that there is more evil than good in God's works. The third, that it is unjust for God to punish us for our sins. The fourth, that God is an accessory to our sins.*

In each case, Leibniz formulates the objection as an argument in three steps—two premises (the first called the major premise and the second called the minor premise) and a conclusion. Then he criticizes one of the premises to show that the argument is unsound. In two cases, his response includes a prosyllogism. Each prosyllogism is a three-step argument meant to prove one of the premises of the main argument under discussion.

Perhaps the most interesting (if most difficult) response is his response to the third argument. Notice that Leibniz grants that human actions are predetermined but denies that they are therefore necessary. Since they are not necessary, God can justly punish us for our sins. Leibniz's treatment of the distinction between the determined and the necessary is one of his most-discussed contributions to philosophy. His major point is this. Human actions are caused by various factors. Given certain causes, a particular action must result. Had the causes been different, another action would have resulted. But if our actions were really necessary, they would occur no matter what came before them. For example, my own inclinations are part of the cause of my actions. If I have good inclinations, I will do good. If I have evil inclinations, I will do evil. My actions can be changed by a change in my inclinations. Therefore, it is not necessary that I act one way as opposed to the other. (In light of the discussions of Part III, we can say that Leibniz is a compatibilist. God can hold us morally responsible for our actions even though our behavior is determined.)

DAVID HUME

Does God Care About Human Suffering?

In short, I repeat the question: is the world considered in general, and as it appears to us in this life, different from what a man or such a limited being would, beforehand, expect from a very powerful, wise, and benevolent Deity? It must be strange prejudice to assert the contrary. And from thence I conclude, that, however consistent the world may be, allowing certain suppositions and conjectures, with the idea of such a Deity, it can never afford us an inference concerning his existence. The consistency is not absolutely denied, only the inference. Conjectures, especially where infinity is excluded from the Divine attributes, may perhaps be sufficient to prove a consistency; but can never be foundations for any inference.

There seem to be four circumstances, on which depend all, or the greatest parts of the ills, that molest sensible creatures; and it is not impossible but all these circumstances may be necessary and unavoidable. We know so little beyond common life, or even of common life, that, with regard to the economy of a universe, there is no conjecture, however wild, which may not be just; nor any one, however plausible, which may not be erroneous. All that belongs to human understanding, in this deep ignorance and obscurity, is to be sceptical, or at least cautious; and not to admit of any hypothesis, whatever; much less, of any which is supported by no appearance of probability. Now this I assert to be the case with regard to all the causes of evil, and the circumstances, on which it depends. None of them appear to human reason, in the least degree, necessary or unavoidable; nor can we suppose them such, without the utmost license of imagination.

The *first* circumstance which introduces evil, is that contrivance or economy of the animal creation, by which pains, as well as pleasures, are employed to excite all creatures to action, and make them vigilant in the great work of self-preservation. Now pleasure alone, in its various degrees, seems to human understanding sufficient for this purpose. All animals might be constantly in a state of enjoyment; but when urged by any of the necessities of nature, such as thirst, hunger, weariness, instead of pain, they might feel a diminution of pleasure, by which they might be prompted to seek that object, which is necessary to their subsistence. Men pursue pleasure as eagerly as they avoid pain; at least, might have been so constituted. It seems, therefore, plainly possible to carry on the business of life without any pain. Why then is any animal ever rendered susceptible of such a sensation? If animals can be free from it an hour, they might enjoy a perpetual exemption from it; and it required as particular a contrivance of their organs to produce that feeling, as to endow them with sight, hearing, or any of the senses. Shall we conjecture, that such a contrivance was necessary, without any appearance of reason? and shall we build on that conjecture as on the most certain truth?

But a capacity of pain would not alone produce pain, were it not for the *second* circumstance, viz., the conducting of the world by general laws; and this seems nowise necessary to a very perfect being. It is true; if everything were conducted by particular volitions, the course of nature would be perpetually broken, and no man could employ his reason in the conduct of life. But might not other particular volitions remedy this inconvenience? In short, might not the Deity exterminate all ill, wherever it were to be found; and produce all good, without any preparation or long progress of causes and effects?

Besides, we must consider, that, according to the present economy of the world, the course of nature, though supposed exactly regular, yet to us appears not so, and many events are uncertain, and many disappoint our expectations. Health and sickness, calm and tempest, with an infinite number of other accidents, whose causes are unknown and variable, have a great influence both on the fortunes of particular persons and on the prosperity of public societies: and indeed all human life, in a manner, depends on such accidents. A being, therefore, who knows the secret springs of the universe, might easily, by particular volitions, turn all these accidents to the good of mankind, and render the whole world happy, without discovering himself in any operation. A fleet, whose purposes were salutary to society, might always meet with a fair wind: good princes enjoy sound health and long life: persons, born to power and authority, be framed with good tempers and virtuous dispositions. A few such events as these, regularly and wisely conducted, would change the face of the world; and yet would no more seem to disturb the course of nature or confound human conduct, than the present economy of things, where the causes are secret, and variable, and compounded. Some small touches, given to Caligula's brain in his infancy, might have converted him into a Trajan: one wave, a little higher than the rest, by burying Caesar and his fortune in the bottom of the ocean, might have restored liberty to a considerable part of mankind. There may, for aught we know, be good reasons, why Providence interposes not in this manner; but they are unknown to us: and though the mere supposition, that such reasons exist, may be sufficient to *save* the conclusion concerning the divine attributes, yet surely it can never be sufficient to *establish* that conclusion.

If everything in the universe be conducted by general laws, and if animals be rendered susceptible of pain, it scarcely seems possible but some ill must arise in the various shocks of matter, and the various concurrence and opposition of general laws. But this ill would be very rare, were it not for the *third* circumstance, which I proposed to mention, viz., the great frugality with which all powers and faculties are distributed to every particular being. So well adjusted are the organs and capacities of all animals, and so well fitted to their preservation, that, as far as history or tradition reaches, there appears not to be any single species, which has yet been extinguished in the universe. Every animal has the requisite endowments; but these endowments are bestowed with so scrupulous an economy, that any considerable diminution must entirely destroy the creature. Wherever one power is increased, there is a proportional abatement in the others. Animals, which excel in swiftness, are commonly defective in force. Those, which possess both, are either imperfect in some of their senses, or are oppressed with the most craving wants. The human species, whose chief excellency is reason and sagacity, is of all others the most necessitous, and the most deficient in bodily advantages; without clothes, without arms, without food, without lodging, without any convenience of life, except what they owe to their own skill and industry. In short, nature seems to have formed an exact calculation of the necessities of her creatures; and like a *rigid master,* has afforded them little more powers or endowments, than what are strictly sufficient to supply those necessities. An *indulgent parent* would have bestowed a large stock, in order to guard against accidents, and secure the happiness and welfare of the creature, in the most unfortunate concurrence of circumstances. Every course of life would not have been so surrounded with precipices, that the least departure from the true path, by mistake or necessity, must involve us in misery and ruin. Some reserve, some fund would have been provided to ensure happiness; nor would the powers and the necessities have been adjusted with so rigid an economy. The Author of Nature is inconceivably powerful: his force is supposed great, if not altogether inexhaustible: nor is there any reason, as far as we can judge, to make him observe this strict frugality in his dealings with his creatures. It would have been better, were his power extremely limited, to have created fewer animals, and to have endowed these with more faculties for their happiness and preservation. A builder is never esteemed prudent, who undertakes a plan, beyond what his stock will enable him to finish.

In order to cure most of the ills of human life, I require not that man should have the wings of the eagle, the swiftness of the stag, the force of the ox, the arms of the lion, the scales of the crocodile or rhinoceros; much less do I demand the sagacity of an angel or cherub. I am contented to take an increase in one single power or faculty of his soul. Let him be endowed with a greater propensity to industry and labor; a more vigorous spring and activity of mind; a more constant bent to business and application. Let the whole species possess naturally an equal diligence with that which many individuals are able to attain by habit and reflection; and the most beneficial consequences, without any alloy of ill, is the immediate and necessary result of this endowment. Almost all the moral, as well as natural evils of human life arise from idleness; and were our species, by the original constitution of their frame, exempt from this vice or infirmity, the perfect cultivation of land, the improvement of arts and manufactures, the exact execution of every office and duty, immediately follow; and men at once may fully reach that state of society, which is so imperfectly attained by the best-regulated government. But as industry is a power, and the most valuable of any, nature seems determined, suitably to her usual maxims, to bestow it on men with a very sparing hand; and rather to punish him severely for his deficiency in it, than to reward him for his attainments. She has so contrived his frame, that nothing but the most violent necessity can oblige him to labor; and she employs all his other wants to overcome, at least in part, the want of diligence, and to endow him with some share of a faculty, of which she has thought fit naturally to bereave him. Here our demands may be allowed very humble, and therefore the more reasonable. If we required the endowments of superior penetration and judgment, of a more delicate taste of beauty, of a nicer sensibility to benevolence and friendship; we might be told, that we impiously pretend to break the order of nature, that we want to exalt ourselves into a higher rank of being, that the presents which we require, not being suitable to our state and condition, would only be pernicious to us. But it is hard; I dare to repeat it, it is hard, that being placed in a world so full of wants and necessities; where almost every being and element is either our foe or refuses us their assistance, we should also have our own temper to struggle with, and should be deprived of that faculty, which can alone fence against these multiplied evils.

The *fourth* circumstance, whence arises the misery and ill of the universe, is the inaccurate workmanship of all the springs and principles of the great machine of nature. It must be acknowledged, that there are few parts of the universe, which seem not to serve some purpose, and whose removal would not produce a visible defect and disorder in the whole. The parts hang all together; nor can one be touched without affecting the rest in a greater or less degree. But at the same time, it must be observed, that none of these parts or principles, however useful, are so accurately adjusted, as to keep precisely within those bounds, in which their utility consists; but they are, all of them, apt, on every occasion, to run into the one extreme or the other. One would imagine, that this grand production had not received the last hand of the maker; so little finished in every part, and so coarse are the strokes, with which it is executed. Thus, the winds are requisite to convey the vapors along the surface of the globe, and to assist men in navigation: but how oft, rising up to tempests and hurricanes, do they become pernicious? Rains are necessary to nourish all the plants and animals of the earth: but how often are they defective? how often excessive? Heat is requisite to all life and vegetation; but is not always found in the due proportion. On the mixture and secretion of the humors and juices of the body depend the health and prosperity of the animal: but the parts perform not regularly their proper function. What more useful than all the passions of the mind, ambition, vanity, love, anger? But how oft do they break their bounds, and cause the greatest convulsions in society? There is nothing so advantageous in the universe, but what frequently becomes pernicious, by its excess or defect; nor has nature guarded, with the requisite accuracy, against all disorder or confusion.

The irregularity is never, perhaps, so great as to destroy any species; but is often sufficient to involve the individuals in ruin and misery.

On the concurrence, then, of these four circumstances does all, or the greatest part of natural evil depend. Were all living creatures incapable of pain, or were the world administered by particular volitions, evil never could have found access into the universe: and were animals endowed with a large stock of powers and faculties, beyond what strict necessity requires; or were the several springs and principles of the universe so accurately framed as to preserve always the just temperament and medium; there must have been very little ill in comparison of what we feel at present. What then shall we pronounce on this occasion? Shall we say, that these circumstances are not necessary, and that they might easily have been altered in the contrivance of the universe? This decision seems too presumptuous for creatures, so blind and ignorant. Let us be more modest in our conclusions. Let us allow, that, if the goodness of the Deity (I mean a goodness like the human) could be established on any tolerable reasons *a priori*, these phenomena, however untoward, would not be sufficient to subvert that principle; but might easily, in some unknown manner, be reconcilable to it. But let us still assert, that as this goodness is not antecedently established, but must be inferred from the phenomena, there can be no grounds for such an inference, while there are so many ills in the universe, and while these ills might so easily have been remedied, as far as human understanding can be allowed to judge on such a subject. I am sceptic enough to allow, that the bad appearances, notwithstanding all my reasonings, may be compatible with such attributes as you suppose: but surely they can never prove these attributes. Such a conclusion cannot result from scepticism; but must arise from the phenomena, and from our confidence in the reasonings, which we deduce from these phenomena.

Look round this universe. What an immense profusion of beings, animated and organized, sensible and active! You admire this prodigious variety and fecundity. But inspect a little more narrowly these living existences, the only beings worth regarding. How hostile and destructive to each other! How insufficient all of them for their own happiness! How contemptible or odious to the spectator! The whole presents nothing but the idea of a blind nature, impregnated by a great vivifying principle, and pouring forth from her lap, without discernment or parental care, her maimed and abortive children!

Here the Manichaean system occurs as a proper hypothesis to solve the difficulty: and no doubt, in some respects, it is very specious, and has more probability than the common hypothesis, by giving a plausible account of the strange mixture of good and ill, which appears in life. But if we consider, on the other hand, the perfect uniformity and agreement of the parts of the universe, we shall not discover in it any marks of the combat of a malevolent with a benevolent being. There is indeed an opposition of pains and pleasures in the feelings of sensible creatures: but are not all the operations of nature carried on by an opposition of principles, of hot and cold, moist and dry, light and heavy? The true conclusion is, that the original source of all things is entirely indifferent to all these principles, and has no more regard to good above ill than to heat above cold, or to drought above moisture, or to light above heavy.

There may four hypotheses be framed concerning the first causes of the universe: that they are endowed with perfect goodness, that they have perfect malice, that they are opposite and have both goodness and malice, that they have neither goodness nor malice. Mixed phenomena can never prove the two former unmixed principles. And the uniformity and steadiness of general laws seem to oppose the third. The fourth, therefore, seems by far the most probable.

GOTTFRIED LEIBNIZ

In Defense of God

Some intelligent persons have desired that this supplement be made [to the Theodicy], and I have the more readily yielded to their wishes as in this way I have an opportunity again to remove certain difficulties and to make some observations which were not sufficiently emphasized in the work itself.

I. *Objection.* Whoever does not choose the best is lacking in power, or in knowledge, or in goodness.

God did not choose the best in creating this world.

Therefore, God has been lacking in power, or in knowledge, or in goodness.

Answer. I deny the minor, that is, the second premise of this syllogism; and our opponent proves it by this

Prosyllogism. Whoever makes things in which there is evil, which could have been made without any evil, or the making of which could have been omitted, does not choose the best.

God has made a world in which there is evil; a world, I say, which could have been made without any evil, or the making of which could have been omitted altogether.

Therefore, God has not chosen the best.

Answer. I grant the minor of this prosyllogism; for it must be confessed that there is evil in this world which God has made, and that it was possible to make a world without evil, or even not to create a world at all, for its creation has depended on the free will of God; but I deny the major, that is, the first of the two premises of the prosyllogism, and I might content myself with simply demanding its proof; but in order to make the matter clearer, I have wished to justify this denial by showing that the best plan is not always that which seeks to avoid evil, since it may happen that *the evil is accompanied by a greater good.* For example, a general of an army will prefer a great victory with a slight wound to a condition without wound and without victory. We have proved this more fully in the large work by making it clear, by instances taken from mathematics and elsewhere, that an imperfection in the part may be required for a greater perfection in the whole. In this I have followed the opinion of St. Augustine, who has said a hundred times, that God has permitted evil in order to bring about good, that is, a greater good; and that of Thomas Aquinas (in libr. II. sent. dist. 32, qu. I, art. 1), that the permitting of evil tends to the good of the universe. I have shown that the ancients called Adam's fall *felix culpa,* a happy sin, because it had been retrieved with immense advantage by the incarnation of the Son of God, who has given to the universe something nobler than anything that ever would have been among creatures except for it. For the sake of a clearer understanding, I have added, following many good authors, that it was in accordance with order and the general good that God allowed to certain creatures the opportunity of exercising their liberty, even when he foresaw that they would turn to evil, but which he could so well rectify; because it was not fitting that, in order to hinder sin, God should always act in an extraordinary manner. To overthrow this objection, therefore, it is sufficient to show that a world with evil might be better than a world without evil; but I have gone even farther, in the work, and have even proved that this universe must be in reality better than every other possible universe.

II. *Objection.* If there is more evil than good in intelligent creatures, then there is more evil than good in the whole work of God.

Now, there is more evil than good in intelligent creatures.

Therefore, there is more evil than good in the whole work of God.

Answer. I deny the major and the minor of this conditional syllogism. As to the major, I do not admit it at all, because this pretended deduction from a part to the whole, from intelligent creatures to all creatures, supposes tacitly and without proof that creatures destitute of reason cannot enter into comparison nor into account with those which possess it. But why may it not be that the surplus of good in the non-intelligent creatures which fill the world, compensates for, and even incomparably surpasses, the surplus of evil in the rational creatures? It is true that the value of the latter is greater; but, in compensation, the others are beyond comparison the more numerous, and it may be that the proportion of number and quantity surpasses that of value and of quality.

As to the minor, that is no more to be admitted; that is, it is not at all to be admitted that there is more evil than good in the intelligent creatures. There is no need even of granting that there is more evil than good in the human race, because it is possible, and in fact very probable, that the glory and the perfection of the blessed are incomparably greater than the misery and the imperfection of the damned, and that here the excellence of the total good in the smaller number exceeds the total evil in the greater number. The blessed approach the Divinity, by means of a Divine Mediator, as near as may suit these creatures, and make such progress in good as is impossible for the damned to make in evil, approach as nearly as they may to the nature of demons. God is infinite, and the devil is limited; the good may and does go to infinity, while evil has its bounds. It is therefore possible, and is credible, that in the comparison of the blessed and the damned, the contrary of that which I have said might happen in the comparison of intelligent and non-intelligent creatures, takes place; namely, it is possible that in the comparison of the happy and the unhappy, the proportion of degree exceeds that of number, and that in the comparison of intelligent and nonintelligent creatures, the proportion of number is greater than that of value. I have the right to suppose that a thing is possible so long as its impossibility is not proved; and indeed that which I have here advanced is more than a supposition.

But in the second place, if I should admit that there is more evil than good in the human race, I have still good grounds for not admitting that there is more evil than good in all intelligent creatures. For there is an inconceivable number of genii, and perhaps of other rational creatures. And an opponent could not prove that in all the City of God, composed as well of genii as of rational animals without number and of an infinity of kinds, evil exceeds good. And although in order to answer an objection, there is no need of proving that a thing is, when its mere possibility suffices; yet, in this work, I have not omitted to show that it is a consequence of the supreme perfection of the Sovereign of the universe, that the kingdom of God is the most perfect of all possible states or governments, and that consequently the little evil there is, is required for the consummation of the immense good which is found there.

III. *Objection.* If it is always impossible not to sin, it is always unjust to punish.

Now, it is always impossible not to sin; or, in other words, every sin is necessary.

Therefore, it is always unjust to punish.

The minor of this is proved thus:

1. *Prosyllogism.* All that is predetermined is necessary.

Every event is predetermined.

Therefore, every event (and consequently sin also) is necessary.

Again this second minor is proved thus:

2. *Prosyllogism.* That which is future, that which is foreseen, that which is involved in the causes, is predetermined.

Every event is such.

Therefore, every event is predetermined.

Answer. I admit in a certain sense the conclusion of the second prosyllogism, which is the minor of the first; but I shall deny the major of the first prosyllogism, namely, that every thing predetermined is necessary; understanding by the *necessity* of sinning, for example, or by the impossibility of not sinning, or of not performing any action, the necessity with which we are here concerned, that is, that which is essential and absolute, and which destroys the morality of an action and the justice of punishments. For if anyone understood another necessity or impossibility, namely, a necessity which should be only moral, or which was only hypothetical (as will be explained shortly); it is clear that I should deny the major of the objection itself. I might content myself with this answer and demand the proof of the proposition denied; but I have again desired to explain my procedure in this work, in order to better elucidate the matter and to throw more light on the whole subject, by explaining the necessity which ought to be rejected and the determination which must take place. That *necessity* which is contrary to morality and which ought to be rejected, and which would render punishment unjust, is an insurmountable necessity which would make all opposition useless, even if we should wish with all our heart to avoid the necessary action, and should make all possible efforts to that end. Now, it is manifest that this is not applicable to voluntary actions, because we would not perform them if we did not choose to. Also their prevision and predetermination are not absolute, but presuppose the will: if it is certain that we shall perform them, it is not less certain that we shall choose to perform them. These voluntary actions and their consequences will not take place no matter what we do or whether we wish them or not; but, *through* that which we shall do and through that which we shall wish to do, which leads to them. And this is involved in prevision and in predetermination, and even constitutes their ground. And the necessity of such an event is called conditional or hypothetical, or the necessity of consequence, because it supposes the will, and the other *requisites;* whereas the necessity which destroys morality and renders punishment unjust and reward useless, exists in things which will be whatever we may do or whatever we may wish to do, and, in a word, is in that which is essential; and this is what is called an absolute necessity. Thus it is to no purpose, as regards what is absolutely necessary, to make prohibitions or commands, to propose penalties or prizes, to praise or to blame; it will be none the less. On the other hand, in voluntary actions and in that which depends upon them, precepts armed with power to punish and to recompense are very often of use and are included in the order of causes which make an action exist. And it is for this reason that not only cares and labors but also prayers are useful; God having had these prayers in view before he regulated things and having had that consideration for them which was proper. This is why the precept which says *ora et labora* (pray and work), holds altogether good; and not only those who (under the vain pretext of the necessity of events) pretend that the care which business demands may be neglected, but also those who reason against prayer, fall into what the ancients even then called the *lazy sophism.* Thus the predetermination of events by causes is just what contributes to morality instead of destroying it, and causes incline the will, without compelling it. This is why the *determination* in question is not a necessitation—it is certain (to him who knows all) that the effect will follow this inclination; but this effect does not follow by a necessary consequence, that is, one the contrary of which implies contradiction. It is also by an internal inclination such as this that the will is determined, without there being any necessity. Suppose that one has the greatest

passion in the world (a great thirst, for example), you will admit to me that
the soul can find some reason for resisting it, if it were only that of showing
its power. Thus, although one may never be in a perfect indifference of equilibrium and there may be always a preponderance of inclination for the side
taken, it, nevertheless, never renders the resolution taken absolutely necessary.

IV. *Objection.* Whoever can prevent the sin of another and does not do so,
but rather contributes to it although he is well informed of it, is accessory
to it.

God can prevent the sin of intelligent creatures; but he does not do so,
and rather contributes to it by his concurrence and by the opportunities
which he brings about, although he has a perfect knowledge of it.

Hence, etc.

Answer. I deny the major of this syllogism. For it is possible that one could
prevent sin, but ought not, because he could not do it without himself committing a sin, or (when God is in question) without performing an unreasonable action. Examples have been given and the application to God himself
has been made. It is possible also that we contribute to evil and that sometimes we even open the road to it, in doing things which we are obliged to
do; and, when we do our duty or (in speaking of God) when, after thorough
consideration, we do that which reason demands, we are not responsible for
the results, even when we foresee them. We do not desire these evils; but we
are willing to permit them for the sake of a greater good which we cannot
reasonably help preferring to other considerations. And this is a *consequent*
will, which results from *antecedent* wills by which we will the good. I know
that some persons, in speaking of the antecedent and consequent will of
God, have understood by the *antecedent* that which wills that all men
should be saved; and by the *consequent,* that which wills, in consequence of
persistent sin, that some should be damned. But these are merely illustra-
tions of a more general idea, and it may be said for the same reason that
God, by his antecedent will, wills that men should not sin; and by his consequent or final and decreeing will (that which is always followed by its effect), he wills to permit them to sin, this permission being the result of superior reasons. And we have the right to say in general that the antecedent will
of God tends to the production of good and the prevention of evil, each
taken in itself and as if alone (*particulariter et secundum quid,* Thom. I, qu.
19, art. 6), according to the measure of the degree of each good and of each
evil; but that the divine consequent or final or total will tends toward the
production of as many goods as may be put together, the combination of
which becomes in this way determined, and includes also the permission of
some evils and the exclusion of some goods, as the best possible plan for the
universe demands. Arminius, in his *Anti-perkinsus,* has very well explained
that the will of God may be called consequent, not only in relation to the
action of the creature considered beforehand in the divine understanding,
but also in relation to other anterior divine acts of will. But this consideration

of the passage cited from Thomas Aquinas, and that from Scotus (I. dist. 46, qu. XI), is enough to show that they make this distinction as I have done here. Nevertheless, if anyone objects to this use of terms let him substitute *deliberating* will, in place of antecedent, and *final* or decreeing will, in place of consequent. For I do not wish to dispute over words.

FOR FURTHER READING

There are many anthologies on the market that cover important topics in the philosophy of religion, including those discussed in the first two chapters in Part VII. The following three anthologies contain classical and contemporary readings: John Hick's *Classical and Contemporary Readings in the Philosophy of Religion* (Englewood Cliffs: Prentice-Hall, 1970), George I. Mavrodes and Stuart C. Hackett's *Problems and Perspectives in the Philosophy of Religion* (Boston: Allyn and Bacon, 1967), and William L. Rowe and William J. Wainwright's *Philosophy of Religion: Selected Readings* (New York: Harcourt Brace Jovanovich, 1973). For an excellent collection of contemporary readings, see Steven M. Cahn's *Philosophy of Religion* (New York: Harper & Row, 1970).

The following, more specialized anthologies are also useful: Donald R. Burrill's *The Cosmological Arguments* (Garden City: Anchor, 1967), John Hick and Arthur McGill's *The Many-Faced Argument* (New York: Macmillan, 1967), Nelson Pike's *God and Evil* (Englewood Cliffs: Prentice-Hall, 1964), and Alvin Plantinga's *The Ontological Argument* (Garden City: Anchor, 1965).

Two useful introductory texts are John Hick's *Philosophy of Religion* (Englewood Cliffs: Prentice-Hall, 1973), and Keith E. Yandell's *Basic Issues in the Philosophy of Religion* (Boston: Allyn and Bacon, 1971). The Hick is the shorter and easier to read of the two.

For Kierkegaard's views on the nonrational or irrational aspect of religious belief, see *Concluding Unscientific Postscript* (Princeton: Princeton University Press, 1941), first published in 1846.

Aquinas's presentation of the cosmological argument appears in his *Summa Theologiae*, Part I, and can be found in *Basic Writings of Saint Thomas Aquinas*, edited by Anton C. Pegis (New York: Random House, 1945). His argument can also be found in the anthologies by Hick, Mavrodes and Hackett, and Rowe and Wainwright.

Well-known criticisms of the cosmological argument are given by David Hume in his *Dialogues Concerning Natural Religion* (Indianapolis: Bobbs-Merrill, 1947), first published in 1779, and Immanuel Kant in his *Critique of Pure Reason* (New York: Macmillan, 1929), first published in 1781. Hume's work also contains his criticisms of the argument from design and his discussion of the problem of evil. Kant's also contains his well-known discussion of the argument from design and the ontological argument.

Anselm's characterization of God and his version of the ontological argument appear in his *Proslogion*. The relevant sections can be found in the Hick and the Hick and McGill anthologies. Another much-discussed version of the ontological argument appears in René Descartes' *Meditations on First Philosophy*, first published in 1641, and available in *The Philosophical Works of Descartes* (Cambridge: Cambridge University Press, 1972), translated by Haldane and Ross. Leibniz's version appears in *The Monadology*, first published in 1714; Spinoza's in *Ethics*, first published in 1677, as well as his earlier *Short Treatise on God, Man and His Well-Being*. See *Leibniz: Selections* (New York: Scribner's, 1951), edited by Philip Wiener, and *Spinoza: Selections* (New York: Scribner's, 1958), edited by John Wild. For Leibniz's discussion of the problem of evil, see *Theodicy* (Indianapolis: Bobbs-Merrill, 1966), first published in 1710, and *Discourse on Metaphysics*, first published in 1686. The *Discourse* and a portion of *The Theodicy* (in which Leibniz summarizes the argument of the book) are available in Wiener.

Pascal's account of his wager appears in *Pensées* (New York: Penguin, 1966). His thoughts on the meaning of life can also be found there. *Pensées* is a fascinating work, consisting of fragments on a variety of topics. Pascal died in 1662 without publishing the work. For William James's views on the rationality of religious belief in the face of inconclusive evidence, see his "The Will to Believe," first published in 1896 and available in a number of sources, including *The Will to Believe and Other Essays in Popular Philosophy* (New York: Dover, 1956).

Another widely discussed justification for belief in God comes from Immanuel Kant, who argued that, although we cannot prove God's existence, we must posit it as a moral necessity. See his *Critique of Practical Reason* (Indianapolis: Bobbs-Merrill, 1956), first published in 1788. See also his less widely discussed *Religion Within the Limits of Reason Alone* (New York: Harper & Row, 1960), first published in 1793.

Among the best-known opponents of religious belief are Friedrich Nietzsche, Karl Marx, Sigmund Freud, and Jean-Paul Sartre. See Nietzsche's *Thus Spake Zarathustra* (in which he announces the death of God) and *The Antichrist*, first published in 1892 and 1895, respectively. Both are available in *The Portable Nietzsche* (New York: Viking, 1968). Marx's views, including his famous remark that religion is "the opium of the people," appear in "Toward a Critique of Hegel's *Philosophy of Right*: Introduction," first published in 1844 and available in *Karl Marx: Selected Writings* (Oxford: Oxford University Press, 1977), edited by David McLellan. In *The Future of an Illusion* (New York: Norton, 1961), first published in 1927, Freud characterizes religion as a neurosis. And in *Being and Nothingness* (New York: Citadel, 1956), first published in 1943, Sartre argues that the normal conception of God is an impossible one.

In the middle of this century, English and American philosophers were asking whether some of the key statements of religious belief (such as "God exists" and "God loves me") are really meaningful statements at all. The most important contributions to this debate can be found in *New Essays in Philosophical Theology* (New York: Macmillan, 1964), edited by Antony Flew and Alasdair MacIntyre. Included is a discussion by Antony Flew, R. N. Hare, Basil Mitchell, and I. M. Crombie entitled "Theology and Falsification," which is also available in the Hick and Cahn anthologies.

For Camus on the absurd hero, see his essay *The Myth of the Sisyphus* (New York: Vintage, 1955) and his novel *The Stranger* (New York: Vintage, 1946). The former contains his arguments against suicide in an absurd world, and the latter dramatizes his view. In a later essay, *The Rebel* (New York: Vintage, 1956), he argues for morality in an absurd world, and the novel *The Plague* (New York: Modern Library, 1948) is an excellent companion piece to it.

Much of the philosophy of Sartre, a one-time friend of Camus, centers on what he calls abandonment. We are in the world here and now for no reason outside of any reason we ourselves supply (hence the term "abandonment"), and it is through our own choices that our lives are given meaning. See *Being and Nothingness*, as well as his novel *Nausea* (New York: New Directions, 1964). Individual responsibility for meaningfulness is also stressed by Nietzsche. See *Thus Spake Zarathustra*.

Wittgenstein presents his reflections on the mystical in his *Tractatus Logico-Philosophicus* (New York: Humanities Press, 1960), first published in 1921. Austin discusses the fallacy of asking about nothing-in-particular in "The Meaning of a Word," available in his *Philosophical Papers* (New York: Oxford University Press, 1970), edited by J. O. Urmson and G. J. Warnock.

Many theologians, of course, have explored the connection between religion and meaning. Among the early church fathers, Augustine is most noteworthy. See his *Confessions* (New York: Penguin, 1961). More recently, the existentialist theologians have been most concerned with the connection. See "For Further Reading," Part IV, for some of the most important works in that tradition.

Finally, there are many great works of literature that deal with the themes discussed in

Chapter 23, far too many to allow any sort of representative list here. Rather than attempt any such list, I shall simply mention two widely noted works that are particular favorites of mine—Fyodor Dostoevsky's *The Brothers Karamazov* (New York: Random House, 1950) and Franz Kafka's *The Castle* (New York: Vintage, 1974).

INDEX

ABOUT THE AUTHOR

Jeffrey Olen is Associate Professor of Philosophy at the University of Wisconsin at Stevens Point. On his way to an undergraduate degree at the University of Pennsylvania, he took four and a half years off to write for newspapers, magazines, radio, and children's television. In 1976, he received his Ph.D. from Temple University. Since then, he has written articles and book reviews for philosophical journals in the United States, England, and Canada.